D1376613

KARL KRAUS
APOCALYPTIC SATIRIST

The scene of writing: Kraus's desk in the Lothringerstrasse

KARL KRAUS
APOCALYPTIC SATIRIST

The Post-War Crisis and the Rise of the Swastika

EDWARD TIMMS

YALE UNIVERSITY PRESS
NEW HAVEN AND LONDON

Copyright © 2005 by Edward Timms

All rights reserved. This book may not be reproduced in whole or in part, in any form (beyond that copying permitted by Sections 107 and 108 of the U.S. Copyright Law and except by reviewers for the public press), without written permission from the publishers.

For information about this and other Yale University Press publications, please contact:
U.S. Office: sales.press@yale.edu   yalebooks.com
Europe Office: sales@yaleup.co.uk   www.yalebooks.co.uk

Set in Bembo by Northern Phototypesetting Co. Ltd, Bolton
Printed in Great Britain by Cambridge University Press

Library of Congress Cataloging-in-Publication Data
Timms, Edward.
    Karl Kraus, apocalyptic satirist: the post-war crisis and the rise of the Swastika/Edward Timms.
        p. cm.
    Includes bibliographical references and index.
    ISBN 0–300–10751–X (cl.: alk. paper)
    1. Kraus, Karl, 1874–1936—Criticism and interpretation. 2. Authors, Austrian—20th century—Biography. 3. Vienna (Austria)—Intellectual life—20th century. 4. Austria—History—1918–1938. 5. Jews—Austria—Vienna—Social conditions—20th century. 6. Vienna (Austria)—Social life and customs—20th century. I. Title: German–Jewish dilemma between the World Wars. II. Title.
    PT2621.R27Z8314 2005
    838′.91209—dc22   2004030067

A catalogue record for this book is available from the British Library

10 9 8 7 6 5 4 3 2 1

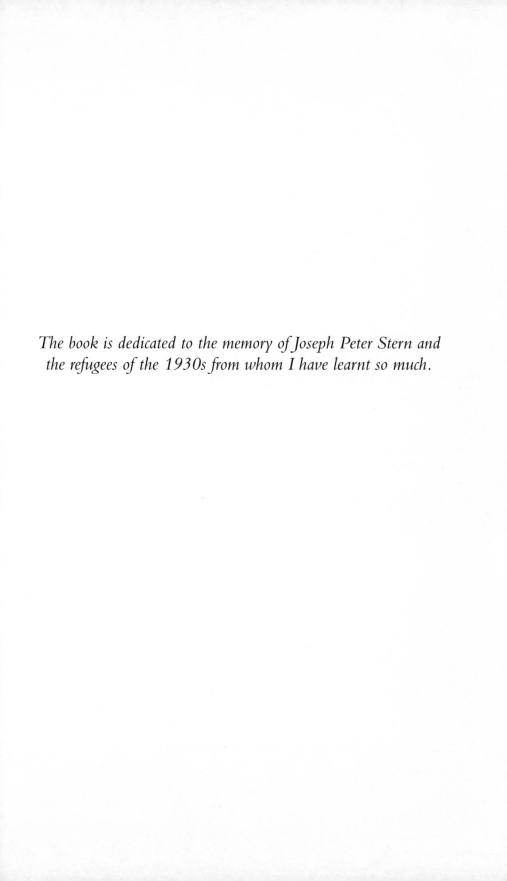

The book is dedicated to the memory of Joseph Peter Stern and the refugees of the 1930s from whom I have learnt so much.

Contents

Illustrations

Preface

When I first encountered Kraus's work forty years ago, his reputation was in eclipse and the magazine *Die Fackel*, which he edited from 1899 until his death in 1936, was virtually inaccessible. But as new editions of his work began to appear in Germany, his critique of militarism and the media struck a chord with a younger generation committed to international reconciliation. The doctoral dissertation on 'Language and the Satirist in the Work of Karl Kraus', which I completed at Cambridge under the guidance of J. P. Stern, presented the satirist as one of the most challenging authors of his day, but it left important issues unresolved. In my attempt to come to terms with Kraus's philosophy of language, I failed to do justice to the full implications of his critique of propaganda and the press. Fortunately, my conception of the role of the satirist avoided biographical simplifications, preparing the ground for a more searching investigation.

The focus of my first volume, *Karl Kraus – Apocalyptic Satirist: Culture and Catastrophe in Habsburg Vienna*, published by Yale in 1986, was on the undertones of war which the satirist analysed during the cataclysmic final years of the Austro-Hungarian Empire. Although relatively little of Kraus's work has been translated, the book helped to popularize his ideas not only in the English-speaking world, but also through Italian, Spanish and German editions. An extended account of his encounter with Freud suggested that they were the two greatest critics of the discontents of civilization to emerge from Habsburg Vienna. The book correlated Kraus's self-appointed mission as a satirist with the dilemma of a Jewish-born journalist who despised both journalists and Jews, longed for a more aristocratic society and converted to Catholicism – and yet became an outspoken critic of the Austrian political elite and the German military–industrial complex.

It has become clear that Kraus's preoccupation with the newspaper press, sometimes dismissed as an obsession, anticipated the pervasive effects of political soundbites and journalistic spin. After tracing the complexities of his anti-war stance, that first volume included a genetic interpretation of his documentary drama of the First World War, *Die letzten Tage der Menschheit* ('The Last Days of Mankind'), a fractured masterpiece that marked the collapse of the old European empires. The book ended with the founding of the Austrian Republic and Kraus's conversion to democracy, suggesting that his new position was that of a disillusioned conservative, rather than an unconditional commitment to democratic politics. Foreshadowing his support for the authoritarian regime of Engelbert Dollfuss, I intimated that this would be 'another story'.

After further years of reading, discussion and research, that story can now be set out in the detail it deserves, chronicling Kraus's engagement with the turbulent developments that linked the two world wars. As a lecturer at Cambridge, my interest in the culture of Vienna prompted me (with my colleague Ritchie Robertson) to found 'Austrian Studies', an annual series launched by Edinburgh University Press in 1990 and continued since 2003 under new editorship by the Modern Humanities Research Association. My research acquired a further dimension after my appointment as professor of German at the University of Sussex, where the Centre for German-Jewish Studies was established in 1994. Consequently, a more explicit emphasis on identity politics and the discourse of race shapes this concluding volume of *Karl Kraus – Apocalyptic Satirist*, highlighting the dilemma of assimilated German-speaking Jews and the destruction of the intellectual and moral culture they embodied. By elucidating a wealth of contextual references, the book presents *Die Fackel* as an indispensable guide to the cultural politics of the inter-war period.

The first section, 'Apocalypse Postponed', shows that Kraus responded to the creation of the German, Austrian and Czechoslovak republics with a defiant hope. Berlin and Prague became almost as significant as Vienna for his defence of republican values, as he invoked the principles of international law against the dual threat of reactionary politics and irresponsible media, and his apocalyptic discourse became increasingly sophisticated, anticipating the ideas of Jacques Derrida and Umberto Eco. To contextualize his polemics against irresponsible journalism, a second section on 'Culture and the Press' maps out the newspaper landscape of Kraus's day and the theory of language that emerged from his critique. His linguistic satire is seen as the link between Popper and Wittgenstein, admired by both without being fully acknowledged by either. If his attack on totalitarian thinking anticipates *The Open Society and its Enemies*, his conception of language as a 'chimera' can be correlated with the duck–rabbit paradox in the *Philosophical Investigations*.

Although his polemics against Jewish-owned newspapers led him to be dubbed a 'Jewish antisemite', Kraus's writings impressed the Zionist Gershom Scholem just as profoundly as the Christians of the Brenner circle. The paradoxes of his position are traced back to his concept of the 'Creative Origin' in a series of chapters dealing with his reflections on childhood, religious faith and erotic love. Personal letters and diaries written by members of his circle throw new light on his emotional life and the poetry it inspired, as well as his rivalry with Franz Werfel and Rainer Maria Rilke. His major polemics of the 1920s are analysed in a central section entitled 'Defending the Republic', which highlights his ambivalent alliance with the Social Democrats as well as his confrontations with the conservative Chancellor Ignaz Seipel, the newspaper magnate Emmerich Bekessy and the Vienna Police Chief Johannes Schober. The frustration of his campaign against increasingly authoritarian tendencies both in Germany and in Austria led him to devote his creative energies to recitals of plays and operettas, from Shakespeare and Nestroy to Offenbach and Brecht. His achievements in this sphere, vividly recalled by Elias Canetti, are assessed under the title 'The Politics of Performance', which shows how the satirist mobilized the resources of 'cultural memory'. Although Kraus claimed to be unmusical, his work proved inspirational for Arnold Schoenberg, Alban Berg and other members of the Second Viennese School.

The legend that Kraus responded to the Nazi seizure of power in 1933 with stunned silence is addressed in the final section of the book, 'Into the Third Reich', which builds on his conception of 'creeping fascism' and of the swastika as the 'twisted cross' of politicized religiosity. Saying an emphatic 'Goodbye to Berlin', he supported the Dollfuss regime not merely as a 'lesser evil', but as an attempt to construct a stable system of government after parliamentary democracy had failed. In *Dritte Walpurgisnacht* ('Third Walpurgis Night', the incisive analysis of National Socialism which he wrote in 1933 but feared to publish, he developed a new style of intertextual satire correlating the Germany of Hitler and Goebbels with motifs from Goethe's *Faust* and the Schlegel–Tieck translations of Shakespeare. My final chapter shows how he took the measure of Nazi ideology by means of an ethics of language that can be clearly differentiated from the ontological speculations of Heidegger. When Kraus finally fell silent, this ethical critique went underground, inspiring incisive commentaries on the events of the Second World War in the diaries of Theodor Haecker and Victor Klemperer.

While contemporaries like Walter Benjamin regarded Kraus as a heroically isolated figure, this book places him within a dynamic field of cultural production, highlighting the social interactions, from the court cases he pursued with his lawyer Oskar Samek to the theatrical projects that earned him the friendship of Brecht. Under the pressures of the inter-war period, the solitude of the author at his writing desk was superseded by new modes of political engagement, reflecting the struggle for control of the streets. In an early aphorism Kraus pictured the scene of writing as a house with many rooms, inhabited by experts on whom the author can call when he needs images from a special discipline: a historian, an economist, a physician, perhaps even a Talmud student who has mastered the jargon of philosophy. Seen in this perspective, his literary career is revealed as a collaborative process in which Austro-German culture reaffirmed its Jewish scriptural heritage.

My own experience of authorship has also been essentially collaborative. All my books have been produced with the help of others, including the

biography of the Turkish poet Nazim Hikmet, co-authored with my wife
Saime Göksu, whose companionship has sustained me in innumerable ways.
The completion of *Karl Kraus – Apocalyptic Satirist* would have been impossible without the support of numerous colleagues, notably Ritchie Robertson,
who read early drafts of every chapter and offered judicious comments on style,
content and structure. A further debt is owed to colleagues with an intimate
knowledge of Kraus's work: to Helmut Arntzen for judicious observations
about research strategies; Gilbert J. Carr and Leo A. Lensing for systematic
advice that has saved me from a number of errors and omissions; Friedrich
Pfäfflin, editor of the electronic version of *Die Fackel* and administrator of the
Kraus Copyright, who has helped with elusive biographical details; Gerald
Krieghofer, an expert on letters written by Kraus under the auspices of his publishing house; Kurt Krolop, whose pioneering research has illuminated many
aspects of Kraus's political writings, not least his links with Czech authors;
Gerald Stieg, whose research ranges from Kraus's alliance with the Brenner
circle to his contacts with the Sorbonne; Christian Wagenknecht, whose
exemplary edition of Kraus's writings is enhanced by such illuminating
annotations; and Sigurd Paul Scheichl, for many years co-editor (with
Wagenknecht) of another important resource, the *Kraus-Hefte*. My debts to
these scholars, as to innumerable published sources, are systematically acknowledged in reference notes and summarized in a select bibliography.

Further thanks are due to numerous friends and colleagues, including
Alexandra Caruso, Dieter Binder, Nicholas Boyle, Amy Colin, Konstanze
Fliedl, Diana and Donald Franklin, Beate Green (née Siegel), Raphael Gross,
Murray Hall, Andrea Hammel, Silke Hassler, Wilhelm Hemecker, Julian
Johnson, Margarete Kohlenbach, Ibrahim Kushchu, William Outhwaite,
Arnold Paucker, Joachim Riedel, John Röhl, Lisa Silverman, Bernhard
Stillfried, Timothy Strauss, Samira Teuteberg, John Theobald, Yusuf Timms,
Joachim Whaley and W. E. Yates. Valuable guidance was received from people
who have sadly not survived to witness the completion of the book: Wolfgang
Bruegel, who recalled the controversies of the 1930s; Julius Carlebach, who
augmented my knowledge of Judaism; Marie Jahoda, who recalled her early
political experiences in Vienna; Kurt Lipstein, who advised on questions of
German law; Joseph Needham, who shared his expertise on the civilization of
China; Erich Heller, who corresponded with me about Kraus's politics; Sophie
Schick, an invaluable guide to archival and biographical sources; and Leopold
Ungar, whose Christian ministry owed so much to Kraus's inspiration.

My research has also benefited from generous institutional support. It could
never have been completed without the study leave and other facilities provided first by the University of Cambridge and Gonville and Caius College,
more recently by the University of Sussex and its Centre for German-Jewish
Studies. Robert Baldock, my editor at the London office of Yale University
Press, has provided patient encouragement for the project throughout its
long gestation, supported by his skilful staff, including Candida Brazil, Ewan

Thompson, Stephen Kent (designer) and Peter James (copy editor). Further support was provided by the Cultural Office of the City of Vienna and by the Internationales Forschungsinstitut für Kulturwissenschaften under the direction of Moritz Csaky and Gotthold Wunberg. The holdings of the Kraus Archive at the Vienna City Library proved an indispensable resource, as did the Tagblatt Archive curated by Eckart Früh. I also benefited from discussions with the staff of the 'Fackel Lexikon', led by Werner Welzig and Evelyn Breiteneder, and with Gabriele Melischek and Josef Seethaler of the Historische Pressedokumentation. In London I consulted the holdings of the Wiener Library, in Prague the unpublished diaries of Sidonie Nadherny at the Statni Oblastni Archive, in New York the Wittels papers at the A. A. Brill Library, and in Washington the letters of Sigmund Freud at the Library of Congress. I am grateful to the Suhrkamp Verlag for permission to quote works by Kraus that are still in copyright, including previously unpublished manuscripts. The result is a book designed to give a comprehensive account of Kraus's career, while not neglecting the friends and foes who inspired him.

Brighton, November 2004
Edward Timms

Abbreviations

Karl Kraus:

BSN   (followed by volume and page number) refers to Karl Kraus, *Briefe an Sidonie Nadherny von Borutin 1913–1936*, ed. Heinrich Fischer and Michael Lazarus, two vols (Munich, 1974)

DW   identifies references to the two editions of Karl Kraus, *Dritte Walpurgisnacht*. Page numbers in roman type refer to the Kösel Verlag edition, ed. Heinrich Fischer (Munich, 1952); page numbers in italics refer to the Suhrkamp Verlag edition, ed. Christian Wagenknecht (Frankfurt, 1989)

F   is the abbreviation for *Die Fackel* (followed by issue and page number)

FS   (followed by volume and page number) identifies references to Karl Kraus, *Frühe Schriften*, ed. Johannes J. Braakenburg, three vols (Munich, 1979–88)

Ib and IN   (followed by inventory number) identify documents from the Manuscript Section of the Kraus Archive, Vienna City Library

P   (followed by volume and page number) refers to *Karl Kraus contra ... Die Prozeßakten der Kanzlei Oskar Samek*, ed. Hermann Böhm, four vols (Vienna, 1995–7)

S   (followed by volume and page number) refers to the twenty-volume Suhrkamp edition of Karl Kraus, *Schriften*, ed. Christian Wagenknecht (Frankfurt, 1987–94). Further details are given in the Bibliographical Note.

Other sources:

ADÖ   (followed by volume and page number): *Außenpolitische Dokumente der Republik Österreich 1918–1938*, ed. Klaus Koch, Walter Rauscher and Arnold Suppan (Munich, 1993)

AST   (followed by date): Arthur Schnitzler, *Tagebücher*, ed. Werner Welzig (Vienna, 1981–2000)

AZ   (followed by date) identifies quotations from the *Arbeiter-Zeitung*

BP   (followed by page number) identifies quotations from *Bekessy's Panoptikum: Eine Zeitschrift gegen Dummheit und Lüge*, No. 1 (April 1928)

GST   (followed by date) identifies references to Gershom Scholem, *Tagebücher nebst Aufsätzen und Entwürfen bis 1923*, ed. Karlfried Gründer and Friedrich Niewöhner, 2 vols (Frankfurt, 1995 & 2000)

M   (followed by page number) refers to *Freud and the Child Woman: The Memoirs of Fritz Wittels*, ed. Edward Timms (New Haven, 1995)

NFP   (followed by date) identifies quotations from the *Neue Freie Presse*

RP   (followed by date) identifies quotations from the *Reichspost*

ST   (followed by date) identifies quotations from *Die Stunde*

PART ONE

APOCALYPSE
POSTPONED

CHAPTER 1

The Post-War German Mentality

Patriotic Germans, brought up with an unshakeable faith in their destiny, found the catastrophe of November 1918 incomprehensible. Economic growth, military power, technical innovation and organizational efficiency had won their country a dominant position in Europe, while the military struggle of the First World War, culminating in the defeat of Russia, opened up visions of a 'Mitteleuropa' under German domination. By March 1918 an area of eastern Europe larger than the Reich itself, stretching from the Baltic to the Black Sea, was under German control, consolidated by the Treaty of Brest-Litovsk. This was followed by a summer offensive on the western front that inspired hopes of final victory before American reinforcements arrived. In mid-September Thomas Mann returned from his holidays in a confident mood. His *Betrachtungen eines Unpolitischen* ('Meditations of an Unpolitical Man'), an elaborate defence of the anti-democratic culture of Germany, was just rolling off the presses in Leipzig, and a diary entry of 12 September shows that his faith in Imperial Germany was still intact. But a few weeks later he was astonished to learn from Maximilian Harden, a journalist with influential connections, that the western front could no longer be held. The government was authorized by the High Command to negotiate a 'capitulation with surrender of Alsace-Lorraine'.[1]

Mann's diaries of the following months reflect the bewilderment of educated Germans at being confronted with the unthinkable: defeat and revolution. Conservative ideologists resolved this crisis of historical explanation by constructing a theory that the German army, 'undefeated in the field', had been betrayed by disloyal elements at home: striking industrial workers, socialists and pacifists, Bolsheviks and Jews. According to this seductive theory, it was not Hindenburg and Ludendorff who were responsible for defeat, but the 'November criminals': Matthias Erzberger, the Catholic who negotiated the Armistice; Philipp Scheidemann, the Social Democrat who proclaimed the Republic; and Friedrich Ebert, the first Weimar President, who was responsible for the signing of the Treaty of Versailles. The abortive attempts at communist revolution in Berlin, Munich and Budapest during the early months of 1919 strengthened the suspicion that the Central Powers had been betrayed by some mysterious enemy within their own camp, rather than defeated by external foes. This feeling that a triumphant nation had been cheated of victory provides a key to the post-war German mentality.

Innocent Victimizers and the Rise of the Swastika

The word 'mentality', popularized by French anthropologists, has been criticized as a definition of collective thinking that ignores individual variations.[2] Kraus disliked the word, putting it into scare-quotes to distance himself from what he regarded as modish jargon, but he used it to equate the so-called 'mentality' with the 'continuing political horror of post-war Germany' (F 787–94, 7). Where 'post-war', in the present book, is used in the general sense of 'after the war of 1914–18', Kraus gives it a specific meaning when applied to Germany and Austria, countries so scarred by the trauma of defeat that they were incapable of adjusting to the new democratic order. The key to this destabilizing 'mentality', noted in another passage of the mid-1920s, is 'self-righteousness' (F 706–11, 35). The belief that military–industrial power had an ethically sanctioned mission inspired the 'bankrupt ideology of German world conquest' (F 514–18, 50).

The pages of *Die Fackel* contain ample evidence of the dream of German domination, and Kraus's essays of the First World War, reprinted in 1919 in the two-volume edition of *Weltgericht*, include a comprehensive critique of war aims. The focus is not simply on the brutalities of modern warfare, but on the propaganda apparatus that sustained it, especially the attempt to clothe the profane reality of war in an 'aura of sanctity' ('Heiligenschein', F 413–17, 19–20). At the heart of that ideology lay the conviction that Germany was fighting a 'defensive war' sustained by ethical ideas – the so-called 'Ideas of 1914'.[3] The invasion of France (it was claimed) began only after French planes had launched an unprovoked attack by dropping bombs on Nuremberg, while the invasion of Russia was also an act of 'defence', designed to pre-empt the Russian High Command. Kaiser Wilhelm II, who was convinced that the Germans had God on their side, greeted victory in the east with words that are highlighted in *Die Fackel*: 'What a transformation through the will of God!' (F 474–83, 155). During a public reading in Berlin on 8 May 1918 Kraus mocked this pseudo-religious rhetoric (F 484–98, 143–4), and in November he was able to turn the tables by applying this phrase to the defeat of Germany (F 499–500, 3).

To intensify his critique of aggressive self-righteousness, Kraus formulated a new psychological insight. Taking up the motif of the 'innocent victim', he inverted it into the 'innocent victimizer' ('verfolgende Unschuld'; F 406–12, 158). This can be linked with the debate about atrocities which dominated the media during the first twelve months of the war. After the German invasion of

Belgium, the western press abounded in stories about the shooting of civilians, accompanied by the wanton destruction of Louvain and other towns. For example, on 26 August 1914 the commander of the Landsturm Battalion Gotha, Major von Hedemann, ordered the execution of 122 Belgian civilians as a reprisal for alleged attacks on German troops. They were killed in groups of ten by firing squads, and the last victims had to climb on the mound of their predecessors to be despatched. Although the shooting of civilians was banned under the Hague Convention of 1907, the Germans were convinced that their actions were legitimate, alleging that those executed were 'francs-tireurs', guilty of treacherous attacks from behind the lines. However, a recent study has revealed that the soldiers shot from behind were almost certainly the victims of 'friendly fire', inadvertently killed by their own side during the chaos of the advance.[4] The myth of the 'francs-tireurs' nevertheless made it possible for military commanders to authorize reprisals with a good conscience, foreshadowing the ruthless actions against 'partisans' during the Second World War.

The belief that you are the innocent party means that aggression can be projected from perpetrator to victim. Hence the complacent accounts of stringing up Belgian civilians by military commanders like Manfred von Richthofen, quoted in Die Fackel in October 1917 (F 462–71, 148–9). Kraus also applies the concept of 'innocent victimizers' to more general aspects of German policy. In February 1918, after the International Red Cross had issued its appeal for the warring parties to cease using poison gas, the German authorities took this as confirmation of the superiority of their own weapons. Although they claimed to be committed to international law, they refused to make any concessions for fear of being 'outmanoeuvred' – further evidence of the physiognomy of the 'innocent victimizer' (F 474–83, 35–6). During the 1920s Kraus repeatedly used this motif to define the German post-war 'mentality' (F 531–43, 78). The self-pity that inspired the ideology of revenge was epitomized by the myth of the 'stab-in-the-back', which enabled Hindenburg to claim that the army, 'undefeated in the field', had been betrayed by defeatists – socialists, pacifists and Jews (Fig. 1).[5] This ignores the fact that in autumn 1918 it was the German army that went on strike, as soldiers 'abandoned their units in their hundreds of thousands'.[6] In an ironic riposte Kraus repudiated this notorious 'Dolchstoßlegende': it was absurd for right-wingers to imply that the army had been stabbed in the back by the socialists, let alone by himself (F 632–9, 8 & 36). In an essay of August 1924, published to mark the tenth anniversary of the war, he recapitulated the deceptions used to legitimate the Central Powers as 'innocent victimizers': the response to the death of Archduke Franz Ferdinand, the legends about bombs on Nuremberg and the myth that Germany was the 'victim of a world conspiracy'. And he ridiculed the claim that 'aggressive' Serbia had forced Austria-Hungary into a war of 'self-defence', showing that it was based on forged documents (F 657–67, 20–6).

This process of projecting aggressive feelings from perpetrator to victim generated the myth of a 'Jewish conspiracy'. If the Germans had failed, it must be

1 'Germans, remember!': cartoon of the alleged 'stab in the back'

because their world-historical antagonists had succeeded. A chorus of influential voices, from Treitschke to Chamberlain, had been proclaiming for decades that 'the Jews are our misfortune' – 'Die Juden sind unser Unglück'.[7] When at last, in 1918, misfortune actually arrived, the explanation was readily to hand, and with the lifting of censorship antisemitism entered the mainstream of German politics. This development was all the more startling because Germany had positioned itself during the war as 'protector of the Jews', challenging both the French chauvinism that had victimized Dreyfus and the Russian penchant for pogroms.[8] The mechanisms of projection now ascribed the German strategy for domination to 'the Jews', a myth disseminated by *The Protocols of the Elders of Zion*, published in German in January 1920 under the title *Die Geheimnisse der Weisen von Zion*. Although this pamphlet was soon exposed as a forgery, it became a best-seller in Germany, since it purported to provide conclusive proof of the worldwide Jewish conspiracy. The Kaiser, in exile in Holland, was convinced that the 'Elders' were responsible for his downfall, while the *Protocols* also served as an inspiration for Adolf Hitler.[9]

It is sometimes claimed that Kraus was blind to the rise of fascism and rendered speechless by Hitler's seizure of power.[10] But to the attentive reader his writings offer an abundance of insights into the fascist mentality and the social mechanisms that promoted it. In December 1917, when victory on the eastern front appeared to have established German military supremacy, he recited his 'Song of the Pan-German' ('Lied des Alldeutschen'), an outspoken satire on the ideology of German domination. It is a mystery why he was not arrested on the spot, as Bertrand Russell was in Britain for more cautious criticisms of the American allies. It was not until November 1918, after the lifting of censorship, that this text could be published (F 499–500, 6–12), and during the following months Kraus repeatedly read scenes from his great documentary drama *Die letzten Tage der Menschheit* ('The Last Days of Mankind'), satirizing the militarist mentality. In January 1920 he included 'Kaiser Wilhelm and the Generals', the scene ridiculing the pathological behaviour of Wilhelm II, at public readings in Berlin and Munich, provoking reactions which he analysed in a further critique of 'German national pride'. Adapting a homely Jewish anecdote, he suggests that 'Pan-Germany', restrained by the policemen of the Entente from committing a public nuisance, is still furtively pissing in its pants, but when the policeman asks: 'Why are you laughing?', the answer is: 'because you think I've stopped' (F 531–43, 20). Kraus read this prophetic anecdote in public on 7 March after his return to Vienna, and within a week the Kapp putsch in Berlin confirmed his worst fears. Although the putsch was defeated by a general strike, the reactionary Gustav von Kahr succeeded in displacing the Social Democratic government of Bavaria, and Munich soon became the centre of Nazi agitation.

Kraus's demythologizing of the figure of Wilhelm II was sixty years ahead of its time, but his contemporaries refused to acknowledge that their revered leader was pathologically irresponsible.[11] Munich in 1920 was teeming with paramilitary groups, and Kraus showed considerable courage in choosing to give one of his readings on the deposed Kaiser's birthday, 27 January. It was less than a year since Kurt Eisner, head of the Bavarian republican government, had been assassinated, and the short-lived communist republic had provoked a violent backlash. The common factor uniting the far right, from the Thule Society to the National Socialists, was the conviction that 'the Jews' were to blame for the collapse of 'Germanic' values.[12] Kraus's plain speaking about the war led him to be singled out for attack in the *Miesbacher Anzeiger*, organ of the Nazi movement in the Bavarian provinces. An anonymous article, published in April 1921 under the title 'Anti-Aryan', incited its readers to physical assault, recalling that Eisner had recently been 'executed', the pacifist Gustav Landauer also 'done in', while the sexual reformer 'Magnus Spinatfeld' (Dr Magnus Hirschfeld) had been severely beaten. Karl Kraus, 'the son of five Polish Jews', was to be next on the list. Responding to this article, Kraus suggested that the person responsible must be Ludwig Thoma, the former contributor to the radical journals *März* and *Simplicissimus*, who in the pre-war period had been one of his staunchest allies (F 568–71, 50–1). This hunch proved correct: the war had transformed Thoma into a fanatical nationalist and an ally of Dietrich Eckart, one of the founders of the Nazi Party. Nothing could illustrate more clearly the brutalization of political discourse than the hundred-odd articles which Thoma published in the *Miesbacher Anzeiger* in his final years, taking precautions to conceal his identity. While *Die letzten Tage der Menschheit* placed Kraus in the front line of resistance against German revanchism, the trauma of defeat had converted Bavaria's leading satirist into a fanatical antisemite.[13]

Kraus's grasp of the political situation is indicated by a comment of January 1921, when he identified Germany as the country 'where the swastika rises above the ruins of the global conflagration' (F 557–60, 59). The post-war economic misery had created a breeding ground for antisemitism, and 'eastern Jews', the favourite target of right-wing agitators, were often the victims of physical assaults, culminating in the Scheunenviertel riots in Berlin on 5–6 November 1923.[14] On 12 November, in the aftermath of the Berlin riots and the Hitler putsch in Munich, Kraus reminded his audience of these prophetic words: the 'devil' he had painted on the wall three years earlier had at last been let loose. In a series of hastily composed strophes in the style of Nestroy, he mocked Hitler, Ludendorff and Kahr. At least among the stars, he concludes, the constellation of the 'swastika' ('Hakenkreuz') is not yet visible (F 640–8, 108–10). The swastika, a symbol with occult origins, made such a strong impression on Kraus's imagination that it was soon to develop into a leitmotif.[15] In *Die Fackel* of the 1920s there are dozens of references to this ominous symbol and the proto-fascist groups associated with it – the 'Hakenkreuzler'.[16] This word, for which the English equivalent would be 'Swastiklers', included members of other right-wing groups as well as the National Socialists.[17] In Austria it was not always possible to distinguish Nazis from the Heimwehr militiamen, whose cockade earned them the name 'Hahnenschwänzler' ('Cockaders'; F 827–33, 43). The fascist threat was difficult to pin down, but Kraus identified it in the Sudetenland as well as Germany and Austria, prompting a Nazi newspaper to describe him as 'a deadly enemy of the *völkisch* idea' (cited F 657–67, 79).

Kraus was particularly sensitive to the infiltration of the legal system. After observing that the typical court official 'usually wears the swastika' (F 613–21, 13), he protested that 'if a Nazi or a monarchist is presiding', they will condemn a socialist for an offence which they condone among their own followers (F 640–8, 136). In 1924 he noted the extreme case of a judge who actually urged a Swastikler to use his revolver – and escaped without reprimand (F 657–67, 210). Kraus had no illusions about the dangers of right-wing violence, which he traced back to the resentments caused by military defeat. This is the theme of his poem 'Immer feste druff!' ('Hit 'em where it hurts!'), a slogan borrowed from Hindenburg. The Germans who are fighting each other with knives on the streets will, Kraus suggests, ultimately plunge the world into another war in the name of 'Deutschland über alles' (F 544–5, 8). He read this poem on a number of occasions, for example on 9 May 1920 in the aftermath of the Kapp putsch and again after the Hitler putsch of November 1923.[18]

Kraus's analysis of fascism can be traced from prophetic aphorisms published in *Die Fackel* of 1915 through comments on the Mussolini cult to his comprehensive critique of National Socialism in *Dritte Walpurgisnacht* ('Third Walpurgis Night'). The starting point is his analysis of the militarization of society during the First World War. For him, as for Hitler, the war had an exemplary function: in one case as a salutary warning, in the other as heroic ideal. Kraus's repudiation of the ethos of military heroism dates from his remarkable address of November 1914, 'In dieser großen Zeit'. During the following twelve months, while the patriotic press was chalking up a string of German victories, his sense of foreboding deepened. The seventy-five pages of aphorisms which he published in October 1915 include the most prophetic of his political observations:

> The returning soldier will nevertheless not readily allow himself to be reintegrated into civilian life. He will break through into the home front and start the real war there. He will grab for himself the successes which have been denied him, and the war will be mere child's play by comparison with the peace that will break out there. May God protect us from the offensive that awaits us then. A terrible activity, no longer constrained by any system of command, will start wielding weapons and pursuing pleasures in every sphere of life, and more death and disease will come into the world than could ever have been contrived by the war itself. (F 406–12, 141)

Written during Kraus's most conservative phase, this prophecy was to be confirmed by the Russian Revolution of 1917, but he was also thinking of Germany. One of his notebooks with comments jotted down in 1915 contains not only the ubiquitous slogan 'shoulder to shoulder', but also the prophetic phrase 'Germany a concentration camp' (Fig. 2).[19]

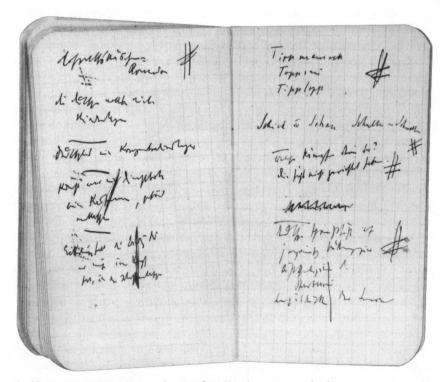

2 'Germany a concentration camp': a page from Kraus's wartime notebook

The prophecy about returning soldiers acquired an even greater topicality by the time it was republished in book form in *Nachts* ('At Night', October 1918) and *Die letzten Tage der Menschheit* (1919 and 1922). The influenza epidemic of 1918–19 did indeed cause more deaths than the war itself, while bloody battles on the streets of Berlin and Munich, Budapest and Lemberg, confirmed his forebodings about civil war. In Austria, too, there was fighting on the streets, and five police officers were killed during an attempted communist putsch in Vienna on 17 April, while twenty demonstrators were shot dead on 15 June.[20] Kraus's concept of the struggle that would dominate the home front anticipates the activities of the right-wing veterans who formed the Freikorps and were instrumental in defeating the Spartacus revolt in Berlin, during which Karl Liebknecht and Rosa Luxemburg were brutally done to death. Moreover, disaffected ex-soldiers provided a primary source of recruitment for National Socialism. The 'experience of battle' ('Fronterlebnis') transformed many a young man into a brutal streetfighter, and in the extreme case, which proved to be prototypical, a sensitive artist emerged from the trenches as a power-hungry demagogue.[21]

Kraus recognized that the Weimar Republic had two faces: the party struggle on the public stage and the twilight of conspiratorial violence. Although he showed little interest in election campaigns, he was aware that legitimate state power was threatened by paramilitary organizations which made 'systematic use of non-legal, extra-state means of violence'.[22] There were numerous spokesmen for this militarized mentality, the most sophisticated being provided by Ernst Jünger in his glorification of the military virtues. Klaus Theweleit has compiled a fascinating study of proto-fascist Freikorps writings and images.[23] But confirmation of the accuracy of Kraus's 1915 prophecy can also be found in documents reprinted in *Die Fackel* itself, since he was tireless in clipping reports about the destructive conduct of ex-soldiers traumatized by the war. The Death's Head Hussars, he observed with reference to events in Germany in 1919, may have been repulsed during the Battle of the Somme, but they are now trying to conquer Germany on the streets of Berlin (F 521–30, 163). Citing a court case of November 1920, in which the accused blamed the war for teaching him how to kill, Kraus suggested that the conflict had brutalized the whole of mankind (F 554–6, 4).

The self-perpetuating criminality of modern warfare led Kraus to direct his most powerful indictment against the officer caste, even though he had numbered several officers among his personal friends and in October 1915, during his conservative phase, had paid tribute to the probity of professional soldiers (F 406–12, 160–3). The horrors of the final years of the war led him to reverse his judgement, as the evidence of atrocities became overwhelming. 'One shouldn't generalize', an army commander had declared in an attempt to minimize his culpability, providing the ironic leitmotif for the twenty-page indictment of the officer corps published in the essay 'Nachruf' ('Valediction') in January 1919. Acknowledging that there are honourable exceptions, Kraus concludes that if only one officer in ten was guilty of maltreating his subordinates, that in itself transforms 'militarism into infamy', converting harmless civilians into 'compulsive criminals' (F 501–7, 25 & 32).

At War with Nature: The Buffalo and the Herd

Kraus contrasts the destructive consequences of militarism with a vision of the natural world which acquires a critical edge at a time when Darwinistic concepts were being used to justify physical brutality. According to this ideology, man is destined by nature to be a 'hunter', driven by his 'blood' to carry out acts of aggression against weaker ethnic groups. For German intellectuals this emphasis on the instincts became conflated with Nietzsche's cult of the superman. Nietzsche's response to Darwin involved a series of sophisticated discriminations, but the publication of his posthumous writings under the title *The Will to Power* helped to confer intellectual respectability on the warlike virtues. These ideas, propagated by war heroes like Manfred von Richthofen, were seminal to the emergence of fascism. Richthofen was a cavalry officer turned air ace, whose book *Der rote Kampfflieger*, published in 1917, presents the killing fields of the First World War as a 'hunting ground'. Shooting down British fighter pilots inspires in Richthofen the same 'thrill of the hunt' that he feels when hunting bison in the forests of Bialowicz. Kraus was so appalled by this celebration of 'Teutonic blood' that he reprinted a photograph of Richthofen and his staff together with excerpts from the book (F 462–73, 148–57).

To counteract this bloodthirsty rhetoric, the satirist invoked the vision of another Germany. Kraus's pre-war writings had celebrated the power of eros, but he now reconfigures nature as an ontological principle. Poets, he notes in November 1916, quoting Schiller's essay on 'Naive and Sentimental Poetry', are the 'avengers of nature' (F 443–4, 13). Kraus's defence of the 'created world' of plants and animals ('die Kreatur') also derives from the Enlightenment, which saw nature as a manifestation of the divine that is threatened by human aggression – the theme of one of his favourite poems, the ballad 'Der wilde Jäger' ('The Wild Hunter') by Gottfried August Bürger.[24] His satire on the First World War highlights the discrepancy between advances in military technology and primitive methods of transport. Its gigantic field-guns had a range of up to fifty miles, but like the war chariots of the Hittites they were still drawn by horses. Motorized traction was relatively rare, while tanks did not make any impact until the final year of the war, and the strategic railway lines could bring men and materials only as far as the railheads. Motive power for the transport of equipment to the front line was provided by horses, oxen, mules, donkeys and dogs. The fate of these animals is repeatedly lamented in *Die Fackel*. In April 1916, ironizing the language of Nietzsche, Kraus suggests that animals are 'the most tragic victims of the will to power', since they bear no responsibility for the system of military conscription (F 418–22, 42). Their sufferings are prominently featured in the visionary sequence that concludes *Die letzten Tage der*

Menschheit: dogs used to tow machine guns into battle; horses forced to carry pieces of artillery so heavy that they cut through the flesh of their backs; oxen dying from exhaustion as they carry refugees through the battle zone; and the 1,200 horses who were drowned when the ship transporting them was sunk by a U-boat, commanded by the vainglorious Count Dohna-Schlodien. The fate of animals victimized on the home front is recorded with equal acerbity. Thousands of dogs were slaughtered because their owners were no longer able to feed them, and in April 1917 Kraus noted that the canine population of Vienna had decreased by 13,000 (F 454–6, 59–60). Among grotesque episodes picked up in *Die Fackel* is a report about a tram conductor accused of having killed and eaten a stray that followed him home (F 426–30, 90–6); and another about a circus artiste unable to find any engagement for her troupe of performing dogs who has killed and eaten them one by one (F 462–71, 9).

Although Kraus at times appears to be losing his sense of proportion, there were grounds for regarding the rights of animals as a political issue. In November 1916 he accused the Social Democratic *Arbeiter-Zeitung* of adopting towards animals a 'pre-revolutionary position', after the paper had mocked a British organization for launching an appeal on behalf of 'our dumb friends'. The socialists' disregard for animals was accompanied by a glorification of the conquest of nature as one of the heroic achievements of the war. Kraus insists that this argument is flawed. Human beings, innocent though they may be individually, are collectively responsible for the machines that are destroying them. Whether at the front or in munitions factories, they are actively supporting the war, whereas animals are being victimized by forces over which they have no control (F 437–42, 30–2). Kraus goes on to suggest that cruelty to animals is the response of people who have themselves been brutalized by war: 'Isn't everything that is going on around us the warmed-up vengeance of superiors who were once subordinates?' (F 457–61, 96). Where Marxists assume that an exploited class will finally turn against its oppressors, Kraus suggests that oppression will merely be extended further down the scale. Next to the animals in this chain of brutalization come the 'enemy' themselves. 'Subaltern cruelty' is linked to an ideology of domination which gives the Germans the right to despise other ethnic groups as inferior species. Russians are vermin to be exterminated as ruthlessly as a cook would crush blackbeetles on the kitchen floor, according to a Viennese pedagogue (cited F 426–30, 63).

In glossing the attitude of the *Arbeiter-Zeitung* as 'pre-revolutionary', Kraus was questioning a technocratic form of Marxism which forgets that nature, not human labour, is the primary source of wealth. At the end of the war he was gratified to discover that his analysis of the chain of brutalization was endorsed by that most principled of German revolutionaries, Rosa Luxemburg. A gifted young woman from a Jewish background in Tsarist-occupied Poland, Luxemburg acquired German nationality through an arranged marriage and emerged around 1900 as one of the leading theoreticians and most charismatic public speakers of the Social Democratic Party. Her campaign against militarism led the Prussian authorities to imprison her for several months in February 1914, and she was taken into 'protective custody' in May 1916 after leading a protest meeting against the war in Berlin with Karl Liebknecht. Her enforced leisure in a fortress prison in Posen provided scope for the rediscovery of her interest in botany, but it was at the women's prison in Breslau that she had her most memorable experience, described in a letter to her friend Sonja Liebknecht:

> Oh, Sonitschka, I have had here a profoundly sad experience, in the yard where I take my walks there are often army waggons, fully loaded with sacks or old military coats and shirts, often blood-stained. They are unloaded here, distributed to the cells, patched, and then loaded up again and delivered to the army. Recently a waggon arrived drawn not by horses but by buffaloes. [. . .] The load was piled so high that the buffaloes were unable to cross the threshold of the main gate. The soldier in charge, a brutal fellow, began to strike the animals so hard with the blunt end of his whip-handle that one of the women warders indignantly took him to task, asking whether he had no sympathy with the animals. 'No one has any sympathy with us humans,' he replied with a malicious smile and struck the animals even harder.

Quoting this passage in *Die Fackel* in July 1920 (F 546–50, 5–9), Kraus suggested that the spirit of this Jewish woman revolutionary, clubbed to death by rifle butts, places her on a level with German nature poets like Goethe and Claudius. The parallels between the positions of Kraus and Luxemburg are remarkable.[25] Both authors invoked a vision of the original harmony in order to challenge the idea of nature red in tooth and claw, so often exploited to justify military conflict and racial domination. Kraus restated his position even more forcefully when he received a letter from an aristocratic Megaera who sneered at Luxemburg as one of those 'hysterical women' who are bound to come to a sticky end if they persist in stirring up trouble. This led him to affirm not only the 'humanity' of Luxemburg's attitude to animals, but also the value of communism as a threat to the 'life-destroying ideology' of the land-owning class (F 554–6, 6–12).

Such ideas about nature were dismissed as 'sentimental' by a generation nurtured on Nietzsche. The numerous comments scattered through the pages of *Die Fackel* suggest that Kraus was one of the few writers of his generation who resisted the philosopher's spell, although there are parallels with Nietzsche's proposition that 'every profound spirit needs a mask'.[26] Kraus certainly admired the philosopher's conception of prose as an artistic medium (F 254–5, 25), but he was hostile to his cult of the superman: 'The superman is a premature ideal which presupposes the existence of mankind' (F 264–5, 24). This formulation presupposes a Kantian conception of autonomous moral beings – an ideal yet to be achieved. In April 1912 Kraus defined himself as an author who 'does not know Nietzsche' (F 345–6, 37). It is possible that his intellectual debt was greater than he was prepared to admit, but looking back over his career in 1934, he described Nietzsche as one of the 'diseases of childhood' that he had miraculously escaped (F 890–905, 46).

The experiences of the First World War obliged Kraus to take Nietzsche's influence seriously, since the philosopher was construed first as spokesman for German imperialism and then as prophet for the Nazi seizure of power. In each phase, his focus is on the propaganda impact of Nietzsche's ideas, rather than their philosophical value. During the war, he showed how slogans like the 'Will to Power' were being exploited for propaganda purposes, while in the post-war period he focused on Nietzsche's style, his moral relativism, his exaggerated polemics, and the inflated rhetoric of *Also sprach Zarathustra* ('Thus Spake Zarathustra'). He never lost sight of the devastating effect on the post-war German mentality of the terms 'superman' and 'will to power', which appealed both to bellicose nationalists and to sophisticated intellectuals. In an essay of November 1921, which includes perceptive comments on Nietzsche's style, he gave a more coherent account of the philosopher's responsibility for the 'disparate cultural evils of German worship of power and German literariness'. This acknowledges that Nietzsche had second thoughts about his 'philosophy of cheerful cruelty' and that German militarism was a 'caricature' of his 'idea of power'. But Kraus cannot absolve him of responsibility for the abuse of his ideas by right-wing pressure groups, since he played into their hands with concepts like the 'blond beast', the 'innocent conscience of the predator' and the despicable 'morality of the herd': 'We have come to recognize, with a painful, indeed physical proximity, that even the morality of herd animals is superior to a morality that treats them merely as beasts to be slaughtered, and that the last will of mankind on its deathbed cannot be the Will to Power.' The concept of the 'superman' deserves to be treated with derisive laughter, while Zarathustra's philosophy is contrasted with that of Kant in the satirical poem 'Der Antichrist' ('The Anti-Christ', F 577–82, 62–5).

A preoccupation with the Kantian concept of 'human dignity' ('Menschenwürde') helps to explain Kraus's hostility to the notion of the 'superman'. The 'categorical imperative', he observes in January 1919, has been perverted into a system of military discipline designed to inculcate the 'will to power' (F 501–7, 113). In October 1925 he engaged with the more sophisticated position of Hans Vaihinger, the philosopher who suggested that Nietzsche's concepts are best understood as 'fictional constructs'. This is the basis of his celebrated book, *Die Philosophie des Als Ob* ('The Philosophy of As If'), an exposition of philosophical indeterminacy which was particularly influential during the inter-war period. Once again Kraus appealed to the values of the German Enlightenment, in this case Schiller, whose principle of 'absolute humanity' is reaffirmed as an antidote to the Nietzschean 'relativity principle of morality'. He recognizes that Nietzsche paid for his critical insights with the 'tragic suffering of a spirit answerable to himself', but Nietzsche is condemned both for undermining moral certainties and for disseminating slogans to fill the vacuum (F 697–705, 115–19). This argument was taken a stage further in October 1932, when Kraus cited Zarathustra's proposition that 'the good war sanctifies every cause'. Such doctrines, he concluded, find their consecration in the swastika (F 876–84, 49–50). This anticipates his critique of the fascist appropriation of Nietzsche in *Dritte Walpurgisnacht*, where the murderous activities of Nazi gangs are equated with the phenomenon Nietzsche abhorred: the 'morality of herd animals' (DW 59–64/72–7).

Creeping Fascism and the German Saviour

Although Kraus was sensitive to the threat of fascism, he preferred to approach politics obliquely – through a snippet of quotation or a revealing turn of phrase. The subtlety of his approach has led even knowledgeable readers to suggest that the satirist may really have had 'nothing to say' about National Socialism.[27] Kraus was conscious of the difficulty of using words to resist physical violence. The most effective polemic against the Nazis, he noted in August 1924, would be 'a bucket of water over their heads' (F 657–67, 81). But if satire is powerless against street violence, it may still illuminate the underlying ideology. Decisive events like the 'March on Rome' in 1922 pass unrecorded in *Die Fackel*, but when fascism begins to become fashionable among intellectuals, he is quick to pick up the danger signals. What interests Kraus is not Italian politics, but the Mussolini cult propagated by the press – the theme of an article published in June 1923 under the title 'The Taming of Mussolini'. In this collage of quotations, interwoven with an incisive commentary, he notes that Mussolini is regarded as 'the man with muscles of iron and a will of iron'. But the dictator could hardly have been more courteous when he welcomed to Rome the Austrian author and opera singer Lucy Weidt. This impressionable visitor reports to her readers back home that Mussolini is a delightful man, who even appreciated her parting gift of a bunch of flowers. Taking up the 'muscles of iron' motif, Kraus draws attention to the political implications of the scenario in which a woman succumbs to the charm of dictators, drawing a parallel with the Hungarian leader, Admiral Horthy:

> She would even have made a hit with Horthy. Even he would have said a polite goodbye, if Frau Weidt had presented him with violets. Why bless you even Hitler could not have suppressed a human impulse. From many an Austrian breast, weighed down by creeping bolshevism, the sigh has been wrung: A Horthy is what we really need, or a Rinaldini, or one of those other stars with muscles of iron who know how to restore order and will not tolerate messy corpses lying around. We now can see that under such a regime even the hearts of the Viennese would be satisfied.

These prophetic words incorporate motifs from Nestroy's *Judith and Holofernes* about the tyrant who cannot tolerate messy corpses. Between Frau Weidt as Judith and this modern Holofernes, Kraus imagines the following exchange: 'They even told me – I can't believe it of such a gentleman – that you eat Jews for breakfast.' 'It's not that bad, I'm simply in the habit of destroying everything.' The suave Mussolini claims to love Vienna, even to have attended a performance of Schnitzler's *Reigen* (*La Ronde*). Presumably, Kraus comments, he must have enjoyed the demonstration by Viennese fascists that disrupted the play (F 622–31, 5–7). Kraus twice read this gloss in public in order to drive home his warning against the blandishments of fascism. During the late 1920s he made only occasional references to the Mussolini cult, which was widespread among western intellectuals. In September 1930 he noted that even Theodor Wolff, proprietor of the liberal *Berliner Tageblatt*, was providing publicity for Mussolini (F 838–44, 42), and two years later he recorded his horror at hearing that the Italian dictator had been awarded the Goethe Medal (F 876–84, 78).

In a period when bourgeois ideologists were obsessed with 'creeping bolshevism', Kraus identified the even more ominous danger of 'creeping fascism' ('schleichender Faszismus'; F 820–6, 16). This phrase suggests that fascism is an amorphous phenomenon that expresses itself in many forms, not least the discourse of charismatic leadership.[28] The Germans, too, were longing for a strong man who would redeem them. As early as May 1920 Kraus pinpointed this messianic discourse. A Christian writer quoted in *Die Fackel* had expressed the longing for a German saviour who will redeem the nation: 'How we long for this *German saviour*! Already we sense his radiant figure in the distance' (F 531–43, 60–2). Kraus italicized the key phrase to show his contempt for the spurious religiosity underlying right-wing politics. During the 1920s it was by no means clear who would emerge as the saviour, and Kraus remained alert to the dangers of 'creeping monarchism' (F 632–9, 168). In August 1924 he published the Kaiser's appalling marginal comments on the proceedings of the Hague Peace Conference: 'I shit on all the agreements!' (F 657–67, 26–7). However, a restoration of the Hohenzollerns seemed unlikely, since the headlines were dominated by military heroes like Scheer and Tirpitz, Ludendorff and Hindenburg, and a typical news item, reprinted in *Die Fackel* in November 1921, reported that Ludendorff had been awarded an honorary doctorate by the University of Königsberg (Kaliningrad). Ludendorff was praised in the university citation as the liberator with an '*iron hand*', indeed as the '*future saviour and avenger of our people*'. Citing these phrases in emphatic type, Kraus reminded his readers that Ludendorff, the man with 'the iron hand and the brazen cheek', had fled to Sweden with a false passport after the German defeat (F 577–82, 94–5). This is one of a number of documents cited to express the longing for a Führer, including a reference of autumn 1923 to a right-wing author named Artur Zickler as '*the first German Fascist*'. To challenge this pretentious nonsense, Kraus asks why Hitler is being ignored (F 632–9, 141).

At this date Hitler was an obscure right-wing agitator, but Kraus was among the first to recognize that when it came to political violence he was in a class of his own. His eye was caught by newspaper reports describing the 'German Days' of September 1923, a patriotic festival held in Nuremberg to commemorate the Battle of Sedan. He cites these reports as a comprehensive picture of the reactionary German mentality. The principal figures at this jamboree, attended by thousands of members of nationalist and military organizations, student federations and church choirs, were Field Marshal Ludendorff and

Prince Rupprecht of Bavaria, but Kraus, discounting these more celebrated figures, highlights a phrase from a speech by Hitler: 'Everyone must be determined to *force the law of love of the Fatherland on others*' (F 632–9, 42). He sensed that in contrast to Hindenburg and Ludendorff, Hitler really meant what he said:

> Hitler is the only one who may have something concrete in mind when he proposes to force the law of love of the fatherland on others, and he probably knows how to set about it. Naturally, the method he has in mind for teaching people to love their fatherland is the rubber truncheon, the only German reality conceivable for these warriors determined to liberate their country. [. . .] In this romantic world [. . .] the truncheon is a weapon that means business (F 632–9, 40–4).

Kraus perceived that for Hitler the idea of *forcing* people to love their fatherland was not simply a metaphor, since Nazi thugs had already been in action on the streets of Vienna with 'rubber truncheons' (F 613–21, 11).

When Kraus published his gloss in September 1923, Hitler was an obscure figure in a mackintosh on the margins of the *völkisch* movement.[29] However,

3   An obscure figure in a raincoat: Hitler in September 1923 at the Nuremberg German Days

within six weeks the Munich putsch had catapulted him into the headlines. The news of Hitler's arrest reached Kraus just as he was putting the finishing touches to his programme for a public reading on 12 November to mark the fifth anniversary of the Austrian Republic. To strengthen his attack on right-wing groups in Germany, he composed an additional strophe on the complicity between Hitler and Kahr, the reactionary state commissioner of Bavaria. This implies that Kahr should also have been locked up, ridicules the role of Ludendorff, and mocks the pretensions of the swastika (F 640–8, 108–10). The swastika motif occurs again in his response to a caricature in the style of George Grosz, portraying a bullet-headed German officer with a broad chest and a double chin, published in Die Fackel in December 1922.[30] Around this figure Kraus weaves his own commentary, concluding with the prophetic phrase: 'Space in front for a gigantic swastika' (F 608–12, 31–2). He saw the Nazi emblem on the patriotic German breast before it actually appeared.

The repudiation of paramilitary violence is fundamental to Kraus's critique of fascism, but he also addresses the psychological factors responsible for the 'spontaneous transformation of the harmless petty bourgeois or the good-natured idiot into a coldblooded fiend'. In December 1926 he reprinted an anecdote from the western front about a Bavarian soldier who felt hungry while on sentry duty. When an English soldier incautiously showed his head, the Bavarian calmly picked him off, clambered through the barbed wire and helped himself to the Englishman's rations. For Kraus this anecdote is 'a cultural symptom of exceptional significance'. The humorous tone forms a horrifying contrast to the content: 'the mechanistic routine of murder' (F 743–50, 22–4). From the jovial Bavarian to the fiend in field-grey uniform there is only the shortest of steps. The fact that this mentality was still so pervasive, ten years after the event, was partly due to the right-wing press, which specialized in such 'Field-Grey Reminiscences'; partly to the reactionary veterans' associations which proliferated all over the German-speaking world. These attitudes also permeated the educational system through a network of student duelling clubs, which cultivated the manly virtues of the officer class. There were scores of these nationalistic associations, with names like Germania, Teutonia and Cheruskia – the group satirized in Die letzten Tage der Menschheit (III/11). In the post-war period they adopted more aggressive names like Stahlhelmkameraden, Wehrwölfe, Wikinger, and their paramilitary activities – as Kraus noted in December 1926 – were far more threatening. Reprinting a report about one such gathering, he italicized key phrases to show that the battles of the First World War were still being fought in the minds of thousands of veterans and their well-drilled young recruits. The principal speaker was Admiral Scheer, hero of the Battle of Jutland, greeted by the throng as their 'Führer' (F 743–50, 20–2).

The first phase of Kraus's campaign against creeping fascism is summed up in the articles he published in August 1924 to mark the tenth anniversary of the war. His theme is the power of political slogans to transform human beings into cannon fodder. Men 'called to the flag' will once more forget that war is fought with grenades and poison gas, but the 'flag' has now been displaced by a more ominous emblem: 'Burnt children plunge into the fire just like chickens running out in front of a motor car, escaping into danger. [. . .] If this were not the case, the attempt by the devil to brand them with the swastika would have failed on the very first day' (F 657–67, 3). Kraus sees the post-war generation as 'branded' with the swastika – a disturbingly physical word which conveys his sense of the compelling power of fascism. It was the blend of religious fervour with physical violence that made National Socialism so difficult to deal with. Moreover the swastika also had sexual associations, as expressed in the primitive sub-culture of graffiti on Austrian lavatory walls ('Abortwänden'). According to Kraus's observations, the wall was often defaced by crude inscriptions lamenting the collapse of the monarchy, followed by abuse of those supposedly to blame. These sequences of scrawls by different hands, expressing 'all the shifts in the political taste of the times', invariably culminated in the claim that 'the filthy Jews are to blame'. Generally (Kraus continues) this conclusion would be embellished 'with the drawing of a sexual organ or with a swastika'. Sex, swastikas and antisemitism become fused into obscene incitements to violence, suggesting that reactionary political movements are 'stronger than is generally assumed', and this 'writing on the wall' provides revelations of 'popular thinking'. Moreover, Kraus demonstrates that this form of 'folk poetry' is not spontaneous, but is promoted by reactionary forms of education (F 640–8, 127–33).

Creeping fascism was an elusive phenomenon, since the early Nazi movement was disorganized and fragmented, overlapping in Germany with the veterans' associations and in Austria with the Heimwehr.[31] In addition to the word 'Hakenkreuzler', Kraus used the word 'Troglodyten' ('troglodytes' or 'cave-dwellers') as a generic term to denote reactionary political groupings.[32] It was difficult to determine where the main threat to democracy lay, although there was a crescendo of Nazi violence during the summer of 1922, at the time of the murder of Walther Rathenau, the German Foreign Minister. Kraus himself received death threats and was warned that it was unsafe for him to visit Germany (BSN 1, 555). Unshaken by these threats, he paid tribute to Rathenau's integrity and condemned 'the unspeakable horror of his assassination' (F 595–600, 1). The attempt on the life of the Berlin journalist Maximilian Harden, Kraus's ancient rival, prompted him in autumn 1922 to define his position more explicitly. After condemning the 'bestiality of völkisch ideology', he suggested that Harden was at fault in refusing police protection, which should be provided in the public interest. It is no answer to the 'legend of Jewish cowardice' to expose oneself unnecessarily to the revolver of an 'Aryan coward', and the writer who receives a death threat proves his courage by continuing to write undeterred. The attempt on Harden's life illustrates the 'bestial climate of ideas in the post-war condition of Germany' (F 601–7, 41–9). Despite these fighting words, it was difficult for writers of Jewish origin

to counteract the threat of fascism, since their arguments were met by antisemitic abuse. Kraus himself was denounced as a 'syphilitic Jew' both by right-
wing newspapers and in anonymous letters.[33] His problem as a critic of Nazism
was to avoid giving the impression that he was defending narrowly Jewish
interests, a defect he identified in a commentary on the Harden affair by
another journalist, Siegfried Jacobsohn, editor of *Die Weltbühne*. Jacobsohn's
otherwise admirable article (Kraus suggests) 'rather too overtly confronts the
swastika with the star of David' (F 601–7, 44). The obliqueness of Kraus's treatment of National Socialism is partly attributable to this dilemma. How is a
Jewish writer to refute antisemitism without giving the impression that he is
merely defending Jewish interests? Kraus, too, found himself trapped between
swastika and star of David, since Austrian culture was pervaded by equally pernicious forms of antisemitism.

CHAPTER 2

Austrian Identity Politics

For seven hundred years Vienna had been the centre of a dynastic realm which, in 1914, extended from Czernowitz to Lake Constance, from Cracow to Dubrovnik. After four years of unprecedented conflict, the frontiers of the Empire were still intact, since the rout of the Italians at Caporetto in November 1917 had stabilized the southern front, while the Treaty of Brest-Litovsk had eliminated the threat from the east. The defeat of Tsarist Russia and the treaties imposed on Romania and Ukraine were a source of particular satisfaction for Austrian Jews, since they appeared to have liberated their brethren from oppressive tyrannies. A study of the Jewish community press suggests that by the spring of 1918 most Jews felt 'that Austria had won the war'.[1] In April 1918 the German advances on the western front raised hopes that the Allies, too, would be forced to sue for peace, and for a moment it seemed as if Austria-Hungary – despite appalling casualties and privations – might still be saved. But the peace negotiations initiated by Emperor Karl I ended in failure, and in the summer of 1918 the German army suffered devastating reverses. In a final attempt to save the dynasty, Karl I issued a proclamation announcing that the multinational Empire would be transformed into a confederation of self-governing nations, but these concessions, coupled with an appeal to President Wilson, came too late. The Armistice of November 1918 signalled not simply the defeat of Imperial Germany, but the end of Austria-Hungary.

Divided Loyalties in 'German-Austria'

Austria, which had triggered the war in 1914, was the principal victim of the peace. The defeat of Imperial Germany resulted in territorial losses to both France and Poland, as well as overseas, but this did not destroy the integrity of the Reich. The position in Vienna was very different, as one by one the Habsburg territories declared their independence. On 16 October 1918 the Hungarians severed all constitutional ties with Vienna, and twelve days later an independent state of Czechoslovakia was proclaimed in Prague. The frontiers of the Empire were crumbling, and Romanian armies, with the support of the Allies, marched into Transylvania and occupied Czernowitz. The retreat on the Italian front turned into a rout, and tens of thousands of Austrian troops were taken prisoner. The conflict with Serbia which had started the war ended with the proclamation of a union of South Slavs in Belgrade, and even the Slovenes of Carinthia attempted to assert their independence, while Cracow was incorporated in the new Polish Republic.

For other Habsburg nationalities, the bitterness of defeat was mitigated by the gaining of sovereignty, and there was rejoicing in Prague and Budapest, Trieste and Sarajevo, but for the Germans of Austria there was no consolation. Morale had been maintained through four years of terrible losses, but there was an appalling price to pay. The Austro-Hungarian army had suffered proportionately heavier losses than any other country. Of 7,800,000 men mobilized, an estimated 1,200,000 were killed in action or died from disease, 3,620,000 were wounded, and 2,200,000 taken prisoner, making total casualties and losses of 7,020,000 – over 90 per cent.[2] The death rate from disease and malnutrition among civilians was also high, and Austrians faced a bleak future. Even the Social Democrats had little cause for rejoicing, since they had nailed their flag so firmly to the German cause. The demonstration of 12 November 1918, which led to the proclamation of the Republic, marked not a triumphant seizure of power, but an 'improvised' revolution.[3] Shots were fired in front of parliament, the red flag was hoisted, and there were rumours of a communist coup.[4] The Hungarian revolutionary Béla Kun arrived in Vienna in December to deliver a personal message from Lenin to Friedrich Adler, the radical socialist who had just been released from prison.[5] But Adler refused to authorize an insurrection, and the socialists maintained control with the support of the police. The result was a 'bourgeois–democratic revolution' organized by a Marxist party.[6]

The politics of 1919 were dominated by the peace negotiations, culminating in the signing of the Treaties of Versailles on 28 June and Saint-Germain on 10 September. The imperial system was replaced by six new republics, Austria, Czechoslovakia, Germany, Hungary, Poland and Yugoslavia, while the territories of Italy and Romania were enlarged. In theory, the frontiers were to be regulated in accordance with the principle of national self-determination, but in practice the treaties left a legacy of bitterness. Kraus, who had no doubts about Germany's war guilt, was among the first to protest about the proposed peace settlement, which he defined as 'the best method of producing a war'. When the terms imposed on Germany were announced in Paris in April 1919, he was appalled to find Paris providing a new home for the 'fundamental evil of nationalism'. Woodrow Wilson, initially welcomed as a moral arbiter, is now censured for permitting vengeance, while Clemenceau is denounced for advocating policies that will sentence 'millions of the unborn from the conquered and the victorious countries to death'. In short, the peace has destroyed the longed-for 'victory over war' (F 514–18, 24–6).

When the terms of the Treaty of Saint-Germain were announced in June 1919, three clauses provoked particular resentment: the ceding of South Tyrol to Italy, the ban on Anschluss with Germany, and the assignment of areas of Bohemia with German-speaking majorities to Czechoslovakia. When the Republic of German-Austria was proclaimed in November 1918, its representatives laid claim to whole swathes of Bohemia and the Sudetenland (Fig. 3).[7] The annexation of these areas by Czechoslovakia blatantly infringed the principle of self-determination, and the incorporation of three million ethnic Germans into the newly created state left a legacy of recrimination. Under these circumstances, it was scarcely possible to describe the events of November 1918 as a 'revolution' in the Marxist sense. The Austrian socialist leader Otto Bauer put the matter very succinctly when he defined events in Poland, Czechoslovakia and Yugoslavia as a 'victory of the bourgeoisie over the dynasties, nobility and military caste [. . .] won on the battlefields of France'. The problem for Austria, as for Hungary, was how to achieve an authentic 'proletarian revolution' under the constraints imposed by an alliance of bourgeois governments and imperialist powers.[8]

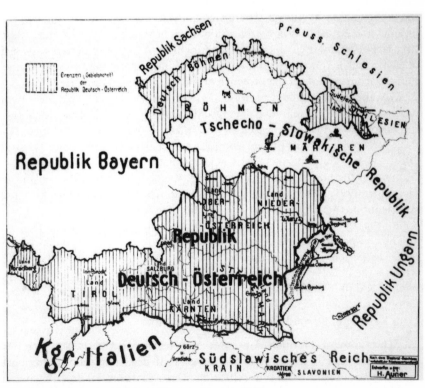

Map showing the territorial claims of German–Austria in 1919

The sole consolation for the German-speaking population of Austria, according to Kraus, was relief at 'no longer being Austrians' (F 501–7, 3). When the Provisional National Assembly met in Vienna in November 1918, the Social Democratic leader Karl Renner proposed a new name: 'Ostalpenlande' – the 'Eastern Alpine Lands' – since 'Austria' denoted the great power that had collapsed. A second suggestion was 'Südostdeutschland' – 'Southeastern Germany'.[9] After some discussion, the new state was proclaimed as the 'Republic of German-Austria' – 'Deutsch-Österreich' – which (as Viktor Adler put it in his speech to the National Assembly on 21 October 1918) was to become part of Germany.[10] Deprived of their ascendancy over the Slav peoples of central Europe, the German-speaking Austrians longed for reintegration into a greater German Reich, not least on economic grounds. Cut off from their traditional hinterland – from access to the Adriatic, the thriving industries of Czechoslovakia and the agricultural resources of Hungary – they faced severe shortages of food and fuel, and union with Germany held out prospect of economic recovery.

The agitation began in Vorarlberg in May 1919, when a referendum was held on the proposal that the province should join the Swiss Confederation. Although the turn-out was modest, 80 per cent voted for union with Switzerland, and the proposal received some sympathy in Berne, but it was realized, both in Vienna and at the League of Nations, that a secession would precipitate the disintegration of Austria. There was an even more vehement agitation for union with Germany. When a referendum was held in Tyrol on 24 April 1921, over 90 per cent of the voters opted for Anschluss. A similar result was expected in Styria, but here the referendum was indefinitely postponed in response to pressure from abroad. In the province of Salzburg, where voting took place on 29 May, the figure in favour of Anschluss exceeded 99 per cent. Given the high turn-out (87 per cent in both Salzburg and Tyrol), there can be little doubt that the majority of Austrians wished to vote their country out of existence, but these referendums were merely consultative and had no immediate political effect.[11] It was only the plebiscites held under the auspices of the League of Nations, in the borderlands of Carinthia in October 1920 and Burgenland in December 1921, which actually altered the frontiers of the Republic, bringing Austria modest territorial gains. The agitation for Anschluss nevertheless made it clear that the question of identity was unresolved.

The composite name 'German-Austria' defined the identity politics of the post-war period. The fundamental question, under international law, was whether the new Republic should be held responsible for the crimes of the old regime, and thus saddled with the stigma of war guilt and the burden of reparations. In a memorandum of 29 November 1918 the constitutional lawyer Hans Kelsen put forward the following propositions:

1   The state of German-Austria is not legally the successor state of Austria, that is to say Austria-Hungary. It does not inherit the legal obligations of the old state, through whose division it came into being at the same time as other national states. [. . .]

2 Hence the state of German-Austria does not inherit any legal obligation for the war which was conducted by the Austro-Hungarian
Monarchy. The state of German-Austria is neutral and emphatically
proclaims its neutrality.[12]

Even Kelsen had to admit the contradiction of claiming simultaneously to be a
neutral state and an integral part of the German Reich, but he argued that
German-Austria should be treated with the same magnanimity as other successor states such as Czechoslovakia. It was with high hopes that the delegation
from German-Austria, led by Renner, travelled to France for the peace negotiations, armed with Kelsen's memorandum, but these hopes were dashed by
the victorious Allies. There could be no doubt that Vienna had been responsible for the ultimatum which led to the war, and Clemenceau insisted that 'the
Austrian people must be compelled to bear their full share of responsibility for
this crime, which brought such disaster upon the world'.[13] Moreover, the
French government was adamant that nothing should be done to strengthen
the German Reich, and union with Austria would have compensated
Germany for its territorial losses. Setting aside the Wilsonian principle of self-
determination, the French vetoed all aspirations for reintegration. Austria,
according to Clemenceau's dictum, would consist of the territories left over
after the creation of the successor states: 'L'Autriche, c'est ce qui reste.'

Under the terms of the Treaty of Saint-Germain, published in July 1919, the
name 'German-Austria' was banned, and the National Assembly was compelled
to identify itself as the government of the 'Republic of Austria'. The new state
was reduced to a rump of German-speaking provinces, hemmed in on three
sides by the successor states and by the rising power of Italy (see map). Otto
Bauer, socialist Foreign Minister in the coalition government, felt compelled to
resign, since his insistence on Anschluss made it impossible for him to continue
negotiations with the French government. However, he remained convinced
that his pro-German policy had created 'a new national ideal', giving to 'the
German-Austrian people, whose body bleeds from a thousand wounds, a soul,
a purpose and a will to life'.[14] A wave of bitterness erupted during the National
Assembly debate of 6 September 1919, which preceded ratification of the
Treaty. Karl Seitz, President of the Assembly, described the Treaty as a 'Diktat',
while Renner lamented the fact that the 'Alpine Germans' were now separated
from the 'Sudeten Germans', with whom they had shared a community 'for
four hundred years'. The Pan-German spokesman Dr Dinghofer claimed that
the Czechs, Poles and Hungarians were really to blame, denoun-cing the
Treaty as an act of 'brute force' that would avenge itself.[15] Faced with an economic blockade, the delegates were compelled to accept the Treaty, but it was
easier formally to renounce Anschluss than to alter the prevailing pro-German
attitudes. Kraus, as usual, was in the minority, since he regarded union with
Germany as a source not of hope, but of danger (F 632–9, 167). Many organizations, including the Social Democrats – as Kraus had occasion to observe

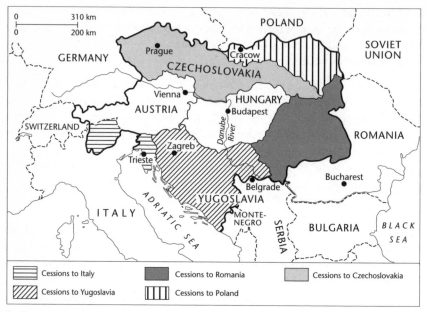

Map showing the disintegration of Austria-Hungary after the First World War

(F 876–84, 21) – retained the phrase 'deutschösterreichisch' in their statutes, even after the name had been repudiated by the Assembly.[16]

The Social Democrats were reluctant partners in the government of a state that no one really wanted. Electors in German-speaking areas of Bohemia, who had overwhelmingly supported the Social Democrats in the last pre-war election, were prevented by the Czech authorities from voting in the Austrian general election of February 1919. This produced an inconclusive result: seventy-two Social Democratic deputies, sixty-nine Christian Socials and twenty-six German Nationalists, together with one Jewish and one Czech nationalist. A coalition government was formed by the Social Democratic and Christian Social parties, and during the next eighteen months it was able to push through a string of constitutional and social reforms, including the dissolution of the House of Lords, abolition of aristocratic titles, confiscation of royal palaces, democratization of the jury system, abolition of the death penalty, reform of the school system, and introduction of an eight-hour working day.[17] A graduated income tax was introduced which effectively transferred resources from the privileged elite to the proletariat, but the economic crisis limited the government's room for manoeuvre, particularly as the moderate socialist leadership shrank from the radical experiments advocated by the newly founded Communist Party. Moreover, the federal police force (Bundespolizei) remained under the control of central government, undermining the power of the socialists in the cities which they regarded as their strongholds.[18]

The achievement of the Social Democrats was to consolidate parliamentary democracy at a time when communists in Budapest and Munich had embarked on abortive attempts at Soviet-style revolution. In Austria, where the majority of the population were conservative in outlook as well as Catholic by religion, the scope for constructing a socialist utopia was severely circumscribed. The new constitution of 1920, drafted by Hans Kelsen, consolidated the power of the central government within a federal system, but the breakdown of the coalition in June 1920 displaced the Social Democrats from power, and they suffered a significant loss of seats in the general elections of October. A coalition was formed between Christian Socials and German Nationalists, and the Social Democrats became the party of permanent opposition. Austria was now divided into two ideological camps: the clerical faction led by Ignaz Seipel, dominant figure in a series of right-wing coalitions during the 1920s, and the Social Democrats led by Otto Bauer, whose revolutionary rhetoric made little impact on practical politics.

The Antisemitic Consensus

Even during the final year of the war, few people in Austria-Hungary had realized that the Empire was on the point of disintegration. Military propaganda had emphasized the need to 'hold out' until final victory was achieved, but shortages of food, fuel and other essentials had left people undernourished and vulnerable to disease, especially the influenza virus that swept across Europe at the end of the war, claiming hundreds of thousands of lives. In Germany, there were an estimated 430,000 influenza-related deaths during the epidemic of 1918–19, causing panic in the major cities.[19] These privations were stoically endured as long as they appeared to have a purpose, but after the collapse of November 1918 the physical shortages were compounded by a far more insidious form of deprivation: a shortage of explanations. The Central Powers had not simply lost the war – the war had lost its meaning. When Italy cut Austria off from the sea, the *Neue Freie Presse* lamented that the Great War had 'lost its final significance'.[20]

Who was to blame? Among foreign enemies the obvious culprits were the Italians, who had been rewarded by substantial territorial gains. The arrival in Vienna of the Italian Armistice Commission, commanded by General Roberto Segre, completed the national humiliation. It might have made even more sense to blame the Czechs, since in 1915 Czech regiments of the Austro-Hungarian army had defected to the Russians. The decisive factor in the dismemberment of the Empire was Thomas Masaryk's insistence that the Czechs should be granted full independence in a state that incorporated Slovakia and the whole of Bohemia. In the eyes of the nationalists there had been a Czech 'conspiracy' to destroy German power, and this view was confirmed by the peace settlement of 1919, which treated the Czechs as most favoured nation. As the government in Prague imposed its will on the German-speaking communities of Bohemia by brute force, reactions in the National Assembly in

Vienna became increasingly heated. On 12 March 1919, after the shooting of German demonstrators by Czech troops, Karl Seitz denounced 'Czechoslovak imperialism' for imposing an 'alien and brutal domination' on citizens who were defending the right of self-determination.[21]

In Vienna there was a Czech-speaking community which, at its height, approached 10 per cent of the population, and if politics had been governed by rational argument, the backlash would have been directed against the Czechs. A total of 81,344 persons gave Czech or Slovak as their language of everyday use in the census of 1923, and there was considerable pressure on them to assimilate to the dominant German culture. However, they were fortunate in having their rights protected by bilateral treaties, and despite references to the 'struggle against Czechoslovak imperialism', anti-Czech sentiment never became a dominant force.[22] It was the prominence of Jews in public life that had excited the greatest resentment ever since the days of the populist politicians Karl Lueger and Georg von Schönerer. Observers from Germany, where Jewish communities kept a lower profile, were astonished by the public success of their assimilated co-religionists in Austria. Jakob Wassermann's widely read autobiography, Mein Weg als Deutscher und Jude ('My Path as German and Jew'), published in 1921, recalls that when he first arrived in Vienna he had the impression that 'the whole of public life was dominated by Jews'.[23] Defeat and revolution resulted in more virulent forms of identity politics, which targeted both the assimilated Jewish community and their orthodox eastern brethren. Rumours of impending pogroms made it increasingly difficult for an author like Arthur Schnitzler to affirm his traditional tripartite identity 'as an Austrian citizen of Jewish race committed to German culture' (AST, 1 November 1918).[24]

The deeply rooted anti-Judaism of the Catholic Church helped to ensure that it was the Jews who became scapegoats both for the defeat and for the ensuing economic hardships. The immediate problems facing the government were how to cope with a potentially revolutionary situation, resolve the economic crisis, and alleviate the shortages of food and fuel. Disease and malnutrition were serious enough in themselves, but irreparable damage was caused when these issues became entangled with the debate about Jewish refugees, who had begun to flee to Vienna in autumn 1914 to escape the Russian advance. At the height of the military crisis the number of refugees in Vienna reached 200,000, and since Galicia was responsible for a high proportion of Austrian cereal production, the arrival of the refugees was followed by a dramatic reduction in food supplies.[25] Once the Russians had been forced to retreat, a repatriation programme began. At the beginning of October 1915, after significant numbers had been returned to their place of origin, there were still 137,000 refugees in Vienna, of whom 77,000 were Jews, 41,000 Poles and 17,800 Ruthenians. The majority depended on financial support from the state, co-ordinated by the Ministry of the Interior and the City of Vienna, with the support of charitable organizations. A new wave of refugees arrived in summer 1916 as a result of the Brusilov offensive, but successful counter-attacks by the Central Powers meant that the programme of repatriation could be resumed during 1917–18. The number of refugees in Vienna registered for state support fell from over 50,000 in September 1917 to just over 20,000 in September 1918.[26]

Just as the practical problems associated with refugees were easing, the political reverberations intensified. Police reports covering the period October 1914 to February 1917 had registered a catalogue of complaints about the refugees, who were denounced as lice-infested layabouts involved in begging and prostitution, causing food shortages and exploiting the black market.[27] They were shunned as carriers of disease – an allegation which gained some plausibility as a result of the crowded and unhygienic quarters in which they were accommodated. The crisis intensified with the arrival of thousands of displaced ethnic Germans and returning prisoners of war, although border controls were imposed with a system of sanitary surveillance. From October 1918 until May 1919 the Austrian Ministry of Public Health was under the direction of the racial hygienist Ignaz Kaup, who was 'keen to exclude racial undesirables in the fight against infectious diseases'.[28] During the final phase of the war, when the actual number of refugees in Vienna had declined, the hostility towards them intensified, and Jews from Galicia and the Bukovina became 'the scapegoats par excellence'.[29] After the lifting of censorship, the 'Jewish question' began to dominate the political agenda. The so-called 'Polish' Jews from orthodox communities in Galicia, with their beards and sidelocks, their long black kaftans and wide-brimmed hats, were a visible presence in the city, but the climate of antisemitism was all the more insidious because it was so self-righteous. The Viennese, it was claimed, had been exceptionally generous towards the refugees, suppressing their feelings of revulsion at the spectacle of 'extremely filthy figures in long kaftans, crawling with every conceivable kind of vermin, wandering through the clean streets and alleys of Vienna'.[30] Now the blighters were allegedly taking over the city and profiteering at everyone's expense.

The number of Jews in Vienna certainly increased during the war, as can be seen from the census figures for 1910 and 1923:

Year	Population of Vienna	Persons of Jewish faith	Percentage
1910	2,020,309	175,318	8.68
1923	1,865,780	201,513	10.80

In this same period 10,129 Jews in Vienna had renounced or changed their religious faith. The increase in the Jewish population (in a period when the birth rate had fallen below the death rate) was primarily due to the refugees, including further groups that fled in 1919 from pogroms in Poland and the Ukraine. In the spring of 1919, Chief Rabbi Chajes estimated that there were 30,000 Jewish refugees in the city, while Rudolf Schwarz-Hiller, who had organized the refugee relief programme during the war, put the figure at a maximum of 20,000.[31] One of the principal tactics of the right-wing press was to exaggerate these figures. On 7 December 1919 the Christian Social newspaper *Die Reichspost* claimed that there were 100,000 refugees in Vienna. The German-Nationalist press was even more alarmist. According to a report of 2 April 1921 in the *Deutschösterreichische Tageszeitung* the population of Vienna included 175,000 Austrian Jews, 198,000 eastern Jews and 210,000 Jews who had changed their religion, making a total of 583,000 – over 30 per cent of the city's population.[32] The effect of this campaign was to identify the economic crisis with the 'Jewish question'. The lack of Austrian self-esteem led to a litany of blaming 'others' – a chain reaction in which each group projected its sense of insecurity on to a convenient scapegoat, the Catholics blaming the socialists, the Social Democrats blaming the refugees.

Even the League of Nations, which set up a High Commission for Refugees in 1921, was powerless to cope with the millions displaced by war and revolution, especially from Russia, Armenia and the Ukraine. Countries like Britain, which introduced an Aliens Restriction Act in December 1919, were far less generous than Austria, while the United States responded to the crisis by restricting its immigration quotas.[33] Moreover, Austrian policy towards Jewish refugees was more liberal than that of Germany, which set a sinister precedent in October 1916 by conducting a census designed to prove that Jewish citizens were shirking front-line duty – the notorious 'Judenzählung'. When a similar census was advocated in Austria, the proposal was firmly rejected.[34] In April 1918 the German government imposed a 'frontier blockade' ('Grenzsperre') to prevent immigration from Polish-speaking areas – in theory to control a typhoid epidemic, in practice to exclude eastern Jews. In 1921 the government of the Weimar Republic took the more radical step of setting up internment camps for 'Ostjuden', condemned by left-wing critics as 'concentration camps'.[35] The authorities in Vienna were more liberal, but the unintended effect of their policies was to intensify the antisemitic reaction. Despite the reforms introduced by the coalition government of 1919–20, there was no underlying national consensus, since the Austrian Republic lacked the cohesion that draws warring factions together at times of crisis. Instead, there emerged an 'antisemitic consensus' that affected all political parties.[36]

Vienna became the scene of an antisemitic crusade. The debate was opened on 4 February 1919, when a Christian Social politician, Anton Jerzabek, introduced a proposal in the National Assembly to prohibit further immigration and expel all refugees. The general election of 16 February should have marked the moment of political renewal, since it was the first fully democratic election ever held in Austria, conducted under universal suffrage with both men and women over twenty entitled to vote. But the campaign was dominated by allegations that Christian-German civilization was under threat from an alliance of Marxists and Jews. While the German Nationalists had never made a secret of their antisemitism, the Christian Socials also mobilized public opinion against the 'Jewish' peril. The tone was set by the most eminent Christian politician, Ignaz

Seipel, a member of the last Cabinet of Habsburg Austria. In the run-up to the election, he delivered a speech to a Catholic organization warning that 'the real Germans' were in danger of becoming the pawns of 'Jewish domination'. He linked this to the allegation that the Social Democratic Party 'unconditionally followed Jewish leadership', so that the Bolshevik danger was a 'Jewish danger'.[37]

These signals from the leadership precipitated an even more venomous campaign at street level. There were valid reasons for fearing a socialist government, since the Social Democrats proposed to liberalize the divorce laws, increase taxes and take key sectors of industry into public ownership, but these issues were subsumed into a fantasy about the 'Jewish' threat to 'German' values. The 'unbelieving red Jews' were allegedly threatening Catholic marriage.[38] The climate is epitomized by an article in the *Reichspost* on 26 September 1919, at the height of the debate about the deportation of eastern Jews. The 'decisive question', it claimed, was 'Jewish Republic or German Republic' (RP, 26 September 1919).[39] The editorialist ignored the fact that the Republic of Austria was actually governed by a coalition of moderate Social Democrats and reformist Christian Socials. But the pragmatists were out-manoeuvred, and the ideological conflict between 'Christian' and 'Marxist' factions became increasingly polarized, with Jews of all persuasions caught in the crossfire. The Social Democrats targeted both the 'rich Jews' who had done well out of the war and the 'unproductive elements' who were scrounging off state benefits. Thus anti-Jewish resentments were cultivated even among socialist workers, while the speeches of the Christian Social workers leader, Leopold Kunschak, amounted to incitements to racial hatred. The eastern Jews, he claimed, in a speech of 29 April 1920 in the National Assembly, were 'locusts' who had stripped the country bare and should be interned in concentration camps. On 31 August 1921 the desperate housing shortages gave him a further opportunity to scapegoat the refugees. To solve the problem it was necessary 'ruthlessly to remove the foreign Jews from the city and thereby cleanse it of a criminal people that lives only by speculation and fraud'.[40] Even Kunschak could not compete with the Deutschösterreichische Volkspartei, led by the publicist Anton Orel, editor of *Der Volkssturm*, a weekly paper that hysterically denounced the 'Jewish dictatorship'. In August 1919 Orel published a long litany blaming the Jews for Austria's 'terrible deprivations'.[41] The impotent rage of the *Volkssturm* may be attributed to the pathetic performance of the Deutschösterreichische Volkspartei in the elections of 1919, and it failed to stir up violence comparable to the Scheunenviertel riots in Berlin. But these groups poisoned the atmosphere through a plethora of antisemitic publications.

An even more ominous development was the founding in August 1919 of the German-Austrian Defensive Antisemitic Federation (Deutschösterrei-chische Schutzverein Antisemitenbund), a coalition of 'German-Aryan citizens of German-Austria'. The obsessive use of the word 'German' reveals how inse-cure they felt about their identity, which could be affirmed only in terms of its

polar opposite: the allegedly 'disintegrative, undermining and strangulating
power of semitic Jewry'. Aggressive politics are presented as legitimate self-
defence, and again we are struck by the self-righteous tone. In theory the law
of association in Austria prohibited the formation of organizations which
incited hostility against other groups, but the Ministry of the Interior decided
not to prohibit the Antisemitic Federation, fearing that a ban might increase
political friction.[42] As a result of this agitation, even the Social Democrats felt
compelled to take action against the eastern Jews. In September 1919, it was
announced that trainloads of Galician refugees would be compulsorily repatri-
ated. The politicians responsible for this decision were the Minister of the
Interior, Mathias Eldersch, and the governor (Bezirkshauptmann) of Vienna
and Lower Austria, Albert Sever, both Social Democrats. On 10 September
1919 Sever published a decree calling on all former subjects of the Monarchy
who did not possess rights of residence in the new republic to leave the territory of German-Austria. This proved a fiasco, since the coal shortage paralysed
the transport system for several weeks, preventing any trains from leaving
Vienna.[43] However, the policy of repatriation was continued by Sever's successor, and Jews from Galicia had to live with the threat of 'deportation'.[44]

The irony is that, despite these efforts, the Social Democratic Party was
repeatedly denounced for being pro-Jewish. The 'Jewish conspiracy' provided
an explanation for the sweeping Social Democratic victory in the Vienna City
Council elections of May 1919: one hundred Social Democrats were elected,
compared with fifty Christian Socials, eight Czechs, three German Nationals,
three Jewish Nationals, and one Democrat. The right-wing *Wiener Stimmen*
responded with a cartoon attributing the victory to voters 'from the east'.[45]
Hatred of the Jews was supposed to be a spontaneous expression of the 'soul of
the common people', but in fact the antisemitic movement was driven by a
flood of pamphlets and periodicals. The crudest of them was *Der eiserne Besen:
Ein Blatt der Notwehr* ('The Iron Broom: An Organ of Self-Defence'), published
by the Antisemitic Federation. To strengthen their fragile self-esteem, Austrian
agitators desperately needed an 'image of the enemy' ('Feindbild') to reassure
them. They showed little interest in the actual socio-economic circumstances
of the refugees, devoting all their efforts to disseminating myths about Jewish
profiteers. There were certainly blatant examples of entrepreneurs who
flaunted their new-found wealth, like Siegmund Bosel and Camillo Castiglioni,
both of whom Kraus was to pursue in *Die Fackel*. But most Jews shared the
hardships of the immediate post-war period, and the impoverished lives of
refugees are reflected in Bruno Frei's documentation of Jewish deprivation,
Jüdisches Elend, published in Vienna in 1920, accompanied by photographs of
the conditions in which they were struggling to survive.[46]

Discussions of the 'Jewish question' in the Viennese press showed scant
awareness of the disorientation which had overtaken established residents as
well as refugees. The majority of the Jews of the Habsburg Empire had felt at
ease with the concept of being 'Austrian' in the pre-1918 'cosmopolitan' sense

of the word: they could be Austrian in Cracow speaking Polish, Austrian in Prague speaking Czech, or Austrian in Trieste speaking Italian, without feeling obliged to deny their Jewish origins. In 1918 this model of multiculturalism collapsed, and it became necessary to create new forms of Jewish identity in the successor states. Dozens of different factions emerged, each with its own spokesmen and its own aspirations to leadership. The dominant ideologies were Jewish nationalism, supporting Jewish minority rights within the secular republic; Zionism, with its programme of settlement in Palestine; and the traditional liberal assimilationists, who in Vienna controlled the Israelitische Kultusgemeinde. Each of these factions had its own competing sub-groups: orthodox versus reform, militants versus moderates, youth groups versus established elites, political activists versus cultural gradualists.

In November 1918 mass meetings were organized in Vienna by Zionist groups. Thousands of Jews took to the streets, and a Jewish National Council was created to articulate their demands. What happened to Austrian Jewry in those November days, according to the Zionist youth leader Robert Weltsch, was 'a genuine revolution'. However, the actual results were modest. The franchise was reformed to make it more democratic, and Jewish nationalists won thirteen out of thirty-six Vorstand seats. The most striking achievements were those of the campaigning journalist Robert Stricker. In January 1919 he helped to launch the first ever German-language daily newspaper devoted to Jewish interests, the *Wiener Morgenzeitung*, in competition with the Zionist weekly *Jüdische Zeitung*, edited by Robert Weltsch, and in February 1919 Stricker was elected to the National Assembly, representing the districts of Leopoldstadt and Brigittenau. When three Jewish nationalists were elected to the City Council in May 1919, this was greeted with great trepidation by the liberal integrationists. The Zionist revival was relatively shortlived, but it made a significant contribution to the Third Aliya of the years 1919–23. A Palestine Office was set up in Vienna in November 1918, and 10,000 Jews, mainly from Poland, registered for emigration.[47]

Citizenship, Self-Hatred and Self-Esteem

The double identity associated with 'Deutsch-Österreich' acquired a further twist for people who were Austrian by citizenship, German by language, but Jewish by religion or (in the new terminology) by race. After the break-up of the pluralistic Empire, in which they had felt rather secure, they faced an intractable dilemma.[48] To be a German-speaking Austrian Jew in an intensely antisemitic society was to experience a fractured identity, especially for liberals proud of having emerged from the ghetto into the enlightened culture of the west. Now that western civilization was in crisis, it seemed that the 'true and authentic Jewish heart' was beating among the migrants from Galicia.[49] The tendency to sentimentalize eastern Jewry was epitomized by Joseph Roth, a journalist with first-hand knowledge of conditions in central Europe. Roth ironizes the 'well-bred, clean-shaven gentlemen in morning coats and top hats, who wrap their prayer book in the editorial page of their favourite Jewish paper'. It is their eastern cousins, he suggests, who have remained 'authentic and uncontaminated'.[50] This nostalgia for a pre-modern simplicity scarcely constituted a viable norm for citizens of the new Republic, and an assimilated Jew like Kraus, whose contrasting of sacred scripture with profane newsprint has numinous undertones, had to position himself within this shifting spectrum.

During the debates about identity politics, those who followed Kraus's example in repudiating all Jewish affiliations were accused of 'self-hatred', notably by Theodor Lessing and Anton Kuh.[51] However, there were so many factions in Jewry, so many possible Jewish 'selves' to choose from, that the concept is unhelpful. Although it tends to be associated with the self-destructive attitudes of Otto Weininger, the origins of 'self-hatred' lie not with Judaism, but with a life-denying Christian asceticism – hence the reference to 'Christian self-hatred' in a passage by Theodor Haecker, first cited in March 1914 (F 395–7, 20). Kraus repudiated the concept of 'Jewish self-hatred' on a number of occasions, dismissing Kuh's arguments as a popularization of the psychoanalytic theory of compensation (F 561–7, 56). For him, as his friend Berthold Viertel observed, 'self-hatred' was not a specifically Jewish phenomenon, but could be applied to other social groups.[52] Indeed, if any nation was denying their identity, it was the Austrians, since the majority were trying to persuade themselves that they were Germans. Even Robert Musil argued that Austria should be 'absorbed into Germany', repudiating the concept of 'Austrian culture' associated with such gifted individuals as Grillparzer and Kraus.[53] The Anschluss movement dominated Austrian cultural politics, from socialist political rallies to nationalist music festivals, leading one historian to speak of a 'masochistic self-loathing'.[54]

Despite the outcry against the Treaty of Saint-Germain, its merits become apparent when we recall the bitter frontier disputes between Hungary and Romania, Poland and the Soviet Union, which unleashed pogroms against thousands of former Habsburg subjects. One of its aims was to regulate the question of citizenship, since the collapse of Austria-Hungary had deprived millions of people of their nationality. For formerly subject peoples, Czechs and Slovaks, Poles and Slovenes, the acquisition of a new nationality may have been a matter for rejoicing, but the proclamation of the successor states plunged the widely scattered German-speaking communities into confusion. Were inhabitants of Lemberg or Czernowitz, who had traditionally owed allegiance to Vienna, now to be defined as Poles, Romanians or Ukrainians? A further mass migration to Austria was scarcely possible, since resources in Vienna were already overstretched. Faced with this emergency, the National Assembly rushed through a new law to regulate citizenship on 5 December 1918. Citizenship was to be restricted to those currently living within the territories of German-Austria, providing their registered place of domicile was in a province that had belonged to the Austrian half of the Monarchy. This excluded those from the Hungarian half, since Hungarians resident in Vienna had always been foreign citizens. The new law specifically denied citizenship to people from the so-called 'refugee areas', including the former crownland of Galicia. It was obvious that this provision was designed to prevent the tens of thousands of Jews in Galicia, who had previously been Austrian subjects, from claiming citizenship of the new Republic. The aim of the National Assembly, as the transcripts of the debates reveal, was to find a formula that would enable them to 'get rid of the Polish Jews' without preventing 'German' officials domiciled in the eastern regions from claiming Austrian citizenship.[55]

Traditionally, the law of citizenship had been governed by the principle of 'Heimatrecht' – the 'right of abode' in a particular locality where one was 'domiciled' ('zuständig'), even if one no longer actually lived there. Thus citizenship in the Habsburg period diverged from the familiar European models: the state-centred French 'citoyen' and the ethnocentric German 'Volksgenosse'. The word 'Heimat' is usually associated with sentimental images of the countryside and a nostalgia for pre-modern modes of existence, but in Austria the concept had legal connotations. 'Heimatrecht' provides the key to sections on citizenship in the Treaty of Saint-Germain, which was promulgated in French, English and Italian (there was no official German text). But one German word does creep into the Treaty: 'Heimatsrecht' (spelt with an 's'), with its Italian equivalent 'pertinenza'. The basic principle, set out in Article 64, was that all those with 'Heimatrecht' within the frontiers of the new republic should be Austrian citizens. Those with 'Heimatrecht' in a territory now belonging to a successor state become citizens of the state in which their domicile now lies. There was one exception to this principle, enshrined in Article 80, which made it possible for members of German-speaking minorities living in remote areas of the former Habsburg Empire to obtain Austrian citizenship by 'option'. The crucial criterion was that they should 'speak the same language and belong to the same race' as the majority of the Austrian population. The link between citizenship and domicile was still retained, since Article 78 specified that anyone obtaining citizenship by option should within one year transfer his place of residence to Austria, unless there were exceptional circumstances. Article 80 left the concept of 'race' undefined, but at first, under the leadership of Renner, this provision was interpreted liberally, as the western representatives at Saint-Germain had intended. 'Language' was taken to be the defining category, while 'race' was interpreted in the sense of 'national affiliation'. A handbook by Lukas Langhoff, published in 1920, exemplifies this interpretation. To establish one's 'adherence to the Austrian people', Langhoff argues, it will probably suffice to show that one has 'completely adapted to Austrian conditions in one's family and civil life'.[56] On this basis it was possible for assimilated German-speaking Jews from the eastern provinces, such as the novelist Joseph Roth, to opt for Austrian citizenship. But for Article 80 of the Treaty of Saint-Germain, that most Austrian of authors would have been Polish, since he was actually 'domiciled' in Brody, his birthplace in Galicia.

During 1921, after the formation of the Christian Social–Pan-German coalition, this liberal application of the 'option' clause was reversed. On 9 June 1921 a decision of the Administrative Court reinterpreted the requirement 'to speak the same language and belong to the same race' in terms that excluded German-speaking Jews. 'Race' was defined by the court as an 'inherent' characteristic, determined 'by physical and psychological factors' that 'cannot be changed by choice'.[57] This judgement enabled the Minister of the Interior, Leopold Waber, to exclude further Jewish applicants from Austrian citizenship. Where the practice of his predecessors had been relatively flexible, Waber decreed that 'not a single option application by a Jew should be approved'. During the six months of Waber's term in office, from 21 June to 23 December 1921, a total of 24,486 Jewish applicants were denied Austrian citizenship on this basis. Since applicants' wives and children were also excluded, approximately 75,000 people must have been affected.[58] Waber enforced the argument that eastern Jews had no right to claim citizenship since they were not 'Germans'. His position was challenged by those who pointed out that one of the aims of the Treaty of Saint-Germain was to protect minority groups. Under Article 63, the Austrian government was obliged to guarantee 'complete protection of life and liberty to all inhabitants of Austria without distinction of birth, nationality, race or religion'. This article prevented Waber from actually deporting those to whom he denied citizenship, but his policy left them in limbo. However, it was still possible to acquire Austrian citizenship by the indirect method of applying for 'Heimatrecht' in one of the quasi-autonomous provinces. Between 1920 and 1930 a total of over 93,000 applicants became Austrian citizens by this alternative method of naturalization ('Einbürgerung'). The majority of these new citizens were domiciled in Vienna, where the Social Democratic administration granted citizenship to 63,970 applicants, of whom 24,891 were Jews. The Christian Social opposition denounced this as a ploy to create new voters, and it is true that in 1923, with both general and municipal elections scheduled for October, almost 15,000 naturalizations were approved in Vienna.[59]

Since Austrian citizenship was dependent on 'Heimatrecht', everyone had to possess a 'Heimatschein'. For those born within the territories that constituted the new republic there was no problem, and pre-1914 migrants like the Kraus family from Bohemia, now part of Czechoslovakia, also had a secure title to citizenship. Karl Kraus had been granted 'Heimatrecht' in Vienna in 1899, after reaching adulthood, and a battered copy of his 'Heimatschein' survives in the Kraus Archive of the Vienna City Library. On paper, his Austrian citizenship seemed indisputable, but during the early 1920s, when Jews without citizenship were being resettled in eastern Europe, he too must have been affected by the climate of hostility. It was no joke to find the antisemitic *Wiener Stimmen* suggesting in the spring of 1921 that Kraus should board one of those trains to the east – 'Ostjudenexporte' (F 568–71, 56). With hindsight, we can see that this plan to deport Jewish migrants set an ominous precedent.

Austrian identity was a contested concept, involving competing ideas about 'patriotism' and 'nationalism', as Prince Starhemberg observed in his memoirs.[60] The standard histories attribute the crisis of the First Republic to a combination of 'economic misery' and 'mental disorientation'.[61] It would be more accurate to say that Austria was the first country to experience the trauma of 'post-colonialism' – the hybridity caused by the migration of formerly subject peoples to the metropolis. The attempts to exclude Jews by defining the Jewish 'race' as a separate entity may have been welcomed by the Zionists, who envisaged emigration to Palestine, but assimilated Jews felt threatened by pressure groups determined to deprive them of their rights. Proposals to create a category of second-class citizenship for Jews were taken up by prominent members of the Christian Social Party, led by Seipel and Kunschak. In November 1919 Kunschak presented a draft parliamentary bill designed to exclude Jews from public office, restricting their access to the professions to a limit set by their proportion in the population as a whole – 10 per cent (the so-called 'numerus clausus').[62] Seipel was aware that the Treaty of Saint-Germain prohibited discrimination on grounds of religion or race, but he shared Kunschak's desire to restrict Jewish influence in public life, and this became a plank in the party programme.

In their campaign to discredit the so-called 'Jewish republic', the Christian Social–Pan-German coalition did succeed in getting the category of 'racial affiliation' ('Rassenzugehörigkeit') included in the official Austrian census forms in 1923. Kraus, who left this space on the census form blank, declared that the one race he did *not* belong to were the Pan-Germans (F 613–21, 11). Religion remained the fundamental determinant of identity for the Catholic majority in Austria, which explains why Seipel (as Kraus noted) was one of the few political leaders to oppose Anschluss (F 632–9, 166). He feared that closer links with Germany would undermine the authority of the Church, and when a distinctive model of Austrian identity began to emerge in the mid-1920s, it was the Catholic press that supported it with greatest conviction. This placed independent-minded critics like Kraus in a dilemma. Kraus's fear of German nationalism led him to distance himself from the Anschluss movement, but he was equally uncomfortable with the cult of 'Austrianness' which came into vogue under Seipel's leadership. In autumn 1922 Seipel succeeded in negotiating a loan with the League of Nations in Geneva, which placed the finances of the Republic on a firmer footing. The currency was stabilized, economic prospects improved, and suddenly conditions in Austria began to look more promising than in Germany, which was still in the grip of runaway inflation.

At this point an emotive form of Austrian local patriotism began to be cultivated, in both the Viennese and the provincial press. The journalism of Stefan Großmann, who made his career in Berlin, exemplified the sentimental gush about Vienna that Kraus abhorred (F 608–12, 60–8). In autumn 1923, after the *Neue Freie Presse* had published a nostalgic celebration of 'Heimat' by Hans Müller, the satirist responded by contrasting this regressive ethos with 'the real

values and successes of republican Austria' (F 632–9, 168). He was even more
severe on an article by Rudolf Hans Bartsch in the *Grazer Tagespost* entitled
'Austrian Self-Esteem' ('Das österreichische Selbstgefühl'). Bartsch, a popular
author from the conservative camp, claims to detect in Austria 'the beginning
of a new, improved people', uncontaminated by the crimes that Kraus had
attacked in *Die letzten Tage der Menschheit*. The Austrians are entitled to feel
superior to the Prussians, providing they cultivate their 'best selves'. Kraus's
scathing rejoinder shows that Bartsch's pride in Austrianness is compromised
by his *völkisch* values, and he exposes the myths cultivated by the Christian
Social–Pan-German coalition as a form of collective amnesia (F 632–9, 1–26).

Austrian Amnesia and the Executions at Kragujevac

The gift for laughter and forgetting is the theme of Kraus's satirical poem of
November 1918, 'Mir san ja eh die reinen Lamperln' ('We're innocent as
fleecy lambs'; F 499–500, 13–14). It is the nasty Germans who are supposedly
to blame for the war, while the Austrians, as Kraus points out in 'Nachruf', take
'pride in their short memory' (F 501–7, 69). 'Lest we forget' became the slogan
of all European nations after 1918, as their military veterans paraded through
the streets, but everything depended on the frame of reference.[63] In England,
the efforts of the British Legion to keep alive memories of 'Our Glorious Dead'
were counterbalanced by a growing pacifist movement, culminating in nationwide support for the Peace Pledge Union in the 1930s. But in Austria and
Germany memories of the war were orchestrated by paramilitary groups like
the Heimwehr and the Stahlhelm, parading through the streets to the rhythm
of strident marches. Remembrance became a political activity, and the myths
of glory competed with the narratives of disillusionment for control of
popular consciousness. A vast apparatus of cenotaphs, war memorials and
remembrance days was created in order to endow the concept of dying for
one's country with an aura of dignity. In a short book about Kraus published
in 1933, the poet Richard Schaukal describes a 'War Heroes Ceremony' held
at the church in Grinzing, enhanced by a male-voice choir. Kraus could not
have appreciated such a ceremony, he argues, because of the 'lack of love'
which inspired *Die letzten Tage der Menschheit*.[64] But Kraus's satire was designed
to discredit precisely the cult of heroism propagated by such ceremonies – a
misremembering of the past that he feared would cost millions of lives in the
future. 'Do not respect the piety of victims for their murderers,' he declared in
November 1920. 'Despise those who have not merely forgotten, but would
also like to discredit memory!' (F 554–6, 55).

The importance of social memory is highlighted by the executions at
Kragujevac. In June 1918 a group of Bosnian veterans, reconscripted into the
Habsburg army after their release from Russian prisoner-of-war camps,
became involved in drunken acts of insubordination, and forty-four of them
were sentenced to death under martial law. Bosnian soldiers were ordered to
shoot from a distance of two paces, but they fired inaccurately, leaving their

victims writhing on the ground. Then the order was given to place the rifle-barrels against the heads of the victims, and 'their brains were shot to pulp'. The officer responsible, Lieutenant-Colonel Suhay, reportedly declared that he would have preferred to execute 300 Bosnians, not just 44 (F 501–7, 68). These words from an eyewitness report are also cited in the corresponding scene at the end of Die letzten Tage der Menschheit, where the officer justifies the executions by saying: 'Drunken orgies cannot be tolerated.' Austrian historians have described the killings at Kragujevac as a legitimate response to acts of insubordination that amounted to mutiny.[65] There could hardly be a clearer illustration of the dictum that those who forget the past are doomed to repeat it, since a similar self-righteousness was to inspire reprisals during the Second World War. In October 1941, after partisan attacks on German troops, Kragujevac once again became the scene of a brutal massacre, as 2,300 civilians were rounded up and shot by the first battalion of the 724th Infantry Regiment, under the command of an Austrian veteran from the First World War, General Franz Böhme.[66] However, after 1945 the phenomenon of national amnesia was to repeat itself, as Austrians connived at the myth that they were the innocent victims of Hitlerite aggression.[67]

Kraus insisted that self-critical forms of public memory are essential to the health of any society. In the first number of Die Fackel published after the Armistice he committed himself to the lifelong task of 'keeping alive the memory' of those who had been so cruelly sent to their deaths (F 499–500, 35). In the following number he emphasized the importance of photographs as evidence of the horrors of war: children in gasmasks and executioners gloating over their deeds. The nations should be willing to forget each other's misdeeds, but 'mankind should not forgive or forget anything that it perpetrated against itself!' (F 501–7, 115–16). His aim is not simply to record the facts, but to reshape public memory by discrediting myths of heroism, and his characteristic method is to confront patriotic slogans with the grim realities they conceal, for example the 'honour' of the officer corps with the use of poison gas (F 501–7, 36). He never tires of reprinting news items about the consequences of war: 'ten million dead, a remnant of twice that number of cripples, and a hinterland of a hundred million beggars, starving, freezing and diseased' (F 521–30, 162).

Even after the trauma of defeat, the nationalist press was unwilling to acknowledge that the military ethos was discredited, and a flood of propaganda sought to consolidate the heroic 'ideas of 1914'. European politics of the inter-war period were dominated by the ideological struggle between conflicting myths of the First World War, designed not simply to recall the past but to prescribe the future. The pacifist movement interpreted the conflict of 1914–18 as 'the war to end wars', while reactionaries cultivated myths of military prowess as the inspiration for a 'conservative revolution'.[68] They remembered the war as they wished it to have been (and as they intended it to be next time round): as a triumph for German military power. To counteract these tendencies, Kraus transformed memory into a performative art, re-enacting the rhetoric of the militarists on the public stage. The greatest impact was made by readings from *Die letzten Tage der Menschheit*. In one of the most striking scenes, he shows how false memories are constructed. A staff officer is dictating a press release about the Austrian fortress of Przemysl, which has just been captured by the Russians. The loss of the fortress, previously regarded as the pride of the Austro-Hungarian army, is now to be played down as insignificant. When this approach is queried by the journalist at the other end of the line, the Staff Officer replies: 'You can make 'em forget everything, my friend!' The corresponding scene in the following act takes place after the recapture of Przemysl. This time the press release reverses the argument, reaffirming the fortress's strategic importance with the same cynical rejoinder: 'You can make 'em forget everything' (II, 16 & III, 22). The comic effect of this scene should not lead us to overlook the sombre truth it embodies. The Officer may appear to be a character from an operetta, but his technique anticipates the Ministry of Truth in Orwell's *Nineteen Eighty-Four*.

Kraus's engagement in the memory wars reached a first climax in Innsbruck early in 1920, when he read scenes from *Die letzten Tage der Menschheit* documenting the Kaiser's sadism. The University of Innsbruck was a hotbed of German nationalism, and the reading was interrupted by a small group that stormed out of the hall. The police banned a second scheduled reading as a threat to public order, and the affair had repercussions in the provincial assembly, parliament and the press which are documented in *Die Fackel*. Kraus was vilified by the reactionary press, which denounced him as 'racially alien'. The real threat to the German people, a professor declared, was 'the Jewish spirit' (cited F 531–43, 60–2, 142–4 & 176). Kraus's friend Ludwig Ficker, who organized the reading, feared for his physical safety.[69] But the satirist himself took a longer-term view, driving home his critique of chauvinism by invoking the internationalism of Immanuel Kant.

CHAPTER 3

International Law and the Clash of Civilizations

Kraus thrived on the intimacy of his relationship with Austria, but after 1918 his horizon was enlarged. Berlin competed with Vienna as a focal point for his creative energies, and the realignments of the 1920s led him to devote more attention to other political centres. He admired developments in Czechoslovakia, as an experiment in multicultural democracy that contrasted with the authoritarian regime in Hungary, but he resisted the fascination with the Soviet Union that was so widespread between the wars. Austrian affairs still provided the staple of his satire, but he made numerous public appearances in Berlin, Prague and Paris in an effort to promote international reconciliation. He welcomed the emergence of a system of international law designed to resolve conflict, while highlighting self-destructive tendencies that led him to look beyond Europe for salvation.

Kant and the International Court of Justice

The most significant paradigm carried over from Kraus's apocalyptic writings into the more sober polemics of the 1920s is the concept of a 'Day of Judgement', redefined in secular terms as a 'World Tribunal', the title of the two-volume collection of his wartime articles published in the spring of 1919.[1] It was Schiller who first suggested that 'world history is the world tribunal' ('Die Weltgeschichte ist das Weltgericht'), but after this idea had been taken up by Hegel in his *Philosophy of Right*, Schiller's ethically inspired concept became an apologia for power politics.[2] Nineteenth-century nationalists equated the 'judgement of history' with military conquest, while Marxists used the claim that 'history is on our side' to legitimize revolutionary violence. In a conversation with students in February 1920, the sociologist Max Weber claimed that 'the world in which we spiritually and intellectually live today is a world substantially shaped by Marx and Nietzsche'.[3] But Kraus's allegiance was to Kant and the principle of 'human dignity', and he reaffirmed the ethical significance of the 'Weltgericht' concept by welcoming the defeat of the Central Powers as a retribution for criminal policies (F 499–500, 1–4). Moreover, he endorsed the proposals for 'Perpetual Peace' in Kant's essay 'Zum ewigen Frieden', a text ignored by German nationalists, who equated the 'categorical imperative' with patriotic duty. In a speech delivered in 1917, Wilhelm II claimed that the 'Lord of Hosts' was on the German side, attributing victory over Tsarist Russia to Kant's ethical and spiritual principles. Kraus responded by printing the Kaiser's effusions side by side with a passage from 'Perpetual Peace' ridiculing those who give thanks to 'the *Lord of Hosts*' for military victories. The conception of the father of mankind, according to Kant, cannot be reconciled with a nation which rejoices 'at having annihilated numerous human beings' (cited F 474–83, 155–6).[4]

Kraus then turned to another of Kant's political essays, 'On the Common Saying: "This May be True in Theory, But It Does Not Apply in Practice"'. Here Kant analyses the relationship between the rights of the state ('Staatsrecht') and international law ('Völkerrecht'), proposing a system of 'international law, based on enforceable public laws to which each state must submit'. The way to counteract the distress caused by wars is to create a 'lawful *federation* under a commonly accepted *international law*'.[5] Writing amid the conflicts of the 1790s, Kant was aware that this idea of a peaceful federation was a distant dream. In a short final section entitled 'On the Relationship between Theory and Practice in International Law', he nevertheless reaffirmed his moral vision: the progress of the human race 'may at times be *interrupted* but never *broken off*'.[6] Kraus quotes a further passage in which Kant affirms his faith in the future:

> Confronted by the sorry spectacle not only of those evils which oppress the human race from natural causes, but also of those which men inflict upon one another, our spirits are still raised by the prospect that things might get better in the future: *moreover* with a sense of unselfish goodwill, since we shall be long in the grave and unable to harvest the fruits we helped to sow.

Kraus's imagination was caught by the phrase 'moreover' ('und zwar').[7] He highlighted it when he printed this commitment to a better future as a motto for his own poem 'Zum ewigen Frieden', which pays tribute to Kant's altruism and offers an eloquent commentary on the madness – 'Wahn' – to which Germany has succumbed (F 474–83, 159–60).

Kant recognized the importance of creating new international institutions. In 'Perpetual Peace' he associates war with the state of nature 'where no court of justice is available to judge with legal authority'. After arguing for a republican constitution guaranteeing equality for all citizens, he suggests that peace may be secured by 'a *pacific federation*' ('Friedensbund').[8] Implicit in these arguments are the concepts of a League of Nations (with the power to regulate disputes) and an International Court of Justice (to punish breaches of the peace). For over a century after Kant's death these ideas remained utopian, but in 1918, in the climate created by President Wilson's Fourteen Points, it was finally possible to put these proposals into practice. Kraus greeted Wilson's 'immortal deed', the liberation of Europe from military tyranny, as the fulfilment of Kant's 'immortal idea' (F 501–7, 113). For a moment it seemed possible to create a system of collective security, but the new democratic order, which depended on American power, suffered a mortal blow in November 1919, when the Senate repudiated membership of the League of Nations. The concept of perpetual peace depended in the last resort on a willingness to wage war against rogue states.[9]

The solution, for Kraus, was to establish an international tribunal with authority to punish political criminals. His support for international arbitration was shaped not only by his reading of Kant, but also by his admiration for the Austrian jurist Heinrich Lammasch. There had been intermittent contacts between the two since the founding of Die Fackel, and they were brought together again during the war, when Lammasch was the only Austrian statesman to argue for a compromise peace. In February 1918 – shortly after the publication of Wilson's Fourteen Points – he urged a settlement that would grant 'self-government' to the different nationalities of the Habsburg Empire. This principled stand earned him a storm of abuse, and Kraus was one of the few to speak out in support of his proposal for a 'dissolution' of the old political structure. At a public reading of 27 May 1918 he praised Lammasch as 'the only teacher of international law [. . .] whose science and conscience were not overrun by the invasion of Belgium' (F 474–83, 47 & 49). Kraus was promptly denounced to the Ministry of War as a defeatist, and an investigation was launched into his allegedly treasonable activities (F 508–13, 81–104).

Lammasch, who had played a leading role at the Hague Peace Conferences, was horrified by the hard line taken by the German representatives. In a passage quoted in Die Fackel in January 1917, he insisted on 'the peaceful resolution of international conflicts' (F 445–53, 66–7). It was Lammasch who transmitted to Kraus the memorandums in favour of a compromise peace drafted by the Austrian industrialist Julius Meinl.[10] Kraus later recalled a conversation in which they had discussed the position of war criminals and 'the problem of responsibility under international law' (F 531–43, 57). They both agreed that those responsible for chauvinistic war propaganda should be liable to 'punishment before an international court of law' (F 521–30, 154). Referring to this conversation again in October 1920, Kraus regretted that the victorious Allies had failed to extradite such criminals and make them answerable in court (F 552–3, 4).

The idea that the leaders of Austria-Hungary and the German Reich should be treated as war criminals was certainly pursued by the Entente. 'Hang the Kaiser' became a popular slogan during the British general election campaign of December 1918, but the government of the Netherlands refused requests for extradition, and Wilhelm II was allowed to live out his days on his Dutch estate. In accordance with Clauses 227–30 of the Treaty of Versailles, the western Allies requested the extradition of a total of 853 suspected war criminals, including Ludendorff, Haber and Tirpitz, but the German government, bowing to right-wing pressure, refused to co-operate. Instead, a small number of army officers, including those responsible for atrocities in occupied Belgium and France, were put on trial in 1921 by the Reichsgericht in Leipzig. It proved almost impossible to secure convictions, since even the U-boat commander who had torpedoed a British hospital ship could claim he was obeying orders, in accordance with the policy of reprisals. In Austria, one of the first actions of the republican government was to set up a Commission for the Investigation of Infringements of Military Duty to investigate offences committed by military commanders. A total of 369 cases were investigated, but the number of convictions was small.[11] The League of Nations was in its infancy, and the leaders of the Central Powers could hardly be called to account by statesmen like Clemenceau and Lloyd George, whose imperialistic policies were equally dependent on military force. By the spring of 1922, at the time of the Genoa Conference, Kraus realized that they were determined to prevent the establishment of a 'world court of justice' (F 595–600, 2). No member of the ruling elite of Imperial Germany or Austria-Hungary was ever put on trial, and it was not until after the defeat of Nazi Germany that an international tribunal was created to prosecute those responsible for crimes against humanity.

In 'Nachruf', his 120-page indictment of the Austro-Hungarian ruling class and their German allies, Kraus insisted that the Austrian attack on Serbia and the German invasion of Belgium were indeed the actions of criminals (F 501–7, 12). But he also identified a more fundamental problem: the discrepancy between the magnitude of the war and the mediocrity of its protagonists. In the drama of modern history there are no characters of tragic stature, but only 'figures from an operetta' (as the Preface to *Die letzten Tage der Menschheit* puts it) whose actions have catastrophic consequences. The disaster of 1914 was instigated by Emperor Franz Joseph, a 'demon of mediocrity' (F 501–7, 6–7). This concept anticipates the analysis of Nazi atrocities fifty years later in terms of the 'banality of evil'.[12] Modern massacres are implemented by faceless bureaucrats, while technology places unprecedented power in the hands of mediocrities. A feeble man sitting at a desk (he observed in May 1918) can blow a whole city sky high (F 474–83, 43). The danger lies not only in the destructiveness of modern technology but also in the facelessness of the man at the desk: 'Everything was anonymous, even the leading personalities. The Chief of General Staff was only his deputy, and the deputy, who signed the reports, read in the evening paper that all was quiet at the front' (F 501–7, 45).

This demonic mediocrity is exemplified by the Foreign Minister responsible for the declaration of war, Count Berchtold, whose jaunty photograph forms the frontispiece of Kraus's valediction. His denunciation of this nonentity anticipates Winston Churchill's judgement that Berchtold was 'the epitome of this age in which the affairs of Brobdingnag are managed by the Lilliputians'.[13] Kraus also ridicules Berchtold's successor, Count Czernin, whose 'paper-thin' character is ludicrously at odds with the role he played in prolonging the war.

Czernin's duplicity – acting like Ludendorff while professing a belief in Wilson – resulted in Austria-Hungary supporting German military victory at a time when the only hope lay in a negotiated settlement (F 501–7, 82–93). These crimes of political judgement were frequently compounded by atrocities committed under martial law, which provided a quasi-legal justification for policies of incipient genocide. Repudiating 'military justice' as a system that translates petty prejudices into appalling crimes, Kraus claims that 11,400 death sentences were carried out by the Austro-Hungarian military authorities during the war (F 501–8, 45). According to the investigation by Georg Lelewer published in 1927, the Archive of the Austro-Hungarian Military Courts contained an estimated 1,500,000 files, covering every conceivable offence from mutiny to fraud. Since a single file may relate to several persons, at least three million people must have been tried by the military courts during the war. Lelewer, himself a senior military judge, does his best to defend the judiciary, referring to death sentences only in his section on soldiers who were court-martialled. According to this account, a total of 754 soldiers were sentenced to death during the war, of whom 737 were executed.[14]

Working in tandem with the *Arbeiter-Zeitung*, Kraus welcomed attempts to make the military answerable to the civil authorities. In October 1918 and again in January 1919 he named the most notorious military judges who had abused their powers: Zagorski, Preminger, Koretz, König, Widmann and Peutelschmied (F 484–98, 151–2 & 501–7, 62). In a series of well-documented cases during the first months of the war, Stanislaus von Zagorski, a lawyer from Lemberg, had sentenced innocent Galician refugees and Ukrainian peasants to death for 'crimes against the military power of the state' ('Verbrechen gegen die Kriegsmacht des Staates'; AZ, 7 February & 27 October 1918). This catch-all provision meant that, in Kraus's terms, everyone was acting under cover: 'the cover of a dossier, of a slogan, of anonymity'. The problem was how to establish responsibility within a chain of command which ensured that crimes authorized from above were carried out anonymously by junior officers. One of the few to suffer retribution was a lieutenant-colonel on the General Staff – Oberstleutnant Oskar Leitner – who committed suicide after being exposed for blatant profiteering (F 501–7, 117–19). This case, reported in the *Arbeiter-Zeitung* on 28 December 1918, forms the basis of a memorable scene in *Die letzten Tage der Menschheit* (V, 47). On 21 December 1918 the *Arbeiter-Zeitung* published the text of an order from a Lieutenant-Colonel Hagauer to the military police under his command: 'Free yourselves from the petty and limited legal scruples which restrict you! Today there is only one justice, that is the welfare of the state.' The paper goes on to report the case of a Ukrainian peasant – shot dead by a police sergeant for making positive remarks about the Russians.[15] Commenting eighteen months later on the acquittal of another notorious Austrian commander, General Kasimir von Lütgendorf, Kraus identifies the failure to hold the military caste responsible for their crimes as an ominous portent for the future (F 546–50, 75–6).

Bolshevism as a Moral Problem

The arguments of 'Nachruf' were so persuasive that an unauthorized edition was published in Hungarian, translated by Gyula Szini with a cover design (by Mihály Biró) that aligned the satirist with the revolutionary overthrow of the Monarchy. Kraus was perturbed by the implication that he supported the revolutionary government of Béla Kun (F 508–13, 27–8), since this could scarcely be squared with his position as the scourge of fellow travellers. Even the critic of quick-change artists was not prepared for the events of November 1918, when poets who had been producing war propaganda experienced a sudden conversion to communism. In Munich the revolutionary movement, led by Jewish intellectuals like Kurt Eisner and Ernst Toller, resulted in the shortlived Bavarian Soviet Republic, while in Budapest the conversion of bourgeois intellectuals to the creed of revolution was even more startling, as the example of Georg Lukács shows.

Lukács was the son of a Jewish banker who had purchased his exemption from military service, enabling him to devote himself to the study of aesthetics. The sudden collapse of the Central Powers in November 1918 cut short his dreams of an academic career, and in December, writing under the title 'Bolshevism as a Moral Problem', he repudiated the idea that a just society could be brought about by violent insurrection. His decision to join the Hungarian Communist Party later that same month, as one member of his circle recalls it, 'took place between two Sundays: Saul became Paul'. He was appointed commissar for education, and when the Romanians invaded Hungarian territory he served on the eastern front as political commissar – 'an earnest little professor in a leather uniform'. He did not flinch from using violence against his subordinates, restoring revolutionary morale by setting up a court-martial and having 'eight men belonging to a battalion that had run away in panic shot in the market place'. Defeat by the Romanians precipitated the collapse of the revolution, followed by several months of White Terror directed not only against the Jewish-led Communist Party, but also against other Hungarian Jews. While some of his comrades were being tortured and executed, Lukács used his father's wealth to have himself smuggled to safety in Austria.[16]

For Kraus, as for Lenin, the antics of these bourgeois intellectuals were a form of 'infantile disorder', while their Marxism was 'purely verbal'.[17] Although he does not mention Lukács by name, he must have been aware of his ambiguous role, since he monitored the activities of the would-be revolutionaries. When Lukács was detained by the Austrian police, the campaign to ensure that he was not extradited to Hungary was led by Thomas Mann and Ernst Bloch.[18] But Kraus had nothing but scorn for 'aesthetes' who transform themselves into 'activists' (F 514–18, 30–3), claiming that these converts to the revolutionary cause were merely indulging in 'role-play' (F 501–8, 82). He was shocked by the violence of Kun's regime in Hungary, which he saw as a threat to Austria, identifying Tibor Szamuely as the most sadistic of the revolutionaries (F 514–18, 2 & 66). There can be no doubt that Szamuely used ruthless measures in his efforts to suppress the counter-revolution, and after the collapse of the regime he committed suicide.[19] Having studied the reports from Hungary, Kraus argued that the Expressionists and Dadaists who supported Kun shared responsibility for the executions carried out by sadists like Szamuely (F 514–18, 51–2). In a passage that was to prove prophetic, he attacked the tendency of the fellow-travellers to turn a blind eye to massacres committed by communists, warning that the crimes committed in Budapest would be seen as a specifically 'Jewish form of violence' ('Gewaltjudentum'), since so many of the would-be revolutionaries were from Jewish backgrounds (F 514–18, 39–40 & 56). Of the twenty-six ministers in Kun's revolutionary regime, twenty were reportedly of Jewish origin.[20] Jews were also prominent in the revolutionary upheavals in Berlin and Munich. 'That is the revolution!' Thomas Mann sardonically noted in his diary of 8 November 1918. 'The ones involved are almost exclusively Jewish.'[21] Kraus predicted an antisemitic backlash, suggesting in July 1919 that the threat of Jewish-inspired 'world revolution' might provoke a 'world pogrom' (F 514–18, 65–6).

The defeat of Béla Kun in August 1919 was followed by a brutal counter-revolution, in which army officers played a leading role. Fanatical groups of 'white terrorists' began to slaughter suspected communist sympathizers and organize pogroms, and hundreds of socialists and liberals were forced to flee the country. In January 1920 Kraus published an outspoken piece condemning Hungary as a 'bandit state' and deploring the counter-revolution as this 'bloody brothel with gypsy music'. He was impressed by the courage of revolutionaries who remained in Hungary to fight for their beliefs, especially Otto Korvin, a political idealist who was arrested and executed (F 521–30, 164). Korvin's behaviour was all the more quixotic because he had a deformed back which made him 'the most easily recognized of all the communist leaders'.[22] Kraus's main target is now the sadistic army-officer type, Géza von Lakkati de Némesfalva et Kutjafelegfaluszég. It was to remove such arrogant monsters from power, Kraus argues, that America went to war. The revolution in Hungary was bound to be a barren business because the ground on which it grew was so messy that this form of revolution could only produce disastrous results. Hence the paradox that Bolshevism, by 'attempting to drive the Devil out through Beelzebub, ensures that he returns through the back door'. Given the brutality of the counter-revolution, the international community had a duty to intervene, the sole action that would give 'meaning to this war' (F 521–30, 162–4). Characteristically, he attributed the existence of Béla Kun to the malign legacy of the Habsburgs (F 552–3, 3).

Kraus's comments were clearly one-sided, since the western powers did intervene by supporting the Romanians, but their aim was to combat communism, not to restore democracy. They then imposed punitive terms on Hungary under the Treaty of Trianon, transferring large tracts of its territory to Romania. If Kraus kept a wary eye on Budapest, it was not because he was an informed judge of Hungarian politics, but because he feared for the stability of Austria. The attempted communist coups in Vienna in April and June 1919, which were backed by the Kun government, prompted him to call for resolute resistance by the Social Democrats, and Erno Bettelheim, the man despatched from Budapest to mastermind the revolution in Vienna, was denounced in *Die Fackel* by name (F 514–18, 72).[23] When the coups were crushed by the police, the Austrian communists were thoroughly discredited, but the next danger, after Admiral Horthy had seized power as regent in Hungary, was the threat of a Habsburg restoration. In April 1921 Karl, the last Habsburg Emperor, returned to Hungary in an attempt to recover his throne, under a plan that was masterminded by General Anton Lehár, brother of the composer.[24] When the coup was frustrated by Horthy's intransigence, Karl was forced to withdraw into his exile on the island of Madeira. Kraus, who could never forgive the Habsburgs for the crimes of the war, analysed this affair in a substantial article embellished by photographs (F 568–71, 1–32). While ridiculing the attempted restoration, he also condemned Horthy's regime for the murder of hundreds of innocents, citing the testimony of the poet Andor Gábor (F 577–82, 71). In October 1921 a second attempted coup ended in farce, discrediting the supporters of the monarchical principle, but Hungary remained in Kraus's words a 'plague-ridden territory' (F 583–7, 27 & 32).

There followed a period of stabilization in Budapest under the prime ministership of Stephan Bethlen, but Kraus had few positive things to say about Hungary.[25] In December 1913 and January 1914 he had visited Budapest to give readings from his work, but after the war these visits were never repeated. Events in Budapest continued to cast a shadow over Austria, where Kun was granted political asylum and Lukács spent the whole of the 1920s, before moving to Moscow. However, it was another Hungarian Jewish refugee who was to figure most prominently in *Die Fackel*, the journalist Emmerich Bekessy. After obtaining Austrian citizenship, Bekessy went into partnership with the financier Camillo Castiglioni and set up a new publishing empire in Vienna. When Kraus launched his crusade against this new style of journalism, he made strenuous efforts to document Bekessy's activities in Hungary, drawing on the archives of the Budapest police. It emerged that Bekessy, although not a communist, had exploited the turmoil of the revolutionary period to promote shady financial deals, providing further reasons to reflect on the effects of the Hungarian Revolution.

Kraus was reluctant to concede to communism the status of a legitimate political movement, and he was later to record that repeated attempts to read Marx had left him unmoved (F 890–905, 43). For Kraus, it is militarism – not capitalism – that is the great adversary, and he condemns the bourgeois world for social injustice rather than economic exploitation. For him, Bolshevism is less a political than a moral problem, and he was shocked by the spectacle of intelligent young men, many from Jewish backgrounds, embracing a creed of violence. True to his Kantian heritage, he could never accept that destructive actions could be justified by idealistic aims. From his reading of 'Perpetual Peace' he was aware of the central principle of Kant's moral philosophy: 'Act in such a way that you can wish your maxim to become a universal law.'[26] Individual human life should never be regarded merely as a means to an end, but always simultaneously as an end in itself. This principle is repeatedly invoked to challenge the idea that 'the end should serve the means and that God first created the producer, after that the consumer and then perhaps the human being' (F 712–16, 5).

Given this subordination of politics to principles, Kraus has no truck with the argument that revolutionary violence might be justified by its results. 'To the devil with its practice,' he declared in a forthright statement about communism in November 1920, 'but God preserve it for us as a constant threat above the heads of those who own big estates and who, in order to preserve them, would like to send everyone else to die at the fronts of starvation and patriotic honour.' The reality of communism is described as the 'inverted consequence' of the life-destroying ideology of the ruling class. It may be more idealistic in origin, but its main value is as a threat to the complacency of reactionaries, like the woman from an aristocratic estate in southern Hungary who sneered at Rosa Luxemburg (F 554–6, 6–12). Since the practical achievements of communism left Kraus unimpressed, the references to the Soviet Union in *Die Fackel* during the early 1920s deal mainly with the great famine, which resulted in millions of deaths. Even in the normally fertile Volga region the 1921 harvest failed. Attacking bourgeois complacency about the consequences of the war in November 1921, he observed that 'Russia is starving' (F 577–82, 98). In March 1922, he criticized the Christians of western Europe, including the newly elected Pope Pius XI, for ignoring the fact that millions of fellow human beings were being forced by the famine to eat the bark of trees and even reduced to cannibalism (F 588–94, 36 & 42). He was scandalized by reports about diplomats, including George Chicherin, leader of the Soviet delegation, wining and dining in Italy during the Genoa Conference of April 1922, while in the Russian province of Buguruslansk 19,500 people starved to death in a single month (F 595–600, 5). His response to this crisis was to embark on a fund-raising campaign in support of the famine-relief programme set up by the charity Künstlerhilfe für Rußland, co-ordinated by the International Russian Relief Commission under the leadership of Fridtjof Nansen. In April and May 1922 Kraus gave a series of readings in Vienna, Berlin and Prague, raising substantial sums, and on several occasions he published the addresses of the fund-raising organizations concerned, urging others to follow his example. He regarded this campaign as 'the most important task which the contemporary world assigns us' (F 595–600, 64–70 & 81–2). The efforts of international organizations, led by the American Relief Administration and the Save the Children Fund, meant that by August 1922 over ten million Russians were receiving food, clothing and medical supplies from abroad.[27]

Kraus's response to the humanitarian crisis was Kantian. He hoped to inspire his readers to make comparable charitable donations, and one of his admirers did indeed contribute a further million Crowns to the fund (F 601–7, 93). However, hostility towards the Soviet Union was so widespread among the middle classes that few people were willing to match this generosity, and the campaign, which was led by the idealistic author Leonhard Frank, was boycotted by the bourgeois press (F 595–600, 66–7). Although it was supported by Friedrich Austerlitz, more radical Marxists regarded charitable giving with scepticism, insisting that rural poverty could be eliminated only through the creation of collective farms. However, the collectivization programme was to bring further disasters, and Kraus was not fooled by the cult of Stalin, later making his attitude clear by bracketing Hitler and Stalin in a single phrase (F 909–11, 27).

Masaryk and Multicultural Democracy

It was not the Soviet Union that provided his model for a new social order, but the Republic of Czechoslovakia. As a student in the 1890s Kraus had briefly fallen under the influence of the German nationalist movement, and in November 1897, at the time of Badeni's pro-Czech language decrees, he had joined the protests against the alleged 'Slav domination of Austria'.[28] But once he had achieved independence through the founding of Die Fackel, he began to sympathize with Czech aspirations, repudiating his position during the Badeni affair (F 285–6, 51–4). He had nothing but scorn for Austro-German representatives who tried to demonstrate the superiority of German culture by disrupting proceedings in parliament, and in May 1904 he repudiated the völkisch idiocy of the German nationalist press, pleading for a more open-minded approach to Czech music and Hungarian literature (F 161, 13–16). The early stages of this affirmative relationship with Czech culture have been analysed by Kurt Krolop.[29] Even more striking is Kraus's political support for the newly founded Republic of Czechoslovakia.

During the First World War he rarely referred to the situation in the Bohemian lands, and he did not give a single public reading in Prague, since the military censorship in Czech-speaking areas rendered it impossible to speak out openly against the policies of the Central Powers. But in May 1918, after the granting of an amnesty to Dr Karel Kramar, the leader of the Young Czechs who had been sentenced to death for treason, Kraus made his sympathies clear (F 484–98, 27). And on 15 and 20 November 1918, after the lifting of censorship, he gave a series of four recitals in Prague, reading scenes from Die letzte Nacht, the epilogue to Die letzten Tage der Menschheit. He also read the essay 'Die Sintflut' ('The Flood'), welcoming the collapse of the Monarchy and quoting a comment by a 'Czech leader' – probably Dr Kramar – that, in the campaign of the Germanic race against the Slavs, his compatriots had not will-ingly sacrificed a 'single drop of blood' (F 499–500, 33). Developments in the Czech Republic now became one of Kraus's most significant themes. He rarely commented directly on political events, disregarding the anti-German and anti-Jewish riots which made life so uncomfortable for contemporaries like Kafka.[30] But he spoke with considerable moral authority, especially as an opponent of imperialism.[31] His reputation was enhanced by over seventy public readings given in Prague and other Czech centres between 1920 and his death in 1936. Reading scenes from *Die letzten Tage der Menschheit* in Prague in December 1922, he recalled that as an enemy of the old regime he had longed for the creation of an independent Czechoslovakia. At the same time he warned the Czechs not to succumb to nationalist euphoria (F 588–94, 66–7).

Although born in northern Bohemia, Kraus had lived in Vienna since the age of three and had only the most rudimentary knowledge of Czech, but he was a regular reader of the German-language press of Prague: the strongly pro-German *Deutsche Zeitung Bohemia*, the more liberal *Prager Tagblatt* and the government-sponsored *Prager Presse*, which numbered Kafka and Musil among its contributors. Thus he kept himself well informed and was outspoken in his criticisms of slanted reporting in the nationalist press, especially *Bohemia*. Feeling that this old-established newspaper was abandoning its original liberal values, he accused it of 'popular mystification' (F 751–6, 110–11). He had a closer rapport with the *Prager Tagblatt*, whose critic Ludwig Steiner he particularly admired, and a further ally in *Sozialdemokrat*, the official organ of the German Social-Democratic Workers' Party of Czechoslovakia. His campaigns against corruption and his efforts to promote international understanding were also supported by leading Czech publications, notably *Tribuna* and *Pritomnost*. An article in *Pritomnost* published in April 1924 under the pseudonym 'Cursor' praised his play *Wolkenkuckucksheim* ('Cloud-Cuckoo-Land') for its portrayal of Austria as a republic without republicans (F 649–56, 93–7). The author was Jan Münzer, a Jewish journalist who was to publish a Czech edition of *Die letzten Tage der Menschheit* in 1933. Kraus's critical writings influenced a whole generation of Czech authors, who revered him as the 'enemy of clichés', from Karel Čapek to the less well-known satirical humorist Karel Polacek.[32] Kraus particularly enjoyed the company of the erudite Ludwig Steiner, according to the reminiscences of Friedrich Torberg, Vienna correspondent of the *Prager Tagblatt*.[33] But he also had contacts with members of the Czech establishment, including Otokar Fischer, professor at the Czech University. His contacts were by no means confined to literary circles, as his correspondence with Sidonie Nadherny reveals. He enjoyed summer holidays in the countryside, motoring through the entrancing landscape and visiting small towns in the Bohemian Forest (BSN 2, 326).

A further significant factor was the stability of the economy. During the immediate post-war period, the unit of currency in Austria was still the Crown (abbreviated as K), as it had been under the Habsburgs, while in Czechoslovakia it was renamed the Czech Crown (čsl. K). Early in 1919 the two currencies were approximately at par, but as confidence in the Austrian economy collapsed the Crown went into free fall, reaching its lowest point in September 1922. A loan from the League of Nations enabled the Austrian government to bring inflation under control, and in December 1924 the more stable Schilling currency was introduced. The presence in 1922–6 of a League of Nations Commissioner in Vienna, the former Mayor of Rotterdam Dr Alfred Zimmermann, ensured that the Crown was never allowed to depreciate to the absurd levels reached by the Mark in Weimar Germany, but the front covers of *Die Fackel*, which print the price in both Austrian and Czech currency, tell their own story. The two-hundred-page number published in May 1920 (F 531–43) carried a notice explaining that increased production costs had made it necessary to raise the price to 'K 16 / čsl. K 12'. So dramatic was the inflation that by August 1924 the cover price of a comparable two-hundred-page number (F 657–67) had risen to 'K 24,000 / čsl. K 15'. The cost of living in Vienna rose equally rapidly, causing widespread deprivation, but the Czech economy had a stronger industrial base, and the Kraus family had reason to be grateful that their paper mills were located at Franzensthal in the Bohemian Forest.[34]

In contrast to other German-language authors, Kraus acknowledged Czechoslovak independence without reservation, since he regarded the founding of the Republic as the consequence of the arrogance of the 'Germans in Austria' (F 521–30, 63–4). In Austria, Masaryk and his supporters were widely regarded as traitors, and in March 1921, when this accusation was made in the Christian Social *Reichspost*, Kraus emphatically repudiated it (F 561–7, 96). He also focused on one of the most controversial episodes in the prehistory of the Republic. In 1915 units of the Austro-Hungarian army, above all the predominantly Czech-speaking Infantry Regiment No. 28 (the Prague Regiment), had surrendered to the Russians.[35] According to an Order of the Day dated 6 June 1915 (cited F 632–9, 35), those Czechs had betrayed their emperor and besmirched the honour of their nation. Quoting this Order during a reading in Prague, Kraus defended the Czechs as a nation forced to participate in a war against themselves, attributing the founding of the Czechoslovak Republic to the criminal policies of the Habsburg government (F 640–8, 102–3).

It is hardly surprising that Kraus was denounced as 'pro-Czech' (F 613–21, 103). He admired a democracy which – by contrast with Austria – was relatively free from reactionary, monarchist and clerical tendencies. In April 1923, at a time of growing right-wing influence in Austria, he even hinted that he might emigrate across the Waldviertel border into Czechoslovakia (F 613–21, 11). He did not ignore the difficulties faced by the German minority under Czech rule, criticizing proposals to compel them to learn the Czech language 'within six months'. A true patriot, he adds, will 'come to meet the foreigner in his own language' (F 546–50, 23). He welcomed the co-operation between German and Czech Social Democrats as the best means of overcoming these problems, criticizing the German nationalist press in Prague for opposing a Czech–German symbiosis.[36] Moreover, he opposed the *völkisch* groups that exploited the alleged superiority of German culture as an instrument of power. His aim, as he emphasized in November 1918, was to transcend all 'national considerations' (F 508–13, 42). This explains why he criticized certain measures introduced by the Czech government, for example the policy of removing German street names in order to give the impression that Prague was an exclusively Czech city. Although incensed by the nonsense about street names, he was reassured by the fact that the new state had an exceptionally cultivated person as its president, Thomas Masaryk (F 697–705, 63–4).

Masaryk exemplified a new form of patriotism that was tolerantly pluralistic. The Czechoslovak constitution of February 1920 even permitted citizens who wished to affirm their Jewish nationality to exercise this right in censuses and elections. Masaryk's attitude towards the Jews was by no means free of ambiguity, as Hillel J. Kieval has shown.[37] But his flexible identity politics, which permitted German-Jewish, Czech-Jewish and Jewish nationalist permutations, formed a positive contrast to the oppressively Christian-Germanic ideology of Austria. His far-sightedness was acknowledged in the earliest numbers of Die Fackel, which praised his 'authentic tolerance'. For more than a decade, Kraus continued, Masaryk had been working idealistically to educate a new generation and achieve his 'idea of the Bohemian people' (cited F 24, 5). This presupposed that Czechs and Germans could live together harmoniously and that the Jews of Bohemia would be fully accepted. During the notorious Polna blood-libel case, Masaryk had denounced the accusation that Jews were guilty of 'ritual murder', and in this context, too, Kraus acknowledged his idealism and energy (F 33, 3–4 & F 36, 25). Masaryk, for his part, welcomed the founding of Die Fackel. Only the previous year, in an essay of 1898, he had complained that 'today's Jews lack the self-criticism of the prophets'.[38] Kraus's satirical spirit was very much to his taste, and he relished his attacks on Habsburg policy towards national minorities. After Kraus had published his trenchant analysis of the Friedjung Case in 1909, Masaryk wrote to congratulate him (letter from Masaryk to Kraus, 8 January 1910, cited F 568–71, 33). Soon after the war Masaryk read Die letzten Tage der Menschheit, praising the work for providing convincing evidence of the cruelty of Austrian policies.[39] In December 1921 a personal meeting between Kraus and Masaryk was arranged by the diplomat Max Lobkowitz, during which Masaryk drew Kraus's attention to an essay on Goethe's Pandora (BSN 2, 306). Hence Kraus's claim that the President of Czechoslovakia had a more authentic rapport with German literature than the Presidents of Germany and Austria, Hindenburg and Hainisch (F 697–705, 64). So impressed was he by certain of Masaryk's writings that he quoted passages from his books, highlighting the dangers of Prussian militarism and the importance of ethical norms (F 697–705, 110–13). Masaryk also anticipated Kraus's critique of the 'Faustian' ethos of modern Germany.[40] For Kraus, writing in 1926, he represented 'a miracle of world history [. . .] namely a combination of statesman and man of honour' (F 726–9, 63).

Czechoslovakia may have provided a model democracy, but there are a number of passages in which Kraus criticized the failings of Czech nationalists.

He was shocked by the events of 4 March 1919, when Czech forces suppressed a series of demonstrations by Bohemian Germans in the disputed borderlands with significant loss of life. These events prompted him to ask whether Prague was becoming the capital of Austria-Hungary (F 514–18, 25). In February 1920 the Czech government promulgated a new constitution together with a language law which restricted the rights of the German-speaking minority in areas where they constituted less than 10 per cent of the total population.[41] For Kraus this represented a continuation of the ancient quarrel between the two nations by the new victors (F 551, 1–2), and speaking from the public platform in Prague on 11 June 1920 he warned that the Czechs were in danger of becoming 'Prussian' (F 546–50, 22).

If Kraus's position was sometimes misunderstood, this was due to his ironic use of quotations. His essay of June 1921, 'Bei den Tschechen und bei den Deutschen' ('Among the Czechs and among the Germans'), recalls an episode in July 1913, when he had criticized the attitudes of a student association which campaigned for the rights of the Germans in Prague. At that date Kraus had alluded to 'German-minded youths in a country where hatred and hypocrisy – among the Czechs – had produced many unfortunate consequences' (F 378–80, 33). The phrase 'among the Czechs' was meant ironically, since the attack was directed against the arrogance of German students, blind to the failings in their own camp. But in 1921 a reader in Prague, completely mis-construing Kraus's intentions, sent him the passage from the pre-war number of Die Fackel with the sneering comment that the 'enemy of the Czechs' of July 1913 had now become a 'friend of the Czechs'. Appalled by this obtuseness, Kraus concludes that the Czechs 'may not understand German, but at least understand it better than the Germans themselves' (F 572–6, 64–8). He was an unwavering opponent of all forms of nationalism, which he defined as a 'dementia' (F 735–42, 67). His complaints about the suppression of the German language became more vocal when a further restrictive language law was introduced in February 1926.[42] In October he repudiated this policy, argu-ing for a pluralistic attitude towards the languages of the Bohemian lands and appealing to the Czechs to respect German as part of their own heritage. His ideal Czech citizen would (like Masaryk) possess a deeper appreciation of German culture than the majority of Germans, and on balance he would prefer 'to speak German with Czechs rather than with Germans'. Best of all would be a 'sign language' that would remove words from the reach of 'human stupid-ities' (F 735–42, 65–8). Shortly afterwards, Kraus received a request from the Prager Tagblatt for permission to reprint the passage about the suppression of the German language – that is only his censure, not his appreciation of Czech policy. The carefully balanced structure of his satire was to be dismantled in the interests of anti-Czech propaganda. His reaction is expressed in a forceful letter to the Prager Tagblatt, emphasizing his intention to repudiate 'national idiocy on both sides'.[43] Here again we are reminded of the affinity with Masaryk. Two years earlier the Czechoslovak President had published a state-of-the-nation address to mark the tenth anniversary of the Republic, stressing that 'in our policy *every form of chauvinism must be excluded. Naturally on both sides.*'[44]

Kraus recognized that more direct methods were needed to combat German nationalism, the most significant being the stage productions of *Die letzte Nacht*. An article published in 1924 in *Ceske slovo* by Otokar Fischer praised the play as a justification for Czech resistance against Imperial Austria (cited F 649–56, 88–93). This helps us to understand why proposals to stage the play in the Czech capital provoked such controversy. After the première in Vienna in February 1923, followed by two guest performances in Brno, German nationalist circles began an intrigue to frustrate a planned production at the German Theatre in Prague. At the centre of this intrigue was *Bohemia*, the bastion of German values in the Czech capital, even though many of its staff were Jews (F 613–22, 131). The president of the board of directors of *Bohemia* was Dr Bruno Kafka, second cousin of the author Franz Kafka.[45] The headlines in the early months of 1923 were dominated by news of the French occupation of the Ruhr, which provoked an intense reaction, since in Czechoslovakia, too, many Germans felt they were under military occupation.[46] The controversy over *Die letzte Nacht*, which reverberated through the pages of the Prague press for several weeks, provides a counterpoint in a minor key. Kraus was attacked in *Bohemia* as an 'author hostile to the German cause', since his play was liable 'to injure the feelings of any German man' (cited F 613–21, 98–105). If the play was staged at the German Theatre, the paper warned, there were likely to be 'incidents' – disruptions by German nationalist and National Socialist students. Faced by these threats, the director of the Theatre felt obliged to cancel the planned performances. There followed a string of reports and retractions, as the deputy editor of *Bohemia*, Ernst Weinert, denied that he had threatened antisemitic violence, while the drama critic, Ludwig Winder, protested his innocence. This claim rang hollow, since – in the aftermath of Kraus's earlier attack on *Bohemia* – Winder had perpetrated what Kraus saw as an act of 'newspaper revenge' (F 546–50, 29). He reacted to this latest intrigue with the comment that German culture in Prague was so deeply compromised that he would prefer to have his play performed in Czech (F 613–22, 128).

Die Fackel devotes almost fifty closely printed pages to the documentation of this affair, which Kraus describes as an insoluble 'puzzle-picture' (F 613–22, 116). It was ironic to find a journalist like Winder, author of the novel *Die jüdische Orgel* ('The Jewish Organ'), identifying himself so closely with the German cause.[47] Kraus's obsession with the irresponsibility of the press led him to conclude that the campaign had been initiated by Winder to settle old scores and that the *Bohemia* had exploited the possibility of Nazi protests for personal rather than political reasons (F 613–22, 145). The government-sponsored *Prager Presse* provided a more perceptive summary when it reported on the affair under the title 'Dohlenpolitik'. This bilingual joke is aimed at readers who know that the Czech for the bird known in German as 'Dohle' ('jackdaw') is 'kafka'. Thus the best translation for 'Dohlenpolitik' would be

'Kafkaesque politics'. Without mentioning Bruno Kafka by name, the *Prager Presse* suggests that he must bear the main responsibility, in his composite role as chairman of the Theatre Committee, President of *Bohemia*, and German member of the Czechoslovak parliament. But the *Bohemia* is not a free agent, since it is under pressure from the more extreme German press of the Sudetenland to prove its nationalist credentials. This is a further variant on the German-Jewish dilemma, seen in a Czech perspective. German-Jewish politicians and journalists in Prague, who might prefer to take a liberal line, feel obliged to become stridently nationalistic in order to prove that they are truly 'German' (F 613–22, 101–3). Bruno Kafka, who was professor of law at the German University in Prague, identified himself with a tradition of German liberalism that could be traced back to 1848.[48] The paradox (as the *Sozialdemokrat* pointed out on 1 March) is that such high-minded men felt compelled to make concessions to their thuggish colleagues (F 613–22, 110–12).

Undeterred by the setback in Prague, Kraus accepted an invitation to stage *Die letzte Nacht* the following year at Teplitz-Schönau in the Sudetenland, as a closed performance for socialist workers. The production was scheduled for July 1924 to mark the tenth anniversary of the Austrian declaration of war. Once again the German nationalist press, led by a Nazi Party official named Josef Watzlik, attempted to have the performance banned. Although no one in the Party had actually read the play, Kraus was denounced as a notorious pacifist and the sworn enemy of *völkisch* thinking, while the Social Democrats were condemned for acting as a 'Jewish defence corps' (cited F 657–67, 78–9). However, the attempted ban aroused so much interest that 12,000 people applied for tickets, helping the socialists to recruit new members. Although there were only two performances, Kraus proudly recorded that this was the only theatrical commemoration of the anniversary of the war, using the episode to expose the grass-roots activities of the Nazis, whom he compares to the Teutonic tribes described by Tacitus. The Sudetens (he concludes) form a mental 'blockage system', which precludes any advance beyond tribal primitivism (F 657–67, 74–85). In March 1925 there was a further performance of the play in Teplitz for German workers from Prague (F 686–90, 47–9). These events form a first climax in Kraus's confrontation with the 'troglodytes' of the Sudetenland.

French Rapprochement and Chinese Dream

Although Czechoslovakia faced severe problems, its frontiers were guaranteed, notably by France, in the context of what became known as the Little Entente. The admission of Austria to the League of Nations in December 1920 was supported by Edvard Beneš, Foreign Minister of Czechoslovakia, and Kraus gave a cautious welcome to this development, although he doubted whether the newly elected right-wing Austrian government, led by Michael Mayr, was fully committed to democracy (F 557–60, 63–72). Even more encouraging was the

Treaty of Lana in December 1921, through which Johannes Schober, who had succeeded Mayr as chancellor, obtained Czech credits for the ailing Austrian economy. In December 1923 Beneš concluded a treaty of friendship with France designed to stabilize the situation in central Europe. For Kraus, the Vienna–Prague–Paris rapprochement seemed preferable to the two most widely canvassed alternatives: Anschluss, the union of Austria with Germany; and the Gömbös plan, which would have aligned Vienna with the regimes of Budapest and Rome.

However, Kraus's attitude towards French culture was ambivalent. He had enjoyed visiting Paris as a young man, savouring the night life with his friend Herwarth Walden.[49] But he regarded French cultural influence with suspicion, arguing in 'Heine und die Folgen' ('Heine and the Consequences', 1911) that the facile writings of French literati had inspired a proliferation of shallow journalism in the German-speaking world. This prompted him to defend German functionalism against the alleged superficiality of Latin nations (F 329–30, 4). The First World War made him think again, developing a schema of international relations in which Russia became associated with spiritual piety and Britain with commercial pragmatism, while Germany, earlier commended for its organizational efficiency, was denounced for its cult of military power. In October 1917, after America's entry into the war, he radically revised his view of the contrast between German and Latin nations, developing a global view of the 'clash of existential principles' ('Zusammenstoß der Lebensrichtungen'). He now welcomes the alliance of Anglo-Saxons (Britain and the United States) and Latins (France and Italy) against the corrupted modern form of German 'Volkstum' (F 462–72, 76–8). But he fears that militarism will triumph, even if Germany is defeated, since the spirit of other nations will be contaminated.

Kraus was not blind to the dangers of French militarism, incorporating in *Die letzten Tage der Menschheit* a scene featuring sadistic French officers with the symbolic names Gloirefaisant, Massacré and Meurtrier (V, 15). He regarded the terms imposed on Germany at Versailles as a disaster and was shocked by the French occupation of the Ruhr in 1923, which he saw as a betrayal of the ideals of Liberty and Fraternity (F 613–21, 55). During the mid-1920s, however, he moderated his view of French policy, now represented by Aristide Briand, the advocate of disarmament and reconciliation. Commenting on a report about the autumn 1929 meeting of the League of Nations, he acknowledged Briand's gifts as a speaker (F 820–6, 110), and in 1931–2, during the controversy caused by proposals for an Austrian customs union with Germany, he supported Briand's offer of a loan designed to strengthen ties with France (F 857–63, 5–7). Personally, too, he made it clear that France was the country where he felt most at home (F 876–84, 12–14).

Writers sensitive to the threat of German nationalism and antisemitism, such as Joseph Roth and Kurt Tucholsky, found the cosmopolitan Paris of the 1920s particularly congenial, and Kraus's reorientation forms part of this pattern. In March 1925 he was invited by Professor Charles Schweitzer of the French

Society for Modern Languages to give a series of readings in German at the Sorbonne, including scenes from *Die letzten Tage der Menschheit* (F 686–90, 36–8). In all, he gave a total of ten such recitals, making a significant contribution to the process of international reconciliation. He set his French listeners exacting standards by reciting not only his own poems and satires, but also Goethe's *Pandora* and a German version of Shakespeare's *Macbeth* (F 726–9, 74–5). He made a special effort to ensure that his anti-war satire was not misconstrued, responding to a protest against his Paris readings by patriotic Germans by stressing the international implications of his work. His critique of war may be expressed in the language and material of the German and Austrian experience. But his theme is the 'tragedy of mankind, hounded to death by its impoverished imagination', and he has 'no fatherland apart from his writing-desk' (F 781–6, 1–9).

The readings in Paris won him influential admirers, and in 1926 Kraus was proposed for the Nobel Prize for Literature by nine professors at the Sorbonne (F 800–5, 56–8). The group was led by Charles Schweitzer and Charles Andler, both from Alsace, the province restored to France in 1918. Schweitzer (as Gerald Stieg has shown) had a political agenda.[50] Fearing a revival of German power, he promoted Kraus as a pacifist and spokesman for anti-imperialist values. A portrait of Schweitzer, as perceived by an impressionable child, can be found in the memoirs of his grandson Jean-Paul Sartre, who emphasizes Schweitzer's love–hate for Germany and the 'patriotic rage' inspired in him by the German annexation of Alsace in 1871.[51] Andler, too, in supporting Kraus's candidacy, hoped to strengthen the prestige of an independent Austria. The proposal was resubmitted to the Nobel Committee in 1927 and 1928, but it was Thomas Mann who received the prize.

The international reception of Kraus's work placed him in a dilemma. How was he to express his admiration for France without appearing anti-German? This charge was levelled against him not only by the nationalists, but also by the liberal journalist Alfred Kerr, and Kraus was obliged to explain that his hostility to German chauvinism did not make him a stooge of the Entente (F 787–94, 179–82). He expressed his internationalism most eloquently by identifying with a German Jew from the Rhineland who had made his career in Paris. It was not Trotsky, Masaryk or Briand who represented his ideal of internationalism, but Jacques Offenbach – German by birth, Jewish by descent, French by nationality. His operettas mocked nationalism, militarism and authoritarianism in every conceivable setting, from Athens to Peru, and Kraus became an inspired advocate of the Offenbach revival, devoting endless hours to retranslating the libretti by Henri Meilhac and Ludovic Halévy. The most delightful of Offenbach's scores, in Kraus's view, was *Die Schwätzerin von Saragossa*, and after reciting this work for the first time he went out of his way to stress its international credentials. Based on a sketch by Cervantes, it was first performed at Ems in Germany in 1862, before having its full-scale première in Vienna. Offenbach (according to an Austrian critic who visited him in Paris)

was 'a Frenchman through and through with a certain Berlin–Cologne orien-
tal expression into the bargain' (F 845–6, 7–13). Kraus quoted such passages in
order to highlight his internationalism, and between 1926 and 1936 he gave
over a hundred Offenbach recitals, offering an antidote to Wagner's Germanic
myths.

Since Kraus's attitude towards Europe was haunted by the threat of militarism, it led him to look beyond Christendom for an alternative, cultivating a
dream of China. His sympathy can be traced back to the Boxer Rising of
summer 1900, when he published an article censuring not the Chinese rebels,
but the hapless western diplomats in Peking. This was the period when western imperialists, led by Kaiser Wilhelm II, were pontificating about the 'Yellow
Peril'.[52] Kraus was sceptical about such sloganizing, converting the alleged
'peril' into a 'Yellow Hope' in the essay 'Apokalypse' (October 1908), which
also alluded to his 'Chinese dream' (F 261–2, 6–7). One source was Oscar
Wilde's essay 'A Chinese Philosopher', published in *Die Fackel* the following
month, which endorsed the ideas of Chuang Tsu as a form of spiritual resistance to capitalism (F 264–5, 5–17). Kraus's image of China was also indebted
to Ku Hung-Ming's *Papers from a Viceroy's Yamen*, published in the aftermath of
the Boxer Rising.[53] The author, a Chinese civil servant, was an outspoken critic
of western militarism and imperialism, publishing a brilliant series of aphorisms
that anticipate Kraus's quotation technique. The arrogance of imperialists like
President McKinley, Wilhelm II and Austen Chamberlain is contrasted with
the humanistic principles of Goethe and Heine, Ruskin and Emerson. If there
is a 'conflict of civilization', Hung-Ming concludes, this is not a 'conflict of the
white race with the yellow race', but a 'struggle on the part of the people
of Europe' to free themselves from the combination of medieval religious
prejudices and modern gunboat policy. To illustrate the hypocrisy of Christian
civilization, he suggests that 'the brains of the people in modern Europe are
divided into two compartments', of which only one is open at any time.[54] This
anticipates another passage where Kraus argues that 'our culture consists of
three compartments, of which two are closed when the third is opened'. He
contrasts this with the 'Chinese jugglers', who master the whole of life
with one finger (F 261–2, 6). There are further striking parallels with Ku
Hung-Ming's book, although it was not specifically mentioned in *Die Fackel*
until May 1924 (F 657–67, 97). Kraus's imagination was also captured by
accounts of Chinese sexual mores, which struck him as far less repressive than
those of Christianity, founded – as he ironically remarks – '500 years after
Confucius' (F 285–6, 16). This telling phrase occurs in his visionary essay 'Die
chinesische Mauer' ('The Great Wall of China'), published in book form
with lithographs by Kokoschka in summer 1914, after appearing in *Die Fackel*
in July 1909.

This interest in China had a political dimension. The essay by Otto Corbach
on 'Proletarians and Coolies', which Kraus published in April 1911, challenges
Marx's assumption (in the *Communist Manifesto*) that capitalist market forces

will 'batter down all the walls of China'. The Chinese, deeply wedded to their traditions, are proving resistant to capitalist penetration. Their frugal agricultural system makes them economically self-sufficient, and coolies enjoy a sense of community unknown to the western proletariat. Moreover, its reservoir of labour makes China potentially a more powerful force than Japan (F 319–20, 24–30). This was a startling proposition, since Japan, victor in the Russo-Japanese War of 1905, was regarded as the most significant force in Asia, while the condition of China in 1911 was described as 'lamentable'.[55] Kraus, who admired the civilization of Confucius, took a longer-term view, presenting the integrated culture of ancient China as a paradigm for the future. This argument impressed the sinologist Joseph Needham, who described Kraus's ideas as 'extraordinarily progressive', particularly the claim that 'China showed how an advanced technology could be developed without suffering its dehumanizing effects'.[56]

The overdependence of western civilization on military power prompted the satirist, on the eve of the First World War, to appeal once more to the 'Yellow Hope', suggesting that the Chinese would teach the Europeans a 'sobering lesson' (F 400–3, 88). He praised the Chinese for having 'worked through the technological apparatus of the modern age in ancient times and kept their life intact'. Indeed, he was convinced that the 'capacity to survive technologized civilization does not grow within the realms of Christendom' (F 406–12, 96 & 127). In January 1917 he cited a collection of Chinese anti-war poems, translated by Klabund (Alfred Henschke), as the testimony of a 'truly cultured people', vastly superior to Europe in their repudiation of the compulsion to kill (F 445–53, 95 & 102–3). He recited four of them in public, including one by Confucius, tactfully ignoring the bellicose quality of Klabund's other writings.[57] This interest in China resurfaced in his letters to Sidonie Nadherny.[58] The most significant passage occurs in a letter of 14 November 1917, in which he shares with her his revulsion at atrocities reported to him by an Austrian officer, Max Lobkowicz:

> M.L. has described experiences which make it impossible for one to share the same part of the world after the war with those involved in them. In Europe, Russia would be the only state which through its spiritual disposition of its inhabitants might grant some form of atonement. But really there remains only China. (BSN 1, 450)

This letter was written in the immediate aftermath of the Bolshevik Revolution and the Russian offer of peace negotiations, but Kraus's idea of Russia as a counterweight to the west was shaped not by Lenin, but by Dostoevsky. He had urged Sidonie to read *The Brothers Karamazov*, and together they had prepared for publication the passages from Dostoevsky's diaries about 'The Jewish Question', emphasizing Christian conduct as a counterweight to 'materialism' allegedly propagated by 'wealthy Jews' (F 413–17, 65; BSN 1, 195 & 308).

It is possible, at the risk of simplification, to present these cryptic arguments in schematic form (Fig. 4). They are restated in Act I, scene 29 of *Die letzten*

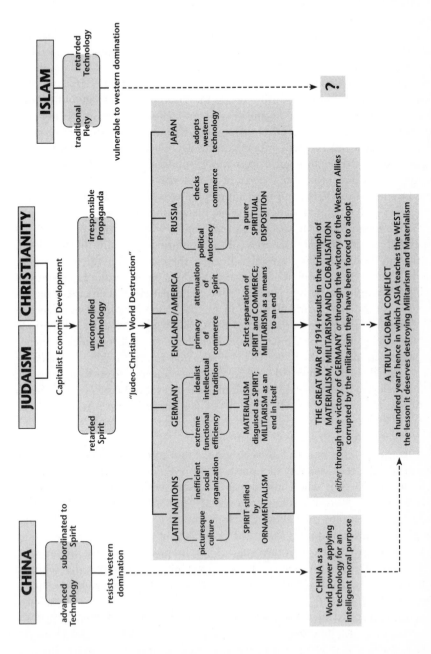

4   The Clash of Civilizations as envisaged in *The Last Days of Mankind*

Tage der Menschheit, where Kraus's spokesman, the Grumbler, predicts a 'war of religion' between Asia and the west. Some alternative must be found for 'capitalist, that is Judaeo-Christian world destruction'. The echoes of Dostoevsky are unmistakable, not least in the suggestion that the Jews are to blame for the ills of modernity, and in the first draft of the play the Grumbler explicitly pays tribute to Tsarist Russia for its resistance to 'Jewish intellectualism'.[59] The target to be destroyed in this future war of religion will be the destructive combination of capitalism, militarism and technology, exemplified by Germany – 'the first militarized people on earth'. When the Grumbler looks beyond Europe for a race strong enough to assimilate modern technology without being corrupted, the Optimist is sceptical: 'Aha, your Chinese; the least warlike race'. The Grumbler, undeterred, anticipates the day when the Chinese will once again acquire the technological apparatus of modernity – in order to cure the Europeans of their affliction. There are Spenglerian overtones to this vision of the Decline of the West, and both authors see western man as enslaved to the machines he has created, denouncing the dictatorship of money.

The impulse to equate specific nations with world-historical principles led Spengler to incorporate a series of deterministic diagrams in his book. Although Kraus's thinking was more flexible, there is also a predictive element in his scheme of the conflict of civilizations, which envisages the ascendancy of China. There are intriguing parallels between the pattern that emerges from his writings of the First World War period and the clash of civilizations envisaged by Samuel Huntington at the end of the Cold War. Kraus anticipates Huntington's suggestion that China's 'Confucian heritage' will influence its hegemonic position, with the potential to create a new international order based on peace rather than conflict.[60] There are obvious omissions from Kraus's vision, which relegates the enduring strength of Islam to a subordinate position. In his writings, for example Act III, scene 19 of *Die letzten Tage der Menschheit*, the piety of Islam serves as a contrast to the arrogance of the west, rather than a force in its own right (cf. F 431–6, 79–83).

Occasional references to China continued to feature in Kraus's vision of the decline of the west, notably in a poem of the 1920s also entitled 'Apokalypse' (F 546–50, 78–80), where the threat associated with 'two hundred million horsemen' alludes to its emergent power (F 552–3, 11). It is unclear whether he kept himself informed about developments in republican China, although in 1922 he made inquiries about the possibility of spending a year travelling with Sidonie to the Far East (BSN 1, 531). In his polemics against the press, he quoted with particular relish a passage by Hung-Ming about the Chinese Emperor who, 2,000 years earlier, had dealt with irresponsible literati by burying them alive (F 657–67, 97).[61] Given that the survival of western 'civilization' depended on racial prejudice and poison gas, the Chinese appealed to him as a race 'superior by nature' (F 697–705, 132), and he cherished the thought that China, unlike Japan, was untouched by western influences (F 838–44, 79). In the final year of his life he commended a study of China by

Julius Tandler, quoting a passage which censures the League of Nations for failing to act against the opium trade for fear of damaging the interests of the colonial powers (F 917–22, 82). Confucius remained one of his guiding lights, and he was particularly impressed by the philosopher's insistence on verbal clarity as the basis of civilized existence (F 852–6, 60). Thus China provided a counterpoint to the configuration he regarded as so fateful for western civilization – the misuse of language, the failure to control technology, and the addiction to war.

CHAPTER 4

Ink, Technology and Death

In April 1919, to mark the twentieth anniversary of *Die Fackel*, Kraus published a seven-page narrative poem entitled 'Nach zwanzig Jahren'. After stressing his commitment to the connection between 'word and being', he lists the themes for which he may be called to account on Judgement Day:

> Geschlecht und Lüge, Dummheit, Übelstände,
> Tonfall und Phrase, Tinte, Technik, Tod,
> Krieg und Gesellschaft, Wucher, Politik,
> der Übermut der Ämter und die Schmach,
> die Unwert schweigendem Verdienst erweist,
> Kunst und Natur, die Liebe und der Traum –
>
> (F 508–13, 7)

> Corruption, idiocy, sex and lies,
> soundbites and phrases, ink, technology and death,
> profit and politics, society and war,
> the insolence of office and the spurns
> that patient merit of the unworthy takes,
> nature and artistry, love and dream –

Lines from Hamlet's monologue (in Schlegel's translation) are blended with Kraus's blank verse, while the assonance of 'Tinte, Technik, Tod' contains a distant echo of Dürer's 'Ritter, Tod und Teufel'. These apocalyptic figures reappear in modern guise in the grimly prophetic epilogue to *Die letzten Tage der Menschheit* as military commander, industrial chemist and media mogul – Knight, Death and Devil.

Diplomats, Telegrams and Lies

On the outbreak of war in August 1914, the patriotic euphoria was so powerful that for a moment even Kraus succumbed. Since he was debarred from military service by his physical disability, a curvature of the spine, his first impulse was to make a financial sacrifice by subscribing to War Loan.

However, in November 1914 he cancelled hi
the realization that supporting the military
the war' (P 1, 284–5). Reacting against the e:
he set out his position in the celebrated decl:
dieser großen Zeit' ('In These Great Times',
on the fanaticism of individual journalists, bu
aganda, culminating in the insight that 'the
like the grenade' (F 404, 12).

The war marked a new phase in the development of mass communications, sustained by innovative technologies. Kraus's reference to telegrams can be correlated with the action of the British navy in August 1914 in cutting the underwater cable across the Atlantic that linked Germany with America. Berlin quickly lost the initiative in the so-called 'cable war', while the Reuters news agency was seen as 'the most powerful weapon of the British government'.[2] The propaganda machine swung into action in every belligerent country, and Kraus was duly sceptical about the reports of German atrocities. The press, in his view, was an 'international disgrace' (F 404, 11), but his main task was to expose the falsifications emanating from German and Austrian sources, especially the Berlin news agency, the Wolff-Büro, and the War Press Department in Vienna. Austro-Hungarian military commanders may have been losing ground on the eastern front, but they were determined to control the hinterland, in collusion with cynical officials and servile hacks. A credulous public clamoured for news of victories, and the propaganda apparatus fed them with morale-boosting despatches from the front.[3]

In autumn 1915, after further reflection, Kraus published a sequence of aphorisms about the relationship between culture, politics, journalism and the war. His opposition had been strengthened by conversations with Sidonie Nadherny, a principled opponent of German militarism. During the month of August, spent in her company at Schloss Janowitz, he drafted the first scenes of *Die letzten Tage der Menschheit*, together with aphorisms oblique enough to circumvent the censorship. Initially, he had highlighted the misdeeds of journalists, claiming that it was they who exploited the diplomats (F 404, 13). Now he arrived at a more balanced judgement, presented in question-and-answer form: '   ade to fight wars? Diplomats tell lies
to jour   see them in print' (F 406–12, 106).
This in   dia-induced false memory: the hypnotic   ans to believe the falsehoods they
themse   is's primary example was the German
govern   had bombed the railway line near
Nuren   78), cited in the Reichstag the following   Bethmann-Hollweg, to justify the
declara   accompanied by equally fraudulent
rumours about 'French gold'. On 5 August the German government reported that twenty-five automobiles carrying eighty million gold francs had entered

the country from the Netherlands en route to Russia. This announcement provoked a frenzied reaction throughout Germany, bringing motor traffic to a virtual standstill. The government itself seems to have believed many of the rumours, and on 9 August its official newspaper, the *Norddeutsche Allgemeine Zeitung*, carried a front-page report that three vehicles loaded with gold had been apprehended. Such reports were promptly reprinted by other news-papers, of which there were over 3,600 in Germany, the most literate country in the world.[4] These government-instigated and media-fed fantasies were not confined to Germany, as it clear from the 'phantom army', created by the British press in September 1914. Rumours that a huge Russian army had landed in France were allegedly confirmed by numerous witnesses, and this collective self-delusion was propagated in the press for a full week, each paper trying to outdo the next with lurid details, before it became clear that the story was a complete fabrication.[5] The phantom army, at least, caused no casualties, but twenty-eight people were shot dead in Germany during the panic about 'French gold', as over-zealous guards intercepted passing vehicles.[6] Kraus found this episode so absurd that in Act I of *Die letzten Tage der Menschheit* he devoted two short scenes to it. Other myths, particularly that of 'Germany's Sole Responsibility for the War', were sustained throughout the conflict with devastating consequences, as Arthur Ponsonby demonstrated in his study of *Falsehood in Wartime*. Lloyd George and Poincaré knew perfectly well that the allegation of sole German responsibility was untrue, but the climate created by their own speeches led them to incorporate the notorious 'war guilt' clause in the Treaty of Versailles, thus sabotaging the post-war settlement.[7]

Kraus was so proud of his insight into the self-deluding nature of statements by diplomats that he rephrased the idea as an epigram in 1925 (F 697–705, 89). During the 1920s he collected further evidence of links between diplomatic manoeuvring and journalistic malpractice, showing how a supposedly free press colludes with the failings of politicians. A telling example was provided by the Economic Conference at Genoa in April 1922, a gathering which exemplified the weaknesses of the post-war European order. The ostensible aim was to discuss international aid for the Soviet Union, but the decision by the Bolsheviks to repudiate the debts of the Tsarist government proved an intractable obstacle. While the western powers were wrangling at Genoa, German and Russian officials met secretly in nearby Rapallo and signed a pact re-establishing diplomatic and economic contacts – a coup masterminded by the German Foreign Minister, Walther Rathenau. For western diplomacy, the negotiations at Genoa proved a fiasco, and Kraus was so incensed that he devoted a twenty-page article to the subjec
ence produced no positive results provided
the statesmen as 'pumpkins', but also to att;
Journalists may claim to be the 'conscienc
coverage of non-events results in a pervas
'what is reported', but that 'something i:

medium is the message. Kraus recalls the irresponsible coverage of the Balkan wars by Austrian journalists in 1913. A decade later, he detects the same self-indulgent tone, with the significant difference that statesmen like Lloyd George are actively colluding in the manipulation of public opinion. Kraus looks in vain for a statesman with the courage to stand on his own feet – only Rathenau has any principles. Tragically, after his return to Berlin, Rathenau was gunned down by Nazi thugs, who hated the idea of a German Jew making peace with Russian communists. Kraus lamented his untimely death in a footnote appended to this polemic (F 595–600, 1–2 & 7–8).

The word 'Lüge' – falsehood or lie – occurs hundreds of time in *Die Fackel*, framed by Kraus's analysis of a self-generating system of mendacity. Lies published in the press about alleged atrocities a
with real atrocities. This leads to an even 1
everything was a lie, including the persistent
and now, plunged into the neurasthenia of h
After condemning the mutual hatreds gene
Kraus turned his attention during the post-w
of mendacity, denouncing the 'fraud of cult
1919 the economic situation in Vienna was s
were needed to pay for imported food, coal a
troversial proposal was that the Flemish tapestries (Gobelins) from Schönbrunn Palace should be pledged to foreign creditors as security. The liberal press, led by the *Neue Freie Presse*, swamped the government with protests, but for Kraus this was sheer hypocrisy. In a period of national emergency, with thousands of
children dying from malnutrition, influenz
the tapestries was justified as a means of alle
to the conclusion that bourgeois culture (
Newspaper readers 'have been spared al
technology of the print medium, which d(
packaged, whatever eternal values they ma
homes'; they are 'accustomed to being comp
loss of vital imagination'. Hence their failu
their neighbours: they experience 'the death of the other as a newspaper report
(F 519–20, 26–7).

Kraus's most chilling prediction was first published in January 1917: 'No, there will be no scar left on the human soul. The bullet will have gone in through one ear and out through the other' (F 445–53, 2). When he repeated this prophecy in January 1920, its truth was already becoming self-evident (F 521–30, 163). By that date Hungary was in the grip of military terror, while Germany was already haunted by the spectre of Nazism. If the military mentality is not discredited, he warned in November 1920, it will lead 'to the dead-certain prospect of new wars' (F 554–6, 8). In October 1927 he denounced those who were longing for a 'greater world war' (F 766–70, 49). By the early 1930s it was clear that the 'war against war' was being conducted not merely against those who had caused the last conflagration, but against those who were planning the next (F 834–7, 20).

Propaganda and Poison Gas

The most prophetic section of *Die letzten Tage der Menschheit* is the epilogue, *Die letzte Nacht*, which distils the dangers of militarism into a sequence of symbolic episodes. This remarkable verse play has tended to be seen merely as a coda, unworthy of close textual commentary.[8] In fact, it was the first part of the play to be published, appearing in December 1918 as a self-contained, forty-eight-page special number of *Die Fackel*, and it has an artistic unity that is lacking in the main body of the play. Kraus wrote *Die letzte Nacht* in a single burst of creativity in July 1917, grieving for the death of his friend Franz Grüner, a young art historian killed by a grenade (BSN 2, 276). He was staying with Sidonie Nadherny in Switzerland at the time, and in Zurich he dictated his manuscript to a typist, disguising certain references so as to reduce the risk of having the typescript confiscated when he returned to Austria that autumn, since its content was treasonable.

The opening lines, spoken by a Dying Soldier, confront military authority with the realities of death and bereavement, echoing the words of a Chinese poem that had been printed in *Die Fackel* with admiring comments (F 445–53, 102). This motif is now reshaped into a denunciation of German militarism: 'Captain, call out the firing-squad! / For the Kaiser I'll not shed my blood!' Since these lines constituted an incitement to mutiny, Kraus replaced the word 'Kaiser' by 'Tsar' in the original typescript so as to divert suspicion (F 834–7, 52). He also omitted this denunciation of the Kaiser when he read scenes from this text in public in December 1917 (F 474–83, 90). The 1918 edition of *Die letzte Nacht* has a frontispiece: a photograph of Wilhelm II against a wintry background, which accentuates the political message. In 1922, when *Die letzte Nacht* was incorporated in the book edition of the drama, the text was left unchanged, but the picture of the Kaiser was dropped and a more poignant photograph added, forming a symbolic coda for the whole play. This shows a figure of the crucified Christ from a wayside shrine, situated near one of the battlefields of the western front. The wooden cross has been shot away, but the figure of Christ remains intact, arms uplifted in a gesture of supplication. The political satire culminates in a religious allegory, and *Die letzten Tage der Menschheit* has been aptly described as a 'post-Christian' tragedy.[9]

The epilogue takes us into the heart of darkness – the ultimate horror that anticipates the Holocaust. Although it abounds in figures from contemporary history – generals and journalists, soldiers and profiteers – its subtext is biblical: the betrayal of Christ by the Christians and Jehovah by the Jews. The epilogue begins with a cluster of stark stage directions: 'Battlefield. Craters. Smoke clouds. Starless night. The horizon is a wall of flames. Corpses. Dying soldiers. Men and women in gasmasks appear' (p. 5).[10] The play is conceived in the mode defined by Kraus as 'topical apocalypse' (F 445–53, 132). The Judaeo-Christian promise of redemption – of messianic expectation fulfilled through the life of the saviour – is retracted in the face of man's revolt against God. The broken cross featured in Kraus's final photograph symbolizes the fractured allegory, since it no longer offers the promise of redemption. In its place, at the apocalyptic climax of *Die letzte Nacht*, the sky is filled with 'a great bleeding cross' (p. 40), symbol of final destruction. If the extinction of mankind can still be pictured as an act of retribution, it is no longer the will of God that is in control. For the sign of the cross is now in the hands of the Anti-Christ, the Lord of the Hyenas, who controls the satanic alliance of 'ink, technology and death' (p. 29). Hence his triumphant boast:

Und der es einst vollbrachte,	The son of man who suffered,
an seinem Kreuz verschmachte,	and on the cross was offered,
wert, daß man ihn vergißt.	deserves to be despised.
Ich tret' an seine Stelle,	In place of life eternal
die Hölle ist die Helle!	now burn the fires infernal.
Ich bin der Antichrist.	I am the Anti-Christ.

(p. 25)

During the twenty strophes of this diatribe, the Lord of the Hyenas reveals his name – Moriz Benedikt, editor of the *Neue Freie Presse*. In 1918 Benedikt had proclaimed that there should be a 'moratorium' on Christ's Sermon on the Mount, demanding the continuation of 'blood sacrifices' (F 474–83, 37). Kraus was also influenced by the fact that the name Benedikt (Benedictus) was identical with that of the new Pope, elected in autumn 1914, and earlier in *Die letzten Tage der Menschheit* (I, 27 & 28) he contrasts 'Benedikt at Prayer' (the Pope imploring the belligerent governments to bring the war to an end) with 'Benedikt at Dictation' (the editor gloating over the deaths of Italian sailors).

There were other candidates for the role of Anti-Christ. In October 1908 Kaiser Wilhelm II was pictured as a figure from the Apocalypse with power 'to take peace from the earth' (F 261–2, 4). But the Kaiser is now subordinated to more sinister forces: the saturation effects of propaganda (represented by the Lord of the Hyenas); the ruthlessness of capitalist expansion (represented by the Hyenas themselves); the sadistic power of German militarism (represented by the Death's Head Hussar); the technology of the cinema, which was transforming war into a spectacle (the Film Crew); and the insidious effects of chemical warfare (represented by the scientist, Dr Abendrot). *Die letzte Nacht* achieves its ideological balance by giving almost equal weight to each of these forces. The press and propaganda may command centre stage, but the militarists are mocked with equal vehemence. The ghastly glamour of the Death's Head Hussar has even more sinister associations, and in the opening lines of this monologue, freely translated, we may catch hints of the sadism of a more recent German military elite, Himmler's SS:

Schneddereng. schneddereng!	Hell and damnation! Damnation and doom!
Die Luft hier ist mein Leibparfeng.	The scent of battle's my favourite perfume.
Wir sind die Totenkopfhusaren,	We shall fight on till our final breath,
in unsrem Handwerk wohlerfahren.	For we are the regiment of death.

(p.16)

There are suggestions in this thirty-five-line monologue that the prototype for Kraus's Death's Head Hussar was the German Crown Prince, Colonel-in-Chief of the regiment, who was later to become an enthusiastic Nazi. On stage, the visual impact is enhanced by the skull-and-crossbones motif on the regimental helmet.

Kraus's aim is to show that the archetypes of the satirical imagination have been given a new lease of life by the mechanisms of modern warfare. The carnival motif of the masked ball is grotesquely updated by the dance of the Gasmasks, male and female, which dominates the opening scenes of the play. Even more menacing are the Hyenas, a motif that can be traced back to another of the classics of anti-war literature, Bertha von Suttner's *Die Waffen nieder!* (*Lay Down Your Arms!*), published in 1889. The finest chapter in Suttner's novel, which anticipates Kraus's own combination of documentary and fictional techniques, portrays the battlefields of the Austro-Prussian War of 1866. Through a telescopic narrative she brings the reader closer and closer to the battlefield of Königgrätz, littered with the bodies of the dead and of those who are still just alive. 'There is one thing [the doctor–narrator continues] even more diabolical than all of this – the most appalling scum produced by the human species in time of war: the hyena of the battlefield.' The doctor explains this phenomenon to his delicately nurtured travelling companion: 'It comes creeping up, this monster that has scented blood and booty, bends down over the dead and those who are still alive and tears their clothes off their bodies. Mercilessly. Boots are pulled off bleeding legs, rings from wounded hands – or the finger is cut off to get the ring', and while 'glorious victory' is being celebrated back home, the battlefield becomes the scene of 'the dance of the hyenas'.[11] Kraus's Hyenas also dance – to the modish rhythms of the tango – but they are not miserable scavengers scouring the battlefield. They are war profiteers, who don't need to get blood on their hands in order to enrich themselves at the expense of dying soldiers:

Wir sagen es ins Ohr euch, ihr solltet uns danken:
dadurch, daß ihr hier liegt, gehts besser den Banken.
Durch die Bank konnten sie das Kapital sich vermehren,
die Fusion mit der Schlachtbank kann man ihnen nicht wehren. (p. 22)

Let us tell you in whispers: you owe us your thanks,
for death during battle brings wealth to the banks.
As our capital grows we spend money like water,
we're making a bid for the business of slaughter.

Capitalism and militarism are destroying the human race, and stockbrokers join the military commanders and media moguls in the apocalyptic chorus.

Kraus is distinguished from other writers of his generation by the fact that he, like Dostoevsky, had a sense of absolute evil. His passion for Dostoevsky coincided with the writing of *Die letzten Tage der Menschheit*, as we know from the fact that he had sent a copy of *The Brothers Karamazov* to Sidonie Nadherny in Switzerland, urging her to read it rather than spend all her time on the ski slopes (BSN 1, 307–8). The Lord of the Hyenas – like the Grand Inquisitor – explicitly defies the love of Christ and dedicates himself to 'the spirit of death and destruction'.[12] But Kraus's vision would be incomplete if he had omitted the most ominous of the angels of death: the demon scientist. By giving this most prophetic of all the figures in *Die letzte Nacht* an emphatically German-Jewish name, Dr Siegfried Abendrot, Kraus decisively enlarges his vision of 'Judaeo-Christian World Destruction'.[13] The spectre of the demonic inventor, which has haunted the western imagination from Frankenstein through to Dr Strangelove, here assumes the features of an industrial chemist:

> Um endlich den endlichen Endsieg zu kriegen,
> und dann also endlich unendlich zu siegen,
> greift ungebrochne strategische Kraft
> in die letzten Reserven der Wissenschaft.
> Was half uns die Kunst unsrer Bombenwerfer?
> Und das Gas, noch so scharf, macht das feindliche schärfer.
> Oft wurde das Angebot von unseren Gasen
> in unsre Linien zurückgeblasen.
> Bei immer wieder vergebnem Beginnen
> muß Wissenschaft endlich auf Abhilfe sinnen. (pp.18–19)

> If we are to gain final victory at last,
> and finally break the constraints of the past,
> the decisive campaign has still to be fought,
> so we'll call upon science for moral support.
> What is the use of the bomb or grenade,
> or the most lethal gases that we have yet made?
> The gases blow back and destroy our own force,
> and the enemy gases affect us far worse.
> The arms race should not be a matter of chance.
> Science must make the decisive advance.

Dr Abendrot then describes a strategy for biological warfare. Once upon a time, he recalls, there was a disease of the lungs that was cured through medical advances. The task of modern science, which has invented a substitute ('Ersatz') for every product of nature, is to invent a 'substitute lung disease' ('Lungenpestersatz'):

> So ersetz'n wa einfach, m. w., auch den Tod
> durch das praktische Mittel Abendrot.

Mit unseren ausgesuchtesten Gasen
jagten wir aus dem Feld nur die falschen Hasen.
Doch fortan, kein Hase bleibt auf dem Platz,
dank unserem Lungenpestersatz!
Die Welt in Spital oder Friedhof zu wandeln,
mußten wir oft zu geräuschvoll handeln.
Nun hoffen wir die Position uns zu stärken,
denn der Feind wird jetzt sterben, ohne selbst es zu merken.
Ein Druck auf den Knopf wird fürder genügen,
über zehntausend feindliche Lungen zu siegen.
Man lebt auf Sandalen und nicht mehr auf Sohlen,
doch der Tod wird sein Opfer geräuschloser holen.   (p. 20)

To cook up a substitute death I'd be willing,
and market it under my name – what a killing!
The gases that we have deployed in the past
affected our own men – that method can't last.
From now on we'll slaughter whomever we please
by means of our substitute lung disease!
No need any longer to make any sound,
as we turn the whole earth to a burial ground.
It's easy to strengthen our front if we try.
Whole armies will perish without knowing why.
One press on the button's enough to expunge
hundreds of thousands of enemy lungs.
We don't need to shout now, we just hold our breath,
and our victims will silently go to their death.

In a phantasmagoric cabaret one does not expect realistic characterization, and Dr Abendrot seems like a grotesque invention, but the figure is brought down to earth by the use of modern slang ('m. w.' stands for 'machen wir' – 'sorted!'). Abendrot was based on a real-life model, Fritz Haber, director of the Kaiser Wilhelm Institute for Physical Chemistry in Berlin. Born of Jewish parents in Breslau (Wroclaw) in 1868, Haber converted to Protestantism so as to avoid discrimination.[14] By 1910 he had established himself as the most success-ful physical chemist in Europe, after synthesizing ammonia from nitrogen and hydrogen to produce artificial fertilizers. The applications of his research were ambiguously poised between life and death, for it was Haber's method of nitrogen fixation that enabled the German munitions industry to maintain pro-duction levels during the First World War, after supplies of natural nitrates had been cut off by the Allied blockade. In 1918 the Haber process produced 200,000 tons of nitrogen compounds, enabling the German army to hold out till the bitter end.[15]

Haber's links with the political establishment made him the key figure in the development of chemical warfare. At the Hague Peace Conference of 1899 twenty-four nations, including Germany, had renounced the use of asphyxiat-ing gases in war, but this did not prevent the German government from setting up an Army Technical Research Centre (Wehrtechnische Forschungsstelle) to explore the military applications of chemistry and engineering.[16] The decisive step towards chemical warfare was taken in 1914, when Haber initiated the development of poison gas, becoming head of the Chemical Warfare Service with the rank of captain, proudly wearing military uniform. As a fanatical supporter of the war, he advocated massed gas attacks in order to break the military stalemate. Having devised a method for releasing large quantities of chlorine gas from canisters, he persuaded the reluctant High Command to deploy it. Such gases are highly volatile, since (as Dr Abendrot ruefully observes) if the wind changes direction you will poison your own men.

There were those in the military establishment, including apparently the Kaiser, who regarded such methods as unethical.[17] But at 4 a.m. on 22 April 1915 Haber's great moment arrived, as the German army launched a gas attack against unsuspecting Canadian and French-African troops near Ypres. The scene has been described by a military historian:

> A greenish-yellow cloud hissed from nozzles and drifted on the wind across no-man's-land. [. . .] Men who breathed it screamed in pain and choked. It was chlorine gas, caustic and asphyxiating [. . .]. Men clawed at their throats, stuffed their mouths with shirttails or scarves, tore the dirt with their bare hands and buried their faces in the earth. They writhed in agony, ten thousand of them, serious casualties; and five thousand others died. Entire divisions abandoned the line. Germany achieved perfect surprise.[18]

Haber (Fig. 5a) was there to supervise operations, as he was on many other occasions. Chemical warfare quickly escalated, as the Allies began to deploy poison gas in reply. When gasmasks were introduced to give protection against chlorine, Haber's research team developed more lethal substances, including mustard gas, known in German as 'Gelbkreuzgas' or 'Lost'. Mustard gas shells, distinctively marked with a yellow cross (Fig. 5b), proved twice as effective as the average gas shell, and nearly five times as effective as shrapnel and high explosive.[19]

From 1916 onwards Kraus repeatedly expresses his horror at the use of poison gas. He does not mention Haber by name, but he must certainly have known about him, since he was by far the most celebrated German scientist of the First World War.[20] The use of chlorine gas prompted Kraus's scathing allusions to Germany's 'chlorious offensive' (F 474–83, 43), and his revulsion reached a climax after the introduction of mustard gas, first used in July 1917 against British positions at Ypres. The attack again came as a complete surprise: 'Shells marked with yellow crosses rained down on the men at Ypres. At first they experienced not much more than sneezing and many put away their masks. [. . .] Though the gas smelled like mustard in dense concentrations, in low concentrations, still extremely toxic, it was hardly noticeable.'[21] Its chemical industry was so advanced that Germany was able to use mustard gas for twelve months before Britain and France could retaliate. This was Dr

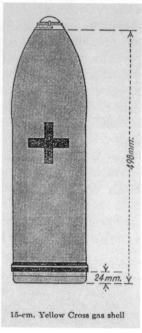

15-cm. Yellow Cross gas shell

5   Chemical warfare: (a) Fritz Haber   (b) Design of a mustard gas shell

Abendrot's most fiendish invention: 'Whole armies will perish without knowing why.'

As the use of chemical weapons increased during the final eighteen months of the war, Kraus's protests intensified. His most incisive essay on this theme is 'The Techno-Romantic Adventure' ('Das technoromantische Abenteuer'), written in the spring of 1918, when the German army's superiority in chemical weapons enabled them to break through on the western front. An appeal by the International Red Cross in Geneva for both sides to renounce the use of gas had been disregarded. German gases (a Berlin communiqué announced on 25 February) were so superior that it would be folly not to use them, and British politicians too disregarded the Red Cross appeal (F 474–83, 35). For Kraus, poison gas represents the most extreme contradiction between the heroic ideology of war and its actual mechanized infamy. How can one speak of 'drawing the sword' in a war where 'chemistry and physiology have fought shoulder to shoulder' and it is possible 'at the touch of a lever to gas a whole front line and extensive areas behind it'? The wider political implications are also made clear: 'The old regime' owes its power to modern chemistry, and it is this that has 'inescapably condemned our victorious civilization to poison itself to death' (F 474–83, 41–5).

Kraus was by no means alone in expressing moral outrage, since Haber's name was on the list of those whom the Allies intended to put on trial as war criminals, and in 1919 he fled to Switzerland. After his return to Germany, he had to face a committee of inquiry set up by the Reichstag, but he was entirely unrepentant, describing poison gas as 'one of the most humane weapons'.[22] The debate continued during the 1920s and 1930s, after Haber, honoured by the Swedish Academy with the Nobel Prize for Chemistry, had once again become a respected member of the international scientific community. The standard textbook on chemical warfare, published in 1937, echoes Haber's claim that poison gas, though very efficient at putting the enemy out of action, is a relatively humane weapon: 'After a close analysis of the casualties produced in the war, we now know the facts concerning the effects of gas and see that much of the alleged horrors of gas warfare were pure propaganda. [. . .] In general, gas causes less suffering than wounds from other weapons.'[23] By this date the United States, following the European example, had set up its own Chemical Warfare Service – with the author of the textbook on its staff.

Kraus foresees that these methods of extermination cannot be confined to the battlefield, and one of the most moving photographs reproduced in *Die Fackel* shows a mother and child in a cottage near the war zone, wearing gasmasks (F 474–83, 129). Another photograph, printed in the 1919 edition of *Die letzten Tage der Menschheit*, shows women Red Cross workers wearing gasmasks (the documentary source for the Female Gasmasks in *Die letzte Nacht*). In 'Nachruf' (January 1919) Kraus recorded his horror at the discovery that a Gas Training School with a lethal stock of two hundred gas grenades had been established in the Leopoldstadt, the Jewish suburb of Vienna (F 501–7, 36–8). Confronted by the phenomenon of poison gas, Kraus refused to acknowledge any justification, insisting that the destruction of the Judaeo-Christian world had been sealed. For centuries Europe had dedicated itself to the vision of Constantine, the first Christian emperor: 'In hoc signo vinces' – 'You Shall Conquer in the Sign of the Cross'. But the new generation emerging from the Gas Schools has been trained 'to conquer in the sign of the Green Cross and the Yellow Cross' (F 501–7, 36). The German army used green and yellow crosses to distinguish phosgene gas shells from those containing mustard gas, and the cross from the wayside crucifix had reappeared on the casing of chemical weapons.

Die letzte Nacht suggests that the alliance between science, propaganda and militarism will transform 'the whole earth to a burial ground'. The paradox expressed through the figure of Abendrot is that a converted Jew pioneered the use of poison gas for the extermination of human beings. In another scene from *Die letzten Tage der Menschheit*, technological advances are specifically linked to the unholy alliance of German imperialists and patriotic Jews. After warning against the dangers of germ warfare, the Grumbler identifies as the source of all evil the 'connection between the Pan-German and the Hebrew drives for existence and expansion' (III, 14). The great mystery (he observes) is how the ethos of military valour can possibly be sustained, when Germany's 'chlorious' victories are in fact due to 'the inspiration of a chemist'. This is the closest Kraus comes to identifying the man who mobilized chlorine gas.[24] Haber's team continued to work on chemical weapons, circumventing restrictions imposed by the Treaty of Versailles. Recognizing that the manufacture of gases for 'hygienic uses' provided cover for clandestine rearmament, he concentrated on the production of defumigants, which were marketed as protection against typhus. In 1924 his group perfected the formula for the delousing agent Zyklon B, an invention that was to claim millions of victims.[25] Several of Haber's relatives perished in the Holocaust – an uncanny fulfilment of the lines Kraus quotes from Shakespeare about 'purposes mistook / Fall'n on the inventors' heads' (F 499–500, 4).

When *Die letzte Nacht* was premiered in Vienna in February 1923, the bleak stage set made a powerful impact, while the effect of poison gas was conveyed through the release of clouds of vapour (F 613–21, 82). Kraus spelt out the implications of this scene after the even more timely Berlin production of 1930, responding to the claim that his apocalyptic vision had been superseded by the wave of realistic novels by front-line veterans. No one, the critics implied, could tell the truth about war unless he had experienced it at first hand, and the communist *Rote Fahne* singled out the pessimism of the Abendrot monologue as a particular weakness. Obsessed with the sunset of the world, Kraus had allegedly failed to grasp that modern science promises a new dawn. But the distanced vision of the satirist, gazing down on war-torn Europe from his Swiss mountain refuge, carried further than the close focus of front-line veterans, and he did indeed regard the invention of poison gas as the 'End of Days'. Replying to his critics, he insisted that 'we are confronted by the possibility of gassing not the front b   f a tap' (F 834–7, 48 & 54). The threat of p   nagination during the post-war period, and l   rpes of gas were being developed (F 686–90   uinea-pigs at research establishments in Engl   s of international reconciliation at the Leas   y of work for 'gas chemists' (F 751–6, 109).   urches for their failure to condemn chemica   when the cartoonist was prosecuted for portraying the crucified Christ in a gasmask (F 806–9, 52). Repeated references to the 'gassing of civilian areas in the next world war' (F 743–50, 49) culminated in the suggestion that there might be a hundred million gas victims (F 890–905, 179).

The lethal combination of innovative technology and regressive ideology is pinpointed through composite images that reinforce Kraus's warnings about 'techno-romantic adventure'. Stirring military marches will doubtless still be played as the earth is transformed into an 'operational space for lethal rays'. Political thinking has failed to keep pace with the destructive power of science, and Kraus laments the 'gigantic gap between technical innovations and traditional ornaments' (F 657–67, 3). This is the context in which he suggests that post-war Germany has been branded with the swastika, but even he failed to

gas that was taking shape in the mind of the
ts in *Mein Kampf,* lost the war only because
rs' will to fight. The sufferings of front-line
ain 'if at the beginning of the war or during
1 of these Hebrew corrupters of the people

The Phrases We're Ruled By

Impenitent militarists provided a blatant target, but Kraus's more subtle satire
focuses on the hidden persuaders: '   1tious
proverbs and outmoded turns of phra   bject,
since the word 'Phrasen' crops up sev   lmost
invariably in a critical context. Lookin   d that
his essential idea had been to identify   fabricated clichés'. Through this process of   e 'the
lethal organization of moral and in{   1ating
events' (F 800–5, 23–5). According tc   done
by the journalistic corruption of langu   diary
entry of 13 April 1918, called 'the phrases we're ruled by'. This seminal insight
inspires her, like Kraus, to portray the destabilization of rationalist language by
modern warfare.[27]

From the perspective of socio-linguistics, clichés may admittedly have a
constructive function, promoting cohesion in an unstable world. During
periods of rapid modernization, we are reminded, clichés 'gain in importance
as fixed points of orientation' – 'reified chunks of past experiences' which help
to fill the 'institutional void'.[28] They organize experience into predigested segments, encouraging predictable and conformist modes of behaviour. Society
could hardly function without a linguistic safety-net of this kind, with nodal
points formed by proverbs like 'Don't throw the baby out with the bathwater'.
Such expressions draw on a homely practical wisdom to establish links between
the domestic and the public sphere – even politicians may require a 'new
broom'. The broad appeal of such phrases is confirmed by the fact that they
are often translatable into other languages, especially when they derive from a
biblical or literary source: 'Don't cast your pearls before swine'. Kraus may
ironize such expressions, but it would be difficult to organize social experience
1ot least', a formula with such all-purpose
1an – including Kraus – commonly use it in

anguage as the repository out of which ideas
1 to be less hostile towards proverbial expres-
etween verbally sensitive individual creativ-
platitudes. Wars occur because irresponsible
1t the will of a nation which they have
most intoxicated with clichés (F 697–705, 113). This would not be possible

without the inherent capacity of clichés to promote patterns of collective thinking that are remote from the realities of political action. From the multiplicity of reflections in *Die Fackel*, the following main objections emerge, illustrated by specific examples. Kraus repudiates the unthinking use of habitual expressions that strike him as:

- pretentious: for example 'into the breach' ('in die Bresche')
- simple-minded: 'hit the nail on the head' ('den Nagel auf den Kopf treffen')
- evasive: 'you shouldn't generalize' ('man darf nicht generalisieren')
- reactionary: 'we need another Bismarck' ('einen Bismarck braucheten wir halt')
- euphemistic: 'protective custody' ('Schutzhaft')
- anachronistic: 'keep the flag flying' ('die Fahne hochhalten')
- sanctimonious: 'with God on our side' ('mit Gott')
- pseudosomatic: standing 'shoulder to shoulder' ('Schulter an Schulter')

The final example is perhaps the most convincing, cited by Kraus more than a hundred times.[29] The politician who proclaims that Austria and Germany – or indeed Britain and the United States – should stand 'shoulder to shoulder' fails on almost every count. This is not simply a cliché but a political slogan, using the tone of schoolboy bravado to distract attention from the realities of modern warfare.

F   . . .   f   ff   )f tonality, developing a conception of
'To   :rn idea of the 'soundbite'. Reviewing
the   reports in September 1911, he claimed:
'Th   undbites. I am convinced that it is no
lon   that function automatically' (F 331–2,
24-   ticizes, but the more subtle seductions of
adv   time he encounters certain phrases, such
as t   e final end'), used in the sense of 'at the
enc   ases discourage us from thinking too rig-
orously about the subject under discussion. His ultimate aim is to convince us that this unthinking use of language may have apocalyptic consequences, and he attributed the disasters of war to a concept of the 'failure of imagination' that echoes the cultural criticism of the German Romantics, familiar to English readers through the writings of Coleridge.[30]

During the 1920s and 1930s, however, there is a change of emphasis as Kraus highlights the significance not merely of anachronistic metaphors, such as 'breaking a lance' ('eine Lanze brechen'), but of mind-numbing slogans. The classic example is the statement by the Viennese Police Chief responsible for the massacre of July 1927: 'throughout my life I have only done my duty because this and nothing else is my duty'. To deconstruct this sententious circular thinking, Kraus published and repeatedly performed a forty-line satirical song in which every other line rhymes with 'Pflicht' ('duty').[31] This provides a

prototype for the authoritarian discourse of fascism, in which slogans like 'duty', 'nation', 'struggle', 'leader', 'loyalty' and 'obedience' are drilled into public consciousness so as to produce automatic reactions. We know from Hitler's observations about propaganda in *Mein Kampf* that this was a conscious strategy: 'All effective propaganda must be limited to a very few points and must harp on these in slogans until the last member of the public understands what you want him to understand by your slogan.'[32] Kraus became increasingly sensitive to the consequences of sloganizing, and, as his theory evolved, the notion of impoverished imagination was replaced by a model of behaviouristic programming through linguistically triggered reflexes, associated with the psychology of Emile Coué. This critique culminated in the incisive account of propagandistic techniques in *Dritte Walpurgisnacht*, written during the summer of 1933. That polemic, to be analysed in a later chapter, shows how Nazi propaganda combined the jargon of modernity with the longing for religious salvation.

Weapons of Mass Deception

Kraus's analysis of propaganda is compelling, and there are few who would defend the record of the patriotic press in disseminating falsehood in wartime. Similar conclusions were reached by the critics of the *Cambridge Magazine*, led by C. K. Ogden, in their polemics against the 'garrulous gerontocracy' responsible for the 'holocaust of young men' during the First World War. The dominant journalistic 'gibberish' reflected a failure not simply of Liberal politics, but of the institutional language of Liberalism, which was incapable of reconciling its progressive rationality with the atrocities of modern warfare.[33] Sadly, those who fail to learn from the errors of the past are doomed to repeat them, and the project of rationalizing the insanities of war is with us still, as can be seen from the media coverage of recent conflicts in the Persian Gulf. The conflict in the Gulf, as a *New York Times* correspondent observed, 'made war fashionable again', but the blame lay 'not with the military but the press,' which 'saw itself as part of the war effort'.[34]

The linkage between the propaganda techniques satirized in *Die letzten Tage der Menschheit* and the media coverage of the first Gulf War was noted by the veteran biochemist Erwin Chargaff, who began reading *Die Fackel* during the First World War at the age of twelve. In his memoirs, written after his emigration to the United States, he recalls that as a student in the Vienna of the 1920s he prepared a lecture in praise of Kraus. The 'Last Days' may have begun in August 1914, he observed almost eighty years later, but they were still continuing in the 1990s, not least in the horrors of the Gulf War.[35] This link is underlined in John Theobald's diachronic study, *The Media and the Making of History*, which combines ideas derived from Kraus with the new discipline of Critical Discourse Analysis. He stresses the connections between journalism and 'mediatised' popular history, which he sees as 'a process of constantly self-replicating distortion or mendacity'. While Theobald recognizes that

counter-hegemonic discourses may challenge the dominant commercial and military imperatives, he highlights the more radical position of the French critic Armand Mattelart, who asserts that 'communication serves first of all to make war' – a connection that is obscured if the study of mass communications is confined to 'the entertainment industry in peacetime'. This idea, Theobald reminds us, is anticipated in *Die Fackel*, where Kraus stressed the continuities between the mindless chat of peacetime journalism and its feeding of the appetite for war.[36]

Kraus attacked the nationalist press during the 1920s for continuing to perpetrate falsehoods comparable to the report that French planes had dropped bombs on Nuremberg, that 'primal falsehood' ('Urlüge') which provided a pretext for the declaration of war (F 787–94, 184–5). The continuities between the propaganda of the First World War and the media strategies of the Gulf Wars have been confirmed by further studies. Noam Chomsky has argued that, despite the commitment to freedom of speech, the *New York Times* sets the spectrum for a political debate in which 'the basic premises of the state propaganda system are presupposed by all participants'.[37] For commentators like Phillip Knightley and Jean Baudrillard, the discourse of war, intensified by television, creates an alternative reality in the minds of armchair observers, who applaud 'surgical strikes' delivered by 'smart bombs', desensitized to human suffering by the slickness of the medium.[38] For the media critic Richard Keeble, the whole notion that an American-led coalition went to war against Iraq in January–February 1991 is a 'myth', since it was not a war at all but a 'series of massacres'. The supposed war was conducted 'in the realms of myth, rhetoric and media spectacle', but in the end there was nothing more than a rout – a 'barbaric slaughter buried beneath the fiction of heroic warfare'.[39] Anti-war voices were systematically excluded from the mainstream media, as Iraq was demonized and the press clamoured for the assassination of Saddam Hussein. The most comprehensive study, *Desert Storm and the Mass Media*, concludes that at times of crisis the 'effective use of words and media' is 'just as important as the effective use of bullets and bombs'.[40] These studies may differ from Kraus in their methods, involving teams of researchers sampling media coverage week by week and using computerized databases to establish correlations with public opinion polls, but their conclusions are similar. His direst prophecies have been fulfilled by the emergence of new forms of 'mediacentrism' controlled by what Keeble defines as the 'media–military–industrial complex'.[41]

Attempts to legitimize air raids that kill civilians provide a striking parallel between then and now. Although the aerial destruction of urban areas was a rare occurrence when Kraus wrote *Die letzten Tage der Menschheit*, his analysis has proved paradigmatic. Experience, the Grumbler observes, should have taught the perpetrators of 'murder from the air' that 'although their intention is to hit an arsenal, they must unavoidably hit a bedroom instead, and in place of a munitions factory, a girls' school'. When the Optimist objects that this is

not done 'purposely', the Grumbler replies: 'No, fortuitously, which is worse! They can't prevent it from happening, but they do it, fully aware of the consequences. They express regret and do it all the same.'[42] This exposes both the criminality of aerial attacks and the hypocrisy of their apologists. Since Kraus's day, there has been an exponential increase in both the scale of destruction and the casuistry used to justify it, but even he never imagined that democratically elected governments would *intentionally* bomb civilian targets like Dresden and Nagasaki, incinerating hundreds of thousands of defenceless people. British politicians of the Second World War spoke of 'obliteration bombing' as they set about the task of destroying Germany 'city by city', a policy condemned by Bishop George Bell.[43] And as hundreds of civilians are killed by 'smart bombs' that have gone astray, the Pentagon speaks of 'collateral damage'. The aerial bombardment of Iraq in March 2003 was presented as a pre-emptive strike against 'weapons of mass destruction'. However, at the end of an unprecedentedly one-sided conflict, the alleged weapons were nowhere to be found, prompting the conclusion that the war was actually attributable to 'weapons of mass deception'.[44] The driving force behind the war was the Anglo-American propaganda machine, disgorging misinformation on behalf of political leaders who insisted on their personal sincerity. Once again, diplomats came to believe their own lies when they saw them in print.

Promotional Trips to Hell

Die letzten Tage der Menschheit offers seminal insights into the workings of military propaganda, and during the 1920s Kraus was never short of material for his critique of the media. While condemning the press for its cliché-ridden coverage of events, he mocks the pretentious language used by advertisers to market meretricious goods. The combined effect is most insidious when it involves a mystification of the sufferings of war, as revealed by Kraus's exemplary critique of battlefield tourism. In autumn 1921 the *Baseler Nachrichten*, a German-language newspaper published in Switzerland, announced to its readers that it was organizing 'Motoring Tours of the Battlefields'. The delights awaiting them are eloquently described: the comfortable automobile in which they will ride along the Ravin de la Mort and visit Verdun, where more than a million men – perhaps one and a half million – bled to death. There will be time for luncheon at the best hotel in Verdun with wine and coffee – everything included in the price. Verdun (the advertisement emphasizes) is 'the battlefield "par excellence"'.[45] The complacent tone of this promotion inspired the most impassioned of Kraus's diatribes, 'Reklamefahrten zur Hölle' ('Promotional Trips to Hell'), which he repeatedly read from the public platform (Fig. 6). This advertisement (he claims) exemplifies 'the mission of the press to lead first humanity and then the survivors into the battlefields'. The press, which for four years had been instrumental in stoking up the conflict, is now repackaging the horrors of war as a tourist attraction.

6   Karl Kraus reciting the anti-war satire 'Promotional Trips to Hell'

Kraus's polemic owes its power to the fact that he reproduces the text of the advertisement word for word. This provides a documentary basis for his devastating riposte:

> You receive your newspaper in the morning.
> You read how comfortable survival has been made for you.
> You learn that 1½ millions had to bleed to death in the very place where wine and coffee and everything else are included.
> You have the decided advantage over those martyrs and dead men of first-rate accommodation and food in the Ville-Martyre and at the Ravin de la Mort.
> You ride to the battlefield in a comfortable automobile, while those men got there in cattle trucks.

CHAPTER 5

From the Jungle of Press Freedom

Looking back over his career in February 1929, Kraus used emphatic type to proclaim that in Austria for the past thirty years '*no other power has ever ruled except the press*' (F 800–5, 22). This is one of those Viennese hyperboles which, although manifestly untrue, have generated a wealth of insight – comparable to Freud's dictum that all dreams are wish-fulfilments, Loos's association of ornament with crime, Weininger's claim that everyone is bisexual, or Hayek's view of Austrian-style socialism as the road to serfdom. Such assertions are untenable, but as Wittgenstein explained in a comment on Weininger's *Sex and Character*: 'The greatness lies in that with which we disagree. It is his enormous mistake that is great'.[1] Kraus's claim that no power had ruled in Austria except the press was clearly mistaken, since the republican government held the upper hand in its dealings with editors, exerting indirect control through the Federal Press Service, whose director, Eduard Ludwig, was a potent influence behind the scenes.[2] But in Kraus's view the laws regulating the press were far too lax, and he would have preferred an enlightened form of censorship, denouncing unrestricted freedom of the press as the 'exterminating angel' destined to destroy true liberty (F 712–16, 99).

The New Journalism

Although it has been claimed that he regarded journalistic phraseology as 'unchanging', Kraus distinguished the high-faluting style of the liberal press from the new journalism of the 1920s, which appealed to the 'lower instincts' of its readers.[3] The Viennese press of the inter-war period no longer possessed the international influence it had exerted under the Empire, and even in domestic politics its status declined. After the national elections of June 1911, Kraus had been able to portray Moriz Benedikt as the true 'victor', since the *Neue Freie Presse* successfully organized an anti-Catholic alliance involving tactical voting by Liberals, Social Democrats and German Nationalists.[4] Real power, Kraus claimed in 1911, lay with those who controlled the press and the

stock exchange (F 326–8, 18). The election of February 1919 for the National
Assembly took place under very different circumstances, as a result of the
polarization of political opinion. The leading liberal papers, *Neue Freie Presse*,
Neues Wiener Tagblatt and *Neues Wiener Journal*, urged their readers to support
the 'bourgeois democratic' slate, a centrist alliance that was both anti-Marxist
and anti-clerical. Although this alliance was lavishly funded, it secured only one
seat in the National Assembly, compared with seventy-two for the Social
Democrats (the party of the *Arbeiter-Zeitung*) and sixty-nine for the Christian
Socials (the party of the *Reichspost*). To maintain circulation, the liberal newspapers had to reposition themselves, drifting steadily towards the right during
the 1920s.[5] In the election of October 1920 the *Neue Freie Presse* supported the
Christian Social Party, which won a total of seventy-nine seats, forming a coalition with the Pan-Germans. Kraus was horrified that Count Czernin, the
diplomat he held responsible for prolonging the war, succeeded in winning a
seat. The fact that Czernin's candidature was endorsed by the *Neue Freie Presse*
led him to denounce the alliance between 'Christian' politics and 'Jewish' press
(F 554–6, 2).

The Christian Social Party set the agenda of national politics, while the
Social Democrats consolidated their control in Vienna. However, it took some
time for Kraus to adjust to this shift in the balance of power and acknowledge
that his favourite targets – the German-Jewish business elite which controlled
the liberal press and the stock exchange – had lost their pre-eminence. The
change of tone is reflected in his comments on the veteran editor of the *Neue
Freie Presse*, Moriz Benedikt, who had wielded such influence in Habsburg
Austria. During that period, according to Theodor Herzl, foreign correspondents were as influential 'as ambassadors' and governments 'negotiated with a
great paper as one power with another'.[6] However, in the Republic, as Kraus
noted in February 1920, newly appointed government ministers no longer
found it necessary to call at Benedikt's office to present their credentials.
Where three years earlier the war-mongering editor had been portrayed as the
all-powerful Anti-Christ, he is now seen as a rather pathetic figure, an 'aged
Job' bewailing afflictions over which he has no control (F 521–30, 52–3). This
proved to be a valedictory tribute, since Benedikt died on 18 March, only a
few weeks after this article appeared. The eulogies by members of the establishment alluded to venomous attacks which the great man had had to endure
from an (unnamed) 'dwarf'. Responding to these comments in a satirical
poem, Kraus insists that death does not transform a sinner into a 'figure of light'
(F 531–43, 207). His most effective riposte was to quote the obituary from
the London *Times* of 20 March, describing Benedikt as 'the evil genius of the
Hapsburg Monarchy in its declining years' (F 544–5, 25).

The death of Benedikt prompted Kraus to redraw his map of journalism.
In February 1920 he had still seen the liberal press as the greatest danger
(F 521–30, 61), but the *Neue Freie Presse* soon ceased to be his principal target.
He certainly made fun of leading articles by Ernst Benedikt, who had succeeded

his father as editor–proprietor, dismissing the paper's editorial content as a 'pre-amble for the financial market, the commercial market and the pleasure market' (F 577–82, 77–90). But he felt that it had become a shadow of its former self, appealing mainly to older readers who would still believe every word 'even if it had been bought up by Pan-German propaganda for the sole purpose of promoting a pogrom against its subscribers'. The paper was 'badly written and utterly lacking editorial direction in every section' (F 595–600, 38). By October 1925 we find him claiming that he samples Ernst Benedikt's editorials only two or three times a year, an exaggeration that indicates the general trend (F 697–705, 15). However, as Kraus's interest in the *Neue Freie Presse* receded, he devoted more attention to its rival, the *Neues Wiener Journal*, which took an increasingly anti-democratic line during the late 1920s, providing a platform for the 'diaries' of Hermann Bahr. The numerous glosses inspired by Bahr may appear light-hearted, as if he were a figure of fun in a satirical 'soap opera', but this ignores the sinister implications of his brand of reactionary Catholicism.[7]

Kraus's account of the Austrian press during the 1920s is far more comprehensive than in the pre-war period. While still denouncing liberal newspapers as a 'global malady', he acknowledges that their discourse – unlike that of the Christian Social press – approaches his intellectual level (F 531–43, 55). The 'banefulness of Jewish journalism' may still make him wince, but the right-wing press represents a greater danger, since the poisonous stupidity of the 'newspaper Christians' combines 'intellectual dishonesty' with 'political depravity' (F 552–3, 2). The editor of the *Reichspost*, Friedrich Funder, is now stigmatized as a war criminal no less culpable than Moriz Benedikt. The Pan-German press, so influential in the provinces, had always been one of Kraus's targets, identified as by far the most blinkered form of factional journalism, and he had included it in his critique of the 'snowball system of stupidity' (F 147, 22–3). The events of the war led him to engage with *völkisch* propaganda more directly, and after the defeat of the Central Powers he hoped that the undefinable species which called itself 'deutschnational' would be swept away. He was dismayed to find republican Austria still swarming with Pan-German agitators, including Karl Hermann Wolf, who had been Schönerer's most vociferous henchman (F 501–8, 79–80). During his lecture tour of Munich and Innsbruck early in 1920, Kraus found himself vilified by German-nationalist newspapers, and he left his readers in no doubt about the dangers. The snowball system has now developed into an 'avalanche system', generating an antisemitic frenzy similar to that which led to the assassination of Kurt Eisner (F 531–43, 3 & 9). In Vienna, too, Kraus recognized the growing danger of the German-nationalist press, especially after the founding of the *Deutschösterreichische Tageszeitung* in April 1921. Its Nazi sympathies led him to describe it as a 'swastika-sheet', whose contributors would prefer to use handgrenades (F 632–9, 39). The weekend edition, which had a pretentious cultural supplement, was a source of great entertainment, while its advertising section revealed that the primary purpose of the 'Germanic ideal' was the 'elimination of price-cutting Jewish competition' (F 668–75, 149–51).

The lifting of political censorship after the founding of the Republic resulted in a flurry of new titles, many of which were shortlived. Where previously newspapers could be purchased only by subscription or from licensed kiosks, they were now sold on the streets by vendors whose raucous cries offended Kraus's ears. The whole 'newspaper concoction' changed, as the journalist Ludwig Ullmann recalls in his memoirs. Front-page editorials printed in a decorous typeface were replaced by bold headlines announcing the 'daily sensation'.[8] *Der Abend*, relaunched in November 1918 under the editorship of Carl Colbert and Alexander Weiss, combined a radical socialist outlook with a sensational popular format. This was followed in March 1919 by *Der Neue Tag*, the paper which inspired Kraus's first denunciation of the 'new journalism'. Speaking from the public platform in December 1919, he borrowed Voltaire's words to denounce the paper's dubious practices: 'Ecrasez l'infame!' (F 521–30, 7–8). This judgement seems unduly harsh, not least because this paper published a series of perceptive essays by Joseph Roth.[9] When *Der Neue Tag* ceased publication in April 1920, it was followed in November 1922 by the founding of *Der Tag*, another left-of-centre paper, edited by Maximilian Schreier. The launching of *Die Stunde* in March 1922 accentuated the sensationalist techniques of the new journalism, and Kraus doubtless had this paper in mind when he bewailed the consequences 'when the sharks are allowed to found newspapers' (F 608–12, 10). The old journalism had at least attempted to preserve a respectable façade, but the new press was shameless in its insolence (F 640–8, 100). With a twinge of nostalgia Kraus recalled the era of Wilhelm Singer (1847–1917), an editor who combined 'tolerant cosmopolitanism' with 'publicistic dignity' (F 649–56, 53).

The new breed of radical journalists, like their liberal predecessors, were predominantly of Jewish descent, but Kraus alludes to this only obliquely (F 514–18, 77–84). An exceptionally virulent form of antisemitism was sweeping through central Europe in the aftermath of military defeat and economic collapse. In December 1919, Kraus's friend Siegfried Jacobsohn, editor of *Die Weltbühne*, warned him that antisemitism in Berlin had become so extreme that he should not include in his forthcoming public readings any passages making fun of Jewish jargon.[10] In Austria, too, antisemites like Anton Orel, editor of *Der Volkssturm*, were blaming the Jews for all the difficulties afflicting the newly founded Republic, and it was awkward for Kraus to find his verses about the dance of the hyenas from *Die letzte Nacht*, which ironize Yiddish-inflected speech, quoted in Orel's paper.[11] The term 'Judenpresse' ('Jewish press') was increasingly used by reactionary ideologists to denounce the whole spectrum of liberal, democratic and socialist journalism, which they saw as part of a conspiracy to achieve world domination – the fantasy propagated by the antisemitic forgery, the *Protocols of the Elders of Zion*, which became a best-seller in Germany during the early 1920s. The situation was not helped by the fact that the two financiers who invested most heavily in the new journalism, Siegmund Bosel (who bought up *Der Tag*) and Camillo Castiglioni (who helped to launch *Die Stunde*), were of Jewish origin. So indeed were the leading socialist journalists, including Friedrich Austerlitz and Julius Braunthal. Antisemitism now dominated the discourse of right-wing ideologists of every stripe, including pious Catholics like Friedrich Funder and Joseph Eberle.[12] If Kraus was to sustain his own independent critique of the press, it was important to avoid the rhetoric of demagogues like Eberle, who included him in their sweeping attacks on Marxists and Jews (F 632–9, 86–7).

Anyone who has studied files of the *Reichspost*, the *Wiener Stimmen* and the *Deutschösterreichische Tageszeitung*, will understand why Kraus was so vehement in his denunciations. Day after day they subjected their readers to a barrage of anti-democratic, anti-socialist, xenophobic and antisemitic arguments and images. Mocking the crudity of 'Christian' journalism, so much less slick than that of their 'Jewish' competitors, Kraus recognized that it amounted to an incitement to violence. This is summed up in a phrase that forms a leitmotif in his satire on right-wing journalism, 'Rrrtsch obidraht', an expletive which he associates with the prejudices of Karl Lueger, the antisemitic Mayor of Vienna. This phrase conveys the thrill experienced by Austrian backwoodsmen at the moment of wringing the neck of some helpless creature that has been hunted down. For Kraus, it is precisely this impulse which animates the hangman gloating over the corpse of the Italian irredentist, Cesare Battisti (F 531–43, 58–8). He also associated the spine-chilling jocularity of 'Rrrtsch obidraht!' with a fanatically antisemitic humorist named Karl Paumgarten, who wrote for the illustrated magazine *Die Muskete* under various pseudonyms (F 601–7, 112). Kraus mistakenly believed that there could be no equivalent for this gruesome expression in any other language, but a right-wing British newspaper caught the same tone of facetious chauvinism in its coverage of the Falklands War in May 1982, gloating over the sinking of the Argentinean battlecruiser *Belgrano*, in which over three hundred men lost their lives, with the banner headline 'GOTCHA!'[13]

Unlike the antisemites, Kraus repudiated journalistic malpractices because they were unethical, not because they were 'unGerman', and his critique of the 1920s develops a more discriminating vocabulary.[14] He may still allude to the 'Jewish press', but this characteristically provides a counterpoint for even more forceful attacks on 'German-Christian', 'Aryan' and 'antisemitic' journalism (F 613–21, 111–12). His polemics, which cover the whole spectrum, may be clarified by means of a diagram placing the Vienna daily newspapers within the left–right ideological spectrum that dominated Austrian public life (Fig. 7). Each paper is assigned a circle whose size reflects its circulation, incorporating the name of the editor. The diagram reflects the position in the mid-1920s, and the leading dailies are located on a horizontal axis from (socialist) left to (conservative) right, adjusted vertically from a baseline of democratic liberalism to the extremes of anti-democratic communism (top left) and

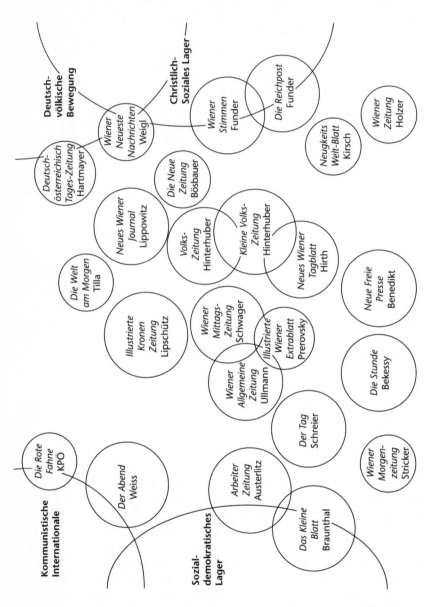

7   Diagram of the Vienna Newspaper Landscape in the mid-1920s

proto-fascist nationalism (top right). The increasingly strident antisemitism of *völkisch* groups (on the anti-democratic right) had the effect of strengthening the Zionist group associated with Robert Stricker's *Wiener Morgenzeitung* (and its successor *Die Neue Welt*). The old-established *Wiener Zeitung*, official organ of the Austrian government, remained a significant factor, reflecting the policies of the right-wing coalitions that formed the government from October 1920 onwards. The majority of Austrian newspapers in this period can be categorized either as 'party' publications ('Parteipresse') or as 'ideologically committed' ('Gesinnungspresse'). The large-circulation *Illustrierte Kronen Zeitung* was unusual in being primarily market-orientated and not supporting any specific political party.[15] Although Kraus concentrated on the Viennese press, his comments on provincial papers like the *Innsbrucker Tageszeitung*, *Grazer Tagespost* and *Linzer Tagespost* are also extremely scathing (F 743–50, 116–17).

Kraus's picture of the press of Weimar Germany is inevitably less comprehensive, given the extraordinary proliferation of print media (forty-five morning papers were published in Berlin alone).[16] His sensitivity to reactionary nationalism led him to censure right-wing papers like the *Münchener Neueste Nachrichten*, the 'most boring newspaper on earth' (F 531–43, 37), and the nationalistic *Kölnische Zeitung* (F 595–600, 6–7). The crudity of Nazi publications like the *Miesbacher Anzeiger* and *Völkischer Beobachter* made them less rewarding targets, since his great theme, as we have seen, was 'creeping fascism', not thuggery in jackboots. So many right-wing newspapers were appearing in Berlin under assorted patriotic titles that Kraus had difficulty in distinguishing the *Deutsche Zeitung* (derided as 'deutschvölkisch'; F 531–43, 28) from the *Deutsche Tageszeitung*, which he described as 'hopelessly Aryan', despite its feeble attempts to emulate the manipulative techniques associated with 'Jewish' journalism. Responding to this paper's distorted account of one of his Berlin public readings, Kraus summed up his view of nationalist newspapers: 'Just as the German God caused bombs to rain down on Nuremberg, so they are continuing to spread their lies and falsehoods' (F 546–50, 20–1). His refusal to forgive the perpetrators of war propaganda led to extended polemics against Alfred Kerr, theatre critic of the liberal *Berliner Tageblatt*, and its editor Theodor Wolff. In Kraus's running battle with the press, waged for more than thirty years, the only paper that earned his respect was the *Frankfurter Zeitung*, which he regarded as unusually objective (F 827–33, 61).

Kraus excelled in analyses of specific journalistic devices, some of which retain their exemplary character long after the occasion has faded into history. In January 1921 he set out the dangers of political manipulation in an article on the phenomenon now known as 'spin'. In German this idea was commonly applied to devious arguments thought to be derived from Rabbinic Judaism – 'der jüdische Dreh'.[17] Kraus turns the tables by using the title 'Ein christlicher Dreh' ('Christian Spin') to introduce his analysis of the coverage of a debate at the League of Nations by the *Reichspost*. A report in this right-wing daily had

attributed Austria's enhanced international reputation to the electoral victory of the Christian Social Party. Citing the full text of the debate, Kraus exposes the report by the *Reichspost* as a 'disgraceful forgery'. Its reactionary mentality, he concludes, should earn Austria admission 'not into the League of Nations, but into a concentration camp' (F 557–60, 63–72). Thus Kraus diagnosed journalistic 'spin' long before this meaning of the word entered the English language.

By highlighting examples of this kind, Kraus demonstrates the power of the media to shape political processes, but he does not confine himself to ideological factions. His target is the daily newspaper as an institution and the global influence it wields. To suggest that the press fabricates an alternative reality, he gives it an ontological status in the opening lines of his 'Song of the Media Mogul':

Im Anfang war die Presse		In the beginning was the press
und dann erschien die Welt.		and then the world was born.
Im eigenen Interesse		Pursuing its own interest
hat sie sich uns gesellt.	(S 11, 57)	the world becomes our pawn.

The echo of St John's Gospel implies that the book of the creation is being rewritten – not by Christian evangelists but by journalistic hacks.[18] That vacuum of empty pages has to be filled every day, whether or not there is any news worth printing. Looking back over thirty years, he declared that the press had been responsible for the 'systematic inversion of all moral concepts'. He associates this with 'the compulsion to transform the materials of life into newsprint every day'. The blank pages have to be filled, whatever the circumstances, and this – he concludes – engenders a frenzied irresponsibility (F 800–5, 24–5). It produces the ubiquitous phenomenon of 'chat' ('Geschwätz'; F 632–9, 74): the transformation of private events and personal opinions into newsprint, as the vacuum sucks endless trivialities into the public sphere. Kraus's pre-war satire had focused on that more elegant form of journalistic chatter known as the 'feuilleton': the dozens of columns devoted by the *Neue Freie Presse* to tittle-tattle about members of the Vienna Male Voice Choir is the classic example. The journalism of the 1920s exacerbated this trend through its coverage of the private lives of footballers and film stars, and Kraus implies that, while fascists may be threatening democracy, the chattering classes are destroying civilization as a whole. Indeed, the two processes may be connected, as the vacuousness of chatter increases the vulnerability of democracy. Kraus sees the cult of 'celebrities' ('Prominente') as one of the most depressing features of the supposedly egalitarian post-war world. The social vacuum created by the demise of the old order had to be filled by gossip columns about 'comedians, film buffs, cabaret artistes, boxers, footballers, parliamentarians, gigolos, ladies' coiffeurs, literary historians'. He attributes this passion for celebrities to the craving for authority figures in the German soul, left 'profoundly homeless' by the Kaiser's departure (F 751–6, 116–19). But his

comments also have a paradigmatic value, anticipating the celebrity chat shows of the television age.

There is no space in the diagram of daily newspapers for the wide-circulation periodical press which featured so prominently in his panorama of villainy. Among Austrian magazines only two earned Kraus's respect: the literary journal *Der Brenner*, edited in Innsbruck by Ludwig von Ficker; and the independent economic review *Der österreichische Volkswirt*, edited by Walter Federn, 'the unique example of a bourgeois journalist with integrity' (F 777, 13). The *Volkswirt* was in the happy position of being able to cover its costs from sales revenues, making it independent of the advertisers who might have tried to influence its policy.[19] Other periodicals are treated with contempt: weekly newspapers like the *Sonn- und Montagszeitung*; humorous weeklies like *Die Muskete* and *Kikeriki*, with their inane texts and crudely antisemitic caricatures; the equally abysmal left-wing humorous magazine *Götz*; the theatre magazine *Die Bühne*, also owned by Bekessy, which in Kraus's opinion pandered to the most trivial need 'for entertainment (F 697–705, 142); the socialist monthly *Der Kampf*, which he regarded as too dogmatic; and far-right magazines like *Volkssturm*, *Staatswehr*, *Deutsche Arbeiter-Presse*, *Das Neue Reich* and *Schönere Zukunft*, which were beyond the pale. The intellectual level of the antisemitic press was so low that there could be no 'bridge' of meaningful communication with such morons (F 531–43, 55). But Kraus was aware of the dangers represented by ephemeral pamphlets like that published by the Austrian Nazi Party in 1925 under the title 'Racial Debasement through Jewry'. However paranoid their assertions about the bastardization of the Teutonic race, such documents could hardly be ignored when they had a print run of 178,000 copies (F 697–705, 9).

Snapshot Photography and Antisemitic Caricature

The fascination exerted by the press over the minds of the barely literate led Kraus to pay particular attention to visual images. The traditional papers were austere in format, using a restrained typography which avoided banner headlines and disdaining the use of photographs, but the reader of *Die Stunde* was confronted by a barrage of photographs and a minimum of text. This trend-setting layout soon had its effect on the more traditional dailies, and in April 1924 even the *Neue Freie Presse* began to print photographs. Imagining how horrified Moriz Benedikt would have been by this development, Kraus scathingly concluded that the text of the newspaper had already made mankind so stupid that they 'cannot understand it any longer without pictures' (F 649–56, 56). For technical reasons the use of photographs as a news medium had previously been confined to the periodical press, and Kraus had taken a critical interest in magazines like *Die Woche* and *Der Weltspiegel*, adapting some of their photographs for his own satirical purposes. It may seem surprising that a writer so obsessed with the printed word should have taken such an interest in visual images, but Kraus was sensitive to the contrived nature of photographic poses and their propagandist potential. The use of photography and the cinema for propaganda purposes during the First World War confirmed the validity of this critique, and he anticipated the techniques for 'staging' images of the battlefield which were to become so widespread in the age of television. The new technology, Kraus claims in May 1918, has not only transformed mankind into a rubbish tip; it also ensures that the rubbish tip is promptly reproduced through the cinema and illustrated magazines. Everything seems to be contrived for the photographer, and images from the world of diplomacy or high society form a façade to distract attention from the grim realities of the war (F 484–98, 123–9).

Where traditional studio portraits had a static and monumental quality, Kraus felt that the new techniques of photojournalism trivialized public events. His essay on 'Snapshot Photography' ('Momentaufnahmen'), first published in 1912, has rightly been praised as a prophetic analysis of the distortions produced by new technology, anticipating the insights of Walter Benjamin's 'Short History of Photography'.[20] The snapshots of press photographers, Kraus argued, transform the activities of politicians into a grotesque dance, reducing fluid movements to a corpselike 'rigidity' (F 357–9, 32–3). In his critique of journalism during the 1920s, the control of the photographic image became a crucial issue, especially after a touched-up photograph from his childhood was published in Die Stunde. He was in at the birth of a new phenomenon – photographers who pursue their prey in order to take snapshots in compromising situations – and he responded to this brave new world by defining the photojournalist as one of the horsemen of his apocalyptic vision (F 357–9, 32). The perspective in which he places the predatory activities of photographers foreshadows the fate of Diana, Princess of Wales – 'death by publicity, with the paparazzi in the role of Aeschylus' Furies'.[21]

Kraus's critique of illustrated papers also addressed the abuse of caricature. He made no secret of his admiration for the great anti-establishment cartoonists of his day, from Thomas Theodor Heine to George Grosz, but he condemned visual crudity, especially the form of antisemitic caricature pioneered by the long-established weekly Kikeriki.[22] Its figures with supposedly 'Jewish' features were so notorious that 'Kikeriki-Jude' became accepted shorthand for such antisemitic caricatures (F 374–5, 32). Kikeriki was supposed to be a humorous magazine, the German-language equivalent of Punch, but in 1925–6 it supplemented its savage cartoons of socialist reformers like Hugo Breitner by publishing weekly instalments from the Protocols of the Elders of Zion. It regarded even the campaign for the decriminalization of abortion as part of a Jewish plot, prompting Kraus's ridicule (F 717–23, 75–6). Readers were subjected to an additional diet of racist cartoons on the front page of the Wiener Stimmen, stablemate of the Reichspost. The most significant of its cartoonists, Fritz Schönpflug, had already figured among the apocalyptic horsemen of Kraus's pre-war satire (F 357–9, 32). Initially, Kraus seems to have been most perturbed by the faulty use of perspective in Schönpflug's cartoons in Die Muskete, which presented army life as a harmless comedy. After the war Schönpflug set about the more serious task of defaming socialists, foreigners and Jews in the reactionary illustrated press. On the front page of the *Wiener Stimmen* he regularly portrayed the figures of the Social Democratic leaders 'twisted and contorted' (as Kraus put it) 'with strange protuberances'. However, Kraus found the work of socialist humorists almost equally crude – a 'gruesome party-political humour' unredeemed by artistic individuality (F 751–6, 32). Austrian caricaturists, denied the imaginative licence that characterizes authentic satire, were expected to follow the party line, reinforcing pre-existing prejudices rather than acting as a corrective to ideological thinking.[23]

In May 1913, after he himself had been caricatured in a Munich magazine, Kraus published a photograph of his well-proportioned features as a 'statement of fact' that discredited the cartoonist's image of a beetle-browed figure with a bulbous nose and jug-handle ears (F 374–5, 32). Four months later he reprinted from *Die Muskete* an equally antisemitic caricature by Schönpflug, portraying him as a hawker of Yiddish tracts (F 381–3, 42). To counteract this pervasive visual racism, Kraus authorized the production and sale of a series of photographic portraits in postcard form, beginning with a carefully posed image by Dora Kallmus in 1908 and continuing during the 1920s with expressive studies by Charlotte Joel, Trude Fleischmann and Lotte Jacobi.[24] His penchant for Jewish women photographers, who portrayed him posing reflectively in an indoor setting, can be construed as an implicit protest against the ideals of outdoor Aryan manliness that were beginning to dominate visual culture. Although these photographic portraits tend to highlight Kraus's expressive hands, there is no trace of the dramatic gestures that punctuated his public readings, and he strenuously objected when a photojournalist took snapshots during one of his recitals, initiating a legal action in order to ensure that the negatives were destroyed (P 3, 280–3). His determination to confront antisemitic distortions with the authenticity of an original photograph reached its climax during the long-running controversy with *Die Stunde*. That paper portrayed him with ape-like features that are absurdly at odds with the photographs by Charlotte Joel taken in the same period (Fig. 8a and b). In a similar spirit Kraus reprinted the paradigmatic confrontation between photograph and caricature from one of his pre-war polemics.[25]

Kraus's verdict is that we would be better off without a journalism that promotes political prejudice, racial stereotyping, personal gossip and intellectual trivialization. In December 1926 he claimed in a legal submission to spend on average not more than 'half-an-hour to one hour per day' reading the newspapers (P 1, 232). This daily dosage was indispensable to his creativity, and his friends would find him sitting in a secluded niche in the coffee-house at a table strewn with newspapers. A grammatical lapse in a press report could spark off animated discussion, and the offending article would be cut out and slipped into his pocket, to be dealt with at his writing desk that same night.[26] For Kraus, the devil lies in the detail, and he cites chapter and verse to sustain

8 (a) Caricature of Kraus as 'Zarathustra's Ape'   (b) photograph of Kraus by Charlotte Joel
from *Die Stunde*

his apocalyptic vision. In a fine passage written shortly before the First World War, he suggested that the 'open book' of the creation had become reduced to 'a much damaged Monday-morning paper, abounding in misprints, legible only in its advertising section, and destined for a cosmic demise' (F 357–9, 32). To sustain this vision of a civilization ravaged by journalism, in which freedom of the press is systematically abused, Kraus offers sheaves of evidence, starting with a clipping from a Monday-morning paper.

Advertising Scams

One of the treasured items in his archive was a copy of the *Sonn- und Montagszeitung* of 14 December 1896, which prefaced its 'Sunday Report' of business trends with the following headings: 'A Favourable Development – Municipal Affairs – Vienna–Berlin – Goldmining Swindle'. The text dealt briefly with the first three topics, but there was no reference to any swindle. Instead, a notice appeared in smaller print commending the prospectus issued by the Fortuna Goldmining Corporation of Transylvania. Leafing through this same edition of the newspaper, Kraus discovered a full-page advertisement – from Fortuna – that gave the game away. Sunday Reports were actually Saturday Reports, so a whole day remained for the process of extortion. After the report of the 'Goldmining Swindle' had been typeset, the proof was shown to

Fortuna, which responded by paying for a full-page advertisement, accompanied by the notice in praise of its shares. The compromising 'Report' was then deleted, but the 'sub-editor and proof-reader forgot the treacherous "heading"' (F 33, 15). This provided a prototype for the incestuous relationship between editors and their advertising departments, but it also created a dilemma. The *Sonn- und Montagszeitung* was a Jewish-owned paper which, at the time of the 'Goldmining Swindle' incident, was resisting the attempts by the Christian Social Party to curb the power of Jewish finance.[27] How could Kraus expose such journalistic malpractices without appearing to confirm the arguments of the antisemites?

This episode revealed the potential for corruption in an economic system where the success of speculative share-issues depended on creating public confidence, and unprincipled editors were in a position to demand protection money in the form of advertising contracts. Kraus recognized that freedom of the press concealed a fundamental problem: the advertising revenues of daily newspapers far exceeded their income from the cover price. Under such a system, he argued, there could be no such thing as independent journalism, uncontaminated by pressures from the advertising department. The 'Goldmining Swindle', to which Kraus reverted in April 1912 (F 347–8, 12), exemplified an institutionalized form of corruption. Newspapers routinely accepted – as 'advertising revenue' – payments that were blatantly intended as bribes, as in the case of the Hungarian Casino affair of winter 1913–14. In a statement to parliament, Prime Minister Tisza revealed that the failed casino company had paid large bribes to the Austrian, Hungarian and foreign press. The Journalists' Association 'Concordia' declared that the payments were for legitimate advertisements.[28] But for Kraus they involved complicity in dubious business deals (F 395–7, 1–3).

The reforms of the republican period promised a more honest style of advertising, introducing in 1922 a new Press Law that outlawed advertisements disguised as editorial comment. The reform was resisted by capitalist newspapers, which derived substantial revenues from this device. They attempted to circumvent the new legislation by a series of manoeuvres, such as printing disguised adverts over the letters 'p.r.', which might be mistaken for the initials of a member of staff, when in reality they meant 'public relations'. Exposing the advertising scams of unprincipled editors was a relatively easy task, but Kraus also argued that the dependence on advertising sets limits to the freedom of expression of even the most respected newspaper. He was particularly severe on the *Arbeiter-Zeitung* for accepting lavish advertisements from department stores, which he saw as a sell-out of socialist principles. He also cited a case where the *Arbeiter-Zeitung* was taken to court by one of its advertisers, a German firm that had arranged for a leaflet publicizing its popular novels to be distributed as an 'insert' in the socialist paper. When the paper printed an article criticizing the novels, the German publisher sued for breach of contract, and the court found in its favour. According to the judgement, a newspaper that accepts a paid advertisement to publicize a product 'also commits itself to avoiding any action that would contradict the aim of the advertisement'. For Kraus, this verdict demonstrates that there is an unresolved contradiction between 'Editorial Office and Production Management' ('Redaktion und Administration'), and that pressure from advertisers curtails the freedom to express critical opinions even in the so-called 'respectable press' (F 873–5, 5–7). The incestuous relationship between journalists and advertisers is further illustrated by his controversy with Willy Haas, editor of the literary review *Die literarische Welt*. In this case Kraus highlights the blurring of the dividing line between reviewing and advertising, forcing Haas to admit that he solicits advertisements by sending publishers a list of titles scheduled for review in forthcoming numbers – the last thing an independent magazine should do (F 838–44, 2–28)! Kraus's authority was enhanced by the fact that he accepted no paid advertisements, and, where most authors use speaking tours to boost the sales of their books, he refused to permit the display of his works at his public readings (F 686–90, 41–2).

Episodes like the 'Goldmining Swindle' may not appear very significant in themselves, but during the First Republic, when the sharks of journalism joined forces with a new generation of war profiteers, such practices resulted in national disaster. Between March and December 1923 dozens of new banking enterprises were founded with the aim of cashing in on inflation through speculative share issues and currency transactions.[29] Since a successful launch depended on favourable publicity, this placed enormous power in the hands of editors, who were in a position to extract protection money. The scope for extortion was so great that, as Kraus put it in another strophe of his 'Song of the Media Mogul':

Sie lesen, was erschienen,	They read all that you publish,
sie denken, was man meint.	they think what you've expressed.
Noch mehr läßt sich verdienen,	But profits are more lavish
wenn etwas nicht erscheint.	when news has been suppressed.

(S 11, 57)

In the process of reciprocal corruption which Kraus describes, businessmen seek to deter adverse publicity by threatening that lucrative advertising may be withdrawn. The Austrian newspapers of the 1920s proliferated with advertisements for fly-by-night banking firms, and the banking crises that destabilized the Republic were exacerbated by irresponsible journalism.[30] In the spring of 1926 it came as no surprise when the editor of *Der Abend*, Alexander Weiss, was arrested, convicted and imprisoned for extortion. The insidious 'covenant' between bribery and corruption – the back-handers offered by Castiglioni and the protection money extorted by Weiss – was analysed by Kraus under the title 'From the Jungle of Press Freedom' ('Aus dem Dschungel der Preßfreiheit'; F 726–9, 10–22). He was even more outspoken in his attacks on links between Castiglioni and Bekessy, to be analysed in a later chapter.

The Misused Miracle

There were, however, more hopeful signs. The world of journalism was transformed during the 1920s by the introduction of broadcasting, creating competition for established newspapers, and the founding of the British Broadcasting Corporation in 1922 set a benchmark for impartial reporting, helping to counteract the salaciousness of the so-called 'dirty *Daily Mail*' period. In September 1924, following the British lead, Austria set up its own broadcasting company, the Radio-Verkehrs-Aktiengesellschaft (RAVAG). In principle, it was to be politically neutral, with programmes monitored by an Advisory Board which included representatives of all the main parties.[31] When broadcasting began, Kraus's comments were predictably sceptical, describing earphones as a 'prosthesis of pleasure' (F 679–85, 25) and radio as a means of linking the 'Viennese concierge with the cosmos' ('F 691–6, 17). However, he soon realized that broadcasting could provide a corrective to tendentious reporting in the press, and in 1929 he even looked forward to the advent of television ('Telescopie'; F 800–5, 28). His Josephinist outlook meant that he was in sympathy with the 'top-down' approach adopted by producers committed to raising educational standards, and he welcomed the opportunity to broadcast his own adaptations of Offenbach and Nestroy.

At the same time, he was sensitive to the trivializing effects of popular broadcasting. He was in at the birth of the chat show, the programme in which celebrities drool away the passing hour. The transcript of a broadcast by the popular singer and entertainer Leo Slezak, published in 1925 in *Die Bühne*, enabled Kraus to analyse this new genre in prototypical form. He feels that the triumphs of the new technology have now been combined with 'an abyss of intellectual and artistic vacuity'. Worse still, the jovial Aryan broadcaster who tells Jewish jokes is quite capable of relapsing into the 'wildest antisemitism' (F 679–85, 19–21). The fact that radio was state controlled meant that it was prone to political manipulation, and it proved impossible to live up to the BBC's idealistic motto: 'Nation shall speak peace unto nation'. It was standard practice for British, German, French and Italian radio services to broadcast their respective national anthems every day – a practice which Kraus denounced as an 'abuse of the aether', indeed a 'musical prelude to poison gas'. This astonishing phrase shows how sensitive he was to the links between music and militarism, insisting that 'Deutschland über alles' was offensive to anyone of international outlook and that playing it nightly on German radio pandered to *völkisch* sentiment (F 751–6, 32–5).

In principle, Kraus supported the new medium, sharing Einstein's hope that radio would serve as a 'means of reconciling the nations', superseding the distorted coverage of the press. But in practice he sadly concluded in March 1932 that its value was diminished by the 'most powerful and most misused application of this true miracle' (F 868–72, 52). It certainly provided new opportunities for developing the art of the spoken word, enhancing the impact of his 'Theatre of Poetry'. And broadcasters were free from the commercial pressures of advertising, which he regarded as the structural flaw of newspaper journalism. But by the same token, national broadcasting companies were vulnerable to centralized political control. Kraus's predictions about the destructive potential of radio propaganda were borne out after the Nazi seizure of power, when German stations broadcast a series of attacks on the Dollfuss government, designed to undermine the loyalty of Austrian listeners.[32] Kraus responded by supporting the attempts by Austrian spokesmen to promote patriotism over the airwaves, reluctantly accepting the need for RAVAG to become more politicized (F 909–11, 59–60).

Power without Responsibility

Freedom of the press had always been a problematic concept in Austria. In the Habsburg period it was an open secret that many journalists received subsidies from the government's 'Dispositionsfonds', designed to shore up loyalty during the final years of the monarchy. During the Republic, the government exerted its influence more discreetly through a subsidy that covered 50 per cent of the cost of newsprint. Newspapers were expected to reciprocate by publishing official communiqués, since the subsidy could be curtailed if they failed to co-operate.[33] Foreign governments, both democratic (in Prague and Berlin) and dictatorial (in Budapest and Rome), also provided subsidies in return for favourable coverage. The Viennese press was indeed 'free' in the sense that anyone could buy himself a newspaper, 'whether he was plutocratic or merely illiterate' (F 751–6, 7). When the well-regarded *Wiener Allgemeine Zeitung* ran into difficulties, it was taken over by the disreputable Camillo Castiglioni, although his ownership was carefully concealed. During the 1920s the paper changed hands four times, causing great distress to conscientious journalists like Ludwig Ullmann, who in younger days had been a contributor to *Die Fackel*. Although Ullmann insists that Kraus's accusations of corruption were unjustified, he concedes that the lack of transparency about ownership was a serious problem.[34] No wonder Kraus insisted that the identity of the financial backers of each newspaper should be disclosed. Reflecting in February 1927 on the collapse of the Post Office Savings Bank, he called for a new law requiring newspapers to print the name of their proprietors in bold type under their mastheads in order to counteract the collusion between politicians, speculators and their hirelings (F 751–6, 6–8). His diagnosis was confirmed in March 1936 by the spectacular collapse of the Phönix Assurance Company. Among the files of the bankrupt company was a comprehensive list of secret payments to influential politicians and public figures, including substantial subsidies to the editors of *Der Morgen* (Maximilian Schreier) and the *Sonn- und Montagszeitung* (Ernst Klebinder).[35]

Kraus had to steer a course between two extremes, distancing himself from reactionary opponents of press freedom, while denouncing those who used it as a licence for fraud (F 691–6, 26). His position emerged most clearly from a vigorous exchange with the journalist who commanded his greatest respect,

Friedrich Austerlitz. In an article in the *Arbeiter-Zeitung* of 24 December 1925, Austerlitz argued that freedom of the press is such a fundamental principle that we must learn to live with its negative consequences, although stricter laws should be introduced to curb extortion and defamation. Kraus, in his counter-argument, insists that Austerlitz's liberal principles are based on a fallacy: freedom of opinion has become confused with the licence to publish 'any infamy'. Freed from the threat of confiscation and even the obligation to testify in court, newspaper editors can get away with every kind of crime. Surely there must be a way to protect the 'right to express political opinions', while curbing the excesses of an irresponsible 'canaille' (F 712–16, 99–100). Kraus was opposed to anonymous authorship, arguing that journalists would show greater responsibility if they were obliged to put their name to everything they wrote. Although the press laws required each newspaper to print the name of its 'responsible editor', Austrian papers systematically circumvented this provision by assigning this function to some junior member of staff. Taking action against a defamatory article, Kraus had to content himself with obtaining court orders against straw-men, who themselves tried to evade responsibility by claiming not to have been in the office at the time. His protracted legal actions were designed to introduce law into the jungle. Press freedom was being 'so frequently abused' that his aim, as formulated in a legal submission of summer 1926, was to prevent it from deteriorating into complete 'press irresponsibility' (P 1, 63).

Kraus's critical glosses contain a wealth of insight, but he undermines his argument through generalizations that are historically untenable. It is true that the laws designed to curb the financial manipulations of journalists were laxly applied, but it was wrong to suggest that 'nominal government' was subordinated to a 'daily more shameless dictatorship of the press' (F 668–75, 9). Kraus acknowledged that in a mature democracy, such as the United States, the press may have a more constructive function, citing a court case in which the *Chicago Tribune* successfully defended its right to criticize the city administration. In Austria, by contrast, experience suggested that the press was more likely to be in cahoots with corrupt administrators (F 577–82, 21). To place this critique in perspective, it is also relevant to recall the situation in England, where the conservative press barons Lord Beaverbrook and Lord Rothermere were trying to dictate the political agenda. After the general election of May 1929, which resulted in the Labour Party leader Ramsay MacDonald becoming prime minister in a minority government, Beaverbrook's *Daily Express* and Rothermere's *Daily Mail* launched a campaign to discredit Stanley Baldwin, leader of the Conservative opposition. They objected to his consensus politics and denounced him for failing to support Empire Free Trade. In a blatant bid for power, they formed their own United Empire Party to contest parliamentary by-elections, and for two years their papers conducted a sustained campaign against Baldwin. Their Empire Crusade stirred up such disaffection within the Party that at the beginning of March 1931 Baldwin was under pressure to

resign. During the Westminster by-election later that month, the Conservatives were challenged by a candidate from the Empire Crusade, but Baldwin rose to the occasion, delivering a speech denouncing the *Mail* and the *Express* and asking 'whether press or party was to rule'. Using a phrase suggested to him by the poet Rudyard Kipling, he declared: 'What the proprietorship of these papers is aiming at is power, and power without responsibility – the prerogative of the harlot throughout the ages.' Two days later, the Conservatives won the by-election, and in the autumn Baldwin led the Party to an overwhelming electoral victory.[36]

Baldwin's words recall the tirades against the 'Whore of Babylon' in *Die Fackel*, but by comparison with Britain the press of inter-war Austria had only limited power, since there were neither mass-circulation newspapers nor by-elections to provide political leverage. However, there were certainly Austrian editors with political ambitions, from Funder of the *Reichspost* at one extreme to Austerlitz of the *Arbeiter-Zeitung* at the other. Thus, to understand the wider implications of Kraus's critique of Viennese newspapers, it is necessary to correlate their activities with those of political pressure groups within the broader field of cultural production.

The Cultural Field

Kraus's aim was to support the Republic without aligning himself too closely with any political party. He endorsed the programme of social reconstruction promoted by the municipality of Vienna under the leadership of the Social Democrats, while vigorously opposing the hegemonic claims of the Catholic and Pan-German camps. Through his public readings for working-class audiences he contributed to the democratization of culture, while insisting on his own artistic and ethical standards. To appreciate the richly allusive quality of his writing, especially his critique of ideological thinking, we need to map the conflictual context within which he defined his own position.

Red Vienna

It was only in Vienna that the socialists were able to implement their programme, after their defeat in the general election of autumn 1920. The introduction of universal adult suffrage in municipal as well as national elections ensured that the city government had a Social Democratic majority in every election from May 1919 onwards, and this led to the creation of 'Red Vienna', an enclave of municipal socialism in the most conservative country of Europe. In 1922 the city also attained the status of a federal province with tax-raising powers and considerable regional autonomy. During the following years the Social Democrats used these resources to fund a remarkable range of social, cultural and educational developments. The housing programme provides the most impressive example. Between 1919 and 1934 the municipality constructed a total of 64,000 new dwellings, mainly in the form of monumental blocks of workers' apartments, providing accommodation for 200,000 people, approximately a tenth of the total population.[1]

The significance of the housing programme, which involved gifted architects like Josef Hoffmann, Margarete Lihotzky, Clemens Holzmeister and Josef Frank, lay both in the dwellings it provided and in the vision of socialism it promoted. Social housing was part of a comprehensive project which involved communal kitchens and bathing facilities, new health services and children's homes, schools and libraries, museums, concerts and exhibitions – all designed to create the 'new human being' envisaged by Austro-Marxist theoreticians.[2] In practice, the paternalistic assumptions underlying this programme of bringing culture to the workers restricted its effect, especially in provincial centres like Salzburg or Steyr, where the pragmatic defence of socialism took priority over the utopian dream.[3] But Austro-Marxism certainly reshaped the intellectual life of the metropolis. The most innovative spirits, from Kraus and Schoenberg to Freud and Schnitzler, strove to maintain their independence, but they could not ignore the pioneering achievements of municipal socialism. From the very beginning the Social Democratic Party had seen education and science as the means of creating a new world order, and anti-authoritarian forms of schooling were introduced by Otto Glöckel, while there was a renewed interest in child development, led by the psychologists Charlotte and Karl Bühler. 'Education is power' became the motto of the Austrian labour movement, and Max Adler, the leading theoretician of Austro-Marxism, saw culture as the key to the creation of a revolutionary working class.[4] This resulted in an alliance between workers, party officials and reform-minded intellectuals.

One by one, the individualists emerged from their isolation, committing themselves to social causes. Robert Musil was appointed by the coalition government to advise on the reform of the army. Adolf Loos drafted a pro-grammatic statement entitled 'Guidelines for an Arts Office', to which Kraus and Schoenberg contributed. The aim was to bridge the 'gulf between people and artist', an awesome task, given Loos's view that, even in the new Austria, the thinking of most contemporaries lagged several centuries behind that of the more advanced artists.[5] It was these discussions which led later that year to the founding of the Social Democratic 'Kunststelle' under the direction of David Josef Bach. This was followed in May 1921 by the appointment of Loos as director of the Office for the Construction of Settlements, and the designer of interiors for affluent patrons started planning terrace houses for workers. How-ever, he resigned in June 1924, since he was opposed to the construction of massive blocks designed to promote the 'party-political spirit'.[6]

The intellectual climate in Red Vienna was very different from that in the capital of the declining Habsburg Empire. Around 1910, cultural innovation had unfolded within a series of inward-looking circles, each centred on a pow-erful personality. The most significant was the Psychoanalytic Society, which met on Wednesday evenings at Freud's house in the Berggasse to discuss a remarkably wide range of subjects. The cross-fertilization between the differ-ent groups generated exceptional creative energy, comparable to that of a condensed system of micro-circuits, but those earlier Viennese circles – unlike their successors in the 1920s – were only marginally affected by the political events of the day.[7] In post-war Vienna the situation was transformed, and the Psychoanalytic Society split into several sub-groups, the most politically committed being the followers of Alfred Adler, who supported educational projects and set up counselling centres in the proletarian suburbs. More formally constituted groups were required to register under the Law of Association, and no fewer than 1,500 such 'Vereine' were linked to the Social Democratic Party, giving its members (as Joseph Buttinger recalls) a sense of collective purpose and cohesive identity.[8] Kraus insisted that he did 'not feel particularly close to the socialist cultural ideal' (F 521–30, 62). But he recognized the need for radical reforms in the fields of welfare, medical care and education. Thus in any map of the cultural field the sphere of influence of Die Fackel intersects with that of the Arbeiter-Zeitung and the Party's pioneering cultural centre, the Kunststelle. Moreover, the convergence of anti-socialism with antisemitism and anti-modernism prompted reactionaries to fantasize about a Jewish take-over of Austrian culture. While David Bach was seen as a 'moderate', the Ostdeutsche Rundschau denounced the artistic bolshevism of the 'extremist Jewish tendency', which it associated with the 'Jews' Arnold Schoenberg (music), Adolf Loos (architecture) and Karl Kraus (literature).[9] In reality, the attitudes of the Jews of Vienna were as diverse as those of any other ethnic group, as can be seen from the documentation of 'Jewish Positions' in a recent comprehensive study.[10] But it was difficult to stand aloof from the ideological struggle between Catholicism and socialism, communism and fascism, as the 'field of cultural production' (to borrow Bourdieu's terms) became inextricably involved with the 'field of power'.[11]

Circles, Clubs and Coffee-houses

The culture of Vienna during the 1920s can be pictured as a network of circles suspended between competing ideological poles (Fig. 9). Some of these groups were inward-looking, like the philosophers who met in the Boltzmanngasse under the aegis of Moritz Schlick, internationally known as the Vienna Circle, but even this group made a public impact through the educational work of Otto Neurath. In 1925, with the support of the Municipality of Vienna, he founded the Museum of Economy and Society, developing an innovative project of visual education. Even atonal composers attempted to reach out to working-class audiences. The concerts organized between February 1919 and December 1921 by Schoenberg's Society for Private Musical Performances were intended for an elite, but his collaborator Anton Webern included avant-garde compositions in the programmes of workers' symphony concerts and the Workers' Choir. Thus the post-war Vienna circles reached out to a wider public, creating a counterculture that challenged the reactionary values of Catholicism and German nationalism. Their members ceased to be outsiders, acquiring resources which enabled them to give their innovative projects a firm institutional basis – a paradoxical form of 'empowered marginality'.[12] It was this that distinguished the Viennese avant-garde from the more esoteric cultural groupings of the 1920s, such as the Stefan George Circle, the Bloomsbury Group or the Fugitive Poets.[13] Even the individualistic Karl Popper was a

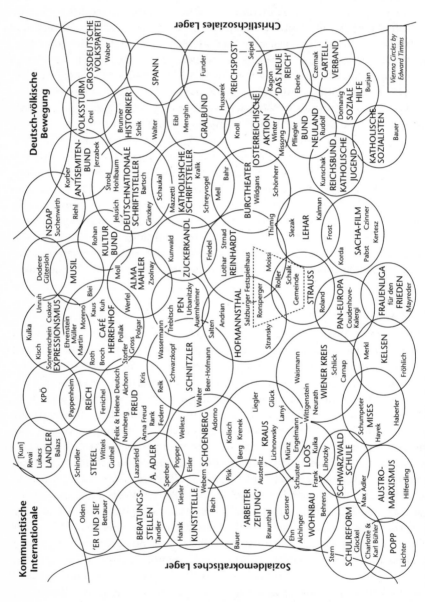

9 Vienna Circles: the Field of Cultural Production

socialist for a time, working as a volunteer in Adler's child-guidance clinics, as well as attending Schoenberg's Private Performances and immersing himself in the ideas of the Vienna Circle.[14] The creative ferment transcended conventional disciplines. David Josef Bach was a musicologist with interests in psychoanalysis, while the philosopher Otto Neurath invented a new picture language and wrote pamphlets in support of socialism. Even Wittgenstein, attracted by the educational reform programme, emerged from his isolation to attend a teacher's training course in Vienna in 1919 and spent several years as a village schoolteacher. Nothing more clearly illustrates the reorientation of the intellectual elite than the fact that Wittgenstein's next publication, after the completion of the *Tractatus Logico-Philosophicus* in August 1918, was a manual for primary schools, *Wörterbuch für Volksschulen*.

This thriving culture was sustained by a network of small publishers, some of which also positioned themselves within the ideological spectrum. The most significant independent publisher on the liberal left was the Anzengruber Verlag, whose list included reformist authors like Josef Popper-Lynkeus and Rosa Mayreder. The leading Austro-Catholic publisher was Verlagsanstalt Tyrolia, while the German-nationalists were spearheaded by the Adolf Luser Verlag, publishers of the *völkisch* family magazine *Der getreue Eckart*, as well as the poetry of Josef Weinheber. Economic constraints meant that Austrian publishers were no match for the German competition, and some of them were essentially cottage industries run from the backroom of a bookshop, like the Verlag der Buchhandlung Richard Lanyi, which published Kraus's adaptations of Shakespeare and Nestroy. The most enterprising firms were Jewish owned, but only two gained an international reputation: the music publisher Universal-Edition, which was responsible for Kraus's Offenbach adaptations, and the Paul Zsolnay Verlag, publisher of best-selling authors like Franz Werfel.[15] The Zsolnay Verlag holds a central position within the field of cultural production, not least because of its links with liberal organizations like the PEN Club.

Repudiating the 'aridities of the two camps' (F 632–9, 66), Kraus also distanced himself from the middle ground. To sum up his position in autumn 1923, he declared that he was 'no friend of club life' (F 640–8, 68). He dismissed the congresses held by the PEN Club and Kulturbund, sociologists and Pan-Europeans as pretexts for boosting the tourist trade (F 743–50, 91–5). And he was particularly hostile towards Concordia, the Vienna Association of Journalists and Authors, established in 1859 during the heyday of Austrian Liberalism. Although it had lost ground as a result of the collapse of the Empire, Concordia still included almost all the leading editors and journalists among its members, apart from those who favoured its 'Aryan' counterpart, the Deutschösterreichische Schriftstellergenossenschaft. Fulsome reports about the Concordia Ball, a highlight of the social season, had provoked Kraus's perennial derision. When this tradition resumed after a six-year hiatus caused by the war, he began to focus on the ideological function of Concordia as a conduit between press, politics and industry. Guests at the ball included not only actors and entertainers, but also Cabinet ministers and business leaders, and the principal speaker was often a politician who held forth about the 'state of the nation'.[16] In 1921 the guests included representatives of the Allied Reparations Commission, prompting acid comments on the contrast between the opulence of the occasion and the message of misery which was supposed to be communicated to the Entente (F 561–7, 5–13).

Inter-war Vienna remained a cosmopolitan city with intellectual life centred on the coffee-houses – a 'public sphere' (in Habermas's sense) free of government control and conducive to rational debate.[17] This was a milieu that inspired witty aperçus and incisively condensed forms of writing, including the witty parodies and polished essays of Alfred Polgar, an author Kraus particularly admired.[18] The Café Herrenhof, favourite haunt of the versatile Franz Blei during his visits to Vienna, formed a hub for cultural gossip and artistic innovation. Heimito von Doderer's diaries of the mid-1920s suggest that he was continuously in and out of coffee-houses, debating with friends like the painter Paris Gütersloh and reading the latest literary magazines. Having been a prisoner of war in Russia, Doderer particularly admired the number of *Die Fackel* published in August 1924 to mark the tenth anniversary of the conflict.[19] Where members of the Berlin cultural elite, such as Count Harry Kessler, liked to meet over breakfast, Kraus's circle would gather in the Café Parsifal at nightfall to dissect the latest news.[20] The habitués of Kraus's circle were not coffee-house intellectuals in the conventional sense, but people with technical and professional skills. In addition to architects and musicians, his circle included a publisher (Franz Glück), a lawyer (Oskar Samek), an art historian (Ludwig Münz) and a mining engineer (Sigismund von Radecki). In the coffee-house they could read not only the Austrian papers, but also the *Prager Tagblatt*, the *Pester Lloyd* or the *Czernowitzer Morgenzeitung*. In cultural terms, as Kraus's friend Friedrich Torberg has argued, the multinational heritage continued to flourish, with Vienna at the vortex of a thriving system of communication.[21]

The city offered a home to numerous exiles, notably the refugees from counter-revolutionary Hungary.[22] Most significant was the communist group led by Jeno Landler, which included Georg Lukács, Josef Révai, Andor Gábor, Béla Balázs and (for short visits) Béla Kun. They held their Sunday discussion groups at the studio of the sculptor Béni Ferency and contributed both to Hungarian exile journals and to left-wing Austrian publications. Interest in Kraus's work is reflected in a series of articles by Andor Németh in *Bécsi Magyar Ujság* and the appreciation of *Die letzten Tage der Menschheit* by Lukács in *Die rote Fahne* (30 March 1923).[23] It was in Vienna that Lukács wrote *History and Class Consciousness* and Balázs his pioneering book on the theory of film, *The Visible Man*. Although their movements were monitored by the police, the Austrian government was remarkably tolerant towards the would-be revolutionaries, turning a blind eye to Lukács's political activities.[24] The communist group had its clandestine headquarters in the Neubaugasse, until in 1928 it was broken up by the police.[25] A number of Hungarian artists, led by Lajos Kassák, also settled in Vienna, where they created a circle around the journal *Ma*, which published Dadaist designs accompanied by visionary texts. The liberals were led by Oskár Jászi, who edited a Hungarian exile newspaper, while the guild socialist Karl Polányi made his name by writing articles for *Der österreichische Volkswirt*. Even the film industry received a stimulus from brief contributions by Alexander Korda (Sándor Kellner) and Michael Curtiz (Mihály Kertés). The openness of coffee-house culture facilitated intellectual exchange, and Balázs and Lukács would meet up with Musil and Soma Morgenstern in the Café Stöckl in Hietzing, and with musical modernists like Alban Berg and Theodor Adorno in the Café Museum.[26]

Some leading figures moved away during the 1920s to more attractive positions elsewhere: Loos to Paris, Schoenberg to Berlin, Wittgenstein to Cambridge, Kokoschka to Dresden, Polgar to Berlin. But the established groups were reinvigorated by the emergence of a gifted younger generation, including the composer Ernst Krenek and the dramatist Jura Soyfer, while there was an influx of migrants from the former Habsburg provinces, including Elias Canetti and Manes Sperber. The network was flexible, and there were significant shifts across the ideological spectrum, especially towards the end of the decade. Both Roth and Werfel were to become monarchists during the 1930s, pleading for a restoration of the Habsburgs. Doderer, who had contributed to leftist papers like *Der Abend* during the 1920s, joined the National Socialist Party in 1933, while the folksy poet Josef Weinheber became an even more fervent Nazi. A few writers, like Schnitzler and Beer-Hofmann, attempted to maintain an 'unpolitical' position, but their Jewish background was an inescapable source of conflict in the prevailing antisemitic climate, and Zionism exerted an increasing appeal, numbering Felix Salten among its converts.

The Christian and Pan-German Camps

The success of the Social Democrats in mobilizing progressive intellectuals provoked a backlash. Social reformers like Hugo Breitner and Otto Glöckel were ridiculed in the right-wing press, while the Christian Social Party strengthened its own institutions in order to resist the advance of socialism. There were over a thousand youth groups associated with the Imperial Federation of Catholic German Youth of Austria, an organization created by the antisemites Anton Orel and Leopold Kunschak.[27] Kraus may have had his doubts about socialism, but he recognized that the combined effect of right-wing societies and the Catholic press was far worse, creating a 'public of men fraternizing in clubs and women selling candles in churches' (F 751–6, 32). The Catholics were less effectively organized in Vienna than in the Austrian provinces, but their control of universities, state theatres and radio enabled them to mobilize writers and thinkers on the conservative side. It was not until after Dollfuss's assumption of power in 1933 that clerical politics dominated Austrian cultural life.

During the 1920s a number of notable figures aligned themselves with the conservative cause, including Hofmannsthal and Reinhardt through their productions at the Salzburg Festival, Anton Wildgans as director of the Burgtheater, Franz Werfel, who gravitated towards Catholicism under the influence of Alma Mahler, and Richard von Kralik through his Catholic Grail Fraternity. Kralik's villa in Döbling became the scene of a regular Tuesday-evening salon, attended by right-wing Catholics like Max Mell, Heinz Kindermann, Hermann Bahr and Richard von Schaukal.[28] The appointment of Richard Strauss as Director of the Vienna Opera in 1919 gave a distinctly conservative flavour to state-subsidized musical culture. Moreover, the Catholic faction had its own Kunststelle, directed by Hans Brečka, cultural editor of the *Reichspost*. Its mission was to promote 'das christlich-germanische Schönheitsideal', as Kraus noted in January 1925, drawing attention to the antisemitic undertones (F 676–8, 16). Although initially less successful than its socialist rival, this Kunststelle für christliche Volksbildung came into its own during the 1930s, when it promoted first the values of Christian Austria and then – still under Brečka's leadership – those of Nazi Germany.[29]

The German-nationalist camp had its own cultural organizations, labelled 'großdeutsch' or 'deutschnational', represented by best-selling authors like Bartsch and Strobl. They made no secret of their anti-democratic and anti-semitic aims, as can be seen from the statutes of the Deutschvölkische Schutz-und Trutzbund. Announcing its programme in the *Deutschösterreichische Tageszeitung* in January 1922, the Trutzbund proclaimed the ideal of German racial purity, insisting on its members avoiding Jewish shops and never consulting a Jewish doctor. Nationalistic gymnastic clubs in Austria were even more determined than those in Germany to exclude Jews from membership, since no 'Jew' could truly be a 'German'.[30] These organizations, which at certain points overlapped with those of the Christian Social Party, provided the primary conduits for popular antisemitism. No fewer than a thousand 'deutschvölkisch' clubs and associations existed in Austria in 1933, according to a contemporary survey.[31] Even the internationally renowned Alpine Club did its best to exclude Jews and bar them from its mountain refuges. The government was inhibited by the Treaty of Saint-Germain from discriminating against minorities, but this restriction did not apply to registered clubs and societies, many of which, following the example of the Austrian student corporations of the 1890s, proudly incorporated antisemitic aims in their statutes.

These right-wing associations represented a physical threat as well as an ideological challenge. In his early satire Kraus had contented himself with mocking the self-importance of 'Aryan' organizations like the Vienna Male Voice Choir, but the First World War opened his eyes to the dangers of the nationalistic grass roots, symbolized by the figure of Paul Pogatschnigg, president of the Federation of German Postal Workers in Austria. This may not sound like a very influential pressure group, but Kraus was quick to spot its significance for the Pan-German movement (F 426–30, 80–1). In one of the most grotesque scenes in *Die letzten Tage der Menschheit* (III, 11), Pogatschnigg appears as president of a German-nationalist drinking club, the Cherusker in Krems, chanting chauvinistic slogans. At first sight this scene reads like a satirical invention, but the incongruously named Paul Pogatschnigg actually existed, and so did the Cheruskia, an association which took its name from the Germanic tribe described by Tacitus. This student society, which had made headlines in 1910 when one of its members was severely wounded in a fencing contest, formed part of a network of provincial associations designed to recruit schoolboys into the German-nationalist movement.[32]

Kraus's satire proved prophetic. Pogatschnigg, whose activities first caught his eye in 1916, became one of the pioneers of the Nazi movement in the Austrian provinces. It was he who arranged for Hitler to visit Krems on 13 October 1920 to deliver a rabble-rousing speech.[33] Kraus's response was to revise the Cherusker scene for the book edition of *Die letzten Tage der Menschheit* so as to make Pogatschnigg's antisemitism more explicit, inserting in one of his speeches a jeering allusion to 'Kohnnationalen'. The real-life Pogatschnigg, who was born in 1873, was a member of a 'Germanen-Verband' named Skuld, which he founded in Innsbruck before the First World War. A prolific contributor to *völkisch* newspapers, he campaigned – unsuccessfully – for election to the National Assembly in 1919, later acting as director of propaganda for the Hitler movement in Austria. A caricature in the *Arbeiter-Zeitung* of 15 February 1927 suggests that he was also involved in creating the right-wing electoral alliance ('Einheitsfront'), which included both Seipel's Christian Social Party and the Austrian Nazi Party (Fig. 10). In this cartoon, clearly influenced by Kraus's satire, the bearded Pogatschnigg is dressed as a member of a Germanic tribe; but when he died in June 1929 obituary notices in the nationalist press portrayed him as a handsome man with a military moustache – the respectable face of Austrian fascism.[34]

This motif recurs in Kraus's later writings, including a text of December 1924 describing a horde of Cherusker emerging from a meeting of the Solo Hunting Buglers Club. In an age when one can fly to America, he ruefully observes, such primitive creatures still dominate Austrian public life (F 668–75, 111–12). His critique of the right-wing press encompassed a whole network of 'Christian nationalist social clubs', including high-minded groups like the Leo Society (Leo-Gesellschaft), the Pius Society (Piusbrüder) and the Brotherhood of the Holy Grail (Gralbund) (F 601–7, 113–16, 123 and 130). But the Pan-German groups impinged on his attention more directly. In October 1927 Kraus received an anonymous letter threatening him with physical violence, written 'in the name of 37 youths' from Elisabethstraße 9, a prestigious address in the First District. He responded by appealing to the courts for protection against the antisemitic associations which had their headquarters there, twelve of which are listed by name in his legal submission, including Antisemitenbund, the Wandervögel and the National Socialists (P 2, 81). The police

Affentierung für die antimarxistische Einheitsfront.
Seipel will Hitler die Sicmetseerlaubnis nach Oesterreich geben.

— Der ist was für Sie, Herr Bundeskanzler; der ist zu allem fähig.

10   'The anti-Marxist United Front': cartoon from the *Arbeiter-Zeitung*

followed up this report by interviewing a young man loitering suspiciously in the street outside Kraus's apartment, but took no further action.

In this battle for hearts and minds there were few neutrals, and even the temperance movement was split into factions: the Social Democratic Arbeiter-abstinentenbund, the Christian Social Verband abstinenter Katholiken, and the Pan-German Deutsche Gemeinschaft für alkoholfreie Kultur. Radio hams were confronted by a similar choice between the Freie Radiobund, the Österreichische Radiobund and the Deutsche Funkhörer-Bund, and even children's chess clubs were drawn into the ideological turmoil.[35] Popular music provided a further field of confrontation, especially after the advent of jazz. Caught in the crossfire between the camps were the exponents of the thriving entertainment industry, centred on the cabaret of Fritz Grünbaum and the operettas of Franz Lehar. As a former band-leader in the Habsburg army, Lehar had impeccable conservative credentials, but many of his collaborators were Jewish. Holding court in the Café Sacher next to the Opera, he would be joined by his fellow composer Emmerich Kalman and the librettists Julius Brammer and Alfred Grünwald.[36] The Empire was still alive in the imaginations of these entertainers, most of whom were forced to flee after the Anschluss, leaving Lehar to enjoy the applause of the Führer.

Similar conflicts occurred in the sphere of gender, since the feminists, too, were split into a Catholic faction (led by Hildegard Burjan), liberals (like Rosa Mayreder) and radical Social Democrats (led by Adelheid Popp). The patriarchal laws of Habsburg Austria had excluded women from political life, but the Republic created new opportunities, and in March 1919 eight women candidates were elected to the National Assembly, seven of them as Social Democrats. Even more striking were the achievements of female pioneers in cultural fields. The most celebrated photographer was Dora Kallmus (Madame d'Ora), who produced portraits of the leading figures of the day (she had photographed Kraus in 1908). Feminism also made an impact on the Psychoanalytic Society, where a younger group, led by Helene Deutsch, challenged the prevailing phallocentric assumptions. One of the boldest innovations was the grammar school for girls founded by Dr Eugenie Schwarzwald, the wife of a senior official in the Finance Ministry.[37] Although the school was denied official recognition, it was supported by Schoenberg, Kokoschka and Loos, and Eugenie's salon became a hub of cultural life. Even Kraus was impressed by some of these developments. In 1920 the Women's League for Peace and Freedom was founded in Geneva, with Rosa Mayreder as vice-president of the Austrian branch.[38] Kraus signalled his approval in 1921 by printing an announcement by the League on the cover of Die Fackel (F 557–60 & F 561–7). Modifying his prejudices against emancipated women, he supported the efforts of his friend Gina Kaus, editor of the magazine Die Mutter, to promote more progressive ideas about child rearing. He also formed an alliance with Mechtilde Lichnowsky, a gifted author who contributed musical settings to his public readings. His scorn was reserved for women who wrote for the daily press: that 'cultural chatterbox' Bertha Zuckerkandl (F 595–600, 100); and the irrepressible Alice Schalek, the war correspondent who continued her career during the 1920s as a travel writer (F 640–8, 24).

This outline of cultural politics may clarify some of the allusions in Die Fackel, but it cannot do justice to the richness of intellectual life in Vienna between the wars. A study of the Vienna Circle has identified a dozen other associated groups, including historians (like Alfred Pribram and Friedrich Engel-Janosi), mathematicians (like Hans Hahn, Karl Menger and Kurt Gödel), sociologists (like Rudolf Goldscheid) and philosophers of science (like Philipp Frank).[39] The fact that intellectual originality thrived in such a conflictual environment intensified the dilemma of German-speaking Jews. One might have expected Viennese students to respond with enthusiasm to such gifted teachers, but antisemitic pressure groups made the university a scene of continuous disruption, with pitched battles between rival factions. The Pan-German duelling fraternities, joining forces with Christian Social student groups, created an atmosphere of intimidation. In Hans Kelsen the University of Vienna had one of the most distinguished jurists of his generation, influenced by neo-Kantian philosophy as well as Freudian psychoanalysis, but this did not protect him from the taunts of antisemites. It was not only Jews who were at risk, but anyone seen as an outsider, including women students who were regarded as a threat to male privileges.

Public Morality and Erotic Revolution

Debates about sexuality constituted the most fiercely contested ideological territory. In turn-of-the-century Vienna the ideas of the most innovative thinkers had been encoded in oblique forms – Kraus's aphorisms, Freud's essays on literature and the arts, Altenberg's prose poems and Schnitzler's psychological plays. Now the advocates of sexual freedom came out of the closet, launching public campaigns with strong political undertones. Although these conflicts were to reach their climax in Weimar Germany, it was in Vienna that the most radical developments originated. In February 1919, members of the Academic Association of Jewish Medical Students, led by Otto Fenichel and Wilhelm Reich, set up the Vienna Seminar for Sexology. Not content with theorizing about the oppressiveness of bourgeois society, they became actively engaged in sex education, establishing sexual advice centres in working-class areas.[40] Developments in the Soviet Union, the first country in Europe to repeal the laws against homosexuality and abortion, were widely admired, leading to attempts at a synthesis of Marxism and psychoanalysis. This culminated in the publication of Reich's *Die Sexualität im Kulturkampf* (*The Sexual Revolution*), which analysed both the oppressiveness of western society and the limitations of the Soviet reforms.[41]

As a young man Reich had been among the students who attended Kraus's readings and regarded him, ambivalently, as 'our god'.[42] His theory of sexuality was indebted to the pioneering arguments of *Sittlichkeit und Kriminalität* and *Die chinesische Mauer*, both of which were kept in print during the 1920s. Kraus himself continued to stress the need for the decriminalisation of abortion and homosexuality in Germany and Austria, and for a relaxation of the divorce laws so as to permit second marriages (F 640–8, 36–7). He was emphatically 'pro-choice', denouncing a law that compelled starving women to bear unwanted children (F 657–67, 218–19). But where earlier he had preached salvation through sensual experience, he distanced himself from Reich's style of sexual revolution, feeling that his arguments had been misunderstood by 'permissive publicists'. This left him disillusioned about 'sexuality as a whole' (F 735–42, 25 & 35), even though the writings of the younger generation were 'spiced with erotic insights from *Die Fackel*' (F 906–7, 16).

There were both personal and political reasons for Kraus's new-found caution, since sexual liberation was perceived as a 'Jewish' agenda. The prominence of Jews in the psychoanalytic movement played into the hands of the antisemites, while the campaign for a repeal of paragraph 144 of the Criminal Code, which prohibited abortion, was perceived as a Jewish-socialist plot. One of Kraus's most trenchant satires analyses the mentality of *völkisch* authors who assume that, if abortion were permitted, Aryan mothers would be particularly at risk (F 668–75, 150). The scandal created by the première of Schnitzler's

Reigen (*La Ronde*), a 'round-dance' of promiscuous relationships, was a further danger signal. The *Reichspost* denounced this affront to morality in an article of 1 February 1921, which contained a clear threat of disruption, and at a mass meeting ten days later Ignaz Seipel protested against 'the performance of a filthy play from the pen of a Jewish author'. On 16 February antisemitic thugs went on the rampage, attacking members of the audience and forcing the cancellation of further performances. Schnitzler, who was present during one of the riots, was chastened by the scandal, which coincided with a personal catastrophe: the breakdown of his marriage (AST, 8–20 February 1921). He decided against further productions of the play and withdrew from public controversy.[43] Kraus's comments show how alarmed he was by the climate of moral rectitude, particularly by a further report in the *Reichspost* defending the behaviour of the rioters as 'an act of self-defence by young Christian men'. He conceded that the time had come for greater discretion (F 561–7, 32–3 & 72–3).

Kraus felt that sexual fulfilment should be pursued in private, not blatantly promoted on the streets, and he was uneasy about the adverts for condoms that were plastered across the city. It was inevitable, in a Catholic society, that the sale of condoms would be promoted by Jewish-owned firms. The leading manufacturer at the turn of the century was Sigi Ernst, and Kraus noted that the words 'SIGI GUMMI' could be read in large illuminated lettering, blazing across the Kärntnerstrasse at night 'like a symbol of Vienna' (F 50, 6), or rather as a solemn warning for punters on their way to the nightclub (F 103, 12–13). The impact was enhanced by alternately flashing electric lights, a device copied from London's Trafalgar Square (F 126, 5). Returning to this theme in 1915 in a cryptic aphorism, Kraus suggested that condoms were now less significant than psychological counselling: 'Sigi Ernst has been displaced by Sigi Freud' (F 406–12, 132). In the post-war period he noted that the SIGI symbol continued to 'illuminate the heavens at night' (F 735–42, 141). Catholics felt that such adverts in the vicinity of St Stephen's Cathedral desecrated the city, while antisemites saw them as further confirmation of the Jewish conspiracy (Fig. 11).

Sexuality became the scene of a bitter ideological struggle, first between socialists and Catholics, later between communists and fascists. In Germany, too, a network of Sexual Advice Centres was set up in the major cities, while Magnus Hirschfeld provoked particular controversy through his crusade on behalf of homosexuals.[44] When he visited Vienna in February 1923 to give a lecture at the Konzerthaus on 'Sexual Crimes', a gang of Nazi youths armed with rubber clubs broke up the meeting, shouting abusive antisemitic slogans and throwing stinkbombs.[45] The *Völkischer Beobachter* attributed homosexuality to 'Jewish degeneration' and promised that in the German state of the future it would be ruthlessly eliminated, even though male sexual bonding was one of the fundamentals of fascism, and the homosexuality of Ernst Röhm's entourage was well known.[46] There are thought-provoking anecdotes in *Die Fackel* about the confusion caused by transvestites on the streets of Berlin (F 649–56, 68).

11   SIGI GUMMI: contraceptive advertisement in the Kärntnerstrasse

In the Austria of the early 1920s the sexual revolution became identified with Hugo Bettauer, the child of Jewish immigrants from Galicia. After a chequered career as a journalist in Germany and the United States, he resettled in Vienna, joining the staff of *Der Tag*. This paper serialized the novels that made his reputation, including *Die freudlose Gasse* ('The Dismal Street'), a sympathetic portrayal of a young woman's experience of the big city, later filmed with Greta Garbo playing the lead; *Die Stadt ohne Juden* ('City without Jews'), a satire on antisemitism, which prophetically imagines how devoid of creativity Vienna becomes after its Jews have been expelled; and *Kampf um Wien*, a vivid portrayal of the 'struggle for Vienna' fought out between competing ideological factions. Bettauer, who had known Kraus since his schooldays, incorporates in this novel a scene paying tribute to the satirist's judgement and integrity. He also introduces his fictional hero to leading political figures like Chancellor Ignaz Seipel and Police Chief Johannes Schober, illuminating the most urgent problems of the day through a blend of topical comment and imaginative projection.

Bettauer achieved sensational success with the founding in February 1924 of the sex-education magazine *Er und Sie: Zeitschrift für Lebenskultur und Erotik*. His first leading article, 'The Erotic Revolution', boldly proclaimed that 'we are living amid the powerful and most decisive revolution of all times'. This revolution, we are told, is far more significant than the economic crises that are making the headlines. Bettauer's article contains attacks on the prevailing 'pseudomorality' that are reminiscent of pre-war numbers of *Die Fackel*. But where Kraus had written for a discriminating elite, Bettauer was preaching sexual freedom to 'the broadest masses of the people'. Within weeks, his magazine was selling 60,000 copies, spawning a gaggle of imitations, including a magazine called *Ich und Du* which became equally notorious.[47] Bettauer's magazine provoked vigorous protests from Julius Tandler, director of the Municipal Office for Youth, who felt it represented a danger to impressionable adolescents. But there was a division of opinion within the Social Democratic camp, and the Mayor, Karl Seitz, who had powers to confiscate publications that threatened the morals of the young, resisted attempts to have the magazine banned. The issue became politicized on 12 March when Ignaz Seipel accused Seitz of encouraging a 'flood of pornography'. After the police had intervened, confiscating thousands of copies of *Er und Sie*, Bettauer launched a new magazine entitled *Bettauers Wochenschrift*. Journalists and politicians of every stripe now entered the fray, and at a meeting of the City Council on 21 March the deputies came to blows, as Anton Orel denounced Seitz for the attempt to 'deprave our children with Jewish poison and Jewish debauchery'. This theme was taken up with even greater ferocity in the Nazi weekly, *Deutsche Arbeiter-Presse*, which denounced the Mayor as 'Seitz-Pollaksohn' and claimed that he must have Jewish ancestry. The Public Prosecutor duly began proceedings against Bettauer and his partner Rudolf Olden for 'offences against public morality'.[48]

The affair provoked further headlines in September when the case came to court and the jury decided in favour of the accused. There was outrage in the Christian Social and *völkisch* press, which alleged that the jury had been packed with socialist sympathizers, while the *Deutsche Arbeiter-Presse*, in an article of 18

October, called for direct action. The editor, Kaspar Hellering, suggested in an article of February 1925 in the Nazi magazine *Grobian* that Bettauer deserved to be 'lynched'. An unemployed dental technician named Otto Rothstock, formerly a member of the Nazi Party, decided to take justice into his own hands. Using a pretext to gain admission to Bettauer's office, he shot him with a revolver, and Bettauer died of his wounds sixteen days later. There was a mixed response to Bettauer's death in the Social Democratic press, where it was alleged that the texts and images of *Bettauers Wochenschrift* must have 'unhealthily stimulated the senses of proletarian youth'.[49] The right-wing press could barely conceal its glee, describing Rothstock as a 'youthful idealist' who had 'carried out the verdict of the people'. Even the *Neue Freie Presse* described him as an honest man who had acted from 'deeply wounded inner chastity'. By this date the affair was making headlines in Germany, and Alfred Rosenberg, the leading Nazi ideologist, published a fifteen-page article entitled 'The Bettauer Affair: A Prize Example of Destructive Jewish Activity'.[50]

When Rothstock was put on trial for murder in October 1925, his lawyer, the notorious Nazi Walter Riehl, entered a plea of diminished responsibility. There was some support for this view from psychiatrists, and although the jury found Rothstock guilty of murder, their votes were evenly divided on the question of responsibility. Technically this amounted to an acquittal, but Rothstock was confined for twenty months to a mental hospital. The *Neue Freie Presse* accepted that Rothstock was 'mentally ill', and only the *Arbeiter-Zeitung* plainly identified the murder of Bettauer as 'the action of a Nazi' ('Die Tat eines Hakenkreuzlers').[51] Kraus refrained from commenting on this furore about themes which he had earlier made his own. Much as he despised the 'policing of morals', he had no sympathy with 'publicity for unrestrained sexual freedom'. To indicate his distaste for Bettauer's journalism he refers to him as the 'well-known pornographic author' (F 649–56, 81–2 & 105). Only in May 1925, after the assassination, did he observe that he was unable to judge whether 'poor Bettauer's attempts at the sexual enlightenment of adults could have confused young people'. Although he had read very little by Bettauer, he now doubted whether he should be regarded as a pornographer (F 686–90, 6–7). This is a grudging epitaph for an author who, according to Robert Musil, had lived and died for his convictions.[52]

Polarizing Tendencies and the Radicalism of the Centre

If the strength of Viennese culture derived from this network of intersecting circles, the fatal flaw lay in a polarization that threatened to tear the country apart. The Bettauer affair revealed the vulnerability of the Republic to the combined power of Catholics and Nazis, while the general election of April 1927 marked a further watershed, as the Christian Social and German Nationalist parties made common cause with the National Socialists in an anti-Marxist United Front. The Social Democrats responded by publishing a declaration of support by the Intellectuals of Vienna, including Alfred Adler,

Karl Bühler, Sigmund Freud, Fritz Grünbaum, Hans Kelsen, Alma Mahler, Robert Musil, Alfred Polgar, Anton Webern, Egon Wellesz and Franz Werfel – but not Kraus, who was becoming increasingly critical of the Party (AZ, 20 April 1927).[53] The satirist distanced himself from the 'interest groups of all camps' (F 691–6, 26). Sensitivity to ideological thinking led him to question the dualistic categories that dominated public life.

Using a language that transcended the antagonisms, Kraus denounced the entire 'Jewish–Christian world' (F 521–30, 61). This implies that the competing ideologies are not as distinctive as they seem, since they are all subject to the same commercial and journalistic pressures. The 'newspaper Christians' do not really despise the 'Jewish press', since they envy its sophistication (F 552–3, 2). The satirist deconstructs the polarized categories of the ideological struggle by attributing 'Jewish cunning' to the Christian *Reichspost* (F 691–6, 63), and he inverts the concept of 'Jewish finance' when he appeals for liberation from 'the disreputable Christian moneybags who dominate our lives' (F 778–80, 18). In his vocabulary, 'Jewish' and 'Christian' denote not races or religions but discourses, shaped by education and social conditioning, and he challenges the view that supposedly 'Jewish', 'Christian' or 'Aryan' ideologies are based on immutable racial differences, demonstrating (in a passage of May 1926) 'how spurious [are] all beliefs in the antagonism between human races, based on nothing but political slogans' (F 726–9, 52).

In his aphoristic writings of the pre-war period Kraus had deployed an antithetical strategy to question received wisdom. He was fond of inverting set phrases, and when this 'inversion of proverbial expressions' was criticized as mechanical he repudiated the charge with vehemence (F 389–90, 38). His satirical aesthetic was set out in May 1912 in the essay 'Nestroy und die Nachwelt' ('Nestroy and the Modern World'), which suggests that satire represents not a fixed 'ideology' ('Gesinnung'), but the penetration, preservation and accentuation of 'polarized tendencies' ('polare Strömungen'; F 349–50, 9). It is this form of delighted mockery, he argues, that underlies a tirade by Nestroy or a melody by Offenbach. The republication of this passage in 1922 in *Untergang der Welt durch schwarze Magie* (S 4, 229) reminded his readers that the most subversive forms of satire play off contradictory attitudes against each other, without identifying with either. If Kraus in the post-war period ceased writing aphorisms, this cannot simply be attributed to his growing fondness for epigrams. He must also have realized that a reliance on antithesis reinforced the dominant dualisms: feminism versus patriarchy, socialism versus conservatism, communism versus fascism, Aryans versus Jews. His antitheses gave way to a multifaceted satire designed to ironize several factions simultaneously: 'jüdisch-deutschösterreichisch' (F 557–60, 64) or 'christlichsozialdemokratisch' (F 759–65, 14). He challenged the binary oppositions that dominated public discourse, developing a polysemic syntax that defied the journalistic urge to reduce politics to punchlines. No ideological faction was immune, and an attack on the shortcomings of the liberal press was likely to be combined with

equally astringent comments on their adversaries. Occasionally, Kraus did succumb to seductive dualisms, as when he tried to prove that poems reportedly
written by a mental patient in Czernowitz were superior to the works of conservative poets published in the Austrian press. It turned out that the matter was
more complex: the patient had memorized verses written by other hands ('Aus
Redaktion und Irrenhaus'; F 781–6, 84–100; 800–05, 75–132). More characteristically, he brackets two targets within a single sentence, attacking both
socialists and conservatives simultaneously (F 735–42, 18). In an attempt to
elude polarized categories, Kraus developed a style of writing that was disconcertingly polyphonic, exploiting the complexities of German syntax to challenge ideological thinking. It was no easy task to define the excluded middle
that resulted from this polarization. Kraus's word for this ethical centre is
'human dignity' ('Menschenwürde'), the principle he affirms as a counterweight to the competing factions with their 'formulas and flags, slogans and
symbols, emblems and masks' (F 697–705, 120–1). His embattled position
amid the competing factions represented (in the words of Ernst Krenek) the
'despairing radicalism of the centre'.[54]

CHAPTER 7

The Scene of Writing

'Culture and the Press' was the title Kraus intended to use for a selection of articles from *Die Fackel*, first announced in 1908 (F 244, 23–4). The repeated postponement of this publication reflected his sense that a balanced account might only be possible from a more distanced perspective (F 341–2, 50), and in practice he found the subject too amorphous for treatment in book form. To tease out the complexities of this subject, it may be best to return to first principles and picture the writer at his desk, as Kraus so often does in passages of self-reflection. It may then be easier to appreciate his unique position within the field of cultural production and identify the most significant features of his work. The apartment in the Lothringerstrasse, where he lived from 1912 onwards, formed a secure base within a conflictual society. Like other original spirits from turn-of-the-century Vienna, notably Sigmund Freud and Peter Altenberg, he staged the act of writing with props from the past. The antiquities on Freud's desk formed the setting for a mind committed to cultural archaeology, while Altenberg's inscribed photos of pristine landscapes and pubescent girls created a more intimate space. But Kraus favoured portraits of authors and actors, so vibrant with emotional associations that they returned to haunt his imagination. From his desk he could see a wall covered with images, centred on a portrait of his beloved Annie Kalmar (Fig. 12). This was no shrine dedicated to vanished cultural formations but an animated theatre of memory, and Kraus (anticipating Derrida) enacts literary production within a scene of writing in which the 'sovereign solitude of the author' acquires a dramatic quality.[1]

Between the Study and the Street

Kraus pictures the scene of writing as a house with many rooms, inhabited by experts on whom the author can call when he needs images from a special discipline: a historian, an economist, a medic, perhaps even a 'Talmud student who has mastered the jargon of philosophy' (F 300, 25–6). This intuition, as we

12   Theatre of memory: pictures on the wall in Kraus's study

shall see, was to be uncannily fulfilled. The writing process is pictured as a nightly vigil – at times devotional, as in the poem 'Gebet' ('Prayer'), at times erotic, as in 'Eros und der Dichter', but the room is alive with faces and voices: snatches of remembered conversation, memories of great actors in their defin-ing roles, hypnagogic hallucinations, pictures that step out of their frames. To counterbalance the seriousness of his public persona, we are also offered glimpses of an author laughing at his desk 'the whole night long' (F 622–31, 97). Self-immersion in the process of writing leads Kraus to repudiate the idea of manipulative authorial control, insisting that ideas are 'created out of lan-guage' (F 267, 41). His numerous observations on this theme anticipate the postmodern conception of the imagination as a site for the intersection of var-ious 'discourses', implying that language speaks through the author, rather than the other way round. But Kraus is loth to abandon the idea of individual agency, and the role he plays as author echoes two different scripts: Mallarmé's self-effacing precept of 'ceding the initiative to words' and Nietzsche's dynamic model of 'philosophizing with a hammer'.[2] The shift towards a more aggressive use of language is signalled by a programmatic statement of January 1920. To engage with the inexhaustible infamy of the day, Kraus feels impelled to call his opponents 'not fools but imbeciles', not 'thieves' but a 'rabble of robbers' (F 521–30, 57). Such hyperboles served both semantic and phonetic intensifi-cation, since their alliterative force enhanced his diatribes from the platform.

The move from poetic contemplation to polemical engagement is expressed through the self-image of a poet distracted by sounds from the street. In 1915 he published an evocative description of the sights and sounds of the Friedrich-strasse in Berlin, with newsboys crying out the titles of the most popular papers (F 413–17, 15–16). In the poem 'Straßenrufe' ('Street Cries'), the raucous 'Extra Edition!' displaces the traditional 'Who'll buy my lavender?' (F 474–83, 119). In October 1920 Kraus gave a fuller account of the tension between 'writing-desk' and 'street' (F 554–6, 5). If only he could remain peacefully in his study, composing those poetic works that the readers claim to admire! But a fight has broken out outside his door, and there is no alternative but to join the fray. This marks a paradigmatic shift in the relationship between writing and politics. Before 1914 Kraus had presented himself as an author inspired by inner vision, proud of the fact that the window of his study overlooked an inner courtyard and that all he could see was a fire-wall (F 338, 16). This emphasis on interiority can be correlated with introspective forms like the aphorism, his favourite mode of writing in the pre-war period. After 1918, his image of the relationship between the courtyard and the street is reversed. An epigram which puns on the word 'Hof', meaning imperial court as well as inner courtyard, culminates in the lines: 'A room with a view of the street / is *certainly* preferable / to one with a view of the court!' (F 551, 16).

For Kraus, after 1918, the street ceased to be the scene of the isolated flâneur and became a forum for responsible citizenship, while militant political action displaced the traditional association of the street with poverty and prostitution. Moreover, the significance of private and public space was reversed. During the nineteenth century, political decisions were normally taken behind closed doors, while the behaviour of crowds was carefully regulated. They were per-mitted to mass on the streets as spectators for royal processions or participants in orderly demonstrations, but not to set the political agenda. However, by 1900 the mobilization of crowds was becoming a significant factor, culminat-ing in the patriotic fervour of late July and early August 1914. The conduct of the crowds in Berlin and other German cities at the outbreak of war has received increasing attention from political historians, offering a differentiated picture of 'war enthusiasm'. The spontaneous demonstrations in Berlin during the weekend of 25–26 July, in response to the Austrian ultimatum to Serbia, were led by patriotic students and reinforced by well-established national rituals. Manual workers were conspicuous by their absence, and during the fol-lowing days the Social Democrats staged their own anti-war demonstrations. The patriotic enthusiasm may have appeared spontaneous, but was actually being orchestrated by the government. Socialist demonstrators were prevented from reaching the city centre, as they had been during the suffrage reform demonstrations of 1910, when the Berlin Police Commissioner, Traugott von Jagow, had mocked the 'right to the streets' claimed by the demonstrators, insisting 'the streets exist for traffic'. However, in response to the surge of patri-otism in July 1914, the police were instructed by the government *not* to enforce the law prohibiting unauthorized public demonstrations. The war enthusiasm was thus the product of a combination of factors: the unwritten script of shared patriotic assumptions, the hidden hand of the government – and above all the sensational headlines in the newspapers, which rushed their 'extra editions' on to the streets and into the hands of the waiting crowds.[3]

After the collapse of 1918, the return of thousands of war veterans created a mood of uncontrollable anarchy, and the boulevards of Berlin, originally designed for imperial pageants and military cavalcades, became a battleground for competing factions. Throughout the inter-war period there were demonstrations on the Vienna Ringstrasse and mass rallies on the Heldenplatz, culminating in Hitler's triumphal return in 1938. In the larger urban centres there were continuous territorial battles between socialists defending their 'strongholds' and right-wing formations determined to reclaim their 'right to the streets' through aggressive counter-demonstrations.[4] In Germany the new wave of political mobilization had equally fateful consequences, as political activists took the struggle to the streets, supported by nationwide networks of political associations and party activists. Patriotic rallies by right-wing pressure groups 'claimed the public spaces that had once been the domain of Social Democrats', and the combined activities of middle-class cultural societies and militant veterans' groups 'provided cover for increasingly militant antiparliamentary politics'.[5] The struggle was waged throughout the 1920s by a proliferation of political militias, each with its own marching songs. The street, as Kraus ruefully observed, 'belongs to those shouting slogans' (F 712–16, 95). It is significant that the dominant motif of the 'Horst Wessel Lied', anthem of the Nazi movement, was control of the streets: 'Die Strasse frei den braunen Bataillonen!' ('Clear the street for the brown battalions!').

Kraus was among the first to put this transformation into literary form. Each act of *Die letzten Tage der Menschheit* begins with crowds on the boulevard, convulsed by the cries of newsvendors. The street had become a scene of writing through a cacophony of competing media: placards advertising political programmes or commercial products, newspapers announcing the latest sensation, marching tunes and popular songs, loudspeakers blaring out propaganda, newsreel cameras recording the urban frenzy. The early-twentieth-century metropolis abounded in messages which passers-by were expected to 'read'. Newspapers provided indispensable guides to the 'hectic rhythms of the metropolis', so that 'not to read the newspaper was to risk losing orientation'.[6] The scene in Berlin on the evening of Saturday 25 July 1914, as the crowds stormed the delivery vans for copies of the *Acht-Uhr-Abendblatt*, was recorded by an eyewitness who concluded: 'Never before has there been so much reading in the streets.'[7] Traditionally, especially in Austria, newspapers had been sold from decorous kiosks or delivered directly to the door, while relatively few were hawked on the streets. But in *Die letzten Tage der Menschheit* the first word we hear in the Prologue is the newsboy screaming, 'Special Edition! Assassination of the Heir to the Throne!' In Act I this becomes the cry of the newsvendor who is selling 'Both Editions!': one reporting news of a sensational event, the other retracting it.[8]

The seismic shift of history portrayed in *Die letzten Tage der Menschheit* involves an inversion of the hierarchy of discourse. A series of ironic reversals exposes the new systems of communication that substitute the slogans of the street for the discriminations of the academy. The Anti-Christ sits in the editorial office, dictating tomorrow's leading article, but his minions are everywhere: from reporters fabricating patriotic interviews to officials doctoring the latest communiqué from the front. Language loses its rapport with reality, and, as the discrepancies between words and actions approach breaking point, the news vendors become frenzied maenads, racing up and down the streets uttering incomprehensible screams (V, 53). The scene is set for the ferocious ideological struggles of the post-war period, and soon even the sidewalks were to be transformed into writing surfaces, with swastikas chalked on the pavement outside Freud's house in the Berggasse and released from tall buildings in confetti-like showers of gilded paper.[9] In *Die Fackel* the tension between the writing-desk and the street generates an astonishing range of expression and performance. At one extreme, Kraus began to compose subtle reflections on language, designed to tease out nuances of style and syntax. At the other, the fervour of his polemics led him to publish sensational posters and provocative broadsheets. The street had become a scene of writing, with official announcements posted next to saucy advertisements, only to be defaced by subversive graffiti. His early treatment of the spurious world created by advertising, the essay 'Die Welt der Plakate' ('The World of Posters'), had humorous undertones (F 283–4, 19–25). But in 1914 this theme acquired a political edge, as he focused on the juxtaposition between facetious adverts and the solemn declaration of war.[10] Kraus included both large posters and small advertisements in his survey of the cultural field, using facsimile techniques to reproduce revealing examples. In April 1932, when a crude advert for margarine disrupted the report in the *Neue Freie Presse* of a speech by the German Finance Minister, he reproduced a section from the offending page. His commentary transforms this 'atrocious image of the commercial spirit' into an allegory of the threat of Anschluss between the Austrian Heimwehr and an increasingly Nazified Germany (F 873–5, 10–12).

During the 1920s the politicization of the streets and the commercialization of public space became entwined, prompting revulsion at the vulgarization of the cityscape. It was not only Kraus who objected to the flashing lights in the Kärntnerstrasse advertising 'SIGI GUMMI' contraceptives. Antisemitic groups exploited the association between 'Jewish' commerce and vulgar advertising by suggesting that German cities were being transformed into a 'Jewish Circus' – the title of a visual juxtaposition of the 'City with Jews' and the 'City without Jews' published in the Nazi magazine *Der Stürmer* (Fig. 13). In Vienna, the Social Democrats attempted to bring greater order into the streets by establishing a new municipally owned bill-posting agency, the Wiener

13   Images of the street: antisemitic cartoon from *Der Stürmer*

Plakatierungs- und Anzeigengesellschaft (WIPAG), priding themselves on the results.[11] Kraus himself was to use the services of WIPAG on a number of occasions, describing his poster of autumn 1927 calling on the Police Chief to resign as the 'sacrifice of a language teacher who takes to the streets' (F 771–6, 15). This public gesture was central to his defence of the Republic, but it also showed that there are limits to what can be achieved by an individual author attempting to set the world to rights by means of the pen – or even a printing press. The absence of group solidarity made the street a lonely place, prompting Kraus to identify with Nikolai Gogol's definition of the satirical poet: 'no sympathy is likely to flower on his street, where he now finds himself alone, a homeless traveller' (cited F 691–6, 35 & 70). The satirist may appeal for solidarity, but he is more likely to experience ostracism or even physical assault.

It is not surprising that Kraus, like other authors of his generation, sought refuge in the coffee-house, which had already become one of the scenes of writing in the 1890s, associated with the bohemian creativity of his friend Peter Altenberg. During the 1920s Kraus held aloof from the characteristic Viennese conviviality, mocking the coffee-house intellectuals in *Literatur oder Man wird doch da sehn* ('Literature or You Ain't Seen Nothing Yet'), his satire on the poets who met in the Café Herrenhof. He no longer found time for the relaxed camaraderie he had shared before the war with kindred spirits like Otto Stoessl in Vienna and Herwarth Walden in Berlin.[12] But he still enjoyed exchanging ideas with intimate friends, meeting at a reserved table in the Café Parsifal, a watering place in the Walfischgasse frequented by musicians. His closest ally was the lawyer Oskar Samek, who would join him at the end of his day's work to discuss the latest legal action, and his circle was open to innovators from different disciplines, as when he was joined on an evening in May 1928 by Anton Webern, the broadcaster Andreas Reischek, the sculptor Josef Humplik, the publisher Franz Glück, and the editor Ludwig Ficker (on a visit from Innsbruck).[13] Kraus habitually carried a little black notebook, which he would produce partly to protect his privacy, partly to jot down his latest inspiration 'between two sips of coffee' (F 279–80, 2). Two such notebooks that survive reveal further links between sociability and creativity: a snatch of conversation jotted down as the germ of an aphorism. Seated in an alcove with a few chairs reserved for his friends, he would scan the newspapers with scissors ready to clip revealing passages in accordance with his motto 'Ausschneiden, was ist!' (F 398, 28). Thus the scene of his writing was inherently social and his glosses incorporate a cacophony of competing voices, comparable to the 'poèmes conversations' of Apollinaire and the Surrealists.[14]

Polyphonic Voices

Between the study and the street lies a further locus of creativity: the platform from which the author declaims polemical texts and performs satirical operettas. Although his writing-desk remains his primary 'home' ('Heimat'), Kraus extends this concept to include any platform where he can count on the assistance of Offenbach (F 820–6, 148). He had become a public figure, appearing on stage in scores of European cities and giving a total of seven hundred recitals. His skilful adaptations amplified the resonance of his monologue satire, enhancing the play of ambiguity. Speaking in the character of Nestroy's misanthropic Herr von Lips, he could introduce additional strophes of his own composition to condemn the French occupation of the Ruhr in January 1923 (F 613–21, 55). While this technique endowed Kraus's voice with the authority of an indigenous satirical tradition, a more cosmopolitan perspective was introduced from 1926 onwards through his Offenbach recitals, achieving a 'merging of both mocking laughters' (F 845–6, 33). Such variations of voice raised complicated questions about authorial responsibility. In September 1928 the critic Alfred Kerr accused Kraus of being anti-German, citing as evidence – in his submission to a Berlin court – the poem 'Lied des Alldeutschen'. This is actually a dramatic monologue in the voice of an imaginary character, the belligerent 'Pan-German', represented in *Die letzten Tage der Menschheit* (III, 40) by the superpatriot Ottomar Wilhelm Wahnschaffe. Thus Kraus was able to argue that the poem expressed not his own opinions, but the 'annexationist spirit' prevailing in Germany (F 787–94, 171–4).

This reluctance to be pinned down to specific political opinions can be linked with Kraus's fondness for oblique forms of discourse, designed to stimulate thought rather than express opinions. One technique was to divide his identity into two separate roles, writing about himself as 'Editor' of *Die Fackel* in the 'function of his secretary' (F 679–85, 61n). This enables him to refer to himself in the third person, as 'Herr Kraus', in letters allegedly emanating from an impersonal publishing house – Verlag 'Die Fackel' ('Torch Publications'). The name of the secretary who actually typed his letters, Frieda Wacha, is not mentioned, since the aim is to achieve an ironic 'distancing of tone' (F 521–30, 136). This engenders a detached mockery, avoiding direct confrontations by placing the author on a different plane from the letter's recipient. There are parallels with the epistolary tone used by heads of state in correspondence with lesser mortals: 'The President of the United States begs to inform you', etc. Kraus composed innumerable letters in this form, printing those which he felt had exemplary value. Legal submissions constitute a further extension of his stylistic range, and he devoted endless hours to drafting legal pleas in consultation with his solicitor, Dr Oskar Samek, many of which were also published. Their innumerable court cases illustrate the 'multivocal' quality of polemical and legal discourse, involving a chorus of competing voices.[15]

Despite these polyphonic qualities, the discourse of *Die Fackel* is held together by a single organizing intelligence. The contrast with Kurt Tucholsky, the leading satirist of Weimar Germany, is instructive. It would be fascinating to compare two authors who developed such differing styles to address a similar range of problems: the failings of the Social Democrats, the bias of the courts, the equivocations of the Jewish bourgeoisie, and the threat posed by the military caste. The house-style of *Die Weltbühne* was bluntly outspoken, while that of *Die Fackel* tended to be teasingly allusive. The most obvious contrast related to narrative voice. Tucholsky's satire was published under five different names – Kurt Tucholsky, Peter Panther, Theobald Tiger, Ignaz Wrobel and Kaspar Hauser. As Tucholsky he became the great adversary of the German nationalists, while as Wrobel he directed his attacks against unrepentant militarists, also publishing witty verses and scurrilous monologues about the foibles of middle-class Jews. In this case the polyphonic impulses of satire are literally expressed through a chorus of different voices, each with a distinct narrative identity. Kraus praised the writings published under the pseudonym Ignaz Wrobel as 'a really effective and courageous anti-war achievement', but he was aware that Tucholsky had to make concessions to the 'constrictions and constraints of publicistic relationships' in Berlin (F 686–90, 61). Writing for *Die Weltbühne*, Tucholsky adopted an increasingly pro-communist stance, but to make ends meet he also wrote for the liberal papers like the *Berliner Tageblatt* and the *Vossische Zeitung*, playing down his political themes.[16] Kraus became suspicious about a writer who seemed equally at home with the 'Vossischen', the 'Mossischen' (Rudolf Mosse's *Berliner Tageblatt*) and the 'Russischen' (the communists; F 847–51, 78). These critical comments do less than justice to Tucholsky's courageous achievements, and Kraus even claimed to find the humorous writings of Erich Kästner superior to those of the man who 'has made five names for himself' (F 868–72, 82). He also had reservations about Tucholsky's habitual use of the first-person plural to express solidarity with left-wing groups.

Kraus's strategy was to sustain a high-profile self-image associated with an exalted conception of authorial responsibility. At times his stance is reminiscent of Kierkegaard, who felt bound by the biblical precept (quoted in *Die Fackel*) that 'a man should bear responsibility in eternity for every improper word he has spoken' (F 706–11, 16–17). In December 1926, challenging the irresponsible techniques of the modern media, he defines himself as 'an intellectually responsible individual self' (F 743–50, 143). At times his embattled monologue may seem too relentless, closing off alternative perspectives through syntactical barricades. But he retains the freedom to modulate into different voices – the lyrical self of the nature poems or the distanced 'Editor' of letters from the Verlag. His saving grace lies in his fondness for 'Glossen', texts suffused with quotations which have an essentially dialogic quality, while his satirical poems evoke a cacophony of voices, as in 'Wien', an acoustic panorama of post-war Vienna (F 595–600, 124–8).

If journalists, according to the suggestive English phrase, spend their lives producing 'copy', what happens when this second-order discourse is copied into *Die Fackel*, forming a patchwork of derivative fragments? A promising approach to this question suggests that Kraus's quotational technique destabilizes the myth that Jews are capable only of mimicry, lacking any 'organic connection with the language they speak', and are therefore 'incapable of creating original art'. The satirist's response is to take the principle of mimicry to its ultimate extreme, creating a kaleidoscope of quotations which – far from being 'Jewish' in any limiting sense – can be seen as one of the defining qualities of literary modernism.[17] In Bakhtin's terms, it could be argued that Kraus's self-immersion in other discourses has elements of 'heteroglossia', those 'centrifugal forces in language' which are continuously at odds with the desire to impose normative meanings.[18] In theory Kraus may distance himself from Jewish jargon and identify with an elevated conception of literary German, but in practice he demonstrates that there is no unitary language, but a chorus of dialects and jargons, transgressions of formal grammar and deviations from cultural norms. His style combines Orwell's polemical radicalism with Joyce's polymorphous wordplay. The fondness for puns endows even individual words with a double-voiced quality, while shifts between registers generate stylistic incongruities within a single sentence.[19] His debt to Viennese popular comedy led him to distance himself from 'literary intellectuals' such as Robert

Musil, who regarded Nestroy as beneath them ('Nestroy und die Literaten', F 595–600, 53–5). At one pole we have an embattled monologue, at the other an entrancing polyphony – the performer capable of reproducing the voices of half-a-dozen different Offenbach or Nestroy characters within a single scene.[20]

Gutenberg and the 'Brungled Imboglio'

Polyphonic satire requires a versatile use of typography. Kraus habitually used a steel-nibbed pen and an ink-well, regarding even the typewriter as an intrusion. When he thematizes 'soundbites and phrases, ink, technology and death' (F 508–13, 7), he is reaffirming the pre-industrial integrity of ink against the automated technology of the rotary press. Hence his denunciation of Johannes Gutenberg for the invention of printing: 'The whole institution is a misprint' (F 384–5, 26). But in practice the scene of writing extended from the study to the printshop, and Kraus developed a passion for movable type, devoting countless hours to correcting proofsheets and perfecting the layout of the printed text. This was facilitated by the services of a dedicated printer, Georg Jahoda, proprietor of Jahoda & Siegel, the firm that between October 1901 and April 1936 produced 335 issues of Die Fackel (the shortest being four pages in length, the longest 315 pages). His poem 'An meinen Drucker' ('To my Printer') pays tribute to Jahoda as his 'creative collaborator':

> der aus dem Wirrsal der unheilgen Schrift
> ein Wunderwerk der Worterscheinung trifft,
> daß dem, der dem Erfinder nie verzieh,
> der Druck erscheint als hellere Magie [. . .].   (F 649–56, 1)

> out of the turmoil of unholy script
> epiphanies are verbally encrypt;
> though Gutenberg I never shall forgive,
> your lighter magic touch makes printing live [. . .].[21]

Such passages make it clear that Kraus is not simply denouncing 'typographic man' in the manner of Marshall McLuhan, but developing a more resourceful use of the printer's art to counteract the effects of linearity.[22] This involved an infinite capacity for taking pains. Jahoda would send his assistant to the Lothringerstrasse to collect the manuscripts and corrected proofsheets on which Kraus had been working overnight. The type would be reset, and that same evening the next set of proofs would be back on his desk, ready for further revision. Every sentence, the author suggests, should be read as many times as it has taken to correct the proofs (F 360–2, 15). The care Kraus lavished over the layout of the individual page was echoed by the design of each issue, and sequences of proofs surviving in the archives show that in some cases more than a dozen sets were required.[23]

Kraus's passion for language embraced the refinements of the printer's art. He defined himself, in his obituary tribute to Jahoda, as an 'author just as intimate with the effects of printing as the printer with the mystery of the word'

(F 743–50, 2). Although his handwriting caused headaches for compositors, Kraus took care to preface his manuscripts with an indication of the typeface to be used: 'petit' (8–point), 'Garamond' (10–point), or 'durchschossen' ('spaced out').[24] He used different fonts to distinguish quotation from commentary, setting the former in smaller type. His scorn for fancy printing, the 'schöner Druck' designed for bibliophiles, did not prevent him from setting exacting standards for 'good' printing – the quality for which Jahoda & Siegel are commended (F 474–83, 75). The original choice of roman type ('antiqua') for Die Fackel, at a time when German print media were predominantly using traditional 'Fraktur', reflects the modernizing principles of Adolf Loos, who designed one of his favourite typefaces. Kraus seems to have felt that 'Fraktur' had backward-looking associations (the only book he published in this font was an adaptation of Nestroy).[25]

When Kraus incorporated a press clipping in his texts, he insisted that the original 'Fraktur' should be reset in antiqua. The result can be seen from the contrast between a manuscript incorporating such a press clipping and the final printed page.[26] Both Kraus's appalling handwriting ('unholy script') and the blotchy press cutting are transformed by the uncluttered elegance of antiqua, and five different fonts are used to achieve a polyphonic effect. Under the lapidary title 'Homecoming and Fulfilment', Kraus reprints a report entitled 'Death from Joy at the Husband's Homecoming from Imprisonment', which records that a woman from a working-class suburb of Vienna has died from a mixture of shock and joy, on hearing that her husband, reportedly killed on the eastern front, has actually survived in a prisoner-of-war camp. The first twelve lines of the commentary consist of verses from King Lear (the King's final dialogue with Kent and Edgar), lamenting the 'image of that horror' – the death of Cordelia. Only near the foot of the page do three lines of larger type introduce the voice of the satirist, whose commentary raises the question of political responsibility by citing further lines from Shakespeare (Act II, scene 5 of Henry VI, Part 3), suggesting that the country will 'ne'er be satisfied!' Responsibility, he concludes, lies with the political leadership: the kings with their 'military commanders, statesmen and journalistic hacks' (F 546–50, 1–2).

This was a period when compositors commonly switched to a smaller typeface simply to save space, but the typography of Die Fackel establishes subtle hierarchies, creating effects that Gershom Scholem described as 'kaleidoscopic'.[27] Scholem (as we shall see) suggested that this technique had theological overtones, and Kraus's use of the word 'Glossen' does indeed echo the Glossa Ordinaria tradition of biblical commentary and Talmudic exegesis. One of his most effective methods was to divide the page vertically, creating a confrontational structure through parallel columns. This contrastive typography was first developed for editions of the Bible that set holy scripture within a framework of scholarly exegesis, and Kraus's use of contrasting fonts to distinguish cited texts from interlinear commentary can be seen as a secularization of that tradition.[28] Moreover, the design of Die Fackel combines tradition with modernity, making innovative use of photography and photomontage. This technique, pioneered before the First World War (F 326–8, frontispiece), becomes increasingly significant in later numbers of *Die Fackel*, where textual and visual quotations are ingeniously juxtaposed. These visual motifs are most effective when an authentic photograph – for example, the Kaiser convulsed with wolfish laughter – is reproduced with a brief but devastating commentary (F 726–9, 58–9).[29]

Kraus's preoccupation with typography involved a love–hate relationship with misprints that can be traced back to his very first publication – a review of Gerhart Hauptmann's *Die Weber*. Checking through his manuscript in April 1892, the editor added a marginal note suggesting that his summary of the plot ought to be 'less skimpy' ('weniger dürftig'). The typesetter took this to be author's copy and printed it as part of the text (FS 1, 9). The memory of this episode rankled, and he mentioned it seventeen years later in a reflection on the role of the typesetter: 'Misprints are the typesetter's resistance against deceit and stupidity, and the typesetter is the first reader' (F 272–3, 37). His horror when misprints crept into *Die Fackel* prompted him on one occasion to destroy a large part of the print run of a forthcoming number (F 386, 8), and his wish to control the printing quality led him to cease contributing to other journals, even when they were as distinguished as *Simplicissimus* or *Der Sturm*. This also helps to explain why from 1918 onwards the book editions of his writings, previously printed in Leipzig, were transferred to Jahoda & Siegel.[30]

Through his exacting mode of literary production, Kraus could aim at the greatest possible stylistic subtlety and typographical perfection, since there was no distracting rush to meet publication deadlines (the magazine appeared at irregular intervals according to the whim of the editor). Everything printed in *Die Fackel* was filtered through hundreds of hours of reflection, and every aspect of the publication process was designed to protect his independence. His increasingly intransigent stance led him to refuse to send out review copies of his books or free tickets for his public readings. Readers were exhorted not to attempt to influence his work by sending him letters, and to distance himself from commercial publishing he insisted that his books should also appear under the imprint Verlag 'Die Fackel'. The miracle is that this little magazine maintained such a substantial circulation, claiming in December 1924 10,000 readers (F 668–75, 72).

Thus the scene of writing includes the print-shop, and Kraus's early aphorisms contain miniature dialogues with compositors who have misread his handwriting. One of his longest letters to Herwarth Walden inveighs against misprints that have been allowed to creep into *Der Sturm*, which fell short of his exacting standards of proof-reading.[31] A good typesetter, he insisted in May 1918, is worth a battalion of war poets, paying tribute to Franz Koch, a seventeen-year-old printer's apprentice who had been conscripted and killed in battle (F 474–83, 77). Kraus pounced on misprints that express the collective psychology of the age, like the misspelling of the German dramatist Lessing as

'Lessner' – the name of a department store (F 431–6, 35), or the decorations which a policeman has reportedly 'slain' – rather than 'gained' ('ermordet', rather than 'erworben'). In such instances, he suggests that it is the typesetter who creates the satire (F 820–6, 107). His favourite example is 'der verbroigte Loibisch', a nonsense phrase allegedly based on a misprint in the *Neue Freie Presse*, which might be translated as 'bungled imbroglio' – or rather 'brungled imboglio'. This is the phrase he used, in a coded telegram sent from Rome in May 1915, to inform a friend of the failure of Austro-Hungarian diplomacy to keep Italy out of the war (F 668–75, 42–5). Lurking behind this phrase are elements of Yiddish ('broigen' in the sense of 'to need') and Italian ('imbrogliare' meaning 'to confuse'), although 'Loibusch' remains a mystery.

Since Kraus's manuscripts caused typesetters such difficulties, it is surprising that he made no effort to improve his handwriting. The answer may lie with his encounter in September 1915 with Raphael Schermann, the celebrated graphologist. Schermann had already studied a sample of Kraus's handwriting without any knowledge of the author, identifying it as that of an aggressive critic with 'nerves overstretched'. When they met for the first time a few days later in the Café Imperial, Kraus produced an envelope addressed to himself by Sidonie Nadherny. He was astounded by Schermann's intuitive reading of her character, sending her a six-page account (BSN 1, 173–4 & 184–7). Since the contrast between the agitated angularity of Kraus's script and Sidonie's sensuously rounded hand apparently confirmed that they were destined for each other, there was little incentive for him to write more legibly. But, once words were set in print, he insisted on the highest possible standards, defining his role as that of a 'teacher of language', whose task is to correct the mistakes of 'grammatical libertines' (F 657–67, 58).

He was particularly concerned with errors of punctuation, pioneering what has become known as the 'zero tolerance' approach.[32] This theme is highlighted in the poem 'Nach zwanzig Jahren' ('After Twenty Years', April 1919), which speaks of 'fulfilling until Judgement Day / the sacred law that commas really count' (F 508–13, 7). It would be wrong to assume that this is mere hyperbole: fifteen years later Kraus did indeed fight a protracted court case over a missing comma, claiming that a line from one of his poems had been mangled (P 3, 325–51). It was not only the integrity of his own texts that he was determined to protect. During the war he denounced a misplaced comma in an edition of Goethe as evidence of German barbarism, while missing apostrophes assumed a political as well as stylistic significance when they became the victims of a policy of melting down metallic type to make munitions. Badly printed modern editions of the classics caused both 'eye-ache' and by implication 'agony for the ears' (F 484–98, 136–8). Kraus really cared about commas and apostrophes, but his interest in punctuation was not mere pedantry, since he was able to show that a missing comma could prolong a war. Did the Austrian Foreign Minister, in the spring of 1918, intend to support a peace settlement based on annexations when he spoke 'of German control of

Belgium', or was he merely proposing a discussion 'of German control, of Belgium' (F 474–83, 4–8)? Kraus was particularly severe on journalists who create confusion by misuse of the comma in reported speech – a practice he stigmatizes as 'das israelitische Komma' (F 445–53, 160). He expected higher standards from Jewish journalists than from reactionaries who wrote 'in Pan-German' (F 781–6, 87).

There were occasions when a misprint inspired trenchant political satire. Manual typesetting meant that sometimes a complete line was misplaced, as in the press report which Kraus reprints under the title 'Das Chaos':

'Reception in the Redoutensaal
On the 21st of the month, under the protection of Federal President Hainisch, there will be an official reception in the Redoutensaal of the Hofburg, profits from which will be devoted to the new hostel for university students which is to be opened in the suburb of Meidling. Members of the State Opera House and the Burgtheater will contribute to the artistic programme of the reception. The event will be attended by the President, the Federal Chancellor, the diplomatic corps, all members of the Cabinet and all official personalities **stabs in the face and in the arm. In response to the cries for help** tickets available in the committee's office in the Third District, Hauptstrasse 1, phone 9577.'

His commentary is wickedly apposite:

Why not? Just as in Vienna it is impossible to conduct a telephone conversation without being interrupted by a crossed line (let alone conclude that second conversation), so too in newspaper reports of local affairs there is a hooking-together and criss-crossing of the spheres, and it is precisely this which reveals a deeper identity. Why not? The violent activities of the Swastiklers, which take place under the protection of placemen, might as well occur before their very eyes for a change, especially in the case of a new hostel for university students. Further down the page there is no doubt a description of crowds lining up to watch the procession of dignitaries brawling in the street. The wrong connections are the true ones. (F 613–21, 12)

Such paradoxes, tucked away in the small print of *Die Fackel*, suggest that there are hidden connections between Christian Social officials and Nazi thugs, especially at a time when the Austrian universities were becoming hotbeds of antisemitism. The images of 'hooking-together' ('haken') and 'criss-crossing' ('kreuzen'), which deconstruct the word 'Hakenkreuz', endow the typographical gaffe with prophetic significance. Kraus anticipated that, under the shadow of the swastika, harmless 'muddle' might develop into a lethally destructive 'mishmash' of deception and murder (F 873–5, 30). This is why, in his theory of language, conceptual muddles form such a fundamental theme.

CHAPTER 8

The Chimera of Language

Kraus's essay on 'Language' ('Die Sprache') contains the delphic statement: 'Language is the only chimera whose deceptive power is infinite, the inexhaustible resource in which life is not impoverished.' The word 'chimera' is usually understood in the sense of 'illusion', as in Nestroy's satirical refrain, frequently recited by Kraus: ''Tis but a chimera, but I find it fun' ('Das is wohl nur Chimäre, aber mich unterhalt's'; S 14, 36–7). But it is difficult to square this conception of language with the claim – in the same essay – that language provides an authoritative 'arbiter' ('Ordonnanz'), which Germans should learn to obey (F 885–7, 3–4). The association of 'chimera' with 'illusion' derives from Greek mythology, where the chimera was a fabulous beast with the head of a lion and the body of a goat – an image that can be correlated with Kraus's binary model of language. In 'Die Sprache' he distinguishes between 'language as communication' ('Sprache als Mitteilung') and 'language as figuration' ('Sprache als Gestaltung'). It is the *same* language in each case, but the honest journalist and the gifted poet use it in different ways. Poetic images have multiple meanings, but journalists should report events in plain words. The charge against journalese is that it deviates from this cardinal rule.

Conceptual Muddles

Kraus sees public life as pervaded by 'conceptual muddle' (F 691–6, 26). He argues for a strict separation of spheres – between art and commerce, literature and journalism, the private and the public. This preoccupation with 'creative separation' was shared by a number of other Austrian critics, including Adolf Loos and Ludwig Wittgenstein. 'What Kraus, Loos and Wittgenstein have in common', observed the architect Paul Engelmann in an influential memoir, 'is their endeavour to separate and divide correctly. They are creative separators.' Loos insisted on a separation between art and crafts, Kraus attacked the journalistic practice of 'mixing news with comment', while the mischief against which Wittgenstein's *Tractatus* is directed is 'the mingling of the sciences with metaphysics'.[1] Hence Wittgenstein's attempt to develop a more rigorous conception of 'picture language'.

The desire to create a language free of ambiguity led another author associated with the Vienna Circle, Otto Neurath, to design the 'International Picture Language' or 'Isotypes'. Neurath was a social reformer who believed that visual statistics would enable people to 'acquaint themselves with the latest sociological and economic facts at a glance'.[2] Hence the programme of visual education which he developed at the Museum of Economy and Society. Public health was a particular concern, and one of his most striking isotypes illustrates the reduction in infant mortality in Vienna between 1901 and 1929, contrasting the rates for poorer families in cramped accommodation with those for the socially privileged. The aim of Neurath and other reforming members of the Vienna Circle, as set out in their programme 'The Scientific World Conception' (1929), was 'to fashion intellectual tools for everyday life'. This was to be facilitated through a picture language capable of representing complex social data in terms which avoid confusion and ambiguity. Thus there is a sign for 'shoe' which is quite distinct from the sign for 'works'; by putting them together it is possible to represent a 'shoe-works' (Fig. 14a). Neurath summarized his aims in the booklet *International Picture Language*, published in basic English in 1936: 'Every ISOTYPE picture has to make use only of such details as are necessary for an account in the language of science.'[3]

Neurath's innovations led, in the longer term, to the global use of picture language for purposes of public information, but in inter-war Austria his work was frustrated. After the banning of the Social Democratic Party in 1934, the Museum was closed and he was forced to continue his work in exile, finding in Oxford the kind of congenial environment that Wittgenstein found in Cambridge. Where Neurath continued to promote his isotypes in the English-speaking world, Wittgenstein became fascinated by the opposite phenomenon: the 'puzzle-picture' ('Vexierbild'). In his posthumously published *Philosophical Investigations* Wittgenstein uses two striking drawings to illustrate the problems of perception raised by puzzle-pictures: the 'duck–rabbit' (borrowed from Jastrow's *Fact and Fable in Psychology*) and the 'double-cross' (Fig. 14b). The problem, in each case, is one of 'ambiguity'. The 'duck–rabbit' would be seen as a rabbit (if surrounded by pictures of rabbits), but as a duck (if surrounded by ducks). There is a 'change of aspect [. . .] as if the object had altered before my eyes'. The double-cross is equally perplexing, since it can be seen either as a white cross on a black ground, or as a black cross on a white ground; but it cannot be perceived as both simultaneously. Such examples lead the philosopher to conclude not simply that the same picture may be viewed under two 'aspects', but that 'the *concept* of seeing is modified'.[4]

For Wittgenstein, in the tranquillity of Cambridge, it was clear that two mutually exclusive perceptions could not occur simultaneously. But this principle did not apply in the topsy-turvy world of 'Deutsch-Österreich' which he had left behind. Kraus attributed the collapse of the imperial order to the

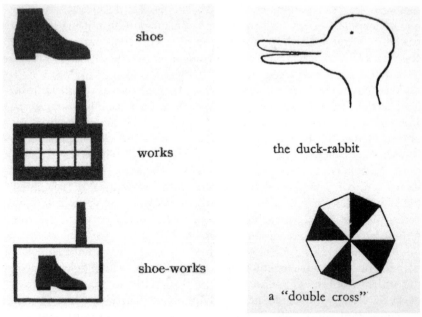

shoe

works

shoe-works

the duck-rabbit

a "double cross"

14 (a) Picture language: Neurath's 'shoe-works' (b) Puzzle-pictures: Wittgenstein's 'duck–rabbit' and 'double cross'

simultaneous existence of anachronistic politics and modern technology. The radicalization of his perspective after 1918 leads him to identify even more disturbing anomalies in post-war society, as the proliferation of extremist ideologies created new contradictions, offering an endless stream of stimuli to the satirical imagination. Like Wittgenstein, he became fascinated by 'puzzle-pictures' – in journalistic form: 'Vexierjournalistik' (F 706–11, 110). He had introduced this concept in May 1903, during his campaign against *Die Zeit*, describing its mystifications as 'puzzle-pictures – you see a landscape and some-where there must be an elderly aunt hidden away' (F 137, 20). In the new journalism of the 1920s the contradictions were even more perplexing. The infighting among German-language newspapers in Prague led him in April 1923 to speak of a 'puzzle-picture' ('Vexierbild'), made 'more complicated by every attempt to solve it' (F 613–21, 116). Journalistic irresponsibility reached its apogee in *Die Stunde*, whose attacks are identified as 'puzzle-pictures', to be retracted a moment later as if they were merely a joke. This paper, flirting with the radical left while condoning the activities of reactionaries, has no pro-gramme that could possibly be pinned down. Since most articles are unsigned, you have to guess who is responsible for the confusions by deciphering the 'stylistic picture-riddles' (F 691–6, 111–13).

The puzzle-pictures that interested Kraus took verbal form. Analysing the hybrid ideologies of his day through the medium of words, he highlighted the significance of compound nouns. German lends itself to the creation of expressive compounds, like 'Schadenfreude', 'Traumarbeit' ('dreamwork') or more balefully 'Würgeengel' ('exterminating angel'). Such concepts may illuminate complex psychological processes, but in ethical terms they are problematic, for they appear to provide a linguistic endorsement for 'the thing which is not' – for lies.[5] During the First World War, Kraus drew attention to the dehumanizing effect of composite expressions like 'Menschenmaterial' ('human material') and 'einrückend gemacht' ('forcibly enlisted'). His critique of dominant ideologies focuses on the series of hybrid expressions that shaped political discourse: 'Verteidigungskrieg' ('defensive warfare'), 'Militärjustiz' ('military justice'), 'Schutzhaft' ('protective custody'), 'Schicksalsgemeinschaft' ('communal destiny'), and above all the German word for 'swastika' – 'Hakenkreuz' (literally 'hooked cross'). In the play *Wolkenkuckucksheim* he shows how visual, verbal and ideological ambiguities are combined as the Christian cross, symbol of Austrian clericalism, is transformed into the hooked cross of National Socialism (S 11, 191). How can a cross, emblem of religious contemplation, coexist with the hook, an implement for cutting and hacking? This insight anticipates the aesthetics of Ernst Gombrich, who was particularly disturbed by the power of the swastika, which he found visually disorientating. Through its blending of symmetrical and rotational effects, he observed, the swastika 'upsets the balance of the mind'. This observation can be linked to the analysis of puzzle-pictures in his study of the psychology of perception, *Art and Illusion*. The starting-point is again the duplicitous duck–rabbit, but Gombrich reproduces further examples in order to prove that we can see 'either a rabbit or a duck' but 'cannot experience alternative readings at the same time'.[6] Kraus, by contrast, shows that words can transmit two contradictory messages simultaneously, and that this tolerance of incompatibilities was typical of the post-war German mentality. Not for nothing had he read Chamberlain's *Grundlagen des Neunzehnten Jahrhunderts*, which proclaimed that the Germanic race was both totally dominant and in terrible danger. Such claims are secure against empirical disproof, since 'events that seem to threaten one part of the fantasy, such as Germany's defeat in 1918, can be taken to support the other part'.[7]

We can now see more clearly why language is a 'chimera'. Kraus was intrigued by the double meanings of concepts of Greek origin, such as 'Aphrodite' – meaning both 'goddess of love' and 'maritime worm' (F 267–8, 42). He must also have been aware that, in scientific usage, the word 'chimera' denotes hybridity: 'an organism consisting of at least two genetically different kinds of tissue as a result of mutation, grafting, etc'.[8] This can be connected with his practice of inventing composite words through a process comparable to 'grafting'. The model, cited by both Kraus and Freud, is Heine's claim that his treatment by the Rothschilds in Paris was 'ganz famillionär', a neologism that wittily grafts on to the word 'Millionär' the prefix from 'familiär' (meaning 'like one of the family'). However, Kraus suggests that this kind of irony may be too 'cheap' ('wohlfeil'; F 406–12, 77–8). His finest examples are better described as 'mutations', as when he refers to Nazi followers of Spengler's *Der Untergang des Abendlandes* as 'Untergangster' (DW 65/78). The suffix '-er' is a familiar semantic mutation, but out of the new formation emerges the startlingly appropriate idea of 'gangsters' emerging from an ideological 'underworld'. His finest neologisms deserve a place in the dictionary, as when he defines government by idiotic nationalists as 'Idiokratie' (F 820–6, 147).

At this point the critique of conceptual muddles acquires a political force comparable to Karl Popper's polemic against totalitarianism. Kraus forms the invisible link between Wittgenstein and Popper, admired by both in the Vienna of their youth without being fully acknowledged by either.[9] He combines Wittgenstein's interest in linguistic 'puzzles' with Popper's pursuit of political 'problems'. Where a muddled concept exists, Kraus cites it – and where it doesn't, he invents it – to highlight the prevailing confusion. In a lighthearted mood he may coin a phrase like 'celebrity bimbos' – 'Prominente Pupperln', the title of an essay on the popular culture of the 1920s (F 751–6, 116–19). His more serious inventions range from 'technoromantisch' ('technoromantic') during the First World War through 'verfolgende Unschuld' ('innocent victimizers') to his denunciation of the cult of rapacious capitalism as 'Metaphysik der Haifische' ('Metaphysics of Sharks'). The care with which he constructed such expressive oxymorons can be traced through the proofsheets of *Die Fackel*. In the original galley proof the title of this essay was 'Die Großmetaphysiker' ('The Great Metaphysicians'), but the image of sharks was substituted to give the attack more teeth.[10] In an even more paradoxical formulation, the deployment of armed police to control socialist demonstrators is defined in *Die Fackel* as 'Polizeikrieg' ('police warfare'). According to the principle of creative separation, the police should be entirely independent of the army, the one protecting citizens at home, the other repulsing enemies abroad. Originally, Kraus had admired the Police Chief, Johannes Schober, because he had protected the rights of civilians against the army. The same logic led him to execrate Schober's police force after the massacre of July 1927 for turning their guns on the civilian population.

There are scores of polemical neologisms like 'Polizeikrieg' in *Die Fackel*, especially in the later years, as the pioneering study by Christian Wagenknecht has shown.[11] Some of them have such verbal subtlety that Wagenknecht elucidates them by reference to the rhetorical concept of 'amphibologies' ('Amphibolien'). But a simpler English word would be 'ambigrams' – the psychologist's term for words that invite 'dual readings'.[12] By contrast with the spasmodic quality of Heine's wordplay, Kraus's has a sustained seriousness, linked to the theory of 'simultaneity'. Around 1910, this concept had been associated with the dynamic worldview of Expressionism. 'We seemed to be in the grip of a new universal awareness,' wrote Johannes Becher, 'namely the sense of the simultaneity of events.'[13] Kraus gives the concept a more critical edge in his anti-war satire, using it to define a situation in which 'the most heterogeneous characteristics of the age coincide' (F 474–83, 41). Thus military valour depends on poison gas – the insight that leads him to graft the words 'glorious' and 'chlorinous' into the phrase 'eine chlorreiche Offensive' (F 474–83, 43). The difficulties of translating such linguistically inspired authors are legion. Indeed, translation becomes a form of commentary, since it is almost impossible to render into English a word like 'Todesfuge' ('Deathfuge') – an 'irreconcilable compound' with Krausian echoes, coined by Paul Celan for the necrophilia of National Socialism.[14]

Kraus's chimeras combine an Orwellian critique of 'double-speak' with the polymorphous playfulness of Carroll's 'portmanteau' words, such as 'slithy' (meaning 'lithe and slimy').[15] Where Orwell's 'doublespeak', as defined in *Nineteen Eighty-Four*, involves crude reversals like 'War is Peace' and 'Ignorance is Strength', Kraus's chimeras constitute a form of 'simultaneous-speak'. Modern weaponry makes the soldier 'simultaneously a hero and a coward' (F 445–53, 13). Anticipating Wittgenstein, he shows that, in the Alice-in-Wonderland world of German-Austria, things *can* be 'red and green all over'.[16] These confusions persisted in the republican period, when he took German nationalists to task for their 'muddling of the concepts Volk, State, Germany, Prussia' (F 632–9, 15). This same ambiguity occurred in official documents, most notably the opening sentence of the German Constitution of 1919: 'The German Empire is a Republic. The Power of the State emanates from the *Volk*.' This confusion of republican values with imperialism, state power and *völkisch* principles was a recipe for disaster.

Faced with such muddles, it was tempting to create a reliable picture-language, in which word and object match. This was the aim of the early Wittgenstein, restated in the introductory section of his *Philosophical Investigations* about the denotative character of nouns like 'table' and 'chair' or 'people's names'.[17] ⸻ ⸻ ⸻ ⸻ ⸻ world in which *res* and *verba* correspond: 'V⸻ connection I have ever aspired to in my lif⸻ ⸻ylic' position, which – in Plato's *Cratylus* d⸻ ⸻tical Hermogenes, who insists on the arbitr⸻ ⸻ suspect the cratylic position may be in the ⸻ ource for writers of comedy, who for centur⸻ and incongruities between name and chara⸻ s are a humorous element, generating a pl⸻ lemical jibes.[19] He draws on the Nestroy tradition to create 'speaking names' for fictional characters, like General Gloirefaisant in Act V, scene 15 of *Die letzten Tage der Menschheit*. A more disturbing form of satire is generated by the fact that the majority of names in that play are historically authentic. Moreover, existential questions are raised by the assumption that a person's name should be a reliable indicator of his character or an author's writings the honest expression of his beliefs. Hence Kraus's perplexity at discovering that 'a perfect line of poetry may have been written by a flawed human being' (F 445–53, 2). His judgement of Franz Werfel's character was originally based on a reading of his poems, but by February 1918 he felt compelled to acknowledge his 'short-sightedness'. There can be no reliable 'correlation between word and being' (F 484–98, 110–11).

Such discrepancies were compounded by a polyglot environment. In the ethnic melting-pot of central Europe, any city might have a plurality of names, and the patronyms of individuals were frequently at odds with their political convictions. In early numbers of *Die Fackel* we already find German nationalists being mocked for having resoundingly Slavonic names like Haluschka, Prochaska and Podgorschegg. To expose nationalism as an absurd comedy, Kraus also remarks that Slovene politicians have German names like Fischer and Mayer. In each case, ideological posturing contrasts with patrilinear descent (F 158, 15). During the 1920s, he points out that German nationalists in the Sudetenland have Czech names like Watzlik – perhaps derived from Watzlawitschek (F 657–67, 85), while Austrian Pan-Germans include Zarboch and Wotawa (F 827–33, 4) and the leading *deutschvölkisch* author is Mirko Jelusich (F 873–5, 35). The satirist is also sensitive to the tendency to change names in order to make them sound more 'Germanic'. If you have an honest German-Austrian name like Jeremias Křiz, why alter it to 'Kreutz' (F 697–705, 114)? He is particularly severe on patriotic Jews who disguise their origins by adopting German-sounding names, substituting Kienzl for Kohn (F 431–6, 31) or, in the case of the author Emil Ludwig, dropping the name Kohn altogether (F 601–7, 84). The fondness of Ashkenazi Jews for animal names such as Wolf and Hirsch ('Hart'), inspired by Genesis 49, forms a further source of onomastic wordplay, but this satire on names should not be confused with the campaign to deny German identity to Jews.[20] Kraus's primary target was exaggerated patriotism, and he regarded the 'German-nationalist Jew' as a contradiction in terms (DW 86/98).

Reanimated Metaphors

If language is a chimeric medium, metaphors introduce further ambiguity. Metaphor is sometimes regarded merely as a linguistic Sunday best, replacing a banal word by a more poetic one: 'ships ploughed the sea' in place of 'ships crossed the sea'.[21] But the case to be argued, according to Kraus, is that metaphors saturate everyday speech, unconsciously shaping our modes of perception. Encountering the phrase 'the case to be argued', few readers will envisage a court of law, with advocates, judge and jury. The source of the idiom has become submerged, but such invisible metaphors permeate our language, indeed our way of life, as has been shown in the more systematic study by Lakoff and Johnson, *Metaphors We Live By*. Their study suggests that fundamental experiences, like love or argument, do not have an intrinsic structure, but acquire one only through metaphorical articulation.[22] Kraus, by contrast, highlights metaphors we may die for – like the slogan 'shoulder to shoulder'. He took the lead in a project of demystification shared not only by Wittgenstein and Popper, but by literary authors like Alfred Polgar, Robert

Musil, Erich Kästner and Bertolt Brecht. Some critics have objected that this
led him in the direction of language fetishism, a form of 'idolatry' divorced
from the political realities; but Orwell, who included 'shoulder to shoulder' in
his list of dying metaphors that can 'corrupt thought', would not have agreed.[23]
For Kraus, words have become weapons through the combined effect of
modern technologies and mass communications. In 1929 a Nazi newspaper
claimed that the triumphant flights of the Zeppelin had earned Germany the
'envy of other nations'. For Kraus, this innocuous cliché was 'a lethal slogan' –
'ein Totschlagwort' (F 820–6, 78). This play-on-words, combining 'Totschlag'
('killing') with 'Schlagwort' ('slogan), is difficult to convey in English, where
the violence inherent in the word 'slogan' is no longer visible.[24]

Kraus's treatment of metaphor moves in two directions, aptly described as
'discrediting' and 'rehabilitating'.[25] He mocks ornamental metaphors that
betray lazy thinking, while resuscitating hidden meanings that reanimate our
sensitivity. When vivid metaphors become empty clichés or hollow phrases,
he emphatically sounds the alarm. Focusing during the Balkan Wars on the
'Catastrophe of Clichés' ('Katastrophe der Phrasen'), he observed in May 1913:
'Now that businessmen avoid submerged rocks and barristers safely reach the
shore, admirals can do it no longer. [. . .] But if the shore is a euphemism for
the shore and the rocks a hollow phrase for rocks – then a war is inevitable!'
(F 374–5, 3). This eccentric approach acquired a new gravity after 1914, when
Kraus took the argument one stage further through a process of reanimating-
in-order-to-discredit. How can one 'earn one's spurs' in the trenches (F
406–12, 107)? Patriotic phrases like 'to keep the flag flying' and 'a place in
the sun' are pursued in Die Fackel with unrelenting irony.[26] The blending
of modern politics with archaic metaphors led Kraus to conclude in autumn
1932 that the 'traditionally most pernicious' of all metaphors, beloved by both
socialists and Nazis, was 'the flag' ('die Fahne'; F 876–84, 3).

Metaphors derived from parts of the body and physical functions, including
the need for food and drink, assume a special significance in Kraus's humanist
perspective. A revealing example occurs in a statement by the British premier
Lloyd George during the Rapallo Congress of 1922, reported in the press in
the following form: 'The peoples of Europe hunger after the results of this conference' (cited F 595–600, 22). To say 'we hunger' for information implies that
there are no physical food shortages. Kraus highlights this phrase so as to draw
attention to the original meaning that has inadvertently resurfaced: the outcome of this unsuccessful conference is that people are starving. The clichés of
diplomats, recycled by journalists, are stigmatized as symptoms of lazy thinking, and this thoughtless use of language led Kraus in June 1921 to devote a
whole number of Die Fackel to reflections 'On the Theory of Language' ('Zur
Sprachlehre'). 'If human beings had no clichés,' he suggests, 'they wouldn't
need any weapons.' Hence his programme of 'reanimating set phrases'. The
remedy for the thoughtless use of metaphors would be to trace the phrases we
use in everyday speech 'back to the root of thought' (F 572–6, 11–12).

Reflections on metaphor thus lie at the heart of Kraus's theory of language, and his critique of worn-out phrases is complemented by a dazzling ability to reanimate hidden meanings. He was well aware that metaphor may have a civilizing function, helping to sublimate the stresses of the physical world by transforming picture-language into figurative discourse. Satire has a special significance in this process of figuration through its symbolic transformation of the 'most physical materials', so that 'physical assault' becomes 'intellectualized' (F 360–2, 4). Metaphors like 'to make a case against someone' help to organize conflictual relationships according to principles of moral responsibility. If war criminals seem likely to escape physical punishment, the satirist arraigns them before a Schillerian 'World Court of Judgement' – 'Das Weltgericht' (F 499–500, 1–5). Kraus had a penchant for the discourse of law, later to be reinforced by a passion for litigation, as the impulse to put his opponents 'in the dock' led to real court actions.

This theory of metaphor may be further elucidated by reference to the data presented by Norbert Elias in *Über den Prozeß der Zivilisation* (1939). As a German-Jewish refugee who found sanctuary in Britain, Elias devoted his researches to two main questions. The most obvious is the containment of violence. Elias felt that historians of the Weimar Republic had not devoted sufficient attention to the 'undermining of the German state from within through acts of terror, through the systematic use of violence'.[27] But his most celebrated work, translated into English as *The Civilizing Process*, concentrates on the gradual sublimation of aggressive instincts over a longer time-span. By documenting the history of manners as reflected in etiquette books of the early modern period, he shows how warriors become courtiers, going on to describe the evolution of civilized norms in the spheres of polite behaviour and public health. One of his key examples is spitting, a universal habit in medieval days which gradually gave way to a culture of self-constraint.[28] Although his evidence is persuasive, Elias fails to elucidate the linguistic changes which accompany the process of socio-psychological adaptation. Lexicographers have shown how the phrase 'I spit on you', originally denoting the expectoration of saliva, gradually evolved into a metaphor for contempt. When Antonio, in Shakespeare's *The Merchant of Venice*, says to Shylock: 'I spit upon thy Jewish gaberdine,' bodily action is still suggested, since the whole plot hinges on physicality: 'a pound of flesh' really means what it says. But gradually, as the modalities of conflict are refined, it becomes merely an expression of disgust to say 'it makes you want to spit' (cited F 462–71, 132). This usage may be contrasted with one of Kraus's most suggestive examples, dating from May 1921: a report about unrepentant nationalists 'physically spitting' on the boundary fence dividing Austria from Germany. The word 'physisch' indicates that, in proto-Nazi circles in Bavaria, metaphorical language has reverted to the realm of brutish action (F 568–71, 50).

Metaphors deriving from bodily functions contain residues of primitive social behaviours, both violent and scatological, historical and infantile.

Although Kraus generally eschews psychoanalytic terminology, we could call
this process the 'return of the repressed'. The idea that bodily metaphors conceal imperfectly sublimated instinctual drives was developed by another author
with psycho-linguistic interests, Ella Sharpe, a British psychoanalyst. Sharpe, in
her seminal paper of 1940, raises the question 'how the process of metaphor,
which is the accompaniment of civilization, evolves'. She goes on to discuss
'the general condition upon which the evolution of metaphor depends', stressing the factor of 'body control'. In place of the physical excretions of our infant
years, adults use the power of speech for the 'discharge of feeling tension'.[29] To
transpose Kraus's argument into conceptual terms, we may combine Sharpe's
evolutionary theory of metaphor with Elias's progressive model of civilization.
Kraus's most telling example of bodily metaphor is the phrase 'rubbing salt in
the wound' ('Salz in offene Wunden streuen'). In primitive societies, before
the emergence of modern medicine, salt served as an antiseptic. When sailors
were flogged for disciplinary offences, salt would be rubbed in the lacerations,
which made them far more painful, but also helped them to heal.[30] After this
practice became redundant, the phrase lingered on as a transferred epithet for
'rubbing in' shame or humiliation. By highlighting this example in his analysis
of the Nazi seizure of power, *Dritte Walpurgisnacht*, Kraus shows that the
mind–body balance inherent in civilized language has been disrupted: Nazi
thugs have plunged the bleeding hand of one of their victims into a sack of salt
in order to exacerbate his pain (DW 123/140).

Linguistic Decay and Mongrel Language

The essays collected in *Die Sprache*, published in 1937, document Kraus's lifelong preoccupation with the subtleties of language. An earlier investigation
examined the various ways in which he conceptualizes language: as 'Symptom,
Cause, Norm, Remedy or Refuge?'[31] His theoretical statements are emphatically logocentric, with language at the centre of a model of rational discourse
that can be traced back to the ethics of Kant and the cultural theory of
Wilhelm von Humboldt. The concept of 'Ursprung' ('origin') endows this
logocentrism with mystical associations, but this 'mystical' element cannot be
separated from the 'practical' activity of the mind, as indicated by the motto
from Humboldt which introduces Kraus's book on language (S 7, 7; cf. F
572–6, 1). To borrow a further distinction from Humboldt: language is best
defined as an activity ('energeia'), not as a system ('ergon').[32] Thus Kraus's invocations of 'Ursprung' are less suggestive than his deployment of the more
dynamic concept of 'Schöpfung' ('creation'), as we shall see in a later chapter.
The tensions between his normative theorizing and his deconstructive praxis
reveal that faith in language is less significant than 'verbal scepticism' ('der
sprachliche Zweifel'; F 885–7, 2).

Kraus's most memorable propositions about language are formulated not as
discursive statements in the manner of Mauthner or Wittgenstein, but as poems
or aphorisms. He emphasizes that the truth content of language used in this

aphoristic way is less important than the imaginative energy which is generated: 'An aphorism need not be true, but it should outrun the truth, as if over-
taking it with a catch-phrase' (F 264–5, 33). This is not linguistics in the
modern sense, but the dramatization of a passion for words. Language, he suggests, is in a state of decay ('Sprachzerfall') – hence the urgency of his task as a
'builder of sentences' ('Satzbauer'; F 554–6, 41). This image draws out the
double meanings by alerting us to the metaphor concealed within the German
word for syntax, 'Satzbau', which is also highlighted in the poem 'Abenteuer
der Arbeit':

In sprachzerfallnen Zeiten	To dwell, when words decay,
im sicheren Satzbau wohnen:	syntactically secure:
dies letzte Glück bestreiten	and find ultimate joy
noch Interpunktionen.	in punctuation pure.

(F 443–4, 6)

Playing on the metaphor underlying the prefix 'Bau', the poem pictures syntax
as a habitat. However, syntax also contains convulsive energies, suggested by
the dynamic secondary meaning lurking in the prefix 'Satz', which also implies
an imaginative 'leap'. Thus 'Satzbau' is another chimeric word – a fortress with
sally-ports from which to counterattack.

The stage is set for a dramatic confrontation between the journalistic corruption of public discourse and the satirist's spirited defence. The house of language becomes a city under siege in another celebrated poem, published in the
same number of *Die Fackel*:

Bekenntnis
Ich bin nur einer von den Epigonen,
die in dem alten Haus der Sprache wohnen.

Doch hab' ich drin mein eigenes Erleben,
ich breche aus und ich zerstöre Theben.

Komm' ich auch nach den alten Meistern, später,
so räch' ich blutig das Geschick der Väter.

Von Rache sprech' ich, will die Sprache rächen
an allen jenen, die die Sprache sprechen.

Bin Epigone, Ahnenwertes Ahner.
Ihr aber seid die kundigen Thebaner!

(F 443–4, 28)

Confession of Faith
You may indeed call me an epigone:
the ancient house of language is my home.

But in this dwelling life attains its worth,
and Thebes will be destroyed when I break forth.

Gone are the ancient masters: though too late,
I'll bloodily avenge the fathers' fate.

Language shall be avenged and justice done
to all of those who speak the German tongue.

Ancestral values animate my mind,
leaving you learned Thebans far behind.

The ancestral figures invoked in the poem include Shakespeare, whose 'learned Theban' forms a cryptic motif in *King Lear* (Act IV, scene 4); and Euripides, who dramatizes the victory of the 'Epigoni' ('Descendants') in *Seven against Thebes*. In German, the word 'Epigone' had acquired associations with 'derivativeness' through Karl Immermann's novel *Die Epigonen* (1836). Against this, Kraus invokes the archaic energies that inspired Greek heroes to avenge the deaths of their fathers – a militant paradigm that should not be confused with cultural conservatism.[33]

Assertions about the decay of language occur in the work of many satirists, from Swift to Orwell, but historical linguists are reluctant to take these claims at face value, since they can be correlated with cultural elitism and nostalgia for childhood. However, there is a qualitative difference between Kraus's media critique and the cultural pessimism of earlier authors, for example Arthur Schopenhauer, whose views on language he is fond of citing. Schopenhauer's 'Aphorismen zur Lebensweisheit' appeared in 1851, when the politics of the German-speaking world were stable and its educational institutions widely admired, but Kraus confronted political convulsions that culminated in two world wars. The predominance of nationalistic and militaristic propaganda gives substance to his claim that 'German is the profoundest of languages, the shallowest of discourses' ('Die deutsche Sprache ist die tiefste, die deutsche Rede die seichteste'; F 406–12, 152). During the First World War, passages of German writing at its most inspired, from Goethe's contemplative poem 'Über allen Gipfeln' to Kant's vision of 'Perpetual Peace', are set against contemporary practices. By clipping hundreds of passages from the press, Kraus creates a corpus of examples to illustrate the shallowness of public discourse, citing strings of xenophobic newspaper headlines (F 406–12, 123). The blend of aggressive policies and empty slogans is exemplified by the appeals to the starving population to 'hold out' ('durchhalten'), while the real aim is conquest and territorial annexation. Kraus anticipated the conclusion which the majority only reached in October 1918: that their government 'had been peddling lies for four years'.[34]

This account of the decay of language becomes more persuasive when it is understood in Peter von Polenz's terms as a 'critique of linguistic usage'. Seen in this perspective, the strength of Kraus's work lies not in abstract assertions, but in the 'concrete political focus' of his critique.[35] Although standing outside the Saussurean tradition, he seems to have had an instinctive understanding of the distinction between the inherent potential of language and specific practices, *langue* and *parole*, a dualism that corresponds to Kraus's more polemical distinction between the profundity of 'Sprache' and the shallowness of 'Rede'. Thus Hans Jürgen Heringer, while questioning the elitist undertones of Kraus's position, praises him for consistently criticising the '*parole* of individuals or particular groups'.[36] Summing up his reputation as a language critic in the light of these discussions, a British commentator has concluded that Kraus and Brecht mark a 'historical highpoint in the development of a systematic, politically engaged *Sprachkritik*'.[37]

This is not to deny that some of Kraus's pronouncements have mystical undertones, linked to a delight in reanimating the root meanings of metaphors, but he would never have endorsed Heidegger's dictum that 'the metaphorical exists only within the metaphysical'. Nor are his reanimated metaphors designed to restore some 'archaic meaning'.[38] The contemporary language is his hunting ground, and the quest is not for an original 'purity', but for the sources of a perplexing 'hybridity'. However, there is a distinction to be made between words which are 'chimeric' (hybrid) and a faith in the moral power of language that may prove 'chimerical' (illusory), and Kraus's attempt to construct an ethics of language is certainly open to question. But there can be no doubt about his skill in teasing subversive mutations out of familiar phrases. The teacher committed to raising standards is also a satirist who delights in transgression. He insists that 'linguistic correctness' ('Sprachrichtigkeit') should be subordinated to 'language usage' ('Sprachgebräuchlichkeit'; F 256, 29). There are closer affinities with the later Wittgenstein, who highlights the concept of 'use' ('Gebrauch'), than with the earlier advocate of a static picture-language.[39]

Kraus may venerate the poetry of Goethe – 'the ancient word' ('das alte Wort'; F 360–2, 16), but this does not prevent him from being fascinated by the opposite extreme: 'mongrel language' – 'Mengselsprache'. This phrase occurs in autumn 1920 in his response to a letter from a young reader complaining that he is using too many 'foreign words' ('Fremdwörter'). Such words should be 'germanized' ('eingedeutscht'), the reader insists, in accordance with the precepts of Eduard Engel's influential publication *Sprich deutsch!* Kraus explains, not for the first time, that words of foreign origin like 'Aversion', 'Adresse', 'Kostüm' and 'Redakteur' are perfectly good German, enhancing the expressive range of the language. He insists that when he uses unconventional words, they are not simply cited as examples of incorrect usage, to be picked up and modified by *Die Fackel* as an 'amplifier'. Defective expressions are also integrated into his own discourse and transformed into a new 'verbal configuration' ('Wortgestalt'; F 554–6, 13–16). The stance of the Germanizers is consistently mocked, from hilarious scenes in *Die letzten Tage der Menschheit* (I, 8) to the polemics of the early 1930s against *völkisch* newspapers. Here again, the focus on words implies a critique of ideologies. Kraus was aware that the proposals for 'pure' German had xenophobic overtones.[40]

Kraus's endorsement of 'mongrel' language impacted on his practice as a writer. The detritus of Viennese dialect, Jewish jargon and Berlin slang provides him with thousands of 'word-scraps', to be picked up and are swept along in his 'linguistic stream' (F 445–53, 41). No inscription on a lavatory wall is too crude to be typographically dignified in antiqua. He may ridicule writers like Felix Salten, who inadvertently allow traces of Yiddish to impair their German (F 820–6, 45–6); but he loved conflating different linguistic registers, and his own practice as a writer is consciously enriched by Yiddish expressions. To portray German intellectual life, he remarks in March 1921, it is necessary to use expressions like 'Chuzpe, Gewure, Mezzie, Rebbach, Nebbich, Ponem, ja sogar Asis-Ponem' (F 561–7, 88). And he goes on to explain how, in the dialogue of *Literatur oder Man wird doch da sehn*, 'Asisponem' ('fat gob') becomes assimilated into a consciously constructed 'Wortgestalt' (F 572–6, 73). Given that Yiddish is pre-eminently a language of 'fusion', incorporating words from other languages, it is particularly suited to the task of adding spice to German prose.

Kraus's sensitivity to dialect and jargon is exemplified by *Die letzten Tage der Menschheit*, where Prussian, Austrian and Jewish idioms are juxtaposed to create incongruous situations and vivid dramatic characters. In the Duden dictionary of Austrian idioms, this drama is given as the source for dozens of expressions which would scarcely have entered the written language if Kraus had not conferred on them the dignity of print.[41] In his satirical glosses he may distance himself from vulgarisms like 'Sakra, Luder, ölendiges', overheard in the provinces (F 657–67, 53) or 'Flatuse' (for 'fart'; F 838–44, 135). But the slang words assimilated into his own satirical discourse included phrases from the street-language of Berlin like 'verhohnepipeln' ('to ridicule'; F 838–44, 75) and 'ne tüchtje Pulle' ('a regular booze-up'; F 838–44, 85). His language abounds in neologisms, created with a Joycean polyglossia. Aristocrats are defined in terms of 'Passletam' – an Austrianization of the French 'passer le temps' (F 622, 163). A sentimental journalist is an 'Untertränenlächler' – a 'laugher-under-his-tears' – while the novelist Hans Heinz Ewers is 'dämondän' – a combination of demonic and mondaine (F 601–7, 24 & 84). Kraus was encouraged in the creation of such new coinings by Sidonie Nadherny, his companion on many adventurous motoring trips, who once remarked that she wished their car had a 'skid-guide' ('Gleitrutsch'; F 445–53, 9). Her mala-propisms were due to being brought up speaking three languages – English, Czech and German – without being entirely at home in any of them.[42]

The pressure of events in Austria led Kraus to push the expressive power of language beyond existing limits, while at the same time avoiding the kind of mystification that Wittgenstein abhorred. In a celebrated passage in the *Tractatus* the philosopher declared: '*The limits of my language* mean the limits of my world.'[43] In the *Philosophical Investigations* he goes on to suggest that running up against the limits of language causes 'bumps' or 'bruises' ('Beulen') to the intellect.[44] One of Kraus's aphorisms, which Wittgenstein may well have known, puts the matter more forcefully: 'When I get stuck, I have bumped against the wall of language. Then I withdraw with a bloody head. And would like to go further' (F 360–2, 16). Where Wittgenstein is circumspect, Kraus is prepared to be transgressive.[45] His syntax, like his use of verse forms, remains conservative, and he criticizes modern literary journalism for 'loosening the bonds of language' (F 484–98, 94). But his lexis becomes highly inventive, responding to new political and cultural situations by creating startling neologisms.

In short, Kraus initiates his readers into an unfamiliar 'word-world' ('Wortwelt'), a concept partly inspired by the experimental language of Goethe's later work (F 640–8, 62). His discourse is further enriched by a rhetoric with its roots in classical languages. Having excelled at Latin during his schooldays, Kraus came to regard this as the staple of his German style, reflected in both his syntax and his lexis. To protect himself from the propaganda of the First World War, he dreams of 'formulating ideas in Latin' (F 445–53, 18). Words of Romance origin are praised for their expressive power – why use 'elend' ('dismal') to describe a translation which is actually 'miserabel' (F 572–6, 4)? And his later style is unmistakably Latinate in its use of extended sentence structures, held together by ingenious appositions, complex subordinate clauses, case-inflections and gender-differentiated relative pronouns. Rarely can there have been such elaborate permutations on *der, die* and *das* – difficult to put into English with its genderless definite and relative articles. Reacting against the punchy style and fractured syntax of journalists like Alfred Kerr, Kraus constructed sentences which sometimes extend for more than twenty lines.

The debt to Greek is reflected in the numerous concepts from classical rhetoric which shape Kraus's reflections on the writing process, especially those that relate to double meanings, such as acrostic, chimera, metaphor, oxymoron and paradox. The delight in constructing sentences that fold back upon themselves leads him to celebrate the figure of 'chiasmus' in the poem 'Abenteuer der Arbeit' ('Adventure of Work'):

In Hasses Welterbarmung
verschränkt sich Geist und Sache
zu weltverhurter Sprache
chiastischer Umarmung.   (F 443–4, 8)

Hate of the world's disgrace
links spirit with the cause
in language like a whore's
chiastic world embrace.

This is the most drastic of the many analogies he draws between language and love-making. The rhetorical inversion associated with 'chiasmus' suggests that – through language – the physical and the spiritual may be brought together in a transformative embrace. He even suggests that in 'chiastische Umarmung' he has found the magic formula to redeem a fallen world (F 443–4, 2). But if language, through its chiastic potential, holds the promise of reconciliation, the apocalyptic impulse proves equally powerful, blending biblical pathos with political prophecy.

Apocalyptic Tone and Mosaic Style

Kraus's style is permeated by biblical allusions – from the 'Mene Tekel' motif in the first number of *Die Fackel* to the vision of the 'Final End' in *Dritte Walpurgisnacht*. This immersion in holy scripture has a significant bearing on his conception of metaphor. In one of the final dialogues of *Die letzten Tage der Menschheit* the Grumbler observes that the wicked are able to mock the judge beyond the stars because his throne is so far away that his arm can no longer reach them (V, 42). This use of a physical motif – the throne – to denote the realm of the divine reflects a tension between physical and spiritual language which runs right through the scriptures, inspiring a wealth of Rabbinic commentary and biblical hermeneutic. 'The Torah', as the Jewish sages observed, 'speaks according to the language of everyday life.' But biblical discourse is at the same time hermetic, since the simplest of phrases – like 'to dwell' (Hebrew 'shakhan') – may contain mysteries. To elucidate the significance of religious metaphors thus requires a *Guide for the Perplexed*, such as the celebrated commentary by Maimonides. It is not simply a question of distinguishing literal from figurative meanings: 'There are also hybrid terms, denoting things which are of the same class from one point of view and of a different class from another.'[46] In another passage, cited by Gershom Scholem, Maimonides stresses the ambiguity of prophetic language: 'Only in the days of the Messiah will everyone know what the metaphors mean.'[47]

This ambiguity reaches its extreme in Kraus's favourite biblical text – the Book of Revelation. So eccentric did this book appear to the scribes who compiled the Greek codices of the New Testament that they hesitated to accept it as a canonical text. Although couched in the form of a letter from John 'to the Seven Churches that are in Asia', the book expresses an unresolved tension between the gospel of hope and the apocalyptic expectations which shaped the world of the early Christians. Indeed, Revelation owes more to Jewish apocalyptic writing than to the Christian message of redemption. Its language abounds in Hebraisms and its narrative is double-voiced, presenting a book within a book. 'Few scholars', notes a commentator, 'would argue that the book was written in Hebrew and translated into Greek, yet most assume that the author writes in Greek as a second language and is still thinking in Hebrew.' Revelation, we are reminded, 'draws on the imagery and language of the Old Testament on almost every line'. The patterns of Hebrew thought in this final book of the New Testament can be traced back to the conflict between 'serpent' and 'woman' in Genesis and the imagery of 'fire' and the 'sword' in Daniel and Ezekiel. In short, it provides an outstanding example of 'intertextuality'.[48]

The book begins with a vision of Jesus as an avenging angel: 'out of his mouth came a sharp two-edged sword' (Revelation 1: 16). Through this image we are forewarned that the language of prophecy, like that of satire, is liable to cut both ways. What follows, as the Seven Seals are opened and the Scrolls unfolded, is war in heaven between the Lamb, the Beast, the Great Whore and the Anti-Christ. These dramatic allegories have inspired a library of eschato-logical writings, in which the biblical prophecies have been adapted to successive political crises, especially in the medieval and early modern periods.[49] However, the preponderance of allegory over more subtle forms of symbolism has diminished the book's imaginative appeal, while the excesses of Christian fundamentalism have discredited it in the eyes of modernists. Even D. H. Lawrence, who valued the Apocalypse for its 'release of the imagination', ulti-mately interpreted the reliance on allegory as a sign of 'emotional impotence'.[50] More recently, however, there has been a revival of interest associated with the post-structuralist turn towards apocalyptic discourse. Distancing himself from the Kantian defence of rational discourse, Derrida, in his essay 'Of an Apoca-lyptic Tone Recently Adopted in Philosophy', confesses to a 'fascination' with this theme. He argues that the 'logic of the current political discourse' can be decentred by the 'mixing of voices, genres and codes' that is characteristic of the apocalyptic tone.[51] This involves not some form of 'doomsday rhetoric', but a 'vigilant scepticism' towards the claims of instrumental rationality, not least with respect to the extremes of 'nuclear-strategic doublethink' identified in Derrida's further essay, 'No Apocalypse. Not Now'.[52]

Thus the traditional apocalyptic tone may be most effective when combined with a radically modern linguistic scepticism, while its rhetoric of crisis forms a legitimate response to propaganda for war. It announces, not a single cata-clysmic event, but an endemic emergency, as indicated by an aphorism of January 1917: 'The condition in which we live is the true end of the world: stabilized catastrophe' (F 445–53, 3). Using the biblical motif of 'the last days' (V, 17) to frame his account of the events of 1914–18 in *Die letzten Tage der Menschheit*, he subordinated the eschatological allegory to a radically innovative form of documentary drama. Only in the epilogue, *Die letzte Nacht*, does Kraus allude to the Book of Revelation more directly.[53] The dangers of an overre-liance on biblical language are illustrated by the contrast between the two very different texts which he published under the title 'Apokalypse'. His essay of October 1908 forms a dazzling collage, intercalating lines from Revelation with a panorama of modern motifs (F 261–2, 1–14). But when in July 1920 he published a second 'Apokalypse', he contented himself with transcribing pas-sages from a German Bible translation into blank verse (F 546–50, 78–80). So closely did he keep to his model that he was accused of plagiarism – indeed of 'desecrating holy scripture'.[54] In his response, Kraus insisted that Revelation is itself a political text, using lines from the translation by Leander van Ess to sug-gest that western supremacy will be superseded by China (F 552–3, 10–11).

Kraus's preoccupation with apocalyptic themes raises the question whether he, like the author of Revelation, is also in some sense 'thinking in Hebrew'. Berthold Viertel compared his philosophy of language with the reverence for 'the Word' in the writings of Hasidic mystics, as described in Martin Buber's *Vom Geist des Judentums*.[55] A more dynamic parallel is suggested by Gershom Scholem, the author who uncannily fulfils Kraus's dream of the 'Talmud student' needed to complement his creativity (F 300, 25–6). From his earliest days as a student in Berlin, Scholem committed himself to learning Hebrew and studying the Talmud. Writing of his early contacts with Walter Benjamin, he recalls their discussions about the derivation of Kraus's style 'from the Hebrew prose and poetry of medieval Jewry – the language of the great halakhists and the "mosaic style"'. The concept of 'mosaic style' ('Musivstil'), which derives from the decorative arts, denotes 'poetic prose in which linguistic scraps of sacred texts are whirled around kaleidoscopelike and are journalistically, polemically, descriptively, and even erotically profaned'.[56]

We know from Scholem's diaries that these conversations with Benjamin took place in 1918–19 in Berne, where the two had found refuge from the war and were studying at the university. Their Kraus-orientated dialogue was to continue intermittently for twenty years (Die Fackel was the only non-scholarly periodical to which Scholem subscribed after his emigration to Palestine).[57] In December 1915, in his earliest reference to Die Fackel, Scholem – a committed Zionist – repudiated Kraus's animadversions about 'the Jews', while endorsing his critique of journalism (GST 1, 204).[58] The 'mosaic style' is elucidated in a series of further diary entries, highlighting 'plays on words' that combine the 'inner self-irony of language' with 'potential references to the words of the bible'. This consists not in a dogmatic appeal to the authority of scripture, but 'in continuous deferral of the canonical word' (GST 2, 367–8). This concept is related to Kraus's aphorism, cited in 1917, about the 'experience of the ancient word' ('das Erlebnis des alten Wortes'), which Scholem encountered not in German, but in Hebrew.[59] Acknowledging that Kraus knows no Hebrew and has never heard of authors of the Jewish Enlightenment (the Haskalah) like the Maggid of Dobno, he still places him in the tradition of Jewish moral preachers. Kraus has committed himself – 'through every pun and every joke and every gloss, even every quotation' – to the quest for the 'canonical element in the German language'. The fact that this is unattainable has unexpected consequences: 'this Jew' – Kraus – discovers in the German language 'undreamed-of Jewish provinces', and it is the resulting creative tension that links his style with the 'mosaic' ('mit dem Musivischen'; GST 2, 468).

This point is clarified in a further text which develops the arguments of Kraus's essay 'Heine und die Folgen'. The journalistic element in Heine's poetry and prose, which Kraus so deplores, is equated by Scholem with 'a mosaic style [. . .] bereft of all its foundations'. The language of journalism is 'mechanical: relative words are further relativized'. Kraus's writings, by contrast, retain that 'religious foundation' which authenticates the mosaic style. This style correlates the specifics of modern experience with the language of the Bible, construed as 'an absolute word which is in principle infinitely interpretable' (GST 2, 586–7). Holy scripture functions not as a fixed set of doctrines, but as a dynamic tradition of interpretation, and Scholem condenses his argument into the neat conclusion: 'The mosaic style is commentary within the text' (GST 2, 356).

Although Scholem does not cite specific examples, he is doubtless alluding to texts like 'Apokalypse', where the 'whirling around' of scraps from sacred texts is most explicit. What fascinated him about Kraus was the convergence between a Jewish style of moral discourse and intuitions about the end of time, and his diaries reveal that Kraus was one of the sources for his 'messianic' conception of language. The messianic impulse, according to an entry of 27 June 1919, arises from 'living in purity among thieves, pimps and whores' – an echo of Kraus's reflections on restoring the virginity of fallen words (F 326–8, 45). In this same entry he goes on to defend Kraus against Franz Werfel's attack in 'Die Metaphysik des Drehs' ('The Metaphysics of Spin').[60] Although Werfel's comments may at one level be justified, they miss the fundamental point: Kraus represents nothing less than '*a messianic movement of language*' ('eine *messianische Bewegung der Sprache* – nichts anders bedeutet Kraus'; GST 2, 462). Thus Scholem, setting aside polemics, sensed the deeper resonance of Kraus's exploration of the expressive resources of German. This intensified his interest in the hidden powers of Hebrew, especially the messianic implications of a language in which past and future appear to be simultaneously present. This is the theme of his remarkable entry of 17 June 1918 headed 'Reflections on Time in Judaism' (GST 2, 235–40). Here he highlights '*waw ha-hippukh*' (the 'conjunction of reversal'), which transforms 'past into future and future into past'. Thus 'the realm of God is *here-and-now*, since it is origin and end' ('Das Reich Gottes ist *Gegenwart*, denn es ist Ursprung und Ende'). This echoes the precept 'Ursprung ist das Ziel' ('Origin is the goal'), which so fascinated Scholem and Benjamin during their discussions of Kraus's *Worte in Versen*.

Although Scholem's reading of Kraus reveals fundamental affinities between their conceptions of language, he fails to acknowledge the divergence between 'apocalyptic' and 'messianic' thinking. Scholem distinguishes between two forms of messianism. The first is 'revolutionary', envisaging the appearance of the Messiah at the end of days, the Day of Judgement and the destruction of the world, leading to the emergence of a '*new creation*'. The second is 'transformative', involving a purification of souls and the inward transformation of nature. This view sees the messianic age as immanent in the here and now: 'the end of days – today' (GST 2, 380). However, Scholem fails to take account of the third possibility, envisaged in Kraus's darkest moments: destruction *without* spiritual renewal. In *Die Fackel* there are no anticipations of a redemptive Messiah, and his writings are free of those messianic longings which inspired contemporary anti-democratic thinkers – on the left as well as the right. There was a spate of Jewish philosophizing about the approaching end of history, initiated in 1918 by Ernst Bloch's *Geist der Utopie* ('Spirit of Utopia') and echoed by the poets of Expressionism. Kraus repudiated this utopian rhetoric, sensing its sinister implications: the longing for a charismatic leader and the subordination of the individual to the collective. Apocalyptic language was indeed a two-edged sword, capable of untold damage when wielded by extremists. During the First World War, apocalyptic motifs were invoked to support the view that Germany, as God's chosen instrument, was destined to be the 'execu-tor of the Day of Judgement'.[61] And National Socialism owes to the Book of Revelation the myth of the 'Thousand-Year Reich'.[62] Kraus distanced himself from this tradition, using motifs from Revelation to suggest that those who rise from the dead 'after a thousand years' will still need to be reminded of the crimes committed in the name of religion (F 546–50, 77).

PART THREE

THE CREATIVE ORIGIN

CHAPTER 9

Childhood, Myth and Memory

Kraus was repeatedly reproached for being able only to 'negate', but for sensitive readers the imaginative impulse underlying his satire was unmistakable, both in his evocative poetry and in his densely textured prose. His own word for this creative impulse, as we have noted, is 'Ursprung' ('origin'), a mystical concept that eludes definition. However, the question may be clarified by a synoptic reading which combines textual commentary with an analysis of biographical sources that remained unpublished during his lifetime. This makes it possible to correlate his aggressive stance as a satirist with the primal experiences of childhood, religious faith and romantic love. If there was to be a successful post-war reconstruction, it had to be based on a return to first principles, and where better to begin than with children? Memories of childhood hold a seminal place in Kraus's writings, and he was a generous supporter of child welfare. To understand the significance of this theme, we must return to the paradigmatic debates about child abuse in the Vienna of his youth and the tensions experienced within his own family. Surviving letters suggest that the childhood so poignantly evoked in his poetic writings was decidedly conflictual. However, by distancing himself from his family, he shaped an image of his youthful self that transforms memory into a creative force, challenging the reductiveness of psychoanalytic models. Kraus, like Freud, was aware that memories may be distorted by 'retroactive construction' ('nachträgliche Konstruktion'; F 285–6, 52).[1] But his sensibility was sustained by images of childhood transposed into mythopoeic terms.

The Battered Child

Child abuse formed a disturbing feature of family life in the early twentieth century, but it was not until sixty years later that there was a clear recognition of the 'battered-child syndrome'. For earlier generations, according to the study by Larry Wolff, 'the very idea of child abuse could not exist', since children were regarded as the 'property of their parents, subject to parental discipline without appeal'.[2] To substantiate this claim, he reconstructs sensational court cases from Freud's Vienna. In November 1899, a working-class couple named Joseph and Juliane Hummel were prosecuted for beating their daughter Anna so severely that she died shortly before her fifth birthday. The mother claimed to have loved her child, while the father insisted that they had merely punished bad behaviour, but after a trial that attracted wide publicity both parents were sentenced to death. The verdict on Joseph Hummel was commuted to life imprisonment, but Juliane was executed. A second case followed a fortnight later, involving the death of a spirited eleven-year-old, also named Anna, at the hands of her father Rudolf Kutschera, a postal official, and her stepmother Marie. In this case, too, both parents were sentenced to death.[3]

Wolff argues that the court proceedings and press coverage constitute 'one of the most significant explorations of child abuse in history'.[4] The hero of this account is the young Karl Kraus, who came closer than any of his contemporaries to grasping the violence inherent in the patriarchal family. The liberal press, led by the *Neue Freie Presse*, responded with incomprehension, claiming that such events could occur only 'on a low level of civilization'. It must be an example of 'atavism' – a throwback to a barbaric age.[5] The paper's correspondent, the poet Felix Dörmann, presented events in melodramatic terms, but Kraus's comments were more judicious. Discussing the Kutschera case, he identified the central paradox of child abuse: the difficulty of distinguishing 'the love that chastises from the hatred that torments'. He concludes that it was a sense of revulsion, when confronted by this paradox of love and hatred, that led the jury to convict the parents of murder, a verdict based on emotional overreaction and class prejudice. They failed to understand that even well-bred parents are liable to overstep the 'limit beyond which crime begins' (F 28, 2–3). Kraus was incensed by the execution of Juliane Hummel, which he saw as a grave miscarriage of justice, resulting in part from sensationalist reporting (F 28, 4–5). He argued that the death sentence on Rudolf and Marie Kutschera should be commuted by the Court of Appeal. Since an intent to kill could not be proved, the child was the victim not of premeditated murder, but of 'grievous bodily harm with fatal consequences' (F 24, 13). The sentence on the Kutscheras was indeed commuted to eight years' hard labour, and Kraus received a letter of congratulation from the eminent jurist Heinrich Lammasch.[6]

It is wrong to assume that, for Kraus, the question of child abuse was merely a 'sideline'.[7] This disregards his subsequent, even more incisive analysis of the sentimental view of the family that makes the problem so hard to conceptualize:

> The age of humanism knows nothing of the rigid paterfamilias who has power over life and death. It recognizes in the sacred institution of the family only a parental *love* – the love that chastises. And since corporal punishment is regarded essentially as an expression of love, just as love is deduced from punishment, there is a law which

permits such punishment and issues a mild caution if it is taken to excess. Then one day, after a child has been chastised to death, it dawned on Justice that there may also be a parental *hatred*. [. . .] The whole problem of parental love was opened up. It was reasonable to expect that moral philosophers, psychologists and sociologists would now follow the leads provided by the Hummel case; after this brutal case, research would focus on the more subtle and most refined forms of child abuse, the loving tortures of education, the processes which lead to a barely noticeable deformation of physical growth and a crippling of the souls of children. (F 88, 1)

This passage shows how precisely Kraus grasped the problem of the battered child. He saw the Hummel case as an opportunity for gaining fundamental insights into violence within the family and called for new laws for the protection of children.

Freud, too, must have been aware of these cases, since they were prominently reported in the *Neue Freie Presse*, but he makes no reference to the subject. If only Freud had taken child abuse seriously, Wolff argues, he could have pioneered the understanding of the battered-child syndrome, just as he could have made the world aware of the sexual abuse of children, if only he had not abandoned the seduction theory. Thus he is held responsible for the fact that, after the glare of publicity created by these trials, the problem of the battered child sank into oblivion. Freud was to make matters worse in the paper "'A Child Is Being Beaten'", which interprets beatings recalled from childhood as masochistic fantasies.[8] This criticism seems unduly harsh, especially when one recalls the pioneering work with children undertaken by his followers, including Siegfried Bernfeld and Anna Freud, who promoted a more enlightened approach to the care of children from broken homes.[9] Moreover, the child abuse cases of autumn 1899 did inspire remedial action: the founding of the Children's Protection and Rescue Society (Kinderschutz- und Rettungsgesellschaft) by the social reformer Lydia von Wolfring, under the patronage of Lammasch and other distinguished public figures. There was an urgent need for reform, since child mortality-rates in Vienna were exceptionally high, figures for the 1890s showing that one baby in five died within the first year.[10] In December 1903 Kraus commended Wolfring for her courage, regretting that her work was being impaired by intrigue and sidelined by the founding of a rival Christian Social organization, the Kinderschutzstationen (F 149, 4–6). He supported her work with a donation of 20 Crowns and was to make further generous contributions in later years.[11]

The passion that inspired his analysis of the Hummel case led Kraus to pursue the issue of child abuse throughout his career, identifying the maltreatment of children as a form of institutionalized violence. Reprinting reports of court cases, he highlighted the oppressiveness of family life, the collusion of neighbours, the ineptitude of the police, the failings of judges, and the irresponsibility of press coverage. Thirty years after the death of Anna Hummel, he devoted several pages to the sufferings of another five-year-old, Mathilde Stodolak. Although the brutality of Mathilde's stepfather was reported by neighbours, the police doctor who examined her injuries on four separate occasions certified that they did *not* constitute '*an infringement of the right to corporal punishment*' (Kraus's emphasis). When Mathilde died from her injuries in April 1928, the Catholic press insisted that the police were not to blame, but Kraus implies that there is a connection between cruelty to children and political authoritarianism (F 781–6, 125–7).

The Habsburg legislators had a vested interest in upholding parental authority, and during the 1920s the ruling Christian Social Party still insisted that parents had the right to chastise their children. The law specified that abusive parents should be cautioned on the first occasion and reprimanded on the second; only after a third offence did they risk prosecution. Kraus insisted that the threat of a reprimand was an inadequate deterrent, leaving children in the care of habitual abusers who claimed to be punishing the child for its own good. Moreover, the provision that severely injured children could be taken into care merely encouraged acts of violence by parents who wished to get rid of their child.[12] He recognized that a primary factor was the birth of unwanted children. The Church's ban on contraception led to unintended pregnancies, which could not be terminated because abortion was also banned, causing resentment towards children who were an emotional and financial burden. The laxity of the law on child abuse was the corollary of the strictness of the law against abortion. The legal protection which is so essential to the child should not, in Kraus's view, extend to the embryo, and he sympathized with proposals to improve access to contraception and liberalize the law on abortion. So strongly did he feel on this point that in February 1907 he devoted a whole number of *Die Fackel* to an article (by Fritz Wittels) denouncing the law against abortion as 'The Greatest Crime in the Penal Code' (F 219–20, 1–22). Almost twenty years later we still find him criticizing the failure to liberalize this law (F 640–8, 36).

The scandal of child abuse became even more blatant during the First World War, when shortages of food led to cases of unbelievable neglect and cruelty. In a typical case cited in 1916, an ex-soldier accused of battering his four-year-old daughter blamed his temper on the effects of front-line service. Extrapolating from this incident, Kraus suggested that all children are at risk from fathers who have been brutalized by the war – or who use the war as an excuse for brutality (F 426–30, 86–7). Hence the scene in *Die letzten Tage der Menschheit* (II, 21) which portrays an ex-soldier working out his frustrations on his ten-year-old son. The boy's body is a mass of wounds inflicted by his father with a bayonet, but the parents are callously unconcerned. Such scenes suggest a correlation between the last days of mankind and the first years of childhood – a point made more explicitly elsewhere. The final pages of the play present images of cruelty towards children which anticipate the atrocities of the Second World War, including the shooting of a twelve-year-old boy before his mother's eyes.

Pedagogic Reform and Education for Humanity

Kraus presents the vulnerable child as victim of an oppressively patriarchal society. Recognizing the violence inherent within the family, he also takes issue with the deformations caused by a chauvinistic education. During the early years of *Die Fackel* he published dozens of articles criticizing barbaric teaching methods, suggesting that errors in the educational system were to blame for driving schoolchildren to suicide (F 41, 29; F 74, 27). The contents of German coursebooks, criticized in one of the earliest numbers (F 11, 11), became a recurrent theme. This system required every class to study a course-book chosen by the head teacher from a list prescribed by the Ministry of Education. It thus provided a touchstone for the ways in which each genera-tion of children was being schooled for adult life. During the First World War the curriculum in German and Austrian schools was revised to reflect the dominant ethos, and in June 1916 Kraus devoted ten pages to reprinting some of the chauvinistic doggerel that was finding its way into school textbooks (F 426–30, 56–65). In October 1917 he reprinted a list of essay topics set in a Viennese grammar school, which included 'Unrestricted Submarine Warfare'. Although there were alternative topics of a more traditional kind, the satirist – in a dreamlike sequence – appeals to the Children's Rescue Society to save the children 'from bombs and school essays'. The brutalizing effects of war put both the physical and the mental health of children at risk. On the following page he prints a report describing how a mother has drowned herself and her six-month-old son because there was no milk for the baby (F 462–71, 30–5).

After 1918 Kraus supported efforts to alleviate the damage caused by the hardships of war. An estimated 180,000 children in Vienna were suffering from malnutrition, and an international campaign was launched to alleviate their plight. This programme had a political as well as a humanitarian dimension, since the Americans, who set up their first relief centre in Austria at the end of May 1919, feared a communist take-over if the population were left to starve. Emergency food distribution was undertaken by American Children's Relief and the Quakers, otherwise known as the Society of Friends, and it was this crisis that prompted the founding of the Save the Children Fund. A survey of the health of 114,947 Viennese schoolchildren undertaken in 1920 showed that 80 per cent were underfed.[13] In February 1921, at the height of the relief programme, 400,000 Austrian children were receiving a free meal every day. In addition, a total of 120,000 children were sent abroad for holidays with temporary foster parents, especially in Switzerland, Denmark and the Netherlands.[14] Kraus was particularly impressed by the work of the Friends and devoted a substantial part of the income from public readings to this campaign. Noting that in Britain and America even poor people had contributed to the fund for Viennese children, he denounced the new rich of Austria as the 'Society of Enemies' (F 557–60, 1–4).

Kraus supported numerous charitable causes, listing his donations in *Die Fackel* so as to encourage others to follow his lead. In May 1921, for example, 32,000 Crowns were shared among four children's charities (F 568–71, 37). Although he continued to support the humanitarian work of the Kinderschutz- und Rettungsgesellschaft, he realized that more radical changes were required, and for over ten years, from October 1917 until June 1928, he systematically supported the Social Democratic Association of Friends of Children (Sozialdemokratische Verein Kinderfreunde). The Kinderfreunde, founded in 1908 in Graz, had branches throughout Austria, and during the Republic it became a major force in the struggle to create an egalitarian society. It was not simply a children's charity, but an organization committed to educating the socialists of the future in a secular and democratic spirit. A programmatic statement by one of its leaders, Felix Kaunitz, argues that socialist education cannot be neutral in the struggle against capitalism and the power of the bourgeoisie.[15] The strength of the Kinderfreunde in industrial centres like Steyr meant that it played a significant role in industrial disputes, providing the financial support for the families of locked-out workers that enabled the Metalworkers Union to obtain a famous victory.[16] Nationally, the importance of the Kinderfreunde may be gauged from the fact that in 1929 it had over 100,000 members throughout Austria.[17] In 1922 the movement was extended to Germany, growing so rapidly that by August 1924 there were over one hundred affiliated groups. The Kinderfreunde outlawed corporal punishment, insisting that children should learn self-discipline by more democratic means. Individual children were designated as group leaders with responsibility for the behaviour of all members of their group, and older children were trained to become teachers in their turn.[18] Catholic groups like Frohe Kindheit, founded in Vienna in 1919, felt forced on the defensive by what they saw as the 'Marxist peril'.[19] In February 1922 the bishops issued a pastoral letter denouncing the Kinderfreunde as a 'revolutionary socialist–communist youth organization' and insisting that Christian parents should not 'spare the rod'. This position was enthusiastically endorsed by the *Reichspost* in an article of 26 February 1922.[20]

In supporting the Kinderfreunde, Kraus aligned himself with the educational reforms that were being implemented by Otto Glöckel in the teeth of conservative opposition. The curriculum had traditionally given prominence to books describing military exploits, and he was horrified by texts which celebrated intrepid fighter pilots and submarine captains. In October 1917 he reproduced from the boys' magazine *Der gute Kamerad* a gruesome picture of soldiers in gasmasks engaged in hand-to-hand combat using bayonets and handgrenades (F 462–71, 13). One of the primary aims of the reform programme was to remove this chauvinistic literature from libraries, and in 1922 a purge was undertaken in Vienna to remove books which glamorized militarism, the Habsburg dynasty and the Catholic Church.[21] Conservative newspapers were horrified by these reforms, but Kraus felt that they did not go far enough, since bloodthirsty war poets like Kernstock and Ginzkey remained

on the list of approved authors. He notes that Kernstock was even congratu-
lated 'by the school reformer himself' – a criticism of Glöckel for not being
more radical (F 588–94, 81–6).

Kraus proposed new texts for inclusion in school coursebooks, recom-
mending the letters of Rosa Luxemburg and emphasizing that her account of
experiences in Breslau Prison had both educational and artistic value (F 554–6,
8; 588–94, 82). In place of the cult of military valour, children should learn
about the debilitating effects of war on the civilian population. Thus he also
commended a passage from the *Arbeiter-Zeitung* of 17 October 1923 describing
the homecoming of a soldier who has lost both his arms and whose child races
across the station platform to meet him, expecting a hug (F 657–67, 11). The
need to educate the next generation in an anti-militarist spirit leads him to
wonder why the socialists have not included any poems from *Die letzten Tage
der Menschheit* in their school anthology (F 588–94, 86); if a version of the play
were published for children, he suggests in December 1924, 'little Aryans,
when they grow up, would not develop into such big Aryans that they can't
wait for a world war' (F 668–75, 58). Recognizing that fascism begins in the
classroom, Kraus was more radically pacifist than the Social Democrats, many
of whom had German-nationalist inclinations. In the summer of 1925 he was
alarmed to discover another article in the *Arbeiter-Zeitung* which stressed that
Austria, as a 'German state', should take pride in German military achievements. Kraus repudiated both this programme of 'military education' and the
concept of the 'nation', citing as an antidote a speech by Otto Bauer on
the barbarism of modern warfare (F 697–705, 1–5).

The most noxious reading material for children, in Kraus's view, was the
daily press. In 1913 he had reacted with horror to a German proposal that
the curriculum should include the reading of newspapers so as to prepare children for practical life (F 354–6, 68). The excesses of wartime propaganda and
the crudity of the new journalism only strengthened his revulsion. He summed
up his position in May 1931, after a questionnaire had been circulated to
several thousand young people between the age of twelve and eighteen by the
German Institute for Newspaper Studies, which revealed that 98.5 per cent of
the sample were at least occasional readers of newspapers. When the *Arbeiter-
Zeitung* greeted this result with enthusiasm under the title 'Children as Newspaper Readers', Kraus pointed out that everything depended on which
newspaper children read. What happens, he percipiently inquired, if the children of Social Democrats prefer to read the *Völkischer Beobachter* (F 852–6,
1–4)? Two months later Kraus clarified his position by quoting a passage translated from Bertrand Russell's *Sceptical Essays* about the need for educationalists
to encourage critical thinking:

> For example, the art of reading the newspapers should be taught. The schoolmaster
> should select some incident which happened a good many years ago, and roused
> political passions in its day. He should then read to the school-children what was said
> by the newspapers on the one side, and what was said by those on the other, and

some impartial account of what really happened. He should show how, from the biased account of either side, a practised reader could infer what really happened, and he should make them understand *that everything in the newspapers is more or less untrue*.[22] (F 857–63, 71–2)

Austrian newspapers provided numerous cases of biased reporting, and the decision of the *Reichspost* to publish a selection of children's verses sent in by Catholic schoolteachers was an eye-opener. The paper found a dialect poem about skinning a cat particularly charming (cited under the title 'How Children become Adults', F 640–8, 128). A few months later, as an antidote to this corruption of the minds of children, Kraus printed a selection of verses written by girls between the ages of nine and thirteen, some of which had appeared in the progressive women's magazine, *Die Mutter*, edited by Gina Kaus. The spirit of the collection is conveyed by the verses 'Wolken über unsere Stadt' ('Clouds above our Town'):

Als der Abend herankam,	When the sun went down,
Und die Sonne unterging,	and evening came nigh,
Sah man, wie ein Wölkchen	we saw little clouds
das andere fing.	come chasing by.
Rosig beleuchtet	In the rosy glow
vom Abendschein,	of the evening light,
Schaute ich entzückt	I gazed into heaven
in den Himmel hinein.	filled with delight.

Contrasting these delicate children's verses with the poetry from the *Reichspost*, Kraus returns to the question 'How Children Become Adults':

The question here is not whether these children will remain poets, but whether they will become murderers and cutpurses. That is decided by the older generation, who teach their fledglings how to sing. [...] With some education for humanity it would be possible to cultivate poetry even in Lower Austria, since everywhere the lyrical impulse is closer to the soul of the child than to that of the professional writer. Here we have an uplifting impulse towards the pure image of man, even if it is later turned to stone by the Medusa of life. For no technological triumph over nature is comparable with this most characteristic miracle of nature: that in the midst of a grown-up world of brutal thugs such tender shoots can sprout. (F 679–85, 27–33)

Such passages take us to the heart of Kraus's view of childhood. In resisting reactionary educational agendas, it was logical to align himself with the Social Democrats, but there is only a partial overlap, and when critics accused him of seeking socialist support, he replied that his guiding principle was 'human dignity' ('Menschenwürde'; F 514–18, 49).

Far from being Marxist in inspiration, his key terms, 'Kinderseele' and 'Phantasie', 'Menschenwürde' and 'Erziehung zur Menschheit', derive from the aesthetic humanism of the late eighteenth century. There is a parallel with idealistic Adlerians like David Ernst Oppenheim, a schoolteacher who saw it as his life's task to 'enlarge knowledge of humanity'.[23] Kraus endorses a concept of child-centred education which can be traced back to Jean Paul, who became a cult figure in *Die Fackel*, as spokesman for spirituality in an age of technological manipulation. It is his ethereal description of Montgolfier's first ascent in a balloon in the 1780s that is cited in 'Apokalypse' in 1908 as a counterpoint to the conquest of the skies by modern aircraft (F 261–2, 1–2). And in 1912 his childlike reverence for mother earth is contrasted with the mechanistic rationality ('mechanistischer Verstand') of the modern age (F 354–6, 68–72). Kraus's readings of Jean Paul's lyrical prose particularly impressed his contemporaries, including Thomas Mann.[24] After 1914 his interest in Jean Paul intensified, as he became aware that the poetic visionary was also a radical pacifist. Jean Paul's work had been marginalized by literary historians, whose dismissive comments are documented on a number of occasions, and Kraus acknowledges that his style is at times insufferably prolix (F 445–53, 105). But he admired his outspoken opposition to the nationalistic fervour of the Wars of Liberation. He thus became a cardinal witness when Kraus launched his campaign against German militarism, quoting in February 1915 an incisive passage from *Dämmerungen für Deutschland* on the insidiousness of war propaganda (F 405, 5–6). Eighteen months later he reprinted an even more extensive attack on militarism from *Levana oder Erzieh-Lehre*, Jean Paul's essay on educational theory (F 443–4, 21–3). By this date he had joined Kraus's pantheon of German poets and philosophers opposed to war, ranking with Goethe and Claudius, Kant and Schopenhauer.

Although Kraus does not comment on the theory of education set out in *Levana*, he endorses the fundamental aim of encouraging individuality, rather than subjecting children to a rigid vocational training. Jean Paul's approach is refreshingly child-centred. 'Children educate us better as educators than any educator', he insists in his preface. Commenting on the socialist reforms of the 1920s, Kraus repudiates the idea that children should be trained to be 'competitive on the world market', preferring the 'inspirational effect of poetic values'. Echoing Jean Paul, he suggests that we should 'have the patience to wait until children succeed in training the right educators' (F 588–94, 86). In short, Kraus found in Jean Paul a combination of admirable qualities: natural piety, spiritual vision and an enlightened view of education linked with principled opposition to war. Small wonder that he included texts by Jean Paul in so many of his readings, describing him as 'one of the most admirable figures of the German world' (F 583–7, 19).

Rewriting the Freudian Script

It is not difficult to understand why Kraus preferred to make the 'journey back to children's land' in the company of Jean Paul, rather than Freud (F 381–3, 73).[25] The reveries of the romantic provided an antidote to psychoanalysis, with its speculative 'dream-readings' (F 354–6, 71). To counteract reductive models of formative experience, Kraus recalls a day from his childhood as a random sequence of stimuli – words and images, sounds and smells, adding that a person with a good brain should be able to recall the fevers of childhood so vividly that their temperature rises (F 241, 10–11). This evocative text dates from the period when Kraus was attending lectures by Freud, whose technique of free association is here adapted to celebrate a recall of childhood that defies schematization. Such texts certainly construct a selective self-image, but it cannot be construed as the idealization of a 'happy childhood'.[26] The emphasis is on vulnerability, dreaminess, solitude and loss, recalling excitements, fears and fevers that return to haunt the mind on the threshold of sleep.

Kraus's autobiographical texts do not offer a coherent narrative comparable to Jean Paul's *Selberlebensbeschreibung*, which paints an idyllic picture of the author's tender years, as a son of a parson–schoolteacher growing up in a sheltered rural community. Jean Paul's autobiography abounds in striking incidents, and the child's inner life unfolds within a social milieu shaped by parents, brothers and schoolfriends. This contextualization of childhood is conspicuously absent from Kraus's reminiscences, and the selectiveness of his memories becomes even clearer when we recall the salient details of his childhood. The eighth of nine surviving children, he was a delicate boy who initially felt overwhelmed by the bustle of the metropolis (he was barely three years old when the family moved to Vienna from his birthplace in Bohemia). He nevertheless grew up in a secure environment with a nanny to escort him to the park and a private tutor to coach him for admission to grammar school. While his father Jakob Kraus was absorbed in running the family business, his mother Ernestine, daughter of a country doctor, lavished particular attention on Karl, the youngest of five boys, who was physically frail as a result of a curvature of the spine.

The rapport between mother and child is stressed in a number of sources, notably the account of Kraus's family background compiled during the 1930s by Germaine Goblot, a French admirer in whom he confided. By contrast, she portrays his father as a no-nonsense businessman who showed little interest in his son's cultural pursuits.[27] Further details of his schooldays are contained in the monograph by Paul Schick, supplemented by an unpublished article by Sophie Schick.[28] The young Karl spent four years, from May 1880 to May 1884, at a Vienna primary school, the Wiener Pädagogium, but his schooling was interrupted by absence due to his delicate health, and during the summer of 1883 he temporarily transferred to the village school at Hadersdorf near Weidlingau, the picturesque village on the edge of the Vienna Woods where the family spent their holidays. Admission to the Franz Josefs-Gymnasium in the Hegelgasse, the grammar school attended by his elder brothers, was also delayed on health grounds, and he found its teaching uninspiring, although he achieved good results. It was here, as a schoolfriend recalls, that he developed his parodistic talent, which enabled him to mimic the idiosyncrasies of his teachers.[29] However, one teacher, Heinrich Sedlmayr, took a special interest in him, later recalling how he helped him to acquire greater confidence in his essay-writing style.[30] When his brother Rudolf, who was eighteen months older, failed to move up to the next grade, the two found themselves in the same class and it was his turn to help his less gifted sibling. Another classmate, the author Hugo Bettauer, recalls that Karl was the 'favourite child of his good, kind, motherly mother'.[31]

During his final years at grammar school the standard of Karl's work declined and his behaviour became so disruptive that his conduct was graded 'less than satisfactory because of disorderly behaviour'.[32] This coincided with the most distressing event of his childhood – the sudden death of his mother, which occurred on 24 October 1891 when he was seventeen. The sense of shock to the whole family is reflected in the formal announcement, which describes her death as 'a terrible misfortune in accordance with the inscrutable will of God'. According to Goblot, his mother's death affected him so deeply that everyone was alarmed by the intensity of his grief. To the end of his life he treasured a lock of his mother's hair and a leaf from her grave, together with the final letter he received from her.[33] But the grief of the seventeen-year-old seems to have been complicated by a further factor which is less easy to explain. Fritz Wittels, in his notorious analysis of 'The "Fackel" Neurosis' (January 1910), alleges that Kraus's relationship with his mother had become so difficult that his brothers blamed him for her death.[34] Wittels, who was the first to interpret Kraus's personality in Oedipal terms, is not the most reliable of witnesses, but during the years 1907–8 he and Kraus had been close friends and may well have exchanged confidences.

Why should Kraus have been blamed for his mother's death? An answer is suggested by the letter she wrote him on 24 August 1891, just two months before she died.[35] Ernestine was holidaying with the family in Bad Ischl, while Karl remained in Vienna in order to give a performance of his satirical sketch about the Court Theatre, 'In der Burgtheaterkanzlei'. Her letter begins by congratulating him on his success:

> Dear Karl,
>   Your letter has just arrived, and I'm very pleased that your wish has been fulfilled and the performance went so brilliantly. I am really sorry not to have been there and congratulate you on your brilliant success, I'm pleased that your dear father was also present. Only, dear Karl, please be reasonable at home, too, so that there really is no rumpus and you don't cause annoyance to your dear father in the evenings. Luise is in any case to give you 2 florins, and when God willing I come home I'll give you something more. Otherwise I've got nothing special to report. [. . .]
>   Your affectionate mother Ernestine

It is clear that he was going through a difficult phase and having rows with his father, not only about pocket money, and making himself unpopular with other members of the family. In a postscript to a further letter written three days later, his younger sister Marie (Mizzi) says how pleased she is that he will not be joining them on holiday. Even more revealing is a sentence written in childish scrawl by his seven-year-old niece Gretl: 'Dear Uncle, please don't come to Ischl.' In his attempts to assert his independence, the seventeen-year-old had evidently become rebellious, and his mother's death, just two months later, coincided with this difficult phase. If his brothers really blamed him for her death, this may have formed part of a 'family script', in which the deviant child becomes the focus for more diffuse anxieties.

After his mother's death, the tensions between Karl and his father continued, and now it was his brother Richard, twelve years his senior, who mediated between them. Jakob Kraus evidently expected his sons to train for business, but Karl insisted on enrolling for a university degree, attending courses first in law and later in German literature. Since he was irregular in his studies, preferring the more stimulating milieu of the coffee-house, it is not hard to understand why his father should have lost patience. Karl's own view of the conflict is summed up in the motto he uses in a letter to Richard on 4 September 1897: 'Father says: I don't want a son with a literary education!' In the following passage he sums up his difficulties: 'Now *I* am the one who is most painfully aware of the lack of any expression of emotional warmth in our family life, even though I decline to give spontaneous and decidedly unctuous expression to such warmth merely on formal occasions.' Richard had evidently been pleading with him to be more tactful towards his father, but Karl's response suggests that it is the 'suppression of feelings that causes embitterment'.[36] In the event, Richard was able to help Karl through this family crisis, encouraging him to strike out on his own by founding *Die Fackel*. There must also have been a reconciliation between father and son, since it was Jakob Kraus who provided the financial guarantee which facilitated the launch.

There is little more that can be added from external sources to this sketch of Kraus's childhood, but at least it is possible to correct certain misconceptions – notably the apocryphal claim that he 'was unable to offer any resistance' against his domineering father and consequently lapsed into 'melancholic self-hatred'.[37] The premise on which this argument is based is manifestly untrue and the conclusion sheer speculation. The claim, advanced in the same context, that the young Karl must have suffered from sibling rivalry after the birth of his younger sister Marie in December 1875 is equally dubious, since their correspondence over many years suggests that she was actually his favourite, and he certainly intended Marie to inherit the precious lock of their mother's hair.[38] An early photograph shows the siblings side by side, his hand resting on the back of her chair in a gesture of intimacy (Fig. 15). During the 1920s he could count on her support during his campaign against *Die Stunde*, after that paper had published that photograph in distorted form, and their continuing affection is reflected in his decision to dedicate volume seven of *Worte in Versen* to her.

More fruitful insights emerge if we consider Kraus's narrative of childhood as a conscious rewriting of the Freudian script. He begins by mocking the

15   Karl Kraus as a child, photographed with his sister Marie

psychoanalytic model of child development – the infant delighted by bowel movements who later fantasizes about raping his mother (F 300, 27). The Oedipal schema is even more effectively challenged as an explanation for the genius of Richard Wagner. If *all* boys are motivated by erotic jealousy and dream of taking their father's place, then the question to be answered is: 'which inclinations and impressions specific only to Wagner prepared him for the composition of *The Flying Dutchman*' (F 376–7, 21)? For Kraus, it is obvious that artistic inspiration cannot be explained by this kind of reductive psychology. The origins of genius are shrouded in mystery, and nothing is really explained by anecdotes about parents or schooldays. It is this conviction that underlies Kraus's autobiographical strategy, leading him to picture his childhood in solitude. There is no trace of the camaraderie of his schooldays, no hint of the bustle of family life and scarcely a reference to either of his parents. His father's name is mentioned only when it becomes necessary to refute calumnies about his business methods, while his mother is never mentioned at all, although one passage in the poem 'Jugend' ('Youth') obliquely alludes to her death (F 462–71, 181). We are almost left with the impression of an only child, since Kraus never voluntarily mentions any of his siblings in *Die Fackel*. This is not simply a matter of protecting his private life. Rather, he rewrites his narrative of origins so as to define his lineage in terms of poetic myth, omitting his family from the script. We know that this is misleading, since Kraus derived a substantial private income from the family firm, run by his brothers after their father's death in 1901. Indeed, his correspondence includes dozens of brief notes asking the firm for financial advances. By creating the persona of an artist without family ties, he sought to reinforce the radicalism of his satire.

The most significant aspect of Kraus's reminiscences lies in what he chooses to forget. Only rarely does he explicitly refer to his schooldays, even though he could still remember the names of all his primary-school classmates forty years later (F 588–94, 82). But this orderly alphabetical sequence merely highlights the randomness of his mode of recall in other contexts: for example, a fragment of poetry from a school anthology like 'Bei einem Wirte wundermild' (F 372–3, 16–18). We look in vain for any account of the gradual shaping of a personality through education associated with the Goethean concept of 'Bildung'. There is scarcely a reference to teachers or mentors, apart from his tribute to Sedlmayer (F 423–5, 39–40). There is no pride in genealogy, no reference to the festivals or rites of passage associated with Jewish family life, indeed scarcely a reference to his religious upbringing, apart from critical comments on David Graubart, the teacher of Judaism at the Franz Josephs-Gymnasium, whose didacticism alienated a whole generation of Jewish boys from the faith of their fathers (F 13, 30). Still more striking is the veil which Kraus draws over his student years, even though they coincided with a dramatic politicization of university life. Experiences that would fill hundreds of pages in a more conventional memoir, such as Schnitzler's *Jugend in Wien*, are distilled in the poem 'Jugend' into a couple of dozen quatrains.

'When I was ten years old,' Kraus recalls in a characteristic aphorism, 'I spent my time in the meadows of Weidlingau exclusively in the company of Red Admirals. I can say that these were the proudest social contacts of my life' (F 241, 9). The reference is to the year spent at the village school at Hadersdorf, but we should not be beguiled by such evocative passages into forgetting that the growing boy actually spent much of his time in the company of brothers, sisters and schoolfriends. The young Karl was certainly not unsociable, and after class, as Bettauer recalls, he would repair with his schoolmates to a nearby cake-shop famous for its creamy éclairs ('Schaumrollen').[39] There are no traces of this camaraderie in Kraus's reminiscences, which picture him in isolation, his social contacts ethereal as the butterflies themselves. The crux of the matter is that in Kraus's self-image, social origins are subordinated to the poetic myth. Butterflies represent not only a childhood idyll, but an image of nature under threat: 'I have observed that butterflies are becoming extinct' (F 241, 9). Amid the turmoil of war, the butterfly remains the emblem of childhood, linked in 'Jugend' with other equally ethereal memories (F 462–71, 182).

The significance of this motif is reflected in the celebrated Kraus portrait painted by Oskar Kokoschka in February 1925, which features a butterfly in flight (Fig. 16). Kraus was sceptical about the artist's literary ambitions, dismissing his Expressionist psychodrama *Mörder, Hoffnung der Frauen* ('Murderer, Hope of Women') as drivel. But this did not affect their friendship, and in 1925 Kokoschka painted this second Kraus portrait, to replace an earlier work (now lost). That first portrait had presented the satirist as a rather forbidding figure, but the portrait of 1925 is far gentler in tone. Delicately conceived in greys and

16 Portrait of Kraus by Oskar Kokoschka

greens, it shows the author seated at a table, his right hand resting on a pile of books and magazines, picked out in red to suggest the cover of *Die Fackel*. The face is irradiated by a yellow light that seems to emanate less from the light bulb, discernible top left, than from the inner resources of the author, who seems poised to recite from the open pages under his hand. We are reminded of the authority associated with the Bible in the iconography of the Reformation, but where portraits of Luther show him holding the good book aloft with unassailable faith, the gestures in this portrait convey a sense of frailty. Indeed, the composition invites us to connect the open pages with the outspread wings of the butterfly, while the faraway expression in the author's eyes seems to be following the insect's flight, suggesting that the pictorial motif is a projection of his imagination. In short, the painting has a 'pictographic' quality, its visual language inviting a discursive reading.[40] Kokoschka was aware of the significance of butterflies in Kraus's writings, quoting in his autobiography the poem 'Reunion with Butterflies', in which the poet celebrates the inspirational return of Red Admirals from his childhood ('Wiedersehen mit Schmetterlingen'; F 462–71, 86–7).[41] But the colours used in the portrait to pick out the butterfly's wings are not the red, black and silver that make Admirals so dazzling, but sombre shades of purple with a bright yellow streak painted diagonally across each wing. This configuration hints at another species from Kraus's writings during the war, the Camberwell Beauty – in German 'Trauermantel' (literally 'Cloak of Mourning'). A short text of October 1918, ironically entitled 'Childhood and Happiness in the Meadows' ('Kindheit und Wiesenglück'), quotes a report that children have been killed while playing in the fields with a handgrenade. The satirist imagines the last surviving Camberwell Beauty following the funeral cortège (F 484–98, 231). In Kraus's text the primal values associated with childhood are invoked through the prism of desecration and loss, while Kokoschka's painting transposes these motifs into emblematic terms.

Dream-Plays and Anal Psychologists

Both Kraus and Freud were writers with a retrospective cast of mind, assuming that adult identity is shaped by childhood, filtered through memory and reconfigured in dreams. But dreams, treated by the analyst as symptoms of neurotic disorder, are treasured by the poet as sources of creative inspiration, while the hypnagogic hallucinations which beset the mind at the onset of sleep become a stimulus for satire. The first chapter of Freud's *Interpretation of Dreams* assigns only marginal significance to hypnagogic sleep, but Kraus develops this motif into a source of heightened suggestibility, devoting to the process of falling asleep some of his most suggestive aphorisms and poems. The most effective way to overcome sleeplessness is to allow the mind to drift, conjuring the most absurd rabbits and ribbons 'out of the magic hat of the subconscious' (F 256, 18). Our apprehensions on the threshold of sleep may be appeased when we are taken back to the 'once upon a time' of our childhood (F 443–4,

33–4). The imaginative energy generated by such fantasies is most strikingly expressed in 'Hypnagogische Gestalten', a poem in which the sleepless imagination is visited by hallucinatory figures from childhood – grotesque images that become a source of inspiration:

Dort ein Mandarine	A man of eastern race,
schneidet eine Miene,	making a funny face,
ruft mir das verlorne Wort ins Ohr.	shouts the missing word into my ear.
Eines Satzes Wendung	The sentence I've selected
wächst mir zur Vollendung,	is gradually perfected,
wenn ich sie bis morgen nicht verlor.	if daylight doesn't make it disappear.
(F 521–30, 89–92)	

Such experiences contribute to the plethora of dream poems published over a twenty-year period. Starting in December 1913 with 'Mein Weltuntergang' ('My End of the World'), Kraus composed such poems in every conceivable register, from apocalyptic vision to poignant elegy. In an entertaining example from June 1920, 'Legende' ('Legend'), the sleeper, wandering through the meadows of childhood, encounters a monstrous Rhinoceros Beetle whose son has run away. Full of sympathy for the grief-stricken father, the sleeper searches high and low until he finally encounters the son – a magnificent Peacock Butterfly. Anything goes in this wonderland, and the secret longings of butterfly and beetle are reconciled through the sleeper's entrancement. This poem, which Kraus enjoyed reciting in public, is a persiflage on the way psychoanalysts conceive the father–son relationship, concluding with an awareness that 'they are interpreting the dream for me' (F 544–5, 36–7). Kraus, as Werner Kraft observed, turns his dreams into a 'weapon against psychoanalysis'.[42]

Dream motifs gain greatest weight when they link memories of childhood with intimations of love. Rational causality loses its power in this timeless realm, as in the poem 'Memoiren', where the advent of spring recalls the intuitions of a ten-year-old for whom everything is a significant 'sign' – even the climbing pole in the gymnasium, which arouses an eternity of sexual longing (F 437–42, 54–5). The imaginative resources released by memory transcend time and space: a dead friend reaches out his hand from a photograph on the wall and the poet is transported back to childhood by the chance recall of a folksong, 'Alle Vögel sind schon da' (F 443–4, 9). The intensity of such experiences transforms them into timeless 'moments of being', comparable to those celebrated by Virginia Woolf, another author who questioned the reductive strategies of psychoanalysis. The apple-trees which Woolf recalls from childhood holidays in Cornwall are comparable to Kraus's butterflies at Weidlingau.[43]

So important was this trance-like recall to Kraus's self-image that in 1922 he made it the subject of *Traumstück* ('Dream Play'), a verse play constructed around the figure of the sleeping Poet, besieged by the attentions of analysts. The title itself implies a challenge to the Freudian conception of dreams – an aim which is confirmed when the 'Anal Psychologists' ('Psychoanalen') make their appearance, propounding their theory of art:

Man glaubt, daß Gedichte	Genius as inspiration
der Genius verrichte,	for poetic creation?
das ist blauer Dunst.	That's wrong for a start.
Privat onanieren	Privately masturbate
und für die Welt sublimieren,	and publicly sublimate:
no ist das eine Kunst?	is that really art?

Freud wisely ignored this attack, although this was by no means the last word in the long-running 'Kraus affair'.[44] But Stekel was mildly flattered, quoting the verses about himself and Freud in a review of scientific literature.[45] Kraus originally intended to dedicate *Traumstück* to Sidonie Nadherny and Mechtilde Lichnowsky, but he changed his mind at the proof-reading stage. Writing to Sidonie, he explained that the shrillness of the sexual motifs in his satire on psychoanalysis might lead some ill-disposed critic to draw the wrong conclusions if he were to dedicate the book to two women who meant so much to him. He had Fritz Wittels in mind, the errant Freudian who had attributed his hostility towards the *Neue Freie Presse* to a 'father complex' (BSN 1, 569–70).

A more subtle challenge to psychoanalysis lies in the Imago sequence which follows. The Poet fears that thieves are about to break in and steal his dreams, but he is reassured by Imago, a figure that steps out of a picture-frame and addresses him in the following lines:

Bevor wir beide waren,	Before we both were born,
da haben wir uns gekannt,	we knew each other well,
es war in jenem Land,	it was in that far land,
dann schwand ich mit dem Wind.	I vanished with the wind.
Dann flog ich mit der Zeit	Then with the time I flew
und keinem ließ ich Ruh	leaving no one in peace,
und blickte stets dir zu	I fixed you with my eyes
und immer war ich fort.	though always far away.

In the following strophes it is suggested that Imago represents a pervasive spiritual force, perceptible to the Poet in every aspect of nature – a blade of grass, a favourite dog, or the haunting tune played by a beggar.

Kraus was aware that *Imago* was the title chosen by Freud and his colleagues in 1912 for their journal devoted to the psychoanalytic study of culture. The title derived from a story by Carl Spitteler, published in 1906, which was admired in Freud's circle for its representation of unconscious processes of self-deception.[46] Under the influence of Jung, the term 'imago' entered the general vocabulary of psychoanalysis, used to denote the unconscious projections which may distort relationships between parents and children: for example, the imago of a terrifying father which might form in the mind of a person whose father was actually rather timid.[47] Kraus's response in *Traumstück* is to reaffirm the spiritual aura the word originally possessed. He was doubtless aware that in classical antiquity the word 'imago' denoted the death mask of an ancestor, placed in the atrium of Roman houses. Such an image stood for thirty years in the corner of his study (Fig. 17): a copy of the bas-relief representing Annie Kalmar, which had been erected in a Hamburg cemetery after her death in 1901. His 'Imago' represents the inspirational female principle that sustains the Poet within a mystically conceived continuity that predates birth and transcends death.

The scene in *Traumstück* where 'Imago' steps out of the picture on the wall echoes the visionary experience recorded by Spitteler's hero Viktor, a philosopher inspired by an ethereal conception of love. In this story the figure of a young woman named Theuda, whom Viktor idealizes even though he scarcely knows her, suddenly appears in the solitude of his study, just as he is contemplating her photograph. This apparition so entrances him that they swear eternal love and are spiritually betrothed, sacrificing all idea of earthly happiness. The philosopher's Muse then blesses their union, conferring on Theuda the name Imago. Her picture remains with him as a timeless inspiration, even though Viktor soon discovers that the real Theuda has married some boring bourgeois and borne him a child. Viktor returns to his home town to confront Theuda with her betrayal and persuade her to resume her ethereal role as his Imago. The following episodes portray the philosopher's pursuit of his spiritual bride in the down-to-earth setting of a Swiss provincial town, subjecting the dreams of an incorrigible romantic to the sceptical insights of

17 'Imago': bas relief of Annie Kalmar (far right) in Kraus's study

modern psychology.[48] However, the image of an idealized woman, which Spitteler treats so ironically, is reaffirmed in Kraus's play as a mystical transformation, and his Poet is immune to the disillusionments inflicted upon the hapless Viktor.

The hostility towards analysis expressed in *Traumstück* was by no means Kraus's final word. He remained sceptical about psychotherapy, including Stekel's interventionist techniques (F 649–56, 66–7), and during the controversy about lay analysis he suggested that the activities of unqualified practitioners discredited the whole profession (F 668–75, 148–9). But, without mentioning Alfred Adler, he recognized the significance of the concept of 'inferiority' (F 514–18, 20). Attempting to reach a balanced judgement, he acknowledged that psychoanalysis might have 'scientific value' (F 735–42, 36), adding that one would be inclined to take it more seriously were it not compromised by 'so much fraud' (F 906–7, 15).

Archetype and Experience

Traumstück celebrates the links between archetype and inspiration. Kraus's syncretic imagination fuses memories of Annie Kalmar with allusions to his more recent attachment to Sidonie Nadherny, and the scene in which Imago steps out of her frame conflates Spitteler's visionary motif with actual photographs hanging in his study. 'Memory is the only paradise from which we cannot be expelled,' Jean Paul observed in one of his most celebrated aphorisms.[49] This idea, picked up by Kraus long before he began to take issue with psychoanalysis, was to resurface in his writings in innumerable ways. Twenty years later, in April 1919, at a time when his generation was confronted by challenging new opportunities, he characteristically turned towards the past in the poem 'Rückkehr in die Zeit' ('Return into Time'):

Mein Zeiger ist zurückgewendet,	My watch-hand points towards the past:
nie ist Gewesnes mir vollendet	that which has gone is never lost,
und anders steh' ich in der Zeit.	thus altering my place in time.
In welche Zukunft ich auch schweife	I care not what the future holds:
und was ich immer erst ergreife,	whatever enterprise unfolds,
es wird mir zur Vergangenheit.	it is the past that's really mine.

New events, the poem suggests, are experienced 'as memory', and even death holds no fears for a poet who feels that he has been blessed by a 'primal image' or 'archetype' ('Urbild'; F 508–13, 72). At this point we may be reminded of psychoanalytic models of memory, although the echoes of Jung are more significant than any debt to Freud.

'Rückkehr in die Zeit' is one of a series of poems that present the mnemonic imprinting of early experiences as paradigms for adult cognition. The associated concepts of 'Ursprung' and 'Urbild' form part of a prelapsarian myth that links childhood memory with poetic imagination. The poet, like the lover, seeks to recover a 'primal image' that has been lost (F 381–3, 69). The 'Ursprung' motif recurs in 'Nach zwanzig Jahren' (April 1919), the most eloquent of Kraus's autobiographical poems, in which the founding of *Die Fackel* is presented as a demonic mission. Here again, poetic myth displaces biographical detail. There is no reference to those who actually supported the launch of the magazine: his elder brother Richard, his father who paid for the paper, his printer Moriz Frisch, or Maximilian Harden, the Berlin publicist who acted as his model. Instead, it is some 'mischievous anti-demon' who summons the poet from the 'origin' and inspires him to pursue his distant 'goal':

Und du, rief dieser Widerpart der Zeit,
bestehe sie, je flüchtiger sie lesen!
Ermüde nicht an ihrer atemlosen
naturentflohnen, zeitverrannten Hast;
dein Weg, vom Ursprung übers Ziel hinaus,
ist länger, darum sollst du nicht ermüden!
Sei Zucht und Strafe, Licht zugleich und Brand;
durch Liebe sind sie nimmermehr zu halten:
so opfere dein Herz den Haßgewalten –
dein Heft, es bleibt als Heft in deiner Hand!

And you, cried this opponent of the age,
don't let your careless readers wear you down,
don't be discouraged by their headlong flight
from nature to distractions of the day;
you shall not tire although your path extends
from primal origin beyond the goal!
Be rod and punishment, both fire and light;
through love their folly you will ne'er abate:
so give your heart up to the powers of hate –
and what you write must surely prove you right!

The calling of the satirist is presented as an act of grace, his curses comparable to prophetic utterance of the Old Testament (F 508–13, 1–5). A similar motif occurs ten years later in another ambitiously autobiographical poem, 'Nach dreißig Jahren' (1929), where the calling of the satirist is presented as a 'fateful gift of nature', while the concept of 'Ursprung' is invoked to differentiate his passionate engagement from the esoteric stance of Stefan George, a poet whose exalted reputation is attributed to empty ceremonial (F 810, 10). The contrast would have been clearer if Kraus had been more specific about the impulse that distinguishes George's mythopoeic imagination from his own: the celebration of the ideal male figure, as opposed to the sensuous woman and the sensitive child. Kraus's concept of a creative 'origin' is most plausible in poems that fuse primal image with erotic encounter. 'Ursprung', for the poet in pursuit of an elusive lover in 1915, is exemplified by water cascading from a fountain ('Vor einem Springbrunnen'; F 406–12, 137–8), while the renewal of erotic experience in the mid-1920s prompted him to associate this motif with the turbulence of a mountain stream ('Der Strom'; F 697–705, 76). But there was an unresolved tension between archetype and experience, since resurgent sexual energies could not always be recuperated into consoling poetic paradigms.

CHAPTER 10

Images of Women and Shadows from the Past

During the 1920s there was a marked change in Kraus's comments about relations between the sexes. The First World War brought about a brutalization of sex life, especially for military conscripts, that was a travesty of his vision of erotic liberation, and in October 1916 he reprinted a passage from a German medical report about the spread of venereal disease and the need to establish brothels with 'impeccable materials under the strictest military control'. This reduction of prostitutes, whose cause he had so eloquently defended, to mere 'materials' led him to declare (echoing a famous song): 'No, this is *not* the freedom I intended' (F 437–42, 86–7). The sobriety of his post-war writings reflects a new sense of responsibility, since he had learnt from personal experience that there was a price to pay for multiple relationships. His friend Elisabeth Reitler committed suicide on 7 November 1917, prompting him to write a letter full of self-reproach to Sidonie Nadherny: 'I didn't see the shadows that had already settled over this life' (BSN 1, 444–7). This motif recurs in his 'Epitaph für Elisabeth R.', published in the third volume of *Worte in Versen*: 'Your ailing heart espoused the shades.'[1] The fate of the 'child woman', Irma Karczewska, cast an even longer shadow, leading him to distance himself from unrestrained eroticism and welcome the companionship of more sophisticated women.

A Private Nemesis

The concept of the 'child woman' ('das Kindweib') was coined in 1908 by the psychoanalyst Fritz Wittels, a pivotal figure in the cultural life of Vienna.[2] The discovery of his memoirs, written in English during the 1940s, has made it possible to reconstruct this complicated story. The first volume of *Karl Kraus – Apocalyptic Satirist* noted that Kraus had 'a short-lived love affair' with Irma Karczewska.[3] It turns out that his involvement with Irma actually lasted for twenty years and that she was the catalyst in a pattern of attachment and rivalry which also involved Sigmund Freud. Wittels, who came from a prosperous

Jewish family, was seven years younger than Kraus, but he made up in impudence for what he lacked in years. In December 1906 he sent Kraus one of his short stories, claiming that it was far superior to the work of Strindberg.[4] This was followed by his plea for the decriminalizing of abortion, published under the pseudonym Avicenna (F 219–20, 1–22), which marked a turning-point in his career, since it won him the respect of Freud. After attending one of Freud's lectures at the General Hospital in the Alserstrasse, Wittels was delighted when the great man approached him and, pointing to the article in *Die Fackel*, said: 'Did you write this? It is like a brief, and I subscribe to every word of it' (M 48).[5] Shortly afterwards, on 27 March 1907, Wittels became a member of the Psychoanalytic Society, and for two years he had the best of both worlds. After completing his duties at the hospital, he would join Kraus and his friends at their favourite restaurant. All kinds of people – government officials as well as artists, actors and attractive girls – would come to his table, and Kraus made them feel they were 'the centre of the universe' (M 54). Freud's circle was less glamorous, and when he qualified in January 1908 Wittels left the General Hospital and opened a private practice in the Graben. He wanted to be closer to the bohemian clique, especially as Kraus had drawn him into the whirl of his private life by introducing him to his mistress, Irma Karczewska.[6]

Irma, born in January 1890, grew up in a petit-bourgeois Catholic milieu with little formal education. As an aspiring actress she caught Kraus's eye (Wittels recalls) because she strongly reminded him of his earlier love, Annie Kalmar. When Kraus staged his production of Wedekind's *Büchse der Pandora* (*Pandora's Box*) in May 1905, Irma played the role of Bob the Groom. She was only fifteen at the time, and had apparently already had other lovers before she became Kraus's mistress.[7] He supported her financially and tried to launch her on a career in cabaret under the name Ingrid Loris (F 203, 18–19). Before long Wittels was himself in love with Irma, and his feelings can be gauged from the letters he addressed to 'Liebes Irmerl' between April and December 1907. In one ecstatic letter, dated 21 July 1907, he reminds her of the moment 'when I dragged you out of Kraus's bed'.[8] This looks like a classic sexual triangle, with the ardent young lover competing for Irma's favours against his mentor, but the ensuing row erupted for very different reasons. Kraus, tiring of Irma, wanted to pass her on to Wittels, since he 'could not stand her chattering'. Nobody could bear her long, although she 'looked more than charming and compensated her lovers in the night for a good deal of what she vexed them with in the daytime' (M 70–1). More serious problems arose when Kraus tried to induce Wittels to marry her. 'All would perhaps have ended better', he recalls in his account of the rupture, 'had I been capable of permanently freeing Kraus of Irma. He wished to get rid of her in good grace' (M 82). Wittels found himself pressed into the ambiguous role of lover and physician, since Irma needed medical care as well as amorous companionship.

An early photograph shows Irma as an appealing young woman with lustrous dark hair (Fig. 18a), but Kraus evidently tried to cast her in a quasi-mythical role – as a 'Dionysian girl born several thousand years too late' (M 58). He groomed her for a life of love, encouraging her to develop erotic refinements reminiscent of the 'hetaera' – the glamorous concubine of ancient Greece as described by Lucian and depicted by Gustav Klimt (Fig. 18b).[9] Irma felt attracted by the glamour of her role: 'She quickly realized that all she had clandestinely practised from early puberty on, to the deep dismay of her petty bourgeois family, was now supposed to represent the sublimest peak a girl could reach' (M 70). Hence she became the model for Wittels's paper on 'Das Kindweib'.[10] Citing Freud's theory of infantile auto-eroticism, he compares her ability to obtain pleasure from any sexual partner to the infant's uninhibited sucking of whatever object is to hand. Although his ideal is the 'hetaera', Wittels is aware that the spontaneity of Hellenistic culture can never be regained, concluding that the child woman is destined to suffer and die young (F 230–1, 14–33).

While Kraus admired this essay, Freud was decidedly critical when Wittels read an early draft to him in private, since he realized that his own concepts were being abused to sponsor what he called a 'perfect ragamuffin [Haderlump]' (M 62). Wittels was persuaded to tone down his argument, which he presented to the Psychoanalytic Society on 29 May 1907 under the title 'Die große Hetäre' ('The Great Courtesan'). The record of the ensuing discussion has not survived.[11] But it is clear that the concept of the 'Kindweib' is a male fantasy which disregards the realities of juvenile prostitution. Irma's charms were enjoyed by other members of Kraus's early circle, including the anarchist Erich Mühsam, who refers to her as 'das Tierchen' – 'the little animal' – from whom he had apparently contracted gonorrhoea. The frequent references to Irma in the letters of Karl Hauer are also rather patronizing.[12] However, Kraus's women friends were more sympathetic. The actress Kete Parsenow inquired sympathetically about her in a long sequence of letters to

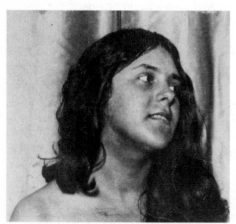

18   Images of women: (a) Irma Karczewska   (b) Klimt's hetaera

Kraus. 'Is her husband with her?' she asks July 1918. 'I really feel sorry for her. Do you still see her often? And how is the Baroness?'[13] Kete was well aware that Kraus's personal entourage included a number of other women, in addition to Irma and Sidonie Nadherny (the Baroness). Her letters frequently mention Helene Kann, the sister of Elisabeth Reitler, who first met Kraus in 1904 and remained 'a loyal companion' until the end of his life.[14]

Kraus had difficulty in keeping these multifarious relationships in equilibrium. We know from his correspondence that in autumn 1908 he succeeded, through the influence of Alexander Girardi, in obtaining an opening for Irma at the Thalia Theatre in Berlin.[15] After her return to Vienna she became engaged, and when her admirer broke off the match, Kraus acted as her intermediary in negotiations with the family.[16] He must have been relieved when she married Albertus (Beppo) Haselhoff von Lich, proprietor of a chocolate factory located at Pottenbrunn in Lower Austria. But the marriage proved shortlived, and we subsequently find Irma living at a number of temporary addresses under a bewildering variety of names. Kraus kept in touch by arranging for his secretary, Frieda Wacha, to send her copies of Die Fackel and other magazines.[17] By 1912 she was listed as Maria Haselhoff-Lich on a register of residents in Vienna, which also records that she was divorced. By 1915 she was remarried, to an engineer named Friese, and she had at least one further husband, Georg Christoduloff, who was Greek Orthodox and came from Tatar Pazardjik in Bulgaria.[18] However, as Wittels puts it, 'Men sooner or later withdrew and she always came back to Kraus, her foster father. [. . .] Moreover he felt responsible for the course she pursued; he had implanted ideas of grandeur in a hussy from the outskirts of the city.' Wittels emphasizes that he 'remained her protector – often against his will – for over twenty-five years, until she died, and I think he will be forgiven all his sins for that' (M 56–7 & 71).

Irma's life reveals the darker side of the erotic sub-culture. She was treated as a plaything by Kraus and members of his circle, but there was no place for her in the more austere post-war world. During her early forties she suffered from physical illnesses accompanied by depression, and on 1 January 1933 she committed suicide. Towards the end of her life Irma recorded her feelings in a handwritten diary. The entries, dated from 8 October 1930 to 23 September 1932, are addressed to Kraus in the intimate 'Du' form, and the diary is a protracted lament for the loss of his affections, interspersed with aphorisms about love and death and allusions to the other men who featured in her life. The solitary reference to Wittels (26 January 1931) expresses chagrin that he is leaving for America with his second wife, while she has to remain behind in her misery.[19] It is difficult to reconstruct a coherent image of Irma from these fragmentary reflections, but on several occasions she recalls that she was only fourteen-and-a-half when Kraus 'took her away from home' (12 October 1930).[20] However, there is no suggestion that she sees herself as the victim of sexual abuse. Recalling the glamour of life in Kraus's circle, she laments her isolation since he broke off contact with her in 1925. Through his solicitor

Oskar Samek, Irma received what was intended to be a final 'financial settle-ment', in return for her agreement to renounce all further claim on him. But she now found herself eking out a living as a landlady renting furnished lodg-ings. Exhausted by household chores, she recalls how Kraus had cherished her as the 'apple of his eye' and eulogized her as a 'literary-historical personality' (30 January 1931). Her attitude fluctuates between gratitude for the happiness they experienced together and an impulse to punish him by selling her story to the press. Her preoccupation with Kraus becomes obsessive as her health deteriorates and she learns that she may require an operation for a tumour (14 May 1932). Her suicide may have been motivated by the fear that she was suffering from cancer.[21] However, grief at being deprived of Kraus's affection was also a factor, since she feels that, just as he once gave her life, so he is now driving her towards death (12 November 1930). We do not know whether Kraus attended her funeral, but he refers in his will to the need to tend her grave. An apt summary is provided by the passage in Wittels's memoirs that – varying a phrase from Nestroy – describes Irma as Kraus's 'private nemesis' (M 71).[22]

Sexual Ambivalence

Irma's claim to be a 'literary-historical personality' relates to Wittels's notori-ous satirical novel *Ezechiel der Zugereiste* ('Ezechiel the Visitor from Abroad'), in which she appears thinly disguised as Mizerl, a glamorous young woman suf-fering from venereal disease, while Kraus is wickedly caricatured as Benjamin Eckelhaft (the name means 'disgusting'). In his memoirs Wittels recalls the strangest episode in this affair: 'One night while hard at the work of writing this novel in which I flayed my former friend, a feeling of intense bitterness and revulsion came over me and, on impulse, I did something which I later com-pletely forgot. I tore off a piece of the sheet on which I wrote and quickly scribbled a few lines to Kraus in which I suggested that we forget all the anger and misunderstanding which had grown up between us and renew our friend-ship. [. . .] A short time later, the tenth anniversary of "The Torch" came around and again I wrote him in a friendly tone.' He was (as he puts it) in 'an ambivalent phase' of 'hate-love or love-hate' (M 95). Kraus made no reply, but filed these affectionate letters away for future reference, later alluding to them as 'love letters' (F 484–98, 140). After completing the novel, Wittels was unsure whether to publish it. A young woman friend induced him to lend her the manuscript and she took it straight to Kraus, who was thus able to read the novel at least twelve months before it was published. 'It was years later,' Wit-tels adds, 'that I learned of this act of treason' (M 95).

Kraus made strenuous efforts to prevent the book's publication so as to protect Irma's reputation – by this date she was Frau Haselhoff, a respectable married woman. A series of handwritten drafts survive from the year 1910 in which he argues that Wittels had a duty to maintain confidentiality about her gonorrhoea, which he had treated as her physician. Instead, through his all too

transparent depiction of her complaint, he had irreparably damaged her reputation. Even before the novel was published, the rumour mill began to turn and
Irma felt obliged to confess to her husband that before the marriage she had had
an affair with her doctor. The outcome (Kraus explains) was that Wittels,
through his authorial indiscretion, destroyed what had originally been a 'happy
marriage'. Haselhoff insisted on a divorce because he feared that the novel's
disclosures would make his social position impossible.[23]

Before the book could be published, Wittels also had to overcome the
authority of Freud, his second spiritual father. Freud was drawn into the
dispute when he was approached by one of Wittels's relatives, the Prague
psychiatrist Alois Pick, whose daughter Yerta had recently become Wittels's
wife.[24] The approach was initiated by Kraus, who argued that Wittels was damaging the reputation of a married woman.[25] His most telling move was to
arrange for Freud to be shown the affectionate letters Wittels had written at the
very moment when he was composing his scurrilous novel. 'One day,' Wittels
recalls, 'Freud asked me pointblank to let him read the printed manuscript. He
read it within twenty-four hours and brought it back and said to me: "I shall
summarize my verdict in one sentence. You lose nothing if you do not publish this book; you lose everything if you do".' When Wittels tried to defend
his cause, Freud 'grew angry and said: "Psychoanalysis is more important than
your silly controversies. Why should I allow it to be damaged by your incon-
siderate book?"' He offered to reimburse the costs Wittels had incurred, if the
book was withdrawn (M 97). Finally Freud declared: 'You are impossible in
my circle if you publish this book.' These words (Wittels recalls) 'settled the
question and made me definitely decide to publish. I was much too obstinate
to let anyone threaten me' (M 98). He resigned from the Psychoanalytic
Society, and *Ezechiel* appeared in the autumn of 1910, with the mocking face
of the picaro emblazoned on its cover.

Wittels had to face legal action which Kraus initiated against him and his
Berlin publisher in Irma's name. In court, Kraus produced the 'love letters' and
delivered a diatribe against Wittels's character. When Wittels himself was
called, he denied that his novel related to real persons, but the allusions were
so transparent that he lost the case and the novel had to be withdrawn.[26] He
responded by making a series of cosmetic changes, and the novel, reset in
roman type, was republished in Vienna later that same year.[27] This time Kraus
failed to retaliate, nor did he fulfil his promise that he would give an account
of the court case in *Die Fackel* (F 311–12, 56). His explanation for this
omission is that further attention would only have nourished his opponent's
feelings of 'love–hatred' (F 484–98, 140). Through an intermediary, Wittels
had let Kraus know that 'Freud had done all he could to prevent the publication of my book' (M 98). This may explain why Kraus, in his polemic against
psychoanalysis, never attacks Freud in person.

The conflict between Kraus and Wittels continued to reverberate during the
1920s. On the basis of his experiences as a medical officer during the First

World War, Wittels wrote a picaresque novel entitled *Zacharias Pamperl oder Der verschobene Halbmond* ('Zacharias Pamperl or The Displaced Crescent Moon', 1923). He decided to cash in on Kraus's reputation by marketing the book with an eye-catching slogan slashed across its cover: '"Die letzten Tage der Menschheit" in Romanform' ('in novel form'). Kraus was furious, forcing the publisher to remove the offending slogan, but his terse reference to this affair in *Die Fackel* does not even mention the title of the offending novel, let alone the name of the author (F 657–67, 94–5). This incident had serious repercussions, producing a chain reaction which obstructed plans to publish *Die letzten Tage der Menschheit* in American translation.[28] Both he and Wittels were haunted by this affair until the end of their days, and as late as October 1932 we find Kraus referring to Wittels's conduct as an 'act of publicistic revenge'.[29]

Although Wittels had in effect been expelled from the Psychoanalytic Society, his early experiences enabled him to write a pioneering book entitled *Sigmund Freud: His Personality, His Teaching, & His School*, first published in German in 1924 and translated the following year. This contains a passage about the 'hetaera' that can be read as a summing-up of his triangular relationship with Kraus and Irma: 'The immense success of women who are ardently desired and greatly loved depends upon homosexual impulses in men,' he observes. 'What a man loves in the hetaera is the other men who have lain and will lie in her arms.'[30] This is a coded reflection on the ambivalent feelings that had linked him with Kraus through Irma. At the end of 1923 Wittels sent Freud an advance copy of the German edition, and Freud replied setting out his objections – especially to the credit given to his rival Wilhelm Stekel. With Freud's permission this letter was published as a preface to the English edition. Kraus's name does not occur in the book, but Wittels's unpublished correspondence with Freud reveals that he *did* originally write a chapter about his own expulsion from the Psychoanalytic Society, dealing with Kraus, Irma and *Ezechiel*. This was omitted from the book, for reasons which Freud approved.

After reading the suppressed chapter about the events of 1910, Freud wrote Wittels a remarkable letter (dated Vienna, 24 December 1923), explaining why the Kraus controversy had led him to expel Wittels from the Society:

> To that I was compelled only when the lawyer told me that you had addressed a certain person with affectionate letters while you were occupied with writing your lampoon. [. . .] You yourself did not deny these letters and claimed the right of acting that inconsistently because your feelings were ambivalent. Your insisting on this point, mixing up the real and analytical worlds, your refusal to correct this mistake, this was the thing that startled me in those days. I always considered Kraus's influence on you very disadvantageous and thought then that you had succumbed to it for good and were prejudiced for ever.[31] (M 104)

After receiving this letter, Wittels realized that he had repressed the memory of those letters to Kraus. His explanation is that he was confused by 'the strange triangular world' in which he then lived (M 105).

Wittels was readmitted to the Vienna Psychoanalytic Society in 1925 – a sign of Freud's special affection. In 1928 he emigrated to New York with Freud's encouragement.[32] He was subsequently to become a leading figure in the New York psychoanalytic community – a defender of Freudian orthodoxy against heretics like Karen Horney.[33] But after he had settled in America the Kraus episode was still not closed, as became evident when Wittels visited Freud for the last time in 1933. They started talking once again about the passages in Wittels's biography which Freud had found objectionable. Suddenly (Wittels recalls) he changed the subject and, growing angry, said: 'It wasn't the biography alone; there are those letters that you wrote to Kraus – regular "love letters", while you were occupied in attacking him. That was very unfair of you, and not only that, it was an act of cowardice.' Wittels was stunned. '"Professor," I said, "do you realize that this was twenty-five years ago?" Freud made a soothing gesture. "I know," he said, "but you were close to me"' (M 143). This final conversation, at a time when Freud was approaching his eightieth birthday, shows how deep the emotions of those original triangles must have run.

Eros, Thanatos and the Poets

The first wave of the erotic revolution ended with the death of Peter Altenberg in January 1919. His correspondence includes an undated letter accusing Kraus and his clique of turning innocent girls into 'sexual animals', doubtless an allusion to Irma.[34] Although Kraus's anti-feminist aphorisms continued to be reprinted in book form, he expressed sympathy for nightclub dancers forced to endure 'crude sexual advances' (F 679–85, 119–21) and girls reduced to bimbos ('Pupperln') perched on the back of motorbikes (F 751–6, 116–19). In his poetry, the theme of sexual pleasure is displaced by that of nostalgic memory: 'mindful of the greatness of yesterday', as he wrote in lines addressed to Sidonie Nadherny (F 544–5, 39–40). He celebrated memory even more eloquently in 'Eros und der Dichter' (F 561–7, 69–71), the poem in which the Poet bids Eros farewell, claiming to be fulfilled:

– noch genießend im Gedenken,	– still delighting in remembrance,
lebt' ich nie die Fülle aus!	riches I could ne'er explore!
Willst du ferner sie mir schenken,	Should you still offer abundance,
so verschließe ich das Haus.	I shall simply close the door.

Although he explores this theme from many angles, Kraus's evocations of remembered love lack the specificity that tugs at the heart in the late poetry of Hardy or Yeats. A further limitation arose from the need for discretion, which led him to clothe passionate feelings in ethereal disguises, since he feared that his affair with Sidonie might be made public by some indiscreet acquaintance (BSN 1, 569). Moreover, the shadows of the past, particularly memories of Annie Kalmar, endow his lyric poetry with an elegiac tone.

However, the claim to be closing the door on new experiences scarcely squares with Kraus's letters of the 1920s, many of which are addressed to women in the intimate 'Du' form. There was a continuing correspondence with Kete Parsenow, his old flame from the Altenberg days, now happily married. She repeatedly sends her greetings to Helene Kann, Kraus's long-standing companion, who now played a more matronly role, while the references to Irma suggest that she was seen as a dependent child. A card which Parsenow sent to Kraus in January 1924 sums the situation up suggestively: 'How are things going with you and your family? You know what I mean.'[35] In addition to supervising Kraus's unorthodox domestic arrangements and creating an archive for his papers, Helene Kann ensured that he was never short of female company. It was she who introduced him to Gina Kaus, former mistress both of the financier Josef Kranz and of the author Franz Blei.

Gina Kaus was a successful author, publishing a dozen dramatic and fictional works during the inter-war period, before being forced into exile. She had close links both with the Social Democrats (her stories were serialized in the *Arbeiter-Zeitung*) and with Alfred Adler's individual psychologists. Her work, like that of her friend Vicki Baum, was promoted by the Ullstein Verlag in Berlin, and she made her breakthrough in the cinema when her novel *Die Überfahrt* (1932), the account of a transatlantic crossing, was filmed under the title *Luxury Liner*. Several of her works were translated into English, including a historical novel about Catherine the Great, and American reviewers praised her fiction as the work of a 'psychological expert in emotional history'.[36] In exile, first in Paris and later in California, she developed a flair for film scripts, including the box-office success *The Robe*, based on the novel by Lloyd C. Douglas. Her autobiography, also written in exile, gives an affectionate account of her relationship with Kraus.

They were introduced in June 1924, at a time when Gina was five months pregnant by her ex-husband Otto Kaus. She was captivated by Kraus's sympathetic attention, and there was an immediate meeting of minds as they began to recite passages from Offenbach's *Blaubart* (*Barbe-Bleue*), which they both knew by heart. She seems to be unaware that Kraus was grieving over his break with Sidonie, which had occurred five months earlier. What he needed, Gina recalls, was 'a very polygamous woman who was a good story-teller and made no demands on him'. He was fascinated by her account of her relationship with Joseph Kranz, and the fact that he had attacked a war profiteer so fiercely in *Die Fackel* may have added spice to the new relationship. Unwittingly echoing Wittels's conception of sexual ambivalence, she concluded that Kraus was erotically stimulated by imagining women in the arms of other men.

Kraus devoted several weeks that summer to taking Gina on trips into the countryside in his newly acquired Tatra motor car, complete with chauffeur, usually accompanied by Helene Kann. They spent a week's holiday together in Sankt Wolfgang – for Gina 'one of the most beautiful weeks of my life'. She recalls how she went swimming with him, feeling proud of her pregnancy, while he experienced the self-immersion in nature as 'a return to his childhood'. The idyll ended unhappily, as there was a minor car accident that left

Gina with cuts on her face, but when Kraus had to return to Vienna, he gave her a passionate farewell kiss. After her baby boy was born in the autumn, Kraus came to visit her at the clinic, but he no longer spoke to her in the affectionate 'Du' form, and it was clear that Helene's attempt to set up a love affair had failed. However, they remained good friends, and he used to phone her every morning after completing his night's work.[37] Several years later, when Friedrich Torberg joined their circle, he formed the impression that Kraus felt most at ease when Gina Kaus was there.

There is scarcely a reference to Kaus in Die Fackel, apart from the passage commending her magazine, Die Mutter (F 679–85, 27). However, Kraus's relationship with Mechtilde Lichnowsky made a direct impact on his work. A member of the German aristocracy who was married with three children, Mechtilde was a strong personality with a multiplicity of talents.[38] In addition to being a successful author, she was artistic and musical, providing satirical cartoons for publication in Die Fackel and musical settings for his Nestroy recitals. Initially, in October 1916, when Mechtilde and her husband Karl Max Lichnowsky, formerly German ambassador in London, first expressed an interest in attending one of Kraus's readings, his reaction was guarded. But they met in spring 1917, and a more intimate relationship developed during house parties hosted by his circle of aristocratic friends: Mechtilde in Kuchelna, Sidonie Nadherny at Janowitz, Mary Dobrzensky at Pottenstein, Gillian Lobkowitz in Raudnitz, and Dora Pejacsevich at Našice. The Lichnowskys had a house in Berlin, where Kraus sometimes stayed, and Mechtilde's presence at one of his readings in June 1920 excited comment in the press (F 546–50, 19). His sixty surviving letters to her offer beguiling glimpses of their intimacy. She shared both his love of animals and his insistence on the precise use of words, and their correspondence contains intriguing reflections on epistolary style, since they both enjoyed letters written 'without overt irony but with ironic undertones'. This coded style stimulated the recipient to read between the lines, while at the same time forestalling the possibility of exposure. The surviving correspondence is fragmentary and one-sided (most of Mechtilde's letters have been lost), but it offers insight into a creative partnership. She gently teased him in verses describing him as 'physically unimpressive, / but spiritually flying high' ('Körperlich nicht übertrieben, / Aber seelisch hoch im Flug').[39] He was proud to be associated with such a gifted woman, repeatedly visiting the Lichnowskys' country estates. The summer of 1921, Kraus suggests, was especially memorable.[40]

He clearly did not 'close the door' on new experiences, although they found only disguised expression in his poetry. The most significant example is the poem 'Du seit langem einziges Erlebnis' ('You whom I owe unwonted ecstasy') (April 1921), of which a manuscript version dated July 1921 bears the inscription 'für Mechtilde Lichnowsky'. This celebrates an encounter which is perceived as inexplicably new, but transposed into a realm of hypnagogic images, and allusions to Mechtilde and Sidonie (Fig. 19a & b) are blended in a

19   Double exposure: (a) Mechtilde Lichnowsky   (b) Sidonie Nadherny

manner comparable to a photographic 'double exposure'.[41] Sidonie assumed
that the poem was written for her, and the tensions within this triangle almost
reached breaking point in November 1921, aggravated by illness. In February
1922 Kraus experienced 'fourteen miserable days' (BSN 1, 533–4), but the
crisis was resolved the following month, which Sidonie spent in Vienna, visiting Kraus every evening and assisting him with proof-reading (BSN 2, 332). In
one and the same number of Die Fackel he published, under appropriate disguises, a poem in praise of Mechtilde, 'An eine Heilige' ('To a Saintly
Woman'), immediately followed by poems addressed to Sidonie, including
'Dein Fehler' ('Your Flaw'; F 588–94, 54–8). Despite the ambiguities of this
double act, the emotional rapport between the two women was so close that
in one of her letters Sidonie refers to her friend as 'meine Mechtsidild'.[42]

There were further emotional fluctuations during the following months,
when Mechtilde temporarily detached herself in a way that Kraus found
baffling (BSN 1, 556). The letters show how jealously he guarded his own role
as 'poet', and one of his most comical misunderstandings with Sidonie
occurred when he imagined that she regarded another poet as his superior,
when in fact the incriminating passage in her letter alluded to a fictional character in Geburt, a novel by Mechtilde.[43] The spectre of jealousy could never be
entirely banished, especially with Rilke lurking behind the scenes (Sidonie had
to reassure him that her relationship with that aesthetically sensitive poet was
'erotically neutral'; BSN 1, 164). An aphorism published in April 1919, during
their first estrangement, suggested that women regard jealousy as a contradic-

tion in terms: 'If it is justified, then it's obviously not justified!' (F 508–13, 77). Kraus was specially protective of his relationship with Sidonie, but in other contexts he suggests that being in love with more than one person may be an enriching experience.

These interactions with Sidonie and Mechtilde were complicated by Kraus's liaison with a third aristocrat from Bohemia, Mary Dobrzensky (Fig. 20a). The three women were close friends, frequently exchanging visits and letters, in which their interactions with Kraus form a recurrent theme. Mary's correspondence with Sidonie and Mechtilde is a significant source, but her long sequence of letters to Kraus is even more revealing.[44] In this case, uniquely, we have letters that trace the evolution of the relationship from the woman's point of view. Born on 26 January 1889, Mary had married in July 1913, becoming pregnant the following year. But her husband, Graf Anton Dobrzensky von Dobrzenicz, was killed in action in September 1915, when their son Franz was barely six months old. Mary emerged from this traumatic experience with a hatred of war and a strong social conscience. Questioning the values of her class, she became a devoted reader of Die Fackel, inviting Kraus in July 1918 to stay for a fortnight at her country estate in Pottenstein (Potstejn), where she organized musical evenings for her guests (BSN 1, 462). After the war she supported the efforts of the American Junior Red Cross to alleviate the sufferings of deprived children, and her generosity led Kraus to dedicate to her a poem entitled 'Einer Geberin' ('To a Woman Bearing Gifts'; F 508–13, 18). During the following years he regularly sent her his publications, and she responded by sharing her own experiences. A few months before the death of her husband, she had received a poignant letter in which he expressed his revulsion at the cruelty of war and the ethos of military valour that sustained it. She later allowed Kraus to incorporate her dead husband's words in one of the most moving speeches of Die letzten Tage der Menschheit (III, 33).[45]

Initially, the tone of Mary's letters is rather formal, but in October 1920 the situation was complicated by a mysterious episode that occurred while both Kraus and Mechtilde Lichnowsky were her guests at Pottenstein. Mary's father Franz Graf Wenckheim, an old-style aristocrat whom they nicknamed 'the swan', caused embarrassment by claiming that he had heard footsteps during the night and seen Kraus slipping back into his room. This implies that Kraus had been paying a nocturnal visit to Mechtilde, and Mary was distressed by such a 'terribly embarrassing matter'. It was months before she succeeded in persuading her father that he must have been imagining things.[46] The tone of her letters gradually became more intimate as she abandoned the formal mode of address, and he responded in autumn 1920 by presenting her with a drawing by Félicien Rops, a clear sign of amorous intentions. Although the title of this work is unknown, the spirit of their relationship is encapsulated in the allegory 'Love Always Inspires Books' (Fig. 20b). She responded by sending him a silver cigarette case for his forty-seventh birthday (letter of 22 April 1921). Mary was a spirited woman with the courage to stand up for her own convic-

20   Amorous intentions: (a) Mary Dobrzensky   (b) 'Love Always Inspires Books' by Félicien
                                                   Rops

tions, and the papers in her literary estate suggest that she was accepted as an equal by some of the leading German and Czech writers of her day.[47] On 17 November 1920 she described to Kraus an aristocratic gathering at the Kolowrats', during which she was taunted as a 'bluestocking' and a 'Kraus groupie' ('Kraus-Verehrerin'). When the assembled company started reminiscing about the good old days of the war, she responded by defending the modern democratic order. Kraus's reply shows how closely attuned he and Mary were politically. He identifies the Kolowrats as members of the landed aristocracy who have enriched themselves through banking transactions during the war: 'They have gobbled everything up and now complain that there is nothing left.' As to the epithet 'bluestocking', he describes it as idiotic.[48] In a letter of 5 May 1925, she challenged Kraus's notorious aphorism about the 'female soul' (F 288, 15), which she found as patronizing as his condescending smile. But she added that when next he came to stay at Pottenstein, she would ensure that her father was out of the way.

Kraus's growing intimacy with Mary coincided with his estrangement from Sidonie Nadherny. In January 1924 Sidonie broke off their relationship, and it was three years before they were reconciled. In a letter of 21/22 May 1924, written after Sidonie had ignored his fiftieth birthday, Kraus tried to reassure her that his sensual experience with others was insignificant compared with the ten years they had spent together (BSN 1, 579). This letter did not reach Sidonie until the following year, and by then it was too late to repair the damage (BSN 2, 349). During Kraus's campaign to drive Imre Bekessy out of

Vienna, Mary offered him resolute support, as well as affectionate company. For her birthday on 26 January 1925, he sent her a necklace with a silver elephant pendant, wrapped in tissue paper (14 February 1925). Since the most passionate phase of this relationship coincided with Kraus's success against Bekessy, the shenanigans in Bohemian country-houses sustained his defence of the Austrian Republic.

These clandestine affairs enhance the complexity of Kraus's poetry. The number of Die Fackel published in July 1925, which opens with a squib against the corrupt financier Camillo Castiglioni and closes with a polemic against Bekessy, also contains lyrics inspired by the relationship with Mary. Her letters reveal that she offered Kraus respite from his battle with Die Stunde, and this helps us to make sense of the lines: 'when fleeing that titanic trial of strength / I found in you unconquerable frailty' ('als ich aus jenes Zweikampfs Kräftemessen / in deine unbesiegte Ohnmacht floh'). In this poem the focus is on a love that transcends individuality, as the title indicates: 'Und liebst doch alle, liebt dich einer so' ('If one man loves you, you love everyone'; F 691–6, 24). But a second poem, 'Das Wunder' ('The Miracle'), suggests that Eros was reasserting his powers in a more personal way, as the gleam in a woman's eye is compared to the light of the original Creation (F 691–6, 23). Sidonie was later to claim that these poems were written for her (BSN 2, 26), but this is most unlikely. During 1925 Mary paid repeated visits to Vienna, staying at the Imperial Hotel and using Kraus's car to make trips to the countryside. It is surprising that Kraus found time to sustain so many love affairs, when the pressure to get Die Fackel into print often led him (as he wrote to Mechtilde in December 1920) to work from early evening right through the night for sixteen hours.[49] To Mary Dobrzensky he explained in a letter of 28/29 May 1921 that it is only once a month that he can spare a few hours for the private affairs that are so dear to him.[50] The fact that these lovers' meetings were so infrequent made them all the more intense. Kraus had an exceptional ability to store emotional energy and draw on its sustenance years after the event.

In July 1925 Kraus reprinted his famous essay on Wedekind's Die Büchse der Pandora, which begins with a quotation from Rops about the fragrance of love in old age. On the facing page he published 'Vor dem Schlaf' ('Before the Onset of Sleep'), the most revealing of his poems on this theme, which anticipates the existential isolation of the moment of death. The last three strophes of this poem compellingly explore the fear of death:

Wer wird in jener Nacht nach diesen Nächten
bei dir sein um den letzten Streit zu schlichten.
Endgültiges dir helfen zu verrichten,
damit sie dort nicht allzu strenge rechten?

Dies war ein Blick aus dem Dämonenauge,
das mich im Dämmern eingenommen hatte.
So prüft das Leben mich, das nimmermatte,
ob nun noch ihm zum Widerstand ich tauge.

Noch wart ich auf das Wunder. Nichts ist wahr,
und möglich, daß sich anderes ereignet.
Nicht Gott, nur alles leugn' ich, was ihn leugnet,
und wenn er will, ist alles wunderbar.

(F 691–6, 42)

In that dark night that comes after these nights
who'll be with you to help you face your end,
fearing that you will find yourself condemned,
and who'll sustain you through that final fight?

This was a glance from that demonic eye
that overwhelmed me as I fell asleep.
Thus life, which never ceases, probes so deep,
testing if you've the courage to survive.

The miracle may happen. Nothing's true,
I wait upon events, my hopes are high.
It is the godless age that I deny,
not God's intent to shape the world anew.

The 'miracle' alludes to that moment of unexpected erotic fulfilment celebrated in the poem 'Das Wunder', but the more sombre diction of 'Vor dem
Schlaf' sets up a tension between faith, hope and love, emphasizing the poet's
vulnerability, as nights of love foreshadow the approach of death. 'Vor dem
Schlaf' is the poem Mary Dobrzensky most admired, as she explains in a letter
of July 1925: 'I never felt your *human* side so intensely as in these lines.' This
is one of the first letters in which she uses the intimate 'Du' rather than the
formal 'Sie', a sure sign of their emotional rapport.[51]

Kraus could not approach death with the equanimity of Rilke. As the two
poets explored the affinities between eros and thanatos, their paths diverged in
a way that Sidonie, who admired them both, must have found disconcerting.
In terms of poetic subtlety there is no comparison, since Kraus's lyrical diction
tends to be abstract, antithetical and alliterative. He eschewed the exploration
of objective correlatives that makes Rilke's *Neue Gedichte* so evocative, dismissing that 'thingliness' ('Dinglichkeit') as a limitation (F 640–8, 54). But the
contrast between the poets proves more instructive when we consider the
developments of the early 1920s. Rilke's *Duino Elegies* (1922), of which
Sidonie received a presentation copy shortly after publication, question the traditional conceptions of love, creativity and death with great originality: 'Is it
not time that in loving / we freed ourselves from the beloved and, trembling,
endured [...] ?' This non-possessive conception of love is complemented by a
vision of an 'eternal torrent' ('ewige Strömung') flowing between the living
and the dead, implying that death is a condition to be accepted, rather than
feared.[52]

It was in the same year that Sidonie received the sixth volume of *Worte in
Versen*, which was dedicated to her and includes several of Kraus's finest poems,

from 'Eros und der Dichter' to 'Todesfurcht' ('Fear of Death'). The contrast with Rilke surfaces most clearly in 'Auf die wunderbare Rettung der Wunderbaren' ('To the Miraculous Rescue of the Miraculous Woman'). This can be read as a riposte to Rilke's most celebrated exploration of the descent into the depths, 'Orpheus, Eurydice, Hermes', first published in the *Neue Gedichte* in 1907. In Rilke's re-enactment of the myth, Orpheus fails in his mission to rescue Eurydice from the realm of the dead not simply because he ignores the precept 'not to look back', but because Eurydice, wrapped in the mystery of her death, has already withdrawn into an inner world.[53] By contrast, Kraus's presents the rescue of a drowning woman as an allegory of salvation through love. The rescuers in his poem have to plunge through the 'death-force' ('Todgewalt') to save the woman from the torrent, and her scream, conceived as a 'final question to God' ('letzte Frage an Gott'), is answered by a miraculous reprieve (S 9, 381). The power of this poem is enhanced when we recall the events that inspired it: a bathing party in the Moldau on 11 August 1921 during which Mechtilde was sucked under by the swirling current and Kraus, aided by Sidonie and Karl Nadherny, succeeded in pulling her apparently lifeless body from the water. Through its repeated use of the word 'wir' ('we'), the poem celebrates human solidarity in the face of an existential crisis. But it understates Kraus's personal courage in wading with his friends into the torrent and plunging under water to rescue her.[54]

For Kraus, death was not a destiny to be fulfilled in a Rilkean spirit of acceptance, but a threat to be defied. Nowhere is this clearer than in 'Todesfurcht', which concludes with the following strophe:

> Todesfurcht ist, daß Natur mich bringe
> einst um alles mir lebendige Grauen.
> Jener ewigen Ruh ist nicht zu trauen.
> Ich will leiden, leben, hören, schauen:
> ewig ruhlos, daß das Werk gelinge!

> Fear of death means one day I'll be bereaved
> by nature of those shocks that help me live.
> There's no redress in that eternal peace.
> I wish eternally to suffer, love, listen and gaze,
> unresting till the work has been achieved!

By contrast with Rilke's subtle modulations, Kraus's defiant lines seem designed for declamation, and Sidonie was in the audience when he read them in public in Prague on 27 December 1921, after they had been published in *Die Fackel* (F 577–82, 67–8). While Kraus pursued Sidonie with a passion she could not fully reciprocate, her relationship with Rilke remained steadfast and undemanding. One of the finest passages in her diaries, written in English on 30 December 1926, records her feeling on hearing of the poet's death: 'He was the only man whose friendship was pure and brotherly.'[55] This was written at a time when Sidonie and Kraus were estranged, indeed it was the news of Rilke's death that prompted them to resume their correspondence (BSN 1, 585).

Acknowledging the fear of death, Kraus conceived writing as a defence. 'When I take the pen in my hand,' he once observed, 'nothing can happen to me' (F 309–10, 44). His sense of supra-personal mission, of complete absorption in his writerly task, led him to remark to Helene Kann that he didn't believe he would have to die: 'The mind must have the power to prevent death.'[56] In fact, the curvature of the spine from which he had suffered since birth resulted in severe circulation problems, which were aggravated by smoking (a habit shared with Sidonie). To correct his postural difficulties he wore a leather corset, which may have made things worse. By the early 1920s Kraus was aware that his health was failing, repeatedly complaining in his letters of sciatica, angina and sleeplessness. On 4/5 November 1921 he writes to Mechtilde that he is feeling weighed down by 'fear of death'. However, illness heightened the effect of his recitations. 'Nothing seems to be better for my voice than angina,' he wrote to Mechtilde on 29/30 March 1922.[57] He was sometimes so ill that it was a struggle to get to the concert platform for his next recitation, but almost invariably he rose to the challenge. The programme note for his last public readings contained the celebrated quip about 'performances through which an illness could be postponed'.[58]

Kraus felt that fate could not touch him once he was up there on the platform with a text to read. Pen in hand, he formulates the paradox in the mystical couplets of 'Bange Stunde' ('Anxious Hour'): 'Let me cling to this chair till my final breath: no longer to live would be worse than death!' ('Nie mögst du von diesem Sessel mich heben. / Lieber den Tod als nicht mehr zu leben!' F 474–83, 79). The fear of death recurs in his finest poems, from the sudden glimpse of a hearse in 'Der Tag' ('Daybreak') to the folksong motif of a bird announcing death in 'Nächtliche Stunde' ('Working through the Night'). In the poem 'Geheimnis' ('Secret'), dedicated to the memory of the dancer Else Cleff, he suggests that dreams may mitigate the fear of the grave (F 800–5, 59). But it was the combination of eros and thanatos that drove him, and his poetry of love has an undercurrent of dread.

How Women Experience Men

Accounts of gender relations in this period tend to marginalize the testimony of women, even though they were making advances in every sphere. Kraus accepted women's suffrage without a murmur, and it is noticeable that during the 1920s he refrained from satirizing the feminists. This was a period when women claimed the right to participate in the public sphere.[59] There was a spate of publications on both social and sexual themes by Austrian women authors, including Rosa Mayreder, Grete Meisel-Hess, Eugenie Schwarzwald, Therese Schlesinger, Helene Deutsch, Hermine Hug-Hellmuth, Anna Freud and Annie Reich, while a new generation of imaginative writers, including Vicki Baum, Anna Gmeyner, Hermynia zur Mühlen, Martina Wied, Hertha Pauli,

Hilde Spiel, Mela Hartwig and Veza Canetti, wrote fictional works from an explicitly female viewpoint. In the sphere of sexual enlightenment, the most radical question was 'How Women Experience Men' (*Wie die Frau den Mann erlebt*, 1931), title of the pioneering study by Sophie Lazarsfeld. Drawing on the work of Marriage Guidance Clinics set up by Alfred Adler, she gives ordinary women a public voice, enabling them to express their difficulties of sexual adjustment, while making allowances for the ways in which women's emancipation generates insecurity in men. She certainly deserves as much credit as her celebrated son Paul for using opinion sampling to explore uncharted territory.[60]

Adapting Sophie Lazarsfeld's question to the study of Kraus, we may ask: 'What did women see in him?' One answer lies in his ability to make his listeners feel that they were the centre of the universe, while communicating to the readers of his letters an enhanced self-esteem. He provided them with a dramaturgy, inspiring them to defy convention and live at the height of their powers. This author notorious for making enemies had a gift for retaining women's loyalty, and Sidonie – no less than Irma – always returned to Kraus. She particularly appreciated his sense of humour: 'He was such fun! He often overflowed with mischievous exuberance & then one couldn't get a serious word out of him for hours on end.'[61] His letters may not be as subtle as those of Rilke, but they sparkle with subversive wit and charged intelligence. It was flattering to receive from him ten closely written pages, a cryptic telegram or a love poem with a personal dedication. It was even more seductive to feel, sitting discreetly in the second row of a packed auditorium, that the words of a satirist are really intended for *your* ear alone. It is significant that Kraus dedicated one volume of *Worte in Versen* to the (unnamed) Sidonie as his 'listener' ('Der Hörerin').

The women in his circle included not only listeners but writers, whose personalities come vividly to life when they put pen to paper to challenge his views. The process began in the pre-war period, when Bertha Maria Denk's intellectual gifts so impressed him that he encouraged her to write her memoirs.[62] In the event, she married Richard Mayr, lead singer at the Vienna Opera, and letters from the 1930s show that Kraus kept in touch with her family, paying tribute to the singer after his death in December 1935 (F 917–22, 35).[63] Although Denk declined to write a confessional autobiography, the flavour of that period is recaptured in the memoirs of Helga Malmberg, *Widerhall des Herzens* ('Echoes of the Heart'), a book which suggests that in the period before 1914 women tended to subordinate themselves to the emotional needs of others (Malmberg was the devoted companion of Peter Altenberg). Her numerous references to Kraus portray him as a 'selfless friend'.[64] The exception to this tendency towards female self-effacement was the poet Else Lasker-Schüler. Although she too had a guru whom she adored, the Berlin bohemian Peter Hille, she developed a distinctive personal voice, reversing the practices of patriarchy by assigning symbolic roles to the men in her life (Kraus becomes the Dalai Lama). In the letters she wrote him over a period of a dozen years, she herself adopts multicultural identities, as Tino von Bagdad and Jussuf von Theben. Much as she appreciated his praise for her poetry and his personal support, she did not hesitate to speak her mind when he declined to fall in with her wishes. In letters written at the turn of the year 1923–4 she bitterly reproached him for his failure to respond to her pleas for help, when her son Paul, an aspiring artist, found himself in difficulties. She felt that Kraus was no longer so well-disposed towards her as he had been before the war.[65] Intermittent contacts continued, and in 1934 she sent him a pen-and-ink drawing for his sixtieth birthday.[66] Kraus's replies have not survived, but the numerous references to her poetry in Die Fackel show that he remained unswerving in his admiration for her work.

In the 1920s the satirist was at last prepared to concede that women can write. Indeed, he began to modify his conception of 'male' and 'female' qualities as polar opposites, conceding that literary creativity may have an androgynous quality that transcends gender roles. This shift was signalled in 1919 by a passage in his obituary tribute to Peter Altenberg, which defines the alternative values embodied in the poet's work as norms 'derived from a primal humanity, from a truly undivided godhead which lives in the sphere of creation, not yet dispersed into the confining activities of gender' (F 508–13, 9). Kraus attached such significance to this tribute that he included it as an afterword in the selection of Altenberg's writings which he published a dozen years later. The idea is illustrated by one of the texts he included, 'Frühling' ('Spring'), the evocation of one of those undifferentiated boy–girls from the poet's personal Eden – a nine-year-old playfully kicking a cardboard box along a lonely road.[67]

It was a similar fusion of supposedly 'male' and 'female' perspectives that appealed to him in the work of Mechtilde Lichnowsky: a blend of bold intelligence and sensitive intuition. These qualities are exemplified by Der Kampf mit dem Fachmann ('The Contest with the Expert'), her most original work, published under Kraus's supervision by Jahoda & Siegel. This delightful book stages a series of encounters between the Expert, who always knows best, and the Layman, whose intuitive understanding leads him – or, more often, her – to question all forms of professional deformation. Kraus was so taken by these ideas that he incorporated certain motifs from the manuscript in his own writings, including the word 'Mausi', which she had coined to ridicule pretentious 'mouseys' (F 686–90, 33).[68] Unfortunately, he failed to clear this with her in advance, and Lichnowsky made no secret of her irritation. 'It makes me wild,' she wrote in English, after discovering that Kraus had used her motif in Die Fackel. 'I have written to Kraus to tell him how I felt. [. . .] he won't do it again: use my things without asking whether he might or not. He ought to know I am a writer – not only a female friend.'[69] Kraus did indeed have a high regard for her writings, using an androgynous word to commend Der Kampf mit dem Fachmann as the work of a 'female fighter' ('Kämpferin'; F 717–23, 37). Small wonder that Lichnowsky proved such a congenial collaborator for musical adaptations of Nestroy that mocked patriarchal authority.

Lichnowsky was the most intellectually distinguished of Kraus's female friends, but there were others whose writings he also commended: Gina Kaus for her publications relating to mothers and children; and Germaine Goblot for her efforts to build bridges between French and German culture. There can be no doubt that his conception of creativity was greatly enriched by his contacts with such gifted women. By contrast with this high-powered company, Irma Karczewska understandably felt marginalized. She seems to have been content with her position as a kept woman, longing to be readmitted to Kraus's circle and once again become the object of his solicitude. Her diary contains no reference to her frustrated career as an actress, although she maintains that she was prevented from pursuing a career by a painful menstrual cycle. Since she never questions Kraus's assumptions about the subordinate role of women, it is hardly surprising that he tired of her.

Almost Too Much Love

Sidonie was far more articulate. The fact that her letters to Kraus have been lost means that she has remained an enigmatic figure, deprived of a personal voice. The editor of her letters to the American painter Albert Bloch sees her as a 'spoilt young woman with unbridled passions', whose freedom was 'dissipated into nothingness'.[70] A more balanced picture is offered by her Czech biographer, who describes her as a 'remarkable' but 'elusive' woman.[71] The most revealing sources are Sidonie's diaries and travel journals, of which only short excerpts have found their way into print.[72] The earliest of the surviving diaries dates from March 1906, and they chart the journey towards self-discovery of an emancipated woman who enjoyed foreign travel, riding, skiing, cycling, motoring and other outdoor pursuits, but was also independent-minded and widely read. Kraus once jokingly suggested that she could relate to only two books, his poems and the railway timetable (BSN 1, 364). But Sidonie was actually a cultivated woman whose mind had been enriched by her contacts with Rilke. They exchanged approximately five hundred letters, showing that, despite self-doubts, she was a gifted stylist with considerable psychological sensitivity.[73] Through Rilke, she was introduced to the work of advanced authors such as Jens Peter Jacobsen and Emile Verhaeren, James Joyce and D. H. Lawrence, Proust and Valéry, and he presented her with copies of his own works, from *Malte Laurids Brigge* to the *Duino Elegies*. Her diaries show that she was familiar with Byron and Tennyson, Novalis and Hölderlin, Dostoevsky and Tolstoy, Ibsen and Strindberg, Hauptmann and Hofmannsthal, Flaubert and the Goncourts, Baudelaire and Nietzsche, Gorky, Wedekind and Wilde. She also read works by contemporary women authors, including Gabriele Reuter, Helene Böhlau, Clara Viebig and Ricarda Huch. A diary entry of 29 July 1917 (Fig. 21) shows how subtly she brought her reading of Kierkegaard to bear on her emotional life. It is misleading to suggest that this bookishness left her with 'a totally unrealistic view of life'.[74] Rilke put the matter more perceptively when he paid tribute to her 'mature inner reality'.[75]

I had a nasty dream tonight: that a Beamter wrote
to me from Polsk, J.R. married a poor fallen girl in
Vienna! - I have written to him to Polsk & to Vienna. -
Pater Method is coming for dinner.   29.7.

I love to read Kierkegaard. For inst. - but here I must
continue in german - er spricht von den thörichten Jungfrauen
u. davon, dass sie die Leidenschaft der Erwartung verloren hatten
Ach, was half es ihnen dann, die Lampen, die ausgegangen
waren, wieder anzuzünden, als der Bräutigam erschien kam.
Er erkannte sie nicht wieder. "Das war keine Bitterkeit vom
Bräutigam, sondern eine Wahrheit." Das glaube ich, muss eine
Todsünde sein gegen das Leben - gegen unsere Seele: die
Leidenschaft der Erwartung zu verlieren! Diese Leidenschaft
muss ewig in uns brennen - als ewige Bereitschaft, als
grenzenloser Muth - sonst verlieren wir das Höchste - den
Bräutigam - den Seger, die Flamme für uns
selbst.
Weiter lese ich, dass die Gewissheit, der Beweis des Glaubens
grösster Feind, die Ungewissheit sein Zuchtmeister, u. es ist
nur aus Eitelkeit, wenn wir Beweisen wollen - was nur
zu glauben ist. Und suchen wir Beweise, dann ist es aus
mit unserem Glauben. Ist es doch auch so mit der Liebe.
Auch hier giebt es kein warum - u. suchen wir eins, dann
ist die Leidenschaft erloschen, denn die Leidenschaft fragt
nicht. Glaube u. Liebe - wir missverstehen sie wenn wir sie
verstehen wollen, "ihre verkannte höchste Leidenschaft: Glaube!"
Der Fischer an Aposteln macht, der Doge versetzen kann - wenn
man ihn hat!" -   Janvic 31.7.18

He has written from Polsk - at last at last, a sweet kind letter, &
he says: "Diana has always remained the same for me."
I lost her all round Milan the whole afternoon   Janvic 2.8.18
with Ch. & a new Seger, returning at 3½ I found the other.

21   'I love to read Kierkegaard': excerpts from Sidonie Nadherny's diary

Although Sidonie, unlike her brothers Johannes (born in March 1884) and Karl ('Charlie', her twin, born 1 December 1885), was denied a formal education, this failed to inhibit her intellectual energy. She conducted – in English – an extensive correspondence with her favourite brother Johannes, in which they shared their ideas about art, life and society. Her willingness to defy conventions is evident from an early letter in which she declares that she is against 'legal marriage' because love is *never a duty*. Love is *born* in freedom only.'[76] At the age of eighteen, she recalls in a diary note, 'science seemed to me the most sacred thing', but her family refused to allow her to attend university. Her father had died in 1895, but her mother, as a compensation for her restricted education, took her on a tour of artistic centres, beginning in 1906 with a visit to Paris. She explains that her mother's company proved irksome to her 'strongly independent nature', and 'after much pleading, I gained from mamma a certain independence'. Working through this relationship involved a great deal of heart-searching, since her mother was seriously ill (she died in July 1910). The outcome was that Sidonie was granted an annual allowance and 'could come & go as I liked' (24 May [1911]). Foreign travel was facilitated by her gift for languages. She spoke English with her siblings, having been brought up by an Irish nanny, Mary Cooney (known in the family as 'May-May'), who remained a lifelong friend. Having grown up in a Czech-speaking area and been educated by German-speaking private tutors, Sidonie could express herself in several languages. In a letter written late in life to the painter Albert Bloch, she observed: 'I really have no native language. English in the nursery, German at home with a teacher, the language of my country never properly. A real "Austrian" bringing up.'[77] Her shaky German grammar and tendency towards code-switching between languages was a source of amusement for Kraus, as Kurt Krolop has shown.[78] But she had considerable gifts of self-expression, in English as well as German, and her diaries contain impressive passages of reflection and self-analysis. She was one of a generation of Austrian women who used the freedom offered by the diary form to develop a distinctively female perspective.

Mechtilde Lichnowsky suggested, in a passage written after Sidonie's death, that there was no meeting of minds between Kraus and Sidonie.[79] The diaries tell a different story, showing that they had a great deal in common, quite apart from the sexual chemistry. Just as she conformed to his ideal of the polygamous woman, so her cosmopolitan outlook appealed to a writer opposed to nationalism in all its forms. The experience of reading Bertha von Suttner's *Die Waffen nieder!* had transformed Sidonie into a lifelong pacifist.[80] And amid the euphoria of August 1914 she was one of the few to keep her head, writing to Rilke that she 'hated' the war and the 'minds of those responsible for it'.[81] Her diary of November 1914 contains an outspoken passage criticizing the destruction of Louvain: 'Löwen, the beautiful, noble old town of the Belgians, burnt down by the Germans! And that is German culture!' There can be no doubt that she shared Kraus's hostility to what she calls 'the German spirit of destroyance'. Her comments in November 1916 on the death of Emperor Franz Joseph are equally radical: 'He ended his reign as he began it: with a bloody war. We have little to thank him for, much to curse him for. May the new Emperor Karl know better' (26 November 1916). Her sympathies lie with the Italian prisoners of war, who are employed cutting down trees in the park.

Sidonie was a cultivated woman with a passion for the arts. Through her brother Johannes she was introduced to artistic circles in Prague, and in 1909 she had her portrait painted by the leading Czech artist, Max Švabinsky. Although she found the portrait unappealing, this encounter resulted in her first passionate love affair.[82] In 1913 she returned to Paris to have her bust sculpted by Rilke's wife Clara. She loved music, especially Beethoven and Mahler, and found an outlet for her feelings at the piano. Playing Chopin's nocturnes lifted her spirits during the darkest days of the First World War: 'How many, many remembrances arise' (28 July 1918). Her contacts with Dora Pejacsevich were enhanced by her friend's exceptional musical gifts, and both Sidonie's diaries and Kraus's letters abound in references to Dora's recitals and compositions, which included settings of two of Kraus's poems.[83] Sidonie's religious life included the rituals of a pastoral community, and a late letter recalls that when the Corpus Christi procession from the village came through the park, she would set up altars bedecked with flowers.[84] Far from being confined to church, her religious faith was displaced into other realms. Her letters and diaries confirm that, through her relationship with Kraus, sex acquired a sacramental quality.[85] Her spirituality was also nourished by aesthetic experience: memories of listening to music with her brother Johannes (Beethoven's Ninth Symphony), self-immersion in artistic achievements (those Italian churches and galleries), and the contemplation of nature (especially the trees in the park). A characteristic passage written on 17 October 1911 illustrates her rapport with nature, transmitted through an expressive English style with an underlying musicality: 'A light nightfrost & a great storm have made the leaves fall of the trees that it was to look upon as a rain of gold & purple; there was a trembling throughout the parc as a beating of pulses. When I awoke this morning the nuttree before my window was naked.' No attempt in the above quotations has been made to correct Sidonie's English, which she described as 'the language of my heart'.[86]

The leitmotif of the diaries is the theme of remembrance. 'K.K., so kind, so good, & I cannot make his life happy – because my thoughts and feelings are in the past,' she writes on 22 July 1915. However, a shared orientation towards the past strengthened their affinity. Sidonie's grief over the death of her beloved brother Johannes, who committed suicide in May 1913, has already been noted.[87] Their earlier intimacy is illustrated by many passages in her diaries, including a recollection of an evening when they were travelling together in a carriage, with nightingales singing in the background, and someone took them to be lovers. Even more poignant are her memories of Josef R, a young man whom she first met in the garden of the Villa Medici in Florence in March 1911. In page after page she grieves over the knowledge that she will never be able to marry him, for reasons that are hinted at by her references to him as 'my darling boy': she was in love with a man who was eight years her junior, Count Josef Rzysczewski-Stadion.[88] The diaries never mention his full name (he is usually 'J.R.'), but they abound in recollections of the moments they spent together, especially their first encounter in the 'wondergarden': 'I entered it as a dreaming child, & left it as a crowned queen' (21 April 1911). It seems as if all her subsequent experiences were tinged with remembrance of that moment.

During this intense relationship, which lasted for two years, Sidonie assures J.R. that she would like 'to walk wrapped in thick veils', so as to avoid the intrusive glances of other men, and 'to keep myself as yours in complete purity' (26 November 1911). The Rzysczewski-Stadion family apparently owned estates in Bavaria, as well as in the eastern provinces of the Habsburg Empire, and on several occasions she and Josef met at Berchtesgaden. During a visit to this picturesque mountain resort in December 1911, she becomes aware of the tensions the relationship is causing, since he is under the pressure of 'fulfilling your duties & your parent's wishes'. She has to ask herself: 'would it really be for your good & your happiness if I were to leave you?' Although fully committed to their love, she acknowledges that they will '*never* marry' (10 December 1911). Reading *Madame Bovary* in his absence, she wonders if one ever 'really grows tired of all those voluptuous pleasures and excitements of the senses', recalling that 'refined voluptuousness' when, sitting together in the box of a theatre, 'he would slip his finger beneath my glove & gently caress the palm of my hand' (20 August 1912). After a further rendezvous in Berchtesgaden in December 1912, Sidonie was assailed by doubts: 'Am I gliding away from you? And yet – oh I love you – even if I see that what is dear & sacred to me, as beauty, nature, art, science, poesy, theatre is nothing to you.' She realizes that they will not see each other again 'for many months'. Despite 'those last long passionate kisses', she has a feeling that, unbeknown to them, it may be 'a farewell to love' (21 December 1912). To fortify her spirit, she writes out the first four lines of the poem by Robert Burns, 'Should auld acquaintance be forgot and never brought to mind' (31 December 1912); but three months later she records that she has written to her lover to renounce their 'golden dream' (28 March 1913).

The suicide of her brother Johannes on 28 May increased Sidonie's sense of isolation. From Rilke she received consoling letters, in which the poet emphasized the need to feel intimately at home in the realms of both life and death. The awareness of death, he insists, endows life with a 'new intensity'.[89] It was less than four months later that she was introduced to Kraus during a visit to Vienna. By this date her attitude towards love had become more sophisticated, and a passage in her diary of 19 September 1913 (translated below from the German), explores the implications of their first encounter:

It is humiliating for a woman to make herself inaccessible in order to stimulate a man's desire. Let him possess me, so that he can discover how inaccessible I am to him. Only then will his longing increase, only then is it directed towards me, and only then is it permissible for me to withdraw from him. We must give ourselves in order to discover what value is attributable to him and what value to his desire. [. . .] How often a man makes himself ridiculous as a lover, for he has to expose himself, & how unworthy is the woman who permits this and spurns his advances, because she fears that she will be loved less as a result. – But I want to share myself, with many people, I want to train them to enjoy pleasure, I want to distribute – illusions to them with a generous hand. – How debased is the woman whose kiss conveys a different message than her body, and whose lips awaken a longing which she fails to assuage. – But this is the reason for my feeling of abandonment and isolation. Where to find the man who will recognize & cherish all the most delicate, silent and remote dimensions of my being?

Such reflections form a striking counterpoint to the aphorisms of Kraus, to whom she had been introduced ten days earlier. During that first evening together, driving through Vienna under the stars, she felt attuned to him in a matter of minutes ('nach 10 Min. gekannt'; 12 September 1913). Her extended reflection of 19 September concludes with the observation that through him she has regained her sense that life was worth living: 'K.K. has opened up a new realm for me, new possibilities.'

During her visits to Italy Sidonie had acquired another aristocratic admirer, Count Carlo Guicciardini, with whom she was contemplating marriage. In 1915 she became engaged, motivated partly by the desire to withdraw from Kraus, partly by the pressure to marry a member of her own social class. However, in May the wedding was forestalled by the Italian declaration of war, and Kraus, unremitting in his efforts to retain her affection, spent the month of August at Janowitz, busily writing aphorisms, poems and early scenes for *Die letzten Tage der Menschheit*. She notes in her diary that, although she no longer loves him as once she did, she reluctantly accepts her role as the poet's muse: 'what more sacred duty can a woman find, than to make a great man happy, & more than that, to know that nearly all he writes, comes to him through me'. Unfortunately, this 'holy duty' obliges her to 'play the dreadful comedy, that he is to me what I to him' (2 September 1915). A fortnight later, while reading Tolstoy, she longs 'once again to live through that wonderful first period of love, when all is trembling, all awaiting, all longing, as I know it so well, & as Anna Karenina lived it through loving Vronski' (15 September 1915).

The diaries reflect Sidonie's skill in maintaining equilibrium amid the turmoil of competing attachments: her mourning for Johannes, her memories of Švabinsky, her longing for Josef R, the maelstrom of correspondence with Kraus, the intermittent attentions of Guicciardini, and her relationship with her eccentric cousin Count Max Thun, the person who had introduced her to Kraus. At the same time she had to cope with the demands of her unmarried brother Karl (Charlie), who lived with her at Janowitz and administered the estate. Charlie initially resented Kraus's presence, competing for Sidonie's attention during his visits. Summing the situation up in a late letter, she observes that she was 'surrounded by almost too much love'.[90] Lurking between the lines of her diary is the wish for a child. 'Shall I never have a child, herewith mistaking a woman's true destiny, as I ever increasingly feel?' she noted on 6 August 1912, during her relationship with Josef R. During her engagement to Guicciardini she again dreamed of having a child, but this was never to be fulfilled. Throughout this period she retained her sexual freedom. On 30 July 1915, at a time when she was planning to marry Guicciardini, she writes: 'Dear Carlo, I wish to marry you, but you must leave me free.' In this same entry she describes (switching to German) an encounter in the overnight train from Vienna to Trieste: 'Elegant gentleman with grey beard – Arab. – Terrific. – What a wonderful night.'

The desire to see J.R. remained so strong that she wrote to him several letters during the war, and on 16 September 1918 they met at the Hotel Sacher. She felt his 'old charm', and the following afternoon 'he came again to me, we had tea together & was it a wonder – with the old passion in our hearts, the old glowth in our blood – that happened, what had to happen?' But she realizes that 'this is not love', and they decide not to meet again. In this same diary entry she records: 'There was goodbye for ever between K.K. & me – he who loves me as no man ever did.' But she goes on to report a further conversation with Kraus, during which she 'told him all that happened'. It is clear that J.R. and K.K. appealed to two sides of her personality. Recalling a Sunday spent with Kraus in the woods at Sievering, she writes: 'His fine spirit & deep soul, built up on passion – I agree with none innerly so well as with him; there is something which freshens my spirit up, something "Geistiges" [spiritual] what I need, & from which J.R. is very distant. But love him I cannot' (1 October 1918).

Sidonie was not the sort of person who could say 'goodbye for ever', and her attachment to Kraus continued – with intermissions – until her dying day. Like Kraus's other aristocratic friends, she supported the newly founded Republic of Czechoslovakia, although the land reforms of the 1920s involved the forfeit of one-third of the 1,075–hectare estate belonging to the Nadherny family.[91] In the published edition of Kraus's letters, there are suggestions that her outlook was coloured by antisemitism (BSN 2, 50–1). However, during several days reading her diaries in a Kafkaesque attic in Prague, I was unable to detect any trace of prejudice against Jews. The conventional antisemitism of her social sphere seems to have influenced her reaction to Franz Werfel, as we shall see in the following chapter. But in Kraus's view it was her brother Charlie who was more likely to make antisemitic remarks (BSN 2, 246). The occasional comments about politics in her diaries suggest that she was tolerantly multicultural, and this is confirmed by her travel journals, which record her impressions of numerous visits abroad, including France, Belgium, Italy, Spain, Tunisia, Egypt, Syria and Palestine. She was determined to see the world with her own eyes, however Kraus might mock her appetite for sightseeing.

Travelling provided an alternative to the tedium of life on the Janowitz estate, and a desire to escape seems to have inspired her shortlived marriage to Max Thun. Meeting her cousin unexpectedly in Prague, she was once again in touch with younger days: 'when we speak to each other, it is as if to some dear remembrance'. She is aware that her depressive mood is causing anxiety to her friends, but she longs to escape to 'strange countries' (26 December 1919). Looking into Thun's eyes, she is sure that the time has come 'to leave my beloved Janowitz' (2 January 1920). Her tone becomes euphoric as her wedding-dress arrives 'direct from Paris', and although her family and friends warn against the marriage, she appears to have no doubts: 'his I am for ever, & I know I can trust him' (spring 1920). But in an entry written on the same page nine months later the tone has completely changed: '1921 New Year's Day. Where am I? Destroyed all dreams, destroyed that strange mysterious love that bound me to M.T.' There follows a breathless outline of the eight months they spent together, between their wedding on 12 April 1920 and her decision 'to leave him for ever' – 'had to flee because mad'. Max Thun had evidently become deranged, and after celebrating his birthday with him on 14 December she escaped to Vienna. By Christmas Eve she was reconciled with Kraus, telling him 'the whole sad story'.

This traumatic marriage undermined the sense of self-worth that had inspired her diaries. 'I never had the heart to write into this book,' she observes on 1 January 1921, 'for everything was so muddy in me, I could see no clear way.' For the first time she expresses doubts about her writing skills: 'I too would like to write my life's story, but I have no talent to express myself' (March 1921). She feels that she is 'untalented' ('talentlos') compared with her friends Dora Pejacsevich and Mechtilde Lichnowsky. Her gifts for self-expression have become completely inhibited, in both words and gestures (6 March 1921). The diary, hitherto so full of thoughts and feelings, becomes little more than a list of dates and activities, including motoring tours with Kraus. Even his attentions fail to raise her spirits: 'K.K. sends me lovely loveletters – but I – cannot love any more. I have only one wish, one longing, & I think of nothing else: to travel into foreign lands, to remain a few years away' (21 December 1921). When he suggested in February 1922 that she should join him on a journey to China, she responded with enthusiasm: 'Shall I really be in China this year?' (12 February 1922). Nothing came of this plan, and by the middle of 1922 the diary virtually fizzles out. She has lost interest in narrating her own experiences, contenting herself with 'copying the letters of K.K. into a nice leather book' (10 April 1922).

The rare diary entries of later date record major events, including the death of her brother in 1931, which leaves her soul 'full of darkness', although she has the consolation that 'K.K. is a true friend.' But, while the diaries fade away, a clear impression of Sidonie as a mature woman can be gained from her correspondence. She was a lifelong letter-writer who, like Kraus, could stay up scribbling all night. Her correspondence with her Czech friend Vaclav Wagner reflects her resilience during the early 1940s, when the SS occupied the house at Janowitz and the park was incorporated in a military training area. Her hatred of militarism became more explicit, as she did her best to defy the 'beastly Germans'.[92] Forced out of her home in February 1944, she could still claim 'the courage of endurance', listening to broadcasts by the BBC as she recovered in hospital from a cycling accident.[93] Even more revealing is her correspondence with Albert Bloch during the years 1947–50, after her return to Janowitz. In the American painter, thousands of miles away in Kansas, she found a listener to whom she could confide the feelings for Kraus that she had cherished for so long. Sidonie showed great fortitude, after the estate was confiscated by the communists in 1948, when she packed her bags and fled on foot across the border to Germany, spending her final years in exile. She emerges from the letters and diaries as a courageous woman who shared with Kraus a relationship of exceptional amplitude, shaping Janowitz into a touchstone for civilized existence.

Within a single lifetime the estate witnessed an extraordinary series of transformations: from Habsburg paternalism and aristocratic privilege to Czech republicanism and land reform, followed by the political and economic upheavals of the 1930s, German occupation and the militarization of the terrain, slave-labour camps and the deportation of the Czech community, the defeat of fascism and the backlash against those with German sympathies, and finally communist collectivization and the confiscation of the estate. The most apocalyptic imagination could never have envisaged the satanic plan to construct a gas chamber in one of the outbuildings at Janowitz, designed by the SS to service the local concentration camp, which was frustrated only by the arrival of the Red Army in May 1945.[94] Sidonie showed astonishing resilience in coping with these upheavals, sustained by her love for the garden at Janowitz, which she tended with such solicitude. She was, after all, not merely a horticulturist, sharing Kraus's vision of the garden as an image of original creation.

CHAPTER 11

The Faith of a Jewish Renegade

Kraus was a renegade in the specific sense of someone who repudiates his religion: in October 1899 he formally left the Jewish community, and on 8 April 1911 he took the more drastic step of becoming a Catholic. Kraus made no explicit reference to his baptism in *Die Fackel*, although he suggested in October 1913 that becoming a renegade may be a form of 'secret altruism' (F 386, 4). His motives in becoming a Catholic cannot be precisely reconstructed, but it was evidently not simple opportunism. An opportunist motivated by the desire for acceptance by the dominant culture would hardly have persisted, as Kraus did, in attacking the Church and satirizing the values of Christianity. He made his name before the First World War through outspoken attacks on Christian civilization, especially its sexual morality, and these attacks continued virtually undiminished after his baptism. After the outbreak of war in 1914 he extended the focus of his satire, denouncing the jingoism of the Churches almost as fiercely as that of the press. During the 1920s his attacks on the combined power of Jewish journalists and Christian politicians became increasingly strident, but it was not until March 1923 that he formally left the Church. The pretext was provided by the staging of Hofmannsthal's *Das Salzburger große Welttheater* in a church in Salzburg, which Kraus saw as sacrilege. For more perceptive readers it was clear that his fundamental motives were political and ethical, as he explains in another context. He could not forgive the Church for 'giving its blessing to bombs and poison gases' (F 613–21, 10).

Kraus thus became a double renegade, rejecting both Church and Synagogue. But sensitive readers were aware of a residual religious dimension, and the composer Ernst Krenek attributed to Kraus 'a Christian disposition [. . .] in the disconcerting guise of a cosmopolitan Jewish journalist'.[1] Despite his hostility towards the Church, Kraus's work appealed to a whole alphabet of Christian commentators.[2] For Leopold Ungar, the decision to convert to Christianity and become a Catholic priest was largely inspired by his encounter with Kraus. Moreover, it was a Catholic publishing house, the Kösel Verlag in Munich, which republished Kraus's work after the Second World War under the editorship of another convert, Heinrich Fischer, and his collaborator on that edition was the devout Gertrud Jahn. More recently, the monumental *Wörterbuch der Fackel* was masterminded by Werner Welzig, a commentator on Catholic sermons.[3]

It is not this Christian dimension that has attracted most attention in Kraus criticism, but the fascination which his work held for authors of Jewish origin: Adorno, Benjamin, Bloch and Canetti through Horkheimer, Kafka, Werner Kraft and Else Lasker-Schüler to Scholem, Torberg, Viertel and Wittgenstein. Even here, however, it is the secular aspects of the subject which have dominated discussion. The question of Kraus's affiliation with Judaism has been obscured by allegations of 'Jewish self-hatred', a slogan that does less than justice to the complexities of identity formation among assimilated Jews. Kraus's critique of destructive elements in the process of modernization has been attributed to 'the personal prejudices of an anti-Semitic Jew', while another critic asserts that there is in his work 'hardly a trace of any discussion of Jewish religion or ethics'.[4] In reality, the absence of serious references to Jewish religion or ethics is a feature of Kraus criticism, not of his own writings.[5] Surveys of secondary literature have little to say on the subject, claiming that Kraus was 'neither a philosophical nor a religious thinker', while acknowledging that Christian authors from the Brenner circle appreciated his 'eschatological orientation'.[6] This fails to do justice to Gerald Stieg's pioneering account of the efforts of members of the Brenner circle to reconcile admiration for Kraus with Christian theology and loyalty to the Church.[7] However, it is above all the biblical motifs in *Die Fackel* that deserve closer attention, if we are to appreciate his transformation of the idea of God into a specific religious discourse, rather than merely 'a generalized ontological reference'.[8]

One of the earliest numbers of *Die Fackel* provides a clue to Kraus's approach to the Bible. Reacting against the dogmatism with which Hebrew classes were taught in Austrian grammar schools, he endorsed the suggestion made by one of his correspondents: 'The profound poetry of the Old and the New Testament can and must be shown to schoolchildren in their mother tongue' (F 13, 29). The passage quoted argues for an opening of the minds of children to the whole range of Old Testament and New Testament scriptures, poetically mediated through translations into the mother tongue. Kraus accepts that the study of Hebrew is a specialized discipline which should be left to philologists and theologians, distancing himself both from Judaism (which privileges the Hebrew text of the Torah) and from Christianity (which insists on the superiority of the Greek New Testament). As an attentive reader of the Bible he was familiar with both the Luther and the Leander van Ess translations, and he repeatedly uses biblical motifs to express his critique of modernity and his sense of the sanctity of the creation. His view of the Old Testament draws a sharp distinction between myths of creation, which he endorses, and narratives of conquest, which he repudiates. But it is nevertheless from the first five books – the Jewish Torah – that he derives the fundamental concepts of his imaginative vision: the act of creation; the indwelling presence of God; the primacy of Law; the people who have gone astray; and the condition of forsakenness.

Forward Striding and Forsakenness

The paradox of faith is expressed in Kraus's memorable religious aphorism: 'The true believers are those who sense the absence of the divine' (F 351–3, 1). The period was marked by a crisis of belief, brought about by the pressures of secular modernism, and his religious response is shaped by a critique of 'progress' ('Fortschritt') – a refusal (to put the matter in more existential terms) to construe life as a process of 'forward striding' ('vorwärts schreiten'). His epigram on the 'Two Runners' ('Zwei Läufer') succinctly expresses the idea that the achievement of external goals involves the loss of 'origin' (F 300, 32). In the first fifteen years of Die Fackel the satire on 'progress' is all-pervasive. Only exceptionally does Kraus allude to progress in a positive spirit, for example in his essay of December 1910 commending the new architecture of Adolf Loos (F 313–14, 5). More typical is his response to the sinking of the Titanic in 1912, which takes the form of a collage of quotations contrasting the boastful claims of modern technology, communications and commerce with the fate of the hapless victims of the disaster: the hundreds of passengers who drowned. It is the flagship of the 'fleet of progress' that has come to grief, and he denounces the optimists of this brave new world for having 'sacrificed God to the machine' (F 347–8, 6).

This conception of godforsakenness assigns a special place to the people who have gone astray. It is not pious Jews that Kraus attacks, but those who have abandoned their faith for a shallow materialism. His hostility towards journalism, advertising, consumerism, sociology, psychoanalysis, financial speculation and war profiteering has an anti-Jewish focus, which is most explicit in his critique of the press. In a review of his position in October 1913, Kraus reflected on the 'condition of Jewry when it had not yet made itself independent of God' (F 386, 3). He went on to declare:

> I am prepared to identify with the development of Jewry as far as the Exodus but decline to take part in the dance around the Golden Calf and from that point onwards am only conscious of possessing those qualities associated with the defenders of God and the avengers of God on a people who have gone astray. (F 386, 3)

It is not the traditional Jew in a kaftan that provokes his wrath, but the modern metropolitan Jew in a dinner jacket – the streetwise city Jew who never goes to the synagogue.

At this stage it is not difficult to see why Kraus earned the admiration of conservative Christians. His view of godless Jews as advocates of 'progress' and 'modernity' is very close to the position of Catholic reactionaries, as articulated in the Reichspost. This was the most conservative phase of his career when he expressed sympathy with pillars of the establishment – aristocrats, officers and prelates (F 386, 4). He hoped that the Church could act as a bastion against secular modernism, appealing to religious faith as a defence against the shallow scientism of the modern world: 'Be Christians in self-defence' (F 354–6, 71). The outbreak of the First World War confirmed his diagnosis of the self-destructive potential of 'progress', and the address which he delivered in November 1914, 'In dieser großen Zeit' ('In this Great Age'), is permeated with religious allusions. However, his indictment was now directed not against godless Jews, but against a whole civilization that had lost its way. In autumn 1914, after the cathedral at Rheims had been bombarded by German artillery, he exclaimed: 'When will the greater age begin when the cathedrals declare war on mankind!' (F 404, 4–5). His aphorisms of October 1915 included the dictum: 'What can be decided through a world war? Only that Christianity was too weak to prevent it' (F 406–12, 97). Kraus repeatedly denounced the Churches for supporting the conflict, intensifying his indictment of Christian-ity in the post-war world – a 'hell on earth', indeed a 'world of murderers after the birth of Christ' (F 561–7, 108). To heighten his attack, Kraus returned to the Old Testament. It was not simply that the Churches had become unchristian; mankind as a whole was living in a 'godforsaken age of torment' (F 443–4, 35). In December 1922 he attacked the alliance between 'freethink-ing Jews' and 'godforsaken Christians' (F 608–12, 6–7). The terms he uses – 'gottverlassen' and 'gottverloren' – may have Christian associations, but they derive from Judaic sources. 'My God, my God, why has Thou forsaken me?' are the words attributed to Jesus on the cross in Matthew 27: 46, but the motif of being forsaken by God derives from the opening lines of Psalm 22.

Like the great satirists before him, Kraus cites Christ against the Church, suggesting that the hostility of so-called Christians on the far right was directed against 'subversives and alien elements like Jesus Christ himself' (F 554–6, 12). This implies that the teachings of Jesus are closer to the values of communists and immigrants than to those of the land-owning class. In 1922 Kraus had placed on the final page of Die letzten Tage der Menschheit the photograph of a wayside crucifix with the figure of Christ still intact, though the cross has been destroyed. In August 1924, while denouncing the rise of the swastika, he printed another photograph from a battle-scarred French cemetery, showing the mutilated figure of Christ dangling from the shattered cross by one arm (Fig. 22). This accentuates his critique of the war guilt of Christian priests, whether French or German, who blessed the grenade that 'shattered the body of Christ' (F 657–67, 3–6).

This same number of Die Fackel, published to mark the tenth anniversary of the outbreak of war, cites the testimony of a Christian pacifist, Friedrich Wilhelm Foerster. The Catholic press during the war, according to Foerster, was far more hostile to Christian values than secular newspapers like the Man-chester Guardian and Le Temps. Foerster specifically condemns the Reichspost for its failure to acknowledge the culpability of the Habsburg ruling class and

22   Shattered crucifix: photograph from the western front

for its insistence that 'Jews, Freemasons, Czechs and Socialists' were exclusively to blame for the collapse of the Monarchy. Articles by supposedly Christian editors, he argues (in a further passage quoted by Kraus), displayed 'the complete absence of a Christian conscience [. . .] nothing was there but repulsive Anti-Christ' (F 657–67, 39–42). By using emphatic type to draw attention to these phrases from Foerster's book, Kraus signalled a significant reorientation in his own position. Five years earlier, in *Die letzte Nacht*, he had identified the Anti-Christ with an individual Jewish editor, Moriz Benedikt, but now he acknowledges the power of the Anti-Christ within the Christian world.

Kraus's critique of Christianity inevitably lost him the sympathy of the *Reichspost*, but the founding of *Der Brenner* created a forum for a more sophisticated debate about the relationship between faith and society. The idea that Christianity has been betrayed *from within* places Kraus in the company of Kierkegaard. The first person to draw attention to this parallel was Theodor Haecker, a contributor to *Der Brenner* based in Germany. In a short book entitled *Soren Kierkegaard und die Philosophie der Innerlichkeit*, published in 1913, he alluded to Kraus's 'unconscious' affinity with Kierkegaard, contrasting his ethical rigour with the spurious religiosity of Franz Blei. Responding in *Die Fackel*, Kraus confirmed that he had never read a single line by the Danish religious thinker (F 395–7, 19–21). But this did not prevent other commentators from pursuing the parallel, which developed into a leitmotif among members of the Brenner circle after the war, when the journal *Der Brenner* became more explicitly Christian in tone, while positioning itself 'outside the official Catholic camp'.⁹ In April 1920, after Kraus's confrontation with the antisemites of Tyrol, the editor Ludwig Ficker equated him with Kierkegaard's prophecy in *Fear and Trembling* about the 'demon' – the avenging angel destined to awaken Christians from their apostasy (F 531–43, 188–91). The following year Carl Dallago, in another *Brenner* article, described Kraus as 'a spiritual and religious person whose attitude towards Christianity simply cannot be ignored'. After quoting Pascal's dictum that true Jews and true Christians have the same religion, he defines Kraus as 'the true Jew [. . .] who strives to return to authentic Judaism and thus reveals incomparably more of true Christianity than all these political "German" Christians'. Dallago also invokes Kierkegaard's principle that the Christian should 'live in a state of struggle', arguing that Kraus's opposition to war 'represented existential Christianity' (F 568–71, 51–5). This argument may be overstated, but the fact that Kraus quotes it at such length, highlighting the passage linking true Christianity with authentic Judaism, reflects a religious faith informed by both Gospel and Torah.

Promised Lands and Chosen Places

During the war Kraus took issue with a more problematic Jewish tradition, the narrative of conquest in the Book of Joshua. He was shocked by what modern scholarship sees as this 'most nationalistic of books', which raises the question 'how a loving God could command the wholesale extermination of nations that inhabited the Promised Land'.¹⁰ In a thought-provoking passage in *Die letzten Tage der Menschheit* (III, 14), his spokesman the Grumbler suggests that only the Jews and the Germans regard themselves as the 'chosen people', guided by their own National Deity. To the astonishment of the Optimist, he compares Hindenburg with Joshua, the victories won by German poison gas with the 'decisive deeds of Jehovah's miracle weapons'. Struck by the similarity between the ancient Hebrew and modern German dynamic of expansion, Kraus made this the subject of a long poem based on the narrative of Joshua's victory at Gibeon, brought about by a miraculous intervention which caused

the sun to 'stand still' (Joshua 10: 12). In this poem 'Gebet an die Sonne von
Gibeon', as has been pointed out in an earlier context, 'Israel' represents a
'Germany which has fallen under malign Jewish influence'.[11] Shortly after the
publication of the poem, Kraus was intrigued to discover that his argument had
been anticipated by Schopenhauer (F 462–71, 67).

It is evidently necessary to discriminate between ethically distinct traditions,
recognizing that there is no definitive form of Judaism which has to be either
accepted or rejected, but a multiplicity of competing paradigms. In the same
scene of *Die letzten Tage der Menschheit*, the Grumbler insists on the fundamental contradiction between the aggression of Joshua and the moral law of Moses,
with its fundamental precept: 'Thou shalt not kill!' And he repudiates one of
the central themes of Old Testament exegesis: the attempt to construe Joshua's
military conquests as the fulfilment of Moses' covenant with God.[12] Kraus was
aware that the books of the Old Testament were written from a variety of
ideological perspectives, and that the deeds of the Creator, with which he
imaginatively identified, belong to a different order from the conquests of
the Lord of Hosts, apostrophized by the Kaiser (F 474–83, 155). For Kraus, the
Book of Joshua lacks the authority of original revelation, indeed its myth of
the 'promised land' appears to sanction imperialism. He returned to this theme
in the aftermath of the war, when he observed Jews promoting another form
of violence, the communist revolutions in Budapest and Munich. The Old
Testament (he observes) provides the 'archetype' ('Urbild') for that syncretic
ideology of 'chosenness' and 'military force' which proved so destructive
during the war and is now threatening the peace. It is in this context that he
formulated the concept of 'violent Jewry' ('Gewaltjudentum'; F 514–18, 56).

Kraus's interpretation of the First World War in terms of a debased form of
Judaeo-Christian theology caused consternation among his contemporaries. A
member of his audience who heard him reciting 'Gebet an die Sonne von
Gibeon' reported that Kraus was blaming the Jews for the war, which
prompted Schnitzler to describe his position as that of 'the most extreme and
cowardly renegade' (AST 25 June 1916). Richard Beer-Hofmann, a poet who
eloquently affirmed his Jewish heritage, found the attitude expressed in Kraus's
poem unforgivable (F 868–72, 1). However, the Book of Joshua 'bristles with
theological difficulties', and recent biblical scholarship has placed it in a critical
perspective, suggesting that its author, the Deuteronomistic historian, was 'carried away with religious enthusiasm'.[13] The balance of evidence suggests that
the Jewish settlement of the Land of Canaan was a process of gradual infiltration, rather than dramatic military conquest.[14] The Book of Joshua, probably
written six hundred years after the events it purports to describe, contains elements of heroic myth-making, designed to raise the spirits of the Jews during
the Babylonian Exile. Theologically, the narrative illustrates the principle that
'obedience to Yahweh's commands will be rewarded with victory and prosperity; disobedience will bring the divine judgment of suffering and failure'.[15]

But historically it constitutes the kind of glorification of military prowess – 'with God on our side' – that Kraus abhorred.

Godforsakenness is presented as a two-way process: as mankind has 'progressed', so God has 'withdrawn'. The forward striding which Kraus associates with modern Jews infringes the covenant, while the crimes of the war have so completely compromised Christendom that God is felt to have abandoned the world that He created. The wicked (the Grumbler declares in *Die letzten Tage der Menschheit*) are able to mock the judge beyond the stars because his throne is so far away that his arm can no longer reach them (V, 42). This lament for a God who has withdrawn from the creation places the satirist in a difficult position. If God is construed as an absence, how is the divine ideal to be transposed into an active imaginative force within the overall narrative of *Die Fackel*? The answer lies with his conception of chosen places. Members of religious faiths attach special value to consecrated buildings, but for Kraus such places become significant only when they are reconsecrated through privileged emotional experience. He attached no special value to the Karlskirche, the grandiose baroque church in Vienna where he was baptized in 1911 with his friend Adolf Loos as his godfather. But it was a very different story in June 1915 when he visited the Catholic monastery of Einsiedeln in Switzerland in the company of Sidonie Nadherny. He was so moved by a biblical inscription on the wall of a chapel at Einsiedeln that when he returned to Vienna he looked it up in the New Testament, checking both the German translations he had to hand, Luther and Leander van Ess. He was sure that the passage occurred in chapter 10 of Paul's Epistle to the Corinthians, the source that he gives when he quotes it on 14 July in a letter to Sidonie (BSN 1, 168): 'I have chosen this place that my heart shall remain there perpetually.' He must have been quoting from memory, since the passage actually occurs in 2 Chronicles 7: 16, relating to the Temple of Solomon. Kraus confused the deeds of Solomon with the epistles of Paul – a suggestive example of misquotation. The notion of an indwelling divine presence is a Judaic conception, associated with the Hebrew word 'shekhinah'. It first occurs in the passage in Exodus 25: 8 where the Lord (anticipating the building of the Temple) says: 'Let them make Me a sanctuary that I may dwell among them.'[16]

There is a further displacement in Kraus's misquotation of Chronicles: 'house' (in the biblical passage) becomes 'place'. His sense of sanctity was not confined to the chapel at Einsiedeln, but embraced the Swiss landscape in which the chapel was located, as we can see from his poetry. More specifically, he associates the idea of a consecrated building with the house and garden of the Nadherny family at Janowitz, as Sidonie recalled after his death.[17] For an orthodox Jew or a Christian fundamentalist, this misappropriation of God's words about the Temple might seem sacrilege; but it reflects Kraus's immanent religiosity – the recovery of the divine through the experience of privileged moments and landscapes sanctified by the heart. His boldest statement about the recovery of religious faith occurs in the poem 'Aus jungen Tagen', published in April 1916 (F 418–22, 59):

Nun bin ich ganz im Licht,
das milde überglänzt mein armes Haupt.
Ich habe lange nicht an Gott geglaubt.
Nun weiß ich um sein letztes Angesicht.

Now I am swathed in light,
which gently radiates round my poor head.
For many years I'd lost my faith in God.
But now I know I'm fully in his sight.

He experienced the relationship with Sidonie as a mystical union which redeemed him from the condition of 'forsakenness'. For both lovers, an intense bereavement had shaken their faith in divine benevolence, and Kraus's poetry suggests that they responded to each other as if to a mystical reincarnation of the beloved person they mourned. For Sidonie, he is to be the emissary if not the replacement for her dead brother Johannes. For Kraus, she has removed the shadow thrown by the death of his first beloved, Annie Kalmar. Love and faith are fused through the 'mysterious radiance of sexuality' (F 418–22, 59).

This is the point of greatest difficulty for the Christian reception of Kraus's work. Ebner and other members of the Brenner circle felt alienated by the absence from his writings of love in the Christian sense of 'agape': spiritual love uniting the soul with Christ. They even denied that he was capable of the kind of 'I/Thou' relationship with another human being which might give access to spiritual transcendence.[18] But for Kraus it is the 'eros' inherent in the most intense 'I/Thou' relationships that gives access to a sense of the divine, and his poems celebrate the indwelling presence revealed through the union of male and female. His attitude towards sex is closer to Judaic sources than to Pauline Christianity. Sexual love, according to an influential Kabbalistic tradition, 'becomes the mirror of divine process on high', making it possible to recover an element of God's presence ('shekhinah') which has been exiled from the unredeemed world.[19] Kraus may not have been a student of the Kabbala, but his imagination was shaped by the myth of the Garden and the encounter between Adam and Eve, and his aphorism about true believers sensing 'the absence of the divine' relates to the creation myth from the Book of Genesis, as interpreted by Strindberg. In Strindberg's view the creation should have been exclusively male, and his quest for faith was frustrated (Kraus argues) because he failed to accept the polarity of 'day and night, man and woman' (F 351–3, 1).

Thus Kraus was haunted by the Old Testament. He certainly admired St Paul's Epistles to the Corinthians, and in July 1915 he even mentioned to Sidonie the possibility of using certain verses from this Epistle as mottoes for his collection of essays *Untergang der Welt duch schwarze Magie*. But in these passages Paul significantly stresses the continuities between Christianity and Judaism:

'Are they Hebrews? So am I. Are they Israelites? So am I. Are they the seed of Abraham? So am I. Are they ministers of Christ? I am more' (2 Corinthians 11: 22–3; BSN 1, 176–8). This is one of many passages in the New Testament which remind us of the 'inherent Jewish character of the Christian tradition'.[20] With this in mind, it is easier to understand why Kraus's writings appealed to both Christians and Jews for whom – in the words of another passage he tran-scribed from the Bible – 'the wisdom of this world is foolishness with God' (1 Corinthians, 3: 19). But Kraus diverges from Christian thinking in not regard-ing the New Testament as an advance on the Old, and in a reflection on what might constitute a 'Jewish characteristic', he mentions his admiration for the Book of Job (F 386, 6). This book expresses an existentialist form of Judaism, exciting a Kierkegaardian sense of fear and trembling that is quite distinct from the Deuteronomistic schema of rewards and punishments. Moreover, the New Testament source which Kraus quotes most frequently is a book saturated with prophetic elements from the Old Testament, the Apocalypse. His view of reli-gion is conservative rather than evolutionary: origins are more significant than advances, and retribution looms larger than redemption.

This attachment to the Old Testament proved an obstacle for Kraus's admir-ers in the Brenner circle. Devout Christians like Ficker and Haecker regarded the prophetic books of the Old Testament as a preliminary stage towards the full revelation of the purpose of God through the life of Jesus, as expressed in the gospels and epistles. They thus had difficulties with the political radicalism of Die Fackel in the aftermath of the war, while Kraus, observing the increas-ingly theological tone of Der Brenner during the 1920s, complained to Ficker that its focus had become too narrow.[21] Kraus may have remarked to a close friend that 'one can after all remain a Christian, without being a member of the Church'.[22] But devout Christians found this proposition questionable, as one can see from Haecker's 'Dialog über die Satire' ('Dialogue on Satire', 1928), a text which suggests that Christianity and satire are incompatible.[23] The prob-lem, once the more radical Dallago had dropped out of the Brenner circle, was how to elucidate the religious dimension of Kraus's aggressive style. Drawing on a passage from Kierkegaard's Fear and Trembling, Ficker presents Kraus as the Jewish 'Dämon', the spirit of negation which may serve to bring about a reawakening of true Christianity.[24] He implicitly endorses the evolutionary paradigm which proclaims that the Christian gospel of love is destined to supersede the Jewish concept of law. Stieg sums the position up succinctly when he observers that, for Ficker and his circle, Kraus the Jew represented the Old Testament, while Der Brenner proclaimed the Christian message of the New. The most rigorous member of the Brenner circle, Ferdinand Ebner, concluded that Kraus was incapable of attaining 'a really understanding rela-tionship towards Christianity'.[25] Ebner's language mysticism is reminiscent of Kraus, but as a thinker preoccupied with the fallen state of man he insisted that the original 'language of creation' ('Wort der Schöpfung') had to be fulfilled through the Christian 'language of redemption' ('Wort der Erlösung').[26]

Artistic and Divine Creation

The first two chapters of Genesis offer contrasting accounts of the creation, both of which feature significantly in *Die Fackel*. In Genesis 2: 6 we read that 'the Lord God formed man of the dust of the ground and breathed into his nostrils the breath of life'. Kraus was fascinated by this idea of the breath of God, and his oblique allusions to the myths of creation are just as significant as his grandiose invocations of 'Ursprung', an ontological concept that ultimately resists interpretation. More fundamental is the concept of 'Schöpfung' ('creation'), which features prominently in his metaphysical poetry. The poem 'Vallorbe', which recalls a visit to the valley of that name near Geneva in May 1917, provides a specific example. The name itself is celebrated in the first strophe as an 'ecstatic word' suggestive of the origin of the world. In the second of the three strophes the harmony of creation is invoked more explicitly:

> Du Sonntag der Natur, hier seitab war die Ruh.
> Ursprung der Zeit! So hat, da alles war geglückt,
> der Schöpfer diesen Kuß der Schöpfung aufgedrückt,
> hier saß der Gott am Weg zum guten Lac de Joux.   (F 472–3, 32)

> On nature's seventh day this was the place of rest.
> The origin of time! The Creator gave this kiss
> to the Creation; here, towards the lake of bliss,
> God sat beside the path, when all things had been blessed.

There are clear allusions to the first chapter of Genesis: the sabbath as day of rest, God as creator, and 'Schöpfung' in the double sense of the process of creation and the product of that process: the awe-inspiring magnificence of the natural world. But the most striking image is that of the creative kiss, which derives from that passage in Genesis 2, where God is said to 'breathe the breath of life' into 'the dust of the ground'. At another level the kiss is the poem itself, composed of words which the creative poet has imprinted on the natural world. The process has strong erotic associations, since the 'Schöpfung' that receives a kiss is an allusion to one created being in particular, the beloved whose invisible presence suffuses the poem. Kraus's letters to Sidonie, together with her own commentary, leave us in no doubt about the mystical sense of union and emotional bliss which they had shared. If Vallorbe was experienced (by both lovers) as 'God's creation' ('Gottes Schöpfung'), it is because each of them perceived the other as 'God's creature' ('Gottes [. . .] Geschöpf'). These are the phrases used by Sidonie in a letter to Kraus, and she later summed her feelings up in her diary in the words: 'The crown of all was sweet Vallorbe' (BSN 1, 439–40; 2, 275–6).

Kraus affirms an erotically inspired poetry that reconfigures the created world and celebrates the lovers' return to paradise, linking the two ideas explicitly in phrases like 'divine and artistic creation' ('die göttliche und die künstlerische Schöpfung'; F 514–18, 33). The poet, in this view, becomes a second creator who reflects through his own activity the mysteries recorded in

Genesis. This idea should not be confused with the cult of the creative genius in German Romanticism.[27] It is not a question of promethean posturing, but of reverent self-immersion in language. There are numerous passages in which Kraus insists on the correlation between divine creation and verbal creation. 'Wortschöpfung' is the concept he uses to describe poems which have this creationist quality, notably Goethe's contemplation of a tranquil landscape at dusk, disturbed by 'scarcely a breath' – 'kaum einen Hauch' (cited F 557–60, 30). For Ferdinand Ebner, this blurring of the distinction between secular poetry and holy scripture was mere aestheticism.[28] What he failed to acknowledge was Goethe's ability to endow a word like 'Hauch' with a sacral quality, comparable to the Hebrew 'ruach' of Genesis 2: 7 – the 'breath' of the creation. For Kraus it is through this heightened use of language that we may apprehend the numinous, as readers of the Bible or indeed of Goethe and Lasker-Schüler. The concept of the 'poetry' of the Old and New Testament which frames the arguments of *Die Fackel* does not imply that religious scriptures are 'only poetry'. They express an ontological conception of the relationship between language and the creation, in which spiritually attuned modern Jewish authors may participate, even though the German nationalists despise them. Else Lasker-Schüler and Peter Altenberg are 'closer to God and language than [. . .] nationalistic German writing' (F 386, 6). Intensity of poetic vision means that even a minor poet like Liliencron may be treated as canonical and read together with the prophetic books of Isaiah, Jeremiah and the Book of Revelation (F 404, 20). This is linked to the idea that the original act of creation was linguistic: 'And God said, Let there be light: and there was light. And God saw the light, that it was good' (Genesis 1: 3–4). According to Jewish tradition the original act of creation was a speech act: 'The world was created by ten sayings.'[29] As a more modern critic puts it: in Genesis the forms of life are '*spoken* into existence'.[30]

The nature of that speaking is analysed in Kraus's most suggestive essay on the relationship between language and the creation, which focuses on what might appear to be the least significant of German words, the neuter pronoun 'es':

> Denn in 'Es werde Licht' ist das 'es' so wahr ein Subjekt, als im Anfang das Wort war. Das stärkste Subjekt, das es im Bereich der Schöpfung gegeben hat, jenes, das Licht wurde, jenes, das Tag wird, jenes, das Abend werden will. (Alles hängt davon ab; alles kann Relativsatz werden.) Es: das Chaos, die Sphäre, das All, das Größte, Gefühlteste, welches schon da ist vor jenem, das daraus erst entsteht. [. . .] 'Und Gott sahe, daß es gut war'. (F 572–6, 49–50)

> For in the phrase 'It shall be light' the 'it' is as truly a subject as the Word was in the beginning. The strongest subject that has ever existed in the realm of creation, that which became light, that which becomes day, that which heralds the approach of evening. (Everything depends on it; everything can become a relative clause.) It: Chaos, the Sphere, the Universe, that which is greatest and felt most intensely, that which is already there before the predicate which first arises from within it. [. . .] 'And God saw that it was good.'

Orthodox theologians, Jewish and Christian, take Genesis to imply a process of 'creation out of nothing'.[31] Kraus's imagination seizes on the particular form that Genesis 1: 3 takes in Luther's German translation: not 'Let there be light' but 'Es werde Licht' ('It shall be light'). This grammatically and epistemologically mysterious 'es' is one of the factors that led him, anticipating Heidegger, to attribute a particular profundity to German. But Heidegger's highlighting of the phrase 'Es gibt' ('It gives'), adumbrated in *Sein und Zeit* (1927) and elucidated in his 'Letter on "Humanism"' (1947), presupposes an ethically neutral ontology deriving from the pre-Socratic vitalism of Parmenides.[32] By contrast, Kraus's thinking about language is rooted in the Judaic tradition, conceiving the original 'Es' as prime mover of 'divine creation' ('Gottesschöpfung'; F 876–84, 151).

Kraus's creative vision can be traced back to an aphorism written in 1912, one year after his baptism: 'There is no antithesis in the creation, for everything within it is free of contradiction and beyond comparison. It is only the distancing of the world from the Creator that makes space for the impulse to find in every contrariety the image that has been lost' (F 360–2, 1). In that same period he coined the word 'gegenschöpferisch' ('counter-creative') to define the religious impulse underlying his satire: 'This counter-creative "And saw that it was not good" – one day this will be understood even by those who are implicated! I invent what exists. [. . .] In saying that, by God, I do not imagine that I am God, but I know that it is my miserable role to gather up the pieces of the falling world from below' (F 343–4, 6–7). In conventional terms, derived from Jean Paul's treatise *Vorschule der Ästhetik*, counter-creative satire is structured according to the principle of the 'inverted sublime' ('das umgekehrte Erhabene'). Taking up this concept, Kraus suggests that the 'inverted sublime' is the product of his own style of satirical wit, rather than the more amorphous phenomenon of humour. In focusing on a specific target, wit 'destroys the finite through the contrast with the eternal idea' (F 577–82, 46).

The principle of counter-creation not only shapes Kraus's prose satire, but also infuses his poetry. Where poems like 'Vallorbe' are radiant with sunshine, there are other texts inspired by nocturnal forces. These poems by an author who habitually worked at night, complement his satirical writings portraying a benighted world. This gives a paradoxical quality to his rewriting of the biblical concept of the creation of night and day. Night may be a time of prayer and vigil, but it is also haunted by demons. Some of his most complex poems express disturbing doubts about a mode of creativity which leaves him wrestling with misshapen beings, notably 'Vergeltung' ('Retribution'; F 691–6, 57), a sonnet about haunted consciousness on the threshold of sleep. The climax comes in the final six lines:

Ein Mißgestaltes hat mir mißgeklungen,
daß ich mich nachtwärts dieser Schöpfung schäme
eh meine müden Sinne ausgerungen.

Und wie ich in das Schreckbild mich bequeme,
hat ein Geräusch mich in den Schlaf gesungen,
damit an Aug und Ohr es Rache nehme.

A grotesque shape produced such raucous noise
that struggling through the night I feel ashamed
of this creation, till my senses find repose.

Absorbing this stark image of my fears,
I'm sung to sleep by an insistent voice
which takes revenge on both my eyes and ears.

The double meaning is again clear: the poet haunted by misshapen beings feels ashamed of *this* creation – his own writing. 'Schöpfung' is a chimeric word capable of numerous permutations such as 'Wortschöpfung' ('verbal creation'), 'Nachschöpfung' ('re-creation') and 'Einschöpfung' ('interpolated creativity'; F 572–6, 61–3). Kraus's self-immersion in language leads him to endow even the most trivial details with mystical undertones, asserting that 'a missing comma could reverse the meaning of the creation' (F 474–83, 4). For a more conventional religious thinker like Carl Dallago, it was not necessarily a merit that he was so attached to the 'perfection of the written word' (F 568–71, 51). But Kraus, undeterred by the vicissitudes of polemical engagement, continued to link language with the 'breath of life', committing himself to an art that 'bears witness to the divine creation by generating form out of the element of language' (F 800–5, 76).

The Long Breath of Language

It was not through the Christian gospel that Kraus sought redemption, but through self-immersion in language. His aim is summed up in a fine passage from the poem 'Nach zwanzig Jahren', published in 1919:

Kunst und Natur, die Liebe und der Traum –
vielfacher Antrieb, sei's woher es sei,
der Schöpfung ihrer Ehre zu erstatten!
Und hinter allem der entsühnte Mensch,
der magisch seine Sprache wiederfindet.

(F 508–13, 7)

By means of art and nature, love and dream,
a diverse impulse, from whatever source,
to give creation back the honour due!
And at the last mankind will be redeemed
through language that's been magically retrieved.

The word 'entsühnt' combines elements of both Christian penance ('Sühne') and Judaic atonement ('Versöhnung'), just as Kraus's reflections on language invoke both Genesis and St John. Echoes of both traditions pervade his polemics against the deformation of the world through the profane language of the media. The abuse of language is a characteristic theme of twentieth-century writing, but Kraus's critique is distinguished from that of secular satirists like Tucholsky, Shaw or Orwell by its religious overtones. He did not regard the debasement of language as a transient phenomenon, stressing, in the 'Song of the Media Mogul', its ontological implications:

Im Anfang war die Presse,	In the beginning was the press,
und dann erschien die Welt.[33]	and then the world was born.

Where the 'word' that was 'in the beginning' fills Christians with hope, Kraus uses its absence to measure the fallen state of the world. Echoing the language of Genesis, he reaffirms the all-encompassing 'breath' of creation, that gift of the linguistic faculty which enables speakers of all mother tongues to apprehend the divine. His own writing attempts to catch the 'breath through which an idea becomes word' – a self-dedication to scripture which he sees as a 'Jewish characteristic' (F 386, 5–6).

Kraus sensed that the German language was being deprived of its spiritual breath: 'Die Sprache athmet nicht' (F 413–17, 108). That is what inspires his polemic against the reformers who were determined to eliminate from modern German orthography the 'Hauchlaut' – the h-sound pronounced with an audible release of breath. In 1915 the modernizers announced that in the interests of economy words like 'Thau' (dew) and 'Thränen' (tears) were to be spelt as 'Tau' and 'Tränen'. Like Schopenhauer, and other philosophers of language before him, Kraus regarded this aspirated 'h' as a 'consecrated character' (F 413–17, 117). Denouncing the spelling reform as a palpable act of barbarism, he responded with an 'Elegy on the Death of a Sound', in which the link with Genesis is explicitly made: 'Ein Tropf ist nur aus Lem, ihm fehlt der Hauch / Von Gottes Segen' ('These dolts are made of cla, they lack the breath / that's blessed by God'; F 413–17, 110). By removing the 'h' from the word 'Lehm' (clay), Kraus takes the policy of the reformers to its logical extreme. The biblical word is deprived of its sonorously elongated vowel and reduced to an abrupt monosyllable (comparable to the effect of removing the 'y' from English 'clay'). The loss of the aspirate signals the destruction of that 'living soul' into which God breathed 'the breath of life' (Genesis 2: 7). In pronouncing the traditional German words for 'breath' with their drawn-out aspirated 'h' – 'Athem' and 'Hauch' – we re-enact that primal exhalation. Hence Kraus's insistence on the sacramental quality of 'Wanderers Nachtlied', the Goethe poem in which the word 'Hauch' is again privileged. This idea echoes the transcendental wordplay of the Romantic period, especially the association of the forcible breathing represented by the letter 'h' with the origins of speech. Seen in this perspective, the efforts of German reformers to introduce a more logical orthography by eliminating the letter 'h' reflect a shallow rationalism, as Johann Georg Hamann had pointed out over a hundred years before Kraus.[34]

At times the biblical allusions in *Die Fackel* may seem rather obvious, as in Kraus's repeated imprecations against worship of the Golden Calf (F 632–9,

147) or his self-identification with Samson slaying the Philistines (F 657–67, 77). But his art of counter-creation is at its most effective when it relies on intertextual allusion. The climax of 'Reklamefahrten zur Hölle' is all the more effective for its vision of a world transformed into a 'den of thieves' ('Mördergrube'), a phrase that echoes both Jeremiah 7: 11 and Matthew 21: 13. These biblical echoes help to explain why Kraus's concept of redemptive literary creation appealed to Christian thinkers like Ludwig Ficker. In a tribute to mark Kraus's sixtieth birthday, Ficker acknowledged the satirist's right to represent the voice of God 'in the image of his own linguistic creation'. He went on to suggest that something of the primal vision may be preserved even in texts which represent hell on earth: 'Time and again Karl Kraus still finds the lost paradise on earth, which he essentially seeks, in the image of his own creation [Schöpfung], even when it reflects hell on earth in a heightened form of realism – a true sign of thought.'[35] This is as far as any Christian thinker could legitimately go in acknowledging the religious dimension of Kraus's work. But after his death in June 1936 there was an exchange of letters between Ficker and the person most intimate with Kraus's spiritual self, Sidonie Nadherny, who tried – in vain – to arrange for him to be buried under the sign of the cross. Ficker comforted her by suggesting that Kraus could be seen as 'a messenger of the Lord', heralding '*the second coming of Christ*'.[36] This reading of his work in terms of eschatalogical Christianity presupposes a more fundamental frame of reference: the messianic Judaism associated with Walter Benjamin and Gershom Scholem.

Origins and Angels

The essay by Walter Benjamin published in the *Frankfurter Zeitung* in March 1931 is one of the most original contributions to Kraus criticism, containing seminal insights such as the paradox of the 'true mask'.[37] But further investigations have shown that his argument is compromised by the use of keywords that are both conceptually unclear and ideologically suspect. Terms like 'Allmensch' ('Cosmic Man') and 'Dämon' ('Demon'), which Benjamin uses as sub-headings, echo the irrationalism of Alfred Rosenberg and Ludwig Klages.[38] Kraus himself was perplexed, although he acknowledged the essay to be 'certainly well intended and presumably also well thought out' (F 852–6, 27). Gershom Scholem was even more sceptical, suggesting to Benjamin, in a letter of 30 March 1931, that the essay was flawed by a 'fantastic discrepancy' between metaphysical insight and materialistic terminology.[39]

Benjamin's essay begins by recalling the 'messenger' in old engravings who 'rushes towards us crying aloud, his hair on end, brandishing a sheet of paper in his hands, a sheet full of war and pestilence'.[40] The motif of the 'messenger' gives the essay its overall structure, setting up a tension between the political and religious realms. Politically, Kraus is seen as 'the messenger of a more real humanism', although his programme has a paradoxically regressive element: 'to reverse the development of bourgeois-capitalist affairs to a condition that was never theirs'. The Marxist terminology is indeed difficult to reconcile with the transformation of the messenger into an 'angel', but the argument is most persuasive when it focuses on processes of communication, especially Kraus's 'campaign against clichés' and his commitment to the 'sphere of law'. Kraus's theory of language and passion for justice are linked with Judaic theology through the suggestion that he reveres 'divine justice as language'. In his indictment of the legal system, as Benjamin construes it, the charge is 'high treason committed by the law against righteousness'. This is achieved through a technique of quotation that sets up a tension between the sacred and the profane: 'Language proves to be the matrix of righteousness through punitive and redemptive quotation'.[41]

Benjamin's use of the word 'Gerechtigkeit' creates difficulties for the translator, since it modulates between secular and religious registers – from 'justice' into 'righteousness'. The theological implications become clear when we trace this tension back to Scholem's early diaries, which record his discussions with Benjamin about the wealth of words relating to the law, both in German and in Hebrew. Scholem transcribed into his diary a short text by Benjamin entitled 'Notes for a Study of the Category of Righteousness'. Here, Benjamin explicitly distinguishes 'Recht' (Hebrew 'mishpat') from 'Gerechtigkeit' (Hebrew 'zedek'). 'Righteousness', Benjamin suggests, is not a virtue like any other, but an all-encompassing condition of existence: 'In God all virtues have the form of righteousness' (GST 1, 401–2). Scholem, who was immersed in the study of the Torah, goes on to link Benjamin's conception of righteousness with 'shekhinah' – the indwelling presence of God: 'The righteous prepare the earth as a place for the divine. That is righteousness: to make the earth the seat of shekhinah' (GST 1, 419). Given this tradition of religious reflection, it is not surprising that Scholem saw Benjamin's Kraus essay as essentially 'theological'.[42]

It is also to Scholem that we must turn if we are to understand the transformation of 'messenger' into 'angel'. His conversations with Benjamin during the early 1920s included discussions of 'Jewish ideas about angels' ('jüdische Angelologie'), with reference to the Talmud and the Kabbala. Looking back on this period many years later, in the essay 'Walter Benjamin and his Angel', he recalls that the angel motif also had a visual source: the watercolour *Angelus Novus* by Paul Klee, which Benjamin purchased in Munich in the summer of 1921 (Fig. 23). During the following years, the reflection of this image in Benjamin's writings underwent a series of transformations, with the angel sometimes representing the 'heavenly self of man', sometimes his darker 'Luciferian element'.[43] Most significant of all is the reversal of time associated with Benjamin's conception of the angel: 'He has plunged forward out of the future and gone back into it again'. This, Scholem explains, is the significance of the Krausian paradox which Benjamin was so fond of citing: 'Origin is the goal' ('Ursprung ist das Ziel').[44]

This paradox derives from the poems 'Two Runners' ('Zwei Läufer') and 'The Dying Man' ('Der sterbende Mensch'), which first appeared in *Die Fackel* before the war (F 300, 32 & 381–3, 74–6). Republished in 1916 in the first

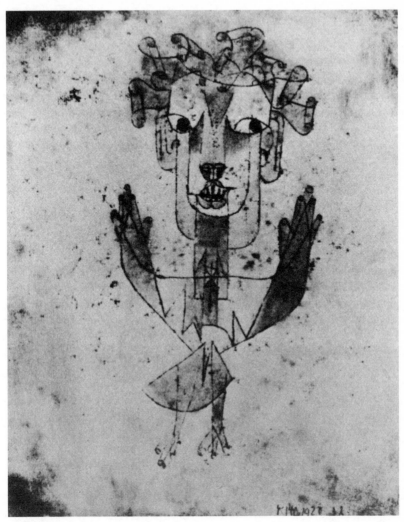

23   *Angelus Novus*, 2002, 32 by Paul Klee

volume of *Worte in Versen*, this motif prompted protracted discussions between
Benjamin and Scholem.[45] My earlier research on Kraus's religious poetry
suggested a link with the idea of returning to the 'origin' ('ursprung') in the
sermons of Johannes Tauler.[46] But Scholem's testimony suggests that Talmudic
sources may also be relevant, especially those that explore the relationship
between secular and messianic time. There are numerous passages in his diaries
which anticipate the idea of turning back to the future. His defence of the retrospective character of Judaism emerged from a complex intellectual debate
with Herzl, Buber, Kraus and Benjamin. The initial enthusiasm for Buber is
displaced, under the influence of Benjamin, by a growing scepticism about

Buber's emotive cult of 'the Jewish experience' (GST 1, 386 & 451). In a series of further entries he takes issue with Kraus's definition of Jewish nationalism as a form of 'regression'. According to Kraus, 'Jewish nationalism should be welcomed as one of those forms of regression which lead back out of a pseudonymous culture to the point where its content is again worthy of becoming a problem' (F 333, 9). Scholem's comment is that Kraus ought to realize that *'to turn back is not to take flight'* (GST 2, 63–4 & 203). This riposte, which makes the Zionist 'return' conditional on spiritual conversion, also forms one of the most fundamental of Scholem's 'Ninety-five Theses on Jewry and Zionism' (GST 2, 303). Distancing himself from the pioneering ethos of the Zionist youth movement, Scholem developed a conception of 'Umkehr' that implies a spiritual rather than physical 'return'.

At the heart of this idea lies the assumption that Judaic culture should situate itself 'outside the European time-scheme' (GST 2, 108). Liberal Judaism has made the mistake of adjusting the concept of messianic expectation to a shallow notion of secular 'progress' (GST 2, 330–1). The 'messianic age' presupposes the non-linear time-scheme expressed through the conjunction of reversal ('*waw ha-hippukh*'; GST 2, 305). In Hebrew, Scholem insists, 'to look backwards is simultaneously to look into the future' (GST 2, 324). It is this deconstruction of linear time that he and Benjamin admired in Kraus's visionary writings. In his study *The Origin of German Tragic Drama*, Benjamin insists that the word 'Ursprung' is dynamic, encompassing both 'development and disappearance'. This leads, in the Kraus essay, to the pairing of 'Ursprung' with 'Zerstörung' ('destruction').[47] It this paradoxical combination that – in the final paragraph – makes it possible for the messenger to overcome the realm of the demonic and emerge as a 'new angel'. The link with Talmudic legend is explicitly suggested.[48]

The debate between Scholem and Benjamin, with its intermittent references to Kraus, continued through their correspondence of the 1930s. It was Scholem who came closest to attaining his goal, immersing himself in the Kabbala and emigrating to Jerusalem, where he became professor of Jewish mysticism at the Hebrew University. Meanwhile Benjamin, in exile in France after 1933, continued to find comfort in Kraus's paradoxical precept. The defining feature in any intellectual rescue operation, he wrote to Theodor and Gretl Adorno on 19 June 1938, 'can never be something progressive; it can be as similar to something regressive as the goal which Kraus calls origin'.[49] The phrase 'Ursprung ist das Ziel' is cited again in Benjamin's posthumously published 'Theses on the Philosophy of History'. But goal and origin proved incompatible for a thinker who tried to combine an attachment to theology with a commitment to communism. In the 'Theses', Klee's *Angelus Novus* underwent a final transformation, becoming the angel of history. With his back to the future, the angel is driven by the storm from paradise, gazing with horror at the ruins created by 'progress'. The tragic circumstances in which this text was written transformed the angel into the symbol of political defeat.

CHAPTER 12

Expressionist Politics and Constructions of the 'Other'

Cultural politics between the wars tended to blur the boundaries between poetic 'vision' and political 'blueprint'.[1] The inflation of political discourse during the Expressionist period influenced a whole generation of German intellectuals, with consequences that were fiercely debated by left-wing authors after they were forced into exile in the 1930s. Some (led by Lukács) saw Expressionism as a source of irrationality in politics, while others (including Brecht) defended its aesthetic innovations. Contributors to this 'Expressionism Debate' now tended to see the movement as an aberration that played into the hands of the Nazis.[2] But their findings had been anticipated in *Die Fackel* twenty years earlier, when the self-indulgence of Expressionist politics became one of Kraus's major themes. In January 1921 he mocked the Berlin Expressionists and Dadaists for acting as if they had 'conquered Germany' (F 557–60, 17). Moreover, his critique of politicized religiosity throws unexpected light on the sources of Nazi propaganda.

Fellow Travellers and the Syntax of Collective Experience

Initially, Kraus welcomed the innovations of the Expressionist generation, opening the pages of *Die Fackel* to a new generation of writers, including Albert Ehrenstein, Ernst Blass, Kurt Hiller, Jakob van Hoddis, Else Lasker-Schüler, Erich Mühsam and Ludwig Rubiner. He also invited left-wing visionaries like Kurt Eisner and Gustav Landauer to contribute (F 601–7, 66–7) and was instrumental in helping Herwarth Walden to found the pioneering Expressionist periodical *Der Sturm*. He was more sceptical about the aims of Franz Pfemfert's *Die Aktion*, the rival journal of the Berlin avant-garde; but even here there were significant affinities, notably a shared hostility to militarism.[3] Kraus enthusiastically praised *Der Brenner*, the Innsbruck magazine that published the poetry of Georg Trakl, and he also promoted the work of Franz Werfel, the most innovative poet from Prague. This phase of fruitful interaction with members of the avant-garde has tended to be overshadowed by the subsequent polemics, but Kraus's programme around 1910 was similar to theirs: 'Art can only come from repudiation. Only from the scream of protest, not from the soothing gesture' (F 360–2, 22). His extensive correspondence with Walden reveals striking affinities in their conception of art, which – as Kraus noted after the successful launch of *Der Sturm* – should have a dimension of 'incomprehensibility'.[4] Introduced by Walden in December 1910 to Georg Heym and the poets of the 'Neopathetisches Cabaret', he was impressed by their innovations. Moreover, his own work won him an ecstatic following, especially his critique of sexual hypocrisy in essays that were reprinted in *Der Sturm*. Trakl was speaking for his generation of radical poets when he eulogized Kraus as 'white high priest of truth'.[5] Reading the bitter attacks on Kraus which occur in the later writings of Pfemfert and Werfel, Ehrenstein, Haas and Brod, one would scarcely imagine that they had earlier been among his most passionate admirers.[6]

By June 1912, however, Kraus was already expressing reservations about the Berlin avant-garde, ironizing the use of collective labels like 'Futuristen' or 'Neopathetiker'. Walden's decision to promote the theories of Marinetti marked the turning-point. The Futurist manifestos, several of which were published in *Der Sturm* during 1912, propounded an ideology of aggression and war, while their prescriptions for poetry involved the destruction of syntax and the random scattering of words on the page. For Kraus, this programme betrayed a 'violent spiritual impoverishment' (F 351–3, 53). In his letters to Walden, he explained why he felt compelled to repudiate the artistic programme of *Der Sturm*. Much as he appreciated his musical compositions, he could no longer support Walden's editorial strategy.[7] However, the more subtle innovations of Expressionism continued to be welcomed, particularly the melodious verses of Else Lasker-Schüler, whom Kraus praised as 'the true Expressionist of all forms inherent in nature' (F 757–8, 35–6).

The outbreak of the First World War marked a decisive caesura. It was only logical for the Futurists, who had celebrated war as 'the world's only hygiene', to clamour for Italy to join the conflict, but in Germany the war was celebrated by writers who had hitherto been pacifists and democrats, including Gerhart Hauptmann and Alfred Kerr. The poets of the Expressionist generation, with few exceptions, were also swept away by the patriotic euphoria.[8] For Kraus, this was a betrayal of the fundamental principle that authentic art should be oppositional (F 360–2, 22), and the treason of the intellectuals became one of his most impassioned themes.[9] The keynote of German poetry became a bloodthirsty religiosity, blending the aesthetics of Marinetti with those of the Kaiser.[10] Richard Dehmel set the tone, drawing Futuristic analogies between machine-gun fire and 'the music of the spheres' (F 418–22, 42). Even poets who attempted to articulate dissent, like Carl Einstein, used an idiom so grotesquely distorted as to be self-defeating (F 454–6, 37). For Kraus this abuse of language is the hallmark of the Expressionists (F 457–61, 59), and he condemns their dislocations just as fiercely as the diffuseness of 'neues Pathos'

(F 484–98, 95). Moreover he notes in 1917 that new Expressionist journals like *Marsyas* are being produced in a luxurious format, designed to appeal to industrialists made rich by the war (F 457–61, 58–61).

Kraus was sceptical about the claim that these poets regarded the war as an atrocity (F 462–71, 89). He was even more dismayed that so many Austrian writers were now working for military propaganda offices like the Kriegsarchiv, Kriegsfürsorgeamt and Kriegspressequartier, including Hofmannsthal, Stefan Zweig, Robert Musil, Alfred Polgar, Franz Werfel, Franz Blei, Felix Salten, Alfred Ehrenstein, Hugo Sonnenschein, Egon Erwin Kisch, Franz Karl Ginzkey, Franz Theodor Csokor, Karl Hans Strobl and Rudolf Hans Bartsch. Some of these, like Zweig and Werfel, were convinced pacifists, but their acceptance of positions in the propaganda machine prevented them from making any significant protest. Even Rilke, a reluctant conscript to the Kriegsarchiv, had contributed to the euphoric mood of August 1914 with a celebration of the god of war in his 'Five Songs' ('Fünf Gesänge').[11] Kraus, as a result of the curvature of his spine, was exempt from military service on medical grounds. His criticisms were resented by authors who had opted for a safe desk job, appalled by the prospect of dying for a cause in which they did not believe. For them this was a strategy for survival, but for the satirist it was a sell-out to the propaganda machine, doubly despicable since they were saving their own skins by urging others to die, and he vowed that he would never allow their conduct to be forgotten (F 474–83, 156–8).

Even Kraus was not prepared for the debacle of November 1918. Caught up in the mood of revolutionary euphoria, a number of poets who had been employed in military propaganda offices experienced a sudden conversion to communism. Discarding their Habsburg military uniforms, Blei, Werfel, Kisch, Ehrenstein and Sonnenschein became supporters of the Red Guard, a revolutionary military unit which was planning the forcible occupation of parliament, banks and newspaper offices. Their efforts were so poorly organized as to have an air of farce.[12] But in Munich the revolutionary movement had more serious consequences, while in Budapest, as we have seen, the communist coup had tragic consequences. In retrospect, it is clear that the posturings of poets like Werfel bore little relation to the realities of power, but Kraus deserves credit for diagnosing the spuriousness of this form of literary politics while it was actually taking place. Two substantial essays on this theme were published in *Die Fackel* at the end of July 1919 under the titles 'Proteste' and 'Gespenster' ('Protests' and 'Ghosts'). By this date both the Spartacus rising in Berlin and the Bavarian Soviet Republic had been defeated with considerable bloodshed. Luxemburg, Liebknecht, Eisner and Landauer had been brutally done to death, while the dramatist Ernst Toller was on trial for his life for his part in the Munich revolution. In the Soviet Union, however, the military defence of the Bolshevik Revolution was being organized by a former patron of the Café Central, Leon Trotsky – an incongruous figure in military uniform, as Kraus observed (F 697–705, 4).

Austrian authors fresh from service in the Kriegsarchiv were prominent in the chorus of revolutionary solidarity. To show up the spuriousness of their proclamations, Kraus cited a letter protesting against the possible execution of Toller, which had been published over the names of a group of radical poets without their knowledge or consent. Instead of denouncing this document as a forgery, several of its purported signatories – who included Blei, Ehrenstein, Gütersloh, Sonnenschein and Werfel – issued a statement thanking the unknown author who had acted on their behalf. Kraus's response was to concoct a hoax proclamation of his own, in which these same signatories acknowledge that they had lacked the courage during the war to make the kind of humanitarian protest which they now so readily endorse. Since they had all then been working for military propaganda agencies, they could not afford to put their own safety at risk by protesting against military executions (F 514–18, 2). The hoax appeared so plausible that it was published in June 1919 by leading Viennese newspapers, including the *Neues Wiener Tagblatt* and the *Neue Freie Presse*. Kraus drove his point home by means of a systematic review of the positions of Viennese intellectuals who were flirting with revolution, including the poets Franz Werfel and Hugo Sonnenschein and the painter Paris Gütersloh. The aesthete Franz Blei exemplifies the ideological instability of the age – 'powder-puff in one hand, holy water in the other, pious and enlightened, sceptic and enthusiast'. As editor of literary periodicals financed by the war-profiteer Josef Kranz, Blei is rightly identified as a pivotal figure in avant-garde artistic circles.[13] His programme in 1919, proclaimed in the journal *Die Rettung* ('Salvation'), contains a slogan cited by Kraus to epitomize the confusions of the age: 'Long live Communism and the Catholic Church!' (F 514–18, 17–18).

Kraus concedes that his satire may have been too harsh on Ehrenstein and Sonnenschein, both of whom published poetry during the war expressing their sense of revulsion (F 514–18, 10–11).[14] But he insists that the undisciplined use of language undermines their work both as poetry and as protest, quoting Sonnenschein's poem 'Ekel vor Europa' ('Disgust at Europe') as an example of self-defeating rhetoric. Six months later, in January 1920, he quoted another purple passage from Sonnenschein's most recent book, *Die Legende vom weltverkommenen Sonka*, a rhapsodic expression of the quest for God (F 521–30, 83–5). Kraus perceived the confusion of religiosity with politics as the central flaw of the Expressionist movement: Sonnenschein was a communist who wrote mystical verses. His political convictions, as Kraus acknowledges, deserve 'respect', but the blending of politics with poetry is a fatal flaw (F 521–30, 81). A similar ambivalence is identified in the writings of Werfel, who in January 1917 had published an influential essay entitled 'Die christliche Sendung' ('The Christian Mission'), repudiating the 'activism' advocated by Kurt Hiller. By November 1919 Werfel had completed a volte-face, making a speech to a potentially revolutionary crowd on the streets of Vienna urging them to occupy the Central Bank and overthrow the capitalist system. Werfel's political transformation suggests that the poets of the Expressionist generation, especially those from Prague, are floating in an ideological void: 'If from the playground of childish feelings one is swept aloft into the misty and wispy realm of ideas, then Communism offers something to hold on to' (F 514–18, l6). Such posturing may have serious consequences, since coups dreamed up in the coffee-house may lead to bloodshed in the streets, if intellectuals like Toller are permitted to 'work off their adolescent hang-ups with machine-guns' (F 514–18, 20). Kraus shows little understanding for the aesthetic experiments of Expressionism, but he rightly censured opportunists like the actor Alexander Moissi for changing their 'ideological shirts' (F 514–18, 14 & 53). The longing for solidarity with a collective, he insists, is politically indeterminate – just as likely to veer towards the extreme right as towards the left. His critique of the communist fellow travellers of 1919 can thus be related to his attack on another Expressionist poet, Gottfried Benn, fifteen years later. Benn's conversion to Nazism in 1933 is perceived in *Dritte Walpurgisnacht* as a mirror image of left-wing radicalism, both responses being rooted in irrationalism. Goebbels, too, is seen as the heir of Expressionism, since his propaganda exploits the 'reduced syntax that Expressionism made available for collective experience' (DW 42/55).

Goebbels and the Emotional Bonds of Community

Joseph Goebbels, who was born in the Rhineland in 1897, had the credentials for a literary career. After showing precocious talent at school, he studied at Heidelberg under Friedrich Gundolf, completing a doctoral dissertation on a German dramatist of the Romantic period. Although he came from a Catholic background, the young man took advantage of the sexually liberated climate of the Republic to enjoy a series of intense love affairs, including one with a Jewish schoolteacher named Else Janke. In 1922–3, while employed in Cologne as a bank clerk, he developed a flair for journalism, contributing articles to the *Westdeutsche Landeszeitung*, in which he contrasted the effete 'system' of the Republic with the undying spirituality of the German 'soul'. At this stage he sympathized with socialism and was neither antisemitic nor anti-Soviet, although his reading of Dostoevsky and Spengler had heightened his sense of the shallowness of modern civilization. His overriding ambition was to join the staff of a national newspaper, and he applied for jobs on the *Berliner Tageblatt* and the *Vossische Zeitung*, both liberal Jewish-owned newspapers. He also applied for a position as editor with the Mosse publishing company, claiming to have studied political economy, the history of the theatre and modern journalism.[15]

Goebbels's self-identification with Expressionism is explicit in his autobiographical novel *Michael*: 'We moderns are all Expressionists. People who wish to shape the external world from within. [. . .] The Expressionist world feeling is explosive. It is an autocratic sense of selfhood.'[16] Readers are invited to identify with the hero's quest for a charismatic leader or a radical cause. The hybrid style blends antiquated diction with abrasive modern prose, but the debt to Expressionism is evident in the fragmented syntax and effusive emotional tone. The disruption of syntax absolves the author of any need for logical argument or connected thought, and certain passages from the first-person narrative read like a pastiche of a poem by Werfel or Rubiner. Attending a public meeting, the hero becomes ecstatic about the principal speaker: 'Revelation! Revelation! A man is standing firm amid the ruins and hoisting the banner to the skies. All at once the people sitting around me are no longer strangers, but brothers.'[17] The Expressionist motifs of messianic leadership and the brotherhood of man are plausibly adapted to a flag-waving ideology, as the reader becomes aware that the man on the platform must be Hitler. Although *Michael* was not published until 1929, it is based on a manuscript written in 1923 at the height of the Expressionist era entitled 'Michael Voormanns Jugendjahre', in which the longing for leadership is an explicit theme, although the reference to Hitler has not yet been inserted. The adaptation of Expressionist ideals to political ends is also indicated by the subtitle of Goebbels's novel. Originally it was to be 'A Human Destiny in the Pages of a Diary'.[18] But in 1928, when he revised his text for a Nazi publisher, it became a 'German Destiny', and the quest is fulfilled by a demagogue with dazzling blue eyes.[19]

Goebbels's rapport with the avant-garde is reflected in his diaries, which include detailed notes about his experiences as a student, showing that during the years 1917–23 his perception of the German collapse was filtered through literature and religion. The spiritual turmoil underlying his political evolution has been the subject of a number of studies.[20] Even more significant is the radicalization of his religious feelings through the Expressionist vision. In a passage dated summer 1919 he links the movement with the 'social question' and the writings of Hasenclever. This reference is linked to two plays he saw on stage as a student in Freiburg: Strindberg's *Dance of Death* and Hasenclever's *Antigone*. That same autumn he began work on 'Michael Voormann', an attempt to write 'my own story from my heart's blood'. His enthusiasm intensified when he moved to Munich, with its abundance of theatres and opera houses, and he developed an insatiable appetite for books and plays, particularly by Tolstoy, Strindberg, Ibsen, Hasenclever and Georg Kaiser. A production of Kaiser's political allegory *Gas* impressed by its artful staging, but he was more strongly drawn to the mysticism of Paul Claudel. His literary studies in Heidelberg during the summer of 1920 acquainted him with more classical styles, from Goethe's *Faust* (both parts) to the poetry of Stefan George (recommended by Gundolf). But his personal taste was for radicals who rejected the liberal consensus, including Dostoevsky and Spengler, Chamberlain and Weininger. As the German political and economic crisis intensified with the occupation of the Rhineland, so too did his longing for radical solutions. In the summer of 1923 he described himself as a 'German communist'.[21] But this did not prevent him, in a diary entry of the following year, from advocating a new form of Christian faith composed of 'religious pain and fanaticism'. Hatred of an allegedly corrupt older generation led him to endorse the Expressionist longing for 'the new man' ('der neue Mensch'). By September, as Goebbels started writing for the right-wing newspaper *Völkische Freiheit* and fell under the spell of Hitler, the political transformation was complete, although the rhetoric was unchanged: 'Ich suche das neue Reich und den neuen Menschen.'[22]

Admiration for the Expressionist theatre led Goebbels to try his hand at the drama of spiritual awakening, and his unpublished early manuscripts include no fewer than five plays.[23] The most significant was the quest drama 'Der Wanderer', which was revised by Goebbels for its first stage production in 1927, and a study of different versions shows how little alteration was necessary to transform Expressionist dramaturgy into Nazi propaganda. In the original version each tableau closed with a proclamation of faith in mankind: 'I will seek the true man. He is not dead but merely sleeping.' In the revised version this is amended to: 'I seek the German people. They are not dead but merely sleeping.' The protagonist of Goebbels's play is the typical Expressionist hero: the poet with a messianic mission, but this now acquires a *völkisch* dimension, especially in the Epilogue, where the poet commits himself not to mankind, but to 'das Volk, die Gemeinschaft'.[24]

Kraus must have been familiar with 'Der Wanderer', since he alludes to this play in *Dritte Walpurgisnacht*. Echoing his earlier critique of the syntax of Expressionism, he shows in an exemplary passage how Goebbels blends Nazi propaganda with an appeal to 'the emotional sphere of the community' ('der Gefühlskreis der Gemeinschaft').[25] Systematic studies of National Socialism have confirmed that it was indeed an 'expressive ideology', clearly distinguishable from systems like liberalism and socialism, which legitimate themselves through rational argument.[26] Moreover, Kraus insists that we shall never understand the seductive power of National Socialism if we operate with the traditional schema of good versus evil: avant-garde poets and liberal journalists confronted by cultural philistines and political reactionaries. The case of Goebbels shows the 'progress' versus 'reaction' model to be a fallacy, and no one who has studied the nuances of his rhetoric is likely to attribute its appeal to the construction of a simplistic friend–enemy model.[27] The Nazi movement would never have captured the support of a highly educated nation if it had not assimilated many of the currents of modernism.

The debt to Jewish models is explicitly acknowledged in Goebbels's diaries, notably in the passage about Maximilian Harden, editor of *Die Zukunft*. Reading a selection of Harden's articles in 1924, shortly before he began to write for *Völkische Freiheit*, Goebbels feels both fascinated and repelled. He notes that *völkisch* writers have a great deal to learn from Harden's dynamic style, especially from his use of sarcasm and satire –'the typically Jewish method of fighting'. He suggests that if the Jews are to be defeated, the only way to do it may be 'with their own weapons'.[28] A further lesson he learnt from the Jewish press was that *völkisch* journalism was too solemn. The articles that Goebbels

contributed to *Völkische Freiheit* may not be on Harden's intellectual level, but they use similar techniques of wit and ridicule, while the strategy of *Der Angriff*, founded three years later, marks a further stage in his adaptation of the 'Jewish' method of mockery and invective. Summarizing the policy of *Der Angriff*, he wrote: 'We tried to outdo the Jewish press in sarcasm and cynical jokes.'[29] The articles he wrote for *Der Angriff*, reprinted in two volumes during the 1930s, represent one of the most remarkable achievements of German political journalism.[30] Thus Goebbels's journalistic style emerged from the intellectual milieu that he later reviled, and his representation of 'the Jew' as the enemy of the German nation concealed a profound ambivalence. So few of his early writings were actually published that there is no reference to him in *Die Fackel* of the 1920s, although Kraus recognized the affinities between such Expressionist proclamations of 'brotherhood' an   He
defined the ideas of leftist fellow trave   ity
which, in precisely the same way as the   rld
conquest, eliminates all reality and all hur   ce
of delusion'. The common impulse (he ar   ith
a collective, regardless of whether it hap   id'
(F 514–18, 50 & 65). Thus for Kraus in V   h,
this approach to politics was a recipe for

Werfel as Inner Antagonist

Kraus was most outspoken in his controversy with Franz Werfel, the leading poet of early Expressionism.[32] After his formative years as a member of the circle of Kafka and Brod in Prague, Werfel settled in Austria, marrying Alma Mahler and developing into a dramatist and novelist of international reputation. He was to achieve even greater success in the 1940s as an exile in the United States. The polemic between Kraus and Werfel, which lasted intermittently for twenty years, weaves together some of the most complex strands of contemporary culture – aesthetic and religious as well as political and ideological, with the problem of Jewish identity at its core. In April 1911, during his talent-spotting phase, Kraus had published the first of several selections of Werfel's poetry, to the dismay of his more conservative readers (F 321–2, 31–3). Nine months later Werfel became an overnight celebrity through the publication of his first volume of poetry, *Der Weltfreund* ('Friend of the World'), and Kraus records the pleasure that he, an 'enemy of the world' ('Weltfeind'), has derived from Werfel's work (F 339–40, 47–51). Both *Der Weltfreund* and his second collection of 1913, *Wir sind* ('Look at Us!'), were advertised on the covers of *Die Fackel*, and the enthusiasm was reciprocated. Werfel contributed a rhapsodic reminiscence of his first encounter with Kraus to the survey *Rundfrage über Karl Kraus*, published in 1913 by Ludwig Ficker in *Der Brenner*, and he arranged for the leading avant-garde publisher, Kurt Wolff of Leipzig, to issue special editions of Kraus's writings. The success of *Der Weltfreund* is easy to understand, since Werfel's style is infused with a secular mysticism in the manner of Walt Whitman (F 484–98, 104). Against the fragmentation of modern experience the poet sets intuitions of a universal harmony, and the freshness of perception, particularly in his invocations of childhood, is balanced by formal control. There is no sign in the verses Kraus singles out for praise of the rhetorical diffuseness of Werfel's later style, but while he praises the 'friend of the world', we soon find him expressing his doubts about his followers. In April 1914 he ironizes the vogue for poetry celebrating adolescent experience, alluding to Werfel rather unkindly as the 'virtuoso of childhood' (F 398, 19–20).

The ensuing polemic owes its fascination to the attempt to construct a symbolic 'other'. Although the decisive break had a personal origin, Kraus treats language as the touchstone of intellectual integrity. Werfel's style after 1913 became decidedly overblown, as he cultivated grandiloquent gestures in the manner of Goethe and Schiller. The neo-classical mode of Werfel's 'Vater und Sohn' ('Father and Son') elicited from Kraus a wicked parody, 'Elysisches' ('In the Elysian Style'), published in *Die Fackel* in November 1916. The parody juxtaposes classical diction with what Kraus now perceives as Werfel's characteristic flaws: eclectic borrowings, Expressionist mannerisms, and Prague colloquialisms with undertones of Jewish jargon. Without mentioning Werfel by name, he laments the willingness of Kurt Wolff to publish such effusions from Prague (F 443–4, 26–7). Werfel, who was now serving in the army as a telegraph officer, wrote to Kraus reproaching him for the crudity of his parody and the tastelessness of his appeal to Kurt Wolff. Kraus responded by publishing the letter in *Die Fackel*, embellished with a fifteen-page commentary entitled 'Dorten' ('Yonder'). Werfel had mistaken the parodistic use of Jewish jargon in 'Elysisches' (particularly the word 'Dorten') for a defect in Kraus's style. His error elicited a devastating rejoinder, described by Kurt Wolff as one of the most brilliant of Kraus's polemics.[33] This disquisition shows that the discrepancy between Schillerian rhetoric and Jewish jargon may be condensed into a single word, since 'dorten' occurs in both registers, the elevated sense of 'yonder' modifying into the gossipy colloquialism 'thataway' (F 445–53, 133–47).

The polemic reached its first climax in 1918, after Werfel had published two further ripostes reproaching Kraus for his self-righteousness: a poem in *Die neue Rundschau* entitled 'Einem Denker' ('To a Thinker'); and an Open Letter in *Die Aktion* entitled 'Die Metaphysik des Drehs' ('The Metaphysics of Spin'). In this perceptive essay, Werfel identifies Kraus's satire as a form of psychic displacement: a tendency to project his 'inner antagonist' ('den inneren Gegenspieler') onto the surrounding world.[34] This provoked Kraus into undertaking his most trenchant analysis of Werfel's style, 'Ich und das Ichbin' ('Self and Selfhood'), distinguishing between poetry based on 'experience' ('Erleben'), vividly recreated in words, and a poetry of vicarious 'participation' ('Mitmachen'). Childhood is acknowledged to be an 'experience' in Werfel's early poetry, but his proclamations of universal solidarity lack this centre of gravity within the self, resulting in 'emotional loquacity' (F 484–98, 93–5). Quoting widely from Werfel's work, Kraus ironizes his borrowings from Goethe, Schiller, Hölderlin, Rilke and Laforgue, concluding that his appeals to the 'brotherhood of man' result simply in sentimentality (F 484–98, 105 & 108).[35] Here Kraus identifies the essential ambiguity of Expressionism as a movement revolving around two diverse impulses, the one political, the other religious. By propagating a fusion of mysticism and activism, Werfel became the spokesman for idealists who hoped that spiritual transformations might help to inspire a political revolution, and even Kafka acknowledged him as the 'leader' of his generation.[36] Indeed, the seminal anthology of Expressionist poetry, *Menschheitsdämmerung* ('Twilight of Humanity', 1920), gives Werfel pride of place as the prophet of a new dawn. The problem (as Kraus sees it) is that Werfel's all-embracing religiosity envelops the reader in a 'metaphysical haze' (F 484–98, 103). The title of Werfel's collection *Der Weltfreund* blurs the biblical distinction set out in the Epistle of St James: 'The friend of the world is the enemy of God' (James, 4: 4). In this sense Kraus and Werfel are indeed antagonists, the effusions of the poetic 'rhapsodist' being set against the scruples of the satirical 'pedant' in an exemplary confrontation (F 484–98, 104–6).

Kraus's strictures have been questioned by critics who commend the Expressionists for their 'disruption of writing conventions'.[37] Expressionist poetry, in its early phase, certainly had exceptional merits, as Kraus acknowledged in his comments on Lasker-Schüler and Trakl, but he subsequently put his finger on a fundamental deficiency – lack of 'concreteness' ('Gegenständlichkeit'; F 514–18, 16). The ideologists of the second Expressionist generation have their eyes fixed on distant horizons, offering abstract visions of mankind in place of the texture of personal experience. They are the antithesis of the English Georgians, whose eye for the nuances of the natural world was to prove such a source of strength during the First World War. There are certainly a number of German war poets who deserve to be better known.[38] But, among the hundreds of poems published in Expressionist periodicals between 1914 and 1918, it is difficult to find any parallel for that direct engagement which distinguishes the poetry of Wilfred Owen. When the challenge of real suffering came, the Expressionists were ill equipped to meet it, since their high-minded moralizing degenerated into 'idealistic humbug', while politically they have been described as 'useful idiots' whose antics played into the hands of the establishment.[39]

Rilke and the 'mentalité juive'

The dialogue between Kraus and Werfel abounds in allusions to a specifically Jewish 'milieu' (F 445–53, 140). Werfel is attacked as the leading figure in a clique of German-Jewish poets, from whom the satirist is determined to distance himself, while the poet's replies reveal that he, too, construes the issue in Jewish terms. His title 'Die Metaphysik des Drehs' attributes to Kraus the 'deviousness' associated with interpretations of the Talmud. Moreover, Kraus's polemic is seen as a 'fencing with mirror images', his targets mere projections – fictional constructs designed to exorcise his own distress. This dualism is attributed to his dilemma as an assimilated Jew – his 'dark compulsion to erase all the traces he has left behind him'. Responding to the charge that his poetry is contaminated by Jewish jargon, Werfel suggests that Kraus is trapped in a psychic 'ghetto'.[40] Kraus's reply avoids direct reference to the Jewish question, but each in his own way was committed to a strategy of assimilation, representing antithetical positions in the spectrum of acculturation. Kraus contrasts the 'expansiveness' ('Weite') of Werfel's intellectual disposition with the 'constraint' ('Enge') of his own, insisting on the need for strict verbal and emotional 'boundaries' ('Grenzen'), which fortify the self within a stable syntax. Werfel's strategy is designed to loosen the constraints of language and embrace a multiplicity of experiences, since he felt that affirmation of the self ('Ich bin') could be attained only through solidarity with others ('Wir sind'). These contending spiritual dispositions recall the general categories of extravert and introvert, but Werfel and Kraus developed their psycholinguistic strategies of 'expansion' and 'exclusion' as responses to an antisemitic environment. Kraus constructs his anti-role as satirist with the aim of eliminating the social accretions of identity, above all the negative characteristics then associated with Jewishness.[41] Werfel responds to the same dilemma with a poetry of universal brotherhood designed to transcend ethnic and religious barriers. Each recognized in the other his psychic antagonist, Werfel responding to Kraus's censoriousness by comparing his gaze to the cutting edge of a 'diamond' ('Glaserdiamant'; F 759–65, 103). Kraus responded with a wealth of metaphors to denote Werfel's amorphousness, denouncing him as a 'sponge' (BSN 1, 28). This phrase occurs in a letter to Sidonie Nadherny, the person who helped to precipitate the controversy, since the problem of assimilation spilled over into their private lives.

This network of emotional relationships also involved Rilke, who was initially entranced by *Der Weltfreund*. He too was eager to meet the prodigy from Prague, and they were introduced in October 1913 at Hellerau near Dresden. The occasion was the German première of *L'Annonce* by Paul Claudel, which Rilke attended in the company of Sidonie. His disappointment at this first encounter with Werfel is vividly recorded in his letters: 'I was really expecting simply to take this young man in my arms,' he wrote to Hofmannsthal, 'but I saw immediately that this was absolutely out of the question. [. . .] I wouldn't have been disturbed by his being a Jew – a Jewish youth, to put it plainly; but what must also have become apparent to me was his thoroughly Jewish attitude to his poetic production, that knowingness about things without having experienced them.'[42] Rilke gives a similar account in a letter to Maria von Thurn und Taxis (this time written in French, with the crucial phrase in German): 'In Hellerau and Dresden I saw a lot of Franz Werfel. It was dispiriting: a "Jew-boy", remarked Sidie Nadherny in dismay (she had come over from Janowitz), and she wasn't entirely wrong.' This leads Rilke to embark on an elaborate analysis of what he refers to as the 'Jewish mentality' ('la mentalité juive'). Werfel's poetry (he argues) has suffered on account of 'a Jewish spirit which is all too familiar with merchandise [. . .] this spirit which penetrates things and nevertheless does not truly possess them, like the poison which enters everywhere taking revenge for not being part of the organism'.[43] It is startling to find the fastidious Rilke using such antisemitic clichés. What he and his aristocratic companion 'immediately' saw cannot have been entirely unprepossessing, since contemporary photographs show Werfel as a handsome young man with regular features. The stereotyping was in the mind of the beholder.

Werfel was taken aback by this encounter, although he later claimed to have been reassured by Rilke's words.[44] Conscious of having been snubbed by Sidonie, he relieved his ruffled feelings by circulating the rumour that she and Rilke were having an affair. When this gossip reached Kraus's ears, he was so enraged that he snubbed Werfel when next they met in Prague. Werfel's attempts to patch up the quarrel included an elaborate letter dated 6 April 1914, apologizing for having spread false reports about an unnamed lady. This letter survives in the Vienna City Library, embellished with vehement underlinings and exclamation marks in Kraus's hand which reveal the strength of his reaction. Another confrontation took place in a Vienna coffee-house in April 1915, when Werfel tried to apologize and Kraus demolished his excuses (BSN 1, 154–5). However insistently he may claim that his concern is with the quality of Werfel's writing, he now acknowledges that the controversy has a personal origin (F 484–98, 110).

In autumn 1913, he had just embarked on his courtship of Sidonie, which he felt was being compromised both by Werfel's gossip and by Rilke's rivalry. In reality, the tone of Rilke's letters to Sidonie is that of a solicitous friend rather than an ardent admirer, but he was so alarmed by the idea that she might marry Kraus that in February 1914 he wrote a closely argued letter designed to dissuade her from the alliance, arguing that it is inconceivable for her to marry a man so essentially 'alien' ('fremd'). Kraus's influence (he continues) may have its value, but only on the condition that 'the distance between you is never for a moment lost, that you sustain between yourself and him, in the spiritual sphere too, some ultimate ineradicable difference'.[45] Although the word 'fremd' hints at the stock antisemitic conception of the Jews as 'alien' or 'other', it has been suggested that Rilke was concerned, not with racial differences, but with incompatibilities of temperament and life-style.[46] He was apparently prompted to write this letter by his wife Clara, the sculptress who was making a bust of Sidonie. After an abrasive encounter with Kraus in Munich, Clara concluded that he was unsuitable as a partner for Sidonie. How could she possibly be happy with a writer whose mind – in Rilke's emphatic words – was an *'instrument sharpened so one-sidedly'*?[47]

The episode with Werfel in Hellerau only four months earlier had alerted Rilke to Sidonie's sensitivity to the 'Jewish' question, and his letter uses a coded language that blends anti-Jewish prejudice with shrewd psychological insight. Although the word 'fremd' frequently occurs in his writings with the sense of spiritual 'alienation', it also featured prominently in the discourse of racial difference. Rilke himself, in his letter to Hofmannsthal, had summed up Werfel's 'Jewish' attitude to his poetic production by saying that everything was ultimately imbued with 'something subtly alien' ('eine feine Fremdheit').[48] Such formulations reflect a cultural antisemitism that was by no means confined to the German-speaking world. Poets of conservative disposition, alarmed at the disintegrative effects of secular modernism, argued that the 'Jewish mentality' was to blame. 'Reasons of race and religion combine to make any large number of free-thinking Jews undesirable,' wrote T. S. Eliot in the 1934 edition of *After Strange Gods*.[49] Rilke acknowledges, in a more careful reflection, that the 'rootlessness' of Jews may lead them to affirm a faith in God, citing Spinoza as an example. More typical, in Rilke's view, is the Jew who 'with a cunning taught him by the need for survival has transformed his free-floating existence from a misfortune into a superiority', thereby becoming 'a pest, an intruder, a disruptive force'.[50]

These ideas can be traced back to Weininger's *Geschlecht und Charakter*, which both Kraus and Rilke had read soon after it appeared.[51] Weininger, like Houston Stuart Chamberlain, drew a distinction between the base Jew, who is at the mercy of his materialistic instincts, and the Jew whose personality has been humanized. 'Jewishness', according to this definition, is a predisposition towards scepticism and relativism which can be transcended by ethical self-refinement. The construction of an authentic 'self', which is essential to Weininger's theory of personality, involves the repudiation of that 'duplicity, indeed multiplicity' which he identifies as the Jewish heritage. Jewish anti-semitism is thus a form of psychic projection with its own inner logic. If a Jew attacks a fellow Jew, it is because his target 'reminds him unpleasantly of himself'. The relevance of this to the Kraus–Werfel–Rilke controversy is clear. It is Weininger's theory of psychic projection that resurfaces in Werfel's 'Die Metaphysik des Drehs', while Kraus's counterattack echoes Weininger's conception of the multiplicity of the Jewish self.[52] There were good reasons for condemning Werfel's rumour-mongering, as the culprit reluctantly acknowledged (BSN 1, 126). However questionable Sidonie's reaction may have been during that encounter at Hellerau, she can scarcely be blamed for those malicious rumours, let alone for the prejudices expressed in Rilke's letters. But the fact that she was the ultimate arbiter in this affair made Kraus hypersensitive. Only this can explain the tone of a letter he wrote her in April 1915, insisting on the contrast between his rigour and Werfel's shallowness: 'A poet like [Werfel] could "express" the splendours of the park in Janowitz a hundred times over. But to imagine him there himself, just once, walking around there, sitting, breathing, even writing poetry – the very idea is suicide' (BSN 1, 155). It is as if Kraus saw the poet as a double who threatened his existence.

While the image of the *Doppelgänger* figures in Kraus's letter only obliquely, Werfel resorted to cruder tactics. His posthumous papers contain the outline of a scurrilous novel, dated 5 July 1920, in which the publicist Karl Kalans is pictured in his elegant apartment, nervously awaiting the arrival of Princess S., who has at last consented to become his mistress. For Kalans this is not simply an erotic conquest, but the longed-for confirmation of his social acceptability. His preparations for the amorous encounter are abruptly interrupted by the arrival of a stranger, who claims to be one of his relatives from the provinces. This mysterious intruder, whose uncouth behaviour echoes the stereotype of the eastern Jew, smoking a filthy pipe and chewing onions, soon makes himself at home, creating chaos on all sides and even helping himself to elegant underwear. Kalans is forced to recognize the affinity when the stranger taunts him about the family deformity concealed beneath Kalans's elegant clothing: a hunchback. In an impulse of despair, Kalans murders his visitor by slipping cyanide into his tea, and hides the corpse in a closet. Only just in time – the Princess is already at the door! But Kalans cannot control his nervousness, the Princess discovers the body, and his happiness is destroyed for ever (BSN 1, 315–18). Werfel's sketch focuses on three of Kraus's most vulnerable points: his repressed Jewish origins, his attachment to Sidonie, and his sensitivity about his misshapen shoulder. Fortunately, Werfel refrained from publishing it, preferring to angle his polemics towards questions of principle. He did not wish his attacks on Kraus to be construed as a vendetta, and when the editors of *Die Selbstwehr* misrepresented his motives, he defended Kraus as a writer with a historical mission, stressing that his approach was a dialogue, not a denunciation.[53] These were two of the most gifted authors of their age, and their interactions culminated in two symmetrically conceived plays: Werfel's *Spiegelmensch* ('Mirror Man') and Kraus's *Literatur oder Man wird doch da sehn* ('Literature or You Ain't Seen Nothing Yet').

Mirror Men

Spiegelmensch, subtitled 'A Magical Trilogy', was published in 1920 and staged in Leipzig the following year. This enactment of the Expressionist quest pivots around the 'Solo' scene in Part III – a persiflage on the founding of *Die Fackel*. When the play was staged at the Burgtheater in 1922, this scene was dropped for fear of protests by Kraus's supporters. However, *Spiegelmensch* should be seen, not as a conventional Expressionist drama, but as a restatement of the dialectic between poetic rhapsody and satirical irony. The theme is the conflict between the true self and the false: Thamal the poet, and Spiegelmensch (Mirror Man), his inseparable companion. Mirror Man, like Mephisto in *Faust*, goads the hero into acts of self-aggrandizement, and the verse dialogue abounds in Faustian echoes. Goethe's idiom is at times mockingly travestied, at times poetically reaffirmed, and this generates an indeterminacy of tone. There are further borrowings from Ibsen's *Peer Gynt* and Strindberg's *To Damascus*, seminal influences on the dramaturgy of Expressionism. These affinities are duly noted in a further polemic published by Kraus in March 1921. His analysis is perceptive, as far as it goes, but he refrains from unravelling all the concealed allusions, in order to 'leave something over for future literary historians' (F 561–7, 62). Critics have been slow to take up the challenge, failing to notice that Werfel's most significant debt is to Kraus himself.

Although ostensibly cast in an Expressionistic mode, *Spiegelmensch* contains scenes that satirize the excesses of the movement. The protagonist Thamal is an ironic self-portrait, exemplifying the ideals of the poet who is 'open to the universe' (p. 37).[54] There are parodistic echoes of Werfel's own early style – that characteristic idiom which had joyously reconciled the 'friends striding arm in arm' in a 'magical unity of being'.[55] The development of the hero echoes the principal stages of the author's own career: the revolt against the parental environment, the desire for universal vision, the misconceived commitment to redemption through political action, and finally a return to religious contemplation. The equivocal aspects of Expressionism are accentuated through the chorus of Admirers, who celebrate Thamal's achievements in lines heavy with irony. They praise as 'virtually Expressionist' a mode of utterance that is caricatured in lines which resist translation: 'Turm-Wort, hah, strammt, du, neuer Mensch, gestemmt!' and 'O Mensch, du bist mein Lebenselixier! Mein Kokain!' (pp. 66–7). This is a pastiche of Werfel's own rhetoric, adulterated with motifs from other poets like August Stramm and Gottfried Benn. The myth of the 'sacrificial act' is also deconstructed, as are the communist ideals which helped to inspire it (pp. 117 & 157). One of the finest tirades by the Admirers ironizes the ideological indeterminacy of the Expressionism:

Vornehm läßt man gern sich blicken	A favourite costume worn this season
Heut als Neokatholiken [. . .]	Is Catholic revivalism [. . .]
Eucharistisch und thomistisch	Eucharistic and Thomistic,
Doch daneben auch marxistisch,	But of course also Marxistic,
Theosophisch, kommunistisch,	Communistic, Theosophic,
Gothisch kleinstadt-dombau-mystisch,	Mystic small-town minster-gothic,
Aktivistisch, erzbuddhistisch,	Buddhist, activistic Maoist,
Überöstlich taoistisch,	Transcendental eastern Taoist,
Rettung aus der Zeit-Schlamastik	Seeking from the age's mulchure
Suchend in der Negerplastik,	Certitude in negro sculpture,
Wort- und Barrikadenwälzend,	Building words and barricades,
Gott und Foxtrott fesch verschmelzend, –	God with foxtrot overlaid.
Dazu kommt (wenn's oft auch ein Last ist),	Another fashion (sad to say):
Daß man heute Päderast ist [. . .]. (p. 130)	The miseries of being gay [. . .].

These lines are worthy of Kraus himself, since they borrow his technique of satirical disjunction. He would have disowned the sneer at homosexuals, but the juxtaposition of Catholicism and communism, books and barricades, comes straight from his article of July 1919, 'Proteste', published a few months before Werfel completed his play.[56]

Spiegelmensch can be seen as a diffuse exploration of the dualism so crisply defined in Kraus's 'Zwei Läufer' (F 300, 32).[57] The 'Two Runners' of that celebrated poem, representing the conflicting claims of material success and spiritual fidelity, reappear as the alternative with which Thamal is confronted by Mirror Man: 'Brüder, laßt uns Läufer sein' ('Brothers, let's be runners', p. 65). The achievements of those who are fleet-footed and agile are contrasted with the lethargy of those trapped by memories of the past, but Thamal is aware that the dualism between action and reflection cannot be so easily resolved: 'Words run to the left, deeds race to the right' (p. 26). This echoes Kraus's critique of Werfel's failure to achieve 'integration of word and being' (F 484–98, 111). Indeed, the whole action is determined by this dualism of words and deeds. For ten years, Werfel's self-image had centred on an ecstatic intensity of vision, but his four volumes of verse, *Der Weltfreund*, *Wir sind*, *Einander* and *Der Gerichtstag*, become progressively more sombre, as the mirror of language becomes clouded by scepticism and self-mockery. *Spiegelmensch* signals the abandonment of his redemptive mission, indeed his implicit acceptance of Kraus's view of his personality as riven by irreducible dualisms. The attempt to build an image of the satirist into his play may be taken as a backhanded compliment.

At first sight, the 'Solo' scene seems artificially grafted on to the play and damaging to its inner consistency.[58] Mirror Man has not up to this point been presented as a character in his own right, but only as an externalization of Thamal's baser aspirations. Suddenly Mirror Man proclaims that he is an author as great as Goethe or Shakespeare. He proposes to found a magazine – an 'acoustic mirror' which will endow small-town gossip with cosmic significance. What should it be called? 'Der Kerzenstumpf? Nein! Die Fackel? Ja!' ('The Candle-End? No! The Torch? Yes!'; p. 189). These digs bring to the surface the concealed dialogue with Kraus, and we become aware that Mirror Man represents the voice of Kraus within the dramatist's consciousness. The introductory scenes of the play propound three conceptions of the self: solipsistic, dualistic and self-transcendent. Werfel's aim is to show that Thamal ultimately succeeds in transcending the dichotomies of experience and destroying his mocking mirror image. Through a voluntary act of self-immolation, he is to gain admission to a higher realm of being, embodied by a legendary religious order, but Mirror Man disrupts this mystical apotheosis by reminding him that it is all 'play-acting' (p. 214). Even with a cast of twenty-six benignly smiling monks, Werfel fails to contrive a convincing denouement.

Spiegelmensch is a play which refutes itself, but Kraus was so provoked that he failed to acknowledge the echoes of his own views. Instead, he responded with *Literatur*, a 'magical operetta' written and published in the spring of 1921. Set in a coffee-house crowded with pretentious intellectuals, the play parodies both the rhetoric of Expressionism and the jargon of the Jewish milieu. Twenty-six journalistic hacks form a satirical counterpoint to Werfel's benignly smiling monks, while two maenads represent the seductive effects of experimental poetry on emancipated women. A number of writers, including Sonnenschein and Ehrenstein, are ridiculed by name, others under thin disguises, including Johann Wolfgang (Werfel), Johann Paul (Georg Kulka), Harald Brüller (Robert Müller) and Brahmanuel Leiser (Ernst Polak), while Kraus reintroduces the figure of the Mirror Man as spokesman for his own viewpoint. One of the highlights of the play is 'The Song of the Media Mogul', sung by the representative of the *Neue Freie Presse* ('Couplet des Schwarz-Drucker'; pp. 59–60).[59] At this point the satire on individual nonentities opens out into a vision of media domination over the whole world. Another impressive sequence deals with the Prussian poet Fritz von Unruh, whose interpretations of battle experience during the First World War culminate in a vision of spiritual revolution. The Maenads go into ecstasies, using a language that appears absurdly parodistic, but is actually based on a eulogy by Bertha Zuckerkandl, published on 23 February 1921 in the *Wiener Allgemeine Zeitung*.[60]

The dialogue of *Literatur* has such verve that it can be seen as the culmination of Kraus's critical involvement with Expressionism.[61] The use of quotation is particularly effective, since it gives the satire a documentary force. However, the focus on a predominantly Jewish milieu seems unduly parochial, while the political implications of the Expressionist revolution are underplayed. So much of the humour depends on contrasts between the effusiveness of the poets and the jargon of their fathers that the play becomes a kind of elaborate Jewish joke. Gershom Scholem recalls how the dialogue caused him and Walter Benjamin to 'choke with laughter'.[62] It was certainly legitimate for Kraus to ridicule the father–son conflict, which recurred with obsessive regularity in the Expressionist theatre (*Spiegelmensch*, too, contains the obligatory parricide). But he creates a heavy-handed caricature of Werfel's family background, with which he was familiar from their pre-war friendship. A further limitation arises from the fact that the coffee-house intellectuals are depicted as participants in a vendetta against a single antagonist. Kraus, as he wrote on 15 March 1921 in a letter to Sidonie, believed that a literary 'mafia' was being organized against him (BSN 1, 495). By making this the dramatic centre of *Literatur*, he reduces the political significance of the satire. Franz Blei does appear towards the end, dressed in the robes of a Catholic monk and the cap of the communist Red Guard, but this is presented as yet another comic turn rather than a portent of disaster. Behind Blei's politicized Christianity lurked the sinister figure of Carl Schmitt, the Catholic jurist who was to become an apologist for National Socialism.[63]

The polemic between Kraus and Werfel culminates in a double paradox. The effect of *Spiegelmensch*, partly conceived as an attack on Kraus, is to confirm the critique of Expressionism undertaken in *Die Fackel*. The effect of *Literatur*, written as a refutation of Werfel, is to show that Kraus's satire does at times degenerate into 'fencing with mirror images'. The moment of truth occurs towards the end, when Mirror Man denounces his adversary Johann

Wolfgang as 'Wolfgang-Doppelgänger' (p. 66). Kraus seems to have felt that Werfel, through his imitations of Goethe, was compromising his own strategy as an author. Self-identification with Goethe was central to the whole process of Jewish-German acculturation, and Kraus was gratified when a 'resemblance to Goethe' was detected in his own poetic style ('Goethe-Ähnlichkeit'; F 472–3, 31). Thus he was haunted by his *Doppelgänger* in the most intimate sphere of linguistic identity-formation. To be acknowledged as 'Goethean' was the ultimate accolade for German-Jewish writers wishing to transcend their ethnic origins. *Literatur* suggests that Mirror Man/Kraus *has* achieved this self-transformation, while Johann Wolfgang/Werfel and his clique are trapped in the jargon of their Jewish milieu. Kraus was aware that his technique of imitating Jewish German ('nachjüdeln') might be identified with 'the well-known phenomenon of Jewish self-hatred' (F 561–7, 56–60). This motif is explicitly ironized in his play (p. 53), as well as discussed in *Die Fackel*. By contrasting Jewish speech-habits with Goethe's elevated diction, he sets up a dialectic that remains unresolved. This point is made by the most perceptive reader of *Literatur*, Franz Kafka. In a letter to Max Brod, Kafka acknowledges the validity of Kraus's diagnosis, suggesting that the adoption of German by Jewish writers is inescapably problematic.[64]

The conflict with Werfel had a coda that accentuates their contrasting attitudes to their Jewish heritage. In Werfel's dramatic legend, *Paulus unter den Juden* ('Paul among the Jews', 1926), which is set in Jerusalem after the death of Christ, the cult of law is ascribed to a sterile Judaic tradition, destined to be superseded by the Christian ethos of love. The play was favourably reviewed by David Bach in the *Arbeiter-Zeitung*, but it elicited vehement objections from other quarters. Freud denounced Werfel's self-indulgent religiosity in an exchange of letters which reduced the playwright to stammering apologies.[65] Kraus, by contrast, seized on his repudiation of the law. Against Paul, the inspired apostle of Christ, Werfel sets the figure of Rabbi Beschwörer ('Rabbi Exorcist'), fanatical adherent of 'das Gesetz' – Judaic Law. The Rabbi is caricatured in terms construed by Kraus as a coded attack on himself. Bach's review (he suggests) has missed the point, and he goes on to quote scenes from the play that reveal the tendentiousness of Werfel's attitude towards Judaism.[66] Far from repudiating the implied identification with the Rabbi, Kraus affirms his own role as law-giver among the Jews:

> I admit that I give the Jews a hard time, making no secret of my wish, which borders on fanaticism, that not only the laws of language but also the laws of the criminal code should be obeyed. Indeed, I wish to mobilize the final pathetic remnants of ruined authority against corrupted freedom. It is the old complaint that in a literature which thrives on give and take I represent the rigid rule of law. [. . .] In general, polemic and satire suffice for my professional needs, but in certain cases of exceptional licentiousness I reserve the right to invoke the protection of the criminal law, however inadequate that protection may be and however problematic the political authority which grants it to the tax-payer. (F 759–65, 106–8).

Dismayed by the conduct of the Churches during the war, Kraus had no confidence in the ideal of Christian love, so blithely espoused by Werfel as he gravitated towards Catholicism. Thus Kraus defended the rule of law as a Jewish heritage with political significance. Traditionally the calling of the prophet was to give the Jews a hard time, setting them higher ethical standards than their non-Jewish contemporaries, but the satirist, as we shall see, mobilizes the law in defence of the republic.

PART FOUR

DEFENDING
THE REPUBLIC

CHAPTER 13

Satire and Social Democracy

Kraus was an incorrigible individualist, hostile to collectives of every kind, and it is this that frames his troubled relationship with the Austrian Social Democratic Party. Although never a Party member, he did on rare occasions advise his readers how to vote, notably during the highly charged election campaign of 1919. On 2 February he gave a public reading that attracted an exceptionally large audience. Setting his scruples aside, he aligned himself with the Social Democrats, even though he felt himself to be the 'anti-politician, for whom the life of ideas only begins beyond communal allegiances' (F 508–13, 31). He urged all voters to support the Social Democrats as the only party to have resisted military tyranny during the war. His tirades against the ruling class provoked a cry of disgust from one member of the audience, but this merely strengthened the solidarity of an audience of 2,000 'unified as if by magic' (F 508–13, 37). For once, Kraus found himself on the winning side: the Social Democrats obtained over 40 per cent of the vote and Karl Renner became Chancellor, leading a coalition with the Christian Social Party. During the election of October 1920 Kraus again implicitly supported the Social Democrats, urging his audience to vote against the reactionary political parties (F 552–3, 27–28). This time the socialists lost, and they were never again to form a government in the First Republic.

The satirist made no secret of his hostility to the Christian Socials, especially during the election campaign of autumn 1923. The programme for his public reading on 5 October featured a series of scathing comments on reactionary Austria, but this time he gave no indication of voting intentions (F 632–9, 84–5). Two weeks later, on 21 October, Seipel's Christian Socials won a sweeping victory, forming a coalition with the Pan-Germans. During the mid-1920s Kraus became increasingly sceptical about Austrian parliamentary politics, objecting to an electoral system which compelled voters to support a party slate, rather than an individual candidate. If it had been possible to delete from the electoral list the names of Social Democrats whom he regarded

as corrupt, he might have been more inclined to vote; but this, as he observed
after the election campaign of April 1927, was precluded by a power-sharing
'electoral subterfuge' ('Wahllist', F 759–65, 2) – a pun on 'Wahlliste' ('electoral
list'). He refused to vote for a slate which included candidates who had
betrayed the ideals of the Party, even though the Social Democrats were faced
with an anti-Marxist alliance of Christian Socials, Pan-Germans and National
Socialists. The contest in April 1927 was so polarized that even Sigmund Freud
signed a declaration urging support for the Social Democrats, but Kraus was so
disillusioned that he refused the sacrifice of intellect.[1] The Social Democrats
achieved their best ever result, with over 42 per cent of the vote, but Seipel
was able to exclude them from power by forming another right-wing
coalition.

A lifelong preoccupation with the integrity of the self led Kraus to construe
politics in terms of the personal qualities of individual leaders. Bismarck provided his model of judicious statesmanship, and his memoirs, *Gedanken und
Erinnerungen*, are repeatedly cited in *Die Fackel* as a source of wisdom. Through
selective quotation he constructed an image of an enlightened Bismarck who
abhorred bloodshed, restrained the Pan-Germans, despised the press and mis-
trusted the Kaiser (F 405, 8–13; 632–9, 45–58). Kraus also admired Ferdinand
Lassalle, the German socialist leader who criticized the press from a Marxist
perspective (F 679–85, 1–9). Austrian socialism did possess one man of comparable distinction, Victor Adler, and despite the reservations about the Social
Democrats expressed in the first two decades of *Die Fackel*, references to Adler
are almost uniformly favourable. Adler, a qualified physician from a cultivated
Jewish background, had converted to Christianity, dedicating his life to building up the Austrian Social Democratic Party. His German nationalism led him
to align the Party with the German Reich during the First World War, but
Kraus admired his efforts at the Stockholm International Socialist Congress
of October 1917 to bring about a negotiated peace (BSN 1, 437). Adler's
sudden death on 11 November 1918, at the age of sixty-six, coincided with the
proclamation of the Republic. In Kraus's 120-page 'Valediction' to Austria-
Hungary, he is commended as a man whose moral example must inspire, even
among those who stand aloof from politics, an enduring respect (F 501–7,
108). Adler's death left the leadership in the hands of a younger generation, led
by Karl Renner, Otto Bauer, Friedrich Austerlitz and Karl Seitz. Recognizing
that they would need support from non-socialist quarters in the process of post-
war reconstruction, the Social Democrats initially welcomed the co-operation
of both reform-minded Catholics and progressive members of the intelligentsia. Thus Kraus was drawn into an uneasy alliance with the Party, although
his attitude was still influenced by the qualities of individuals.

Friedrich Austerlitz and the Capitalist Press

Kraus had much in common with Friedrich Austerlitz, editor of the *Arbeiter-
Zeitung* and a member of the National Assembly. The *Arbeiter-Zeitung* was a

'unique paper', as Julius Braunthal recalls, 'a daily magazine of political and cultural affairs'. Its staff 'were not journalists in the English or American sense; they were rather essayists, and most of them were brilliant'. Above all of them towered the powerful figure of Friedrich Austerlitz, editor from 1895 until his death in 1931. Although Austerlitz has never been the subject of a systematic biography, Braunthal has left a memorable pen-portrait:

> He was one of the rare sort of European journalists who felt profoundly the great responsibilities of their office. He held, and never tired of preaching, that because journalists wielded such tremendous power for good or evil, their intellectual and moral integrity required a particularly high standard. [. . .] He regarded the careful cultivation of the language as the supreme task of the journalist. [. . .] A trivial phrase, or a wrong comma, would evoke his white-hot rage; he would burst into the cubicle of the careless writer and passionately dissect the wrongly applied expression, often revealing a new meaning of words and phrases which had become petrified by their thoughtless use.

Braunthal, who joined the *Arbeiter-Zeitung* in 1919 and went on to become editor of the more popular socialist newspaper *Das kleine Blatt*, adds that Austerlitz was an insatiable worker – a bachelor with no private life who spent twelve hours a day in the office.[2]

It is hardly surprising that Kraus felt such an affinity with Austerlitz, paying tribute to his ethical stance during the war (F 462–71, 141) and endorsing his campaign against the tyranny of 'military justice' (F 501–7, 108). The satirist's denunciations of monarchy and militarism, capitalist press and complacent bourgeoisie were closely attuned to the programme of the *Arbeiter-Zeitung*, and personal friendship reinforced the ideological alliance. Kraus would occasionally visit Austerlitz during the night at his office in the Rechte Wienzeile, as Sidonie Nadherny records (BSN 2, 332). He received the *Arbeiter-Zeitung* daily, until in April 1926 he became so disenchanted that he cancelled the subscription, still paying tribute to Austerlitz, the beating 'heart' within the Party apparatus (F 726–9, 79 & 84). Both men loved working through the night, and it was an open secret that they enjoyed nocturnal telephone conversations.[3] A letter to Austerlitz dated 6 November 1924 provides a glimpse of their relationship at a time when Kraus was becoming disillusioned with other members of the Party. The tone is cordial, even though Kraus acknowledges that their discussions – both by phone and face to face – have become almost too 'animated'.[4]

In February 1920 Kraus quoted a speech delivered by Austerlitz in the National Assembly attacking the press as an 'instrument of capitalism'. He insists that his priorities are quite distinct from those of the Social Democratic Party, although he respects Austerlitz's 'whole-hearted commitment to a cause'. By contrast, Kraus's hostility to dehumanizing forms of propaganda does not preclude a certain 'conservatism of natural values'. Thus there are regressive undertones to his critique of the media, and his relations with the *Arbeiter-Zeitung* involved complex discriminations on both sides. Although

Kraus repudiated faith in any political party, in the case of socialism he was willing to engage in a 'political dialogue' (F 521–30, 50, 58 & 62–3). This dialogue
became most effective in 1922 during the campaign against disguised advertising in the bourgeois press. Austerlitz piloted through parliament the measure
designed to outlaw advertisements disguised as editorial comment, and it is
likely that Kraus had a hand in drafting the proposals. Their dialogue was continued by the article in the *Arbeiter-Zeitung* of 24 December 1925, in which
Austerlitz suggested that the satirist attached too much significance to printed
paper that 'disappears almost as soon as it sees the light of day'. The laws against
blackmail and defamation should certainly be strengthened, but it would be
wrong to take too seriously a newspaper that is merely a 'waste-product of the
bourgeois-capitalist world'. Kraus's reply insists on a more fundamental 'moral
principle': no newspaper is entitled to delve into people's private lives and
spread rumours about adultery, masturbation or homosexuality all over its
financial pages (F 712–16, 92 & 97–8).

Kraus repeatedly condemns the 'capitalist press' (F 649–56, 52) and the
'atrocity of the capitalist spirit' (F 712–16, 10). But it is the excesses of capitalism that he repudiates, not the whole economic system – not firms (like his
father's) that manufacture a useful product and market it at a fair price, but speculators who corner the market in commodities in short supply, forcing up prices
for an inflated profit. His satire exposes the unacceptable face of capitalism:
unproductive middlemen responsible for price inflation and black-marketeer-
ing; corrupt officials, who accept bribes or back-handers; and war profiteers,
who enrich themselves by exploiting shortages of essential goods. The war
revealed that aggressive economic expansionism was one of the motors of
German militarism (F 406–12, 112), and Kraus denounced a mercantile war in
which 'markets' have been transformed into 'battlefields' (F 404, 4). The most
spectacular profits were made by armaments manufacturers. In January 1917 he
recorded the names of eight directors of the Styrian Munitions Factory with the
enormous dividends they had received for the year 1915–16, and in May 1918
he noted that the Manfred Weiss Munitions Company in Budapest had
announced a profit of 11 million Crowns on a working capital of 35 million.

Despite these attacks on capitalist profiteers, Kraus's own position was not
free of ambiguity. Responding to the revelation that he owned a motor car, he
had to concede that his life-style was 'not quite as anti-capitalist' as people
imagined (F 691–6, 101). Moreover, the focus of his satire, especially in *Die
letzten Tage der Menschheit*, is distorted by an assumption that Jews are particularly to blame for the ills of capitalism. Early in the play his spokesman the
Grumbler refers to 'Jewish-capitalist world destruction' (I, 29), unwittingly
echoing arguments that had been popularized by the antisemitic demagogue
Georg von Schönerer several decades earlier.[5] However, it is not possible to
draw a clear line between Kraus's satire and the supposedly more 'scientific'
critique of Marxism, since even Marx, in his essay on 'The Jewish Question'
(1844), had identified capitalism with 'the Jewish spirit'.[6] The prominence of

Jews in Austrian banking and commerce had led Victor Adler to acknowledge, at the 1897 Party Congress, that in Vienna the capitalist bourgeoisie had a 'Jewish complexion'. It was not the Party's fault (he explained) that they kept finding 'Jews in their soup'. In Austria, another speaker observed, the terms 'Jew' and 'capitalist' had become 'synonymous'.[7]

The position was complicated by the fact that so many socialist leaders were of Jewish descent, including Otto Bauer, Friedrich Austerlitz, Hugo Breitner, Julius Tandler, Robert Danneberg, Julius Braunthal, Oskar Pollak and David Bach, as well as the Adler family. Moreover, the Party enjoyed overwhelming electoral support from the Jewish population of Vienna.[8] The problem was how to refute right-wing allegations that there was some sinister Jewish conspiracy against the German people, in which Marxists and capitalists were colluding. Social Democrats felt obliged to distance themselves from allegedly 'Jewish' practices in banking and the stock exchange by adapting antisemitic arguments to their own purposes. This was a tactic of self-defence, not an expression of self-hatred. They did not want the party of social justice, whose leaders happened to be Jewish, to be discredited by association with big business, where Jews were also prominent, so they too, from a socialist perspective, denounced 'Bankjuden', 'Börsenjuden' and 'die jüdische Presse'.[9]

Otto Bauer and the Bourgeois World

Social justice was indeed the primary aim, but the Austrian bourgeoisie resisted radical economic reform, especially the programme of 'socialization', designed to take large sections of industry into public ownership.[10] This policy was promoted by Otto Bauer as a first step towards the creation of a classless society in which workers would no longer be subject to capitalist exploitation. In his book *Die österreichische Revolution* ('The Austrian Revolution') Bauer describes socialization as the key to the economic reform programme of 1919, recalling with pride the pioneering legislation which set up works councils, to give workers a voice in industrial management, and co-operatives, linking the interests of producers and consumers.[11] The socialization programme initially acquired strong momentum, since it was supported by bourgeois economists like Joseph Schumpeter, Minister of Finance in the first coalition government. The proposals were launched by Bauer in a series of articles in the *Arbeiter-Zeitung* between 5 and 28 January 1919. On 14 March the Assembly set up a Socialization Commission, with Bauer as chairman, and for a time it enjoyed the support of the Christian Socials, who recognized that concessions were necessary to avoid the revolutionary violence that was occurring in Budapest and Munich. A government announcement of 21 May declared that coal mining, electricity, iron and steel, and forestry would be the first sectors to be nationalized. At this point Bauer's account of events diverges from that of later historians, who have shown that the primary obstacle lay with the Austrian legislature. Any new law would require the support of the Christian Socials in both the National Assembly and the provincial governments, but once the danger of a communist coup was past, they began to backtrack. The Deputy Chancellor Jodok Fink later admitted that he had 'jumped on the revolutionary bandwagon only in order to apply the brakes'.[12]

Bauer, by contrast, attributes the failure of the socialization programme to the operations of international capitalism. The most obvious candidate for public ownership, he explains, was the Austrian iron industry, centred on the Alpine Montangesellschaft, and it should have been relatively simple to take this industry into public ownership, since its shares, almost entirely in Austrian hands, had fallen so sharply. However, without informing other members of the government, Schumpeter gave permission for the banker Richard Kola to purchase a large package of Alpine Montangesellschaft shares on behalf of Italian investors. Although this brought precious foreign capital into the country, it blocked the socialization programme, since it was impossible to impose public ownership on foreign shareholders. Bauer recalls these events in terse, unemotional prose. Schumpeter's action 'led to a vigorous conflict within the coalition government', with the result that the Finance Minister was sacked. But Bauer's Marxist schooling leads him to place the blame not on individuals, nor indeed on his coalition partners, but on international capitalism. The adverse balance of trade in 1919 made it 'inevitable' that Austrian industry would be penetrated by 'foreign capital', and he quotes Marx's 'Class Struggles in France' in order to explain that it is impossible to introduce socialism in a country that is dependent on foreign credits. Hence his conclusion that the socialists were compelled to abandon their revolutionary proposals for the 'expropriation of the expropriators'. The necessity of capital inflows was to blame for the failure of the nationalization programme, just as French imperialism was for blocking Anschluss with Germany.[13]

Kraus was clearly in sympathy with the socialization programme, and four years later he described the failure to dispossess the 'plutocrats' as incomprehensible (F 632–9, 20). But his satire on the fiasco of autumn 1919 offers a different perspective from that of the Social Democrats, insisting that Schumpeter should be held personally responsible for his misdeeds:

> Little Schumpeter flutters past, a butterfly above the skulls of the dead. Is he in ladies' lingerie? No, he's a Finance Minister who's really making a splash. A favourite among women who'd appeal to men as well. A coalition of commitments to every political party, please delete where inappropriate. An exemplary republican, ready to play the lion's part, only he forgot his lines and touched his cap to his Lordship when Rothschild entered the theatre. An exchange professor with variable convictions, extending from those members of society who are scouring the rubbish tips for their children's food to those who can pay 6000 Crowns for a box in the theatre on New Year's Eve – a better crowd, don't you know. A man, take him for all in all, with more ideologies than strictly necessary for his advancement. (F 521–30, 158)

Schumpeter, after emigrating to the United States, was to become one of the most celebrated economists of the western world, but the devious role which he played in Austrian affairs is well documented. He led an ostentatiously hedonistic life, driving down the Kärntnerstrasse in an open carriage with a blonde prostitute on one knee and a brunette on the other.[14] Kraus's image of the social butterfly hovering over the skulls of the dead, adapted from baroque religious painting, contrasts this life-style with the devastating influenza epidemic of 1918–19, which caused thousands of deaths. Schumpeter's offence was to combine a plurality of interchangeable ideologies in a single person. Indeed, his next move was to become chairman of the old-established Biedermann Bank, where his speculative deals helped to precipitate a further crisis.[15]

Although references to Bauer in *Die Fackel* of the 1920s are relatively sparse, Kraus was familiar with the socialist leader's ideas both from the *Arbeiter-Zeitung* and from *Die österreichische Revolution*, a book presented to him by the author with a handwritten dedication.[16] He has little to say about Bauer's political theories, but the contrast between their perspectives helps to explain why the relationship between satire and Social Democracy proved so difficult. Bauer was well aware that a Soviet-style dictatorship in Austria had no chance of success, for reasons which he set out in a letter to Béla Kun on 16 June 1919. The proclamation of a Soviet dictatorship would result in the Austrian provinces seceding from Vienna, and the city would be starved into submission, even if it was not occupied by the military forces of the Entente.[17] This diagnosis led him to develop the 'two-phase' model of revolution. Eschewing the destructive violence that had occurred in Russia, where for three years he had been a prisoner of war, Bauer saw the first phase as *political* revolution: the overthrow of the Monarchy and the establishment of democratic government. The second phase, *social* revolution, required a longer-term strategy, in which the Social Democrats would win an overall majority at the polls.[18] They placed their faith in the 'economic laws' that predicted that capitalism would succumb to its own contradictions. Thus he campaigned, not for violent revolution, but for the achievement of socialism through the ballot box. Once a majority of 51 per cent had been achieved, the capitalist system would be dismantled. The process would be non-violent, although a transitional period of working-class 'dictatorship' might still be necessary to break the final resistance of the bourgeoisie.[19]

Kraus's critique of capitalism, by contrast, was directed against 'bourgeois' values, not against the economic system. This ambiguity can be traced back to a celebrated exchange of January 1906, during which Robert Scheu had argued that satire and socialism have a common enemy: 'the bourgeois' ('den Bourgeois'). Kraus's response was to insist that his definition of the 'bourgeoisie' was quite different from that of the Social Democrats. He believed that 'in the struggle to destroy the artistic personality every collective becomes a "bourgeoisie" [. . .] regardless of whether it consists of bourgeois or proletarians' (F 194, 2 & 8). This repudiation of socialism in the name of artistic individuality led him, in the final years before the First World War, to denounce the levelling-down tendencies of 'democracy' (F 261–2, 8). But the horrors of war forced him to revise his position and to acknowledge, in October 1917, that it was no longer legitimate for the artist to seek 'secure protection for his inner life'. In an oblique allusion to the Social Democrats he affirmed that he had never repudiated 'the party of human dignity' (F 462–71, 76–8).

However, a fundamental ambiguity underlies his attitude towards 'revolution'. The violence of Béla Kun's revolution in Hungary filled him with apprehension, especially during two attempts at a communist coup in Vienna – on 17 April and again on 15 June 1919. Kraus supported the efforts of the Social Democrats to forestall revolutionary action in Austria, urging the Secretary of State for the Interior (Mathias Eldersch) and the Vienna Police Chief (Johannes Schober) to clamp down on the communists and their ideological supporters (F 514–18, 67–72). In this emergency, with the irresponsibility of the Entente apparently driving central Europe towards bolshevism, he even found himself – to his dismay – expressing solidarity with his own social class: 'the German-Austrian bourgeoisie' (F 514–18, 81). The coalition led by the Social Democrats stood firm against the threat of insurrection, and Kraus emphatically supported this policy, scathingly condemning the communist agitators and their intellectual fellow travellers. After the hunger riots of 1 December 1921, when communist-led demonstrators converged on the Ringstrasse and wrecked the bar of the Hotel Bristol, he showed greater sympathy for the militants, suggesting that next time they should demolish the newspaper printing presses, rather than a few worthless pictures and mirrors (F 588–94, 3–7). But the crucial question, formulated by the communist author Hugo Sonnenschein, was whether Kraus, despite his radical gestures, was not objectively a defender of the status quo.[20]

The contrasting critiques of the bourgeois world represented by satire and socialism can be traced back to the antithesis between Marx and Heine. Marx established the words 'der Bourgeois' and 'die Bourgeoisie' as signifiers of a socio-economic category – the property-owning capitalist class, while Heine's primary target was 'der Spießbürger' ('the philistine'). When Kraus, addressing a working-class audience in December 1925, denounced 'bourgeois society' ('die bürgerliche Gesellschaft'; F 712–16, 10), he was using the phrase to denote not a socio-economic category, but a spiritual disposition: complacent, hypocritical and narrow-minded.[21] For Kraus, being bourgeois was a mindset, class-specific only in so far as it implied financial greed and hostility towards manual workers, and he particularly despised 'Spießbürgertum' in the erotic sphere (F 649–56, 81). Further difficulties arise over the adjectival equivalent for the German noun 'der Bourgeois'. Only occasionally, when he was trying to force the issue, did Kraus use the German loan-word 'bourgeois' as an adjective (F 706–11, 66). More commonly, 'bürgerlich' has to do service both for the socialist struggle against capitalism and for the satirical crusade against the philistines. Kraus clearly stands on the cultural side of the divide, as is evident from the echoes of Heine in his satirical poetry. Towards the end of his life he emphasized that repeated attempts to read writings by Marx had left him cold, although he had no reason to regret his own 'critique of the bourgeois world' ('Kritik der bürgerlichen Welt'; F 890–905, 43).

Kraus, in short, was anti-bourgeois but not anti-capitalist. Indeed, he was a beneficiary of the capitalist system, having inherited a private income from his father Jakob Kraus, a manufacturer of packaging products and dye-stuffs. The firm of Jakob Kraus survived the First World War, continuing to prosper during the upheavals of the 1920s. Although its head office was in Vienna, the factory was situated in financially stable Czechoslovakia, earning Kraus, as he acknowledged in December 1921, a secure income of a thousand Crowns a month (F 583–7, 50). An agreement with his brothers drawn up after the First World War gives further details of his income from the family business.[22] Thus the satirist who repudiated 'materialism' in all its forms, particularly the corrupting effects of the cash nexus, was himself cushioned from material need. To put the matter politely, he was 'a man of independent means' – 'selbständig' – the word applied to the Grumbler in the 1919 edition of Die letzten Tage der Menschheit (III, 3), but later deleted. In Marxist terms he was profiting from the sweated labour of the poor, and his frugal life-style did not alter his basic socio-economic position. It is not the concept of 'surplus value' that inspired his attacks, but the Shakespearean idea of 'superfluity'. Introducing, at a public reading of November 1923, his denunciation of 'the bourgeois' in the poem 'An den Bürger', he quoted from the opening lines of Coriolanus: 'If they [the patricians] would yield us but the superfluity while it were wholesome, we would guess they relieved us humanely' (F 640–8, 107). 'Humane relief' in the form of generous donations to charity was more important for Kraus than social revolution. In the eyes of orthodox Party members, Kraus's position was suspect, and Oskar Pollak argued, in a penetrating article published in March 1923 in Der Kampf, that Kraus's achievements were limited by his preoccupation with cultural 'façades', leaving him ill equipped to confront the realities of class conflict and economic exploitation. Moreover Kraus had 'never written a line for the workers' and was allegedly 'unpopular' among them. Three years later Pollak returned to the attack, arguing that Kraus's influence on Party members was divisive: he was so preoccupied with 'corruption' that he failed to understand capitalism. Austerlitz, by contrast, praised the satirist in the Arbeiter-Zeitung as a 'true revolutionary' (F 649–56, 105–8). He also stressed in Der Kampf the importance of Kraus's critique of the 'superstructure' of capitalism.[23]

Karl Seitz, Ghosts and Parasites

It was practical socialism that appealed to Kraus, not the abstract rhetoric of Marxism, and he made no secret of his admiration for the 'social achievement' of the Municipality of Vienna (F 632–9, 168). Hence his admiration for Hugo Breitner, the Finance Director, whose graduated taxation system achieved a redistribution of wealth, providing the basis for the construction of hospitals, children's homes and social housing.[24] While Breitner, a banker committed to public service, became a hate figure for the bourgeois press, Kraus responded by describing him as one of the few people in Vienna who was working 'unflinchingly for the common weal' (F 691–6, 25). He approved of Breitner's policy of charging a substantial tax on entertainment, including the cinema, since the revenues were devoted to 'socially useful purposes' (F 743–50, 128–9). It was these revenues that enabled Julius Tandler to create child-care facilities in Vienna that attracted worldwide admiration. Tandler, Kraus concluded, was 'a more useful and courageous socialist' than radicals of the Otto Bauer type (F 917–22, 83).

He also respected another pragmatic socialist, Karl Seitz, first President of the National Assembly and – from 1923 until 1934 – Mayor of Vienna. Having been orphaned at a tender age, Seitz knew the poverty that afflicted workers' families, and as a young teacher he had challenged the regressive policies of Karl Lueger, making headlines in March 1901 when he was suspended for being too outspoken. By that date his flair for public speaking had won him a seat in parliament as one of the first Social Democratic deputies. He was an evolutionary socialist in the mould of Eduard Bernstein, and his aim, as set out in an article in *Der Kampf* in 1915, was to promote 'countervailing tendencies' within the capitalist system that would lead to a new social and international order. His organizational ability led Victor Adler to describe him as 'the best horse in my stable', and it was he who – after Adler's premature death – proclaimed the Republic from the steps of parliament. After piloting the National Assembly through the crisis months of 1919, when he was formally head of state, Seitz became the presiding genius of Red Vienna, gaining a popularity that extended well beyond Party members, although his aquiline features, caricatured in the Nazi press (Fig. 24a & b), exposed him to taunts from the antisemites.[25]

Kraus had followed Seitz's early career with interest, defending him in March 1901 against the educational authorities (F 72, 28–9). As a long-standing reader of *Die Fackel*, Seitz wrote to him on 1 May 1919 to mark its twentieth anniversary. Every republican, he affirmed, would gratefully acknowledge Kraus's contribution to the 'expulsion of the ghosts of the past' (F 514–18, 21). Five years later, in a letter to mark Kraus's fiftieth birthday, Seitz wrote in even more complimentary terms, thanking him for all he had done to counteract the prejudices generated by the 'capitalist social order' (F 649–56, 148–50). The tone of these letters suggests a real affinity, while the reference to 'ghosts' recalls one of the most famous scenes in Ibsen, where the sins of the past return to haunt a younger generation. The essay 'Gespenster' ('Ghosts'), in which Kraus responded to the first of these letters, acknowledged that the rulers, diplomats and generals had been deprived of much of their power. But there was reason to fear the return of the ancient ghosts, as long as there were journalists to legitimize their activities. Far from creating a new European order, the vindictive terms imposed by the Versailles peace

24   Karl Seitz as Austrian President: (a) photograph (b) caricature in a Nazi newspaper

settlement seemed designed to strengthen the 'nationalist demon' among both victors and vanquished. Moreover, the collapse of conservatism in central Europe had left a vacuum that was being filled by new forms of irresponsibility. The essay denounces monarchists and bolsheviks with equal fervour, insisting that the 'belief in ghosts' will prove to be justified if, after a thousand murderers have been pensioned off, their power has been usurped by 'ten activist writers' (F 514–18, 22, 25–9, 32 & 50).

Kraus was equally severe on journalists who were compromising the socialist cause, denouncing radical papers like *Der Abend* with exceptional vehemence (F 514–18, 77–84). The issue became more acute after the founding of Bekessy's *Die Stunde*, a left-of-centre newspaper with an aggressively modern style. The Social Democrats in City Hall had granted Bekessy Austrian citizenship, and he in his turn gave their programme favourable coverage. When Kraus attacked Bekessy's sensationalist reporting, he received no support from the *Arbeiter-Zeitung*, since his ally Friedrich Austerlitz was prevented by the Party hierarchy from intervening. This led him to appeal directly to the Mayor of Vienna to distance himself from Bekessy's activities. Citing Seitz's words in praise of his satirical crusade, Kraus asked why the city tolerated 'parasites of capitalism', just because they displayed 'radical left-wing views' (F 691–6, 124).

This appeal formed the climax of the attack on *Die Stunde* launched from the public platform on 25 June 1925 and repeated in similar terms several months later, calling on the Social Democratic Party to combat the opportunism of its own supporters on the supposedly liberal left – 'the parasites of freedom' (F 712–16, 74). Seitz replied that he was precluded from making a public statement by his 'circumscribed rights and duties'. After initially acknowledging Seitz's position, Kraus came to believe that it was actually determined by 'Party tactics' (F 732–4, 50). Their willingness to make tactical compromises hastened his disillusionment with the Social Democrats, and Seitz's 'third letter' ultimately became a sign of the Party's 'intellectual and moral decay' (F 811–19, 16). Their political manoeuvring during the constitutional crisis of 1929 ('on the one hand [. . .] on the other hand') led him to incorporate the mayor's name in a mischievous misprint: 'einerseits [. . .] andererseitz' (F 820–6, 122). But a poem addressed to an (unnamed) 'Social Democratic Dignitary' expressed residual sympathy for a man obliged to participate in events he disdained (F 834–7, 45).[26]

David Bach and the Socialist Cultural Ideal

Recognizing that the war had left a legacy of nationalist resentment and social deprivation, Kraus was drawn into the political struggle. The aim must be to defeat the reactionary forces which threaten mankind with a repetition of the cataclysm of war. 'This and nothing else', he declared, 'is my socialism!' (F 554–6, 4–5). It was in the sphere of culture that he became most directly involved with the Party, setting aside his doubts about the 'socialist cultural ideal' (F 521, 62). In March 1919, and again in March 1920, he accepted invitations from Social Democratic groups to give readings to working-class audiences. These links were formalized in the spring of 1920 when he was invited by the central organization of the Social Democratic Party to give two readings 'for the workers of Vienna' (F 544–5, 14–15). The second of these took place on May Day, the international festival of Marxism, and the following year he was invited to participate in the festival to commemorate the founding of the Republic on 12 November. On this occasion he gave two readings 'for the workers of Vienna' in the Hofburg, erstwhile residence of the Emperor, organized by the Cultural Department of the Social Democratic Party – the Kunststelle (F 608–12, 49). This organization arranged for Kraus to give further readings on May Day 1923, in the council chamber of the Vienna City Council (F 622–31, 113); and in November and December 1923, again in the Hofburg (F 640–8, 108 & 111). Kraus's public readings, together with his polemics in *Die Fackel*, made a significant contribution to socialist cultural politics, as members accustomed to the tedium of Party meetings were roused from their slumbers by his captivating performances.

Kraus shared the Austro-Marxist view of 'Bildung' (culture and education) as a force for social renewal. The programme of his public readings encompassed some of the classics of anti-establishment satire and socially conscious literature, including Offenbach, Nestroy, Gogol, Ibsen, Strindberg, Hauptmann, Wedekind, Luxemburg and Brecht. These were also 'readings' in the interpretative sense: indications that the work of Goethe or Shakespeare could be mobilized against the dominant ideologies. His gift for composing topical verses, inserted into songs by Nestroy or Offenbach, revived one of the most potent of popular traditions, using satirical stanzas or hard-hitting epigrams to clinch the connection between culture and politics. This creative alliance with the Austrian Social Democrats continued for almost seven years, with a final May Day reading in the Hofburg in 1925 (F 686–90, 46). Altogether, Kraus gave over twenty readings specifically for working-class audiences, but the majority of his recitals, organized by the Richard Lanyi Bookshop, took place in more conventional locations, including the Konzerthaus and the Musikverein.[27] The revenues from these readings were frequently donated to radical social causes, including the Social Democratic militia, the Schutzbund. Thus Kraus's readings formed a bridge between middle-class intellectuals and the organized working class.

The person who facilitated this alliance was the director of the Kunststelle, David Josef Bach, a gifted organizer who has rarely received the credit he deserves, either in studies of Kraus or in general histories of Red Vienna.[28] Born in 1874 into a Jewish family, he was by vocation a musicologist. His wide-ranging cultural interests are evident from the library which he brought with him into exile in England, after the Nazi occupation of Austria.[29] Although the classics of European literature are well represented, Bach was receptive to the avant-garde, supporting artists like Kokoschka, who made him the subject of a

vivid line drawing (Fig. 25). Bach was one of the early members of Schoenberg's circle, and also, from 1906 to 1911, a member of the Vienna Psychoanalytic Society.[30] From 1905 to 1933 he was on the staff of the *Arbeiter-
Zeitung*, and it was he who initiated the celebrated Workers' Symphony
Concerts, which formed a notable feature of Viennese cultural life from 1905
onwards. In Red Vienna he expanded this programme, hiring Anton Webern
in 1922 as director of the Workers' Choir. Bach exercised considerable powers
of patronage, since the Kunststelle was responsible for the block-booking
of tickets for musical and theatrical events on behalf of workers' cultural organizations. He was thus the pivotal figure in the interactions between Social
Democracy and the avant-garde.

25   David Josef Bach: drawing by Kokoschka

Given his organizational energy, Bach was the ideal person to become director of the Kunststelle, when it was formally constituted in 1919. His success in getting Kraus involved is a tribute to his diplomatic skills, and the fact that the relationship ultimately ended in acrimony should not obscure this achievement. For five years Bach sustained the creative interaction between the idiosyncratic satirist and the Party apparatus, and Kraus responded by presenting him with a signed copy of *Wolkenkuckucksheim* in October 1923.[31] He also contributed a handwritten copy of the poem 'An den Bürger' to the collection of manuscripts by writers, artists and musicians which was presented to Bach to mark his fiftieth birthday on 13 August 1924.[32] Kraus had reason to be grateful to the Kunststelle, since Bach organized twelve performances of *Die letzte Nacht*, epilogue to *Die letzten Tage der Menschheit*, at the Neue Wiener Bühne in February 1923 (F 613–21, 62). In April 1924 the Kunststelle also sponsored the Viennese première of Kraus's poetic dramas, *Traumstück* and *Traumtheater*, directed by Berthold Viertel, with music conducted by Paul Amadeus Pisk, the music critic of the *Arbeiter-Zeitung* (F 649–56, 128).[33] Bach's success in gaining the satirist's confidence is shown by the fact that Kraus, who refused to allow *Die letzten Tage der Menschheit* to be performed in the commercial theatre, gave permission for him to stage the play for a working-class audience at the Vienna Carl-Theater. This idea, described by Bach as 'the dream of his life', was never realized, since the Carl-Theater project, after staging *Lenin* by Ernst Fischer, ran into financial difficulties and had to be abandoned. Kraus was subsequently scathing about Bach's approach to staging the play, but his willingness to contemplate this production reflects his respect for Bach's abilities (F 795–9, 38–9).

The activities of the Kunststelle were not simply icing on the cake of socialism, since the frustration of the Party's hopes for political power led it to intensify its efforts to conquer hearts and minds. Socialist culture was to succeed, where political propaganda had failed, in weaning the Austrian electorate from conservative prejudice and Catholic superstition. The climax of Bach's career was the Music and Theatre Festival which he organized in autumn 1924, the year of his fiftieth birthday. The ambitious programme was accompanied by an exhibition at the City Hall showcasing the vitality of Viennese popular theatre. Conscious of Kraus's renewal of this tradition, Bach offered to display the manuscripts of two topical strophes written by Kraus for the Comet Song from Nestroy's *Lumpazivagabundus*.[34] He also welcomed his suggestion that one of Nestroy's neglected plays, *Eine Wohnung ist zu vermieten*, should be revived at the Lustspieltheater under the direction of Josef Jarno. The production proved a success, and Kraus, who acted as artistic consultant, could claim some of the credit (F 668–75, 64–6). However, he was disappointed with the exhibition at the City Hall, which also featured popular entertainers like Ralph Benatzky and Josma Selim (F 668–75, 40–1). After noting that the exhibition, which ran from 13 September to 16 November, had attracted 26,738 visitors, he claimed that it demonstrated the bankruptcy of the Viennese theatre – the displacement of Nestroy's authentic comedy by trivial modern operettas (F 679–85, 17).

A more serious conflict was provoked by the International Exhibition of New Theatre Technology, which Bach organized at the Konzerthaus. The most daring modern designs were on display, including a full-scale model of Friedrich Kiesler's 'Raumbühne', a spiral stage construction designed to be viewed in the round, which was erected in the Konzerthaus. Popular scepticism is reflected in a cartoon in the *Kronenzeitung* mocking the spiral stage and the constructivist costumes (Fig. 26). Such designs were calculated to provoke the wrath of a satirist hostile to gimmickry, and Kraus ridiculed the suggestion, put to Kiesler in an interview, that a *Faust* production on the 'Raumbühne' would involve Gretchen zooming up on a motorbike to recite her verses (F 668–75, 39). On 5 October 1924 Kraus reclaimed his territory by booking the large hall of the Konzerthaus for a public reading to mark the tenth anniversary of the outbreak of war. In a forthright declaration he denounced those who were turning the theatre into a mixture of 'motor-racing track and boxing ring'. Chief among the culprits was the avant-garde director Karlheinz Martin, an outspoken advocate of experimental theatre (F 668–75, 61 & 88).

26   Cartoon of the 'Raumbühne' by Ladislaus Tuszynsky

The Festival of 1924 marked the beginnings of the quarrel that alienated the satirist from the Social Democrats. Kraus was irritated by the administrative inefficiency of the Kunststelle, including its failure to provide accurate documentation about donations transmitted to charitable causes. This prompted him to send Austerlitz that letter of 6 November, objecting (without mentioning Bach by name) to the unprincipled way in which he organized the Party's cultural programme. Reading between the lines, it is clear that Kraus is alluding to the 'Raumbühne'. The letter alleges that Bach had disowned in private a project which he had publicly promoted, had then promised to revoke his position in public, but failed to keep this promise.[35] Austerlitz must have promptly picked up the phone, since the following day Bach wrote to Kraus apologizing for the most recent administrative oversight (a donation to the Jewish Institute for the Blind had not been properly attributed). Significantly, he also insisted that the promised article about the 'Raumbühne' would soon appear.[36] Kraus was further incensed when Seitz, ignoring his complaints about the Kunststelle, delivered a speech in praise of the Music and Theatre Festival containing an unmistakable dig at the satirist (F 668–75, 40).[37] The quarrel with Bach rumbled on for years, fuelled by Kraus's 'personal annoyance' (F 712–16, 78). In December 1925 he published a lengthy account of his reasons for declining to participate in the Festival of the Republic. By this date, his wrath was directed not simply at socialist cultural politics, but at the failure to support his campaign against *Die Stunde* (F 706–11, 63 & 67).

Kraus's judgement on Bach seems unduly harsh. It took a bold man to introduce avant-garde stage technology to conservative Vienna, as historians of the theatre have noted. Admittedly, the 'Raumbühne' proved impractical, since the scaffolding tended to obscure the sight-lines and prevent the audience from following the action. Only one play, *Im Dunkeln* by Paul Frischauer, was actually staged on the structure in the Konzerthaus, and this proved a flop. But Kiesler was one of the most imaginative designers of his generation, whose work now enjoys international renown.[38] Bach's weakness (in Kraus's eyes) lay in the attempt to cater for all tastes. Put more positively, his aim was to create a cultural consensus that would draw performers from different factions into his orbit. His first great success was the Music Festival of June 1920, in which he involved church choristers as well as the Workers' Choir, high mass in St Stephen's Cathedral as well as Schoenberg's 'Gurrelieder'. The Festival, which was underwritten by the Vienna City Council, actually made a profit, and over 125,000 Crowns were donated to a fund for the relief of tubercular children. This elicited from *Der Volkssturm* the acid comment that 'in the hands of Jews everything becomes a money-making business'.[39] Even Arthur Schnitzler had reservations about Bach's approach to the arts, which he found 'unclear, party-orientated, self-important' (AST, 23 October 1920). But Bach continued to promote consensus politics, and the productions during the Festival of 1924 included not only Fischer's *Lenin*, but also a mystery play by Richard Kralik, the doyen of Catholic culture. This is the context in which to interpret Kraus's strictures (in his letter to Austerlitz) on Bach's 'complete lack of conviction [. . .] in the conduct and promotion of matters to which, in contrast to your party, I assign the highest priority'. Austerlitz, while doing his best to defend Bach's position, had to concede that on this point Kraus was right.[40] The satirist was by no means alone in his criticism, since there were radical spirits within the Party who shared his view that Bach was selling out to the bourgeoisie.[41] The slide towards embourgeoisement became one of Kraus's most insistent themes, and once he had broken off his relationship with Bach, he repeatedly denounced the Kunststelle, above all in the devastating attack delivered to a working-class audience in December 1925. Instead of providing for the cultural needs of the proletariat (he alleged), it was 'propping up the collapsing culture-industry of the bourgeoisie' and fobbing the workers off with trivial operettas (F 712–16, 2 & 8). Thus Bach found himself in an impossible position, caught between Kraus's unattainably high standards and the radicalism of younger members of the Party, who accused him of ignoring the workers in the industrial suburbs.[42]

Marxism on Moral Foundations

The polemic against Bach formed part of Kraus's campaign against the 'infamy of embourgeoisement' (F 712–16, 2). His critique was most effective when he focused on the hollowness of socialist rhetoric, with Otto Bauer's martial metaphors a favourite target. In the triumphal parades of the socialist masses he detected nationalistic overtones, especially when militants from Austria were demonstrating solidarity with their comrades in Berlin. Kraus abhorred the reactionary politics of right-wing German leaders like Friedrich Ebert and Gustav Noske, preferring the Austrian working-class movement with its 'simultaneously more humane and more politically radical outlook' (F 697–705, 120). But he was no more successful than Bauer in explaining how a classless society could be created without revolutionary violence. In December 1922 he suggested that the failure to act decisively in November 1918 constituted the 'historical guilt of the socialist party' (F 608–12, 7). But he appeared to have forgotten that he had supported its defence of stable democratic institutions. The plutocrats may have been 'trembling' (F 632–9, 20), but there was never any chance of depriving them of power by parliamentary means. After the breakdown of the coalition, the influence of the Social Democrats was restricted to Vienna, and – as Danneberg observed – 'Capitalism cannot be abolished from the Town Hall'.[43] By the mid-1920s Kraus's condemnation of the Social Democrats grew increasingly strident as he became convinced that, politically as well as culturally, they were selling out to the establishment. Despite its revolutionary rhetoric, the Party was making deals behind the scenes with Chancellor Ignaz Seipel, while dubious business transactions were being arranged with capitalists like Siegmund Bosel in order to bail out socialized industries. Worse still, the *Arbeiter-Zeitung* was making concessions to consumerism by accepting advertisements from large department stores. These tendencies led Kraus in

December 1925 to denounce the compromises of 'right-wing socialist politicians' who were responsible for 'the transformation of the socialist into the capitalist world' (F 712–16, 2).

Politically, the tactics of the Socialist Democrats did indeed lead to disaster, while their social and cultural reforms were only partly successful.[44] But Kraus's critique betrays a fundamental inconsistency.[45] He wanted radical social reform without the revolutionary seizure of power, and he blamed the Social Democrats when this proved impossible. In an intemperate poem he denounced them as 'parvenus intoxicated with bourgeois poison', who had embarked on the path of collaboration by means of 'furtive zigzags' (F 743–50, 4). This may have applied to opportunists on the right of the Party, for example Franz Gruener, the property speculator who acquired a castle in the Tyrol (F 743–50, 31–2).[46] But Bauer and Seitz, whatever their miscalculations, were men of probity who would have endorsed Kraus's concept of a 'Marxism on moral foundations' (F 743–50, 152). He implicitly acknowledged this in October 1926, after the Social Democrats had finally come out in support of his campaign against *Die Stunde*. In the euphoria of victory he defined himself as an 'outsider who is nevertheless the ally of a great cause', alluding to the Party as 'the last hope for the future of humanity' (F 735–42, 59).

Further disillusionment was to follow as the political and economic situation deteriorated and another antagonist, Johannes Schober, became chancellor of Austria. Kraus did not entirely lose faith in the socialist movement, since he maintained close links with the German Social Democratic Party in Czechoslovakia, which supported his campaign against Schober (F 800–5, 66–8). But he repudiated the compromising tactics of the Austrian Party, and in September 1930 he attacked Otto Bauer's rhetoric in another satirical poem mocking his 'zigzag course' (F 838–44, 120). The German nationalist undertones in Bauer's speeches struck him as particularly problematic, since he feared that Anschluss with Germany would lead to a renewal of international conflict (F 857–63, 3–4). There were moments, in the crisis years around 1930, after the strategy of the Social Democrats had manifestly failed, when Kraus turned towards communism as the 'final hope born of despair' (F 876–84, 6).[47] Amid the chaos of Austrian politics around 1930, he denounced the attempts of the Social Democrats to arrive at an accommodation with the Christian Socials, but events were to discredit his assertion that, in contrast to the zigzags of socialism, he himself was treading a straight and narrow path (F 743–50, 4). Faced in 1933 by the threat of Nazi terror, he felt compelled to reverse his position, blaming the Social Democrats for their failure to support Dollfuss. On the slippery slope of inter-war politics Kraus never found a firm footing, but it was precisely because socialism had raised such high hopes that he felt so profoundly disillusioned.

CHAPTER 14

The Twisted Cross

Austrian politics were shaped by the competing ideologies of clericalism and Marxism. At first the Social Democrats seized the initiative, and during the coalitions of 1919–20 the Christian Socials led by Ignaz Seipel co-operated in a series of radical reforms.[1] To forestall the threat of bolshevism, they accepted proposals for universal suffrage, the eight-hour working day, state support for the unemployed, holidays with pay, restrictions on child labour, the confiscation of Habsburg property, and the extension of state ownership. But the goal of creating a secular society threatened the hegemony of the Catholic Church, since the socialist reform programme proposed to abolish religious education, while the liberalization of divorce undermined the sanctity of marriage. Worse still, the Social Democrats began a campaign to persuade their members to leave the Church.[2] This resulted in a *Kulturkampf* even more ferocious than that fought against the Catholics by Bismarck. Drawing on its strength in the provinces, the Christian Social Party was soon re-established as the dominant force, and in a series of coalitions with other right-wing parties it dictated the terms of national policy, while the Social Democrats consolidated their hold in Vienna. The resulting polarization left the Republic poorly equipped to defend itself against fascism.

The struggle was fuelled by ideological divergences, since each faction represented a comprehensive worldview, the Marxist vision of a classless society challenging the Christian conception of a divinely ordered hierarchy. One faction believed it had History – the other, God – on its side. The clergy became politicized, while the bishops declared that the Social Democratic programme contradicted Christianity.[3] During a series of hard-fought elections, the appeal to the voters developed into a contest about every aspect of social life, from birth control to burial practices. Each faction sought to mobilize members of the intellectual elite, and Kraus's respect for Christian piety did not deter him from condemning clerical politics. There were three main segments to his critique: the tendentious reporting of the newspaper Christians, led by Friedrich

Funder; the unholy alliance of religion and politics represented by Ignaz Seipel; and the high-minded discourse of the Catholic cultural elite, led by Richard Kralik. The polemic was reinforced by *Wolkenkuckucksheim* ('Cloud-Cuckoo-Land'), an adaptation of Aristophanic comedy that can be seen as a response to the revival of Christian theatre at the Salzburg Festival.

Friedrich Funder and the Newspaper Christians

The axis of the ideological struggle was the confrontation between the *Arbeiter-Zeitung* and the *Reichspost*. Since Kraus's stance was shaped by his radical pacifism, the bellicose rhetoric of the *Reichspost* – in both war and peace – became one of his principal targets. In October 1920 he recalled a conversation with the Catholic jurist Heinrich Lammasch about the war guilt of the Austrian press. Moriz Benedikt (Kraus had argued) should be put on trial by an international court, to which Lammasch replied: 'Funder, too!' (F 552–3, 4; cf. 657–67, 42–3). Dr Friedrich Funder, the dominant figure in Austro-Catholic journalism, had joined the *Reichspost* in 1896 after finishing university and was appointed editor in 1902 at the age of thirty. He belonged to the right wing of the Party, and his militant Christian principles echoed the antisemitism of Karl Lueger. During the war he advocated the consolidation of Habsburg power through military conquest, and after the founding of the Republic he became an outspoken opponent of socialism.

Kraus's attacks on the *Reichspost* were concentrated in the years 1920 to 1927 – the period when Seipel dominated Austrian politics with Funder's vociferous support. The *Reichspost* became a crucial instrument in the campaign for the 'salvaging of souls' ('Seelensanierung'), which Seipel launched in the wake of his restructuring of the economy, but between Funder and Seipel there was a significant difference of tone. Seipel was a pragmatist, aware of the need to temper his authoritarian vision to the requirements of international politics, since he could not afford to alienate the League of Nations, but Funder had no such inhibitions. Although the *Reichspost* claimed to be a quality paper with an extensive cultural section, its pages overflowed with anti-socialist propaganda and antisemitic smears, rooted in a theology that was widely disseminated in Austria.[4] Catholic doctrine held the Jews responsible for the crucifixion of Jesus, and every schoolchild reciting the catechism was reminded that the Jews had betrayed the covenant. Indeed, anti-Judaism formed an integral part of Catholic doctrine until the Second Vatican Council of October 1965, when it was repudiated in the declaration *Nostra Aetate*. During the 1920s there was no risk that the Church would restrain Funder's excesses, since the Vatican took a similar line on the threats to Christian civilization. The conciliatory policies of Pope Benedict XV, whose stance Kraus had commended during the war, did not result in any modification of anti-Jewish dogma, and the Catholic press in Rome, led by *Civiltà cattolica*, regarded Judaism as 'a permanent danger for the world'. During the early 1920s this paper ran a series of articles on Austria, alleging that a 'swarm of Polish Jews' had dissipated the country's riches, while the 'ceaseless violence' of the socialists, working under the 'cunning direction' of the Jews, was transforming Vienna into 'a Judaic city'.[5]

Religious prejudice combined with economic resentment to sustain an Austro-Catholic ideology that was to have catastrophic consequences.[6] The antisemitism of the *Reichspost* covered a broad spectrum. The front-page carried lofty editorials about the sanctity of Austria's Christian heritage, but its illustrated evening supplement, the *Wiener Stimmen*, featured vicious caricatures of stereotyped Jews. The paper's election coverage in autumn 1920 exploited a remarkable range of registers: Seipel defending 'strict Catholic principles' and Kralik eulogizing 'true Austrian culture' (September 23); Funder denouncing the Social Democrats as 'racially alien deceivers of the people' (16 October); and Christian Social Party advertisements attacking the Social Democrats as 'Jewish parasites' (16 October). The pervasive antisemitism included a travesty of Goethe's 'Wanderers Nachtlied' ridiculing the Jews for speaking German with a Yiddish accent ('Warte nur, balde / Mauschelst du auch', 2 October); and an attack on eastern Jews as a 'swarm of locusts' (22 September). The most explicitly racist language was reserved for a series of full-page advertisements funded by an unidentified 'German-Austrian' pressure group, which attacked the eastern Jews as the cause of Austria's sufferings and identified the Social Democrats as agents of an international conspiracy. The advertisement of 15 September set the tone with denunciations of the 'judaized' Social Democrats and imprecations against the 'eastern Jews': 'Hinaus mit allen Ostjuden!'

The task of refuting this pernicious propaganda fell primarily to the *Arbeiter-Zeitung*, which published documents suggesting that the mysterious pressure group was funded by the Hungarian government, intent on discrediting socialism and undermining democracy. After a series of bitter exchanges, Funder acknowledged his links with the Hungarian embassy, although he denied receiving a bribe.[7] Kraus played an active role in this campaign, denouncing 'this whole godforsaken gang of newspaper Christians'. Early in October he gave two public readings, ridiculing the *Reichspost* for the cretinism of its antisemitic campaign (the Goethe parody and the attack on the eastern Jews as 'a swarm of locusts' particularly caught his eye). Endorsing the charge that Funder and the Christian Social Party were in the pay of the Hungarians, he accused them of a 'betrayal of the Republic'. This number of *Die Fackel* included vehement appeals *not* to vote for any of the right-wing parties (F 552–3, 1–2 & 27–8).

Kraus saw the First World War as the turning-point in the brutalization of public discourse, not least by the Churches, and the action of *Die letzten Tage der Menschheit* is punctuated by carefully documented scenes in which priests bless the guns and altars are constructed from grenades. In an article of August 1924 he reiterated his indictment of 'the prostitution of theology for the glory of slaughterers'. The conduct of the priesthood during the war had compromised religion so completely that the only remedy would be a 'mass defection

from the Church to God' (F 657–67, 5–6). In peacetime, as in war, it is not
Christian religious faith that Kraus attacks, but its perversion into a Christian-
Germanic ideology with racist undertones. Despite these counterattacks, the
propaganda of the *Reichspost* proved effective. The Social Democratic Party,
vulnerable to antisemitic smears because of the prominence of Jews in its leadership, obtained less than 36 per cent of the vote, while the Christian Socials won
almost 42 per cent, becoming the dominant force in parliament.

Kraus saw this election as a watershed, signalling the return to power of
the reactionary forces responsible for millions of deaths during the war. Speaking in public three days after the election, he denounced the Christian Social
Party and its supporters for their 'corrupted Christianity' (F 554–6, 1–5). He
redoubled his attacks on the *Reichspost*, which displaced the *Neue Freie Presse* as
his principal example of journalistic malpractice, since he recognized that
Catholic chauvinism had become a greater danger than the liberal press. It is
true that Kraus shared certain of Funder's assumptions about the disproportionate influence of Jewish journalists and entrepreneurs, and at times he had
difficulty in distinguishing his own position as 'a better class of antisemite' from
the 'cretinism' of the *Reichspost* (F 552–3, 2). But he was clearly shaken by the
propaganda campaign of autumn 1920, which amounted to an incitement to
racial hatred. If the voices of Jewish journalists were given undue prominence
in the original version of *Die letzten Tage der Menschheit* in 1919, Kraus made
amends through the revisions which he introduced in the book version of the
play three years later. In the first version, the chauvinism of the Catholic press
had formed a minor motif, but the post-war backlash prompted him to accentuate this theme, linking the militarism of the *Reichspost* with its insidious
racism. The scenes satirizing 'Admirers of the *Reichspost*' were expanded, and
in Act IV, scene 1 he inserted the following exchange, using dialect to express
the gut-reactions which the *Reichspost* exploited:

First Admirer of the *Reichspost*: When the next offensive begins, just you wait –
gotcha!
Second Admirer of the *Reichspost*: And then we'll deal with the Jews – smash-
'em-to-pulp!

He went on to construct a composite portrait of the typical reader of the
Reichspost, Kasmader – Cheeseworm (F 622–31, 174). This expressive name,
which he stumbled on by chance, apparently belonged to an Austrian postal
worker, but for the satirist it captured the spirit of reactionary Austria like a
'magic spell' (F 501–7, 80). Kasmader blends Catholic piety with German
nationalism and antisemitic resentment, and in *Die letzten Tage der Menschheit*
this is the name given to one of the fanatical members of that Austro-German
patriotic organization, the Cherusker. A jocular passage in *Die Fackel* attributes
the birth of the *Reichspost* to a late-night encounter between Kasmader and
a prostitute (F 601–7, 110). Kasmader is the dunderhead who, reading the
headline 'Contaminated Sources', leaps to the conclusion that the Jews have

poisoned the wells. This kind of ignoramus may appear to have little in common with the Catholic intellectuals, but Kraus suggests that the combination of Kralik's cult of the Holy Grail with Kasmader's hatred of the Jews is capable of precipitating violence on the streets (F 622–31, 173–5).

The right-wing press had repeatedly called for restrictions on the right of Jews to study at universities – the so-called 'numerus clausus' campaign.[8] Since Jews had high educational aspirations, there was a high proportion of Jewish students in some faculties, notably medicine and law. At the end of 1922 the president of Vienna University, Dr Karl Diener, denounced what he called the 'Levantization of Vienna', calling for a reduction in the number of eastern Jewish students.[9] The Vienna Technical University then imposed a 10 per cent quota designed to exclude Jewish applicants who were not Austrian citizens. These moves were criticized in the liberal and socialist press, with the *Neue Freie Presse* arguing that Diener's antisemitism disqualified him from holding office, since a university president was not entitled to 'speak in public as an antisemitic party representative'. Holders of public office had to accept certain 'limitations'. The *Reichspost* responded to this conception of academic impartiality with the perverse counter-argument: 'Does not this principle justify us in demanding that a Jew should not be entitled to speak in public as a university president?' At this stage Kraus joined the fray, responding to this absurdity with the riposte: 'Well, no actually. [. . .] He is entitled to speak as a Jew, just as he is entitled to speak as a Christian.' He was even more scathing about the further assertion in the *Reichspost*: 'If an office imposes "limitations", why shouldn't semitism be subject to the same limitations as antisemitism?' This time Kraus responded with bitter irony:

> The introduction of the concept of 'semitism' clears up the whole confusion! For of course antisemitism is something positive, either as the expression of Christian faith or as the consciousness of Aryan descent. Even if it were not something positive but perhaps in reality a programme of attack, well, wouldn't it still have at least the same rights as Jewish descent, for this must after all be something negative, i.e. an attack on Christianity or on Aryanism. Jews are not simply semites, but they also propagate semitism. But what is semitism? Semitism is not simply, as the word itself indicates, a campaign against antisemitism, but also against Christianity and Aryanism. (Repeat that after me!) So now it's clear that when a Jew speaks in public as a university president, by definition the university president must speak as a Jew, and we all know what that means. The Jewish university president is a semite, as such he propagates semitism, consequently he would naturally express in public his regret that science, for the time being, is still determined by ability and not by Jewish descent, although he would prefer to exclude native-born applicants from academic appointments and only accept foreigners. (F 606–12, 15–17).

Through a series of ironic inversions Kraus exposes the absurdities of this campaign, comparing the antisemites to a hunting club and the Jews to an association of deer. Following the logic of the *Reichspost*, a hunting journal would presumably claim that huntsmen feel threatened by the existence of deer.

Kraus's decision to side with the *Neue Freie Presse* shows how radically his position had shifted. He now recognized that the cretinism of Catholic journalism posed a greater threat than the sophistication of the liberal press, and during the mid-1920s he moderated his own critique of 'Jewish' influences.[10] Although the *Reichspost* was not a mass-circulation newspaper, it set the agenda for a counter-revolutionary movement which extended from the pulpit to the classroom, from the policies of the Cabinet to the programme of the Burgtheater. The theatre critic of the *Reichspost*, Hans Brečka, was also the director of the Christian Kunststelle, the organization responsible for adapting Nestroy to the tastes of Christian Socials (F 676–8, 16–18). Thus Catholic culture constituted a nationwide network, and it was even worth sampling a journal as parochial as the *Wiener Kirchenblatt* to see how the younger genera- tion was being prepared for adult life (F 608–12, 12–13). The examples Kraus quotes may appear harmless, but Catholic parish magazines persistently reinforced the antisemitic stereotypes.[11]

At the centre of this *Kulturkampf* was the question of educational reform. Proposals for a secular curriculum were fiercely resisted by the Christian Socials, and the reformer Otto Glöckel was repeatedly attacked in the *Reichspost*. The paper provided a forum for Catholic teachers, publishing exam- ples of their work that revealed how racial stereotypes were being transmitted in the classroom. In January 1924 Kraus reprinted a selection of children's verses from Lower Austria, sent in to the paper by two teachers and a priest. They included passages abusing gypsies and inciting cruelty towards animals, as well as the following taunt: 'Jüdale, Jüdale, hepp, hepp, hepp, / Schweine- fleisch, das macht's Jüdale fett!' ('Little yid, little yid, hop, hop, hop, / Roast pork fattens the little Jew up!'). For Kraus this is comparable to the graffiti found on lavatory walls, usually embellished with sexual organs or swastikas, blaming everything on the 'filthy Jews'. He takes such scrawls seriously, seeing them as 'writings on the wall which reveal the popular mentality'. Reinforced by the school system, this kind of 'folk poetry' perpetuates the primitive attitudes which lead to crimes of violence: this is how 'children become adults' (F 640, 127–33). A further example of lavatorial graffiti, which Kraus recalls while reading the *Wiener Stimmen*, relates to eastern Jews: 'Polish Jew, / Drink the dregs of the brew, / That's good for you, / Polish Jew'. This jingle, recalled from his childhood, is identified as one of the sources from which 'Christian journalism derives its slogans' (F 679–85, 71).

Ignaz Seipel and the Salvaging of Souls

Despite the shameful record of the *Reichspost*, the Catholic cause was led by men of intelligence and ability, whose contributions to public life should not be underestimated. Seipel was a liberal theologian who had risen to eminence in the Church before embarking on a political career, and throughout his life he was a prolific author, contributing to a wide range of Catholic publications in addition to the *Reichspost*. Another distinguished contributor was the veteran

Habsburg politician Max Hussarek von Heinlein, Professor of Canon Law, who campaigned like Kralik for a revival of Catholic culture. Conservative positions were strongly represented in the Austrian universities, notably by the advocate of the 'corporate state' ('Ständestaat'), Othmar Spann, whose authoritarian political model was taken up by Seipel during the late 1920s and finally implemented by Dollfuss.

Seipel's politics underwent a series of transformations, as the loyal monarchist evolved into a shrewd parliamentarian. When appointed chancellor in May 1922, his immediate task was to resolve the economic crisis. His mission to Geneva in autumn 1923 enabled him to negotiate a loan from the League of Nations which stabilized the currency. The conditions imposed by the League were that Austria should reduce state expenditure, accept foreign financial controls, and renounce Anschluss with Germany. These policies were implemented by Seipel's new Finance Minister, Viktor Kienböck, who in earlier days had been Kraus's solicitor, but they were denounced by the Social Democrats as a betrayal of Austrian interests to international finance. They rightly predicted that Seipel's austerity measures would place a heavy burden on the working class and increase unemployment.[12] Kraus evidently shared this view, since in October 1923 he suggested that the stabilization of the currency had been achieved 'through a national sell-out' (F 632–9, 166). However, Seipel was able to exploit his economic success at the parliamentary elections of 21 October, when the Christian Socials won 45 per cent of the vote and were only one seat short of an overall majority.

By the end of 1923 Seipel had consolidated his power, but his reputation was compromised by the Jewish question. He made no secret of his anti-Judaism, although he tried to present it in ethical terms. As early as March 1921 Kraus picked up a reference in one of Seipel's speeches to the need to combat 'pernicious Jewry' (F 561–7, 50). While execrating subversive left-wing Jews, Seipel welcomed the support of the Jewish elite, some of whom – notably the banker Gottfried Kunwald – were among his advisers. Once Seipel had ceased to advocate state ownership, the Christian Socials could also count on the support of Jewish-owned newspapers like the *Neue Freie Presse*. Kraus was disgusted to see Seipel campaigning 'shoulder to shoulder' with Ernst Benedikt (F 608–12, 6) and winning the support of Jewish voters during the October 1923 elections (F 640–8, 10). Moreover, the Christian Social Party received financial backing from the leading organization of Viennese industrialists, the 'Hauptverband der Industrie'.[13] Kraus noted that the attacks in the *Reichspost* on 'Jewish' finance did not deter the banks from supporting the paper by means of lavish advertising (F 532–9, 29–30). Borrowing a motif from the gospels, he went on to suggest that the money-changers whom Christ drove out of the temple have been reinstated by the *Reichspost* (F 632–9, 60).

The Jewish issue became more acute in November 1926, when the Christian Social Party included in its programme a clause attacking the 'predominance of destructive Jewish influences'. The phrasing is characteristic of

Seipel, who had defined the Jews in an article of 1919 as a 'zersetzendes Element'.[14] According to his biographer, this antisemitism was essentially 'defensive' and 'ethical', in contrast with the racism of the Pan-Germans.[15] But antisemitism was the common denominator which united the right-wing parties, and in April 1927 Seipel made an electoral pact which resulted in the Christian Socials campaigning on the same 'Unified List' ('Einheitsliste') as the overtly racist Pan-Germans and the fanatically antisemitic National Socialists. The electoral frenzy led a right-wing paper to call for the assassination of prominent Jews, including Kraus himself, prompting the public prosecutor to intervene. After all, the satirist observed, Seipel had a duty as chancellor to protect the rights of all Austrian citizens and did not want to forfeit the votes of his 'dear Jews' (F 759–65, 100).

Seipel exploited his political success as the basis for a moral crusade: 'Seelensanierung' – the 'salvaging of souls'.[16] This concept is ironically identified in Die Fackel as the only idea Kraus has ever found in Seipel's speeches (F 640–8, 41). Given his preoccupation with the phenomenon of duplicity, it is hardly surprising that he denounced the Chancellor for blurring the line between religion and politics. Seipel habitually wore a cassock in public, something that Kraus found offensive in a politician whose primary task was to stabilize the currency (F 608–12, 6). Moreover he was fond of being photographed – and even filmed – performing acts of Catholic piety. Seipel epitomized the aspirations of Austrian clericalism to undermine secular democracy and reconstruct the state according to Christian principles, and Kraus's polemics focus on the problem of charismatic leadership. He attributes this to a complex process of manipulation, showing that Seipel enjoys the support not only of the Church hierarchy and the Christian Social Party, but also of anonymous Jewish bankers. The hacks of both the liberal and the Catholic press combine to eulogize his achievements, and once the movie cameras arrive to film the statesman conducting an open-air mass, his ascendancy is assured. The picture is completed by pious reports that, after his labours at the Chancellery, Seipel retires to the austerity of a monastic cell. Photographs of Seipel making political speeches in clerical garb provoked the conclusion: 'If ever clothes made the man, then God knows in this case the cassock made the statesman' (F 640–8, 42).

Kraus scarcely does justice to the Chancellor's political skills, and even in the summer of 1924, after Seipel had narrowly escaped an assassination attempt, his comments remained astringently ironic (F 657–67, 48–51 & 90–93). The programme of 'salvaging souls', coming from a representative of the Church that had hailed the 'spiritual renewal' of the First World War, left him unconvinced, as is clear from the poem 'To a Prelate' ('An einen Prälaten'; F 691–6, 16). This is by no means the most memorable of his epigrams, but Kraus repeatedly read it in public as a challenge to the Seipel cult. He also mocked the 'salvaging of souls' in satirical verses interpolated into his Nestroy and Offenbach recitals. His suspicions were confirmed by the events of the late

1920s, when the conflict between government and workers resulted in bloodshed on the streets. The ruthlessness of Seipel's policies, as Kraus observed in October 1927, flatly contradicted his Christian principles (F 766–70, 1–2 & 53–4). Seipel's support for republican institutions was dictated by tactics rather than conviction, and his concept of 'true democracy', as defined in his speeches of 1928–9, was virtually a euphemism for 'dictatorship'.[17] It is perhaps an overstatement to suggest that Seipel's ideal society amounted to 'a military dictatorship in which the Church and the capitalists would enjoy unlimited power'.[18] But by the time he finally resigned as chancellor in 1929, he had prepared the ground for the anti-democratic regimes that would destroy the Republic.

Richard Kralik and the Christian-Germanic Ideal

Seipel was supported by a chorus of literary authors. In the aftermath of the war, mainstream writers 'turned to the Catholic heritage for inspiration, as they tried to provide comfort for the defeated populace and a cultural identity for the new Austrian Republic'.[19] The most prestigious figures included Hermann Bahr (a confidant of Seipel), the dramatists Hugo Hofmannsthal and Max Mell, the novelist Franz Werfel, the poets Anton Wildgans and Richard Schaukal, and the popular women authors Enrica Handel-Mazzetti and Maria Eugenie delle Grazie. Since the compilation of literary histories was ideologically slanted, it is not difficult to produce lists of authors who were in favour with the government. Kraus ridiculed one officially sponsored publication of the mid-1920s, *Neu Österreich*, which presented 'the Parnassians of the *Reichspost*' as the leading poets of Austria (F 622–31, 76). This lavish volume gave prominence to authors like Bartsch, Strobl, Ertl, Nabl, Lux, Ginzkey, Greinz, Kolbenheyer and Hohlbaum.[20] These authors, many of whom had strong Pan-German sympathies, blended cultural conservatism with political nostalgia, and although Bartsch and Strobl were third-rate novelists, their sales ran into millions. Kraus also monitored the writings of Max Hussarek, who used his column in the *Reichspost* to argue for a restoration of the 'legitimate' rights of papacy and monarchy (F 557–60, 59) and for the creation of a Danube federation (F 561–7, 96–7). When the American author Upton Sinclair criticized Austrian clericalism in his book *The Profits of Religion*, Hussarek responded with libellous comments. During the ensuing court case Hussarek was forced to retract and pay a fine. Kraus was all the more vehement in his comments on this case because he felt an affinity with Sinclair, whose crusade against corruption in public life included a critique of the capitalist press, notably in *The Brass Check: A Study of American Journalism*, translated into German as *Der Sündenlohn* (F 622–32, 23–8).

Kraus's favourite target among the literary supporters of the Church was Hermann Bahr. Some critics have seen these attacks as a personal vendetta, but ideological factors were equally important. Bahr, after his return to the Catholic fold, had published a chauvinistic volume of essays in praise of the 'Blessings of War' (*Kriegssegen*, 1915), and during the 1920s he became an eloquent supporter of Seipel's policies. His shifting ideological allegiances ceased to be a personal foible and acquired political significance. In a prophetic passage of October 1917 Kraus had warned supporters of the Austrian Catholic revival against accepting Bahr as one of their mentors (F 462–71, 25–9). And he never tired of mocking the religiously tinged cultural column which Bahr wrote for the *Neues Wiener Journal*. Some of these glosses are as ephemeral as the journalistic utterances which they ironize, but the strategy of treating Bahr as a representative figure was by no means misconceived. For Bahr's folksy patter concealed the sentiments of an unrepentant militarist, who by the early 1930s was already welcoming the approach of another war (F 876–84, 48–50). Even Kraus could not keep track of the baroque convolutions of his political creed, which combined nostalgia for the Counter-Reformation with a proto-fascist longing for a 'Führer'.[21]

The leading figure in the Catholic revival was Richard Kralik, a prolific author whose themes ranged from religion, philosophy and history to politics, literature and the theatre. He emphasized the continuities between classical antiquity and Germanic mythology, the Christian Church and European humanism. Kralik was a proselytizer, ceaselessly writing prologues and prefaces, pamphlets and articles, poems, stories, plays and folkloristic pageants; but, by contrast with that of Bahr, his work was founded on a single, all-embracing dogma: the authority of the Catholic Church. Rejecting the liberalizing ten-dencies of *Hochland* (the review founded in 1903 by Carl Muth in Munich), Kralik founded a journal of his own, *Der Gral* ('The Grail', 1906). This pro-vided a forum for the fundamentalists associated with the Grail Fraternity (Gralbund). In his *History of Austria* (1913) Kralik defended the Catholic mis-sion of the Habsburgs against the Protestant upstarts of Prussia, and during the First World War he wrote a stream of pamphlets designed to prove that the Central Powers had God on their side. His Austro-Catholicism had militant political undertones, and in 1922 the seventieth birthday of this 'Master of Catholic Romanticism' was marked by eulogies in the *Reichspost* and effusive publicity leaflets (Fig. 27). The Kralik Society, founded in 1922, which met at his villa in Döbling, provided a rallying-point for Catholic authors and politi-cians.[22]

Kraus had ignored Kralik's pamphleteering during the war, even though his articles in the *Reichspost* argued that the war had been 'sent by God to try and test us'.[23] After 1918, however, he clearly perceived the dangers of this blend of Christian Socialist and German nationalist ideology. In the essay 'Kralikstag' ('Kralik Festival'; November 1922) he attacked the reactionary fraternity led by this epitome of conservative Austria: 'Dilettantism as an intellectual alignment, illiteracy as an artistic principle'. Their antisemitic tendencies are clearly identified, and he goes on to ridicule the blend of nationalism, religiosity and mystification that characterizes Kralik's writings, a variant on that 'Christian-Germanic ideal of beauty' which he had attacked during the war. This ideal has

Das katholische Österreich feierte am 1. Oktober 1922
den 70. Geburtstag des großen Österreichers
und Meisters der katholischen Romantik!
Richard Kraliks Werke soll jeder Österreicher kennen!
Richard Kraliks Werke sollen in keiner Bücherei fehlen!

27 'Master of Catholic Romanticism': Richard Kralik

now been superseded by Kralik's 'synthesis of antiquity, Christianity and Teu-
tonism'. He even (as Kraus notes with derision) wrote a history of literature
purporting to prove that the greatest writers, including Goethe and Schiller,
had been Catholics at heart. Taking the measure of the infrastructure sustaining Catholic cultural life, Kraus cites the organizations in which Kralik played
a leading role, including the Piusbrüder, the Leo-Gesellschaft and the Gralbund, suggesting that there is little to choose between them and the rabble-
rousing Cherusker (F 601–7, 111, 113, 118–19 & 126).

Kralik made no secret of his proselytizing zeal, even including Egon Friedell on his list of potential converts, a performer (Kraus suggests) more inclined towards spirits than the spiritual (F 622–31, 54–7). The Catholic Church, according to another Kralik dictum, was the 'true continuation of classical Greek and Roman culture', and its liturgy defined the significance of Goethe's *Faust*. Kraus would scarcely have devoted so much attention to such nonsense if he had not sensed that Kralik was advancing hegemonic claims for Catholic culture and mobilizing nationwide support.[24] The Association of Austrian Catholic Authors was reorganized under his leadership, and by the beginning of 1925 Kralik could claim that it numbered over six hundred members, all of them acknowledging the authority of the newly elected Pope (F 679–85, 117).

The Catholic revival involved not only sophisticated authors like Kralik and Hussarek, but also rabble-rousing poets from the provinces. From the very first year of *Die Fackel* Kraus had been aware of the 'most extreme pathological wing of the Christian Social faction' (F 24, 7). He hoped that more pragmatic leaders would counteract the fanaticism of racists like Ernst Schneider, the most obsessive antisemite of the Lueger period. In the inter-war period he registered a similar dualism. The most extreme examples of the pathological tendency were two regional poets who were also Catholic priests, Ottokar Kernstock from Styria and Anton Müller from the Tyrol. Müller, who wrote under the pseudonym Bruder Willram, represented Austrian provincialism at its worst – 'the darkest region of Christian-Germanic literary activities'. His verses, cited by Kraus as examples of the Christian-Germanic ideal of beauty, wallowed in images of bloodshed. The satirist feels overwhelmed with shame when he contemplates these 'German-Aryan literary products' (F 531–40, 158–62), aware of the antisemitic overtones of Willram's blend of Catholicism and 'Volkstum' (F 632–9, 28–30).

Even more sinister was the poetry of Ottokar Kernstock, the 'Styrian nightingale'. There are dozens of references to Kernstock's folksy verses in *Die Fackel*, and a whole scene is devoted to the poet and his awestruck admirers in *Die letzten Tage der Menschheit* (III, 32). The blatant contrast between his supposed Christian principles and the bloodthirsty xenophobia of his war poetry made Kernstock a sitting target. Worse was still to come during the republican period, when Kernstock was awarded an honorary doctorate by the University of Graz and his poetry made prescribed reading in schools. For Kraus, Kernstock's bucolic poems about his Styrian 'Heimat' are just as suspect as his celebrations of military heroism. How can a poet notorious for stirring up 'feelings of hatred' possibly be recommended as a formative influence for the younger generation (F 588–94, 81–4)? The answer is that Kernstock's cult of blood and the soil fulfilled the aesthetic needs of Austrian Catholicism. In July 1923, on the occasion of his seventieth birthday in July 1923, Seipel praised the poet for his contribution to German 'Volkstum' (F 632–9, 30–1). Given this weird blend of reactionary Catholicism and *völkisch* nationalism, it is hardly surprising that, even after the poet's death in 1928,

Kraus continued to inveigh against a culture shaped by Kernstock's verses, including the poem 'Sei gesegnet ohne Ende / Heimaterde wunderhold' ('Let the earth of our lovely homeland / blessed be eternally'), which was formally adopted in December 1929 as the Austrian national anthem (F 834–7, 45). However, it seems that Kernstock's most notorious work escaped his attention. In 1923 the Styrian nightingale composed a poem for his local National Socialist group, the 'Song of the Swastika' ('Das Hakenkreuzlied'):

Das Hakenkreuz im weißem Feld	The swastika on a white field
Auf feuerrotem Grunde [. . .]	With a flame-red divide [. . .]
Wir fürchten Tod und Teufel nicht,	To death and devil we'll not yield,
Mit uns ist Gott im Bunde.	For God is on our side.

Kernstock may have had reservations about Hitler's programme, but his career confirms the links between reactionary Catholicism and grass-roots National Socialism.[25]

Kernstock epitomized the *völkisch* wing of Austrian Catholic culture, but there were also more moderate authors in the conservative camp, notably the dramatist Anton Wildgans, who became a kind of poet laureate for the First Republic. His patriotic poetry during the First World War combined military fervour with Catholic religiosity, adding Pan-German overtones that even his mentor Hofmannsthal found hard to take.[26] In 1921, after making his reputation with a series of social-critical plays, he was appointed director of the Burgtheater, prompting Kraus to recall that he had made his reputation by poetry that blended patriotism with prayer. His most celebrated poem, quoted in *Die Fackel* several times, was 'Das große Händefalten: Ein Gebet für Österreichs Volk und Kämpfer' ('Folding the Hands in Prayer for Austria's People and Warriors'). This suggests that the Austrians will be redeemed on the Day of Judgement, not by their piety, but by their musical gifts:

Denn immer noch, wenn des Geschickes Zeiger
Des Schicksals große Stunde wies,
Stand dies Volk der Tänzer und der Geiger
Wie Gottes Engel vor dem Paradies.[27]

Whene'er the hour of Destiny may ring,
Announcing that we all must meet our Fate,
This people that knows how to dance and sing
Stands like God's angels before Heaven's Gate.

In Kraus's view this was one of the emptiest strophes ever written (F 561–7, 91), but he acknowledged the appeal of Wildgans's verses and paid him the compliment of subjecting his poetry – particularly the motif of 'Volk der Tänzer und der Geiger' – to stylistic analysis (F 572–6, 53–60). In March 1922 Wildgans was a member of a delegation sent to France on a mission of reconciliation. Recalling the xenophobia of his war poetry, Kraus sardonically inquired why Austria was sending to Paris 'one of the wildest of its bards of war', recalling Wildgans's notorious line hailing the moment 'when God summoned us to the great task of slaughter' (F 588–94, 101). He went on to question the work of a poet who had become part of the Austrian establishment, only too willing to compose doggerel for fund-raising events organized by the Christian Social Party (F 640–8, 46–9). In a judicious summing up, published in 1931 after the celebrations to mark the poet's fiftieth birthday, Kraus acknowledged Wildgans's integrity, but lamented that his achievements had been distorted by their 'publicistic echo'. However, he did not doubt that Wildgans, who had published his celebrated 'Rede über Österreich' ('Speech about Austria') the previous year, was a patriot (F 852–6, 67–75).

Hofmannsthal, Reinhardt and the Salzburg World Theatre

Clerical Vienna offered little scope for artistic innovation, and it was in the provinces that Kraus encountered the two most significant manifestations of the Catholic cultural revival: the Brenner circle and the Salzburg Festival. The Festival was launched in August 1920 with Max Reinhardt's production of Hofmannsthal's *Jedermann*, an adaptation of *Everyman* designed to recreate the medieval morality as a modern dramatic spectacle. In England the play had been revived in 1901 in a production by William Poel, and it was Poel's text and stage-design that stimulated Hofmannsthal to start on his own version of the play. It was not completed until 1911, but it rapidly became the most popular of all his plays, frequently being staged in the open air. The aim was to continue the tradition of popular Christian spectacle, a revival initiated in the 1890s by open-air productions of Calderón's *El gran teatro del mundo* in an adaptation by Kralik. At that date Kraus had responded with respectful interest, although he recognized the political agenda lurking behind the attempt to recreate Spanish piety (FS 2, 77–8). But when Reinhardt became the impresario of the Catholic revival, his comments became far more scathing. To stage the Berlin première of *Jedermann* in 1911 Reinhardt hired a circus arena with over 3,000 seats, and he had an even greater success later that same year with *Das Mirakel* ('The Miracle'), a religious pantomime by Karl Vollmoeller with music by Engelbert Humperdinck. Reinhardt's scenic imagination knew no bounds, and for the London première he had the Exhibition Centre at Earl's Court transformed into a cathedral.

The Vienna production of *Das Mirakel* in autumn of 1912, shortly after Kraus's conversion to Catholicism, provoked a diatribe against the perversion of Christianity by a counterfeit 'miracle' designed for a world which no longer believes in God. This first attack on Reinhardt coincided with what Kraus calls a 'Kulturkampf' (F 354–6, 71–2). This alludes to the debate about the influence of the so-called 'Jewish spirit', which German nationalists found so threatening. The phrase 'Kulturkampf' acquired a new twist during the debate triggered by Moritz Goldstein's article 'The German-Jewish Parnassus', published in March 1912 in *Der Kunstwart*, the journal edited by Friedrich Avenarius. The phrase was used by Avenarius to describe the struggle for cultural supremacy between Christians and Jews.[28] Kraus's allusion to this debate is oblique and ironic, but he too was sensitive to the prominence of Jews in public life, seeing Reinhardt as the leading example.

Reinhardt's productions for the Salzburg Festival provided ammunition for those who claimed that the 'Jewish' spirit was contaminating Christian-Germanic ideals. The Festival combined religious revivalism with an attempt to reaffirm Austria's cultural identity in the aftermath of military defeat. From the start there were close links between Church and theatre, and Reinhardt's production of *Jedermann* in 1920 was staged in the cathedral square with the baroque façade of the cathedral as a backdrop. In 1922 he took the even bolder step of transforming the interior of one of Salzburg's finest baroque churches, the Kollegienkirche, into a temporary auditorium. A stage was constructed in front of the high altar, and in this setting Reinhardt produced the most ambitious of Hofmannsthal's religious allegories, *Das Salzburger große Welttheater*, based on Calderón (Fig. 28). This provoked the most extreme of Kraus's polemics against Reinhardt and Hofmannsthal, 'Vom großen Welttheater-schwindel' ('The Great World-Theatre Swindle').

Hofmannsthal's adaptation of Calderón gives such weight to the religious allegory that it precludes any serious engagement with the economic and social conflicts that shaped the post-war world. Kraus indicates that he was familiar with only a single scene from the play (F 601–7, 5).[29] But it is not hard to understand why he condemned the discrepancy between the sufferings of the created world ('das Leid der Kreatur') and the facility of Hofmannsthal's religious verse ('gottgefälligen Vers'; F 601–7, 4–5). In *Das Salzburger große Welttheater* the themes of class conflict and social deprivation are assimilated into a traditional religious scheme with neo-Platonic undertones. It is both dramatically and ideologically implausible for the Beggar, who speaks with the aggrieved voice of the proletariat, to undergo a conversion, withdraw into the forest and become an anchorite. The action pivots on the notion of 'order'

28   The church as a theatre: *Das Salzburger große Welttheater*

('Ordnung'), which is invoked by the Rich Man in his confrontation with the Beggar. The order of human society, we are told, is rooted in the harmony of nature and sanctioned by the will of God. But what the play in fact represents is not order but fixity: it is the Beggar's predestined role always to be poor. This deterministic view of social identity precludes those unpredictable movements of the wheel of fortune which we encounter in earlier versions of the *theatrum mundi*, and it is grotesquely at odds with the collapse of the old order which characterized republican Austria.[30] Hofmannsthal's form of Catholic revivalism was politically tendentious, as clear-sighted Catholics acknowledged. In autumn 1922 *Der Brenner* published a critique by Ferdinand Ebner that was just as outspoken – from a Christian perspective – as Kraus's polemic in *Die Fackel*.[31]

The main thrust of Kraus's attack was directed against the use of the church as a theatre. This was the last straw for a satirist who had become thoroughly disillusioned with Catholicism because of its support for the war, prompting his announcement that he was leaving the Church. His fondness for paradox combined with his hostility to Reinhardt led him to declare that his decision was motivated 'primarily by antisemitism' (F 601–7, 5). This implies that the Church has succumbed to the 'Jewish' spirit represented by Reinhardt's production style and box-office success. The fact that tickets for the Festival fetched inflated prices – 500,000 Crowns for admission to a première – certainly gave cause for concern in a period of economic deprivation.[32] Politically, however, Kraus was on shaky ground, since he disregarded the climate of antisemitism in the Austrian provinces. Salzburg, too, had an Antisemitic League that was conducting its own campaign against the 'Reinhardt circus' as a 'falsification of German art by Jewish dilettantes'. When *Der eiserne Besen*, the radical antisemitic weekly, denounced the performance as a 'desecration of the church by Jewish actors', it was echoing the arguments of *Die Fackel*.[33] However, Kraus failed to acknowledge the convergence between satirical malice and popular agitation.

'Cloud-Cuckoo-Land'

In June 1923 Kraus returned to the attack on the Salzburg Festival with one of his wittiest poems, 'Bunte Begebenheiten' ('Colourful Antics'), mocking members of the Austrian cultural elite and the tourists who are flocking to attend the spectacle. The packaging of piety for profit leads him to repudiate a festival that gives 'glory to God / in the highest prices' (F 622–31, 65–7). That same month he sat down to write a play designed as an antidote to Hofmannsthal's Christian mysteries, *Wolkenkuckucksheim*, an adaptation of Aristophanes' satirical comedy *The Birds*. The Greek demotic ethos, with its irreverent allusions to the gods, forms an implicit contrast to Calderón's theocentric dramaturgy. Written at a crucial stage in the development of the fledgling Republic, Kraus's political allegory explores the tension between a harmonious republic of birds and the menace of destructive predators. He uses a colourful menagerie of avian characters to represent the factions contesting power in Austria, including Social Democrats and Clericals, monarchists and militarists, but his most remarkable feat is to anticipate the force that was to sweep them all away.

Formally, *Wolkenkuckucksheim* is a rather traditional play composed predominantly in rhyming pentameters. In the first two acts, which follow Aristophanes rather closely, we see the birds – led by Ratefreund and Hoffegut, two disreputable characters from Athens – defying the gods and setting up their own kingdom in the clouds. The animal fable is wittily adapted to contemporary circumstances, with an abundance of ingenious puns and oblique allusions to life in Vienna. The German translation by Emil Schinck, from which this adaptation derives, suppressed the ribaldry of the original, and Kraus's jokes, for example the parodies of Expressionist poetry, are also rather cerebral.[34] But his emphasis on the physical appearance of his characters, human figures cavorting in birdlike costumes, makes it clear that the play was designed for performance. He thought of it as a 'republican Festival Drama', and made no secret of his disappointment that it was never staged (F 827–33, 82–4). The planned studio production by the Berlin Theater am Schiffbauerdamm was frustrated by events (F 806–9, 27).

The reluctance to stage the play may be attributed to an unevenness of tone, light-hearted at one moment, sententious the next, with hard-hitting topical satire diluted by whimsical flights of fantasy. The most startling change occurs in the final act, which forms a powerful climax. Here the mood darkens as Kraus, departing from his source, portrays the bird-brained community in the grip of war psychosis. The satirist is in his element, transposing the militaristic rhetoric of *Die letzten Tage der Menschheit* 'into a more ethereal realm' (F 800–5, 64). Cloud-Cuckoo-Land is under threat because the gods are angry, and the birds are on the point of surrender when two 'Helpers' appear, offering radical solutions, a monarchist and a fascist. The monarchist advocates the restoration of the dynasty, urging the birds to reinstate the Double-Headed Eagle, while the fascist propounds a programme of hatred and violence. Speaking 'from an Aryan viewpoint', he insists that members of alien species with 'hooked beaks' must be expelled, preferably after being beaten to death. Drastic action is also needed to forestall the threats of the 'red guard' – the robins and the redstarts, in league with the red-headed finches. The symbol he unveils is far more potent than the Double-Headed Eagle:

> Fascist (Second Helper):
>   You hear his words; now listen while I speak.
>   There is a sign that guarantees we'll win
>   and devastates the enemy within.
>   Attach this cross to every twisted beak,
>   grab rubber truncheons and begin to fight:
>   the alien menace must be put to flight.
>   To clarify my plan, let me repeat:
>   it's terror tactics that we must defeat.

The best defence is a pre-emptive strike,
Wielding your clubs as wildly as you like.
          Behold, out of this twisted form
          the sacred swastika is born.
Ratefreund: The sign exerts a magic force,
          I'm really hooked on your black cross.
Fascist: No mortal being can resist
          the cross that's clenched into a fist.
          You'll win your victory in style.
          Just kill them while we shout Sieg Heil!

The phrasing is even more powerful in the original German text:

Der Zweite Helfer:
     Ihr habts gehört; so hört nun meinen Plan.
     Es gibt ein Zeichen, das den Sieg verbürgt
     und auf den innern Feind zerschmetternd wirkt.
     Bringt ihr's auf sämtlichen Kreuzschnäbeln an,
     dann greift ihr von selbst zu den Gummiknütteln,
     um die Reste der Fremdherrschaft abzuschütteln.
     Wenn ihr es noch nicht wißt, sei's euch gesagt:
     der Terror ist es, was wir stets beklagt;
     und um ihm noch beizeiten vorzubaun,
     braucht man mit Knütteln nur herumzuhaun.
          Ihr werdet sehn, es wirkt enorm,
          das Kreuz gewinnt die Hakenform.
Ratefreund: Der Haken wirkt und man schlägt drein,
          das muß ein wahrer Zauber sein.
Der zweite: Unwiderstehlich ist der Reiz,
          die Haken richten sich zum Kreuz.
          So wird euch spielend leicht der Sieg zuteil.
          Ihr schlägt sie tot, wir rufen Heil!

This scene dramatizes Kraus's insight that it is the swastika, not the Christian cross, that has arisen out of the ruins of the world war (F 557–60, 58–9). The verses are reminiscent of the darkest passages in Goethe's *Faust*, as the fascist advocates a genocidal war to be waged with 'swastikas, rubber truncheons and poison gas'.[35]

Kraus recognized, as early as summer 1923, that the appeal of the swastika defied rational explanation. His formulations, in this verse play as in his political prose, draw attention to its visual impact, the 'hooked cross' element which is ever present in the German word 'Hakenkreuz'. In his imaginative vision the cross is twisted so violently that it becomes the symbol of aggression, visual equivalent of the coshes and cudgels used by Nazi thugs on the streets. Moreover the parallelism between the two crosses also implies that reactionary clericalism may be one of the sources of Nazism – a diagnosis which had particular relevance to Austria. In certain scenes Ratefreund, who finds it difficult to resist the 'magic force' of the swastika, is endowed with the features of Ignaz Seipel, the Austrian Chancellor, and Kraus also alludes to the 'Rassenzugehörigkeit' clause in the census form of 1923, a measure that Seipel supported but which the play associates with expulsion and genocide.[36] Kraus recognized that conservative Christianity was not diametrically opposed to Nazism but partially congruent with it, a consequence of the convergence of anti-democratic, anti-Marxist and anti-Jewish ideas. Hence the connection which he makes, in *Die Fackel* as well as in the play, between the 'two crosses' – the symbol of Christian piety, distorted by anti-Judaism, and the 'hooked cross' of Nazi tyranny (F 640–8, 139). This insight was to be tragically confirmed in the 1930s, when the Churches in both Germany and Austria colluded with Nazism.[37] The prophetic verses of *Wolkenkuckucksheim* anticipate the culminating image of Kraus's indictment of the Nazi seizure of power, *Dritte Walpurgisnacht*, written ten years later: 'a comet, like that cross of which it is written that – twisted to the right – it signifies decline, dissipation, death' ('ein Komet, dem Kreuze gleichend, von dem die Bücher schreiben, rechtsgeflügelt bedeute es Niedergang, Vergehen, Tod'; DW 291/*326*).

Since *Wolkenkuckucksheim* was published in October 1923, a few weeks before the Hitler putsch, its warnings could hardly have been more timely. But the play ends on an optimistic note, as the two Helpers are disgraced and peace is made between Athens, the gods and the birds. The spokesman for militarism, Flamingo von Fahnenfeld, may insist that the army has been 'stabbed in the back', but his claims are discredited, and the lark has the final word:

> Wir sind erwacht. Behüten wir das Glück.
> Wir träumten Macht. Wir leben Republik! [. . .]
> So heimzukehren ist der größte Sieg;
> so stehn wir auf zum Schwur: Nie wieder Krieg![38]

> At last we are awake. We bless the happy hour.
> The life of the Republic destroys the dream of power! [. . .]
> The victory we've won lies in the oath we swore
> and steadfastly repeat: Never again a war!

The fascist threat may be dispersed by the republican dawn, but the message of the final act is clear, and Kraus repeatedly read in public this allegory about the combined threat of unrepentant militarism, reactionary Catholicism and militant Nazism.

CHAPTER 15

The Contest for the Law

Defective judicial systems place a special onus on the satirist, and Kraus's polemics draw extensively on the rhetoric of prosecution and judgement, prompting Elias Canetti to criticize his approach as excessively judgemental.[1] But the satirist's preoccupation with justice was not merely a quirk of temperament. 'Considering the defectiveness of our laws,' wrote Jonathan Swift in an exemplary formulation, 'it is possible that many great abuses may be visibly committed which cannot be legally punished. [. . .] I am apt to think it was to supply such defects as these that satire was first introduced into the world.'[2] The application of this dictum to the situation after 1918 is clear. So ineffective were the courts, particularly in their treatment of right-wing political criminals, that for Kraus in Vienna – as for Tucholsky in Berlin – the essential task was to strengthen the administration of justice. However, the two critics reached very different conclusions.

Since the founding of *Die Fackel* Kraus had been committed to the 'contest for the rule of law' (F 657–67, 150), a concept deriving from the jurist Rudolf von Ihering, who delivered a lecture under this title at the University of Vienna in 1872. Frequently reprinted, *Der Kampf ums Recht* became a standard text for students, and Kraus doubtless read it when he enrolled at the Law Faculty in December 1892. He soon lost interest in law as an academic subject, switching after eighteen months to philosophy, and he was later to deny that legal studies had influenced his style (F 679–85, 59). But there can be little doubt that Ihering's principles contributed to his overall strategy. For Ihering, law is not a rigid system, but the dynamically evolving product of a contest between interest groups, and the health of the system depends on the active participation of citizens. The individual who enforces his rights through the courts is motivated not simply by self-interest but by his duty to society, since he serves the whole community in affirming the rule of law. Observing that Austrians appear reluctant to stand up for their rights, Ihering urges every citizen to become 'guardian and executor of the law within his own sphere'.[3] Kraus was influenced not only by these general principles, but by a specific concept cited by Ihering from Roman law, the 'actiones populares' ('Popularklage'). In an early number of *Die Fackel* he defined the aims of his magazine in precisely these terms: 'Because popular accusation is unknown to our oral form of public criminal prosecution, I have founded the "Fackel" for the purpose of *popular actions made public in writing*' (F 46, 20). The institution of 'actiones populares', as Ihering explains in his lecture, entitled any public-spirited citizen to appear in court and call offenders to account.[4] This was the principle that Kraus adopted, speaking out against miscarriages of justice and initiating innumerable legal actions of his own.

The Rehabilitation of Justice

During the Habsburg period Kraus's attitude towards the courts had been predominantly critical. Reacting against the oppressiveness of antiquated institutions, his satire was primarily directed *against* the judiciary, particularly in *Sittlichkeit und Kriminalität* (1908), where he attacked the enforcement of morals by reactionary judges operating an anachronistic legal code. He recognized that the authoritarian legislation of the nineteenth century was losing its validity in a period of rapidly changing social and sexual mores. The failure to adapt legal precedents to new cultural norms is attributed not only to the hypocrisy of bourgeois society, but also to the constitutional chaos of the multinational empire. The introduction of more enlightened legislation (Kraus notes in May 1904) is being frustrated by disputes between national factions. Consequently, court decisions which are technically 'correct' may be just as objectionable as judgements which are manifestly 'faulty' (F 163, 9). These critical essays were widely read, not least by aspiring lawyers. An article published in 1924 in the law journal *Das Tribunal* recalls how aspiring public prosecutors would surreptitiously read *Die Fackel* in court, concealed behind their legal briefs. Kraus came to be regarded as 'judge of the judges', creating through *Die Fackel* a 'revolutionary tribunal' (F 649–56, 112). But, if his attacks on judges at times appear revolutionary, his writings also betray sympathy with the Josephinist tradition, which assigns authority to an enlightened elite, rather than a democratic consensus. Even in his most radical phase, Kraus had little sympathy with the Marxist view of the courts as a system of class justice, and he offended both socialists and liberals through his critique of the jury system.

Kraus insisted that Austrian juries could not be relied on to grasp questions of legal principle, and during the first decade of *Die Fackel* the prejudices of jurors form almost as significant a theme as the arrogance of judges. This culminates in July 1913 in a critique of the Austrian jury system, during which he aligns himself with the conservative jurist Heinrich Lammasch. Trial by jury, he argues, presupposes an educated electorate and a consensus about moral norms. But the system is unworkable in a state riven by faction, where the verdict may depend on whether a juror is 'Jew or Christian, antisemite or freemason, Czech or German, German Nationalist or Pan-German, landlord or janitor, coffee-house owner or customer' (F 378–80, 8). Moreover, a jury system that is dependent on property rights, not education, subordinates complex judicial and ethical questions to the verdict of butchers and grocers. 'Ignorance of the law', according to a celebrated axiom, may be 'no defence against punishment', but it is certainly not a qualification for 'passing judgement' (F 378–80, 1–10).

Lammasch was by no means Kraus's only mentor, since he also had significant contacts with the leading liberal jurist Franz von Liszt. These interactions are explored in the study by Reinhard Merkel, which argues that, under the influence of Liszt's reformist theories, Kraus came to see criminal law as a 'protective measure' for society, not as a punitive system based on moralistic principles.[5] In the pre-war period Kraus also benefited from the advice of two practising lawyers, Viktor Kienböck in Vienna and Hugo Heinemann in Berlin. Heinemann, a pupil of Liszt's, was a Social Democrat with a particular interest in the rights of workers. He and Kraus were on friendly terms, and it was he who conducted the case against Fritz Wittels, obtaining the injunction banning the publication of *Ezechiel der Zugereiste*. Kienböck, who represented Kraus with mixed success in a number of cases between 1901 and 1918, was a lawyer with political ambitions, who became Austrian finance minister in autumn 1922, successfully implementing the reforms required for the stabilization of the currency. Although these jurists belonged to different camps, they all regarded the law as a constructive rather than coercive force.

In the Habsburg era, when legal institutions appeared to be moribund, the thrust of Kraus's satire had been directed against the enforcement of morals through the courts, ridiculing anachronistic verdicts and prejudiced juries. His critique of justice exposed what has aptly been described as a 'crisis of legitimation'.[6] But during his reactionary phase around 1912 he found it difficult to imagine a viable alternative, since his repudiation of an anachronistic judicial system was at odds with his desire for a 'consolidation of the conservative will' (F 354–6, 70). In October 1915 he noted with satisfaction that not only parliamentary government but also trial by jury had been suspended for the duration (F 406–12, 104). This satisfaction was shortlived, for the First World War precipitated new forms of legal tyranny by military prosecutors who abused their emergency powers. In the threatened frontier areas of Austria-Hungary, martial law was enforced with a ruthless disregard for civil liberties, especially for the rights of dissenting minorities. Kraus soon realized that if military courts are permitted to operate without restraint, the rule of law itself is at risk. His awareness of this danger was reinforced by the campaign in the *Arbeiter-Zeitung* against the iniquities of military justice, which he emphatically endorsed (F 501–7, 108). By the end of the war it had become clear to him that civil law was fundamental to the defence of freedom.

In 1919 the legislators of the Austrian Republic embarked on a programme of constitutional reform, sweeping away the privileges of the traditional elite (including titles of aristocracy) through legislation that strengthened the rights of all citizens. The abolition of the death penalty marked a decisive break with the punitive principles of the past and a shift towards remedial conceptions of justice. Court procedures were made more democratic by extending the system of trial by jury so that all citizens had the right to act as jurors, and a Constitutional Court, under the guidance of the liberal jurist Hans Kelsen, was established to protect civil rights against arbitrary authority. The redrawing of political frontiers had eliminated the clash between nationalities that had frustrated earlier attempts at reform, and Social Democratic leaders like Renner, Bauer and Danneberg joined hands with prominent Catholics like Seipel, Fink and Mayr to lay the foundations for a democratic republic. The laws they passed had an enduring value, satisfying a need for social reconstruction which was recognized by politicians in both camps. Responding to this enlightened legislation, Kraus revised his own position, insisting that the law should be enforced against forces that threatened the Republic.

The reforms of the post-war period laid the foundations for a new social order, and Kraus became an outspoken republican, condemning the 'daily barrage of abuse against the Republic through newspapers, administrators and so-called judicial pronouncements' (F 632–9, 168). He continued to campaign against pedantic judges, arguing that the Social Democrats should have taken more radical action to remove those 'fossils' from the Habsburg judiciary (F 640–8, 38). Too often, the judgements they pronounce 'in the name of the Republic' are compromised by the arrogance of the imperial era (F 668–75, 11–12). However, in certain respects Kraus could now feel that he had the courts on his side, welcoming the Press Law of 1922, which was piloted through parliament by Friedrich Austerlitz. This legislation fulfilled one of Kraus's lifelong aims, since paragraph 26 made it mandatory to distinguish paid advertisements from editorial comment. It also enshrined in paragraph 23 (the 'Berichtigungsparagraph') the citizen's right to compel newspaper editors to correct misleading news items, a paragraph that Kraus was to invoke on many occasions. During the debate about this new legislation he insisted on 'obedience to the law' (F 601–7, 65). However, when the legislation came into force on 1 October 1922, devious editors attempted to circumvent paragraph 26 by continuing to publish disguised advertisements. Austerlitz led the campaign against these practices with a series of articles in the *Arbeiter-Zeitung*, naming and shaming the culprits, who included Ernst Benedikt and Friedrich Funder (AZ, 5 October 1922, p. 4). There followed a series of court cases in which the editors were convicted and fined, but at the end of November these judgements were reversed by the appeal court under a presiding judge named Rudolf Wessely. This provoked further attacks in the *Arbeiter-Zeitung* and a diatribe in *Die Fackel* denouncing the justice system for condoning a 'flagrant breach of the law' (F 608–12, 3). This campaign had its effect, and five months later the appeal-court decision was annulled.[7] Kraus greeted the successful implementation of these reforms in June 1923 as a 'rehabilitation of justice' (F 622–31, 13–20).

We now find the erstwhile scourge of judicial malpractice aligning himself *with* the courts, rather than pitting his wits *against* them. This change of attitude was reflected in Kraus's growing fondness for litigation. The court actions instigated during the first twenty years of *Die Fackel* were relatively infrequent and never central to his strategy. His confidence in the ability of the courts to support his satirical crusade had been undermined by his humiliating defeat in the libel case initiated against him in 1901 by Hermann Bahr and Emmerich Bukovics, when the jury found against him and the judge imposed a swingeing fine (F 69, 1–22). During the following dozen years Kraus had shown little appetite for litigation, but after 1918 his strategy was transformed and he became the living embodiment of Ihering's citizen committed to the struggle for justice. In January 1920 almost forty pages of small print were devoted to two cases arising from his critique of patriotic propaganda (F 521–30, 9–47), and the favourable outcome suggested that the satirist might find an ally in the public prosecutor. In March 1926, at the height of his campaign against Bekessy, he was to hail the judicial system as the one institution capable of setting things to rights, when all other forces in the state had failed (F 717–23, 130–1).

The contrast with the situation in the Weimar Republic is instructive. There had been no attempt at a reform of the German judiciary, and, although judges prided themselves on their independence, they were predominantly nationalistic in outlook, treating left-wing political violence with great severity while turning a blind eye to numerous murders committed by right-wing extremists, thus foreshadowing developments during the Third Reich.[8] The political bias of the courts, compellingly documented by the statistician Julius Gumbel, provoked Kurt Tucholsky in September 1921 to publish an outspoken attack on the 'disgrace of our judiciary'.[9] This was to develop into one of his most urgent themes in *Die Weltbühne*, as German judges persistently displayed their contempt for democratic principles, while making allowances for the 'patriotic' motives of right-wing criminals, like those who tried to assassinate Harden in July 1922. The case against Harden's assailants was conducted so ineffectually that Tucholsky grimly concluded 'We no longer have any justice'.[10] As Gumbel continued to monitor the verdicts of the courts, his findings earned him the hatred of nationalistic students, who tried to deprive him of his university post.[11] The events of the following years did little to improve the picture, and in April 1927 Tucholsky published a devastating critique of 'German Judges', denouncing a form of justice 'exercised by one class over other subjugated classes'.[12] He convincingly identified the social factors responsible for the reactionary attitudes of the judiciary, but the sweeping nature of his attack betrayed an increasing sympathy with communism.[13] The contrast with Kraus, who had not yet lost faith with republican institutions, could hardly be clearer. It was in May 1927 that he published one of his strongest endorsements of the criminal code (F 759–65, 108).

Oskar Samek and the Art of Correction

This commitment to the courts was reinforced by Kraus's friendship with Oskar Samek, who became his lawyer in 1922. Born in 1889, Samek was a specialist in press law with a doctorate from the University of Vienna. Like Kraus, he was an assimilated Jew, although he observed major festivals like Yom Kippur. After front-line service as a lieutenant during the First World War, he opened an office on the Schottenring with the backing of his father, the owner of a furniture business. Samek quickly gained Kraus's confidence, and during the next fifteen years they were involved together in over two hundred court actions. They became close friends, meeting regularly in the evenings to review the latest developments, and this alliance transformed both Kraus's satirical strategy and his literary style. His attitude towards judicial proceedings before 1914 had been anti-establishment, satirizing court proceedings with Shakespearean verve.[14] Now we find him writing in the style of a public prosecutor, setting out the indictment with a rigour he associates with Torquemada (F 759–65, 109). This passion for litigation is reflected in the multitude of legal submissions produced in collaboration with his lawyer. When Samek fled to the United States in September 1938, he took those precious files with him, and after his death they were bequeathed to the Vienna City Library, which has published extensive excerpts in four volumes.[15] The collaboration between Kraus and Samek was frequently so close that they must be regarded as joint authors of these remarkable texts. Their favourite tactic, facilitated by paragraph 23 of the Press Law, was to compel newspapers of every stripe to retract misleading statements, and they developed this technique of 'correction' into a fine art. The aim was both personal and exemplary: to protect Kraus's reputation from malicious gossip, while exposing the distorting effects of the media. Recalcitrant editors who failed to follow the letter of the law would be pursued through a series of instances, resulting in a 'chain of corrections' (F 847–51, 51). A favourite target was the *Reichspost*, which in January 1923 had to print a retraction after misrepresenting Kraus's attitude towards Catholicism and Zionism. The lengthy submissions about this affair survive in the form of a printer's proof, indicating that they were originally intended for publication (P 1, 2–24). Court cases provided a rich source of copy for *Die Fackel* throughout the 1920s. In some instances publication signalled an exemplary triumph, while in others the failure of a legal plea led to the publication of submissions claiming a moral victory. The attempt to prove that Alfred Kerr, a professed pacifist, had published numerous xenophobic poems during the First World War, resulted in a protracted series of inconclusive court actions, and the patience of Kraus's most loyal readers was tested in September 1928 by a mammoth number devoted exclusively to this affair (F 787–94, 1–208). The voluminous legal submissions show how much weight these disputatious authors attached to the courts as arbiters in the public sphere.

The submissions drafted in consultation with Samek offer revealing biographical insights, even when they were not actually published. In a draft of

January 1927 intended for the *Neues Wiener Journal*, Kraus compiled a list of his favourite reading, which included – between Spinoza and Swift – the Austrian Criminal Code (P 1, 233). He not only immersed himself in the minutiae of legislation, but also created new case law relating to publication rights for photographic images. This involved intriguing contradictions, especially on the question of photomontage. Kraus insisted on the right to protect his photographic image from 'falsifications' (P 1, 64), repeatedly invoking the law protecting images (P 3, 280–3). But when he himself clipped photos from the press and republished them in *Die Fackel*, he justified them as 'visual quotations' (P 2, 155–64). To carry the day in such cases required the finesse of an erudite lawyer combined with the verve of a sophisticated stylist, and Kraus's polemics were increasingly cast in a forensic mode, appealing to readers 'schooled in criminology' (F 771–6, 102). When a judge named Christoph Höflmayr tried to dismiss these actions as mere 'squabbles', Kraus responded by suggesting that he was out of his depth, lacking the sensitivity of his predecessor, Carl von Heidt (P 1, 97–80). In many cases the plaintiffs, defendants and advocates were all of Jewish origin, which enhanced the sophistication of the debate. However bitterly contested such cases may have been, they at times have the air of a civilized fencing match between opponents with a shared respect for the rules. This created a 'culture of argument', in which authoritative texts are invoked not simply to settle disputes, but to 'maintain a community, defined by its practices of language'.[16] A very different language was involved in Kraus's actions against National Socialists, since he insisted that there should be no compromise 'if [the offender] turned out to be a Nazi' (P 1, 125).

Kraus's income enabled him to initiate actions for defamation that would have been beyond the means of the average citizen, while the self-effacing Samek kept his fees to the minimum. Costs were frequently awarded against their opponents, and substantial sums received in damages were donated to charity. Kraus was able to build up a litigation fund, but innumerable court actions meant that by January 1929, according to a letter from Samek, the fund was completely exhausted (P 2, 139). This may help to explain one of the less edifying dimensions of the Samek files – the pursuit of debtors, which at times degenerates into Dickensian farce. Kraus was well-known for his generosity towards aspiring writers and artists, and in the early 1920s he made substantial loans to support the theatrical enterprises of Berthold Viertel, Peter Lorre and Ernst Aufricht. However, during the financial crisis of 1930–1, when his own position was under pressure, Kraus instructed his lawyer to obtain repayment of those debts. Both Viertel and Lorre were ultimately able to meet their obligations, since they had new sources of income from the film industry, but Aufricht was ruined as a result of the collapse of the Theater am Schiffbauerdamm, where he had been one of Brecht's collaborators. The ruthless streak in Kraus's recourse to the law became apparent when bailiffs were sent to confiscate Aufricht's furniture and auction off his possessions – two hats, four suits, eight pairs of shoes and a revolver (P 3, 71–8).

Wall of Judgement and Despairing Righteousness

The distinctive quality of this commitment to the law emerges from the contrast with other authors of this period. Kraus's position is that of the 'legislator', with the courage to present his own values as 'absolutely binding', while Kafka represents the perspective of the 'interpreter', portraying life under conditions of 'incurable uncertainty'.[17] Kraus emphatically affirms the rule of law, gaining spectacular successes through the courts, while in Kafka's writings the law recedes into an impenetrable labyrinth. The heroes of *The Trial* and *The Castle* are trapped in a maze of interpretations which can never lead to ultimate truth, while in his most celebrated parable the radiance ('Glanz') of the law is unattainable. Kraus responded to the same dilemma in the opposite way, creating (as Elias Canetti puts it in an essay of 1965) the impression of 'an established, absolutely certain and inviolable law'. When he spoke from the public platform, his audience experienced a vision which Canetti describes in words which are strangely reminiscent of Kafka's parable: 'For the incomprehensible and unforgettable thing (unforgettable to anyone who experienced it, even if he lived to be three hundred) was that this law *glowed*: it radiated, it scorched and destroyed.'[18]

Kafka's job at the Workers' Accident Insurance Institute in Prague had taught him that contradictions can develop within a supposedly unified legal system, and his first substantial publication analysed the 'dangerous confusion about relations of law' that had arisen as a result of a series of inconsistent court judgements.[19] If we reconstruct his position in terms of the wider debate about principles of justice, it becomes clear that he was caught up in an intractable conflict of laws, involving five dimensions: family law (which placed him under the authority of his father); Judaic law (in which he was schooled at the synagogue); civil law (the system in which he was trained at the German University in Prague); 'Volksrecht' (the theory that law should discriminate on the basis of ethnicity); and finally existential legitimation (the Kierkegaardian imperative). His characters have difficulty in distinguishing between these different codes, which form intersecting planes of narrative. Josef K, the hero of *The Trial*, assumes that he has been arrested under civil law, when perhaps he should be attempting to justify himself in existential terms. The chapter 'In the Cathedral' dramatizes the disjunction between traditional religious law, with its claim to absolute authority, and modern secular society, with its variable systems of legislation. Kafka's sense both of the grandeur of traditional law and of its inadequacy is condensed into another of his most memorable stories, 'The Great Wall of China'. The inhabitants of his fictional kingdom lead a 'life which is subject to no contemporary law, and attends only to exhortations and warnings that come to us from olden times'.[20] The 'Great Wall' is pictured as a structure which has lost its unifying function and no longer affords any protection. This has been compared to the loss of the authority of the Talmud and the 'insecurity of life in the Diaspora'.[21]

Canetti probably had Kafka's story in mind when he pictured Kraus at work building his own 'Great Wall of China'. The encounter with Kraus was the most significant of Canetti's formative experiences, as recounted in his autobiography. At the first public reading he attended in 1924, he was amazed by the power of Kraus's voice and the applause with which he was received. For a year and a half, Canetti records, he attended every public reading: 'I was filled with him as with a Bible. I did not doubt a single word he said. [. . .] It was only in him that you found justice – no, you didn't find justice, he *was* justice.'[22] With the passage of time Canetti became more critical, as he explains in his essay of 1965. The atmosphere at those public readings is now compared to a court of law in which offenders were subjected to a 'process of annihilatory punishment': 'All charges were presented in a strangely cemented diction that had something of legal paragraphs'.[23] This account goes on to identify a self-righteousness that is ultimately seen as sterile: 'Sentence joins sentence, piece joins piece into a Great Wall of China. It is joined equally well everywhere, its character is unmistakable everywhere; but no one knows what it actually encloses. There is no empire beyond this wall [. . .] and eventually, one could readily fear that the erection of this indestructible wall of judgments had become the true purpose of life.'[24] Canetti's critique is persuasive up to a point, since there are indeed passages in *Die Fackel* that are excessively judgemental. But he fails to acknowledge the political and the religious implications of Kraus's conception of law, so sensitively analysed by Walter Benjamin. In the inter-war period the defence of the law was not a personal idiosyncrasy, but a strategy for excluding the barbarians. There really was another 'empire' looming beyond the wall – the Third Reich.

Benjamin's interpretation emerged from his theological debates with Gershom Scholem, which highlighted the links between Kraus's quotational style and the language of the halachists. Writing in the *Frankfurter Zeitung* in 1930, Benjamin famously asserted that every aspect of Kraus's work was conceived 'within the sphere of law' ('in der Sphäre des Rechts').[25] This argument is taken a stage further in one of his aesthetic fragments:

> In Kraus, halachic writing breaks magnificently through the mountainous landscape of the German language. [. . .] This man's linguistic and moral pedantry does not mean that he always insists on being in the right. It forms part of the truly despairing righteousness of an investigation in which words and things, seeking to save themselves, concoct the most duplicitous alibis, which must continuously be discredited through observation or naked logic. This man is one of the rapidly diminishing minority that have a conception of freedom, but he can only serve freedom by becoming senior prosecutor. Precisely this mode of existence is today the most passionate prayer for redemption that passes through Jewish lips.[26]

Such formulations remind us that, for German-Jewish writers of this generation, the law had theological undertones, as well as enshrining their hard-won civil rights. The Criminal Code becomes blended with the commandments of Moses when Kraus insists that one 'should not bear false witness on behalf of a fellow journalist' (F 759–65, 108). The courtroom imposed different rules from the editorial office, and witnesses taking the stand, unlike journalists at their keyboard, were liable to imprisonment if they failed to tell the truth. The sense of public responsibility derived from Roman law converged in Kraus's practice with the rigour of his Jewish heritage, while the finesse with which he and Samek teased out the implications of legal testimony led one exasperated opponent to describe them as 'the Talmud–Torah people' (P 1, 84).

In the Name of the Republic

While Kraus, in the Habsburg era, had mocked the purported 'majesty' of the law, he now conducts his arguments 'in the name of the Republic'. This inspired him in 1921 to defend the 'return of lawful thinking' ('Wiederkehr des Rechtsgedankens') against the 'concept of violence' ('Gewaltbegriff'). The law itself is discredited, he concludes, when the courts acquit Nazi students who have committed violent crimes (F 557–60, 59). Like Tucholsky, he was aware of the bias of the German judiciary, a disturbing sign of the times that revealed the failure of the revolution to eliminate 'German barbarism' (F 697–705, 121–3). In Austria, too, he noted that court officials were observed wearing swastikas as early as April 1923 (F 613–21, 13), adding in January 1924 that even the Minister of Justice has Nazi sympathies (F 640–8, 36). Moreover, monarchists are being acquitted for actions that would have landed socialists in jail (F 640–8, 136). In August 1924 Kraus joined the *Arbeiter-Zeitung* in condemning a judge for inciting a Nazi sympathizer to use a revolver (F 657–67, 210). The fact that the courts offered such inadequate safeguards made it all the more important to monitor their decisions, and the protection of the law was essential in a situation where outspoken authors ran the risk of being assaulted. On several occasions Kraus had to ask for police protection, and in December 1924 he gave a detailed account of the threats he had received over a two-year period from a group of 'aspiring terrorists', led by an eccentric monarchist named Stefan Padajaunig.[27] After an article threatening to abduct him to Hungary had been published in the journal *Die Monarchie*, he had to endure a barrage of threatening phone calls and anonymous letters. The news that Karl I had died in exile in April 1922 intensified this campaign, since Kraus was regarded as the 'Emperor's murderer'. The limit was reached when the stalker, accompanied by two right-wing thugs, accosted him as he was sitting alone at night on the terrace of the Café Imperial. The police were called, and Padajaunig was arrested. A significant feature of the ensuing court case was that the accused, who had publicly abused Kraus and one of his female companions as 'Republic Jews', repudiated the authority of 'republican justice'. Although psychiatric reports confirmed that the man was unstable, he was sentenced to two months' imprisonment. In his commentary on the trial, Kraus praised both the public prosecutor and the judge, who had resisted the forces of reaction by passing judgement 'in the name of the Republic' (F 668–75, 104–10).

The concept of republican justice, offering equal protection to all citizens, was under threat at every level, from stormtroopers on the streets to conservative jurists in the universities. In Weimar Germany the position was even more parlous, since verdicts were passed 'im Namen des Volkes' – a formulation that opened the door to *völkisch* distortions of jurisprudence, as Tucholsky grimly observed.[28] No wonder the Berlin satirist ridiculed the dignity of the courts so fiercely, in both word and image (Fig. 29a), in his book *Deutschland, Deutschland über alles* (1929). The position was complicated by the fact that in both countries the rule of law was attacked as a 'Jewish' creation. Jurists of Jewish origin had made an exceptional contribution to Austrian jurisprudence in the late Habsburg Empire.[29] During the First Republic they dominated the legal profession to an extraordinary degree, and statistics published in Vienna during the mid-1930s suggested that 85 per cent of the city's lawyers were of Jewish origin. These figures were exaggerated, but estimates by modern scholars still put the figure at over 60 per cent.[30] For antisemites, the republican legal system appeared to be part of that 'Jewish conspiracy' which had supposedly led to the defeat and humiliation of the German race. A typical cartoon in *Der Angriff*, the Nazi paper edited by Goebbels in Berlin, showed a German worker heroically defying the machinations of Jewish lawyers (Fig. 29b). Thus the rule of law was under attack from both the Marxist left and the *völkisch* right.

One of the slogans of the National Socialists, prominently displayed at the University of Vienna in the mid-1920s, was 'The Law of the *Volk* takes precedence over the Law of the State'.[31] This concept of 'Volksrecht' was originally formulated to define localized judicial systems within the Roman Empire, which resisted the universalizing principles of Roman law.[32] It was

Unſer das Recht — euer die Juſtiz!

29   Ridicule of the courts: (a) montage by   (b) cartoon by Mjoelnir from *Der Angriff*
     John Heartfield from *Deutschland,*
     Deutschland über alles

subsequently exploited by nationalists, both in Austria and in the German Reich, who claimed that rights enjoyed by Aryans should not be extended to 'alien' races.[33] The study of law at universities became polarized first between nationalists and liberals, later between racists and universalists. In Austria, the key figure was Hans Kelsen, whose adjudications as a member of the Constitutional Court, particularly on the question of divorce, exposed him to attack from both Catholic and antisemitic factions. It was not only the fanatics who were dreaming of sweeping away the institutions of the 'Jew Republic'. Respected figures at the University, notably Othmar Spann, were devising schemes for the suspension of individual liberties and the establishment of a corporate state.[34] While liberals like Kelsen argued that the principles of law should be universal, reactionary jurists insisted that Jews and other ethnic minorities should be treated as 'aliens' and subjected to discriminatory forms of 'alien legislation' ('Fremdengesetzgebung'). This concept featured in the original programme of the Nazi Party (paragraph 5), and the distinction between 'Fremdenrecht' and 'völkisches Recht' was systematically invoked to legitimize the persecution of the Jews after 1933.[35]

The threat to republican justice reached its climax in the controversy between Kelsen and Schmitt. Schooled in the traditions of the multinational Habsburg Empire, Kelsen was committed to international law, while he promoted constitutional law as a means of reconciling competing ethnic and social groups.[36] Where Kelsen's theory was integrative, Schmitt's was confrontational, driven by his theory of opposition between 'friend' and 'foe'. He insisted that the interests of the state took precedence over constitutional laws, which could be set aside in a national emergency. During the crises of the early 1930s, Schmitt advocated rule by presidential decree, supporting the policies of Brüning and Papen. But after Hitler's appointment as chancellor he shifted his ground, arguing that 'decisionist' laws are sanctioned not simply by the state, but by the ethnic community ('Volksgemeinschaft'). In an article of May 1933, written to welcome the Nazi seizure of power, Schmitt praised the new regulations concerning civil servants, doctors, lawyers and schools for guaranteeing the 'purity of German stock' and purging public life of 'non-Aryan foreign elements'.[37] Schmitt was hostile to heirs of the Enlightenment who used the words 'Menschheit' and 'Menschenwürde' in a Kantian sense to develop a normative conception of human rights, and he regarded Kelsen as a 'zealot of blind normativism'.[38] His hostility to liberal universalism is encapsulated in the notorious dictum: 'Whoever uses the word mankind is trying to deceive' ('Wer Menschheit sagt, will betrügen').[39] Although there is no direct allusion to *Die letzten Tage der Menschheit*, it is likely that Kraus was at the back of Schmitt's mind, since he had clandestinely published a malicious caricature of 'Die Fackelkraus' a few years earlier.[40]

Kraus showed no interest in the abstract debates about the philosophy of law which preoccupied the professors (Schmitt is not mentioned in *Die Fackel* and there are only fleeting references to Kelsen). But his practical activities placed him firmly in the liberal camp, which construed the law as a defence of republican values. Although he had an acute eye for the prejudices of reactionary judges, he assigned to the law a status above factional politics, mobilizing it against irresponsible journalists, left-wing anarchists and right-wing thugs. In 1928 in Munich, he even took Hitler and the *Völkischer Beobachter* to court, successfully claiming damages (F 800–5, 50; P 2, 90–102). He thus made a significant contribution to the campaign to resist National Socialism by means of legal sanctions.[41]

Hangman's Justice

The alternative to the rule of law was the 'hangman's justice' practised by the military courts during the First World War, which still operated in Horthy's Hungary (F 557–60, 59). Kraus was a principled opponent of the death penalty, describing it in his early essays as a 'legislative atrocity' (F 148, 20), since he saw 'legalized killing' as a contradiction in terms (F 207, 29). His revulsion was all the stronger because in Habsburg Austria the death penalty had a human face – that of the hangman, Josef Lang. Even before the First World War this jovial character, commandant of the Simmering Fire Brigade, had become a popular hero. The press reported that he wore a top hat and velvet gloves when reporting for duty (F 77, 8), and there was a lively demand for picture postcards of him eating a hearty breakfast in a café near the prison, after carrying out a hanging (F 114, 11–12). During the war his services were much in demand, and his features are immortalized on the frontispiece of *Die letzten Tage der Menschheit*, in the photograph that shows him gloating over the body of the Italian irredentist Cesare Battisti. In 1920, after the abolition of the death penalty had put him out of a job, Lang published his memoirs, a gruesome concoction of anecdotes later serialized in *Die Stunde*.[42] Kraus responded by describing Lang as the 'prototype of the laughing hangman' (F 632–9, 5). Even for those guilty of political murders, he observed in 1919, the death penalty is 'despicable' (F 514–18, 65), and the reimposition of the death penalty by the Dollfuss regime in November 1933 provoked further agonized reflections (F 890–905, 267). While judging is civil and legitimate, killing is militaristic and abhorrent. Worst of all for Kraus was the combination of the two, exemplified by the Austrian courts operating under martial law, which reportedly passed 11,400 death sentences during the First World War (F 501–7, 45). He gives no source for this astonishing figure, but Merkel suggests that it is not unreasonable.[43] Kraus shows prophetic insight into the kind of judicially sanctioned massacre that is conceivable under an authoritarian regime. His critique anticipates developments in Germany after Hitler's seizure of power, when – as he observed in words borrowed from Goethe's *Faust* – 'lawlessness predominates as law' ('Ungesetz gesetzlich überwaltet'; DW 273/*299*).

It was this belief in a political system based on violence that inspired the rise of fascism. 'Legal system?' sneers a patriotic German in one of the closing scenes of *Die letzten Tage der Menschheit*: 'We have poison gas!'[44] Writing in

Mein Kampf two years later, Hitler complained that deserters from the German army had been treated far too leniently, since relatively few had been executed by the military courts. The only way to maintain discipline, he insisted, was the 'ruthless application of the death penalty'.[45] This threat was carried out during the Second World War, when approximately 30,000 German soldiers were executed by their own side. It was not only the military courts that participated in this frenzy of extermination. The civil courts imposed the death penalty for the most trivial of crimes, such as stealing an overcoat or making a defeatist remark, and the number of civilians executed has been estimated as 'at least 40,000 to 50,000'.[46] A whole generation of German jurists, trained to uphold the independence of the courts, colluded in legalized murder. To understand this contradiction, one would have to penetrate the unconscious dimensions of Christian jurisprudence, which (following the example of Carl Schmitt) saw in the constitutional rule of law the 'secularized arch enemy of Jewish origin'. Schmitt invoked the Protestant concept of 'nomos' as a theological basis for repudiating 'Jewish legal thinking'.[47] After 1933, the universalism enshrined in liberal civil rights was superseded by a system of 'Volksrecht' that exposed ethnic minorities to endemic persecution. The German judiciary lined up behind the Nazi Party with indecent haste, and efforts to identify judges of the Third Reich who refused to serve the regime have yielded a 'grand total of one'.[48]

It will now be clear why Kraus followed Kant and Kelsen in supporting the universalizing principles of civil law and international justice. This prompted him to set aside his own version of the Monroe Doctrine, which normally restricted his 'watchfulness' to the European continent, leaving American affairs outside his sphere of interest (F 743–50, 47). In the summer of 1927 he attempted to intervene in one of the most celebrated of American legal controversies, the Sacco–Vanzetti case. Two Italian immigrants, Nicola Sacco and Bartolomeo Vanzetti, had been sentenced to death in August 1921 for allegedly committing murder during a payroll robbery. Since the two men had socialist sympathies, their supporters argued that they were the victims of hysteria about the alleged 'red peril'.[49] After a protracted appeal process, during which new evidence emerged that would have justified a retrial, the death sentences were confirmed in April 1927. The blatant miscarriage of justice provoked worldwide protests, and Kraus was so incensed that he took the unusual step of writing to the President of Czechoslovakia, Thomas Masaryk, asking him to appeal for clemency. The international campaign had no effect, and on 23 August the two men were electrocuted, provoking Kraus to denounce their executioners as 'monsters' (F 766–70, 55). Drawing parallels with the ruthless suppression of working-class demonstrators in Vienna, he identified the deaths of Sacco and Vanzetti with the 'martyrdom' that results when constitutionally guaranteed judicial processes are subordinated to the 'authority of violence' (F 771–6, 18).

Kraus regarded the rule of law as the cornerstone of republican government. Before the war he had felt able to take for granted the hard-won constitutional rights of the liberal era, and his satire concentrated on the failings of the legal system. But the collapse of the old order led him to alter his position, and in a programmatic statement of July 1926 he insisted that during a period of political upheaval it is essential to uphold 'moral basic laws' ('moralische Grundgesetze'; F 730–1, 4–5). This phrase conflates his ethical crusade with the principles of the Basic Law on the Rights of Citizens, the *Staatsgrundgesetz über die allgemeinen Rechte der Staatsbürger*, which had abolished discriminations against Jews. Kraus's construction of a wall of judgement may have obsessive elements, but in the eyes of his Jewish admirers it acquired a special significance, especially during the Bekessy affair. For he highlighted the dangers emanating not simply from anti-republican fanatics, but also from a new generation of lawless Jews, whose conduct – as we shall see – compromised the position of their law-abiding fellow citizens.

CHAPTER 16

Sharks in the Danube

The most formidable of Kraus's antagonists was Emmerich Bekessy, editor in chief of *Die Stunde*. This polemic runs to five hundred pages, from his indictment of the 'metaphysics of sharks' in October 1923 to the 'hour of judgement' almost three years later. To achieve a balanced view, we must take account of the arguments of Kraus's opponents, which fill many columns of *Die Stunde*, not to mention a 250–page publication entitled *Bekessy's Panoptikum: Eine Zeitschrift gegen Dummheit und Lüge*. The dispute also had visual dimensions, involving acrimonious exchanges about photographs. Kraus's siblings found themselves dragged into the controversy, while its impact on Bekessy's family is reflected in the memoirs of his son Jansci, who was a schoolboy at the time.[1] The documentation from the Samek archive fills dozens of folders, while the need to consult police records in Budapest gave the affair an international dimension. A shadowy role was played by members of the Austrian political establishment, including the Mayor of Vienna, Karl Seitz, and the Chief of Police, Johannes Schober. Most elusive of all were the 'sharks' themselves: Castiglioni, Bosel and Bekessy.

Born in 1887 in Budapest, Bekessy was a self-made man from an impoverished Jewish family, who had converted to Calvinism shortly after his marriage to Irma Maron, a primary school teacher. He was equally fluent in Hungarian and German, and his chequered career began in Budapest on the eve of the First World War.[2] After enlisting in the Austro-Hungarian army, he found military service so traumatic that he feigned mental illness, obtaining his discharge in 1915. He returned to Budapest and founded the Komertia Company, a supplier to the armed forces which proved highly profitable, but his dubious business methods resulted in charges of fraud and profiteering. In 1916 the profits from Komertia enabled him to found a weekly stock-exchange journal, the *Börsenkurier*, but in 1919 he switched sides, putting his communication skills in the service of the Hungarian revolution with responsibility for the provincial press. After Béla Kun's defeat he was briefly imprisoned, and the following year he escaped to Vienna, hiding with his wife and child in the hold of a Danube steamer.[3] However, he was not strictly speaking a political refugee, being (in the view of another Hungarian journalist) 'far too cynical and intelligent to be a communist'.[4] The decision to leave Budapest was prompted by a series of unresolved court cases and financial scandals. During the post-war economic crisis the Austrian capital provided unprecedented opportunities for self-enrichment, and Bekessy was among those who cashed in on the inflationary spiral. His most influential associates were Siegmund Bosel, a self-made man from a lower-middle-class Jewish background in Vienna, and the flamboyant Camillo Castiglioni, the son of a rabbi, who had migrated from Trieste. These two men dominated the financial markets during the inflationary years 1919–23, and from the frenzied scramble for survival Castiglioni and Bosel emerged as multi-millionaires.

Masters of Vienna

Bekessy has left his own record of Castiglioni's meteoric career: the take-over of the Depositenbank, which enabled the Italian financier to challenge old-established banking families like the Rothschilds and the Siegharts; his magical gift for transforming zeros into thousands; his skill at tax avoidance, which prompted the Austrian parliament in autumn 1922 to introduce stricter controls (the so-called 'Lex Castiglioni'); the coup he brought off during the stock-market bubble of 1923 by masterminding an immensely profitable share issue for the country's largest industrial concern, the Alpine-Montangesellschaft; the failure of his attempt, in collaboration with the reactionary Governor of Styria, Anton Rintelen, to create a new business empire in Graz; and finally the collapse of the Depositenbank in May 1924, which ruined thousands of investors and forced Castiglioni to flee to France in order to avoid arrest (BP 83–123).[5] During his years of glory Castiglioni was a leading patron of the arts, amassing a lavish collection of paintings at his residence in the Rennweg, and it was he who financed the restoration of the Theater in der Josefstadt under the direction of Max Reinhardt. The reopening of this sumptuously redecorated theatre on 2 April 1924 was followed only a week later by the suicide of one of his business partners (BP 121).

Castiglioni, an Italian citizen with influential supporters in the Austrian government, was never put on trial, even though he was guilty of 'blatant infringements of the law'.[6] Long before the scandal broke, Kraus had identified his interest in culture as a strategy for tax evasion (F 608–12, 9), and he was scathing about the leniency of the courts towards this 'Patron of the Arts' ('Der Mäzen'; F 691–6, 1–2). The existence of these 'sharks in the Danube' was due to 'the moral poison of the inflation period', which had undermined the authority of the state (F 771–6, 90). But Kraus's analysis was incomplete.[7] In reality, it was inadequate state regulation that allowed the banking system to disintegrate. The run on the Crown was a direct result of an enormous budget deficit combined with a reluctance to introduce currency controls, and the

Ministry of Finance issued new banking concessions with a blissful disregard for the consequences. In 1924 there were sixty-one banks registered as limited-liability companies in Vienna, compared with twenty-six in 1913, and this disproportionate expansion of the banking system is highlighted in even the most sober studies of the crises that undermined the Republic.[8] The account by Karl Ausch draws attention to the extraordinary proliferation of unregistered banking institutions.[9] A further factor was lack of regulation at the stock exchange, which permitted an epidemic of insider trading. The favourite technique was to launch new share issues, assigning substantial packets to privileged investors at a preferential price, to be redeemed at a future date. As the share price rose, the speculators were able to cash in their shares at a vast profit. Castiglioni, during his period as president of the Depositenbank and majority shareholder in Alpine-Montan, became the master of this art. His example was followed by thousands of others, keen to invest money they didn't actually have in shares whose value was expected to rise.

The decline of the Crown prompted ordinary citizens to purchase shares in a desperate attempt to protect their savings. In a diary entry dated 25 November 1919, Anna Eisenmenger noted: 'Everywhere one sees new banks opening, and people who have succumbed to the lure of speculation stand in large groups before the lists of quotations and discuss their chances. Market-women with their fruit baskets rub shoulders with young men about town; shop-girls and servant-girls elbow fashionable ladies. They all want to buy and sell shares.'[10] These small investors were at the mercy of sharks like Castiglioni, who were able to transfer their profits abroad. The stabilization of the currency in 1923 boosted the investment fever, but between January and July 1924, partly as a consequence of ill-advised speculation against the French franc, shares on the Austrian stock market lost 60 per cent of their value. In September 1924, Castiglioni's illicit dealings were exposed. As president of the Depositenbank he had syphoned off profits from Czech-based Spiritus Syndicate to the Investment Trust Company in Zurich, in which he was the sole shareholder.[11] When a warrant was issued for his arrest, he and his associates slipped out of the country. His departure enabled Siegmund Bosel, who had close links with the Post Office Savings Bank (Postsparkasse), to expand his financial empire, but he too overreached himself during the speculation against the franc, leaving the bank with enormous foreign currency debts when he fled to Switzerland.[12] After his return to Austria, he was able to stall the inquiries of a parliamentary commission, continuing to manipulate public opinion through his newspaper *Der Tag* (F 751–6, 6–8).

These events provided a field-day for antisemitic agitators, who drew a distinction between productive 'Aryan' capital, invested in factories to create jobs, and parasitic 'Jewish' speculators. The gross national product certainly fell dramatically in the territories of the Austrian Republic: from a benchmark of 100 per cent in 1913 to 66.4 per cent in 1920.[13] But there were plenty of fraudulent 'Aryan' banks, and it was a myth that the speculators were predominantly of Jewish origin. The Nordic Austrian Bank, which was to feature in Kraus's campaign against Bekessy, made its pitch to investors by declaring that all its directors and employees were Christians.[14] Moreover, members of the right-wing government were heavily implicated in banking scandals: Bosel could not have impoverished the Post Office Savings Bank without the complicity of the Minister of Finance, Jakob Ahrer. It was the collusion between government and banks, stock exchange and press, which allowed the system to run out of control. The failure of the old-established Biedermann Bank provides the most instructive example. To increase its participation in the speculative frenzy of 1923, the bank exploited its contacts with the Christian Social Foreign Minister, Heinrich Mataja, and with Viktor Kienböck, Ahrer's predecessor as minister of finance. It took several years to disentangle these transactions, which involved substantial unsecured state loans, but in 1926 Mataja was forced to resign and the bank went into liquidation.[15]

These banking failures had serious consequences. When the Depositenbank collapsed, 1,500 employees lost their jobs and perhaps as many as 40,000 investors lost their savings.[16] Between 1919 and 1925, the savings of the middle classes were wiped out, while thousands of professional people were forced to retire on meagre pensions. The economic disciplines imposed by the Geneva Agreement of October 1922 may have stabilized the Crown (to be replaced in January 1924 by the Schilling), but this resulted in a credit squeeze and stagnating state expenditure. Low investment in both state and private sectors caused chronic unemployment, which during the 1920s affected a higher percentage of the working population in Austria than in Germany. The number of registered unemployed rose from 103,000 in 1922 to 188,000 by the end of 1924 and to 220,000 by the end of 1925.[17] This resulted in a schizophrenic economy, with a flourishing minority sector producing luxury goods, while the majority population suffered privation.[18] Kraus condemned the resulting social injustices, but his critique, unlike that of the *Arbeiter-Zeitung*, does not identify flaws inherent in the capitalist system, nor does he offer the close analysis of malpractices undertaken by the *Österreichischer Volkswirt*. His theme is the collusion between banking and the press, and Castiglioni fades into the shadows as Bekessy emerges as the villain.

It was Castiglioni, handsomely profiled in *Bekessy's Panoptikum* (Fig. 30a), who launched Bekessy (Fig. 30b) on his career in journalism by backing *Die Börse* ('The Stock Exchange'), which began publication in November 1920. Castiglioni was a major shareholder in the Kronos Verlag, Bekessy's publishing house, which on 1 March 1923 also launched the new daily paper, *Die Stunde* ('The Hour'). The aim, as the financier himself put it in July 1923, was to build up a newspaper empire that would make them the 'masters of Vienna' ('die Herren von Wien'; BP 122). *Die Börse*, a cross between scandal sheet and investors' chronicle, was outspoken in its approach to financial affairs, challenging the hegemony of highbrow journalism like the 'Economist' section of the *Neue Freie Presse*. Bekessy was a hands-on journalist of exceptional energy,

30   Sharks: cartoons of (a) Castiglioni and (b) Bekessy

who could spend hours with the compositors in the print-shop.[19] The success of *Die Börse* was due to his entrepreneurial skills and the close links which he formed with financial institutions, many of which relied on him for journalistic support. *Die Börse* backed Castiglioni and Bosel in their attempts to increase the value of their holdings, and its pages were filled with advertisements for fly-by-night banks. By making regular payments to the Kronos Verlag, nominally for advertising, the banks could count on obtaining editorial support, or at least avoiding embarrassing disclosures, but Bekessy was an unpredictable ally. On two occasions, in August 1922 and again in the summer of 1923, he published attacks on Castiglioni. His critics interpreted these moves as attempts to obtain further money by extortion, while Bekessy himself claimed that they demonstrated his editorial independence (BP 93–6 & 101–4). But his papers supported Castiglioni even during the scandal at the Depositenbank, where his culpability was clear.[20]

Bekessy, whose profile also features in *Bekessy's Panoptikum*, saw himself as the spokesman of 'youthful capitalism' (BP 86). But his style of financial journalism blurred the line between independent analysis and the tendentious manipulation of the market, and this incensed Gustav Stolper and Walter Federn, the editors of the *Österreichische Volkswirt*. Bekessy suggested that their hostility was motivated by fear of competition: the *Volkswirt* was losing circulation to *Die Börse*. But there is circumstantial evidence to suggest that he was guilty of obtaining money by extortion, threatening advertisers with adverse publicity if they did not pay up. The legislation against these practices was clear, but the problem was how to get Bekessy into court, and those who advertised in *Die Börse* were reluctant to testify for fear of counter-charges of attempted bribery. The links with Castiglioni, on whom Bekessy had allegedly made improper demands, could be clarified only by getting the financier to testify against him, but Castiglioni had compelling reasons to protect his ally and was soon to place himself outside Austrian jurisdiction. The only alternative was to provoke Bekessy into taking court action by denouncing his manipulations in print.

An article in *Österreichische Volkswirt* on 7 July 1923 described Bekessy as a liar and swindler who published news items that were invented and untrue (cf. F 697–705, 170). Stolper and Federn further accused him of demanding and accepting payment in return for articles designed to promote the interests of his clients or boost the value of their shares. Bekessy issued a writ for defamation, thus providing an opportunity to bring his murky record before the courts. Stolper and Federn prepared a dossier of his alleged misdeeds, including the text of a 'police report' compiled in November 1923 in preparation for the court proceedings, giving details of fifteen cases in which Bekessy, while still in Budapest, had been accused of blackmail, extortion and related offences. This report, while conceding that he had not actually been convicted on any of the fifteen charges, summed up his guiding principles. Just as the lawyer or the doctor receives a fee from his client or patient for services rendered, so too – in Bekessy's view –'the journalist is entitled to claim remuneration from people for whom he has provided a service, through either the publication or the suppression of news'. When challenged on this point, Bekessy emphasized (in a passage also reprinted in *Die Fackel*) that a newspaper 'is not a moral institution, [but] a business' (F 691–6, 87). Acknowledging his 'theory that the services of journalists are for sale', he attempted to turn the tables by accusing Gustav Stolper of corruption. It became increasingly difficult for Bekessy to justify his position, and on 13 November 1923 he withdrew his action, preventing his opponents from substantiating their charges. He also succeeded in extricating himself from a second court case, brought against him in January 1924 by Stolper and Federn on the basis of defamatory allegations in *Die Börse*. When the issue of Bekessy's dependence on Castiglioni was raised, his defence lawyer came clean: 'Castiglioni is [. . .] the financial backer of the magazine *Die Börse*. There is a certain dependence of *Die Börse* on its backer, but despite this Bekessy's personality ensures that this dependence is reduced to a minimum' (F 691–5, 95). When asked how much Bekessy had received from Castiglioni, the lawyer replied that the sums reported were actually an understatement.[21] There was laughter in court at this disclosure, and some wit subsequently concocted a fictive 'correction' for a false press report, put into the mouth of Bekessy: 'It is untrue that I received a thousand million from Castiglioni. The truth is rather more' (F 691–6, 92). Those who attended the court case in January 1924 were dumbfounded when, on the morning of the second day, Bekessy suddenly announced that he was withdrawing his allegations and offering an apology, while his opponents were abandoning their action. Only later was it revealed that he had obtained a private letter written by Stolper containing embarrassing details about his recent divorce. By threatening to publish this letter, Bekessy obliged them to accept an out-of-court settlement.[22]

Bekessy shrugged off the adverse publicity attracted by the Stolper–Federn cases with disarming cynicism. The success of his papers had made him a wealthy man, with a palatial house in the Wienzeile, three automobiles, and a posse of journalists at his disposal. They included such talented writers as Karl Tschuppik, editor of *Die Stunde*, and Hans Liebstöckl, who edited Bekessy's third publication, the popular entertainment magazine *Die Bühne*. The publisher also had an eye for budding talent, hiring an eighteen-year-old named Samuel ('Billie' or 'Billy') Wilder as a cub-reporter. Bekessy's charisma also won him admirers in the Social Democratic camp. Since the political stance of *Die Stunde* was left of centre, Bekessy had connections with leading socialists, including the former Chancellor Karl Renner and the Mayor of Vienna, Karl Seitz. On 11 July 1923, at the height of the controversy with Stolper and Federn, Bekessy was granted the coveted 'Heimatrecht' (Right of Domicile) in Vienna, which enabled him to claim Austrian citizenship without forfeiting his original Hungarian nationality. The Social Democrats overruled the doubts about his business ethics which were expressed by Johannes Schober at Police Headquarters (BP 199 & 205–11; F 771–6, 39).

Austrian citizenship strengthened Bekessy's position, forestalling efforts to have him deported to Budapest. Stolper was so disillusioned by the failure of his action that in September 1925 he moved to Berlin, but Bekessy made the mistake of provoking a more resourceful antagonist. In an article in *Die Börse* of 29 October 1923 he invoked the words spoken by the Duke of Vienna in Shakespeare's *Measure for Measure*, which Kraus had quoted twenty years earlier to legitimize his campaign against corruption: 'My business in this state / Made me a looker-on here in Vienna, / Where I have seen corruption boil and bubble, / Till it o'er-run the stew' (F 115, 1). This implied that Bekessy had taken over the mantle of the satirist, and some of his attacks on the harassment of prostitutes by the police do indeed read like footnotes to the pioneering essays in *Sittlichkeit und Kriminalität*. Assuming that Kraus would sympathize with his aims, he sent him this number of *Die Börse* (F 732–4, 23). After all, they had a number of enemies in common, especially the journalistic establishment exemplified by the *Neue Freie Presse*, which Bekessy, too, denounced for its hypocrisy.

The Metaphysics of Sharks

The launching of *Die Stunde* transformed the climate of Viennese journalism just as radically as *Die Fackel* had twenty-five years earlier. The established morning newspapers in Vienna were technically as well as politically conservative. Their news coverage was lugubrious, with few headlines, virtually no photographs, heavy Gothic type and monotonous columns of newsprint. Bekessy, by contrast, was an innovator – the first Austrian publisher to exploit human-interest stories, and in 1923 he visited London in order to familiarize himself with the techniques of illustrated journalism (BP 119). *Die Stunde*, an afternoon paper sold on the streets of Vienna, brought a breath of fresh air into Austrian journalism, using roman type and a modern layout with eye-catching headlines. Frequent cross-heads made for easy reading, while the visual impact

was enhanced by a lavish use of photographs. From February 1925 onwards
virtually the whole of the front and back pages was taken up by news photographs, enlivened by ironic captions and incongruous juxtapositions. *Die
Stunde* launched a craze for crossword puzzles and promoted sporting events
and new forms of popular entertainment, especially radio and cinema. Thus the
paper marked a turning-point in the history of Austrian journalism, introducing techniques comparable to those of the popular press in other countries.[23]
Kraus put the matter more wittily when he defined the new journalism as a
blend of 'murder, sport and crossword puzzles' ('Mord, Sport und Kreuzwort';
F 679–85, 136).

Politically, too, *Die Stunde* appeared progressive. Although critical of
Breitner's taxation p   1 the Social Democrats,
defending Vienna a   provinciality of conservative politicians. 1   d favourable coverage,
while the good faith   uently questioned. Karl
Tschuppik, the edi   t who wrote trenchant
leading articles, son   book form.[24] The paper
was critical of Pan–   agitation for union with
Germany, and outs   ocialism. It criticized the
activities of the swa.......   ned the streets of Vienna
and terrorized Jewish university students, while the tendency of the Christian
Social Party to equivocate about antisemitism was also condemned. Thus *Die
Stunde* had its merits as a modern, democratic newspaper, but it was compromised by sensationalistic reporting and dubious business practices. It specialized
in divorces, bankruptcies and suicides, showing a flair for salacious gossip, but
the aim was not merely to divert the reader. The threat of adverse publicity
helped to attract lavish advertising from members of the business community.
In the summer of 1923 the paper launched a provocative series of pen-portraits
under the title 'How to get rich' with the clear implication that businessmen
who wished to protect their reputations should contact the advertising man-
ager. Bekessy had excellent sources of information, and those who had
emerged as millionaires from the traumas of war and inflation were only too
likely to have guilty secrets.

For six months, Kraus observed the operations of *Die Stunde* in silence. His
first attack, which took an oblique form, appeared in October 1923 under the
title 'Metaphysics of Sharks' ('Metaphysik der Haifische'). This denunciation
of the profiteers of the inflationary period, which does not mention Bekessy
or his newspaper by name, is built around a series of quotations from an
unidentified newspaper, celebrating financiers like Castiglioni and Bosel who
speculated against the Crown. 'I didn't follow the herd,' one of the new-
minted millionaires is quoted as saying. 'We bought up their factories, their
jewellery, their shares, their carpets.' Kraus's target is *Die Stunde*, which was
attempting to transform Castiglioni and Bosel into popular predators. This
attempt to glorify 'the will to financial power' is denounced for using

arguments from the 'gutter of Nietzschean thought' (F 632–9, 150–8). The new journalism is analysed more explicitly in an article of January 1924 entitled 'Bekessy's Mission' ('Bekessys Sendung'). Taking as his starting-point those lines from *Measure for Measure* which had been quoted in *Die Börse*, Kraus ironizes Bekessy's Shakespearean posture of self-righteousness. Though he concedes that Bekessy has good reason for despising the liberal press, he is even more strongly repelled by the corruption and sensationalism of *Die Stunde*. Where the old journalism had concealed its financial interests behind a 'cultural façade' ('kulturelle Fassade'), Bekessy's papers are shamelessly rapacious. The 'waltz' of Viennese corruption has been displaced by a 'jazz-band of seething depravity' ('Jazzband überschäumender Verderbnis'). Despite this hard-hitting language, Kraus's article ends on a note of equivocation. Confronted by the Bekessy press, his inclination is to 'dream his way back' into the less disturbing nightmare of the past (F 640–8, 84–101). This publication of 'Bekessy's Mission' was followed by an uneasy truce, which lasted for almost a year. Kraus was uncomfortably aware that the editor of *Die Stunde*, Karl Tschuppik, was developing ideas adopted from *Die Fackel*, and he resolved to treat him with 'extreme reserve', not mentioning Tschuppik by name until August 1926, after he had been forced to resign as editor of *Die Stunde* (F 732–4, 33–5).

In November 1924, a combination of factors inspired Kraus to return to the attack. The first was the role played by *Die Stunde* in promoting the Nordic Austrian Bank. Kraus's suspicions had been aroused by the prominent display of adverts for this bank on its title page (F 657–67, 133), and he noted that, during the final days before the bank collapsed, it was still lavishly advertised in *Die Stunde* (F 668–75, 6–9). The second factor was the paper's treatment of a tragic incident in which a young boy, who had climbed the fence of a wealthy man's garden to find shelter for the night, was torn to pieces by ferocious watchdogs. An editorial in *Die Stunde*, entitled 'Die Planke' ('The Fence'), used this episode as an analogy for the fate of Castiglioni, who had dared to climb the fence protecting 'old-established wealth', only to be confronted by (metaphorical) 'watchdogs'. What kind of imagination, Kraus asks in horror, could treat the corpse of a child as 'symbol for the stranded shark'? Echoing the language of Schiller's *Die Räuber*, he declares: 'This ruthlessness borders on genius!' (F 668–75, 158–60). *Die Stunde* responded by publishing, on 30 January 1925, a malicious article entitled 'A Fraternal Quarrel in the House of Kraus' ('Ein Bruderzwist im Hause Karl Kraus'). This was a characteristic distortion, which had to be corrected two days later (ST, 1 February 1925, p. 4). There was no quarrel, but the introduction of the new Austrian currency meant that the private income which Kraus derived from the family's paper-manufacturing business had to be revalued (at 400 Schilling, in place of 1000 Crown, per month).[25] This process, which was finalized by a court decision of 27 March 1925 in Graz, provided *Die Stunde* with a pretext for ridicule, contrasting the activities of 'Fackel-Kraus' with those of his brothers:

'Sackel-Kraus' (Rudolf, who manufactured paper bags), 'Packel-Kraus' (Josef, who was in the packaging industry), and 'Lackel-Kraus' (his 'lanky' brother Alfred; ST, 30 January 1925, p. 3).

The article, written by Anton Kuh in consultation with Karl Tschuppik, was submitted for Bekessy's approval before publication.[26] But this joke at the expense of the family touched a raw nerve, and in March 1925 Kraus launched a sustained attack. His point of departure is a story in Die Stunde about another successful Jewish family, the Reitzes (ST, 17 February 1925, p. 5). The wife of Baron Reitzes had travelled to Paris to dispose of a piece of furniture (a secretaire), and Die Stunde, seizing on this story, reported that she had eloped to Paris with 'the young secretary of the Baron'.[27] This characteristic blend of facetiousness and scandal prompted a scathing rejoinder in Die Fackel. This does not imply that Kraus had any brief for Reitzes, whose name crops up on a number of occasions in Die Fackel in the context of dubious business transactions. The fundamental principle is that smears about people's private lives should not be used to discredit their professional achievements, and Kraus denounces Die Stunde for pandering to the public. Vienna, he observes, is at last 'in possession of a sexual organ'. Using words that seem designed to provoke an action for defamation, he denounces Bekessy both for 'avid sensationalism' and for supporting Castiglioni, that 'monster who has emerged after the flood'. The paper's claim to be reporting things 'as they really are' is denounced as a fraud, indeed its headlines make 'the naked truth a lie' (F 679–85, 126–40).

The Bekessy press combined a salacious interest in private lives with a campaign for greater sexual freedom and more liberal abortion laws. The police, the courts and the puritans were repeatedly ridiculed in a style of investigative journalism that explored the bedroom as freely as the boardroom. Die Stunde provided a platform for the ideas of Hugo Bettauer, one of whose novels it serialized. During the sensational anti-pornography case against Bettauer in autumn 1924, Die Stunde was one of the few papers to defend him. When Bettauer was assassinated by Otto Rothstock, the paper condemned the crime, while other supposedly liberal papers condoned Rothstock's action. The article in the Neue Freie Presse, describing Rothstock as an 'honourable' man, elicited from Die Stunde a vituperative attack on the Benedikt family, which suggested that Ernst Benedikt was sexually degenerate and a compulsive masturbator (ST, 15 March 1925, p. 3). This episode only served to intensify Kraus's opposition. Given his commitment to the cause of privacy, he was even prepared to make common cause with Benedikt or Reitzes in defence of 'the integrity of other people's genitals' (F 691–6, 79).

Stigmatization

Bekessy responded with his most notorious exploit: the publication, on 25 March 1925, of a front-page photograph of Kraus as a child together with his sister Marie Turnowsky. Lifted from the monograph by Leopold Liegler, this photo was touched up so that Kraus's boyish features acquired jug-handle ears, a bulbous nose, an elongated mouth, and feet about double actual size. A caption was added containing the erroneous information that on 18 April Kraus would be celebrating his fifty-first birthday and that he was embroiled with his sister in a dispute about their inheritance. Bekessy issued precise instructions about how to falsify the photograph so as to make Kraus look as 'ugly' as possible (P 1, 53); but he lived to regret this traducing of the image of a child. For fifteen months Kraus devoted himself unremittingly to the task of discrediting *Die Stunde* and driving its publisher out of Vienna. His first move was to invoke paragraph 23 of the Press Law, which imposed on newspapers the duty of printing 'corrections' of false reports. Few of those misrepresented in *Die Stunde* had ventured to use this device, for fear of incurring further ridicule, but in March 1925 Kraus applied to the court for the right to 'correct' his own photograph, and the ensuing hearings made legal history. Through a series of pleas the Kronos Verlag tried to evade its responsibilities, but Kraus and Samek were implacable.

On 17 April *Die Stunde* was obliged to print on its front page the distorted image of Kraus and sister together with the 'correction': the authentic photograph from Liegler's book, supported by an explanatory text signed by Samek and approved by the court. As a gesture of defiance, Bekessy's staff introduced further distortions into the reprinted photograph, as well as altering the agreed form of words. Samek promptly obtained a further court order, and on 29 April *Die Stunde* was again compelled to print the correction, together with both photographs, adding a sardonic headline to their involuntary lead story: 'Was Karl Kraus a pretty child?' (Fig. 31). Once again, a tiny error crept into the text, and on 28 July Samek once again compelled them to print the two photographs together with the formal retraction. It seems incredible that they should have failed to get it right on this third occasion, but another word was misplaced, and on 10 October *Die Stunde* was again obliged to print the two photographs on its front page, repeating the mocking headline: 'Was Karl Kraus a Pretty Child?' This war of attrition over a photograph provoked further attacks in *Die Stunde*, and readers perusing their evening paper on the journey home must have been baffled. Five times they had been confronted with a front-page photo of Kraus as a child, embellished with huge feet, ugly ears and a mouth distorted into a demonic leer, and four times it had been accompanied by a 'correction'. Kraus was willing to expose himself to the stigma of antisemitic caricature in order to reveal the paper's inhumanity, himself reprinting the scurrilous distortions (F 686–90, 12–13 & 86–7).

Confronted with this series of court actions, none of the staff of *Die Stunde* could remember who had taken the decision to publish the incriminating photograph, and when Samek put them in the witness box, they repeatedly perjured themselves to protect their boss. It was only with difficulty that he was able to exact a financial penalty from Dr Fritz Kaufmann, the person formally responsible for the contents of the paper. Kaufmann, a lawyer by training,

31   'Was Karl Kraus a pretty child?': touched-up photo with the 'correction' in *Die Stunde*

vigorously defended himself in court, claiming that in 1911 Kraus had set a precedent for the satirical exploitation of touched-up photographs by publishing his photomontage of 'The Victor', Moriz Benedikt. He also asserted that the touched-up photograph was not subject to correction under paragraph 23, since it was not a 'statement of fact' but an 'expression of opinion', analogous to a caricature. In his court testimony, as reported in *Die Stunde*, Kaufmann summed up the 'opinion' which the photograph was intended to convey: in early childhood Karl Kraus was already 'an exceptionally ugly little git' – 'ein ausgesprochen mieser Bocher' (ST, 28 April 1925, p. 6; cf. F 691–6, 85). The expressions 'mies' and 'Bocher', both Yiddish in origin, underscored the antisemitic intentions of the touched-up photograph.

Desperate to discredit Kraus by any means available, *Die Stunde* published a further sequence of photographs and caricatures during 1925. On 24 May their front-page included a snapshot of Kraus's motor car (Fig. 32a). Ownership of an automobile was restricted to a privileged elite, and the caption implied that the satirist was a wealthy parasite. This was followed two days later by a photomontage which took a portrait photograph of Kraus and reprinted it against a nightclub background under the heading: 'An Orgy, or It's Only a Short Step from the Private Car to the Bar' ('Mulatschag, oder vom Privatauto zur Bar ist nur ein Schritt'; Fig. 32b). The caption suggested that Kraus had a

32   Images from *Die Stunde*: (a) Kraus's motor car (b) 'Orgy, or it's only a step from the car to the bar' (photomontage) (c) cartoon of Oskar Samek (d) riddle caricature of Kraus

taste for gypsy music and that his favourite drink was Hungarian mineral water. The use of photomontage was designed to evade paragraph 23, but Samek took *Die Stunde* to court for infringing copyright on the original Kraus photo, once again securing a conviction accompanied by a substantial fine, damages and costs (P 1, 58–67). The sketch of Samek published in *Die Stunde* was relatively respectful (Fig. 32c). But during the summer of 1925 the paper ran a series of visual riddles, in which readers were given a verbal clue and invited to guess the identities of those who were caricatured. Kraus was featured on 3 June in 'Riddle-Caricature No. 5' together with an insulting anagram of his name on a 'visiting card' (Fig. 32d). An even cruder caricature of a hunchback with a lemur-like face accompanied a further attack on Kraus on 28 July. The stigmatization of the satirist also included references to his misshapen shoulders, which allegedly became ludicrously visible when he rose from his chair to denounce Bekessy in public (ST 23 April 1925, p. 6). Kraus responded with fury to this use of body-language, which implied that his campaign against the evils of his age was attributable to his 'hunchback'. Returning to the public platform on 25 June, he appealed for the 'stigmatization' of this scandalous behaviour (F 691–6, 80).

Frontal attacks on *Die Stunde* featured in more than a dozen of Kraus's public readings between October 1923 and August 1926. In this war of words, humour was one of the most effective weapons, and Bekessy became the target of a coruscating series of epigrams (F 691–6, 65–7). Bekessy's papers, too, were entertaining, especially the magazine *Die Bühne*, a cheerfully hedonistic publication which gave lavish coverage to his parties (F 697–705, 139–44). Its editor, Hans Liebstöckl, had to redeem himself for an earlier indiscretion, when he let slip the remark that *Die Stunde* had become an 'unadulterated gangster paper' ('das reine Banditenblatt'). When this found its way into *Die Fackel* (F 691–6, 12), he emphatically denied it (F 706–11, 71–84), and the ensuing dispute had to be settled in court (P 1, 125–34).

The real joker in the journalistic pack was Anton Kuh, a charismatic public speaker with an appetite for controversy (Fig. 33a). His irreverent style of journalism placed him in the opposite camp to Friedrich Austerlitz, another target of caricature in *Die Stunde* (Fig. 33b). Playing on the English equivalent of his name, Kraus alluded to Kuh as one of Bekessy's 'cowboys' (F 697–705, 148). Kuh possessed a wicked wit, and his entertaining public performances won him many admirers. After publication of the photo of Kraus's motor car, the satirist tried to defend himself, claiming that it was essential for his trips abroad to give public readings. If he used it for his own pleasure, it was only to escape into the countryside and listen to the song of the nightingales (F 691–6, 100). Kuh responded with a piece entitled 'Kraus, the Friend of Nightingales', which mocked his romanticism. He claimed to have observed Kraus in the Café Imperial engaged in a more mundane pastime: 'swallowing in quick succession fifteen chocolate eclairs' ('fünfzehn Indianerkrapfen en suite zu schlucken'; ST 18 July 1925, p. 5; F 697–705, 151). Thus Kraus was castigated

33   Adversaries: cartoons of (a) Anton Kuh and (b) Friedrich Austerlitz

by the 'cowboys' for a fondness for 'Indian Muffins'. These polemics resulted in a series of libel actions. In an article in *Die Stunde* Kuh had responded to the 'cowboy' taunt by alluding to Kraus as a 'performing ape' (ST 11 October 1925, p. 5). During the ensuing court case Kuh put up a spirited defence. Why should it be an offence to insult Kraus, when Kraus's own insults counted as 'German literary history'? However, Samek secured Kuh's conviction, and he was ordered to pay costs totalling over 1,100 Schillings (P 1, 74–87).

Kuh's fondness for abusive animal imagery acquired a further twist on 25 October, when he delivered an impromptu diatribe from the public platform under the title 'Zarathustra's Ape' ('Der Affe Zarathustras'). This event had been given a tremendous build-up in *Die Stunde*, and Samek arranged for shorthand transcripts to be made as a basis for possible legal action. The two versions in the Kraus archive differ on points of detail from the text published by Kuh himself.[28] He took his title from a section in Nietzsche's *Thus Spake Zarathustra* entitled 'Of Passing By', which describes the prophet's encounter at the gate of a great city with a fool whom the people called 'Zarathustra's ape'. The fool launches into a series of imprecations against the evils of the city, but Zarathustra quells him with a gesture of disdain: 'Where one can no longer love, one should – *pass by!*' Adapting Nietzsche's concept of resentment, Kuh denounces Kraus's followers as 'intellectual plebeians', using an antisemitic vocabulary that is all the more remarkable when one recalls that Kuh himself was of Jewish descent. Responding to a barrage of interruptions, he denounces Kraus's supporters as 'Judenbubeska' ('Jewish bums') and as an 'Itzigseuche' ('plague of yids'). For Kuh, the copy of *Die Fackel* in the pocket of the typical Viennese intellectual is not the red badge of courage, but 'the successor to the yellow patch from the age of the ghetto'.[29] This intemperate language again provoked Kraus to sue. Kuh had the hearing postponed, claiming that he was suffering from appendicitis, but Samek's sleuths discovered that, on the night when he claimed to be in a sanatorium, Kuh – a noted drinker – was actually in the Renaissance Bar (P 1, 140–2). Kuh responded in *Die Stunde* on 9 June 1926 by denouncing Kraus and Samek for 'incredibly complicated deceptions in the style of Sherlock Holmes'. The case was concluded on 11 November, when Kuh was convicted and fined, but the costs were well beyond his means, and he vanished abroad to evade Austrian jurisdiction (P 1, 146–55).

The Law of Inertia and the Hour of Judgement

Meanwhile, Kraus had embarked on the more challenging task of getting Bekessy into court. The publisher of *Die Stunde* rarely allowed articles to appear over his own name, and it seemed impossible to curb his activities without a reform of the law. Speaking in public on 16 April 1925, Kraus claimed that parliament and the judiciary were helpless, since no law prevailed in Austria apart from the 'law of inertia' (F 686–90, 18). *Die Stunde* responded with a sardonic comment, suggesting that Kraus, in league with Ernst Benedikt and Rudolf Sieghart, was setting up a committee to promote a 'Lex Bekessy' (ST 23 April 1925, p. 6). This joke prompted one of Kraus's admirers, an unemployed author named Leo Schmidl, to launch a petition designed to pressurize parliament to curb the activities of *Die Stunde*. This petition, dated 1 July 1925, was widely circulated and reprinted in *Die Fackel* (F 697–705, 106–7). The centre for the collection of signatures was the Richard Lanyi Bookstore in the Kärntnerstrasse, which acted as a box office for Kraus's public readings. The news that Lanyi was displaying the Schmidl petition provoked *Die Stunde* to retaliate on 17 July with the headline 'UNMASKING OF A PORNO-GRAPHIC BOOKSELLER', accompanied by a report that Lanyi was being prosecuted. The story of a police raid on his premises was completed by a cartoon of Lanyi in his crowded bookshop (Fig. 34) with the anti-Krausian caption: 'Morality and ethics in the shop window, filth under the counter' (ST 17 July 1925, p. 3; cf. F 697–705, 49–59).

The tactics adopted against Leo Schmidl were more radical. On 23 July an anonymous advertisement was inserted in a number of Viennese newspapers claiming that Schmidl was willing to make substantial payments to anyone who could provide him with names and addresses in support of his petition, if they called at his flat at Koppstrasse 39 in the sixteenth district, on Friday between 9 and 10 a.m. As a result the hapless Schmidl was besieged by hordes of importunate visitors, demanding money in exchange for addresses. This jape attracted adverse comment throughout the Viennese press, and Austerlitz was incensed because unemployed workers had been taken in by the hoax. In the *Arbeiter-Zeitung* of 26 July he denounced Bekessy for this tasteless practical joke, stinging him into an incautious reply. In an article published over his own name he denounced Austerlitz for the unfairness of his attack, adding a few abusive remarks about Schmidl – one of those miserable 'yids' ('Itzige'; ST 28 July 1925, p. 5). Libel actions were expensive, and Schmidl was in no position to respond to a relatively mild sneer, but Samek realized that here at last was a

Doppelte Buchhaltung

Zeichnung von Carl Josef

— Man muß sich's nur einzurichten wissen ; vorne Sittlichkeit und Ethos, hinten die Schweinerei !

34   'Double book-keeping': cartoon of Richard Lanyi's bookshop from *Die Stunde*

chance to 'unroll the whole Bekessy case' (F 771–6, 57). He agreed to represent Schmidl without payment, mobilizing the law against Bekessy.

Samek's submissions to the court, particularly his plea of 26 February 1926, make remarkable reading.[30] Taking the Schmidl affair as his pretext, he reopened the whole question of Bekessy's 'police report' of November 1923, gaining access to previous court files, including records of the Stolper–Federn case. Forced on the defensive, Bekessy now disowned the idea that the journalist is 'entitled to claim remuneration' for 'the publication or the suppression of news' (P 1, 204–5). However, Samek had reason to believe that he had substituted a 'doctored' report for the version originally compiled by the police (P 1, 211). The action for libel thus opened up the prospect of criminal proceedings, raising the question whether Bekessy's Austrian citizenship had been obtained by fraud. Samek proposed to summon forty-eight witnesses to testify about Bekessy's journalistic practices, including Gottfried Kunwald and Louis Rothschild, as well as Siegmund Bosel and Camillo Castiglioni. Bekessy was not initially informed of the steps that were being taken against him, but as details filtered through to the coffee-houses, he developed a sense of persecution (BP 53–4).

To make Bekessy's position untenable required intense activity behind the scenes. Samek undertook a number of visits to Budapest to interview potential witnesses, and when this news reached the staff of Die Stunde, they fabricated another story, reporting that one of Kraus's representatives, Dr Miksa Rosenberg, had attempted to bribe officials in Budapest in order to obtain incriminating material (ST 30 October 1925, p. 5). Rosenberg was in fact in Vienna at the time, and he immediately forced Die Stunde to print a retraction (ST 31 October 1925, p. 6; cf. F 706–11, 107–17). Further court proceedings revealed that it was the Budapest correspondent of Die Stunde, Geza Bekessy, who had made improper approaches to the Hungarian authorities (P 1, 91–104). At Samek's suggestion, Kraus called on the Police Chief, Johann Schober, on 21 October 1925 to expedite inquiries about the court cases in which Bekessy had been involved in Budapest. Two weeks later Kraus met Schober again, this time at the Police Chief's request, and they had a further meeting at the end of January 1926. Schober had supported Kraus during an earlier crisis in 1918, when he was threatened by the military authorities, and now, too, he gave him a sympathetic hearing. But during this same period Schober and his assistant Bernhard Pollak were also receiving approaches from the Bekessy faction. Kraus's outrage on discovering Schober's duplicity is reflected in a detailed account of these behind-the-scenes manoeuvres in Die Fackel of December 1927 (F 771–6, 45–112), and this episode was to inspire one of the most effective scenes in his documentary drama, Die Unüberwindlichen ('The Invincibles').

It was not only the Police Chief who was involved in double-dealing, since the Social Democrats were also compromised. Austerlitz, who supported Kraus's campaign with a number of hard-hitting articles, had also started court proceedings in response to Bekessy's article of 28 July, but there were others in the Party who valued their alliance with Die Stunde. Apart from providing the Social Democrats with editorial support, Bekessy had found other ways of placing the Party in his debt. In the summer of 1923, he had provided them with information about insider trading which enabled their spokesman for economic affairs, Heinrich Allina, to launch a devastating attack on the Christian Social Finance Minister, Viktor Kienböck (BP 104–5). And when the Social Democrats got into financial difficulties over the Hammerbrotwerke, a bakery owned and managed by the Party, they were bailed out by Bekessy's associate Siegmund Bosel – on condition that they refrained from supporting the campaign against Die Stunde.[31] Bekessy now began to pull strings in order to have Austerlitz silenced. His link-man was Dr Anton Eisler, a Social Democratic member of parliament. On 20 October 1925 they had a private meeting, during which Eisler declared that the Social Democratic Party was 'fed up to the back teeth' with Kraus. Since they had no wish for their relationship to be poisoned, this meeting resulted in a 'truce' between Bekessy and the Arbeiter-Zeitung (BP 197–8). Under pressure from the Party leadership, Austerlitz was obliged to withdraw his libel action and discontinue his attacks, so that Kraus again found himself isolated. Indeed, he was now fighting a war on two fronts. His public reading of 14 November consisted of an outspoken denunciation of Bekessy and an even fiercer attack on the Social Democrats (F 706–11, 94). This was followed on 9 December by a tumultuous public meeting in the suburb of Favoriten, at which Kraus addressed a mainly working-class audience. His criticisms of the Social Democrats were so outspoken that an outraged Party official lowered the curtain midway through his address, while Kraus's supporters vociferously endorsed his campaign ('Nachträgliche Republikfeier'; F 712–16, 1–18 & 35–7).

By the spring of 1926 Bekessy appeared to have consolidated his position, obstructing judicial inquiries through a number of diversionary manoeuvres (F 771–6, 58–65). He had divided the opposition, placated the Social Democrats, squared Schober, silenced Austerlitz, and intimidated Ernst Benedikt and the bourgeois press. Gustav Stolper had left for Berlin, depriving Vienna of the only commentator capable of challenging Bekessy on his own ground.[32] However, Kraus found a new ally in an unexpected quarter – Ernst Spitz, the only member of Bekessy's staff to break ranks. Spitz was sacked in February 1926 for questioning the ethics of a colleague in conversation with Billy Wilder, who reported him to the management.[33] After his dismissal, he published a pamphlet entitled *Bekessy's Revolver*, suggesting that it was not only big business that felt obliged to pay tribute to Bekessy. *Die Stunde* also provided publicity for small shopkeepers and restaurants, and photographs of newly opened coffee-houses formed a regular feature. Spitz described how members of staff would tour the cafes and restaurants of Vienna to collect protection money known as 'Bekessy's Coffee-House Tax'.[34] This allegation was supported by the testimony of the owner of the Café Ankerhof, Josef Heller, who was told that, if he did not pay up, *Die Stunde* would promote the opening of a new coffee-house adjacent to his own.[35] Bekessy responded to these allegations by suing Spitz for libel and attempting to have *Bekessy's Revolver* confiscated (P 1, 216–19). This case was overshadowed by a new banking scandal involving the left-wing paper *Der Abend*, edited by Alexander Weiss, which diverted attention from Bekessy's peccadilloes. While Weiss was arrested and charged with extortion, Bekessy still basked in the favour of leading politicians. On 1 June 1926 *Die Bühne* published a photograph of him relaxing in the company of Josef Kollmann, the newly appointed Minister of Finance, at a dinner in the holiday resort of Baden (F 730–1, 12). This was to be followed on Sunday 11 July by an even more opulent Beach Party on the Danube at Klosterneuburg, at which 10,000 spectators were expected.

It seemed that the law of inertia would prevail, since Samek's investigations were proceeding desperately slowly. Kraus kept up the pressure with further polemics in *Die Fackel*, but he had lost the support of Austerlitz – a 'sensitive heart among tacticians' (F 717–23, 126). When the news broke in March 1926 that Weiss had been arrested on charges of extortion, no one was willing to act against Bekessy (F 726–9, 1–9). But three months later the public prosecutor

finally intervened, and on 26 June *Die Stunde* reported that Harry Weller-
O'Brien, a member of the Advertising Department of the Kronos Verlag, had
been arrested on charges of extortion in connection with the Nordic Austrian
Bank. At this point, the staff of *Die Stunde* made their fatal move. Fearing
that Austerlitz would break the truce, they reverted to the tactic of going for
the genitals. On 29 June, under the heading 'Bedränger kleiner Mädchen'
('Molester of Little Girls'), *Die Stunde* printed a report about an elderly bespec-
tacled gentleman who had been observed on the streets of Vienna pursuing
little girls. His name, they added, was being kept secret because he was 'a political personality'. On 3 July they printed a follow-up article entitled 'Wer ist's?'
('Who is It?'), threatening to disclose the man's identity. Bekessy later disclaimed responsibility for these items (BP 242–3), but if the authorship is
unclear, the consequences were dramatic. For readers attuned to the art of
innuendo, it was not hard to identify the target, since Austerlitz had repeatedly
been portrayed in *Die Stunde* in derogatory terms. He was a bachelor wedded
to his desk, but no one had ever questioned his personal integrity. By publishing what was taken to be a smear against Austerlitz, Bekessy finally alienated
the Social Democrats, and the *Arbeiter-Zeitung* returned to the attack. Kraus
responded by sending Austerlitz a telegram expressing his sympathy.[36]

According to Bekessy's account, the Party apparatus now swung into action.
The initiative was taken by Hugo Breitner, who administered the advertising
tax paid to the municipality by all Viennese newspapers. This revenue was usually collected at the end of the financial year, which meant that papers like *Die
Stunde* were allowed extended credit. In the summer of 1926, according to
Bekessy, this credit was suddenly withdrawn, and his papers were required to
make immediate payment in full, a demand that threatened the Kronos Verlag
with bankruptcy (BP 61–3). This account was later challenged by Kraus, who
denied that 'Breitner taxes' had played the decisive role (F 890–905, 182).
Instead, he gave credit to the Public Prosecutor, who finally responded to the
repeated calls for legal action. A warrant was issued against the advertising man-
ager of *Die Stunde*, Eugen Forda, and on 12 July he was arrested at his office
on charges of extortion. Twelve months earlier, in July 1925, Kraus had named
Forda as the man primarily responsible for the strategy of extortion, identifying the Nordic Austrian Bank as one of his victims (F 691–6, 78 & 94–5).
Forda had extracted advertising revenue from the bank, paid with a view to
obtaining favourable press coverage, at a date when it was on the verge of collapse. After protracted investigations, a director of the bank named Otto
Waldegg finally agreed to testify that he had been subjected to extortion
(F 735–42, 10).[37]

During the early months of 1926, the atmosphere in the Bekessy family
became fraught with tension as their home in the Linke Wienzeile was
thronged with solicitors and soothsayers. But by the time the scandal broke,
Bekessy was taking the waters at Bad Wildungen in Germany, since the stresses
of the campaign had aggravated a kidney condition. The grief of his family still

resonates through the memoirs written thirty years later by his son.[38] A final attempt at self-justification appeared under Bekessy's name in *Die Stunde* on 8 July. He remained defiant, denouncing Kraus and Austerlitz for attempting to intimidate 'fearful public prosecutors or ministers'. Tipped off that a warrant was to be issued for his arrest, he found refuge in France, and it was here that he heard the news of Tschuppik's resignation (announced in *Die Stunde* on 14 July). He also received an ultimatum from his board of directors, insisting that he sell his shares in the Kronos Verlag in order to save the concern. Bekessy consulted Castiglioni, who was also in France and still owned a substantial packet of Kronos shares, but his former ally refused to bail him out (BP 64–8). Faced with this disaster, Bekessy was forced to relinquish control of *Die Stunde*. Even the elements appeared to be conspiring against him. The Beach Party at Klosterneuburg had to be postponed because of torrential rains, finally taking place on Sunday 18 July, and fulsome reports in *Die Stunde* and *Die Bühne* could scarcely conceal the debacle. Four days later, on 22 July, *Die Stunde* carried the formal announcement that Bekessy had resigned as editor in chief and the paper had been taken over by a rival firm.

Thus Kraus's campaign culminated in an astonishing victory. The suggestion by Robert Musil that his critique of the press merely expressed the 'objectivized bad conscience' of sloppy journalism, with no practical consequences, proved way off target.[39] To picture Kraus's achievement in modern terms, we might imagine a satirical journal like *Private Eye* conducting a campaign against the most notorious British tabloid, the *Sun*, and driving its proprietor Rupert Murdoch out of London.[40] A slim number of *Die Fackel*, published in July after Forda's arrest, celebrated the 'Hour of Judgement' ('Die Stunde des Gerichts', F 730–1, 1–32), but it was only on 3 August, after Bekessy had fled to France, that Kraus could claim complete success for his 'solitary struggle' (F 732–4, 3). He was puzzled why a writer as gifted as Tschuppik should have provided the 'brothel music' for a strategy of extortion.[41] But there could be no doubt about Tschuppik's editorial responsibility: it was he who had brought about the 'prostitution' of Vienna 'in the name of a free spirit' (F 732–4, 33–4). Samek received confidential reports suggesting that Tschuppik was dependent on cocaine and that he and Kuh were lovers.[42] But Kraus, true to his principles, made no reference to their private lives. His aim was to purify the public sphere, presenting his victory as a vindication of the rule of law. Hence his tribute to his solicitor: since the campaign began in April 1925, Samek must have spent 1,600 hours on the case, while Kraus himself – working for up to sixteen hours at a stretch – laboured for approximately 6,700 hours (F 732–4, 44). He also gives credit to the investigating judge, Oberlandesgerichtsrat Dr Katlein, who signed the order for Bekessy's arrest on charges of fraud and extortion (F 771–6, 80).

The Redemption of the City

Victory is celebrated as the fulfilment of an archetypal mission: the defence of the polis. Austrian citizenship, as we have seen, depended on the principle of 'Heimatrecht' ('Right of Domicile'). Habsburg law had discouraged social mobility, placing special constraints on the migration of Jews, and when in the 1860s those restrictions were lifted, every citizen was required to have a registered place of domicile ('Zuständigkeit'). After 1918, the possession of 'Heimatrecht' in a community within the borders of the new Republic provided the most secure basis for citizenship. Those who became citizens by 'option' under the Treaty of Saint-Germain had a less secure legal status, since they were liable, if convicted of an offence, to be deported to their original domicile, which might now be located in Poland or Romania. The threat of 'deportation', popularly known as 'the push' ('der Schub'), was one of the hazards of life in inter-war Vienna, and Kraus questioned its use for minor misdemeanours (F 632–9, 138).

In the case of Bekessy, however, Kraus endowed the process of expulsion with archetypal overtones. Echoing the language of Attic tragedy, he defines his aim as the 'redemption of the city' (F 691–6, 123) so that Vienna is 'freed of the plague' (F 730–1, 26). Bekessy is defined as the insolent intruder, a 'buccaneer from abroad' (F 691–6, 119), wafted into Vienna 'by a wind from the Levant' (F 640–8, 91). Forced on the defensive, Bekessy tried to deny that he was a Hungarian intruder, claiming during the Stolper–Federn case that he had spent his childhood in Vienna.[43] He had to face a barrage of witticisms about 'Budapestilence' – the 'journalistic plague that has taken control of Vienna' (F 679–85, 128 & 137). This plague can only be overcome by expelling the usurper, but how is Bekessy to be deported if he can legitimately claim 'Heimatrecht' (F 691–6, 75)? Kraus challenged the Social Democrats to acknowledge their complicity: by granting Bekessy the right of domicile in Vienna they had established his 'immunity to deportation' (F 697–705, 149). His aim is to prove that those rights were 'obtained by fraud' (F 691–6, 124), and thus bring about the 'liberation of Vienna' (F 706–11, 105).

Kraus's own citizenship was based on almost fifty years of continuous residence, but he had been born in Jičín, a small manufacturing town now located in the Czech Republic. Die Stunde seized on this anomaly in a long article designed to discredit his origins. His father Jakob Kraus (the anonymous author claimed) owed the fortune he built up in Jičín to the exploitation of convicts, who were forced to manufacture paper-bags for miserable wages (ST 27 May 1925, p. 5). Kraus defended his father's reputation in a furious rejoinder (F 691–6, 104–6), but he could hardly deny that he was born in Jičín (F 697–705, 166–7). A further attempt to present Kraus as the outsider occurs in Anton Kuh's 'Der Affe Zarathustras'. Where the native Viennese (Kuh claims) feels at home in his environment, this man from Bohemia has the 'eyes of an alien'. Kraus's arguments are reminiscent of 'the brilliant Jewish advocates', while his complex style betrays a 'Jewish brain'.[44] These insinuations reveal a further subtext underlying the debate about citizenship: the problem of Jewish assimilation.

The principal antagonists, with the exception of Tschuppik and Liebstöckl, all came from Jewish backgrounds, and a crude summary would be that 'the

Jew Kraus attacked the Jew Bekessy'.[45] A more differentiated view is offered
by Bekessy himself, who was aware of a hierarchy of acculturation. Eastern
Jews were regarded in Vienna as the least welcome of migrants, while Jews of
Hungarian origin were one step up the social scale, envied for their commercial acumen. Greater prestige was enjoyed by migrants from Bohemia, who
were noted for their intellectual gifts, but Jews actually born in Vienna could
claim to be most securely at home, especially if they could trace their lineage
through several generations. This explains why Kuh, a native of Vienna, felt
justified in denigrating Kraus as an 'alien' and his followers as 'yids'. Kraus in
his turn could feel that Bekessy was an interloper from a less civilized stratum
of Austro-Hungarian society, while Bekessy felt entitled to despise migrants
from Galicia like Baron Reitzes, ridiculed in *Die Stunde* as an 'eastern Jew' (ST
28 June 1925, p. 5). A constant refrain in *Bekessy's Panoptikum* is that neither
Kraus nor Austerlitz should be regarded as authentically Viennese, since they
belonged to the 'stratum of German-Bohemian Jewish intellectuals'. By contrast, Bekessy's supporters in the Social Democratic Party, like Karl Renner,
had both feet firmly on authentic 'Austrian soil'. The group which destroyed
Bekessy's links with the Party, he concluded, represented a 'hysterically Jewish
intellectuality' that was 'unViennese' (BP 189–93). While Bekessy attributed
his defeat to a vendetta by Jews from Bohemia, Kraus transposed it to an
ethical plane, invoking the tribute paid to him by Karl Seitz, Mayor of Vienna,
on his fiftieth birthday. Seitz had declared that the 'city of Vienna can be proud
to count you among its citizens' (F 649–56, 148–50). It is citizenship, defined
by ethical principle not ethnic origin, that Kraus invokes against Bekessy
(F 691–6, 125–6). The paradox is that Seitz was himself responsible for the
decision to grant Bekessy 'Heimatrecht' in Vienna, and that he was inhibited
from supporting Kraus by 'Party tactics' (F 732–4, 50).

Kraus resurrects the ethic of citizenship in order to defend the polis against
the offender. His campaign is prefigured in the classical myths with which he
was familiar since his schooldays, but he also invokes paradigms from Scandi-
navia. The Great Boyg (from Ibsen's *Peer Gynt*) provides an eloquent symbol
for the inertia of public opinion (F 730–1, 1–2). Even more significant are the
diaries of Kierkegaard, which record the activities of an earlier muck-raking
journalist, Meir Goldschmidt, editor of the *Corsair*. Goldschmidt, a young man
who had initially been one of Kierkegaard's admirers, joined forces with the
critic Peder Ludvig Möller in ridiculing Kierkegaard's aesthetic philosophy,
his deformed physique and his unhappy love affair with Regine Olsen. The
Corsair, notorious for its 'anonymous, gossipy, and at times libellous invasion of
privacy', was the largest-circulation journal in Copenhagen.[46] In a series of
articles published between January and April 1846, Goldschmidt humiliated
Kierkegaard by means of ironic squibs and malicious caricatures, which accentuated his deformed shoulders and spindly legs. In the diaries Kierkegaard
records that he was made the laughing-stock of the city, but he also undertakes
a pioneering critique of journalism. Moreover, he takes upon himself the task

of redeeming the community from this blight, responding with an affirmation of Christian values that finally induced Goldschmidt to leave the city. Kraus, reading Kierkegaard's diaries in Theodor Haecker's translation, was astonished by this 'miracle of recurrence', and at a public reading on 14 November 1925 he read substantial passages, citing Kierkegaard's prophetic definition of the new journalism: 'Here people are demoralized in the shortest possible time, on the largest possible scale and at the cheapest possible price' (F 706–11, 24, 95 & 99). In January 1926 Kraus again reflected on this 'prefiguration', noting that Goldschmidt bowed to Kierkegaard's moral authority, while he would have to mobilize the law. Inspired by this parallel, he predicted that Bekessy, too, would soon be obliged to give up his 'Corsair' and leave town (F 712–16, 69–70).

Like Goldschmidt, Bekessy was to be expelled from the city because he is corrupt – not because he is Jewish.[47] A close reading shows that Kraus consistently avoided identifying Bekessy as a Jew, alluding to his origins so obliquely that the casual reader must have been startled to learn, long after the campaign was over, that he was 'a Hungarian Jew'.[48] On the rare occasions when the matter is alluded to, Kraus's aim is to show that Bekessy's attitudes are *not* those associated with Jewishness – he is not inhibited by the traditional Jewish pieties (F 691–6, 77). Moreover, the polemic has a subtext which transforms it into a critique of antisemitism. In his public reading of 25 June 1925 Kraus introduced the slogan that was to shape his whole subsequent campaign: 'Throw the villain out of Vienna!' (F 691–6, 122). Its effect can be judged from an account of his reading on 14 November, which describes how an audience of nine hundred people, responding like the chorus of an antique drama, joined him in declaiming the words: 'Hinaus aus Wien mit dem Schuft' (F 706–11, 100). He even set the phrase to music, adapting a Nestroy song to include the words: 'In Vienna we all shout / "Throw the villain out!"' (F 706–11, 87). The slogan was echoed by others who despised the new journalism. Theodor Adorno, who was studying music in Vienna during the mid-1920s, recalls Kraus's reading of 'Hinaus aus Wien mit dem Schuft!' as an 'unforgettable experience for everyone who was present'.[49] And when Billy Wilder was sent to interview Sigmund Freud, the great man, on discovering that he represented *Die Stunde*, pointed to the door and said '*Raus!*'[50]

Like so many of Kraus's turns of phrase, 'Hinaus aus Wien mit dem Schuft' is a montage of concealed quotations. For decades the most notorious slogan of the antisemites had been 'Hinaus mit den Juden!' Kraus shows great daring in reformulating this slogan in ethical terms: 'Hinaus aus Wien mit dem Schuft!' is designed to drive Bekessy out of Vienna – but not by using the arguments of the antisemites. Kraus's imperative appeals to the reader's moral imagination. Like the great satirists before him he cultivated complexity of discourse, expressing – like Swift – a disconcerting 'quantity of ideas per square inch'.[51] His imperative, which does indeed form roughly a square inch of text, is a montage of motifs from three different registers:

Hinaus	contemporary slogan
aus Wien	defence of the polis
mit dem Schuft!	literary paradigm

The only characteristic that Kraus felt he shared with Bekessy was that they were 'both familiar with Shakespeare' (F 706–11, 106). His prototype for Bekessy is Paroles, the lying braggart in *All's Well That Ends Well*, who 'out-villained villainy' ('den Schuft überschuftet'; Act IV, scene 3; cited F 686–90, 18). This Shakespearean image, supplemented by the ethics of Kierkegaard, provided Kraus with an elevated register of imprecation.

This campaign coincided with an upsurge of antisemitism, triggered by the Fourteenth International Zionist Congress, which opened in Vienna on 21 August 1925. In the run-up to the Congress there were violent antisemitic demonstrations, as reactionary political groups, with financial backing from Germany, intensified their campaign against the alleged world Jewish conspiracy. Thousands of antisemitic broadsheets were distributed, and the predominantly Jewish district of Leopoldstadt was terrorized by gangs of swastika-flaunting youths spoiling for a fight. In the city centre, too, there were frequent assaults, directed against premises that were thought to be Jewish owned. On 17 July a Nazi gang raided the restaurant in the Stadtpark, Hübners Kursalon, chanting, 'Beat the Jews up, throw the Jews out!' ('Haut die Juden, hinaus mit den Juden!'). The opening of the Congress provoked further demonstrations, but the Austrian government, under pressure from abroad, acted with considerable firmness. Police units backed by security forces were deployed to protect the Konzerthaus, where the plenary sessions took place, and the Congress, which received lavish coverage in the Austrian press, was regarded as a success.

Die Stunde, too, was opposed to antisemitism, running a series of editorials condemning the Nazis at the time of the Zionist Congress, but its position was compromised by its journalistic practices, since its addiction to scandal, sensation and graft seemed to confirm the accusations against Jewish migrants. Such practices played into the hands of the antisemites, just as the crookedness of the *Sonn- und Montagszeitung* had done twenty years earlier. Kraus summed up his argument in October 1925, after the turmoil accompanying the Congress had subsided, by arguing that *Die Stunde* 'could even confer something like the legitimacy of an irresistible compulsion upon that lamentable revolt of primitive emotion which challenges the meaning of life by brandishing the swastika' (F 697–705, 175). In short, Kraus attacked the paper both for promoting a predatory form of capitalism and for provoking anti-Jewish reactions. The phrase 'Hinaus aus Wien!' was designed to ensure that both the journalistic villain and the antisemitic slogan were rejected by the community.

After taking refuge in France, Bekessy experienced such a severe depression that he made the first of a series of suicide attempts. However, he still had allies in Hungary, and the following year he returned to Budapest to rebuild his career as a newspaperman. He and his wife survived the war in America, returning to Hungary in 1947 with a renewed enthusiasm for communism. However, within a few years they had become so disillusioned that in July 1951 they both committed suicide. An overview of Bekessy's career is provided by his son, who also became a journalist after changing his name to Hans Habe. He, too, escaped to the United States, writing a number of successful novels and making a name for himself in post-war Germany as a political commentator. His memoirs show that he could never escape the shadow of the Kraus–Bekessy affair. In a striking passage he records how he was haunted by the word 'extortion' ('Erpressung'), which he seemed to hear in the 'melody of railway wheels, of murmuring waves and subdued voices'.[52] Castiglioni was more fortunate. After rebuilding his financial empire in Weimar Germany, he emigrated to America in 1934, returning to Italy after the war to continue his banking career. He remains a shadowy figure, although his early life was made the subject of a colourful film.[53] Both Gustav Stolper and Walter Federn survived the war in exile, continuing their careers in the English-speaking world. Karl Tschuppik moved to Berlin, writing a series of fine political-historical studies, including a nostalgic biography of Emperor Franz Joseph and a hard-hitting critique of Ludendorff. When he died in Vienna in 1937, his friend Joseph Roth penned a tribute, recalling that 'towards the great Austrian Karl Kraus he had been not only unjust, but also insolent'.[54] The most curious footnote is provided by the career of Billy Wilder, who also moved to Berlin, developing a passion for the cinema and writing film reviews for the *Berliner Zeitung*, before emigrating to the United States. Traces of the irreverent wit of *Die Stunde* can be found in his Hollywood comedies *Some Like It Hot* and *The Apartment*, while *Irma la Douce*, although set in Paris, echoes the intrigues of inter-war Vienna. As for Kraus, his attempt to stem the tide of tabloid journalism was to prove in the longer term as quixotic as that of Kierkegaard.

CHAPTER 17

The Destruction of Justice

The politics of the Republic were compromised by shady deals between government and finance, especially under the chancellorship of Rudolf Ramek. During the Savings Bank scandal, the Finance Minister, Jacob Ahrer, abruptly disappeared, resurfacing a few weeks later in Cuba. He claimed that he had left Austria 'for family reasons', but the parliamentary investigation revealed a morass of corruption and inefficiency. It was clear that taxpayers and small savers had been systematically swindled by the collusion between financiers like Siegmund Bosel and politicians like Anton Rintelen, Governor of Styria, while even Castiglioni, after making a deal with the tax authorities, had resumed operations in Vienna. The Social Democratic Party was compromised by its own connections with Bosel, who had saved the socialist-owned Hammerbrotwerke from collapse. Worse was to follow in autumn 1926 when the Party, disregarding its revolutionary programme, made secret deals with the right-wing government. After Ramek's discredited administration was forced to resign, Seipel again took over as chancellor, striking a bargain with the Social Democrats. If they agreed to remain silent about financial corruption, he was willing to adopt their proposals for a reform of old-age pensions and disability payments. The leadership swallowed the bait, and Seipel was able to extricate his party from a compromising situation 'with the connivance and participation of the Socialists'.[1]

Zigzag Tactics

This deal between the two main parties was not made public at the time, but Kraus had excellent sources of information, and this double-dealing inspired him to write a poem denouncing the opportunism of the Social Democrats, 'Weg damit!' ('Cut it out!'):

> Die ihr errungenes Gut geschändet habt,
> bezwungnes Böses nicht beendet habt,
> der Freiheit Glück in Fluch gewendet habt;
> Hinaufgelangte, die den Wanst gefüllt,

vor fremdem Hunger eigne Gier gestillt,
vom Futtertrog zu weichen nicht gewillt;
Pfründner der Fortschritts, die das Herz verließ,
da Weltwind in die schlaffen Segel blies,
vom Bürgergift berauschte Parvenüs,
die mit dem Todfeind, mit dem Lebensfeind
Profit der Freiheit brüderlich vereint,
die freier einst und reiner war gemeint –
mein Schritt ist nicht dies schleichende Zickzack,
mein Stich ist nicht dies zögernde Tricktrack:
er gilt politischem Paktiererpack!

(F 743–50, 4)

You who have desecrated every gain,
spared the antagonist you should have slain,
and turned the joys of freedom into pain;
your bellies stuffed with food, your heads with pride,
you gorge yourselves while others are denied,
and cling to office till you're satisfied;
you parasites of progress whose hearts quailed
when global tempests blew through your slack sails,
now faced with mortal foes your courage fails;
drunk with the poison of the bourgeoisie
you've lined your pockets with our liberty,
that fine ideal which should have set us free –
my stride avoids these slimy zigzag tracks,
while you procrastinate, my pen attacks
that gang whose politics consist of pacts!

This poem made a powerful impression when he declaimed it on 20 November 1926 at his four-hundredth public reading.[2] But satirical poetry is no substitute for effective politics, and the question remains whether there was any alternative to the compromises he condemned. Although no one is mentioned in the poem by name, Karl Renner, who led the reformist wing of the Party, was the principal target. Referring in the same number of Die Fackel to an incident during the Party conference at Linz, Kraus expresses his sympathy with a veteran socialist who had protested against the antics of the leadership: 'shimmy-dancing tribunes of the people and dining companions of the biggest black marketeers' (F 743–50, 153). The 'dining companions' doubtless included Mathias Eldersch, one of Bekessy's toadies whom Kraus despised, as well as a right-wing Social Democrat from the Tyrol named Franz Gruener, whose profiteering he described as an 'abomination in the sight of the Lord' (F 743–50, 31–2). The shimmy-dancing tribune was the portly Karl Renner, and this dig at the revered leader provoked a riposte in a socialist magazine, resulting in another legal action (P 1, 234–45).

The Social Democrats were struggling to adapt to changing circumstances, as the balance of power tilted to the right throughout western Europe, with a loss of revolutionary momentum and a consolidation of authoritarian regimes. The defeat of the General Strike in Britain had shaken confidence in the power of industrial action. In Hungary the government of Horthy was tightening its grip, while the situation in Italy was even more ominous, since Mussolini's dictatorship impinged on Austria both directly, through Italian membership of the Allied Control Commission, and covertly, through the financing of proto-fascist militias. The growing strength of these militias in the Austrian provinces led the Social Democrats to review their policies during the annual conference held in Linz in autumn 1926. This resulted in the Linz Programme, one of the most significant documents of Austrian socialism, a skewed compromise between the revisionists (led by Renner) and the radicals (represented by Max Adler). The main emphasis was on achieving power through the ballot box, but Otto Bauer, in an important speech, addressed the question of revolutionary violence. Although he was opposed to the use of force, the final text of the Linz Programme acknowledged that a 'dictatorship' might be necessary to defend socialism against the forces of counter-revolution. If the bourgeoisie succeeded in destroying democracy, then the working class 'could only seize power in a civil war'.[3]

The contradictions of the Linz Programme confirmed Kraus's view of the 'zigzag' tactics of the Social Democrats, and his poem 'Weg damit!' anticipates the consensus which has emerged in recent years about the weaknesses of Austro-Marxism. Committed in principle to the creation of a classless society, they failed to use their electoral strength to construct an effective centre-left coalition. The basic contradiction (as a historian of the Party puts it) lay in 'the conflict between theory and practice, between radical slogans and craven retreat in challenging situations'.[4] At crucial junctures the leadership accepted half-hearted compromises: with Seipel in 1919–22 and again in 1926, and ultimately – in 1929 – with Schober. Kraus's hostility was increased by his knowledge of their dealings with Bekessy, as is clear from a second text included in his four-hundredth public reading, 'Ich und wir' ('I and We'). There was good reason to remain alert, since Bekessy still had influential friends in the socialist camp and there was a risk that he – like Castiglioni – might defy his critics and return to Vienna. To forestall a comeback, Kraus monitored Bekessy's movements during the years 1926–9, obtaining reports from both Paris and Budapest (P 1, 165–81 & 216–25). The news that Bekessy was planning to re-establish himself as a newspaper publisher prompted Samek to obtain German translations of articles in the Hungarian press. The aim was to ensure that, if Bekessy ever returned to Vienna, he would be arrested and put on trial, but it was not until 14 June 1927 that the warrant was issued for his arrest (F 771–6, 80). In the spring of 1927 Bekessy's allies in the Social Democratic Party embarked on a manoeuvre to exonerate him, proposing to revoke his Austrian citizenship so that the material against him would be transferred to Budapest, thus protecting him from further proceedings in Vienna. Kraus was so alarmed that in May 1927 he printed a poster denouncing this as

a 'legalization of crime'. But WIPAG, the organization set up by the City
Council to regulate bill-posting in Vienna, refused to display the poster, claiming that the references to Bekessy might be defamatory. The ban was later
withdrawn, after Kraus had circumvented it by arranging for the poster to be
displayed in bookshops and newspaper kiosks and mailed to leading politicians.
He also reprinted the text in Die Fackel (F 759–65, 117–40).

Although Kraus had reason to distance himself from the Social Democrats,
it was incongruous to condemn them for having missed their revolutionary
opportunity, when we recall how vehemently he had urged them to resist
communist insurrection seven years earlier. Moreover he failed to acknowledge – until it was too late – that under certain circumstances 'pacts' may have
a positive value. The cardinal weakness of Austrian politics was a preponderance of dogma. Both the Marxists and the Christian Socials were committed
to doctrines of political redemption which left little scope for compromise, and
the greatest threat to freedom arose from the polarization between left and
right, which ultimately rendered the republic defenceless. In their programme
published at the end of November 1926, the Christian Socials denounced not
only 'class dictatorship' but also 'Jewish influences'. Since his party relied on
the banks for financial support, Seipel was obliged to explain that his hostility
was anti-socialist rather than anti-capitalist. He pointed out that the leaders of
Austrian socialism (like those of Russian Bolshevism) were 'mostly Jews',
which explained 'the antisemitic bent of popular opinion'.[5]

During the elections of April 1927 for the National Assembly and the
Vienna municipal government, the country became divided into two camps.
Abandoning his conciliatory tactics, Seipel transformed the campaign into a
crusade against the Red Peril, merging the right-wing parties into an anti-
socialist United Front ('Einheitsliste'). In this election the anti-Marxist
rhetoric of the Christian Social Party coalesced with the anti-democratic and
antisemitic propaganda of the Pan-Germans and the National Socialists. The
Social Democrats responded by mobilizing the liberal intelligentsia, publishing
an impressive declaration of support by the 'Intellectuals of Vienna' in the
Arbeiter-Zeitung of 20 April. The list of distinguished names included both
Freud and Adler, but Kraus (as we have noted) was conspicuous by his absence,
since his hostility to such declarations was notorious (F 781–6, 47–8). There
are signs that he might have been willing to vote for the Social Democrats, if
the ballot paper had allowed him to strike out the names of candidates he
despised, but in the event he abstained from voting (F 759–65, 2). Setting for
the Social Democrats a higher standard than for any other faction, he restated
his criticisms of those who had compromised the Party, notably Mathias
Eldersch, a man admired by Bekessy for his easy-going attitude towards public
morality, such a contrast to the 'hysterically Jewish intellectuality' of other
Social Democrats (BP 190–2). In April 1926, at the height of the polemic
against Die Stunde, Kraus had identified Eldersch and Renner as self-indulgent
politicians who had betrayed the austere ideals of Wilhelm Liebknecht

(F 717–23, 76–7), and this helps to explain his refusal to vote for the socialists. Thus Kraus stood on the sidelines in April 1927, while the struggle between left and right was being fought out with unprecedented vehemence. He was equally sceptical about both factions, which for him formed a 'bourgeois–social-democratic United Front' (F 759–65, 3). On 23 May he again read the poem 'Weg damit!' in public, clarifying his position by insisting that he still supported 'the cause of the workers', although never a Party member (F 781–6, 47). In the event, the Social Democrats made significant gains in the elections, consolidating their control of Vienna, where they obtained 60 per cent of the vote. Although they increased their share of the national vote to over 42 per cent, they were far less adept at constructing pacts than Seipel, who formed another right-wing coalition government. The socialists were forced on the defensive, frustrated at the ballot box but flinching from the barricades.

The Burning of the Palace of Justice

The reference to 'civil war' in the Linz Programme of 1926 had to be taken seriously, since both the main political parties were backed by organized militias: the Social Democratic Schutzbund (Defence Corps) and the right-wing Heimwehr or Heimatwehr (Home Guard). Each faction had caches of weapons, which they tried to conceal from each other, as well as from the Allied Control Commission. The Heimwehr, a collective term for regional militias set up in 1919 to defend Austria's frontiers, had developed into a proto-fascist movement modelled on the organizations of Mussolini. It had close links with the Austrian Nazis and other right-wing groups like the Front-line Veterans' Association (Frontkämpfervereinigung). The Schutzbund, created to protect the interests of the Social Democrats, was an auxiliary police force rather than a revolutionary militia, since its main function was to provide marshals for mass demonstrations. Both organizations regularly took to the streets, and there were numerous clashes, often resulting in bloodshed.

In January 1927 a confrontation of this kind occurred in Schattendorf, a village in the politically sensitive province of Burgenland on the Hungarian border. The competition for control of public space, which was such a feature of city life, was echoed in the provinces by tussles for control of the village street and even the pub.[6] In Schattendorf, where there was only one street, three members of a right-wing veterans' association, provoked by a demonstration of the Schutzbund, opened fire from the windows of a pub, killing a veteran socialist and an eight-year-old child. The culprits claimed to have acted in self-defence, and right-wing newspapers, led by the Reichspost, did their best to exonerate them. The chances of an impartial trial were further compromised by the choice of the leader of the Austrian Nazi Party, Dr Walter Riehl, as counsel for the defence. A lawyer representing the victims of the shooting successfully challenged the selection of jurors who were known to be right wing, but the jury that was finally empanelled proved to be irreconcilably divided. After a fourteen-day trial, the foreman announced their verdicts. By nine votes to three the jury acquitted the accused of unprovoked violence. On the second charge of grievous bodily harm they were equally divided. Only in the case of one of the accused was there a narrow majority (seven votes to five) on the minor charge of threatening personal security. Under Austrian law a minimum of eight votes (a two-thirds majority) was required for a conviction, so these verdicts signified an acquittal.[7]

The case destroyed the 'precarious equilibrium' of the political system.[8] The socialists were caught in a dilemma, since the principle of trial by jury was fundamental to their programme. Members of the Party Executive decided at a hastily convened meeting not to organize any official protest nor to mobilize the Schutzbund. The meeting broke up, leaving Friedrich Austerlitz to write the leading article for the *Arbeiter-Zeitung*. Like Kraus, he was committed to the rule of law, denouncing the acquittal of the Schattendorf killers as 'the denial of justice'. His main target was the manipulation of the jurors both by the Nazi defence lawyer and by the right-wing press, especially the *Reichspost* and the Pan-German *Wiener Neueste Nachrichten*. The anti-socialist propaganda of the government (Austerlitz argued) was as much to blame as the jurors themselves, but towards the end of his editorial his pen ran away with him. 'The bourgeois world', he concluded, 'is always warning us about civil war. But is this blatant, this provocative acquittal of men who killed workers, because they killed workers – is it not in itself already civil war?' (AZ 15 July 1927, p. 1). Around midnight on 14 July a delegation of electricity workers arrived at Party Head-quarters, demanding action. Otto Bauer, who was still in the building, slipped out through the back door, revealing the 'helplessness and incompetence' of the leadership.[9] The workers were received by Austerlitz, who informed them that the Party had not authorized a strike, but they resolved on a power stoppage, to start at eight o'clock the following morning. This brought the factories and public transport system of Vienna to a standstill, acting as a signal for workers in all parts of the city to down tools and join an improvised march on parliament. The news of the Schattendorf verdict spread rapidly through the city, although it was not reported on Austrian Radio, and by 9 a.m. protesting workers were converging on the Ringstrasse. Elias Canetti was breakfasting in a coffee-house in the suburbs when he read the news of the acquittal, sanctimoniously reported in the *Reichspost*. He leapt on his bicycle and raced downtown to join the demonstration.

The antecedents of this momentous day included social deprivation, unemployment, and resentment at 'class justice', exacerbated by socialist rhetoric.[10] If the police in Vienna had been under municipal control, as they were in other socialist strongholds like Steyr, the demonstration would have been handled very differently. As commander of the Federal Police Force, Schober misjudged the situation, dismissing his special police units and leaving parliament underprotected. This was the first of a 'chain of mistakes' by the authorities.[11] Schober was the most significant figure in the ensuing disaster, but at every stage his decisions were geared to the responses of politicians, both Christian

Social and Social Democrat. The key figures were Chancellor Seipel, Interior Minister Hartleb and Army Minister Vaugoin, but he was also in touch with Karl Seitz, as governor of Vienna, and Julius Deutsch, Commander of the Schutzbund. Since the Social Democrats had not planned the demonstration, there were initially no Schutzbund marshals on duty to assist the police in controlling the crowds, which made the position even more hazardous.

By the time the politicians were roused from their slumbers, the situation was out of control. Shots were fired as the mass demonstration passed the university, and a small detachment of mounted police charged the demonstrators as they approached parliament around 9.30 a.m. The workers reacted by throwing paving stones and constructing barricades with materials from a building site. The situation turned ugly as individual policemen began to open fire with their revolvers, and the workers stormed a sub-police station and wrecked the editorial offices of the *Reichspost* and the *Wiener Neueste Nachrichten*. Forced back from parliament by police cordons, they began to besiege the Palace of Justice, situated on the adjacent Schmerlingplatz, and this building, although not connected with the Schattendorf trial, became the symbolic target of their protest against class justice. As police opened fire from inside, some of the demonstrators broke into the building, looting it and setting it on fire. So enraged were the crowd that they refused to allow fire engines to approach the building, even when implored to do so by Seitz and Deutsch. It was only with difficulty that hastily assembled Schutzbund units were able to save the lives of those trapped inside the burning building (Fig. 35).

Fearing anarchy on the streets of Vienna, Seipel authorized Schober to put down the riot by force. Responsibility for security in Vienna was divided between the federal police and the municipal administration. Schober consulted the Governor of Vienna about the possibility of calling in the army, and if Seitz had been responsible for policing, the situation might have been brought under control with a minimal loss of life.[12] Instead, the Police Chief took the fateful decision to arm the police with rifles obtained from military barracks, authorizing them to open fire. After mounted units had failed to disperse the crowds, police detachments fired on demonstrators in front of the burning Palace of Justice, and dozens of people were killed, including children and innocent bystanders, while hundreds more suffered injuries caused by gunfire, batons and swords. The panic-stricken crowds retaliated, but only one policeman was killed that day, caught in a salvo fired by his own men.[13] The draconian methods of the police succeeded in dispersing the crowds, although sporadic clashes continued in the suburbs for several days, and three more policemen were killed. The Social Democratic leaders, who had done everything in their power to avoid bloodshed, belatedly called a general strike, but it proved ineffectual, since they had little support in the provinces, where the Heimwehr were emerging as the dominant force. These events left the Party in complete disarray. In theory they were dedicated to the overthrow of

35   *The Burning of the Palace of Justice*: painting by Hugo Löffler

bourgeois society, but in practice they did everything in their power to restrain the fury of the crowds. Seitz and Bauer had a series of secret meetings with Seipel and Hartleb, failing to obtain any concessions, while Deutsch deployed the Schutzbund to supplement the efforts at crowd control. Having failed to protect their supporters from armed police on the rampage, the socialist leaders were open to the charge that they had betrayed the working class.

The post-mortem within the Party followed a predictable zigzag course. Should they campaign implacably for the resignation of Seipel, or should they join him in a government of national reconciliation? Renner, in an article of 12 November 1927, argued for a coalition, a move denounced by Kraus as an obsequious 'readiness to sneak inside' (F 771–6, 13).[14] The arguments in favour of a coalition were discredited only when it was pointed out that this would mean 'climbing over corpses into ministerial armchairs'.[15] After the collapse of the general strike all the cards were in Seipel's hands, and, having crushed what he regarded as a revolutionary insurrection, he was in no mood for compromise. No government representative attended the funeral of any of the demonstrators, whereas the four policemen were buried with military honours. Deprived of political options, the Social Democrats fell back on empty rhetoric, failing even in their bid for a parliamentary inquiry. Their hostility to Seipel prompted them to organize a campaign for mass defections from Catholicism, and between 1 and 10 August a total of 2,734 people left the Church, causing the Chancellor great distress.[16]

In treating Seipel as their bogeyman, the socialists played down the responsibility of Schober and the officers under his command. In the annals of policing in the western world, there is no massacre of comparable magnitude.[17] Thus Kraus was hardly exaggerating when he referred to it as 'the greatest crime of all civilized eras' (F 777, 5). In a mature democracy Schober's resignation would have been inevitable, but the government, supported by the bourgeois press, threw its weight behind him. Even on the Social Democratic side the calls for Schober's resignation were muted, since the Party was inhibited by discussions behind closed doors. During the events of 15 July, Schober had maintained contact – either by telephone or in person – with Seitz and Deutsch, who co-operated with him in the hope of avoiding bloodshed. Their public-spirited action implicated the Social Democrats in a massacre they had been powerless to prevent. Deutsch subsequently recorded that Schober had agreed to delay the order to open fire, so that the Schutzbund could make a final effort to bring the demonstration under control, but Schober's messenger (according to this account) failed to get through.[18] The position of the Schutzbund was indeed unenviable, since they were exposed to the violence of both police and demonstrators. Of the eighty-five people shot dead by the police, eleven belonged to the Schutzbund.[19] On the following day, Saturday 16 July, Seitz called on Schober three times for further negotiations. His plan was to set up an auxiliary police force under the control of the municipality, but its primary task, like that of the Schutzbund, was to control the workers rather than to protect them against police brutality. Schober showed considerable sympathy with the Social Democrats, and during one of his meetings with Seitz he suggested that the Party should demand his resignation in order to appease the rank and file. Seitz replied that this was 'out of the question'.[20] The record of this conversation shows how completely the Social Democrats were trapped by their own tactics.

Mediocrity Drunk with Power

Kraus had no such inhibitions. In mid-July he was preoccupied with a court case against the *Arbeiter-Zeitung*, and if – following long-established habit – he was sleeping at his apartment on the morning of 15 July, he must have been woken by gunfire, since the Lothringerstrasse is within walking distance of the Palace of Justice. His immediate reaction was to withdraw the court action, urging the *Arbeiter-Zeitung* to concentrate on documenting the 'disgraceful actions of the police' (P 2, 55–6). Unlike the Social Democrats, Kraus had consistently campaigned against the jury system, since in Austria there was no ethic of responsible citizenship to sustain it. His doubts were spectacularly confirmed by the perverse verdict in the Schattendorf case, which he described in autumn 1927 as an 'abomination', inconceivable if the case had been left to 'professional judges following the letter of the law'. Liberal illusions about the impartiality of jurors had succeeded in 'making realities unrecognizable through slogans' (F 766–70, 65). The following months, during which he formulated his own response, proved exceptionally stressful, although at the end of August he had the consolation of a reunion with Sidonie in Bavaria. His letters explain that he has 'not had any summer, not an hour with calmed nerves' (BSN 590–1). The 'terrible pressure of these days' reminded him of the fateful events of the First World War (BSN 1, 590–1).

Kraus was sickened by the reactions of the government and the media, which celebrated the events of 15 July as a victory. Chancellor Seipel praised Police Headquarters as the 'strongest bastion of the state order', while President Hainisch decorated the police commanders responsible for the shooting of civilians. Schober responded with a sanctimonious speech to his officers about the happiness that results from 'duties conscientiously fulfilled' (cited F 766–70, 1 & 40). Meanwhile, the right-wing coalition used its majority to block demands for a parliamentary inquiry, entrusting the task of compiling an official White Paper on the events of 15 July to the very man responsible for the massacre, Schober himself. Seitz reacted by instigating an inquiry by the Municipality of Vienna, conducted by Robert Danneberg.[21] Kraus characteristically compiled a dossier of his own – a forty-eight-page documentation, supported by a polemical commentary, published towards the end of October under the caustic title 'Der Hort der Republik' – 'The Bastion of the Republic'.

In autumn 1927 Kraus launched his campaign to discredit Schober and resist the slide towards a police state. On 17 September hundreds of copies of a poster (Fig. 36a) were displayed in Vienna with the boldly printed text:

> To the Police President of Vienna
> JOHANN SCHOBER
> I call on you
> to resign.
> KARL KRAUS
> Editor of 'Die Fackel'

The layout of the poster intensified its impact, as the poet Erich Fried, who was a schoolboy at the time, recalled many years later.[22] But while Kraus's proclamation was welcomed by socialists, it also provoked a spate of anonymous hate-mail denouncing him as a 'filthy swine' (F 766–70, 47) and a 'Jew-boy infected with syphilis' (F 806–9, 69). Right-wing thugs threatened to disrupt his next recital, scheduled for 9 October, and 'beat him to pulp' (F 806–9, 56–9). With considerable courage he went through with the recital, which featured a new version of Offenbach's Madame l'Archiduc, ignoring the threats of 'assault or death' (F 766–70, 82). He was undeterred by the pro-Schober poster published by his adversaries in an attempt to discredit his own (Fig. 36b).

36   Schober campaign: posters: (a) by Kraus (b) by Winkler

Kraus's relations with Schober form a complex story which can be traced back to their contacts between 1914 and 1918. At the end of the war he had commended Schober as one of the few men in Austria who had had the courage to stand up to the High Command (F 514–18, 98–9), and he emphatically endorsed his resolute action against the threat of a communist putsch in 1919 (F 514–18, 69–71). The references to Schober during the early 1920s, when for a short time he held the office of chancellor, are cautiously complimentary. In October 1923 Kraus appealed to him as a 'cultivated man' to curb police action against prostitutes (F 632–9, 136). Initially he regarded Schober as an ally during the Bekessy affair, and it was not until the summer of 1926 that he began to express his doubts (F 732–4, 51–5). The massacre of July 1927 transformed the situation. Aligning himself with the Social Democrats he had so recently condemned, Kraus sought to discredit Schober by every possible means. His hostility is attributed by one historian to his revulsion at the 'weakness and prevarication' of the Police Chief in allowing Bekessy to escape from Austria. According to this account, Schober's role in the riots of July 1927 provided the satirist with an opportunity to 'pay off an earlier score'.[23] This overpersonalizes the most political of Kraus's polemics. His fundamental theme is the militarization of the police force during a massacre perpetrated by 'mediocrities drunk with power' (F 766–70, 49 & 62–4).

THE DESTRUCTION OF JUSTICE

Militarization 'brutalizes decent average blokes and makes them into murderers' (F 766–70, 63). By highlighting the capacity of ordinary men to
commit horrendous crimes, Kraus sets up connections with a wider context.
The war, he argues, has produced a new personality type that longs for human
slaughter 'without being capable of hurting a hair on the head of a fly'. This
conflation of clichés recalls the conclusions about the 'banality' of evil which
he had drawn from the First World War (F 501–7, 102), and which he was to
intensify under the impact of National Socialism.[24] In her celebrated analysis of
Eichmann's complicity in the Holocaust, Hannah Arendt emphasizes the gap
'between the unspeakable horror of the deeds and the undeniable ludicrous-
ness of the man who perpetrated them'.[25] This echoes a passage from Die Fackel
of October 1927, which she may have had at the back of her mind: 'What
makes our great atrocities so unbearable is the fact that they are the responsibility of such tiny human beings' (F 766–70, 62). Schober was no evil genius
of the Eichmann type, but the bestiality of his police force on the streets of
Vienna, as documented by Kraus, bears a striking resemblance to that of
the police battalions deployed in Nazi-occupied Poland, as described by
Christopher Browning and Daniel Goldhagen. 'Orders are orders,' insisted the
commander of Reserve Police Battalion 101, as he briefed his unit of 'ordinary
Germans', middle-aged men from Hamburg, for the task of shooting Jews in
July 1942. Similar units were recruited in Vienna, as we know from the records
of Police Battalion 322, despatched to Poland on 8 June 1941. On arrival in
Warsaw, their commander lectured them on the need for 'unquestioning
obedience, a sense of duty and unswerving loyalty'. The language echoes the
platitudes of Schober, but the massacres that followed were even more horrific.
Their posting to Bialystok involved them first in the 'evacuation' and then the
'liquidation' of hundreds of Jews, meticulously recorded in the battalion diary
in the spirit of duty conscientiously done. Thus on 14 August 1941 the diarist
notes: '282 Jews were shot.' Kraus prophetically identified this capacity for
state-sanctioned violence in the conduct of the police in supposedly peace-
loving Vienna.[26] Issued with rifles and authorized to open fire, Schober's
officers succeeded in killing eight-five civilians in a single day. For Kraus, the
'police-war' betrayed a hidden truth about the post-war world: the longing for
a 'greater world war' (F 776–70, 49). Seen in this perspective, the conduct of
the police in July 1927 provides the missing link between the brutalizing effects
of the First World War and the atrocities committed by the execution squads
of the early 1940s.

The Wounded Republic

'Der Hort der Republik' is Kraus's most important political polemic of the
1920s, comparable to 'Prozeß Friedjung' (December 1909) in its analysis of the
self-destructive potential inherent in a whole political system. His documentary technique is radically democratic in the sense of giving a voice to the
common people, creating a polyphonic collage in which tendentious official

pronouncements and dishonest newspaper editorials are challenged by eyewit-nesses. In the first forty-eight pages we hear approximately a hundred different voices, from the screams of girls pursued by mounted policemen with drawn swords to Schober's poetic platitudes. Wengraf, president of Concordia, defends the 'bestiality' of the police in the name of private property, while right-wing political parties clamour for the reintroduction of the death penalty (F 766–70, 7–9 & 40). Kraus does not attempt to give a balanced picture, rely-ing heavily on testimony from the municipal inquiry, the *Arbeiter-Zeitung*, *Das kleine Blatt* and *Der Abend*. In his documentation there is little trace of the 'violent crowd' led by foreign agitators, whose 'excesses' are described at such length in the police White Paper.[27] His eyewitnesses describe helpless people fleeing from volleys of gunfire and policemen screaming abuse as they inflict life-threatening wounds. The acoustic collage reaches its climax in the cry of outrage with which the crowd responded when the police opened fire: 'P – f – u – i!' (F 766–70, 53).

Amid all this sound and fury, two statements stand out as the testimony of foreign observers who have no political axe to grind. Kraus quotes an authority on crowd control, writing in the *Berliner Tageblatt*, who identifies the inadequate organization of the Viennese police as the main cause of the catastrophe. This view is confirmed by G. E. R. Gedye, a British foreign correspondent who was an eyewitness of events. Gedye's analysis, published in the *Contemporary Review* of September 1927, is cited by Kraus in some detail. 'This much is certain,' Gedye writes, 'that up till the moment when bullets and stones began to fly, no one had intended violence. [. . .] Suddenly one saw in the distance a detachment of mounted police ride through the tail end of the procession – apparently an unnecessary lapse from the tact usually charac-teristic of the Vienna police. [. . .] When incendiarism began, the police resorted to volley firing into the crazy crowds, at first with revolvers and then with rifles' (F 766, 20–1).[28] Gedye, who had contacts at Police Headquarters, makes it clear who was to blame for allowing events to run out of control, providing a judicious summary in *Fallen Bastions*, his classic account of the destruction of Austrian democracy. At the root of the trouble (Gedye writes) was Schober's 'blunder' in allowing the police to disperse at 6 a.m., leaving par-liament inadequately protected. The second blunder was barring the line of march to the hundreds of thousands of workers, instead of keeping them moving round the public buildings and so back towards the factory areas in the outer suburbs as the marchers had planned. Immediately 'the whole temper of the demonstrators changed. Whether the police drew their revolvers or the workers threw stones first, was never definitely settled and is not important. The vital point is that the nervousness of several police commandants with insufficient forces at their disposal turned a peaceful protest demonstration into bloody street-fighting.' Gedye confirms that the police, 'firing indiscrim-inately', used target ammunition that inflicted 'terrible wounds', and he exposes the cover-up in the press, instigated by Schober's assistant Bernhard

Pollak, which attempted to conceal the blunder over the use of the wrong ammunition.[29]

The image of the Austrian elite that emerges from *Die Fackel* is as devastating as the caricatures of the German ruling class by George Grosz. But if Kraus's documentation is equally partisan, this is not due to distortion. Far from inventing his quotations, he has assiduously cut and pasted them, accentuating the political fanaticism and moral vacuousness of Seipel, Schober and their supporters. He devotes relatively little attention to the question: Who was responsible for the riot – *Arbeiter-Zeitung*, Social Democrats, communists or anarchists?[30] Taking issue with the notion of irresponsible 'elements', he attributes 'the symbolic destruction of justice' to the demonstrators' outraged 'sense of human rights' ('Rechtsgefühl'). He goes on to argue that the legal system has repeatedly failed, allowing the well-attested crimes of individual police officers to go unpunished and refusing even to permit private prosecutions (F 766–70, 45 & 50–4). His main focus is on the willingness of the state to legitimize violence against its citizens. The Chancellor, Ignaz Seipel, responded to the massacre by congratulating Schober on his outstanding 'success' and declaring in parliament that no one should expect him to 'show mercy to the victims and culprits', for that would be cruelty 'to the wounded Republic'.[31] These statements, reprinted on the first two pages of *Die Fackel*, are incisively deconstructed in Kraus's collage of quotations, which includes eyewitness statements showing that the conduct of the police was just as anarchic as that of the demonstrators – and far more lethal. Responding to Seipel's rhetoric about the 'wounded Republic', he deconstructs the metaphor, documenting the real wounds inflicted on both demonstrators and bystanders by wild volleys of gunfire. The word 'verwundet', denoting wounds inflicted in warfare (as opposed to accidental injuries), occurs a score of times, often highlighted so as to draw attention to the horrific consequences, including a wounded man lying in the Ringstrasse, executed by a police inspector in cold blood, and a nurse shot through the back of the head as she tended the wounded (F 766–70, 33 & 42).

Kraus also responds to the crocodile tears shed by Seipel and Schober for the 'Republic'. If the police really were the 'bastion of state order', he argues, parliament would 'have to commit suicide' – a prophetic comment. Seipel is in the absurd position of supporting a 'massacre among passers-by' as a means of saving 'republican honour'. In reality, he is a 'reactionary who wishes to inflict damage on the Republic'. In his polemic against Seipel and Schober, Kraus suggests that their real aim is to transform the Republic into an 'authoritarian state' ('Obrigkeitsstaat'; F 766–70, 69).[32] Before publishing this text, Kraus made repeated revisions, later explaining that he was reluctant to commit himself to print until his ideas were fully worked out (F 806–9, 56). This can be confirmed by a comparison of proofsheets in the Kraus Archive with the published text. In an early draft he ironized the Police Chief for 'guaranteeing the security of the Republic, as long as no one happens to be crossing the Ringstrasse'. In the final version this becomes: 'as long as no republican happens to be crossing the Ringstrasse'. The impersonal word 'man' has been replaced by the more forceful epithet 'Republikaner', emphasizing that the existence of the Republic is at stake. In this text he is writing not simply as a satirist, but 'as a republican' (F 776–70, 69 & 91).

There were strong reasons for demanding Schober's resignation, but Kraus's commentary goes further, denouncing him for waging war against defenceless and innocent people. Confronted with the misdeeds of 'a few stone-throwers, arsonists and looters', the police grotesquely overreacted. The use of firearms for crowd control (he insists) is justified only as a last resort, if a policeman believes that his life is in danger. Since demonstrators can be dispersed by means of water-hoses, the firing of salvoes into panic-stricken crowds is indefensible (F 766–70, 49–56). The job of the police is to catch pickpockets and traffic offenders, not to massacre passers-by (F 766–70, 69). The passion of Kraus's polemic is reminiscent of his campaign against the inhumanities of war, and his most scathing comments, in 1927 as in 1914, are directed against the apologists of massacre. Instead of admitting that the police lost their heads, the government decorates them as if they were 'war heroes'. The alliance between 'state authority and bourgeois media' is so complete that the Austrian press applauds this 'bestiality'. No independent voice is raised to condemn Schober for his brutal methods or Seipel for his intransigence (F 766–70, 52–6). Kraus cites specific examples to substantiate these claims. It is hardly surprising that the *Reichspost* was guilty of tendentious reporting, since its offices had been wrecked. More compromising was the conduct of the *Neue Freie Presse*, which (as Kraus noted) omitted from its report of Seipel's parliamentary speech any reference to his refusal to show mercy '*towards the victims*' (F 766–70, 2).

The reactions to his protests confirmed Kraus's worst suspicions about the decay of democracy. Shortly after the publication of his poster, Schober was confirmed in office by Chancellor Seipel and his Cabinet (F 766–70, 46–7). Far from achieving practical results, the poster exposed Kraus to abuse and ridicule. A few days later that second poster was published calling on Schober *not* to resign. The person responsible for this ploy was Ernst Winkler, a shopkeeper known as the 'Goldfüllfederkönig' ('King of the Golden Fountain-Pens').[33] Its effect was to suggest that Kraus's attitude to Schober carried no more authority than that of any other member of the public, although Winkler later confessed that his action, far from being a spontaneous act, was prompted 'from above' (F 781–6, 91). Representatives of the police also issued a statement denying Kraus the right to express 'the will of the population of Vienna' – as a 'private person' he has no political standing. To these arguments Kraus responded by denouncing the moral lethargy of Austria and claiming for his own position 'the authority of moral example' (F 766–70, 48 & 71). The impact of Kraus's poster on those with greater sensitivity is recorded in the memoirs of Canetti, who witnessed the burning of the Palace of Justice. This experience was to shape his whole career, culminating thirty years later in the publication of *Crowds and Power* (*Masse und Macht*, 1960). The events of July

1927 still reverberate in the second volume of his autobiography, published in 1980. 'Fifty-three years have passed,' he writes, 'and the agitation of that day is still in my bones.' The blend of fascination and fear inspired by the riot and massacre was followed by weeks of utter dejection, but his one consolation was a 'specific public deed': Kraus's poster calling for Schober's resignation. Kraus, he recalls, 'was alone in this demand; he was the only public figure who acted in this way. And while the other celebrities, of whom Vienna never had a lack, did not wish to lay themselves open to criticism or perhaps ridicule, Kraus alone had the courage of his indignation. His posters were the only thing that kept us going in those days. I went from one poster to another, paused in front of each one, and I felt as if all the justice on earth had entered the letters of Kraus's name.'[34]

It was this concern for justice that gave Kraus's campaign its authority. In 'Der Hort der Republik' he denounced a system of justice which sides with the victors and is enforced by random gunfire (F 766–70, 50 & 54). In the following number of Die Fackel he condemned the 'prostitution of legal norms' (F 771–6, 18). It is not personal hatred, but an insistence on the indivisibility of justice that leads him to link Schober's culpability for the massacre with his duplicity in the Bekessy affair. This second theme develops into the main thrust of the subsequent polemic, as Kraus attempted to overcome the inertia of public opinion by challenging the myth of Schober's integrity. He felt that Schober's decision to arm the police with rifles was grotesquely at odds with his cowardice when confronted by Bekessy's revolver, and this paradox constitutes the subtext of Kraus's poster (F 771–6, 110).

For three years he campaigned to get Schober into court, hoping that 'judicial moves' might once again provide a way out of the 'moral labyrinth' (F 766–70, 71). Since there was no chance that Schober would ever be put on trial for unlawful killing, Kraus accused him of 'abuse of official powers in protecting a blackmailer' (F 778–80, 8). He hoped to provoke an action for defamation, so that he could substantiate these allegations in court, but Schober, unwilling to be cross-examined under oath, ignored the challenge. This provoked an impassioned denunciation entitled 'Das Ereignis des Schweigens' ('The Occurrence of Silence'), which Kraus read in public on 13 January 1928, before it appeared in print. The controlled fury of this attack is attributable to the death of a sixteen-year-old youth named Hans Erwin Kiesler, one of those passers-by shot by the police on 15 July. Lying on the ground awaiting medical attention after being hit by a stray bullet, he was shot at close range by a sadistic policeman. Kraus was so affected by Kiesler's death, after six agonizing months in hospital, that he threw discretion to the winds, denouncing the police as 'murderers' whose actions should not remain 'unavenged'. Although aware that this exposed him to prosecution for 'incitement' (F 777, 8–9), he was determined to have the matter tested in court.

For Kraus, the bastion of the Republic was an impartial judiciary, and he lamented both the failure of the courts to punish crimes committed by the

police and their harshness towards the rioters. Although he joined the Social
Democrats in condemning this 'July justice' (F 771–6, 17), he was reluctant to
endorse the Marxist critique of the courts as a bourgeois institution. The more
blatantly the rule of law was threatened, by brutal policemen, prejudiced juries
or vindictive judges, the more tenaciously he pursued his cause through the
courts. Frustrated in his campaign to discredit Schober for the suppression of
the riot, he fell back on more oblique tactics, which seemed to offer the only
chance of practical success against this 'symbol of bourgeois power' (F 795–9,
23). It was certainly possible, he wrote in February 1928, explaining his appeal
to the law, for 'citizens to make use of this civil institution' (F 778–80, 7). The
problem, implicit in the ambiguity of the word 'Bürger', was whether the
universal rights of the citizen could be wrested from the control of the bourgeoisie. The nearest Kraus came to getting Schober into the witness box
was in April 1928, when he himself initiated an action for defamation after
Schober had incautiously referred to irresponsible attacks on the police,
but Schober denied that he had the satirist in mind. Kraus's response reveals a
sophisticated grasp of legal principle, particularly the implications of attacks on
unnamed persons (F 778–80, 15–28); but the outcome confirmed his suspicion
that Schober's faction was 'invincible' (F 777, 12).

Beyond Morality

The crusade against Schober was the most political of all Kraus's polemics. He
may insist that his 'partisanship' for the victims of 15 July cannot be seen as a
'party matter' (F 766–60, 51), but by taking up the cause of the demonstrators
he made common cause with the socialists. Seipel's refusal to show 'mercy'
towards the victims and culprits of 15 July became a leitmotif of socialist propaganda, earning him the title of 'prelate without mercy' ('Prälat ohne Milde').
This lack of Christian charity also forms a refrain in Kraus's polemic, which
pictures Seipel as a man whose face has hardened into a 'rigid mask' (F 776–70,
57). Meanwhile Austerlitz, whose inflammatory editorial helped to inspire the
demonstration, escapes censure. When right-wingers at the Party conference
of October 1927 criticized the editorial as an infringement of discipline, Kraus
praised the 'impulse for justice' ('Rechtsgefühl') which inspired it. For him, the
errors committed by the Party on 15 July were due to 'the failure of its leadership', by which he meant Renner and Bauer (F 771–6, 13).[35] In his critique it
is possible to detect affinities with the position of the Communist Party, which
argued that the leadership had betrayed the workers through a failure of nerve
in 1927, repeating the errors of the potentially revolutionary years 1918–19.[36]
Here Kraus found more radical allies, and on 23 October he gave a public reading to raise money for the victims of 15 July, organized by Rote Hilfe ('Red
Support'), an offshoot of the Communist Party. According to the report in
Rote Hilfe, the journal of this organization, the audience responded to Kraus's
indictment by singing the 'Internationale'.[37] Further evidence of communist
support can be found in the report on the massacre of 15 July published by

Rote Hilfe, which reproduces eyewitness accounts of police brutality from *Die Fackel*.[38] The following year, on 17 November 1928, Kraus gave a second reading for Rote Hilfe (F 800–5, 53), including the 'Schober-Lied', a satirical song about constabulary duty which makes the Police Chief look like a musical-comedy character from *The Pirates of Penzance*.

Kraus had also recited the 'Schober-Lied' to a Social Democratic audience in the suburb of Hietzing in May. He had hoped the Party would help with the distribution of this musical broadsheet through its network of cultural organizations, but it declined to co-operate. This made him even more reliant on the support of Rote Hilfe, which helped to sell about 19,000 copies of the song (F 795–9, 27–9). Proceeds from the sale of this broadsheet, published in July 1928, were again devoted to helping the victims of 15 July. At the end of July the police confiscated copies of the song and banned its sale on the streets, moves which Kraus resisted through the courts (F 806–9, 1–4). In August, when Rote Hilfe members were selling the 'Schober-Lied' at a workers' musical festival, they were harassed by Social Democratic officials. Disputed accounts of this incident, which further alienated Kraus from the socialists, led him in the spring of 1929 to reproduce a long statement defining the aims of Rote Hilfe, insisting that it was a 'non-party proletarian organization' whose members were not exclusively communists (F 806–9, 17–21). Kraus was also vigorously supported in his campaign against Schober by the communist journal *Rote Fahne* ('Red Flag'), which paid tribute to him on 17 February 1929 as a 'revolutionary writer and artist'.[39]

The Social Democrats, as Kraus had foreseen, were ready to compromise with the class enemy, undermining his campaign against Schober just as they had in the case of Bekessy. But without their support he could hardly hope for 'practical success' (F 795–9, 9–11). The political dynamics of the years 1927–30 made the failure of Kraus's polemic all the more spectacular. The Police Chief's forceful tactics transformed him into a key figure in right-wing politics and, with Seipel in ailing health, Schober emerged a possible successor – the strong man capable of restoring stability. His suppression of the riots was admired in conservative circles abroad, and in April 1928 his prestige was enhanced when his agents uncovered a Hungarian communist cell in the Neubaugasse and arrested Béla Kun, who was living there under an assumed name.[40] For Kraus this achievement could not erase Schober's responsibility for the bloodshed of July 1927 (F 778–80, 44). Throughout 1928 he kept up the pressure on Schober to resign, although he was also preoccupied by his quarrel with Alfred Kerr. On 14 June 1929 he denounced Schober once again, coupling his name with that of Karl Zörgiebel, the Police Chief responsible for the shooting of demonstrators on May Day in Berlin. Schober, who was holding a grand parade to mark the sixtieth anniversary of the Austrian Police Force (Fig. 37), is ridiculed as a 'mediocre civil servant', strutting around the streets of Vienna as if he were a 'generalissimo' (F 811–19, 5). The summer of 1929, however, marked a watershed in Austrian politics. Seipel resigned as chancellor in April,

37   Schober celebrating the sixtieth anniversary of the Viennese Police Force

leaving his successor Ernst Streeruwitz to cope with the growing menace
of the Heimwehr. Backed by fascist groups in Italy and Hungary as well as
Austrian industrialists, its leaders Pfrimer and Steidle were threatening a putsch.
In the incipient crisis, Schober was seen as the authority figure who might construct a new coalition government and introduce a reformed constitution, and
on 29 September, less than two months after the publication of Kraus's latest
attack, he was once again appointed chancellor. Judged by Kraus's ethic of
citizenship, Schober was discredited, but in terms of practical politics he
was vindicated.

Schober's government provided a rallying-point not only for the right-wing
coalition, but also for the socialist opposition. The Heimwehr assumed that
Schober would fulfil their demand for an authoritarian constitution along
Italian lines, but for the Social Democrats his leadership offered the chance of
saving democracy, since they had reason to believe that he would bring the
Heimwehr to heel. The socialists thus welcomed Schober's government as a
lesser evil. Kraus grimly noted in October 1929 that *Das kleine Blatt*, the Social
Democratic tabloid edited by Julius Braunthal, which had earlier supported his
campaign, greeted Schober's administration as a 'government against a coup
d'état'. Even Robert Danneberg, author of the City Council's inquiry into the
events of 15 July, made conciliatory gestures (F 820–6, 15–21). Kraus found
himself virtually isolated, although the communist *Rote Fahne* continued to
regard Schober as a 'fascist bloodhound'.[41] Schober went on to achieve some
notable successes, both at home and abroad. Despite the vulnerability of the

Austrian economy after the Wall Street Crash, he remained Chancellor for over a year, achieving a breakthrough at the Hague International Conference of January 1930, when he renegotiated the indemnity clauses in the Treaty of Saint-Germain which had placed such a burden on Austria. Schober was granted financial support by Britain and France on the understanding that he would curb the extremist groups which threatened Austrian democracy. His decision in May 1930 to disarm all paramilitary forces provoked violent protests by the extreme right, but Schober responded by deporting Waldemar Pabst, a German fascist who acted as the Heimwehr chief of staff.

Schober's successes transformed him into a national hero, and he consolidated his reputation in the spring of 1930 through visits to Rome, Berlin, Paris and London. The *Daily News*, a British liberal newspaper, actually described Schober as 'the best policeman outside London' (F 838–44, 2). Registering these developments in May 1930, Kraus conceded defeat. His campaign against Schober had been overtaken by events, and in a succinct five-page statement he acknowledged that he had no option but to follow the example of other opposition groups and 'draw a line under the past'. He now acknowledges that 'ability in the field of international politics is defined beyond the moral and intellectual criteria' that had inspired his polemic (F 827–33, 39). It made no sense to continue his campaign, if even the western powers were willing to support Schober as the saviour of Austria. This marks a turning-point in Kraus's approach to politics, hitherto conceived in ethical terms. His approach now became more pragmatic, as he adapted to situations where it was necessary to choose the lesser evil. Schober's duplicity, seen during the Bekessy affair as a moral blemish, proved to be a political asset, as he negotiated behind closed doors first with the leaders of the Heimwehr, then with the Social Democrats. In private discussions with Rintelen, Steidle and Pfrimer, he promised that if they supported him as chancellor he would push through a new, authoritarian constitution that would represent a final 'reckoning' with the Marxists. During secret meetings with Seitz and Danneberg a few days later, he reassured them that his government would protect the Social Democrats from the threat of a Heimwehr coup. This 'double double-game' (as his biographer puts it) proved remarkably effective, consolidating his position as chancellor.[42] But Kraus, who had insisted on the need for moral principles in public life, felt obliged to retire to the sidelines, contenting himself with symbolic victories in the sphere of stage performance.

PART FIVE

THE POLITICS
OF PERFORMANCE

CHAPTER 18

Theatre against the Modern Age

In Germany the 1920s were the era of 'Zeittheater' – topical theatre for the modern age. The aim as defined by Heinrich Fischer, a close collaborator of both Kraus and Brecht, was 'to stage contemporary problems with factual accuracy as bare document'. But Fischer singled out *Die letzten Tage der Menschheit* for special praise as prototype for a 'theatre *against* the modern age'.[1] Kraus's innovative achievements as a political dramatist are hard to reconcile with his nostalgia for the old Burgtheater and his cult of the theatre as locus of cultural memory. The aesthetic experiences of his youth led him to combine Schiller's model of the stage as a tribunal with Goethe's conception of a theatre of poetry, but this did not prevent him from writing dramatic satires as subversive as those of Brecht or Piscator. To understand this paradox, we need to recall his debt to two divergent sources: the pathos of the Habsburg court theatre and the irreverence of Jewish vaudeville.

The Good School of the Burgtheater

As a young man Kraus had an insatiable appetite for the theatre, and his early reviews form a cornucopia of names, dates and productions.[2] He claimed that great actors may be seen to best advantage in lightweight plays, and a performance by Alexander Girardi and his partner Helene Odilon at a provincial theatre receives almost as much attention as Adolf von Sonnenthal and Charlotte Wolter in Goethe's *Faust* (FS 1, 26–7 and 76–7). Indeed, *Charley's Aunt* and *Trilby* seem to rate more highly than the tragedies of Hebbel and Grillparzer, and he praises Gilbert and Sullivan's *Mikado* just as enthusiastically as Mahler's production of *Lohengrin*. He was fascinated by fringe theatres, including the café–theatres of the Prater, and reports amusingly on the latest musicals, not to mention a slapstick featuring a boxing kangaroo (FS 1, 98). After the founding of *Die Fackel* he used the theatre as a means of measuring the 'temperature of life' (F 391–2, 33).

Although he repeatedly contrasted the 'old' Burgtheater with the 'new', it is wrong to suggest that Kraus experienced the closing of the venerable building on the Michaelerplatz as a traumatic loss.[3] According to the memoir by Germaine Goblot, it was 'around the age of fifteen' – that is, around 1889 – that he became consumed by a passion for the theatre.[4] Kraus himself, writing in March 1912, speaks of 'twenty-five years' of knowledge of the theatre, which would date his earliest experiences back to 1887 (F 343–4, 20). Since the old Burgtheater closed its doors on 12 December 1888, this suggests that he attended only a handful of performances in that building. On that final night Sonnenthal delivered a valedictory oration after a performance of Goethe's *Iphigenie auf Tauris* in which Konrad Adolf Hallenstein, as Thoas, spoke the celebrated parting words: 'Lebt wohl!' Although Kraus later attached special significance to these words, there is no evidence that he was actually present.[5] After the closing of the theatre on the Michaelerplatz, many of its productions were revived in the monumental new building, whose acoustics required greater clarity of diction. It was only through declamatory speeches that the actors could communicate with the distant galleries, displacing the art of subtle 'conversational speaking' cultivated in the older, more intimate auditorium.[6] It was primarily the style developed in the *new* building that Kraus had in mind when he recalled the 'good school of the Burgtheater' (F 138, 15). Here he first saw Sonnenthal in his most celebrated classical roles – as King Lear (1889) and Henry IV (1890) – in addition to more modern plays.[7] During the 1890s (as he later recalled) he became a regular visitor to the fourth gallery, finding the distance from the stage no impediment (F 546–50, 37–9). However, there was no uniform house-style ('Burgtheaterton'; F 43, 20), but a blending of the traditions established by the mid-century directors, Heinrich Laube and Franz von Dingelstedt. These are sometimes seen as irreconcilable opposites: 'Laube, denying all spectacle, placed sole emphasis on the word, while Dingelstedt accentuated physical appearances.'[8] The system of retaining successful productions in the repertoire for decades makes it impossible to draw a clear line between one era and the next. Laube ceased to be director several years before Kraus was born, but his cult of the spoken word left an 'indelible imprint' on the work of the ensemble until the end of the century.[9] Similarly, the Dingelstedt tradition of spectacular stage design was continued by Burckhard and Schlenther. As late as January 1901 we find Kraus complaining about the persistence of 'Dingelstedt's intellectually lethal pomp' – 'not the best Burgtheater tradition' (F 65, 26). These comments were occasioned by a revival of Shakespeare's *Henry IV* which retained features from Dingelstedt's opulent sets, reconstructing the palaces of Tudor kings in supposedly authentic detail.[10]

During the 1890s the grand style co-existed with the modernizing tendencies of Max Burckhard, who introduced naturalism into the repertoire. The ensemble was still that of the old Burgtheater, but the repertoire included provocatively modern problem plays by Ibsen, Hauptmann and Schnitzler.[11]

Such innovations, as Kraus observed in August 1892, affronted the traditionalists, who preferred the salon comedies of Sardou and Scribe (FS 1, 16–18).
Looking back over these events six years later, in January 1898, he concluded
that Burckhard had presided over the 'seven lean years of the Burgtheater' (FS
2, 161–2). This judgement, reiterated in December 1908 (F 269, 28), shows
how difficult it is to take his theatre criticism at face value, for he had actually
welcomed Burckhard's innovations, mocking the traditionalists who saw them
as a sign of 'decline'. He praised Hauptmann as the 'apostle of modernism' and
was fascinated by the 'titanic' Ibsen (FS 1, 17–21). In April 1891 he hailed the
production of *The Pretenders* as an unforgettable experience (FS 1, 48), later
recalling that it was he who had prompted Burckhard to stage this play
(F 546–50, 35). If Kraus, who described himself as one of Burckhard's 'most
passionate admirers', had any reservations at that date, it was because the
director's innovations were not radical enough (FS 1, 104).

In February 1893 Kraus travelled to Berlin to attend the première of *Die
Weber*, being so impressed that he gave public readings of the play later that year
(F 521–30, 98). In February 1894 he defended Burckhard's productions of
both *Hanneles Himmelfahrt* and *Einsame Menschen* against the traditionalists who
regarded the staging of such plays at the Burgtheater as sacrilege (FS 1, 183–4),
and in later life he repeatedly returned to that production of *Hannele*, listing the
cast as reverently as a liturgy (F 885–7, 17). The last of Burckhard's productions to gain his approval was Ibsen's *The Wild Duck* – 'a virtually flawless
production' (January 1897; FS 2, 16). A significant shift occurred in May 1897,
when Kraus published an article on the Berlin actor most closely associated
with the modern style, Emanuel Reicher, contrasting his 'external naturalness'
with the inner qualities of 'our unnatural Sonnenthal' (FS 2, 59–61). The
appointment of the stolid Paul Schlenther as Burckhard's successor in 1898 led
him to reassess his experiences, and his enthusiasm for the moderns was
swamped by a wave of nostalgia.

Where conventional memoirs abound in colourful anecdote, Kraus relies
on synecdoche, using a single attribute to characterize an actor's style:
Matkowsky's 'volcanic' temperament (F 200, 19), Baumeister's 'elemental'
passion (F 222, 15), Wolter's 'scream' and Sonnenthal's 'tears' (F 462–71, 183).
Theatre historians have been unable to make much of such apodictic judgements, based on 'general impressions' rather than 'critical analysis'.[12] They
require the contextual support provided by the two-volume edition of
Sonnenthal's correspondence published in 1912, which records an extraordinary range of achievements. Between 1856 and 1908 Sonnenthal appeared on
the stage of the Burgtheater in over four hundred different roles, working with
seven different directors. Initially, he played in social comedies, and it was only
later that he embarked on the great classical roles from Hamlet and Faust to
Wallenstein. He won glory for the Burgtheater by transcending its limitations,
and there was nothing provincial about an actor who could move audiences
in New York and Chicago, just as he did in Berlin and St Petersburg. If

Sonnenthal was the 'leading German actor of the age', this was due to the universality of his appeal.[13] Although initially hostile towards Burckhard's modernizing tendencies, the innovations of the 1890s provided Sonnenthal with new opportunities – as Doctor Stockmann in *Enemy of the People* and Weiring in *Liebelei*, followed in 1899 by the title role in Hauptmann's *Fuhrmann Henschel*. When traditionalists were scandalized to see this lowlife drama at the Burgtheater, he defended the play's poetic qualities.[14]

The eulogy which Kraus published in January 1914 gives the impression that Sonnenthal had always been his hero, but twenty years earlier he had described him as 'rather colourless' in the title role of *Faust* (FS 1, 77). In May 1893 he observed that Sonnenthal, for all his merits, was incapable of doing justice to the role of Lear, while in March 1894 he added that he was insipid as Wallenstein (FS 1, 115 and 197). In January 1901, he expressed grave reservations about his acting in *Henry IV* (F 65, 26–7), while in May he again criticized his performance as Lear – 'every inch not a king' (F 78, 22). In December 1905 he distinguished between the power with which Sonnenthal delivered certain speeches by Lear and his failure to do justice to the role as a whole – 'just as insipid as his Wallenstein' (F 191, 22). Even at the time of the actor's death in April 1909 Kraus's response was very subdued, and it was not until five years later, after reading the correspondence, that he endowed Sonnenthal with mythic status. A passion for the actors of the past, as he half admits, 'idealizes what one remembers' (F 391–2, 36).

Sonnenthal's correspondence, described as a monument to the 'passing of a noble stage culture' (F 391–2, 38), illuminates the career of a man who started life in Budapest as a Jewish tailoring apprentice, yet developed into the presiding genius of the Vienna court theatre. In him Kraus admired the convergence of aristocratic and middle-class traditions, represented by an acculturated Jew who actually fulfilled the promise of his family name ('Sonnenthal' in the sense of 'sunlit valley'). The actor had redefined the terms of exchange between artist and society 'so that the parson could learn a lesson from a comedian, the aristocrat from a Jew, the man of the world from a tailor's apprentice' (F 391–2, 32). Kraus, who in this period routinely associated the Jewish bourgeoisie with commercial values, sees in Sonnenthal a more humane alternative: a form of acculturation that transcends religious and ethnic barriers. In January 1905 he repudiated the 'infernal stupidity' of the antisemitic press, which treated Sonnenthal 'as a complete bungler', but reviewers who praised his acting out of a spirit of Jewish solidarity were equally suspect (F 174, 21). His eulogy of 1914 attempts to strike a balance:

> Antisemitism, which denies an Adolf Sonnenthal the respect he deserves, is replete with its own emptiness, and liberal ideology reaches its limit when it starts to lay claim to the actor who embodies its still unexhausted humanism – an actor who was a human being before the merchants came into the world. His voice received a different consecration than the temple music which they have usurped. (F 391–2, 37)

Here, Kraus is trying to find a middle way between the reactionary anti-semitism of the Christian Social Party and the progressive liberalism of the Jewish commercial bourgeoisie with its mimicry of Christian practices in the reformed synagogue.

To resolve this dilemma, he invokes the values of the Enlightenment, appealing to a concept of the 'human being' ('Mensch') which carries echoes of both Lessing and Kant. In 1895 Lessing's celebrated plea for religious toleration, *Nathan der Weise*, had been reintroduced into the repertoire of the Burgtheater with Sonnenthal in the title role. Kraus was certainly familiar with this play, which uses the famous Parable of the Three Rings to suggest that the truth of the three religions, Judaism, Christianity and Islam, manifests itself through the moral conduct of their adherents. In Lessing's play the word 'Mensch' is endowed with an exceptional moral charge, particularly in the speeches of Nathan, the enlightened Jewish merchant who challenges religious dogmas. The words he addresses to the young Knight Templar in Act II, scene 5 are characteristic: 'Are Jews and Christians more Christians and Jews / than human beings?' Kraus echoes this antithesis in attributing to Sonnenthal a 'human value' ('Menschenwert') that transcends religious affiliations (F 391–2, 37). Lurking behind these formulations is the Kantian association of the sublime with the ethical heritage of Judaism. In the *Critique of Judgement*, Kant suggests that there is 'no more sublime passage in Jewish Law' than the ban on graven images. This subordination of sensual perception to an abstract idea is seen as a primary source of 'the predisposition within us for morality'.[15] Judaism, as a religion of words and hearing rather than images and seeing, becomes secularized in Kraus's celebration of a style of performance which privileges the spoken word, as opposed to visual spectacle. This helps to explain why Sonnenthal's art can be seen as a 'consecration' superior to that either of the Church or of the reformed synagogue which has adopted Christian practices. Acting the classics becomes a liturgy, with Sonnenthal fulfilling his mission as if he were 'the last remaining image of God' ('das letzte Ebenbild Gottes'; F 391–2, 32–7).

Life Enhancement and Cultural Memory

Looking back in July 1920 on his formative experiences in the Burgtheater, Kraus defined them as an enduring 'life enhancement' (F 546–50, 37). To understand this suggestive phrase, we need to consider his attitude more closely, especially his emotional response to Sonnenthal's rendition of the speech in Act I, scene 4 of *King Lear* where Lear curses his daughter Goneril. Kraus repeatedly praised the actor's delivery of this speech, even when questioning his interpretation of the role as a whole (FS 1, 115).[16] A passage from Sonnenthal's correspondence helps us to understand why Kraus was so fascinated by this scene. In November 1889, after one of his aristocratic admirers had suggested that the curse should be delivered in a harsh voice without any trace of passionate feeling, Sonnenthal replied:

Your view, gracious Princess, that the scene should be played 'coolly' (to use the artistic expression) would certainly be a great relief for me, above all physically, but this is something I could never do and shall never be able to do. I have to give my all and I believe, my dear Princess, that the poet demands it at this moment. It is less the king in Lear than the tormented heart of a father that causes him to pronounce the terrible curse on an ungrateful child. Before the curse begins, he cries: 'Ingratitude, thou marble-hearted fiend, more hideous when thou show'st thee in a child', etc, and he concludes the curse: '. . . That she may feel how sharper than a serpent's tooth it is to have a *thankless* child.' And while speaking he sheds 'hot tears'. Thus everything suggests that the curse must be delivered with passionate feeling [. . .].[17]

We know that Kraus, like the Princess, attended this performance, although he was only fifteen at the time, and that he returned to see Sonnenthal as Lear seven times during the following years. There is a mystery here, since in May 1893 he insisted that Sonnenthal was too soft, 'soft as a baby's nappy' ('windelweich'), to do justice to the role of Lear, while asserting in the same breath that his cursing of Goneril was 'one of the most magnificent, most powerful acting achievements' (FS 1, 115).

The mystery can be resolved if we correlate Sonnenthal's rendition of the 'thankless child' speech with the psychological trauma unfolding within the Kraus family. After his mother's death in October 1891, it was (as we have seen) the seventeen-year-old Karl who was blamed, and his relations with his father were strained. The tension continued during the following years, leading him to complain in his letter of 4 September 1897 to his brother Richard about the 'lack of any expression of emotional warmth in our family life'. The theatre clearly helped to fill that emotional void, with Sonnenthal expressing through the voice of Lear the feelings of an ideal father. This scene also left an imprint on Kraus's creativity by establishing a conjunction between 'curses' and 'tears'. The association of Sonnenthal with the 'father' motif also reverberated in Kraus's mind at a metaphorical level. In June 1890 Sonnenthal appeared in the title role of *Henry IV* (Part 2), a performance to which Kraus responded by highlighting a single line, spoken by the King to his son: 'Thy wish was father, Harry, to that thought.' Prince Harry's 'thought' that he will never see his father again is motivated by the desire to succeed him to the throne, hence the stress should be on the word 'wish'. But in 1901, when Kraus attended a reprise of the Burgtheater production, he noted – not for the first time – that Sonnenthal displaced the emphasis on to the word 'father'. He was carried away by the 'melodic colouring of a poetic phrase', but no one in the audience minded, since 'everyone was weeping' (F 65, 26–7).

Theatre offered a formative psycho-drama enabling the young Kraus to experience conflicting emotions in an intensified form while maintaining aesthetic distance. His ability to surmount personal crises was strengthened by a series of aesthetic enactments: the wrath of an injured father in *King Lear*, the sufferings of a sensitive child in *Hanneles Himmelfahrt*, the death of a beloved actress in Offenbach's *Tales of Hoffmann*, the encounter with uninhibited sexuality in Wedekind's Lulu plays, and – as we shall see – the dilemma of Jewish assimilation in Eisenbach's vaudeville. But, as Kraus approached the age of forty, he ceased to be dependent on the theatre for emotional nourishment. The passionate theatre-goer of the 1890s had by 1910 become a disillusioned armchair critic, preferring his table in the coffee-house to a seat in the stalls. His method was to review the reviews, pointing out contradictions in the reception of productions he had not actually seen. In March 1912 he observed that he hadn't visited any Viennese theatre for the past two years (F 343–4, 20). In January 1917 he recorded that it was ten years since he had last been to the Burgtheater (F 445–53, 62), and on the rare occasions when he was tempted back he felt repelled by its 'mediocrity' (F 457–61, 78). His later writings on the theatre blend judgement with nostalgia, as experiences recalled from younger days become the norm against which he measures modern develop-ments, and there was an element of invented tradition in his reminiscences. To castigate a shoddy production of *King Lear* in April 1935, he recalls that per-formance of 1889 with Sonnenthal in the title role (F 906–9, 12–14). This reactivation of memory involved not simply the 'conservation' but the 'inten-sification' of vividly remembered voices from the 1890s, as Kraus observed in 1932 after a public reading of Hauptmann's *Die Weber* (F 885–7, 17).

Although the impressions of his youth had an enduring value, Kraus's claim to prodigious powers of memory tells only part of the story. He consolidated his cult of the old Burgtheater by reference to the treasured volumes of theatre history in his library, including pen-portraits by Ludwig Speidel, doyen of Austrian theatre critics.[18] His repeated references to the final scene of Goethe's *Iphigenie auf Tauris* exemplify this process. When Heinrich Anschütz, playing Thoas, spoke the concluding 'Farewell' – 'Lebt wohl!' (according to an account quoted in *Die Fackel*), he condensed a whole life into a single dramatic gesture. Anschütz had died a decade before Kraus was born, but his heritage was transmitted through the memoirs of another reveared actor, Josef Lewinsky (F 640–8, 55). Thus the theatre, initially valued as an emotional resource, became the locus of 'cultural memory' ('Kulturgedächtnis'; F 912–15, 32–3). This anticipates the theory that cultural traditions are constituted through 'sites of memory'.[19]

Jargon Theatre and the Dilemma of Assimilation

Nathan the Wise does not figure in Kraus's list of Sonnenthal's great roles, since he regarded the Parable of the Three Rings, when promoted by the liberal press, as an expression of 'humanitarian schmaltz' (F 279–80, 33). Indeed, his antithetical cast of mind led him to contrast Lessing's Nathan with a disrep-utable namesake. In June 1906, the fiftieth anniversary of his first appearance at the Burgtheater, Sonnenthal was fêted by Jewish organizations after choos-ing *Nathan the Wise* to mark his jubilee. Kraus responded by suggesting that if Sonnenthal had chosen any other play, members of the audience would have asked: 'Wot's keeping Nathan tonight?' ('Wo bleibt Nathan heint?'; F 205, 26).

This allusion to one of the longest-running plays of the jargon theatre, *Die Klabriaspartie* ('The Game of Cards'), sets up a contrast with a further inspirational source: Jewish vaudeville.[20] Historians of the Yiddish theatre, which had its heyday in the period 1880–1930, tend to repudiate the use of Jewish-accented German, suggesting that this 'gibberish was crippling for both plays and players'. In Vienna, one had to obtain a licence for full-length dramas, so there was a preference for vaudeville shows 'chopped up every few minutes by songs, dances, or acrobatics'.[21] This hybrid form was perfected by the Budapester Orpheumgesellschaft, a troupe of comedians whose performances in smoky suburban hotels, such as the Hotel Central in the Praterstrasse (Fig. 38), were condemned by assimilated Jews, feeling that they pandered to racial prejudice.[22]

Kraus, by contrast, was exhilarated by their performances, claiming in June 1911 that they were superior to the productions of Alfred Berger (director of the Burgtheater) and Max Reinhardt (at the Deutsches Schauspielhaus). In a

38   Programme of the Budapester Orpheum, featuring Heinrich Eisenbach

cryptic phrase he credited the Budapesters with 'the unique artistic representation of a cultural formation' (F 324–5, 23), adding that, as the most gifted
ensemble in Vienna, they should take over the Burgtheater. Their distinctive
achievement is to present 'cultural images of petit-bourgeois Jewry' in such a
way that the conventional identification of Jews and commerce is 'dissolved
into art'. Jewish jargon ('mauscheln') becomes an artistic medium, and actors
like Herbert Eisenbach and Max Rott are able 'to portray the travelling salesman in such a way that one would like to embrace him' (F 341–2, 7–8). This
was not simply a slap in the face for public taste. Kraus's admiration for the
Budapesters can be traced back to March 1896, and Eisenbach had been praised
as a 'quick-change artist' in one of the earliest numbers of Die Fackel (F 20, 5).
   The Budapesters performed in the Leopoldstadt, the predominantly Jewish
quarter to the east of the Danube Canal. As a member of the cultural elite living
in the affluent city centre, Kraus normally avoided the Jewish quarter, except
when he had to despatch proofsheets from the Nordwestbahnhof, the station
for Leipzig.[23] However, he did frequent the Hotels Stephanie and Central in
the Taborstrasse, where the Budapesters performed on makeshift stages in large
rooms lined with tables.[24] Their skits on current affairs provide a striking parallel with Kraus's essays. For example, Eisenbach's Jewish-accented mockery of
the exploits of the polar explorer Frederic Cook, 'Eisig Cookeles Polarreise
zum Polareise', forms a hilarious counterpoint to Kraus's reflections on this
theme, 'Die Entdeckung des Nordpols' (F 287, 1–14).[25] Moreover, the audience were permitted to drink and smoke – a further advantage over the
Burgtheater, where the fire regulations prevented him from lighting up to
alleviate his boredom (F 341–2, 8). Such was his passion for this theatre that he
shared it with his friends Adolf Loos and Oskar Kokoschka. 'It is impossible to
forget those performances, full of originality and fantasy,' Kokoschka recalled
sixty years later. 'The music and dances, the solo numbers and duets had so
much sheer theatrical verve, and the Jewish humour was so wild, that one did
not know whether to laugh or cry'.[26]
   In his own appreciation, Kraus cites Hamlet's aspersions on players who
have 'neither the accent of Christians nor the gait of Christians' (Hamlet, III,
2). The Budapesters, by contrast, have 'the accent and the gait of Jews', while
Eisenbach is a 'farceur who needs less than a step to reach the sublime':

> It would be impossible to imagine anything greater than the figure of the Jewish
> father who experiences the humorously intended proof that his three sons are not
> his own children as a tragedy, were it not for the fact that Eisenbach also appears in
> a virtuoso sketch involving a succession of six masks. [. . .] As an English entertainer
> who cannot find the words to convince the judge that he has a chimpanzee at home,
> he experiences a spasm and starts ambling around the stage as a chimpanzee. He's
> wearing the clothes of the English entertainer, only it's the hide of an ape, he has
> human skin only it's changed colour. He has the limbs of a chimpanzee and stares
> with the eyes of a chimpanzee into a world out of which the soul of an actor seems
> to stare into a prehistoric realm. As he crosses the stage he undergoes an evolution-
> ary regression, as if it were his mission to put the reliability of scientific knowledge

to the final test. The casual ease with which he represents the inner life of an ape, without costume or mask, shows how completely this singular actor has established his psychic ascendancy over everything organic, without a trace of forced technique. (F 343–4, 19–20)

Eisenbach's gifts, like those of Girardi, enable him to transform the most trivial materials – in this case probably the sketch *Der Wüstling* (*The Roué*) by Josef Armin.[27]

Kraus was captivated by a troupe that enacted the experiences of semi-assimilated German-speaking Jews. By reconfiguring their dilemma through art, Eisenbach showed that Jewishness is not a destiny but a discourse, since the gait and accents of Jews are subject to so many transformations. Kraus's response was equally multi-faceted. As moralist, he attempted to purify the language of the tribe by reference to the most elevated model – Sonnenthal's consecrated voice. But as a satirist he adopted the opposite strategy, absorbing the jargon of Eisenbach's dialogues into his own imaginative theatre. It has been suggested that Kraus's ideal was 'a language purified of the curse of *mauscheln*'.[28] In fact, his admiration for Eisenbach inspired him to transform *mauscheln* into an artistic medium. 'In art everything depends on *who* is using Jewish jargon,' he wrote in the context of his tribute to the Budapesters (F 343–4, 21). Shortly after praising the Budapesters, he published a satirical dialogue in which snippets of German-Jewish jargon are combined with a collage of pompous pronouncements from the liberal press (F 326–8, 1–18). It was at this stage in the evolution of his style that he famously defined his own work as 'theatrical performance in writing' (F 336–7, 41). The evidence suggests that he had the Budapesters in mind, although their influence, unlike that of the Burgtheater, was not openly acknowledged.[29] There is a clear connection between his praise of the Budapesters and his decision to start writing and reciting dialogues in German-Jewish jargon, notably the two long scenes set in newspaper offices, composed towards the end of 1912. Introducing the first of these readings, Kraus suggests that this mode of dramatic satire makes journalists speak the dialect of 'their soul' (F 360–2, 53–5), juxtaposing pompous editorials against the slang spoken by their authors. In these early satires, the dialogue is still printed as continuous prose, but the typographic conventions of drama were introduced two years later when he began to sketch similar scenes for *Die letzten Tage der Menschheit*, notably the dialogue of the Jewish social climbers Hofrat Schwarz-Gelber and his wife (F 423–5, 1–11).

If Eisenbach's jargon forms one end of the stylistic spectrum, Sonnenthal's 'tearful curse' provides the other. This is evident from the very first speech by the Grumbler in *Die letzten Tage der Menschheit*, when the jargon-flavoured dialogue of social climbers attending the funeral of Archduke Franz Ferdinand is interrupted by blank verse invoking the 'tears of God' ('Gottes Thräne'). This same blend of grief and imprecation characterizes the long monologue at the end of Act V. The medium may now be prose, but the cadences of the Burgtheater can still be detected as the Grumbler denounces a system which has brought death and destruction. These two monologues frame a multiplicity of soulless dialects, from Prussian arrogance to Austrian whimsy, and the use of Jewish jargon reaches a climax in the coffee-house of Act V, scene 25, where profiteers have animal names like Wolf and Hamster. However, where Kafka's speaking animals have endearingly human traits, Kraus's become ferocious caricatures, culminating in the Dance of the Hyenas.[30]

Kraus's debt to Jewish actors invites comparison with the 'Jargontheater' episode recorded in Kafka's diaries: the encounter in 1911 with the Yiddish theatre group of Jizchak Löwy in Prague. This marked a turning-point in Kafka's career, leading him to redefine both his attitude to eastern Jewry and his approach to writing. There is a gain in physical immediacy and scenic enactment, resulting in a synthesis of two literary forms: the German *Novelle* and the Yiddish family drama.[31] The plays performed by Löwy's troupe on an improvised stage in the Café Savoy, including Jakob Gordin's *Got, mensh un tayvl*, were little more than melodramas, but it is clear that they 'touched some deep emotional response in Kafka that dimmed his critical faculties'.[32] When Kraus and Kafka use the word 'Jargontheater', they are referring to two distinct phenomena: Löwy's troupe performed in Yiddish, Eisenbach's in mongrel German (there is no evidence that Kraus attended the Yiddish theatre that also flourished in the Leopoldstadt).[33] Kafka made a determined effort to understand the language, although his knowledge was not advanced enough for an appreciation of nuances. He was fascinated by a style of acting that relied on gesture, just as Kraus was impressed by the physical immediacy of Jewish popular theatre. Moreover, they both responded to a self-mocking irony tinged with sadness that has been described as 'peculiarly Jewish'. In the eyes of the purists, such third-rate performances were merely *shund* (trash).[34] But Kraus gained from Eisenbach, Kafka from Löwy, a heightened awareness of the incongruities of Jewish identity in a society that simultaneously demanded and frustrated assimilation.

The influence of the Budapesters is most pronounced in Kraus's 'magical operetta' *Literatur oder Man wird doch da sehn* ('Literature or You ain't seen nothin yet'; 1921). The debt is signalled by his subtitle: the phrase 'Man wird doch da sehn' derives from the jargon theatre (F 324–5, 23), while the musical scores that accompany four of the songs are also reminiscent of the Budapesters. The figure of the perplexed Jewish father, so compellingly performed by Eisenbach, now reappears in a literary milieu, speaking a homely idiom far removed from the exalted discourse of the Son. The play combines two forms which appear to be incongruous: satire on the pretensions of coffee-house intellectuals and Jewish family drama. The resulting juxtapositions between poetic pastiche, intellectual cant and Yiddish-flavoured idioms are rich in intertextual nuances.[35] Kraus, who repeatedly recited the play in public, did not intend the jargon to be a source of cheap humour, pointing out that the characters who speak it belong to a more honourable older generation who make no secret of their commercial motives. When the Distant Relative,

who sits phlegmatically playing cards, scornfully addresses one of the verbose
littérateurs as 'Asis Ponem' ('ugly gob'), his use of the colourful Yiddish
epithet forms a positive contrast to the affected language of the younger
generation. The comedy is generated by the gulf between the two incompatible forms of existence, expressed though a complex 'verbal configuration'
('Wortgestalt'; F 572–6, 73). Max Brod was to denounce this use of jargon as
a malicious caricature.[36] But this ignores the dilemma of aspiring intellectuals
struggling to detach themselves from the commercial values of their parents.

Brod might have recalled a letter received from Kafka, which analyses
Literatur in detail. Far from dismissing the play as a caricature, Kafka recognizes
that Kraus represents a 'principle'. It is his 'delicate feeling for language' that
enables him to get to the heart of the matter:

> The wit lies primarily in the *mauscheln*, and there is no one who can *mauscheln* like
> Kraus, even though in this German-Jewish world hardly anyone can do anything
> else but *mauscheln*, taking the concept in its widest sense, as indeed it inevitably must
> be taken, that is as the noisy or silent or indeed self-tormenting usurpation of an alien
> possession. [. . .]

Through its representation of the conflict between fathers and sons, Kafka
continues, *Literatur* expresses the dilemma of Jewish intellectuals who seek
salvation through self-identification with German, a language that is 'alien' to
them:

> What pleases me in this case more than psychoanalysis is the recognition that the
> father complex, from which many people draw spiritual sustenance, relates not to
> the innocent father but to the Jewishness of the father. To get away from Jewishness,
> usually with the vague assent of their fathers (this vagueness was what was so infuri-
> ating) – that is what most people who started writing in German really wanted, they
> wanted it, but with their hind legs they were still clinging to their father's Jewish-
> ness and with their front legs they had not found any new ground. Despair about
> this situation was their inspiration.[37]

Kafka's use of animal imagery adds poignancy to his reading of the father–son
conflict. In this same letter, he defines 'mauscheln' as 'an organic combination
of paper German and the language of gesture', illustrating this by citing specific
examples from *Literatur*: 'how plastic is the phrase: "Which way he's got
talent?" or accompanied by a lurching upper-arm and jutting chin: "That's
what *you* think!"' His response to Kraus's dialogue enables him to supply his
own imaginary stage directions, guided by a shared sense of the physicality of
Jewish speech. The awareness of body language which Kraus and Kafka
derived from the Jewish theatre leaves a marked imprint on their creativity.
'Everyone is talking at once, gesticulating wildly,' we read in the opening stage
direction of *Literatur*.[38]

The gestures in Kafka's stories accentuate discrepancies between speech and
body language, and when the reader seeks connections, the text turns away
with a mysterious gesture, like the policeman in the story 'Give It Up' ('Gib's

auf'). Kafka takes this discrepancy between physical presence and speech act to the ultimate extreme in stories that transform humans into animals, leaving their powers of communication unimpaired. This motif is intensified in his story 'Josefine die Sängerin oder das Volk der Mäuse', where a mouse holds her audience entranced through recitals that consist merely of shrill whistling. This story was interpreted – in a book by André [Andor] Németh – as an 'allegorical representation of the interactions between Kraus and his predominantly Jewish public', while another critic has linked the mouse's unmusical whistling with Kraus's enactment of 'mauscheln', the language of Jews caught between emancipation and Zionism.[39]

Kafka was a compulsive reader of Die Fackel during his final years, thanking his friend Robert Klopstock for sending him copies of the magazine, which he defined as 'the sweet nourishment of all good and bad impulses'. In November 1923 he also thanked him for 'the Kraus book', probably Wolkenkuckucksheim.[40] Given his interest in speaking animals, it is not surprising that he found Kraus's battle of the birds 'entertaining'. Writing from Berlin in February 1924, he reports spending the whole evening reading Die Fackel, experiencing the familiar 'enervating orgies'. Kraus was giving a series of recitals in Berlin, including Literatur with its persiflage on 'mauscheln' and its mocking songs. One of the recitals was attended by Kafka's partner Dora Diamant and his uncle Siegfried Löwy. They were 'delighted', he reports, although 'probably differently delighted from me'.[41] Discussions after the recital must have stimulated Kafka to further orgies of reflection about the problematic relationship between artist and audience. It was at the end of March, after his return to Prague, that he wrote 'Josefine die Sängerin' – with its echoes of the satirist's idiosyncratic performances. On 28 April 1924 Kraus, who was at the height of his fame, celebrated his fiftieth birthday, and the publication of Kafka's story in the Prager Presse on 20 April can be seen as an ambivalent birthday tribute.

Berlin Theatrical Affairs

A critic hostile to visual razzmatazz was unlikely to be attracted by the avant-garde theatre of Berlin, the scene during the 1920s of radical experiments: the symbolic dramas of Expressionism, the constructivist stage designs of Jessner, Fehling and Martin, and the political theatre of Piscator and Brecht. But Kraus longed to extend his influence to Germany, and in 1909 he had attempted to establish an office of Die Fackel in Berlin with the help of Herwarth Walden, who organized Kraus's first public readings in January 1910 and supported him in the columns of Der Sturm. After two tempestuous years Kraus had to acknowledge that his German readership was too small to justify the additional distribution costs, and in January 1912 the Berlin office was closed.[42] But in May 1918 he formed a new alliance with Siegfried Jacobsohn, editor of Die Schaubühne (now renamed Die Weltbühne). It was Jacobsohn who obtained clearance from the censors, enabling Kraus to read outspoken texts like the attack on Kaiser Wilhelm II in 'Ein Kantianer und Kant', as well as plays by Shakespeare, Nestroy and Hauptmann. The political tensions of the post-war period led Jacobsohn to warn him that antisemitism in Berlin had become 'so insane' that he should not include in his recitals any examples of Jewish-accented German ('Mauschelton').[43] Kraus responded, in the reading which took place on 20 January 1920, by concentrating on scenes from *Die letzten Tage der Menschheit* which satirized right-wing nationalists. His reading was particularly praised by Kurt Tucholsky in the *Berliner Tageblatt* for the telling use of north German dialect (F 531–43, 23–5). In the post-war period Kraus regularly received *Die Weltbühne*, which announced his public readings and praised his work, and it was through Jacobsohn that he was introduced to Sigismund von Radecki, an author who had spent several years as a Russian prisoner of war.[44] Kraus (as we have seen) commended Tucholsky's articles as a 'courageous anti-war achievement', remaining neutral during the protracted dispute between Jacobsohn and another left-wing journalist, Wilhelm Herzog. However, in May 1925 he finally lost patience, announcing that he no longer wished to be sent copies of the magazine, since he was unable to reconcile his admiration for Jacobsohn's 'literary achievement' with the deviousness of the polemic against Herzog (F 686–90, 54–69). For Kraus, as he indicated in a brief obituary tribute, the sphere in which Jacobsohn excelled was theatre criticism (F 743–50, 69).

Disillusioned by the provinciality of the Austrian stage, especially the 'Christian-Germanic' agenda of Herterich at the Burgtheater, Kraus felt drawn to the bright lights of the Kurfürstendamm, keeping an eye on 'all Berlin theatrical affairs' (F 806–9, 64). His first incursion into the Berlin theatre occurred in 1922, when he supported the founding of 'Die Truppe' by Berthold Viertel. Born in 1885, Viertel had begun to read *Die Fackel* as a fourteen-year-old, sending in a letter which was published over the initials *B-d. V.* (F 15, 31). It was the theatre that brought them together, since they met in May 1905 on the occasion of Kraus's production of *Die Büchse der Pandora*.[45] By 1910 Viertel had become a regular contributor to *Die Fackel*, and their friendship was to last thirty years. He served as a lieutenant on the eastern front, publishing patriotic poetry which earned him a rebuke in *Die Fackel*, but by May 1916 he had come to recognize the futility of the war, acknowledging that Kraus had been right all along (F 423–5, 22–3). In 1917 he published a series of articles about the satirist in *Die Schaubühne*, later reprinted in book form. After the war, his passion for the theatre led him to enlist Kraus's help in setting up his own theatre company. The launching of 'Die Truppe' in 1923 was facilitated by the substantial loan which Kraus advanced to Viertel and his co-director Ernst Josef Aufricht, with Kraus's friend the art historian Ludwig Münz providing a further guarantee (P 2, 84–5). Although the company survived for only two years, it provided a springboard for talented actors like Fritz Kortner, Rudolf Forster, Sybille Binder and Heinz Hilpert. Its literary adviser was Heinrich Fischer, introduced by Viertel to Kraus.[46]

'Die Truppe' stressed the importance of ensemble playing, as opposed to the cult of stardom that was being promoted by the cinema. This theatre with its 'roots in the ensemble' was to stage 'works of genius by world dramatists'.[47] This ambition is reflected in an exacting repertoire, inaugurated in September 1923 by Shakespeare's *Merchant of Venice*, with Kortner as Shylock.[48] The aim, as Kraus put it in January 1924, was to reaffirm the traditions of the old Burgtheater 'in wildest Berlin' (F 640–8, 56). In March 1924, to mark Kraus's fiftieth birthday, Viertel staged *Traumstück* and *Traumtheater* at the Lustspielhaus in Berlin, and the following month the production transferred to Vienna. There was a total of fourteen performances, seven in each city (F 649–56, 70). Kraus, who participated in the rehearsals, expressed his gratitude in an extended tribute to Viertel. He also thanked Ludwig Münz for his support, reiterated his admiration for Oskar Homolka, and praised Fischer as the 'faithful custodian of verbal treasures' (F 649–56, 5–9). The sceptical response of reviewers to Viertel's productions led to a heated exchange between Kraus and Herbert Ihering, theatre critic of the *Berliner Börsen-Courier* (F 657–67, 145–63). Viertel's project proved too utopian to survive cut-throat competition, although it had an exemplary value.[49]

The programme of 'Die Truppe' had initially been welcomed by Jacobsohn in *Die Weltbühne*. In an article of 15 March 1923 on the bankruptcy of the established Berlin theatres, he had praised Viertel's artistic temperament and literary judgement; but during the following winter he was scathing about the shortcomings of 'Die Truppe'. In a series of private letters, Kraus tried to persuade him to take a more positive line. A long reply from Jacobsohn dated 12 February 1924 makes it clear that he has lost faith in Viertel's work, preferring the experimental productions of Ludwig Jessner, particularly his staging of Shakespeare's *Othello* and Grabbe's *Napoleon*.[50] The resulting differences of opinion contributed to the rupture with Jacobsohn in May 1925 (F 686–90, 54–69). This episode prompted Kraus to take a more sceptical view of Tucholsky, later to be characterized as the 'prototype of the left-wing radical journalist with certain pugnacious merits' (F 827–33, 75). During the spring of 1924 he spent two whole months in Berlin, giving a series of recitals under the auspices of 'Die Truppe', but he found the atmosphere uncongenial, speaking of the 'nervous torture of this Berlin exile' (F 649–56, 4). After 'Die Truppe' was forced to close, he temporarily lost interest in the German scene, although he gave a further series of readings in Berlin in March 1925. This was followed by a three-year interval during which Kraus was so absorbed in the controversies with Bekessy and Schober that he found no time to give any readings in the German capital. But then his attention switched back to Germany, and by 1928 there were rumours that he was planning to settle in Berlin. He now engaged in a series of further controversies, questioning the innovations of avant-garde directors like Erwin Piscator and challenging the authority of the leading theatre critic, Alfred Kerr of the *Berliner Tageblatt* – a rivalry that provoked an amusing cartoon in *Simplicissimus* (Fig. 39a).

Launching his polemic against Kerr from a public platform in Berlin, Kraus claimed to be able to 'throw the scoundrel out of any city' (F 781–6, 10). The aim was to expose Kerr's lack of integrity by contrasting his pacifist stance with the chauvinistic poems he had written under various pseudonyms during the war, and the ensuing exchanges consumed reams of paper, as the two traduced each other in print and in court (F 787–94, 1–208). Kraus pinned down the inconsistencies in Kerr's attitude towards militarism – sword in one hand, olive branch in the other, as in the cartoon by Koffler (Fig. 39b). But he was less successful in his critique of his role of the theatre critic. On hearsay evidence he suggested that, when Kerr was hired by the *Berliner Tageblatt*, he was compelled to abandon his hostile attitude towards Reinhardt, a close friend of the proprietor, Theodor Wolff (F 781–6, 204). When this rumour was repudiated, Kraus sued Wolff for defamation in an attempt to substantiate the charge (F 795–9, 81). Research has confirmed that there was indeed an 'extreme change of attitude towards Reinhardt' in Kerr's later criticism.[51] But it was not possible to prove that he had succumbed to improper influence, and Kraus's case was dismissed (P 2, 155–210).

These polemics show how keen Kraus was to consolidate his reputation in Berlin. He wished to establish himself as a 'German writer' (F 781–6, 9), while avoiding the over-identification with Germany that was so characteristic of the German-Jewish elite. Despite his preoccupation with Austrian affairs, Kraus looked increasingly towards Berlin for intellectual stimuli, and in the years 1928–32 he gave more recitals in Germany than in Austria.[52] There was an extraordinary theatrical flowering in the Berlin of the 1930s, which formed for the impressionable young Marcel Reich-Ranicki a counterweight to the Nazi

39   Cartoons of Alfred Kerr: (a) with Kraus as a caryatid supporting Piscator's theatre, by Th. Th. Heine (b) as a militarist belatedly converted to pacifism, by Osio Koffler

threat.[53] Kraus, too, experienced not only 'dilettantism' and 'humbug', but also 'authentic impressions of the theatre', singling out several actresses for special praise, including Friedel Schuster in Reinhardt's production of Offenbach's *La Belle Hélène*, and Käthe Haack and Blandine Ebinger in Zuckmayer's *Der Hauptmann von Köpennick* (F 864–7, 25). For a brief period he enjoyed Berlin social life, gathering around him a circle that included not only Viertel and Fischer, but also Peter Lorre, Friedrich Kortner, Sigismund von Radecki and Elias Canetti. 'After every public reading about eight or ten of us used to go to a little café,' Fischer recalls, 'and there he would talk enchantingly, evidently very relieved that he could postpone his night's writing for a few hours.'[54] Berlin was no longer a place of exile, and after giving eight public readings in spring 1928 Kraus felt invigorated like 'Antaeus on foreign soil' (F 781–6, 82). He was, however, increasingly aware of the polarization of German politics, and this strengthened his hostility towards Jessner and Piscator, that 'mafia of literary swindlers and manipulators of the theatre market'. They failed to recognize that their desecration of the classics was likely to provoke a violent – and indeed well-deserved – reaction 'in the realm of the swastika'. Jessner staged *Hamlet* on a series of intersecting staircases, transforming King Claudius into a caricature of the Kaiser. So disgusted was Kraus by this affair that he felt impelled to defend both Shakespeare and Wilhelm II against this 'Expressionist directing swindle' (F 751–6, 26–8). This did not prevent him from attending further Jessner productions, including Hauptmann's *Die Weber* and Sophocles' *Oedipus der Herrscher*.[55] His interest in Shakespeare prompted him to see Elisabeth Bergner in *Twelfth Night* at the Lessingtheater, as well as Jürgen Fehling's *Much Ado About Nothing* at the Staatstheater, but he was clearly out of sympathy with these productions (F 668–75, 88–93).

Even more significant was his confrontation with Piscator, a communist who created a scandal in 1926 by transforming *Die Räuber* into a plea for revolutionary action. Kraus, who attended the première at the Deutsches Staatstheater, was incensed to see Schiller's subtle reflections on the legitimacy of revolutionary action reduced to a barrage of political slogans. Piscator had tendentiously rewritten Schiller's play, transforming Spiegelberg, the most radical of the robbers, into the figure of Trotsky. In an extended polemic entitled 'Mein Vorurteil gegen Piscator' ('My Prejudice against Piscator'), Kraus denounced this project, expressing satisfaction when the director was dismissed after a row about his politicization of another play, Ehm Welk's *Storm over Gottland*, described by Kraus as 'topical kitsch with a communist "perspective"' (F 759–65, 54). The poem 'Berlin Theater', written as a reaction to the travesty of *Die Räuber*, suggests that the satirist can't wait to get away from Berlin (F 743–50, 88–9). After this outburst, it seemed unlikely that he would attend another production by Piscator, but his passion for the theatre was stronger than his hostility to modernism, and he saw at least two further controversial productions. The most radical was Piscator's staging of Ernst Toller's *Hoppla, wir leben!*, which used film projections to explore the politics of Weimar

Germany in a style that Kraus found too crass to be convincing (F 781–6, 25). The theme of war resurfaced in Piscator's version of *Die Rivalen*, based on a play by Maxwell Anderson. Here the stage gimmickry included the use of a conveyor belt to show German soldiers marching resolutely off to the front. The result was the reverse of what Piscator intended, since it was interpreted as a 'glorification of war'.[56] Kraus was appalled by both the crudity of the play and the jingoistic reactions of the audience (F 847–51, 75).

Whatever his objections to Piscator's style, Kraus could hardly fail to notice that *Hoppla, wir leben!* was inspired by the principle of 'documentary dramatization' which he himself had pioneered (F 781–6, 23). The debt was even more obvious when Piscator staged a play about the First World War, *Rasputin*, based on a text by Alexei Tolstoy and incorporating a wealth of documentary material. One reviewer reported that the scenes featuring the Emperor Franz Joseph and the German Kaiser had actually been lifted from Kraus (P 2, 83). There can be no doubt that Piscator was indebted to *Die letzten Tage der Menschheit* – he would have welcomed the opportunity to stage the play, if Kraus had not resisted his approaches (F 759–65, 68). Kraus recognized that the bourgeois theatre could convert the most radical drama into an entertainment for affluent consumers, and his most penetrating comments relate to Piscator's audience, which enjoyed the spectacle while remaining impervious to the message (F 781–6, 25). But to see the Kraus–Piscator relationship only in confrontational terms ignores the continuities, which were clearly recognized in autumn 1928 by Heinrich Fischer, now working at the Theater am Schiffbauerdamm under the direction of Aufricht. In an article in *Das Stichwort*, the house magazine, he emphasized the ability of both Kraus and Piscator 'to seize the present moment in documentary form'. But Kraus's superior sensitivity to language, he continued, enabled him to transform documents into symbolic figures of the age. Fischer singled out *Die Unüberwindlichen* ('The Invincibles') for special praise, announcing that it would shortly be staged at the Theater am Schiffbauerdamm.[57]

The Scene as a Tribunal

In February 1925, as a prelude to his campaign against Bekessy, Kraus recited 'Die Kraniche des Ibykus' ('The Cranes of Ibykus'), Schiller's ballad about guilt and retribution, which reaches its climax in the line 'Die Szene wird zum Tribunal' (F 679–85, 50). He had originally hoped to obtain the verdict of a real tribunal, and after Bekessy had fled abroad he envisaged a parliamentary inquiry into the disgraced editor's political dealings (F 732–4, 47–8). It was the failure to get Bekessy, Castiglioni and Schober into court which led him to write *Die Unüberwindlichen*, the political drama that deploys a documentary technique against three of the most powerful figures of the post-war world, thinly disguised as Barkassy the newspaper tycoon, Wacker the Police Chief, and Camillioni the international financier.[58] Although temporarily disgraced, Bekessy was a wealthy man who was about to return to Hungary to re-establish his newspaper business, while Castiglioni controlled an industrial empire in Germany and Schober enjoyed considerable international prestige. The play abounds in references to other figures from the political establishment, including Ignaz Seipel and several of his ministers. Kollmann, notorious for his heavy drinking, becomes Vollmann, while Ahrer, the Finance Minister who absconded to Cuba, is referred to as Drahrer. The financier Bosel figures as Lobes and the journalist Salten as Salzmann, while Kraus himself lurks behind the anagram Arkus and his lawyer Samek becomes Maske. The blackmailer Sandor Weiss is referred to by his own name, and only in the case of Schober's assistant, Bernhard Pollak, does Kraus opt for a symbolic name, Veilchen.

Die Unüberwindlichen has features of the well-made play, with recognizable social settings, but the plot is less significant than the power of individual scenes. There is a tendency towards static tableaux with a stark visual impact and characters incapable of real development, since they are transfixed by their own words. In the first act we are taken inside the office of Barkassy the newspaper magnate, before his expulsion from Vienna. He is portrayed as a nervous character whose immense power conceals an inner insecurity – an Austrian (or rather Hungarian) Citizen Kane. His position is threatened by the disclosure of his past misdeeds, but he has good contacts with Wacker at Police Headquarters, which forms the setting in Act II. Here the stage is divided into two sections which are alternately illuminated in a style reminiscent of Piscator. First we see Wacker receiving Arkus and promising to pursue the investigation against the notorious blackmailer Barkassy; then the spotlight switches to the adjacent office, where Barkassy is trying to win over Veilchen by a mixture of threats and compliments. The alternating focus exposes the double dealing of the police, and it appears that Barkassy's manoeuvres will be successful when Vollmann intervenes by telephone on his behalf. In Act III the scene shifts to Paris, where the millionaire Camillioni is relaxing in his boudoir. His temporary absence from Vienna, where he is revered by journalists like Salzmann as a patron of the arts, is due to the fear that he might be subpoenaed. He cannot evade his compromising connections, especially with Barkassy, who knows too much about the origins of his financial empire. His calm is disrupted by the arrival of Barkassy, who confesses that the threat of arrest has caused him to lose his nerve and flee from Vienna. The dialogue reveals the contempt the two men feel for Austria, which they see as a republic riddled with debt and corruption. During the ensuing struggle of wills Barkassy reasserts himself, using the threat of disclosures about Camillioni's younger days to extract from him 300,000 francs.

In the final act, set five months after the massacre of 15 July, we are back at Police Headquarters, where the genial Wacker is presiding over a Christmas party, surrounded by his henchmen. There follows a series of confrontations in which the stage is transformed into a tribunal and Wacker's subordinates begin to recite documentary statements about the massacre, as if they were witnesses compelled to tell the truth under oath. The cold-blooded shooting of children and innocent passers-by is recalled with chilling precision, as Wacker vainly tries to restore the festive spirit (Fig. 40). The editor of a Nazi newspaper intervenes to denounce 'the Jew' who is threatening Christian-German civilization by means of a mixture of abortion and jazz. Wacker, whose pretence of jovial impartiality sits uneasily with his defence of German 'Volkstum', announces that he is dismissing his deputy Veilchen, whose Jewish descent has become an impediment. The crudest form of antisemitic abuse is directed against Arkus himself, while a thuggish policeman named Ramatamer gloats about the 'young Hebrew' he has shot and other Jews put through the 'flogging machine' at the police station. Finally, Barkassy himself returns to reassert his power, and the band strikes up 'Silent Night, Holy Night' as the curtain falls on Christmas at Police Headquarters.

This is the most political of Kraus's post-war plays, showing exceptional prescience. He ignores the failings of the Social Democrats, recognizing that they have become a marginal force in Austrian politics, attacking instead the pillars of bourgeois capitalism: the press baron, the police chief and the financier. The satire on antisemitism suggests that the combination of 'Christian' and 'German' ideologies is a recipe for a Nazi take-over, while the Jewish milieu, so prominent in Kraus's earlier plays, is relegated to the background. The most distinctive feature of Barkassy's dialogue is not Jewish jargon, but snippets of Hungarian, while Camillioni speaks as an educated man of the world and Veilchen has a fondness for Latin tags. The target is conservative

40   The Policemen's Christmas party: scene from Act IV of *Die Unüberwindlichen*, photographed by Lotte Jacobi

Austria with its 'fascism mitigated by muddle', a prophetic phrase put in the mouth of Camillioni, who is funding the Heimwehr. The claim that the Jews are 'undermining' German values is propounded by the sanctimonious Wacker and his sinister Nazi supporters, while the focus on Christmas develops into an outspoken attack on the politicization of religion. The setting of the final act has a documentary basis, for the genial Schober really had presided over a Christmas party for policemen's families five months after the massacre (F 781–6, 127–8). Clipping a newspaper report about this event, Kraus transforms it into a compelling symbol through a stage set dominated by a Christmas tree and a machine gun, the one surrounded by colourful gifts, the other limbered up for action. This vivid scene anticipates the authoritarian state that was to turn its guns on the workers five years later.

Die Unüberwindlichen was designed for performance, as can be seen from the detailed stage directions. It has been claimed that the construction of this play is 'dilettantish' and Kraus's handling of plot and character 'weak'.[59] This ignores his ability to transform documents into vivid scenes and powerful characters, especially in the case of Barkassy, the newspaperman whose lust for power is undermined by a neurotic disposition. The play, which appealed to some of the most gifted actors of the day, was premièred in Dresden in May 1929, but this production was incomplete, since Castiglioni obtained an injunction preventing the performance of Act III, which he regarded as defamatory. The complete play was performed at the Volksbühne in Berlin on 20 October 1929, a Sunday matinée notable for the wealth of acting talent: Peter Lorre as Barkassy, Kurt Gerron as Camillioni, and Ernst Ginsberg as Arkus. Even more compelling, according to Walter Benjamin, was Hans Peppler as the jovial Police Chief who is capable of the greatest infamy.[60] The success of this production, which attracted an audience of 2,000, is attested by dozens of reviews. Berlin, too, had an embattled Chief of Police, a Social Democrat named Karl Zörgiebel, who had ordered his men to fire on May Day demonstrators earlier that same year, and the German courts had just exposed the activities of the Sklareks, corrupt Jewish businessmen in cahoots with City Hall.[61] Thus there were obvious parallels with the political situation in Berlin, and Kraus was praised by a communist critic for using the 'stage as a battleground' and 'words as weapons' (F 827–33, 17). Even Ihering, who had earlier dismissed his work as parochial, acknowledged that the play had caught the mood of the moment, predicting that it would rate a hundred performances if transferred to the repertoire, since Germany lacked topical plays with this 'penetration, courage and precision' (cited F 827–33, 32). However, the Volksbühne decided against any further performances, succumbing to political pressure. Schober had just been reappointed as Austrian chancellor, and the cancellation was due to interventions from Berlin Police Headquarters and the Austrian embassy (F 827–33, 31–4). Moreover, the Social Democrats, who controlled the Volksbühne, were perturbed to see the play interpreted as an attack on *their* man, Zörgiebel, and Kraus accused them of 'strangling' a successful play (F 868–72, 13).

Three months later, on 15 January 1930, *Die letzte Nacht* was staged at the Theater am Schiffbauerdamm with almost equal success, directed by Heinrich Fischer with music by Hanns Eisler. Kraus seemed poised to make a major contribution to political theatre, since *Die Unüberwindlichen* was accepted by the Frankfurt Schauspielhaus for the 1929–30 season. In the event, the play proved too topical for its own good, exposing the machinations of the ruling class at the moment when the capitalist system experienced its greatest crisis. On Thursday 24 October, four days after the Berlin première, the Wall Street Crash occurred, plunging Germany into deep recession. Theatres and concert halls were soon recording a crippling fall in receipts, and on 2 June 1930 the Schauspielhaus wrote to Samek to explain that the Frankfurt première would have to be postponed. Kraus reluctantly agreed that it should be held over until the following season, but on 17 October 1930 the Nazis, hitherto a negligible force in Weimar politics, gained a stunning victory in the general election, winning over six million votes. The director of the Schauspielhaus might defy the Austrian embassy, but he could not ignore the destabilization of German democracy. *Die Unüberwindlichen*, the overnight sensation of autumn 1929, had by January 1931 become an embarrassment 'as a result of the altered economic and political situation' (P 2, 264). Kraus himself was affected by the economic downturn, which drastically reduced his earnings, after an exceptionally successful year in 1929.[62] But he persisted in his efforts to have the play staged, and the correspondence between his lawyer and the theatre management fills seventy pages. The Schauspielhaus evaded its contractual responsibilities by arranging a one-night guest performance by the Leipzig Komödienhaus on 10 February 1932. This provoked a hostile reaction from the audience, some of whom walked out during the final act in protest against the attack on Christian values. The satire on Schober was particularly resented, since proposals for a customs union between Germany and Austria had transformed him into a national hero. Given the polarization between left and right in the crumbling Weimar Republic, Kraus's anti-establishment satire was beginning to look like bolshevik subversion.[63] Thus *Die Unüberwindlichen* was overtaken by the tendencies it satirized, and Kraus was obliged to withdraw from the theatre and concentrate on his one-man shows.

CHAPTER 19

Dramatic Poetry from Shakespeare to Brecht

K---- ---d Shakespeare through Goethe's eyes, emphasizing poetry rather than
I   inest dramatic verse eluded physical enact-
r   he most subtle forms of drama appealed to
t   tion was less significant than 'spiritual utter-
a   the Burgtheater in January 1901 (F 65, 27),
l   ; principle for his own Shakespeare recitals,
i   *Athens*. His primary objective was to create
a   iration' (F 426–30, 47), counteracting the
l   f visual spectacle; but it would be wrong
to see these recitals as an --------vely literary affair, since he also sought a
dramaturgy commensurate with world events.

Visual Spectacle and Theatre of Poetry

In a polemic extending over thirty years, Kraus challenged the productions of
Max Reinhardt, the most celebrated impresario of the age. Their acquaintance
dates back to a student production of Schiller's tragedy *Die Räuber* ('The
Robbers') in January 1893, when Reinhardt played Spiegelberg, while Kraus's
failure in the role of Franz Moor put an end to his acting ambitions. Recognizing Reinhardt's acting gifts, Kraus helped to launch him on a theatrical
career by commending him to the Berlin director Otto Brahm. After gaining
experience in a variety of roles, Reinhardt made his name as a director at the
Kleines Theater, and Kraus followed his early career with interest. In 1903,
when Reinhardt captured the headlines with an innovative production of
Gorky's *Lower Depths*, he praised the depiction of the low-life milieu, while
expressing reservations about the acting (F 138, 14–17). But from 1905
onwards Kraus's comments became increasingly sceptical, as Reinhardt staged
the dramatic spectacles which made him famous, and the sniping intensified as
the press coverage transformed the director into an international celebrity.

There have been a number of attempts to explain this antagonism between two men who had so much in common, not least their passion for Shakespeare. Reinhardt claimed that Kraus was motivated by a personal grudge resulting from the humiliation he had suffered during that student production of 1893.[2] This ignores the fundamental opposition between the satirist's passion for words and the director's love of images. Kraus's conception of the theatre was aural and verbal, while Reinhardt's was visual and gestural. As a director, he 'was concerned with realizing the word – spoken or written – as image. The use of non-verbal means of artistic expression enabled him to materialize human feelings and experiences that cannot be expressed by words or by words alone'.[3] Kraus invokes this same dualism in an extended reminiscence in 1936, relating Reinhardt's career to the divergent traditions of the Burgtheater – Laube's 'passion for the word' and Dingelstedt's obsession with 'stage design'. Reinhardt is seen as a descendant of Dingelstedt, poised to conquer Hollywood through his command of the decorative principle. He may devote endless time to rehearsals with the aim of making his actors word perfect, but he fails to do justice to what Kraus values most – the 'verbal configuration' (F 912–15, 40 & 51–2). Admittedly Reinhardt, too, had learnt his trade at the Burgtheater, picking up the echoes of a great acting style from his seat in the fourth gallery (F 138, 15; 305–6, 52). But Reinhardt recalled that the acoustics of the Burgtheater made it so difficult for him to follow the dialogue that he had to rely on his imagination.[4] What he found most unforgettable about the acting of Sonnenthal was a visual gesture: 'How he drank chocolate on stage'.[5] By contrast, Kraus's sensitive ear enabled him to hear every word, and he had no patience with those who complained about the acoustics (F 546–50, 37–9).

While Kraus's aesthetic predestined him for broadcasting, Reinhardt inclined towards cinema. His most celebrated project was *A Midsummer Night's Dream*, staged before the First World War with real trees on a revolving stage (Fig. 41). The Berlin première in February 1905 caused a sensation, even though (as Kraus noted from the reviews) the dialogue was scarcely audible (F 175, 20). When *A Midsummer Night's Dream* transferred to the Theater an der Wien, Kraus recalls, he was disconcerted to see real grass being delivered to the stage door (F 912–15, 53). The 'symbolic completeness' of Reinhardt's stage design has been praised by theatre historians.[6] The most that Kraus was willing to concede was that the forest performed 'better than the rest of the cast' (F 601–7, 9). The satirist failed to acknowledge the achievements of a versatile genius who has been described as 'the most progressive force in German theatre' in the early twentieth century, but he anticipated the judgement that Reinhardt's main concern was with the 'challenge of scenic realizations in new venues and environments'.[7] This one-sided polemic, intensified during the 1920s by Kraus's attacks on the Salzburg Festival and his mockery of Reinhardt's relaunching of the Theater in der Josefstadt, reached its climax with the filming of *A Midsummer Night's Dream* by Warner Brothers under Reinhardt's direction, with Mickey Rooney as Puck. Kraus gleefully quoted

41 'The forest performed better than the rest of the cast': stage set for Reinhardt's 1905 production of *A Midsummer Night's Dream*

reviews suggesting that the film reduced Shakespeare to a blend of 'Babes in the Wood' and the 'Crazy Gang' (F 917–22, 13).

Through his emphasis on the spoken word, Kraus distanced himself from both visual spectacle and constructivist experiment, developing his own Theatre of Poetry ('Theater der Dichtung'; F 712–16, 43). His solo recitals affirmed the value of continuity, as memories of the productions of his youth became fused with the programme of his next public reading. Like every performer, he had to prepare his recitals, shortening dramatic works in order to intensify their impact, although he rejected the suggestion that his readings were 'rehearsed' (F 706–11, 94). A polemical tone was introduced by references to recent productions through which some great work had allegedly been desecrated, presenting the reading as a 'rehabilitation' (F 885–7, 17). The framework was defined by the carefully researched programme notes, to which he attached such importance that excerpts were regularly reprinted in *Die Fackel*. They included quotations designed to assist the audience's understanding, such as Goethe's comments on *Faust*. These notes were replete with reminiscences, including cast lists of earlier productions, transforming the printed sheet into a mnemonic space. A characteristic example lists the cast of the 1889 Burgtheater production of *The Winter's Tale*, with Charlotte Wolter as Hermione. The facing page of *Die Fackel* emphasizes the continuities by recording the cast list of Kraus's 1930 Berlin Radio production of *La Grande Duchesse de Gerolstein*, with Cäcilie Lvovsky as Wanda (F 838–43, 127–9).

Book in hand, Kraus promoted a reverence for literary masterpieces reminiscent of the Burgtheater of his youth. Although his audience clamoured for his own writings, he schooled them to appreciate a broader stylistic spectrum ranging from Shakespeare's darkest tragedies through the satirical comedies of Nestroy to the songs of Brecht. He had a special flair for bringing the imaginative drama to life through an economical use of gesture.[8] While attuning his listeners to the poetic qualities of classical theatre, he accentuated the dramatic qualities of German poetry, notably the ballads of Bürger, Liliencron and Wedekind. He also revived neglected poets of the eighteenth century like Friedrich Hagedorn and Günther von Goeckingk.[9] Of his 700 public readings, only 260 were exclusively from his own work, while over 300 were entirely devoted to the work of others, and this self-immersion in literary tradition enhanced the resonance of his own writings. Fragments of dramatic verse are incorporated in his satirical poetry and polemical prose through the technique of quotation which he defined as 'Einschöpfung' ('interpolated creativity'; F 572–6, 61–3). This denotes the splicing of literary allusions into modern discourse to create a complex intertextuality, setting up a tension between documentary materials, culled from the press, and an extraordinary range of literary and musical motifs, from the Bible, Kant and Schopenhauer through Offenbach, Nestroy and Ibsen to Altenberg and Wedekind. When Kraus incorporates a line from Shakespeare or Goethe in one of his satires or poems, we are reminded of the allusions to Dante and Baudelaire in T. S. Eliot's *The Waste Land*. Responding to what they saw as an immense panorama of futility and anarchy, both authors use fragments from the past to shore civilization up against its ruins. Like Eliot, Kraus had a lively sense of the 'presence' of the past, linking individual talent with literary tradition.[10] His literary favourites included the devout Matthias Claudius and the reverential Jean Paul, but satire was also strongly represented. In June 1925, at the height of his campaign against the Bekessy faction, he gave his first reading of Nikolai Gogol's *The Government Inspector* (*Der Revisor*). In the programme note he endorsed Gogol's claim that the satirist's most effective weapon is the 'fear of ridicule' (F 691–6, 33–5 & 68). He later described Gogol's play as 'the most powerful dramatic satire of world literature' (F 838–44, 127).

In a mood of uncharacteristic optimism Kraus announced in November 1929 a plan to create a company to be known as 'Theater der Dichtung', appealing for a total of 500,000 Marks to finance this project (F 827–33, 77). The aim was to retrain actors so as to create an ensemble capable of expressing the resonances of dramatic verse. A group of supporters set to work raising funds, registering themselves in March 1931 as the 'Theatre of Poetry, Karl Kraus, Preparatory Organization' – a charity with an account at the Postal Savings Bank. The appeal for funds was endorsed by forty distinguished figures, including Alban Berg, Otto Erich Deutsch, Ludwig Ficker, Heinrich Fischer, Jascha Horenstein, Ernst Krenek, Adolf Loos, Otto Rommel, Richard Schaukal, Otto Stoessl and Anton Webern. As their motto they chose

Wedekind's tribute to Kraus's exceptional gift for the theatre, defining him as the person 'who could show actors the way to the art of performance which our age demands'.[11] It would be more accurate to say that the idea was to mobilize the theatre *against* the fashions of the modern age, but the practical obstacles proved insurmountable. After the appeal had been publicized in the *Frankfurter Zeitung* (24 June 1931), Kraus distanced himself from the project, questioning its 'realizability' (F 857–63, 56). The economic crisis frustrated the idea of leasing a theatre in Berlin, and in July 1934 the charity was dissolved.[12]

While Kraus's project languished, Reinhardt succeeded in founding a school for actors at the Schloss Theater in Schönbrunn, launched in November 1928 with government support. Far from insisting on the primacy of the spoken word, the curriculum of the Reinhardt Seminar covered every branch of the thespian arts, including speech training and ensemble playing as well as directing and stage design. Reinhardt's international commitments meant that he was not personally involved in teaching, which may have been a blessing in disguise, since the staff offered a plurality of approaches, led by Emil Geyer, a director who shared Kraus's scepticism about Reinhardt's emphasis on visual effects.[13] However, it was Reinhardt's prestige that kept the school afloat through the economic crisis of the early 1930s, and Kraus was undoubtedly the loser in this long-running feud.

While Reinhardt was able to mobilize a cast of thousands, the Theatre of Poetry remained a one-man show, and it was only through the radio that Kraus was able to achieve his wider aims. When broadcasting began in 1924, his initial response was guarded, but he soon began to appreciate the artistic potential of the medium. His friends included leading figures from Berlin Radio like Hans Flesch and Alfred Braun, and with their assistance he was able to realize his dream of presenting plays and operettas which appealed to the ear, above all the works of Offenbach. Some of these broadcasts took the form of Kraus reading a complete text before the microphone, but he also worked with actors on more ambitious productions, coaching them in subtleties of expression. The series began in March 1930 with his adaptation of *Madame l'Archiduc* (F 834–7, 35) and included Shakespeare's *Timon of Athens*, with Kraus both directing and playing the title role (F 844–6, 27–8). Looking back in July 1931 on his first dozen broadcasts, he described them as 'more enjoyable and artistically productive than working with any permanent ensemble', adding that the 'acoustic scenery' created a purer theatrical atmosphere (F 857–63, 59).

The Unknown Goethe

Harking back across the centuries with a remarkable generosity of spirit, Kraus brought to life a tradition of dramatic poetry centred on Goethe and Shakespeare. This was a period ˸ ympian sage, not least by German-speaking ˸kel far more frequently than any other autl ˸ account of the Kraus–Goethe relationship ˸ shown how radically the satirist challenged the conventional image of Goethe, mobilizing the poet *against* his people.[14] Madame de Staël had apostrophized the Germans of the age of Goethe as 'le peuple des poètes et philosophes' – 'das Volk der Dichter und Denker'. Kraus transforms them into 'Richter und Henker' – not 'philosophers and singers', but 'judges and killers'. This formulation was first published in January 1908 in the context of a critique of the criminalization of homosexuals (F 242–3, 11). It can be linked to a pervasive scepticism about modern civilization with its interlocking ideals of sexual repression and technological advance. The clichés of the prevailing Goethe cult, with its emphasis on Faustian striving, are seen as an alibi for a society obsessed with power and dominated by mass communications. Modern printing presses, Kraus claimed in 1915, do more *against* culture in a single day than the value *for* culture of Goethe's complete works. Cossacks, he implies, have a closer rapport with Dostoevsky than Prussian infantrymen have with Goethe, even though the latter are better educated (F 406–12, 101 & 153).

Reacting against the propaganda of the First World War, Kraus mocked the philistinism of the 'nation of Goethe' ('Goethes Volk'). He was especially severe on popular travesties of the poem 'Wanderers Nachtlied' concocted in the name of politics and commerce, like the version published during the war in praise of German U-boats (F 454–6, 1–4). An earlier example, sent in by a reader, dates from a meeting of the Austrian Farmers' Federation in 1894, when some antisemitic wag had used this paradigm to mock members of the stock exchange (F 649–56, 87). Few branches of commerce could resist the temptation to use Goethe's haunting lines about the peace of forests and mountains to advertise their products, from farmers and tailors to manufacturers of central-heating systems, washing-machines, shoe-polish and margarine. Would-be humorists even adapted the poem to the task of complaining about inadequate transport services in provincial cities, and it was used as an epitaph for banks and businesses which had collapsed and a concert agency threatened by the competition of radio. For Kraus, these perversions amounted to a declaration of cultural bankruptcy (F 857–63, 117).[15]

To illustrate the gulf between Goethe's values and the dominant ideology, he quoted passages from Eckermann's *Conversations with Goethe*, in which the poet sets out his conception of patriotism: 'to combat disgraceful prejudices, to eliminate insensitive opinions, to enlighten the spirit of his people'. It is only among primitive peoples, the quotation from Goethe continues, that one finds violent forms of 'national hatred' (F 443–4, 18–20). The hollowness of 'German self-cultivation' ('deutsche Bildung'), which became so blatant during the war, is systematically analysed in November 1919 in the essay 'Brot und Lüge'. The belief that great poetry, like that of Goethe, has an ennobling effect on its readers is rejected as a 'contrived fable'. There is too large a gap between the peaks of German literature and the 'flatland' ('Flachland') inhabited by most of the population. In other cultures, by contrast, literature holds a 'middle position', nourishing 'the artistic strength of the nation'. Recalling the treason of the intellectuals during the war, he concludes that the claim to be the nation of Goethe serves for the 'embellishment of every kind of cultural and humanitarian atrocity' (F 519–20, 12–14). To counter this kind of misappropriation, Kraus mobilizes a more radical Goethe, creating challenging forms of intertextuality. The final page of 'Nachruf' (F 501–8, 120), his settling of accounts with the Central Powers, culminates in an indictment of the 'Faustian' military commanders, reinforced by imprecations from the Classical Walpurgisnacht (*Faust II*, lines 7660–75).

It is the unknown later Goethe that Kraus most admired, not the creator of the lovesick Werther, the swashbuckling Götz von Berlichingen or the impetuous Faust of the Gretchen Tragedy. The plays that he cited – and recited – most frequently are *Iphigenie auf Tauris*, the dramatic fragment *Pandora*, and *Helena*, the central act from *Faust II*, published separately in 1827.[16] He was certainly not immune to the appeal of Goethe's early nature poetry, describing 'Wandrers Nachtlied' as the nation's 'most sacred poem' (F 454–6, 2). Other poems singled out for praise are 'Nachtgesang', 'An Schwager Kronos' and 'An den Mond' (F 583–7, 28–9). But in principle he prefers a dimension of Goethe's poetry that is more intellectually exacting and imaginatively charged: 'to earthly outstretched hands unreach- / able', according to lines from *Pandora* cited in the programmatic essay 'Die Sprache' ('irdisch ausgestreckten Händen unerreich- / bar'; F 885–7, 3). In this convoluted poetry, as Goethe acknowledges in a phrase repeatedly quoted by Kraus, the words are 'wedged into each other' ('ineinander gekeilt'; F 554–6, 24).[17]

Pandora is celebrated as 'the greatest and most unknown German poem' (F 868–72, 68). The text did indeed baffle many readers, who regarded its style as 'unGoethean'.[18] Eduard Engel's comprehensive study, *Goethe: Der Mann und das Werk*, described the use of Greek metrics in *Pandora* as an 'artistic disaster' (cited F 640–8, 61). Worse still in Kraus's eyes was the insensitivity of scholarly editors, exemplified by their handling of the following lines from Goethe's manuscript of *Pandora*: 'Auf! Rasch Vergnügte! Schnellen Strichs!' ('Arise! Swiftly assuaged! Quick as a flash!'). The publisher Kurt Wolff, recalling a private conversation in Munich, described Kraus's fury on discovering that the Insel Verlag had smoothed out the irregularity of Goethe's verse by printing: 'Auf rasch! Vergnügte! Schnellen Strichs!' ('Arise swiftly! Assuaged! Quick as a flash!').[19] After denouncing this 'infamous alteration' (F 484–98, 138), Kraus traced it back to the Weimar Edition, whose editors evidently 'regarded linguistic profundity as a slip of the pen' (F 519–20, 11–12). Since both variants occurred in versions of *Pandora* published during Goethe's lifetime, the issue was one of aesthetic judgement rather than textual scholarship.[20] Taking issue with attempts to make Goethe's later poetry more reader-friendly, Kraus praised its 'entrancing profundity' (F 583–7, 28).

Reading Goethe in private was clearly not enough. Germany's humanistic heritage had to be reactivated, since modern readers preferred the memoirs of war heroes like Manfred von Richthofen to *Pandora* or the *West-östlicher Divan*

(F 519–20, 10–11). The cult of 'Faustian' dynamism tended to obscure the later Goethe's warnings about the dangers inherent in the pursuit of 'wealth and speed'.[21] To remind his audience of that more reflective Goethe, Kraus read *Pandora* not only in Berlin, Vienna and Prague, but also in provincial centres like Dortmund, Essen and Mährisch-Ostrau (Ostrava). This does not mean that Goethe is idealized. He has harsh words for plays like *Der Bürgergeneral*, a response to the French Revolution that reveals a defective political imagination, while Goethe's toadying towards the aristocracy makes him the target for a satirical epigram (F 577–82, 66). Kraus points out that the Germans, who have no knowledge of the poet's highest achievements, are equally ignorant of 'Goethe's lowest'. Thus he quotes the embarrassingly obsequious poems which Goethe wrote in praise of the Austrian royal family – a dimension of the oeuvre that had previously been unknown to Kraus himself (F 583–7, 15–30). He also ridicules the Goethean posturings of contemporaries like Hauptmann, Rilke, Hofmannsthal, Werfel and Bahr (F 583–7, 3–4). A collage of platitudes from the dictionary of literary quotations forms the basis of the extended poem mocking these 'Goethe Apes' ('Die Goetheaffen'; F 622–31, 126–8).

The language of *Pandora* resists this kind of facile appropriation, inspiring Kraus to construct an alternative tradition in which the classicizing dimensions of Goethe's poetry are given precedence over its roots in German folk tradition. He rejoiced in Goethe's use of phrases like 'pyrophic splendour' ('pyrophische Pracht'; F 640–8, 60–6), based on the Greek word for 'fire', and had no truck with the *völkisch* assumptions implicit in Engel's repudiation of the 'alien versification' of *Pandora*.[22] He also valued *Helena* for the way it dramatizes the tension between 'Greek' and 'Germanic' diction. But *Pandora* represents the extreme case, wedging classical metrical patterns into the dactylic–iambic rhythms of conventional verse. Moreover, its elegiac flavour transforms the myth about a gift from the gods into a symbolic drama about the power of memory, set against the archetypal conflict between shepherds and warriors. Although Goethe included the figure of Pandora in his list of characters, he published the work as a fragment, leaving the audience – like that of a Beckett play – waiting for a godlike figure that never appears.

The opening scene is dominated by the antithesis between the two brothers, Prometheus, bringer of fire and warfare, and Epimetheus, the bereaved husband of Pandora, who represents pastoral values. In contrast to the titanic energy celebrated in Goethe's youthful poem about Prometheus, the centre of sympathy is now the ageing and reflective Epimetheus, meaning 'the one who thinks back'. The contrast between action and reflection is intensified in the next generation: the ardent young Phileros (son of Prometheus), and the fragile daughters of Epimetheus, born of his marriage with Pandora: Elpore (whose name suggests Hope) and Epimeleia (Solicitude). The play invites a feminist reading by questioning the violence of Prometheus and Phileros, while associating the female characters not simply with the erotic heritage of Pandora, but also with redemptive qualities. The grieving Epimetheus is consoled by Elpore in a dream. Longing for Pandora's return, he reluctantly acknowledges that this is possible only in a 'dream world'. Phileros, after attempting suicide, is purged of his aggressive pursuit of Epimeleia by being reborn from the sea under the aegis of Eos, the goddess of dawn. The gendered discourse of the play is underscored by Goethe's unusually varied and experimental verse. While he uses a weighty six-stress metre for the philosophic exchanges between Prometheus and Epimetheus, the speeches of Elpore and Epimeleia have a dithyrambic quality, culminating in the use of a kind of sprung rhythm ('ionicus a minore') for Epimeleia's anguished confession that she inadvertently provoked Phileros's violence. Kraus made use of this same metre in 'Die Flamme der Epimeleia', his poetic tribute to Goethe's dramatization of a 'woman-power' ('Weibmacht') – contrasted in May 1918 with the forces responsible for the cataclysmic 'world-crash' ('Weltsturz'; F 474–83, 85–6).

Even in this ethereal play Kraus detects a dramaturgy relevant to world events. He found it especially significant that Prometheus is converted by the final scene to a more reflective frame of mind, so that the play reaches its climax in a restatement of the theme of memory. Through his repeated readings of *Pandora*, Kraus was urging his audience to remember a play about remembrance. In a collage of quotations published in August 1924 to mark the tenth anniversary of the outbreak of war, he cited that final speech by Prometheus censuring the human race because 'it only apprehends today's events, / rarely recalling those of yesteryear' ('Freilich frönt es nur dem heut'gen Tage, / Gestrigen Ereignens denkt's nur selten'). Cultural memory should serve as a corrective for the trivial obsession with today's events, but the context in which he places this precept gives it a political edge, suggesting that Germans have to choose between Goethe and the swastika (F 657–67, 3 & 6). Six years later Kraus was able to reach out to a wider audience by broadcasting a complete reading of *Pandora* on Berlin Radio. In the fragmentary recording that survives, he can be heard laying exceptional stress on the need to be mindful of 'yesteryear'.[23]

By 1932, the centenary of Goethe's death, it was clear that the wrong choice had been made. At public readings in Berlin on 11 January and Vienna on 6 February, Kraus analysed the gap between the poet and his purported admirers under the title 'An der Schwelle des Goethe-Jahres' ('On the Threshold of the Goethe Year'). Of the total German population (then approximately eighty million), less than a thousand – he suggests – have read *Pandora*. The majority are familiar with only one Goethe quotation: Götz's notorious message, to the commander of the imperial troops besieging his castle, that he can 'lick my arse' ('am Arsch lecken').[24] The true state of culture can be construed from German toilet walls, scene of all the people's 'political, spiritual and erotic endeavours'. Echoing the phrase about 'electrically illuminated barbarians' which he had first used during the war, he now identified the Germans as 'cave-dwellers wired-up with electricity' (F 868–72, 1–5). His comments on Austria are less severe, and on 17 February he broadcast a reading of *Pandora* on Radio Vienna, having already allowed himself to be photographed for their house magazine. He also celebrated the centenary in Czechoslovakia, reading *Pandora* first in Mährisch-Ostrau and then at a cross-cultural event in Prague. Indirectly, this was a tribute to Thomas Masaryk, whose enthusiasm for *Pandora* prompted him to draw Kraus's attention to an article about the play during an audience at Hradschin Castle. The reading in Prague, organized by the Modern Philology Club in November 1932, began with an introduction in Czech, delivered by Professor Otokar Fischer (F 885–7, 5–10). This was the moment when Hitler was poised to seize power in Germany, and the tone in which Kraus recited Prometheus' final words had the impact of a 'political testament'.[25]

Dialogues with Music

It was not simply the spoken word that moved Kraus's audiences, but the combination of poetry and music. Over half of his seven hundred public readings involved some form of musical accompaniment, with a pianist partly concealed behind a screen, and this involved him in a complex process of rehearsal. He may claim that the harmonizing of words with music was due 'more to happy improvisation than to the fleeting rehearsal' (F 706–11, 94). But it is clear from other sources that this was a simplification. The collaboration with Viktor Junk, his regular accompanist during the early 1920s, involved numerous visits to the composer's home in the Third District, since Kraus did not own a piano. What may have started as an improvisation, based on the satirist's own 'suggestions', ended with the composition of original scores which he had to commit to memory, since – although he performed with the text in his hand – he could not read music. Similar accounts of this process of collaboration have been left by his other principal accompanists, Otto Janowitz, Franz Mittler and Georg Knepler.[26] Far from insisting on the purity of poetry, he went to great lengths to enhance his dramatic readings by musical interludes. This mixed mode formed an integral part of the Austrian popular tradition, exemplified by his Nestroy recitals, and music also enhanced his readings of the comedies of Raimund, the first of which, on 9 June 1914, included songs from *Der Alpenkönig und der Menschenfeind*, accompanied at the piano by Otto Janowitz (F 400–3, 47–8). In this case, as in subsequent recitals, he was able to use the original music by Wenzel Müller (1767–1835). A recording made in Berlin in May 1931 includes his performance both as the misanthropic Rappelkopf and as the impoverished Charcoal Burner's family, singing as they are forced to leave their cottage: 'So leb' denn wohl, du stilles Haus'.[27]

Kraus also used music to underscore his readings of German classics, especially the *Helena* act from *Faust II*, read for the first time in April 1918 'with musical accompaniment'. Kraus later provided a more detailed justification for this musical enhancement, citing Goethe's insistence that the latter part of *Helena* is to be conceived 'operatically'. His gift for 'Sprechgesang' enabled him to recite complex passages, including the Euphorion sequence inspired by the death of Byron, to 'improvised music' (F 917–22, 34–8). Music in a different key accompanied his recitals of *Hannele Matterns Himmelfahrt*, Hauptmann's dream-play about the religious visions of a girl in a workhouse. So accomplished was Kraus's performance that it was broadcast on Berlin radio, and he can be heard singing the lullaby 'Schlaf, Kindchen, schlaf!' in the fragmentary recording that survives.[28]

It is clear that Kraus, working closely with his pianists, developed a flair for matching words with music. In his early Shakespeare readings his approach had been rather conventional. Music by Carl Nicolai (1810–49) inspired by *The Merry Wives of Windsor* accompanied his reading of that play in April 1916 (F 426–30, 47). Later he became more inventive, particularly when working with the talented Franz Mittler, who wrote the score for Kraus's adaptation of *The Winter's Tale*, a comedy in which song and music play a particularly significant role (F 838–44, 127–8). Shakespeare's setting of certain scenes in Bohemia prompted Mittler to compose a polka for piano solo entitled 'Böhmische Dorfmusik' for the dance of the shepherds in the fourth act.[29] Kraus allowed himself even greater freedom in the choice of music for his adaptation of *Troilus and Cressida*. For his first recital of this play in February 1926 he borrowed the overture and interval music from Offenbach's *La Belle Hélène*, also performing Pandarus' song from Act III, scene 1 ('For O love's bow / shoots buck and doe') to one of Offenbach's mocking tunes (F 717–23, 105). This is one of seven Shakespeare plays that Kraus adapted for publication, in editions designed 'for listeners and readers'.[30] In his introduction to this 'most captivatingly threatening of all Shakespeare dramas' he argued that a stage production using Offenbach's music would bring out the affinities between two closely related theatrical worlds (S 15, 549–51).

He also introduced music into his readings of Shakespearean tragedy, including *Timon of Athens* – with introductory and interval music by Mozart and Gluck, and dance music during the banquet scene improvised by his pianist, Viktor Junk (F 668–75, 51–2); *Coriolanus* – the overture by Beethoven, played by Eduard Steuermann (F 743–50, 77); and *Macbeth* – with music by Franz Mittler (S 15, 374). An unusually wide range of music accompanied his readings of *King Lear*, especially the so-called Tent Scene in the final act, where the Doctor calls for louder music to rouse Lear from his slumbers. In the Shakespeare folio of 1608 there is only a brief reference to music, and it is dropped altogether in the quarto edition.[31] But Kraus's melodic conception of the theatre led him – in a magisterial summing-up – to insist that the whole dialogue of that scene is 'guided by music' (F 906, 24–5). For his first reading of *King Lear* in May 1918 he used music composed and played by Viktor Junk, together with introductory and interval music by Mozart and Bach (F 484–98, 134–5). During the following years he read the play more than twenty times with a variety of accompanists and musical interludes.[32]

This orchestration of dialogue is reflected in Kraus's own plays. *Literatur* was published with musical settings, scored by Viktor Junk in accordance with the author's suggestions. Recitals of *Wolkenkuckucksheim* invariably had a piano accompaniment, while both the stage productions of *Die Unüberwindlichen* and his readings of the play were enlivened by catchy tunes: jazz for the cynical newspaper editor, the Police Chief's song set to the Radetzky March, the echoes of Offenbach in the scene at the Paris hotel, and 'Silent Night' as an ironic finale at the policemen's Christmas party. The extreme case is *Die letzten Tage der Menschheit*, which uses music for both documentary authenticity and satirical effect. A detailed analysis has identified over a hundred musical motifs, confirming the suggestion that they 'cry out for performance'.[33]

Kraus also welcomed the use of music in productions of *Traumstück*, the dream-play that highlights his post-war disillusionment and ridicules the reductiveness of psychoanalysis. The printed text specifies the use of music at just two points: a foxtrot to accompany the allegory of Securities dancing with the Interest Rate (Valuta and Zinsfuß); and music from the Olympia Act of Offenbach's *Tales of Hoffmann* to introduce the figure of Imago. However, the Berlin production of March 1924 had a more elaborate musical score composed by Heinrich Jalowetz, a member of Schoenberg's circle who made his career as a conductor.[34] For Kraus, the involvement of Jalowetz with this production was an exceptional 'highlight', while the Imago episode, performed by Cäcilie Lvovsky, left him with a vibrant 'melodic memory' (F 649–56, 6–8). Although the score has apparently not survived, we know that it also included a trio for the Anal Psychologists. When this production transferred to Vienna the following month, the music was directed by another of Schoenberg's pupils, Paul A. Pisk. Muffled drums announced the appearance of the profiteer Gabardine (Gürtelpelz), while the dance of the Securities was set to a shimmy entitled 'Kitten on the Keys'. Lvovsky's performance was commended as a 'half-sung recitative', while Pisk's musical direction was widely praised (F 649–56, 128–47). Thus Kraus made a virtue of hybridity, combining modalities that might appear incommensurable, were it not for the musical language that legitimizes them: the entrancing verses of Imago and the cacophony of the Anal Psychologists. So impressed was he by Jalowetz's music that he repeatedly used it for his solo recitals of *Traumstück* (F 657–67, 97) and his less frequent readings of *Traumtheater* (F 691–6, 27). The piano remained an essential instrument in Kraus's theatre of poetry until the end of his life, and in April 1936 he performed Jalowetz's setting of the 'Anal Psychologists' during his last public appearance.

In sum, the function of music in Kraus's dramaturgy is to accentuate the extremes of the expressive spectrum, both satirical and lyrical. In works like *Troilus and Cressida* and *La Belle Hélène*, he suggests that the two extremes are melodically combined to form a kind of 'double identity' ('Doppelnatur'; S 15, 551). Above all, he introduces music to articulate the transition between waking and sleeping and the onset of dreams – the theme prefigured in *Pandora*. Thus music is heard as the Poet in *Traumstück* dreams at his desk; as Hannele begins to hallucinate; as Lear is roused from a traumatic sleep; and as

Hermione awakens in *The Winter's Tale*. Through his musically enhanced recitals and adaptations, of drama as well as operetta, Kraus draws us into imaginative worlds that subvert reductive rationality. Moreover, by mobilizing a repertoire that links Offenbach with Brecht, his Theatre of Poetry acquired a political dimension.

Epic Theatre, Masks and Songs

The melancholic satirist may appear to have little in common with the brash exponent of epic theatre, and Kraus's early comments on Brecht were hostile. However, Brecht had begun to read works by Kraus in September 1921, a few months after the publication of *Literatur*. He does not specify which texts he was reading, but there are striking parallels between Kraus's satire on the poetry of Expressionism in *Literatur* and the opening scenes of Brecht's first play, *Baal*, published in 1922 and premièred the following year. He also recognized the importance of Kraus's campaign against the press, even if he could not fully endorse it.[35] What brought the two together was a shared passion for the use of song as a dramaturgical resource. After *Baal* had been staged in Berlin and Vienna in the spring of 1926, Kraus received favourable reports about Brecht's work from his friend Ludwig Münz.[36] His curiosity aroused, he found the opportunity in August 1928 to observe Brecht's practice at first hand. This visit to Berlin coincided with preparations for the première of *Die Dreigroschenoper* at the Theater am Schiffbauerdamm, where Heinrich Fischer was working as assistant to Ernst Josef Aufricht:

> While we were rehearsing the *Dreigroschenoper*, Kraus [as Fischer recalls] suddenly asked me whether he could watch Brecht working without being seen. He sat out of sight in a box and was at once enthusiastic about the way Brecht worked over the dialogues with the actors. Very shortly afterwards Brecht was introduced to Kraus. From then on both, together with a few friends, met every evening in a little beer hall in Friedrichstrasse. Brecht was almost shy in the presence of Kraus – he frequently told me he considered him one of the greatest writers. But there was soon a very natural bond of understanding between the two of them, although both of them stuck to their own points of view. Kraus, as nearly always in his private life, was very charming to Brecht and tactfully avoided antagonising him, and if he now and again talked disparagingly about Piscator, he would add with a sweet smile, 'Your friend', and there was nothing of the bitterness that there was in his writing about Piscator. Brecht, in his turn, would smilingly answer with a quotation from the *Dreigroschenoper*: 'Ja, die Verhältnisse, die sind nicht so' (Sorry – the force of circumstances).[37]

Aufricht's account of the rehearsals adds that Kraus, after listening to the 'Jealousy Duet' sung by Polly and Lucy, contributed an additional strophe, which was incorporated in the script.[38]

This friendship with Brecht has been described as a sudden and astonishing turn of events.[39] Elias Canetti, who joined their circle in summer 1928, could hardly believe his eyes when he saw Kraus, epitome of an uncompromising

morality, treating the cynical Brecht with such indulgence: 'He treated everyone at the table with tenderness; however, he treated Brecht with love, as
though Brecht were his son, the young genius – his *chosen* son.'[40] There were
distinct artistic and temperamental affinities, since both of them aimed to
challenge the comforting illusions of the bourgeois entertainment theatre,
transforming the stage into a forum for social criticism. Brecht admired *Die
letzten Tage der Menschheit* as a critique of ruling-class attitudes which complemented Jaroslav Hašek's down-to-earth account of the survival strategies of
ordinary soldiers in *The Good Soldier Schweik*.[41] And when Heinrich Fischer
staged *Die letzte Nacht* at the Theater am Schiffbauerdamm in January 1930,
using songs and masks to heighten the impact, Brecht was actively involved.[42]

In further comments Brecht observed that Kraus's critical strategy presupposed 'the construction of a space in which everything becomes a judicial
procedure'.[43] Comparable judicial procedures occur in his own most characteristic plays and operas, including the comic trial scene in *Aufstieg und Fall der Stadt
Mahagonny*, which Kraus particularly admired. Their aim may have been
didactic, but both were aware that comedy is the most effective weapon for the
social critic, especially when enhanced by song. When it was announced in
autumn 1928 that *Die Unüberwindlichen* would be staged at the Theater am
Schiffbauerdamm, Brecht must already have been familiar with the play. He was
particularly captivated by Kraus's use of wit to punch home his message, citing
a passage from Act I in which the corrupt newspaper editor reveals his favourite
method of blackmail. 'Don't disturb me,' Barkassy tells his secretary at the
beginning of the act, 'I'm writing a very important article which is *not* intended
for publication, and what's more *tomorrow!*' In conversation with Kraus and
Fischer, Brecht described this sally as 'wittier than ten German comedies'.[44]

It was Alfred Kerr who provided the stimulus for Kraus to declare his
support for Brecht. In 1929, after the publication of the songs from *Die
Dreigroschenoper*, Brecht was attacked by Kerr for not acknowledging K. L.
Ammer's translation of verses from Villon as one of his sources. Although
Brecht conceded that he had been careless about copyright, Kraus sprang to his
defence, praising his 'passion for the theatre' (F 811–19, 129). When Brecht
and Weill's second satirical opera, *Mahagonny*, was staged in Berlin in December 1931, Kraus attended the première. He was particularly impressed by the
acting of Lotte Lenya, although he had his doubts about the demonstrative use
of placards and slogans, which in his view obscured the poetic qualities of the
play. Three weeks later, on 11 January 1932 he included two texts from the
play in a Berlin public reading – the courtroom scene and the poem 'Kraniche
und Wolken' ('Cranes and Clouds'). He was accompanied at the piano by Kurt
Weill, playing music from the opera. Kraus admired *Mahagonny* for its combination of topical and enduring qualities, endorsing Brecht in ringing tones as
'the only German author' who 'really counts today' (F 868–72, 33 & 36). This
implies that *Mahagonny*, with its idiosyncratic use of music, came closer to
doing justice to the incipient anarchy in Germany than any well-made play.

Those beer-hall discussions stimulated a minor dramaturgical revolution. While Brecht was inspired to extend the use of interpolated songs into an explicit form of epic theatre, Canetti responded by writing a series of texts based on 'acoustic masks', including the black comedies *Hochzeit* ('Marriage') and *Komödie der Eitelkeit* ('Comedy of Vanity') and the novel *Die Blendung* ('Auto-da-Fé'). In his account of these early works, Canetti made no secret of his debt to Kraus, particularly to the technique of 'acoustic quotation' that inspired *Die letzten Tage der Menschheit* and suffused his public readings.[45] Canetti's characters, too, in both novel and plays, are transfixed by communicative stereotypes, resulting in a mask-like rigidity. The school of listening created by Kraus's recitals prompted Canetti to take the idea of theatre *against* the modern age to its logical extreme, exploiting the parallel between the voices of humans and hyenas.[46]

The delight in alternative dramaturgies sparked by his contacts with Canetti and Brecht prompted Kraus to explore the murkier districts of Berlin theatrical life and reflect on their political implications. He felt there must be some connection 'between the sadism required of the prostitutes walking the Tauentzienstrasse in high, red leather boots, some with whips in their hands, and the viciousness of SA-troops marching through Berlin'. Heinrich Fischer recalls a characteristic episode:

One day Kraus asked me to go with him to a tiny music hall, the Stettiner Sänger, in one of Berlin's northern suburbs. At that time – 1931 – many of these little music halls were already staging very nationalistic productions, an additional attraction being that all female parts were played by men, to cater for transvestite tastes. We saw a one-act play – an indescribably cheap offering – about an old, blind pianist who had been robbed of his savings by a Jew. But he had two grown-up daughters who in the end saved him from disaster. Now these two girls were played by two enormous heavies, each weighing about seventeen stone, wearing simple German dresses, two blond guaranteed Aryan plaits and no make-up. At the happy end, as the two girls danced around their father, their skirts flew up revealing massive masculine thighs, and as the curtain fell the old blind father said, his voice trembling with emotion: 'As long as Germany has *girls like this*, she will never be defeated!' The audience was deeply moved, and Kraus and I nearly died laughing. But he said, 'Believe me, it might not be as funny as it looks now.'[47]

Kraus's account of this episode stresses the hurricane of applause that greeted the punchline: 'Ein Volk, das solche Mädels hat, kann nicht untergehn!' (F 759–65, 52). Given his awareness of the Nazi threat and his disenchantment with Social Democracy, it is not surprising that he was drawn towards the communist alternative, but this was by no means the primary motive for his friendship with Brecht. Their passion for performance brought them together, just as Kraus's hatred of gimmickry kept him apart from the equally left-wing Piscator. To speak of him forming an 'alliance' with communist groups in Berlin is misleading.[48]

Where Brecht and Kraus diverged was in their attitude towards cinema. As the economic crisis of the early 1930s brought theatres to the brink of collapse,

new opportunities arose from the movies. Given his indifference to visual spectacle, it is hardly surprising that Kraus showed little interest in the silent screen,
which was already attracting mass audiences. However, the advent of sound led
him to modify his position, and he sat through kitschy films featuring such
gifted actresses as Elisabeth Bergner, Lucie Mannheim and Dolly Haas (F
857–63, 57; 864–7, 25).[49] Brecht, by contrast, was an enthusiast, and after the
filming of *Die Dreigroschenoper*, released in February 1931, he tried to transform
cinema into a revolutionary medium by making *Kuhle Wampe*, a communist-
inspired film produced by an artists' collective. Equally revolutionary is his
play *Die heilige Johanna der Schlachthöfe* ('St Joan of the Stockyards'), which
dramatizes the conversion of a Salvation Army woman to the cause of the proletariat. Although Kraus expressed reservations about Brecht's political and
artistic doctrines (F 847–51, 77), he was moved by Carola Neher's performance, praising her sensitive recitation of passages from the play in December
1931 (F 864–7, 26). He must have attended rehearsals, since his comments
appeared four months before it was premièred as a radio play in April 1932.

This interest in radio marks a further convergence between Kraus and
Brecht, but the fundamental affinity lies in their use of music to break the
theatrical illusion, a Brechtian technique foreshadowed by Kraus. The prototype was provided by the 'Song of the Media Mogul' in *Literatur*, where
Schwarz-Drucker steps out of character to sing an incisively critical song about
the machinations of the press. Equally effective was the 'Schober Song' from
Die Unüberwindlichen, which was reissued as a political broadsheet. Through his
recitals of Nestroy and Offenbach, Kraus had transformed satirical songs into
an instrument of social criticism. Between 1928 and 1932 he gave twenty-two
Offenbach recitals in Berlin, and in March 1931, when he was supervising a
production of *Perichole* at the State Opera, Brecht attended the rehearsals.[50] He
was doubtless familiar with Kraus's programmatic essay identifying 'double
tonguing' – the ironic disjunction between text and music – as Offenbach's
inimitable achievement (F 757–8, 47). In the mixing of song and dialogue
there was a meeting of minds, and one of the sources for the ironic function
assigned to music in Brecht's 'Notes on Mahagonny' was surely Offenbach, as
interpreted by Kraus. A further point of convergence was their shared passion
for Shakespeare.

Re-creating Shakespeare

Shakespeare had been an inspiration for Kraus since the earliest days of *Die
Fackel*, since his work seemed so prophetically to interact with the follies and
disasters of the twentieth century. The plays are seen as fragments of a master
plot, linking arrogance with humiliation, ambition with moral retribution,
although at different times he foregrounds different texts. *Measure for Measure*
provides the analogies for his early satire on sexual hypocrisy, not least because
it is set in Vienna. The First World War represented a more extreme challenge,
since Kraus, as he sketched the first scenes from *Die letzten Tage der Menschheit*,

found it hard to decide 'which play' was 'actually being performed' (cited F 423–5, 12). The final monologue of the Grumbler in *Die letzten Tage* suggests that he saw himself as Thersites, who rails against vainglorious Greek heroes like Achilles in *Troilus and Cressida*. But the defeat of the Central Powers prompted him, both in the preface to the play and in *Die Fackel*, to invoke a more hopeful Shakespearean dramaturgy in which political crimes are subject to cosmic retribution. Hence his allusions to *Hamlet*, the tragedy of a state so corrupt that the royal house has to be overthrown and order restored by Fortinbras, the representative of a new power. This role is assigned to Woodrow Wilson, while Kraus speaks in the voice of Horatio, bearing witness 'to th'yet unknowing world / how these things came about' (F 499–500, 4).

During the 1920s Kraus invoked a multiplicity of Shakespearean motifs in his polemics, finding a paradigm for Bekessy in Paroles, the lying braggart in *All's Well That Ends Well* who 'out-villained villainy' (F 686–90, 18). The most systematic study of Kraus's debt to Shakespeare, written in Portuguese, lists over three hundred allusions to *Hamlet* alone, evenly distributed throughout his career.[51] During the late 1920s his interest in Shakespeare was temporarily subordinated to his passion for Offenbach, whose spirit he so resourcefully mobilized against the troglodytes. But by October 1930 a growing disillusionment with Austrian politics, especially after the failure of his campaign against Schober, led him to declare – while introducing a cycle of Offenbach songs – that 'things are now becoming Shakespearean'. This phrase signals a disillusionment so profound that it can be conveyed only through the language of bleakest tragedy, borrowed from the final act of *Timon of Athens*. Disgusted with human civilization, Timon has turned his back on the city and taken refuge in the woods, but Athens is threatened by the military power of Alcibiades, and two senators come to plead with Timon to return and organize the defence of the city. Timon replies (in words that express Kraus's attitude to the situation in Austria): 'If Alcibiades kill my countrymen, / Let Alcibiades know this of Timon, / That Timon cares not.' Alcibiades is to be understood as Prince Starhemberg, the Heimwehr leader who was threatening to overthrow the Republic. Kraus responded with resignation, suggesting that the only option is to 'take refuge in things of the spirit' (F 845–6, 2–3). The following month, the audience that flocked to the Konzerthaus in response to a poster announcing that Kraus would be reading from his 'own works' had to sit through his adaptation of *Timon*, prefaced by a scathing indictment of their lack of interest in Shakespeare (F 845–6, 30–6).

To the consternation of admirers who expected greater political engagement, Kraus now devoted most of his energy to adapting the existing German translations of Shakespeare for his Theatre of Poetry. He particularly admired the so-called Schlegel–Tieck translation, discovering that two of the plays that most appealed to him, *Timon of Athens* and *The Winter's Tale*, had actually been translated by Dorothea Tieck, the granddaughter of Moses Mendelssohn, and that she had also contributed to the standard version of *Macbeth*. However, he felt that the existing versions of Shakespeare in German were unwieldy in length and often faulty in their versification. In addition to *Timon von Athen* (1930), he published his own adaptations of six other plays in two handsome volumes (1934–5), and two further collections were planned. Using existing translations as his raw material, he also produced a 'poetic re-creation' ('Nachdichtung') of Shakespeare's sonnets, which was published in March 1933. Given that he had virtually no knowledge of English, these projects were highly problematic, but in his comments on existing translations, including the version of the sonnets by Stefan George, he claimed that his re-creations were closer to the spirit of Shakespeare. These claims were challenged by Richard Flatter, a rival translator who had the advantage of knowing English, but whose German – according to the satirist – betrayed traces of Jewish jargon (F 845–6, 5–6). Flatter responded with an eighty-five-page pamphlet analysing Kraus's linguistic errors, especially in his version of the sonnets, and showing how his approach to *Macbeth* reduces the raw energy of the Witches by making their speeches too poetic.[52] Subsequent critics have also questioned his treatment of the plays, suggesting that his adaptations – even of *King Lear* – reduce the action to a series of 'emotional high-points', omitting not only incidental stage business, but also passages essential to character development.[53]

It was, of course, absurd for Kraus to suggest that his re-creations might be 'more Shakespearean' than the originals (F 885–7, 49). But in the long history of Shakespeare reception, the liberties he took were relatively modest. Goethe, in adapting *Romeo and Juliet* for the Weimar Court Theatre, had reduced the length of the play by one-third, transforming its violence and discord into a spiritually elevating harmony, while Schiller's translation of *Macbeth* superimposed a sense of sublime order on the unmitigated evil of the action.[54] There are certainly traces of that Weimar tradition in Kraus's approach, and it is no coincidence that he sought to legitimize his Theatre of Poetry by once again quoting Goethe's precept that Shakespeare appeals to 'the mind's eye', so that his living word is best transmitted by 'reading aloud' (F 847–51, 59–60). Since his adaptations were primarily designed for listeners, they created a decorum far removed from the rumbustiousness of the Elizabethan stage. To heighten the poetic effect, he introduced both rhyme and alliteration at points where there is no trace of them in the original, rendering the opening lines of *Macbeth* more mellifluous.[55] By this means he achieved his basic aim of making the plays more accessible – by condensing the action, harmonizing the style and intensifying individual scenes.

Thus Kraus became an active participant in the 'battle for Shakespeare', which at the same time was (in Gundolf's phrase) a struggle to define the 'German spirit'.[56] Distancing himself from both Romantic tradition and Expressionist experiment, he sustained a didactic approach with political implications. To counter the charge that his readings were elitist, Kraus emphasized Shakespeare's sensitivity to the 'nobility of proletarian humanity' (F 890–905, 246). His critique of military heroics was reinforced by readings of *Troilus and*

Cressida, a text which, after centuries of war, still reminds us how 'heroic myth is created out of murder'.[57] And when Kraus turned to the history plays, he highlighted not the battle scenes, but the sombre reflections on war by two soldiers in *Henry V*. His reading in Vienna on 25 January 1933 included the following speech (reprinted in *Die Fackel*):

> But if the cause be not good, the King himself hath a heavy reckoning to make, when all those legs and arms and heads chopped off in a battle shall join together in the latter day. [. . .] I am afeard there are few die well that die in a battle, for how can they charitably dispose of anything, when blood is their argument? Now, if these men do not die well, it will be a black matter for the King that led them to it – who to disobey were against all proportion of subjection. (F 909–11, 9)

The warning could hardly have been more timely. Four days later, Hitler was appointed German chancellor, and the era of total subjection began.

During the previous years Kraus had made a final effort to influence listeners in Germany, projecting his Theatre of Poetry over Berlin radio. Through these broadcasts, which included Shakespeare, Goethe, Nestroy, Raimund and Hauptmann as well as Offenbach, he reaffirmed his humanistic concept of cultural memory, while pioneering that democratic form of drama known in German as 'listening plays' ('Hörspiele'). The broadcast on 15 December 1931 included his poem 'Zum ewigen Frieden', condemning the 'German madness' of militarism while celebrating that 'German miracle' of Kant's vision of peace (F 868–72, 27). This series of broadcasts was building up a powerful momentum when it was cut short in 1932 by Papen's emergency decrees, which suppressed democratic institutions in Prussia, preparing the ground for Hitler. To socialists, Kraus's self-immersion in Shakespeare seemed mere escapism. When he announced an ambitious cycle of play readings for January–February 1933, one of them objected that 'Shakespeare in daily doses / won't cure the world's neuroses' ('Die Welt hat andere Sorgen / Als Shakespeare heut' und morgen'). Kraus responded by suggesting that the world would be in a less desperate state if Shakespeare were taken more seriously. The connection would be clear to anyone who seriously reflected on the 'dramaturgy of world events' (F 909–11, 13). This phrase alludes to the crisis of historical understanding that erupted during the 1930s. Both liberalism and Marxism, in their different ways, presupposed a pattern of evolution in human affairs, while Christian thinkers discerned a providential purpose. With the collapse of the economy and the triumph of the dictators, these beliefs were profoundly shaken. The crisis is reflected in the introduction to a *History of Europe*, published in 1936 by an influential British historian: 'Men wiser and more learned than I have discerned in history a plot, a rhythm, a predetermined pattern. These harmonies are concealed from me. I can only see one emergency following upon another.'[58]

Kraus's intensified preoccupation with Shakespeare and Goethe can be seen as a response to this dilemma – an attempt to discern a rhythm in world events.

The misanthropic defeatism of Timon was by no means his final word. For some time he had been pondering the difficulties of adapting *Macbeth* for his Theatre of Poetry, finding the existing German translations – especially of the opening scene on the Heath – so inadequate that he began to draft versions of his own (F 724–5, 1–44). The threat to Austrian independence after the Nazi seizure of power in Germany prompted him to take up this project again, since *Macbeth* provided striking analogies with the dilemma of a nation at the mercy of a ruthless upstart. Between February 1933 and November 1934 he read the play four times, drawing explicit parallels with events in Austria. As European politics became sucked into the German vortex, Kraus devised a new drama-turgy, combining – in his polemic against the Third Reich – the tragedy of *Macbeth* with the phantasmagoria of Goethe's Walpurgis Night.

CHAPTER 20

Heine, Nestroy and Satirical Verse

Kraus belongs to a generation of poets who challenged traditional aesthetics by giving poetry a political function through the medium of *Zeitstrophen* ('Topical Verses').[1] In July 1931 he specifically compared his work with that of left-wingers like Kurt Tucholsky, Erich Kästner and Walter Mehring (F 857–63, 65). The political cabaret of the Weimar Republic mocked the bourgeoisie and ridiculed the nationalists, combining the radicalism of Marx with the irony of Heine. Kraus adopted a more conservative stance, defending traditional poetics against the onslaughts of modernism and questioning Heine's influence. Set against Goethe's resonant nature lyrics, Heine's poetry is dismissed as facile, while his journalistic prose is contrasted with Nestroy's profounder imagination. However, this does not preclude the possibility that Kraus, as a satirical poet, may have owed both Nestroy and Heine a significant debt.

Heine's Versified Journalism

Hostility towards Heine forms one of the leitmotifs of *Die Fackel*, inspiring a number of Kraus's most incisive literary essays, notably 'Heine und die Folgen' ('Heine and the Consequences'). Focusing on the perennially popular *Buch der Lieder*, he holds Heine responsible for a trivialization of the German literary tradition, describing his poetry as 'versified journalism' (F 329–30, 22). Kraus attempts to give his critique an ontological foundation by opposing two conceptions of language, the one reverently attuned to the harmony of nature, the other cynically manipulative. As a journalist Heine 'loosened the bodice of the German language' so that every travelling salesman could finger her breasts. As a poet he was a 'Moses who struck the rock of the German language', only to produce not water but eau de cologne (F 329–30, 11 & 33). These formulations may remind us of the attacks on 'Jewish' attitudes to language which date back to Richard Wagner and were intensified by literary historians like Adolf Bartels.[2] But Kraus distanced himself from the 'narrow-minded

hatred directed against Heine as a Jew' (F 329–30, 19), declaring that 'if Herr
Bartels should understand a single line of my Heine essay, I take it all back'
(F 315–16, 50).

Kraus had no truck with *völkisch* conceptions of culture, repudiating both
German nationalist and Jewish revivalist variants, and denouncing those who
regard Heine as a 'sacred Jewish national possession' (F 45, 22). The spokesman
of this school was Gustav Karpeles, who in 1906 had described Heine's songs
as the expression of the 'soul of the Jewish *Volk*'.[3] For Kraus, the antisemitic
diatribes of Bartels and the philosemitic Heine-cult of Karpeles both presup-
pose a problematic Jewish essentialism, and he denounces them both because
their judgement of Heine the poet depends on their conception of Heine as a
Jew (F 329–30, 31; 315–16, 50). The pressures on German-speaking Jews,
during the fiercely contested process of modernization, provoked both Kraus
and Heine to distance themselves from Judaism.[4] Antisemitic prejudices
exerted a malign influence, and in a notorious poem about the 'New Jewish
Hospital in Hamburg', quoted with some astonishment in *Die Fackel* (F 87,
20–1), Heine identified the three most grievous afflictions as 'poverty, physical pain and Jewishness!'[5] Traces of this medical imagery can also be detected
when Kraus describes Heine's facile style as the 'French disease' imported into
German writing (F 329–30, 7). It has been argued that his attacks on Heine
represent 'an over-compensation for his own Jewishness'.[6] But he makes a
determined effort to focus on literary style, not racial stigma. If we are looking
for a parallel for Kraus's discrimination between Heine's contrived poetic
moods and Goethe's more inward contemplation of nature, we should turn not
to Bartels, but to F. R. Leavis's comparison of the poetry of Shelley and
Wordsworth. Here Shelley's 'sentimental commonplaces' are contrasted with
Wordsworth's 'grasp of the outer world', which unobtrusively transforms the
'outer' into the 'inner'.[7] It is only fifteen-year-olds who are intoxicated by
Shelley, Leavis insists, while Kraus sees the passion for this kind of poetry as one
of the diseases of childhood (F 329–30, 16–19). The aim, for both Kraus
and Leavis, is to challenge this immaturity of judgement and teach people to
read in a more discriminating way – indeed to 'create readers' (F 329–30, 3).
Asserting that Heine's writings pander to the taste of an emergent newspaper-
reading public, Kraus holds him responsible for a form of journalism, the
'feuilleton', which subordinates factual reporting to a self-indulgent subjectiv-
ity. Hence the 'consequences' identified in 'Heine und die Folgen': a
journalistic civilization in which poetry is displaced by pastiche and news is
swamped by opinion.

Although Kraus's conclusions are far too sweeping, a more balanced picture
emerges if we acknowledge that he (like Leavis) may be right in his aesthetic
discriminations, but wrong in his moral conclusions. The Heine cult of the late
nineteenth century tended to bracket Goethe and Heine as the greatest
German poets. Kraus demonstrates, through a series of illuminating examples,
that the language of Heine's poetry is fundamentally different from that of

Goethe – more flexible and innovative, playful and irreverent. He also makes telling observations about the modernity of Heine's prose, describing him as 'truly the forerunner of modern nervous systems' (F 329–30, 30). It is at the point where stylistic analysis becomes the basis for moral judgement that Kraus's argument must be challenged, for he fails to establish a nexus between Heine's playful experiments and the awesome consequences ascribed to them. Such innovations appear morally reprehensible only if we adopt a position of linguistic conservatism and cultural pessimism, as Kraus did in the final years before the First World War. When Heine's letters to the Rothschild family were published in 1915, he interpreted them as further proof of the poet's duplicity (F 406–12, 52–93).

At times Kraus seems determined to discredit his predecessor by fair means or foul, mobilizing misquotations and echoing the stereotypes which he claims to despise.[8] Thus his polemic has provoked a polarized response, with some critics endorsing his scathing judgements, while others repudiate them. The one camp insists that Kraus was right to conclude that Heine was not truly a poet.[9] The other presents Heine as a progressive author who had the courage to engage with politics, unlike Kraus, the reactionary who banished from his conception of art all consciousness of the disruptive pressures of the age.[10] In an attempt to avoid such polarized positions, Theodor Adorno suggested that Heine's strength lies in his polemical prose. Echoing Kraus's critique, Adorno transforms the idea that Heine was not fully 'at home' in the German language (his 'Heimatlosigkeit') into a merit, expressing not merely failed Jewish emancipation, but a universal modern condition.[11]

The critical literature tends to ignore the shift in Kraus's position between 1910, when he denounced Heine's stylistic and thematic innovations, and 1920, when he began to assimilate them into his own practice. During the First World War, when Kraus redirected his attack against German nationalism, he retracted his assertions about the shallowness of 'Latin' culture. Where earlier he had repudiated Frenchified influences and defended the 'sanctity of authentic German', he now denounced Germany as the 'intolerable conqueror of a place in the sun' (F 462–71, 76–8). The anachronisms of German public life are satirized in a critique of the 'Techno-Romantic Adventure' that displays striking affinities with Heine's writings of the 1840s. It was Heine who identified the romanticizing of evolving political institutions as the central problem of German ideology, and in Kraus's anti-war satire this theme underwent an unprecedented intensification.[12] The crimes of the militarists led Kraus to renounce his conservative sympathies, and during the 1920s he became an outspoken critic of both reactionary Germany and clerical Austria. Moreover, he began to write 'Zeitgedichte' – 'topical poems' in the Heine tradition which are difficult to reconcile with the concept of an irreconcilable antagonism between them. In theory Kraus continued, even in the 1920s, to subscribe to a traditional conception of aesthetic harmony, associated with an ontological conception of 'origin', and some of his poems can indeed be construed within this paradigm.[13] However, only about one hundred of his poems (barely a tenth of the total) fall into this category. Moreover, even his most poignant poems about love and nature, memory and death have satirical and elegiac undertones. The self-identification with the language of Goethe may enhance Kraus's persona, but it characterizes only a small segment of the poetry he published.

Rhyme, Resistance and Rapport

Kraus's theory of rhyme appears to place him and Heine in opposite camps. The conventional view is that he insists on the harmonizing function of rhyme, whereas Heine develops a poetics of dissonance.[14] His critique of the facile rhymes in 'Heine und die Folgen' is indeed taken a stage further ten years later in an essay entitled 'Von Humor und Lyrik' ('On Humour and Lyric Poetry'), which broaches the question of disjunctive rhyme. Citing a quatrain from *Deutschland. Ein Wintermärchen* ('Germany. A Winter's Tale'), he denounces Heine's 'clattering strophes':

Von Köllen bis Hagen kostet die Post	To get to Hagen from Cologne
Fünf Thaler sechs Groschen Preußisch.	you pay a Prussian price.
Die Diligence war leider besetzt	The coach was full, and so I had
Und ich kam in die offene Beichais.	to take the open chaise.

Kraus emphasizes the impossibility of forcing 'Beichais' to rhyme with 'Preußisch', condemning Heine for his 'careless handling of language' (F 577–82, 50). This discordant strophe nevertheless made such an impression that he cited it again several years later in his essay 'Der Reim' ('Rhyme'). Here the point of departure is a couplet from one of his own poems, also entitled 'Der Reim', first published in November 1916 (F 443–4, 31–2):

Er ist das Ufer, wo sie landen,	When two ideas land on the shore
sind zwei Gedanken einverstanden.	of rhyme, they reach complete rapport.

At first sight the reader might imagine that Kraus is advocating 'purity' of rhyme, but as the argument unfolds it becomes clear that his theory depends on an erotically tinged conception of resistance ('Widerstand'), courtship ('Werbung') and conquest ('Eroberung'), leading to a consummation ('Paarung'). Words, he suggests, have an inherent disposition towards rhyme, but at the same time they resist their potential 'rhyme partners', hence the 'erotics of the world of language'. The thrust towards rhyme inherent in the word 'landen' finds fulfilment in overcoming the obstacle created by the prefix '*einver*standen' (just as 'shore' has to overcome the resistance of '*rap*port'). The emphasis is on the capacity of rhyme to resolve this aesthetic tension through the transformative power of sound, which in its turn discloses an unexpected affinity of ideas. Purity of rhyme, such as that cultivated by Stefan George, results in a hollow formalism, if no tension of sound and meaning is generated and no underlying affinity revealed. Quoting a wealth of examples, Kraus pursues the implications of this theory in this finest of his essays on poetry. The erotic subtext is accentuated by lines from the scene in *Faust II* where Helena (Helen of Troy) is initiated into the mysteries of rhyme (F 757, 16):

Faust: Und wenn die Brust von Sehnsucht überfließt,
           Man sieht sich um und fragt –
Helena: – wer mitgenießt.

Faust: After the heart by longing has been captured,
           one looks round to discover –
Helena: – who's enraptured.

Kraus's theory of rhyme is simultaneously an allegory of love. We are invited to assent to a series of analogies between the tensions of poetic language and the relations between emotional partners. Not surprisingly, this whole mode of argument has been dismissed as unscientific.[15] But the erotic parallels in Kraus's poetics, like the archaeological analogies in Freud's psychology, offer imaginative insights into processes which elude rational categories. The reliance on such controlling metaphors does not prevent either author from using other analogies when the fancy takes them. Kraus also associates writing with building work and the sieving of crude materials, law-giving and religious contemplation.

There appears to be a gulf between Kraus's insistence on harmony regained and Heine's 'clattering strophes', but when we consider the arguments of 'Der Reim' more carefully, we may detect a shift of attitude. Although the tone is still hostile, he concedes that Heine's verses are occasionally 'verbally tight' ('wortdicht'). In a further allusion to *Deutschland*, he commends the effect in Caput 14 of the refrain 'Sonne, du klagende Flamme' ('Sun, you accusing flame'). He adds that in the context of satire it may even be possible to justify a forced rhyme like 'Wohlfahrtsausschuß' / 'Moschus' (from Caput 26). Such a disjunctive combination can be legitimized in so far as it is 'acoustically plausible' (F 757–8, 20 & 25).

Political Poetry and Acoustic Plausibility

The concept of acoustic plausibility illuminates a dimension of Kraus's work that has received little attention.[16] He may claim almost to be able to judge the quality of a poem 'from its graphic layout' on the printed page (F 757–8, 22), but the ultimate sanction lies with the ear, not the eye. What matters is not that a rhyme should look aesthetically pure, but that it should sound acoustically plausible. Words that look very different on the printed page are actually well adapted to his theory, since lexical divergence accentuates the semantic tension, which has to be resolved through an unexpected harmony of sound. Repudiating puristic arguments, Kraus specifically defends combinations which sound similar but are spelt differently, like 'crying and sighing' ('Tränen und sehnen'; F 757–8, 11). The decisive factor is not the shape of words but their sound. Kraus goes on to argue that even the most forced rhymes may be legitimate if they achieve 'the effect of caricature' (F 757–8, 9). This type of rhyme,

although only mentioned in passing, is as fundamental to his practice as a satirical poet as it is for Heine. The theory of harmonious rapport tells only one
side of the story. If we look more closely at Kraus's practice, we find that it
implies a kind of anti-theory of rhyme, through which any kind of cacophony
can be justified in a satirical context. In a blatant example from November
1916, the mock-heroic poem 'Elysisches' ('Elysian Fields', F 443–4, 26–7), he
ridicules the exalted pretensions of Franz Werfel and the poets of the Café Arco
in Prague:

in das Café Arco,	writers who gather in the Arco
dorten, Freunde, liegt der Nachruhm stark o	thataway, friends, lies fame, hark o

The rhyme with which the poem concludes is even worse:

wer nur am Worte reibt sich,	any poet who hypes it
wird gedruckt bei Drugulin in Leipzich.	gets printed by Drugulin in Leipzig.

When reproached by Werfel for publishing such trash, Kraus responded by
developing a theory of satirical rhyme – not as harmonious rapport, but as a
'forbidden consensus' between two ideas. The aim (he explains) is to confront
the crude colloquialisms of the Prague poets, which are permeated by Jewish
jargon, with their literary pretensions. Add in the distorting effect of Saxon
dialect, and 'Leipzich' can even be made to rhyme with 'reibt sich' (F 445–53,
137–40). In his satirical verse, with its undertones of parody and caricature,
Kraus is thus prepared to deploy the most contrived rhymes and blatant dis-
junctions. On the printed page they look just as forced as any rhyme in the
work of Heine, with whom there are obvious parallels. Kraus's rhyme on
'Leipzich' is just as forced as Heine's 'Preußisch', while the 'Arco' / 'stark o'
rhyme echoes one of Heine's 'Zeitgedichte', in which 'Apollo' is made
to rhyme with 'toll, o'.[17]

The impact of such disjunctive rhymes is evident from a poem which Kraus
recited on 16 December 1917, as part of his campaign against fanatical German
nationalism. This 'Song of the Pan-German' was published in November
1918, immediately after the lifting of censorship, and later incorporated in *Die
letzten Tage der Menschheit* (III, 40). It exemplifies the move towards a radical
style of political poetry, using satirical rhyme to show up the contradictions of
German ideology and incorporating a childish tune to underline the irony. The
unholy alliance of patriotism, religiosity and commerce is ridiculed through
disjunctive rhymes and registers:

Ich geb' mein deutsches Ehrenwort:	This is the German's sacred oath:
wir Deutsche brauchen mehr Export.	we live for economic growth.
Um an der Sonne 'nen Platz zu haben,	To gain our own place in the sun,
gehn wir auch in den Schutzengraben.	into the trenches we must run.
Zu bessrer Zukunft Expansionen	Accepting the ensuing pains
hilft uns so unbequemes Wohnen.	will guarantee us future gains.
Einst fragt' ich nicht nach Gut und Geld,	Who cares for homely goods and chattels,
der neue Deutsche ist ein Held.	what modern Germans love are battles.
Der neue Deutsche ist ein Deutscher!	The modern German is a German!

The elevated concept of a 'sacred oath' is yoked to the mercenary ambitions of 'economic growth', just as Heine once mocked the 'German delight in quarrel' by associating it with the enormous 'Heidelberg wine barrel' ('Germanen [. . .] Haß' / 'Heidelberger Faß').[18] Kraus's radicalism is evident from the fact that in another strophe of the 'Song of the Pan-German' he even yoked the name of Goethe to a strikingly impure rhyme, forcing 'Goethen' to rhyme with 'beten' (F 499–500, 10). This sounds as sacrilegious in German as if an English poet were to rhyme 'Shakespeare' with 'fakes prayer'. Since the poetic voice in Kraus's poem (as in Heine's) is that of a pompous German patriot, the function of this kind of rhyme is clearly 'caricatural'. Kraus was to become a master of this form of facetious name rhyme, creating dozens of examples. To identify the prototype for this satirical topos, we need only turn back to *Deutschland. Ein Wintermärchen*, where Heine rhymed 'Romantik' with the names of the poets 'Uhland, Tieck'.[19] Kraus's fondness for such rhymes shows that resistance to Heine does not preclude an underlying rapport.

In the early 1920s Kraus was just as strongly committed to the creation of a new social order as Heine in the early 1840s, and his use of satirical verse was just as radical. Attacking the failure of an Austrian judge, Rudolf Wessely, to enforce legislation which prevented newspapers from disguising advertising copy as editorial comment, he even perpetrated the following:

> Daß die Presse sich vom Pressegesetz losmacht,
> kein Wunder: vis major und sechste Großmacht.
> So ungefähr reimte sichs Wessely,
> der sein Interesse jenem der Presse lieh.
>
> > (F 622–31, 21)

> The massive power of the press
> places the courts under duress.
> For this rhyme or reason, Wessely
> prostrates himself like press jelly.

This too is a poem written for performance – Kraus read it in public on 12 May 1923 in the course of his successful campaign to get Wessely's decision reversed. Although he seems to be sacrificing poetic quality to political effect, producing the 'versified journalism' which he had condemned in Heine, he defends the 'Wessely / Presse lieh' rhyme as 'pure lyric poetry'. Poetry does not depend on elevated diction, for it is possible to shape the 'image of contemporary life from the most trivial language' (F 622–31, 70–2).

Kraus claimed that 'any pile of shit' ('Kuhmist') could stimulate him to write poetry (F 561–7, 57). That this was no idle boast can be seen from a strophe from 'Luxusdrucke', a poem mocking the 'Luxury Editions' published by the Expressionists:

> Auf den Inhalt kommt es weniger an,   As to the contents, you can tell 'em
> wo die Aufmachung der Ruhm ist.   it's packaging that makes the hit.
> Man wickelt in Kaiserliches Japan   Just wrap up in imperial vellum
> den ungeformtesten Kuhmist.   the most shapeless pile of shit.
>
> > (F 472–3, 22)

Since such rhymes were designed to be aesthetically offensive, it is absurd to claim that Kraus was a purist. The assertion that he was a lifelong opponent of Heine's anarchic plays on words could hardly be further from the truth.[20] Kraus's satirical verse engages with the ideological conflicts of the 1920s through the most ingenious rhymes and puns, exploiting differences of register to accentuate his vision of an age that is out of joint. Challenging the oft-quoted axiom from Goethe's *Faust* that 'political songs are nasty songs', he defiantly builds this motif into one of his own poems (F 551, 16). His style defies both the aesthetes, who feel that poetry should be refined, and the bourgeois, who think its subject matter should be elevated. This position is neatly encapsulated in the opening couplet of the poem 'Die Bürger, die Künstler und der Narr' ('The Bourgeois, the Artists and the Fool'):

> Unter einem Künstler verstehen sie einen,
> der sich nicht abgibt mit solchen Schweinen
>
> Their view of the artist is different from mine.
> They think he should hold aloof from such swine

(F 588–94, 107)

Kraus does not hold aloof. In a select group of lyrical and elegiac poems he may indeed offer intuitions of a timeless harmony, but the bulk of his verse is unashamedly topical. Distancing himself from the folksy Austrian ethos of his day, he insists that an authentic lyric poet need not write about luminous meadows and frolicking butterflies. He claims to be able to create 'an image of divine creation' by writing about 'bedbugs' – journalists and politicians (F 743–50, 141–2).

Contemporaries like Alfred Kerr noted the Heinesque element in Kraus's poetry (F 787–94, 21), and Soma Morgenstern tried to convince his friend Alban Berg that Kraus was a 'Heine imitator'.[21] He does indeed deploy a range of Heinesque techniques that include satirical wordplay, the ironic treatment of metaphorical and proverbial expressions, a focus on food and drink as a means of discrediting idealistic cant, and the use of animal imagery to accentuate asinine behaviour. Politically, too, the two poets have many targets in common: clericalism, monarchism and militarism, antisemitism and the vagaries of Jewish assimilation, reactionary politics and romantic nationalism, social oppression and economic exploitation. The most obvious parallels can be found in their poems on the monarchy. Heine has fun at the expense of Friedrich Wilhelm IV of Prussia and Ludwig of Bavaria, while Kraus's targets are the Emperors Franz Joseph and Karl I of Austria and the German Kaiser, Wilhelm II. Where Heine transforms Frederick Wilhelm into the king of the donkeys, Kraus mocks Franz Joseph through the voice of a parrot (F 508–13, 49).

Given these affinities, it is hardly surprising to find occasional passages where Kraus praises the achievements of his predecessor. In an essay of June 1923, he explicitly acknowledges the validity of Heine's 'political outlook', which he

sees as being 'more vital than his lyric poetry' (F 622–31, 156). This suggests
that Kraus was willing to revise his view of Heine as a 'political' author – a poet
who ridiculed the 'Teutomanen' of the nineteenth century just as fiercely as
Kraus did the 'Troglodyten' of the twentieth. In this attack on their most formidable antagonists, they both use the resources of the German language to
subvert the dominant forms of German ideology. The parallel is particularly
striking in the use of forced rhyme for caricatural effect. One of Kraus's
favourite devices is to pair off familiar words with concepts of foreign origin,
like 'reward your patience' / 'through annexations' ('lohnen' / 'Annexionen';
F 474–83, 50). Such rhymes are so close to the Heine tradition that he might
well have recalled that prototypical poem from the Buch der Lieder: the satire on
a pretentious tea party which rhymes 'ästhetisch' with 'Teetisch' (comparable
to 'aesthetes' who 'eat sweets'). When Kraus alluded to this example in 'Heine
und die Folgen', his tone was dismissive (F 329–30, 16), but later we find him
developing this type of rhyme with unprecedented versatility. He may still
repudiate Heine in principle, but he certainly echoes him in practice – at times
quite consciously. The discordant rhyme on 'Jakobs Töchter' / 'Gelächter'
('Jacob's daughters' / 'mocking laughter'), which he uses in June 1923 to
accentuate the motif of the dance around the Golden Calf (F 622–31, 75), is
borrowed from a poem on a similar theme in Romanzero.[22] Kraus was aware
that such incongruous rhymes also occur in Nestroy, but the echoes of Heine
are far more unexpected.

Implicit in Kraus's acoustic theory of rhyme is the concept of poetry as
performance. During the First World War, when censorship inhibited direct
political comment, he began to write and recite satirical verse as a more oblique
means of expression. The Heine model is evident in his fondness for the quatrain with its characteristic 'abab' rhyme pattern. In November 1916 Kraus's
epigrams ('Inschriften') were still mainly composed in this mode (F 443–4,
24–5). But a year later, when he devoted a whole number to satirical verse, he
introduced sequences of rhyming couplets, exemplified by the opening lines of
'Shortages' ('Knappes Leben', F 472–3, 7):

Ich wollte in einem Kaffeehaus Kaffee;
da sagte der Kellner: 'Gar ka Idee!'
So bat ich ihn um zwei Zigarren:
da sah er mich an wie einen Narren.
Ich hatte zum Glück noch eine bei mir:
da sah er mich an wie ein Wundertier.
Nun wollt' ich sie rauchen, da brauchte ich Feuer:
da schien ich ihm vollends nicht geheuer,
er sprach: 'Ja, was fällt Ihnen ein, lieber Herr,
wo nehmen denn mir ein Strafhölzl her?'

I ordered a coffee in the café,
but the waiter's reply was simply: 'No way!'
So I asked for a couple of cigars instead,

and he looked at me as if I were mad.
Fortunately I had one to spare:
then he gave me a most peculiar stare.
Now I wanted to smoke it and asked for a light,
but the very question gave him a fright,
and he said: 'You must be dreaming, sir,
how'll the likes of us find a lucifer?'

These are lines written for performance, and Kraus recited this poem in public on 17 October 1917 before it actually appeared in print. He was beginning to revive that more dramatic form of satirical verse associated with the Viennese popular theatre.

This process of transition is registered in a letter by Ferdinand Ebner, a young Catholic philosopher who was working during the war for the Red Cross. On 17 October 1918, when Ebner attended one of Kraus's readings for the first time, the programme included 'Mir san ja eh die reinen Lamperln' ('We're innocent as fleecy lambs'). This witty sequence of fifteen four-line strophes makes extensive use of dialect to suggest that 'we Austrians' are unwilling to accept any responsibility for the war:

Im Ernstfall wär'n wir ja geschnapst,   And if we're really in the soup,
die Welt soll Österreich nicht verlieren!   why, Austria must still survive!
Drum wird, so hoffen wir, der Papst   After all, why can't the Pope
uns doch beim Wülson protegiern.   make Wilson give us an easy ride?

                                                                    (F 499–500, 13)

In a note recording his impressions, Ebner expresses some reservations, but what really captivated him was the way Kraus recited this poem: 'He imperceptibly glided over into the tone of singing a satirical song, sustaining that tone for a few lines and then abruptly breaking off and reverting to a speaking voice – that had a barely credible effect, and the end result was that I too was utterly swept away.'[23] This gift for making transitions between the spoken and the singing voice predestined Kraus to become a performer of satirical 'Couplets' in the style of Nestroy.

Topical Strophes in the Spirit of Nestroy

In May 1912 Kraus paid tribute to this Viennese tradition in 'Nestroy und die Nachwelt' ('Nestroy and his Heritage'), praising Nestroy for questioning the progressive ideologies of his day and constructing 'verbal barricades' against the onslaughts of banality (F 349–50, 16). While his linguistic sensitivity enabled Kraus to identify the qualities of Nestroy's finest dialogue, political prejudice led him to attach undue significance to a passage from *Lady und Schneider* (1849), in which the common people ('das Volk') are defined as 'a giant in the cradle' which 'wakes, gets up, staggers around and kicks everything to pieces, and finally collapses somewhere even less comfortable than the cradle' (cited F 349–50, 56). Ten years later, after the collapse of the old order, Kraus conceded that he might have 'gone too far' in dissociating Nestroy from liberalism. Citing another Nestroy passage on the aspirations of 'das Volk', he demonstrates that it was not 'anti-democratic' (F 613–21, 52–3). These discriminations reflect the more progressive conception of satire which he associated with Nestroy in the 1920s.

This reorientation is reflected in his view of *Judith und Holofernes*, described in 1912 as a 'far more significant work' than *Judith*, the play by Hebbel which inspired Nestroy's parody (F 351–3, 31). Five years later he set out in greater detail his reasons for regarding the verbally sensitive parody as superior to the intellectually contrived original. His decision to include *Judith und Holofernes* in the programme of two successive public readings in April 1917 was inspired by his sense that 'the grandiose dimensions of heroism and usury in the parody [would be] familiar to the contemporary audience' (F 457–61, 53–7 & 63). This implies a correlation not only between the vainglorious Holofernes and the bombast of German militarism, but also between the jargon spoken by Jews in Nestroy's play and that of modern war profiteers (F 457–61, 1–19). Five more years were to pass before he gave his next reading of *Judith und Holofernes* as part of a cycle of Nestroy plays presented in January 1923. Now the change of perspective was even more radical, as he distanced himself from Nestroy's mockery of the Jews for their alleged money-mindedness and lack of martial valour. Nestroy's Joab mocks 'our people' because they 'don't like fighting in wars', but Kraus commented that the waging of wars is the greatest form of cowardice (F 613–20, 42–3). His problem was how to respect the artistic integrity of Nestroy's work while counteracting its political tendency. He resolved this dilemma by composing an additional ten-line strophe which is stylistically congruent with the original but morally opposed to it. Adapting the song to post-war circumstances, he redirected Nestroy's irony against Christian militarism: 'God forbid that these murderers we should deride! / They're all of them Christians with God on their side!' ('Denn sie sind nicht bloß Mörder, Gott verhüte den Spott! / Sind doch auch Christen und glauben an Gott!'; F 613–20, 45). Shortly afterwards he borrowed words from Holofernes to satirize Mussolini (F 622–31, 5–7) – an idea that finds its visual equivalent in a costume design from the early 1920s by Harry Täuber (Fig. 42).

The satirist who had earlier been concerned to rescue Nestroy from the liberals now sensed that he might be transformed into a folksy humorist by the reactionaries. In autumn 1924 Kraus paid one of his rare visits to the Burgtheater to see *Einen Jux will er sich machen*. He was horrified to find the witty comedy devalued by slapstick designed to appeal to a 'sturdily Aryan audience' (F 668–75, 65). He went on to describe how an actor got a cheap laugh by bending down to pick up a stone and pretending to have handled a turd. Kraus questioned the slant given to the programme of the Burgtheater by its director Franz Herterich, recognizing that the appeal to an Aryan audience had antisemitic connotations. When he returned later that year to see a new production of *Lumpazivagabundus*, directed by Karl Zeska, he was quick to detect the *völkisch* undertones. The Viennese press welcomed this revival of

42   Topical Nestroy: costume design for Holofernes by Harry Täuber

Nestroy's celebrated comedy about three unemployed journeymen, Knieriem the cobbler, Zwirn the tailor and Leim the carpenter, who are tempted by Lumpazi, an evil spirit from the nether world, with wealth obtained by winning the lottery. Kraus, too, had long admired this comedy of character, especially the touches of metaphysical humour in the 'Comet Song', where Knieriem's intoxicated imagination reaches out towards the stars. But the 1924 production provoked a forty-page polemic entitled 'Nestroy und das Burgtheater', lamenting the failure to match the performances by Josef Lewinsky and Josef Kainz in 1901. Kraus's comments on that original Burgtheater production had raised questions about the casting of individual actors, especially Kainz (F 88, 21–2). But now he condemned the attempt to give the comedy an antisemitic slant – 'with a nudge and a touch of swastika'. He denounced Zeska for

presenting Lumpazi in the opening scene as a Nazi sympathizer and transforming the seller of lottery tickets into a Jewish pedlar – a caricature so crude
that it would have 'turned Hitler into a philosemite' (F 676–8, 26–7).

Kraus recalled that Zeska had introduced a similar caricature of 'Jewish'
money-mindedness into *Einen Jux will er sich machen*. The metaphysical
humour, he observed, was being reduced to the level of the *Wiener Stimmen* –
the evening paper notorious for its antisemitic ribaldry. To make matters
worse, this tendentious production was rapturously received by the audience,
and Hans Brečka, writing in the *Reichspost*, welcomed the spectacle of Jewish
attitudes being caricatured on stage. Since Brečka was the director of the
Christian Social Kunststelle, his comments carried additional weight. One of
the functions of the Kunststelle was to organize block bookings for the party
faithful, and Kraus may have been close to the mark when he observed that an
audience which appreciated this kind of humour must have consisted mainly
of Party members (F 676–8, 17–18 & 26–8). To explain the favourable notices
in the liberal press, Kraus concluded that Jewish critics, surrounded by the rap-
turous faces of members of the 'other race', must have been intimidated by 'fear
of a pogrom' (F 676–8, 7 & 19). This exemplifies his view of the theatre as an
indicator of the temperature of life. In 1917 the newly appointed director,
Max von Millenkovich, had announced that he was placing the Burgtheater
in the service of the 'Christian-Germanic ideal of beauty' – a phrase with antisemitic undertones (F 457–61, 80). Kraus felt that this tradition was being
continued by Millenkovich's successors in the 1920s, since the travesty of
Lumpazivagabundus was so obviously aimed at the 'Christian-Germanic cultural
constituency'. Turning the tables on the right-wing reviewers, he suggested
that Nestroy's subtleties were far more likely to be appreciated by Jewish
audiences than by the 'art-goys' (F 676–8, 5 & 16).

The non-Jews whose approach he questioned included his friend and biographer Leopold Liegler, who in 1924 launched a misconceived Nestroy edition
which transcribed the dialogue into broad Viennese dialect.[24] In an extended
note acknowledging Liegler's good intentions, Kraus criticized him for eliminating the tension between formal diction and the vernacular that enriches
Nestroy's dialogue. These comments deal primarily with stylistic nuances – the
linguistic 'Sunday best' ('Feiertagsg'wandl') in which Nestroy characters clothe
their discourse (F 676–8, 26). But the dispute also had ideological undertones,
as Kraus's musical accompanist Viktor Junk recalls in his memoirs. Looking
back on this episode from the perspective of the early 1940s, Junk suggests that
Kraus repudiated the attempt to transpose Nestroy into a homely dialect
because he sensed – 'as a Jew' – that the project had nationalistic implications.[25]
As a result of Kraus's intervention, Liegler's well-intentioned project was
discontinued.

Kraus mobilized the spirit of Nestroy against numerous adversaries, featuring his texts in over a hundred public readings. The first occasion when he
inserted one of his own topical strophes into a Nestroy play was during his

recital of *Tritschtratsch* in October 1921 (F 577–82, 73–4). In the following decade he enriched these recitals with almost two hundred new strophes (well over 1,500 lines) in the form of rhyming couplets rounded off by a punchy refrain. The function of these 'Zeitstrophen' is neatly defined in lines which were added to *Der Talisman* in January 1923:

> Der Nestroy'sche Geist durch die Zeiten erglänzt:
> Das zeigt sich noch, wenn sein Couplet man ergänzt.
> Was immer heut g'schieht, ihm kann nix geschehn –
> Er bietet die Spitze mit seinem Refrain.   (F 613–21, 51)

> The spirit of Nestroy transcends his own times,
> so one can augment his satirical rhymes.
> The events of today wouldn't leave him nonplussed,
> since his punchlines provide an effective riposte.

The aim was not simply to give these verses a 'topical slant', but to achieve an 'extension of Nestroy in a highly personal sense' (F 676–8, 21).

The effect of such 'Zeitstrophen' is very different from the 'Zeitgedichte' in the manner of Heine. There Kraus was speaking with an individual voice, while here he articulates the concerns of a community. The spirit of Nestroy, he insists, speaks 'out of the heart of the common people' (F 676–8, 7). Hence the divergent function of the rhyme patterns: the Heinesque rhyme tends to be spiky and unexpected, while the Nestroyan refrain is rounded, although not necessarily reassuring. The challenge arises from the ingenuity with which a disconcertingly modern theme – for example, transvestites on the streets of Vienna – is integrated with the familiar pattern. It may seem incongruous to devote several strophes to an escapologist named Breitbart, who drew crowds to the Kärntnerstrasse to watch him chewing his way through chains, but this provides Kraus with an analogy for his own performance (F 613–21, 49 & 56). The chains that enable him to dramatize his art are those of strophic form.

In 1912 Kraus had recited a passage from *Höllenangst* ironizing the concept of 'equal rights' that had inspired the Revolution of 1848 (F 349–50, 42). His reorientation after the First World War led him to foreground songs reflecting the tensions of social change. Thus in June 1922 an addition to *Der Talisman* links the refrain 'Ja, die Zeit ändert viel' ('Times ain't what they've been') to an attack on war profiteers:

> Jetzt sieht man Gestalten in unserem Wien,
> Die sind g'wiß von der Hölle direkt ausgespien.
> Bevor diese Erde in Brand aufgegangen,
> Hab'n s' irgendwo unten ganz klein angefangen.
> Jetzt sind sie obenauf und vom Felde der Ehre,
> Wo die andern begraben, beginnt ihre Karriere.
> Jetzt sitzen s' in Logen, fahren im Automobil.
> Ja, die Zeit ändert viel.   (F 595–600, 78)

In our Vienna the most ghastly sight
is figures spewed up from the depths of night.
When all over Europe the lights went out,
their business was nothing to brag about.
But when others were slain on the field of glory,
that was the start of their success story.
Now they drive to the theatre by limousine.
Times ain't what they've been.

The phrase 'our Vienna' conveys a new sense of social solidarity. Like Nestroy, Kraus directed his rhymes against the privileged classes, updating traditional refrains to take account of the latest social scandals and to challenge the reactionaries at home and abroad: ex-Emperor Karl after a restoration attempt in Hungary; Hitler and Ludendorff after their abortive Munich putsch; Admiral Horthy, the Hungarian dictator; the leadership of the League of Nations; the Austrian Chancellor Ignaz Seipel and Vaugoin, his Minister of War; disreputable Christian Social ministers like Kollmann and Ahrer; wheeler-dealers like Castiglioni and Sandor Weiss; the antisemites Jerzabek and Hartleb; and, not least, the right-wing student rowdies and Nazis with their stinkbombs.

By blending political commentary with comic song, Kraus devised a flexible mode of satire to supplement his polemics. Nestroy's satire on hypocrisy has timeless applications, and Kraus made particularly effective use of the refrain from *Der Zerrissene*: 'Sich so zu verstell'n, na, da g'hört was dazur' ('Hiding your feelings, well, that's asking things'). At a reading for the Workers of Vienna in the Hofburg on 12 November 1923, he redirected Nestroy's motif against the ambiguous policies of Chancellor Ignaz Seipel:

Wir haben einen kleinen, aber gemütlichen Staat,
Den saniert jetzt ein Kanzler, der is ein Prälat.
Als Prälat zelebriert er des öftern die Messe,
Und als Kanzler verfolgt er dasselbe Intresse.
Doch halt. . . man muß ja auch der Presse und vor allem
Den Juden, versteht sich den reichen, jetzt g'fallen.
Man gibt Gott, was Gottes, und daneben den Banken,
Was ihnen gebührt, und sie können Gott danken,
Der wieder den Kaiser erhalten soll in einer Tour.
So all's zu sanieren, na da g'hört was dazur!

(F 640–8, 109)

We live in a small but congenial state
controlled by a chancellor who's a prelate,
He celebrates mass in a manner sublime,
and his politics follow a similar line.
But wait. . . he must keep on good terms with the press,
and the Jews, if they're wealthy, require great finesse.
He gives homage to God, a free hand to the banks,
so it's really to God they should offer up thanks,

who's supposed to protect the divine right of kings.
Fixing all factions, well, that's asking things!

The dactylic lines have a lilting, songlike quality, while the metrical irregular-
ities convey an air of improvisation. These lines encapsulate Austria in the mid-
1920s: the confusion of religion and politics, the unregulated banking system,
trade-offs between government and press, ambivalence towards Jews, and a
lingering attachment to the monarchy.

This strategy climaxed in the campaigns against Bekessy and Schober, helping him to supplement personal invective with artistically orchestrated ridicule.
During a cycle of plays that included Shakespeare, Goethe and Gogol as well
as Nestroy, Kraus inserted in *Eine Wohnung ist zu vermieten* the following lines:

> Einer hat eine Zeitung, die ist interessant,
> Da gibt's kein Geheimnis, er macht alles bekannt.
> Er sagt's wie es ist, und den fettesten Lohn
> Den bringt der Skandal und die Sensation.

(F 706–11, 91–2)

> There's a man with a paper that's really appealing
> He just states the facts and it's all so revealing.
> There's simply no secret that he wouldn't print:
> through sensation and scandal he's making a mint.

These verses can be seen as perlocutionary acts within a 'total speech situation',
fusing the resources of the popular theatre with the rhetoric of criminal justice
in order to laugh the villains out of court.[26] This radicalization of the spirit of
Nestroy anticipates the political cabaret of Jura Soyfer, the communist poet
whose satires were staged in the cellar theatres of the 1930s.[27]

Kraus's renewal of popular tradition is very different from his cult of the old
Burgtheater. Instead of commemorating a culture irretrievably lost, he was
now mobilizing satirical comedy behind a campaign for social justice. In
Tritschtratsch Nestroy had used a proverbial refrain to express resigned disbelief:
'One feels one would like to sink into the earth'. Kraus's variations convey a
spirit of defiance, prompted by the massacre of July 1927 to present a bleaker
vision:

> Wir haben jetzt die Freiheit. Und das ist das Wort
> für die weitere Willkür von Raub und von Mord.
> Nie herrschte frecher die herrschende Kaste,
> nie gab's einen grimmigern Hohn der Kontraste.
> Wie die Wahrheit sie schänden, wie die Lüge sie schminken,
> da möchte vor Scham in die Erde man sinken.
> Ich hab' mich als Feind dieser Ordnung erklärt –
> [:sie hat's gehört, und sie hat sich mit Kuschen gewehrt!:]

(S 14, 217)

> Now we've got our freedom. And that's an excuse
> for robbery, murder and every abuse.

There never was such an oppressive regime,
nor injustices taken to such an extreme.
They're cheating and lying for all they are worth,
one feels one would like to sink into the earth.
This system's the target I want to attack;
[:there's no way they'll stop me from answering back!:]

The mood is no longer even remotely 'gemütlich', but the strategy is still the same: to integrate satirical protest with the values of the community.

The Educated Audience and the Wild Hunt

Although accounts of Kraus's recitals tend to emphasize his heroic isolation, the musical accompaniment invited the audience to hum along. He used time-honoured melodies by Adolf Müller and other composers from Nestroy's day, but when the original music could not be traced he drew on the support of gifted collaborators.[28] Although Viktor Junk held decidedly right-wing views, the two developed a partnership that lasted from 1918 until 1927. Responding to the rhythm of Nestroy's strophes, Kraus would declaim them with his 'admirably emphatic accentuation and drastically emphasized so-called verbal melody', and Junk would transcribe these improvisations into musical notation.[29] This collaboration left it unclear who was actually the composer, leading to a dispute when Kraus proposed to publish some of these musical settings in his volume of Zeitstrophen (1931). Reluctant to be involved in a publication that he regarded as 'anti-German', Junk applied for the return of his manuscripts, only to be informed that Kraus claimed 'authorial property of the musical idea'.[30]

A further significant contribution was made by Mechtilde Lichnowsky. The first reference to her music occurs in July 1922, after Kraus had recited songs from Der Zerrissene, Die schlimmen Buben and Die Papiere des Teufels to her settings (F 595–600, 65 & 77). Although she did not accompany him in public, they rehearsed together, and on 4 December he gave a recital of Weder Lorbeerbaum noch Bettelstab, stimulated by her musical score, which he described as a 'miracle of empathy' (F 608–12, 54). That same night he wrote to her to describe the impact: 'At the end I had to take at least 28 curtain calls – on behalf of the composer [. . .] It was one of the most beautiful evenings ever.'[31] Reviewing one of these Nestroy recitals in Prague, the critic Ludwig Steiner commended Lichnowsky's 'spiritually congenial music' (F 595–600, 74). However, her settings of Kraus's topical poems in the manner of Heine were more controversial. The most significant example was the poem 'Wohnungswechsel', in which Kraus used the theme of 'moving house' as a metaphor for repudiating the monarchy (F 551, 15). This was one of a number of poems recited on 5 October 1923 to Lichnowsky's music (F 632–9, 85). A fortnight later, he felt obliged to defend these settings against the criticisms of a 'well-intentioned' musician who felt that this music acted as a 'fetter' on the spoken word (F 640–8, 102). Lichnowsky's setting of 'Wohnungswechsel' regularly featured in his repertoire, but in April 1924 he read the poem without any accompaniment, leading the unnamed critic to assume that he had won the argument about Lichnowsky's music. Forced on the defensive, Kraus claimed that the music made an impact comparable to the carmagnole, one of the songs and dances of the French Revolution (F 649–56, 83–6).

By contrast, the texts and melodies composed to accompany the Nestroy recitals won unqualified applause both from working-class audiences and from sophisticated scholars like the Nestroy editor Otto Rommel and Nestroy's biographer Franz Mautner.[32] Even reactionary critics, writing in papers with National Socialist sympathies like the Klagenfurt *Freie Stimmen*, conceded that his versions of Nestroy were more authentic than those of the Burgtheater. Kraus responded with the suggestion that the Nazis should acknowledge that one of their despised Jewish fellow citizens – 'ein Kohnnationaler' – had achieved more for Nestroy than the advocates of the Christian-Germanic ideal (F 679–85, 87–9). The appeal of these 'Couplets' lies in Kraus's construction of a collective subject: 'we Austrians', 'our Vienna', 'the Republic', 'our freedom', and even 'the likes of us' (the vernacular 'mir'). Where Heine stood for monologue satire, Nestroy represented the dialogue of social solidarity – not simply among the characters on stage, but more significantly between performer and audience.

In 'Nestroy und die Nachwelt' Kraus had used the word 'we' negatively – to signal the breakdown of tradition and the 'retreat of the spirit' (F 349–50, 1 & 23). But his verses of the 1920s are presented in more constructive terms, as 'the reaction of the spirit of Nestroy to the circumstances of a later age' (F 595–600, 77). In March 1922, after a particularly successful recital, he reported to Lichnowsky that their setting of a Nestroy song was being sung by the 'whole of Vienna'.[33] This sense of community is the theme of the essay written in 1924 to mark his two-hundredth public reading in Vienna, 'Zweihundert Vorlesungen und das geistige Wien'. The phrase 'das geistige Wien' was usually applied to the cultural elite, including writers and journalists who were among his favourite targets. Denouncing that 'gang of intellectual fakers', Kraus reclaimed the term for the audience of his own recitals, 'proud to be able to prove that if there is any such thing as a Viennese cultural community, it is assembled here in this hall between the table on the platform and the most distant standing place' (F 676–8, 59 & 68).

Kraus printed this essay as a counterpoint to 'Nestroy und das Burgtheater', indicating that he was trying to construct a cultural community more authentic than the right-wing establishment, and he substantiated his claims by giving recitals in the Middle Hall of the Konzerthaus with a capacity of almost nine hundred. On special occasions, for example when he gave his three-hundredth public reading in the Large Hall of the Konzerthaus, there was an audience of 2,000 (F 649–56, 84) – greater than the capacity of the Burgtheater. Even the Small Hall, which he used for more intimate readings, held over four hundred people.[34] The Konzerthaus was the forum where the pressure groups of the First Republic competed for hegemony by staging public meetings, concerts and artistic events. The record of bookings for the period 1913–38 shows that Kraus's appearances were far more frequent than those of any other group or individual: he gave a total of 161 recitals in the Konzerthaus, compared with the 91 Workers' Symphony Concerts organized by the Social Democratic Kunststelle and a mere 51 events sponsored by its Catholic rival.[35]

Kraus's appearances were not normally advertised in the press and he refused to court publicity by means of complimentary tickets for reviewers. Had he announced the programme of his recitals in *Die Fackel*, the size of his audience would have been less surprising, since the magazine reached approximately 10,000 readers. But details of his recitals were recorded in the magazine only after the event, and advance publicity was handled by Richard Lanyi, whose bookshop acted as box office. Kraus had reason to pride himself on his attendances, although it was tactless to point out that, when his old rival Felix Salten announced a public reading for charity, only two tickets were sold and the event had to be cancelled (F 676–8, 65). Reading the essay 'Zweihundert Vorlesungen und das geistige Wien' on 1 January 1925, Kraus acknowledged the links with his listeners, and two years later, while remonstrating with those who showed no interest in linguistic subtleties and always laughed in the wrong place, he paid tribute to his audience for participating in a unique form of 'cultural collaboration' (F 751–6, 80).

This dynamic rapport is perceptively described by Canetti, who attended Kraus's three-hundredth reading in the Large Hall of the Konzerthaus in April 1924. He recalls that as a nineteen-year-old, returning to Vienna to study chemistry, he was sceptical about the satirist's reputation, although his friends assured him that Kraus's audience was not a 'decadent clique of aesthetes à la Hofmannsthal', but the 'true Viennese cultural community'. He should not be put off by the enthusiasm of the listeners, for Kraus had 'educated' his audience so that they were sensitive to the subtlest allusions. In the event, he felt bewildered to find himself among an audience that applauded so fanatically: 'A hall that was packed to the aisles fell under the sway of a voice whose influence persisted even when it fell silent, but the dynamics of such an auditorium can no more be described than the Wild Hunt of ancient legend'. He was so captivated that he attended approximately a hundred Kraus recitals, including no doubt the programme of 5 March 1927, which featured the ballad 'Der wilde Jäger' by Gottfried August Bürger, a dramatization of the frenzy of the hunt (F 759–65, 26). Canetti felt there was something uncanny about Kraus's ability to galvanize his audience, transforming them into a 'baying pack of intellectuals'. For him the real Kraus was 'the *speaker*', who brought to life the voices of others with compelling power, and he welcomed the 'schooling' he received from the Nestroy recitals.[36] However, his conception of the 'conscience of words' understates the importance of music, both for Kraus's dramatic readings and for his recitals of Offenbach. The satirist's reflections on the 'consonance of words and tones' presupposed a musically cultivated audience with access to a piano (F 868–72, 44).

CHAPTER 21

The Crisis of Musical Culture

The authors of inter-war Vienna included gifted performers, notably Arthur Schnitzler.[1] Kraus, by contrast, professed to be musically 'completely uneducated' (F 370–1, 18). Living through the age of Mahler and Schoenberg, he disclaimed any ability to evaluate their innovations; but members of the Second Viennese School regarded *Die Fackel* as a 'cultural beacon' and their attitude towards Kraus verged on idolatry.[2] The testimony of Schoenberg and Webern, Berg and Krenek reveals that he acted as a catalyst for a musical revolution, even though, as Krenek observed, he was a 'stranger in the land of music'.[3] An early aphorism suggests that he preferred firmer ground: 'Music washes against the shores of thought. Only those who have no ground under their feet dwell in music' (F 229, 12). Banal tunes, he implies, may stimulate brilliant ideas, but the balance is disturbed by compositions overloaded with erudition, such as the tone poems of Richard Strauss.

This argument was further developed in an essay on 'The Nature of Music' by Karl Hauer, a member of Kraus's pre-war circle. For Hauer, music reinvigorates the nervous system through the rhythm of marches, religious incantations and work-songs. It achieves more subtle effects through song settings which endow simple texts with rich layers of semantic and emotional ambiguity, so that even the average person may gain a sense of the sublime. So-called 'absolute' music, which no longer relies on the human voice, transposes ideas and feelings on to a plane of abstraction. It provides a medium through which both performers and listeners can get in touch with emotions and phantasies that would normally be censored, for example in the erotic sphere (*Tristan* or *Salome*). But Hauer warns against the narcotic consequences of an over-indulgence in music, which may tempt people to regress into a trance state. In conclusion, he endorses Kraus's idea of music that 'washes against the shores of thought': you need to stand on your own feet, if you are to resist being swept away by emotion (F 246–7, 11–19). Thus both Kraus and Hauer felt more secure in the coastal zone between the terra firma of reflection and the surge of musical feeling – the realm of song.

King Lehar and the City of Songs

Kraus may have been musically untrained, but he was able to draw on a rich repertoire of 'melodic memory' (F 649–56, 8). The Vienna of his childhood was celebrated as 'Die Stadt der Lieder', the title of the song by Oskar Hofmann which he associated with his favourite performer, Alexander Girardi (F 270–1, 3). Kraus's writings abound in musical reminiscences, from ballads learnt at school like 'Jung Siegfried wa-a-ar ein tapferer Held' to melodies churned out by the hurdy-gurdy such as 'Nur für Natur' from Johann Strauss's Der lustige Krieg (F 241, 10–11). In the changing musical tastes of his day he detected the symptoms of a more fundamental crisis, which he analysed at various levels: the evolution of operetta from Lanner to Lehar; the controversies about Mahler as director of the Vienna Opera; the scandals provoked by the innovations of Schoenberg; and the ideological implications of works by Wagner and Offenbach. Avoiding the temptation to essentialize the German passion for music (in the manner of Thomas Mann or Romain Rolland), Kraus repeatedly reminds us that musical identities are *constructed* – by choral societies and music festivals, radio and the entertainment industry.

The 'Wiener Lieder', with their celebration of transient pleasures and nostalgia for the good old days, are often regarded as 'unpolitical'.[4] But in periods of ethnic conflict and social mobility, popular music acquires ideological overtones. The composing of the 'Blue Danube' by Johann Strauss coincided with the transformation of Vienna into a modern metropolis through the construction of the Ringstrasse. The original text written for this waltz suggests that the Viennese no longer feel at home in their own city, since Jewish investors in real estate are transforming it into a 'new Jerusalem'.[5] Such prejudices tended to be subtly encoded, as in the introduction to the collection of Wiener Lieder und Tänze published under the auspices of the City Council in 1912. The editor feels that 'folksy' ('bodenständig') music is being diluted by the 'arrival of alien elements'.[6] In practice, Viennese music benefited from the migration from the provinces, which gave it a cosmopolitan flavour. Gifted composers like Franz Lehar hailed from Hungary, while it turned out that the creator of the waltz, Johann Strauss Senior, had a Jewish grandfather, a detail which the advocates of *völkisch* music were anxious to conceal.[7] Some of the most poignantly 'Viennese' songs were written by immigrants, many of them of Jewish descent, including Gustav Pick, Alexander Krakauer, Leo Fall, Paul Abraham, Emmerich Kalman and Fritz Beda-Löhner. This Austro-Jewish musical symbiosis is exemplified by Krakauer's 'Du guter Himmelvater', a ballad that portrayed Vienna as a 'paradise', much to Kraus's disgust (F 343–4, 12). A further example is Pick's 'Fiakerlied', sung by a cabbie who claims to be a 'true child of Vienna' (Fig. 43). This song with its intimations of mortality, first performed by Alexander Girardi in 1885, was felt even forty years later to epitomize Vienna, although (as Kraus observed in a gloss directed against the pseudo-religiosity of the Reichspost), 'both text and music of this folksy song were composed by a Jew' (F 697–705, 7–8).

43 'Text and music by a Jew': Gustav Pick's 'Wiener Fiakerlied'

The documentation by Robert Dachs shows how deeply Viennese culture was indebted to composers and entertainers of Jewish origin.[8] But the anti-semitic politics of Lueger left an indelible imprint, and the process of Jewish assimilation was reflected in popular song, most notably 'Der kleine Kohn', a ballad mentioned in *Die Fackel* on a number of occasions from 1903 onwards (F 137, 17):

Haben Sie nicht den kleinen Kohn gesehn,	Hasn't little Cohen caught your eye?
sahn Sie ihn denn nicht vorübergehn?	Haven't you just seen him passing by?
In der Volkesmenge	Caught up in the throng,
kam er ins Gedränge,	things start going wrong,
da hab'n Sie nun den Schreck:	now you're in a funk:
der Kohn ist weg!	Cohen's done a bunk!

The context is mildly humorous: Kohn has taken a girl out one evening to enjoy the bright lights, but he slips away after his wife appears. The bewildered girl asks a policeman: 'Hab'n Sie nicht den kleinen Kohn gesehen' – a refrain which is taken up by the onlookers.[9] This ballad was analysed at one of the first meetings of the Vienna Psychoanalytic Society. Stekel suggested that such songs provide a harmless discharge for popular resentments, comparable to the expression of anti-Czech feelings in 'Servus Brezina', but Freud took a sterner view, emphasizing the infantile character of recurrent refrains and the anger they express. The most perceptive comment (by Max Kahane) drew attention to the bonding function of popular songs, however nonsensical: 'Idiocy creates a bridge from person to person.'[10] Surprisingly, the speakers ignored the Jewish subtext, although the surname 'Kohn' was a marker of Jewish difference that had acquired a strong antisemitic charge.[11]

Kraus was fascinated by the politics of performance, seeing Vienna as a community defined by its favourite melodies and trying to identify the 'definitive acoustic expression for Austria' (F 632–9, 25). He implies that hedonistic songs from the wine-bars, like 'Jetzt trink' ma noch a Flascherl Wein', are setting the tone for a whole society, while there are numerous references to Johann Strauss, whose *Fledermaus* is recognized as a turning-point in musical history, marking a shift towards 'drawing-room operetta' (F 270–1, 12). He had a certain affection for this musical comedy with its celebration of insouciance: 'Glücklich ist, wer vergißt, / was doch nicht zu ändern ist' ('Happy is he who can forget / the things that can't be changed'). But in the post-war austerity period, cheerful chansons, like those by Ralph Benatzky and Josma Selim (F 601–7, 31), seemed less appropriate than the sober resignation of 'Verkaufts mein G'wand' (F 657–67, 68). Kraus even noted a song about women's bobbed hair – the 'Bubikopflied' (F 668–75, 116), while he felt that the double act of Hermann Leopoldi and Fritz Wiesenthal epitomized the trivial journalistic ethos of the 1920s (F 691–6, 37). At a more serious level, nostalgia for the Habsburg era was reflected by the reintroduction into the republican army of traditional military marches, experienced by Kraus as a torture (F 632–9, 20–1).

During the mid-1920s it was Fritz Löhner-Beda's saucy version of the American banana song, 'Ausgerechnet Bananen', that caught the public mood – not without justice, as Kraus observed (F 649–56, 86). For now it is the 'jazz bandits' who call the tune (F 730–1, 29), although the tinkling libretti of Brammer and Grünwald, set to music by Kalman, can also claim to express 'the tempo of the new age' (F 726–9, 31). The spectacle of male-voice choirs performing slushy songs like 'Mei Muatterl war a Weanerin' in honour of the

Austrian President made him long to emigrate (F 795–9, 17). In the early 1930s this feeling was intensified by the advent of film music, exemplified by 'Wien und der Wein' from *Der Kongreß tanzt*, described as an 'interminable, execrable song' (F 868–72, 75–6). In May 1935 Kraus composed a collage of reports of trivial musical entertainments, including a performance by the Vienna Philharmoniker of the nostalgic 'Adieu, mein kleiner Gardeoffizier', conducted by the composer Robert Stolz (F 909–11, 35–7). But even he could not resist the captivating melancholy of songs like Josef Hornig and Ludwig Gruber's 'Es wird ein Wein sein, und wir wer'n nimmer sein' ('There'll be wine and we'll be gone'). Towards the end of his life, he described this as 'the Austrian national anthem' (F 876–84, 149), indeed a distillation of the Viennese 'Weltanschauung' (F 917–22, 47).

In a period when tenors enjoyed greater public esteem than football players, musicals shaped the consciousness of a whole community. Although Richard Heuberger's *Opernball* (1898) is set in Paris, its song 'Komm mit ins Chambre Séparée' set the tone for night-life in Vienna. Kraus later claimed to have understood everything without needing to endure a complete performance (F 876–84, 124–5). The most seductive expression of Austrian identity was the work of Lehar, whose blend of folksy bonhomie and military élan led Kraus to describe him as the 'musical sergeant-major' (F 270–1, 7). He recognized that the triumph of *The Merry Widow* in 1905 marked a watershed in Austrian culture, though he was so appalled by the first production at the Theater an der Wien that he walked out during the interval. In January 1909 he set out his arguments against this new form of entertainment in the seminal essay 'Grimassen über Kultur und Bühne' ('Grimaces about Culture and the Stage'), objecting to the introduction of modern psychology into a genre which had traditionally inhabited a realm of fantasy. Lehar has created a modern form of 'drawing-room operetta', so infused with the 'spirit of the man-about-town' that its main function is to stimulate the consumption of champagne. The commercial success of *The Merry Widow* was associated with Louis Treumann, who played the role of Danilo, but who in Kraus's eyes embodied 'the dancing sales executive'. He felt that the predominance of dancing led to a loss of the verbal wit, while Lehar's lush instrumentation appeared at odds with the trivial dance routines (F 270–1, 3–7 & 12–13). He also comments on Viktor Leon, the librettist whose dialogue gives *The Merry Widow* its 'modern' flavour (F 270–1, 4–5). Like so many librettists, Leon came from a Jewish background – hence the jocular comment that 'the ghetto leads straight to the libretto'. But at least he is plying an 'honest trade', marketing his texts without claiming to be a poet, thus satisfying Kraus's principle that there should be a 'clear separation between economic and artistic objectives'. This is not the case with Hofmannsthal, whose libretto for *Der Rosenkavalier* aspires to 'literary' status (F 311–12, 49–53).

Kraus recognized that the success of *The Merry Widow* had altered 'the map of Europe' (F 313–14, 15). He insisted on the parallel between light music and atmospheric journalism, attributing to both the capacity to 'drown the suspicions of the people in music' (F 363–5, 72). Lehar carried his audience with him when he shifted in key from an idealization of Balkan folk culture ('Vinya, oh Vinya') to a glamorization of champagne-cork-popping Paris ('Dann geh ich zu Maxim'). An operetta culture glosses over logical contradictions, encouraging a willingness to dance to the music of time regardless of who is calling the tune. When the world comes to an end, Kraus observed in January 1908, orchestras in all European cultural centres will still be playing the song 'Dummer, dummer Reitersmann' ('You silly little horseman') from the *Merry Widow* (F 241, 15). The tone of his comments on light music became more astringent as localized conflicts in the Balkans signalled the approach of a larger catastrophe, defining the cultural configuration which has become known as the joyful apocalypse. In 1910 three new operettas by Lehar were playing simultaneously in Vienna, while a total of 2,200 performances of his works took place that season in the German-speaking world.[12] Kraus felt he had the 'measure of the age' when in May 1912 he came across a garbled item in a newspaper announcing a production of '*King Lehar*. Tragedy by W. Shakespeare' (F 347–8, 7). The advent of the gramophone made Lehar's tunes inescapable, and five years after the première of *The Merry Widow* songs like 'Vinya' were still being played in every late-night café (F 274, 18). 'Theatre agents are proud because they are managing the end of the world,' Kraus concluded in February 1912 with reference to Lehar's latest successes (F 343–4, 8). In December 1912 he denounced Habsburg Austria as an 'Operettenkultur' on the brink of self-destruction (F 363–5, 71); and he borrowed musical motifs from a nightclub to define the public reaction to the assassination of Archduke Franz Ferdinand (F 400–3, 8).[13] At first sight, this seems preposterous, as if George Bernard Shaw had attributed British jingoism to the productions of the Windmill Theatre. But it is relevant to recall that the word 'jingoism' actually derives from a British music-hall song of 1878, written to whip up hostility against Russia.[14] Moreover, songs like 'Keep the Home Fires Burning' helped to sustain the morale of British troops throughout the First World War, while rhythmical marches created a sense of solidarity for soldiers 'singing all together with their throats bronze-bare / [. . .] swinging on to glory and the wrath out there'.[15]

The role of Austrian popular music during the war confirmed Kraus's worst suspicions, as schmaltzy songs were exploited for political purposes. 'Draußen in Schönbrunn', the song by Ralph Benatzky and Fritz Grünbaum glorifying Emperor Franz Joseph, is cited in Act II, scene 25 of *Die letzten Tage der Menschheit* as the epitome of political sentimentality. Kraus noted that the most poignantly patriotic Austrian song, 'Österreichisches Reiterlied', set to music by Lehar, was written by a Zionist (F 418–22, 43).[16] During the year 1916, as the casualty figures mounted, he recorded with incredulity the success of Lehar's *Fürstenliebe*, a love story set in Greek bandit country, Kalman's *Csardasfürstin*, an aristocratic extravaganza set in the nightclubs of Budapest and

Vienna, and Eysler's *Ein Tag im Paradies*, which had just reached its two-hundredth performance (F 426–30, 25). Kraus's primary focus may be on Vienna, but he also notes the mobilization of popular music in support of German imperialism. It was Lehar's music that accompanied the German armies into occupied France and Belgium. Between 1914 and 1918 he composed numerous military marches and patriotic songs, notably the cycle 'Aus eiserner Zeit', dedicated to Kaiser Wilhelm II. Further Lehar songs celebrated military operations in Poland, Italy and the Carpathians, while he travelled the length and breadth of the territories controlled by the Central Powers, from Lille to Constantinople, to conduct concerts for the troops.[17] In Lille he prefaced a performance of *Der Graf von Luxemburg* with a patriotic 'song of defiance' dedicated to the Kaiser – scarcely a strategy likely to impress the French (F 431–6, 91–2). He even went to Zurich in an effort to win over the neutrals with his latest hit 'Der Herrgott lacht' ('The Lord God is Laughing') – an episode glossed with astringent irony (F 462–71, 99–101).

The war effort was sustained by a thriving nightclub industry, designed to satisfy the appetites of war profiteers and to drum up custom for callgirls. One of Kraus's most brilliant satires reviews the night-life of Berlin in 1915, creating a potpourri of snippets from songs like 'Rosa, wir fahren nach Lodz!' and 'Puppchen, mein Augenstern' (F 413–17, 11–18). Back in Vienna, the population was being diverted from the horrors of the war by a further stream of operetta productions. Between 1914 and 1918 there were an average of twenty-five premières in Vienna every year, almost as many as in the pre-war period.[18] Kraus repeatedly drew attention to this phenomenon, especially the popularity of escapist entertainments like Berté's *Das Dreimäderlhaus*, a sentimentalized version of the life and music of Schubert (F 437–42, 95). He was not the only one to see the success of works like *The Merry Widow* as a 'pathological symptom'.[19] But his distinctive achievement was to orchestrate the events of the First World War as an operetta, blending German sentiment with Austrian insouciance.

The triviality of popular music and the savagery of war are repeatedly brought together in *Die letzten Tage der Menschheit*.[20] The most frequently cited song, 'Ich hatte einen Kameraden', based on a ballad by Ludwig Uhland, forms a leitmotif, with its poignant refrain (addressed to a fallen comrade): 'In der Heimat, in der Heimat, da gibt's ein Wiedersehn'. A dozen different songs are alluded to in the Vienna Nightclub scene that forms the climax of Act III, from saucy chansons and patriotic marches to the blending of macho sexism with military conquest in 'Rosa, wir fahren nach Lodz'. The musical motifs reach their climax in Act V, scene 55, where sadistic army officers are entertained by a dance band over dinner at military headquarters. The effect of this scene can be judged from the recording made by Austrian Radio, incorporating words and music from many of the songs. 'Sag Schnucki zu mir' (from Leo Fall's operetta *Die Rose von Stambul*) forms a sprightly counterpoint to patriotic songs like 'Heil dir im Siegerkranz' and 'Die Wacht am Rhein', while references to the soldiers at Kragujevac, who were executed as mutineers, are accompanied by a spirited rendering of 'Jetzt trink mir noch a Flascherl Wein'. The retreat on the Italian front is ironized through the introduction of 'Braunes Isonzomädel', a sentimental ditty by Egon Schubert, and the drunken climax is punctuated by cheery waltzes like 'Jessas na – uns geht's guat', as the Empire collapses in ruins.[21]

In short, Kraus presents the operetta culture of central Europe in apocalyptic terms. The success of *Walzertraum* (by Oscar Straus) was one of his pre-war portents (F 261–2, 6), although Straus himself is treated gently in *Die Fackel*, perhaps because Kraus had affectionate memories of his contributions to cabaret.[22] The apocalyptic paradigm even finds its way into his private correspondence. In July 1918, after listening to a piano recital which included works by Josef Lanner, the presiding genius of Metternich's Vienna, he suggested to Sidonie Nadherny as a theme for a polemical essay: 'From Lanner to Lehar: Narrative of the End of the World' (BSN 1, 440). Not surprisingly, Kraus's account has been challenged, most notably by the historian Moritz Csaky, who defines Viennese operetta as a multicultural art form which helped to reconcile the nations of the Habsburg Monarchy. Since the genre reflected significant social transformations, Csaky concludes that Kraus was wrong to identify it with the spirit of the mindless man-about-town.[23] However, the idea of music as a means of reconciling the nations was already a cliché before the First World War. Kraus noted that Germans block their ears when they encounter the music of Dvořák or the lyrics of Machar (F 161, 14–15). The nationalists of the Monarchy, gathering with their brethren from the Reich for a 'Sängerfest' in Nuremberg, certainly feel united through song, as he observes in August 1912 under the ironic title 'Art Builds Bridges' ('Die Kunst verbindet'). But such effusions leave the Czechs and the Hungarians cold. Moreover, beer glasses are liable to start flying when Jews intone Heine's 'Lorelei', Social Democrats the 'Workers' Marseillaise' and antisemites 'Die Wacht am Rhein' (F 354–6, 34–9).

On one point, however, Csaky and Kraus are agreed: light music deserves to be taken seriously, since popular songs create a 'cultural code' which shapes the behaviour of social groups. Moreover, Csaky concedes that, after the collapse of the Empire, operetta lost its critical function and became a locus for nostalgia.[24] This is confirmed by the more detailed analyses of Martin Lichtfuss and Stefan Frey, which endorse Kraus's view of Viennese operetta as an escapist art form. Frey's study of Lehar acknowledges his innovativeness, but stresses that the operetta of the 1920s became predominantly nostalgic.[25] Lichtfuss shows that the composers of the inter-war period invited their audiences to escape into a comforting realm of illusions, exploiting the longing for a restoration of the traditional social order.[26] During that period two hundred operetta premières were staged in Vienna, including international successes like Oscar Straus's *The Last Waltz* (*Der letzte Walzer*, 1920), Kalman's *Gräfin Mariza* (1924) and *The Circus Princess* (*Die Zirkusprinzessin*, 1926), Lehar's *Paganini*

(1925), *Der Zarewitsch* (1927), *Friederike* (1928) and *The Land of Smiles* (*Das Land des Lächelns*, 1929), and Benatzky's *White Horse Inn* (*Im Weißen Rößl*, 1930). Despite the financial difficulties which confronted theatre directors in a period of increased taxation and unemployment, intensified by the competition from cinema, this was the 'silver age' of operetta. Its popularity represented the typical Viennese response to the disorientation of the post-war period and the pressures of modernity. Kraus lamented the artistic decline of operetta as a 'nightmare which oppressed his dream of a sunken theatrical world without being able to destroy it' (F 876–84, 124). But he claimed to be so attuned to contemporary music that if someone suggested to him a line like 'Mädel du, nur du', he could immediately set it to one of the current musical idioms, differentiating between the styles of Lehar and Kalman, Abraham and Benatzky (F 876–84, 125).[27]

More significant than the tinkling tunes was the underlying ideology. Since the most successful works were set in the period before 1914, they offered a musical version of the 'Habsburg myth' replete with nostalgia for aristocratic elegance and imperial glory.[28] Kalman's *Zirkusprinzessin*, which was premièred in March 1926, offered a typical example, with its idealization of the officer type – the hussar who (as Kraus put it) 'has emerged so victoriously from the World War' (F 726–9, 31). He was acutely aware of the ideological implications of this revival of a 'realm of dreams' – stirring images of infantry barracks and the annexation of Bosnia-Herzegovina (F 838–44, 54–5). Since Jewish authors were responsible for so many libretti, he felt that the culture of the Republic, no less than that of the Monarchy, was a blend of 'Emperor's beard' and 'Jewish librettist's gob' (F 876–84, 120). He was especially severe on Lehar's *Friederike*, a dramatization of the young Goethe's love affair with Friederike Brion, based on a text by Fritz Löhner-Beda and Ludwig Herzer.[29] The attempt to incorporate passages from Goethe's poems resulted in a travesty of the original (F 820–6, 50). The popularity of Richard Tauber, who sang the role of Goethe, provoked paroxysms of indignation. Attending a performance of Lehar's *Zarewitsch* in Berlin, with Tauber in the title role, Kraus felt revolted when this 'schmaltzy tenor' responded to the adulation of the audience with five encores of the love song 'Komm und mach mich glücklich'. Even before the première of *The Land of Smiles*, he was warning his readers that the worst was still to come. In 1929, twenty-five years after Lehar had resigned his original position as a military bandmaster, his music is still dismissed as 'the strains of an Austrian musical sergeant-major' (F 820–6, 51–2).

Lehar, who sensitively explored a Jewish theme in his early operetta *Die Rastelbinder* (1902), could hardly be accused of racial prejudice. His wife was Jewish, as were his most gifted librettists. After the Nazi seizure of power in Germany, he continued to work with Löhner-Beda, co-author of his last great success *Giuditta*, which was premièred at the Vienna Opera in January 1934. The Nazis, according to a report compiled by Alfred Rosenberg's office in November of that year, were scandalized by the fact that Lehar's social contacts were 'almost exclusively in Jewish circles' and his libretti, concocted by Jews, were 'devoid of all German feeling'.[30] But Lehar had an influential admirer. As a young man in Vienna, Adolf Hitler had been captivated by *The Merry Widow*, sitting enthralled through the same production from which Kraus had walked out. Hitler was fascinated by Louis Treumann's suave performance in the role of the diplomat Danilo, and Lehar's music remained one of his passions. In November 1936 the composer was summoned to Berlin to meet the Führer, and in 1940, on the occasion of his seventieth birthday, he was celebrated by Goebbels's propaganda machine as 'the master of the German operetta'. Lehar's music was given pride of place at the Nazi-sponsored Salzburg Festival, and throughout the Third Reich his operettas were continuously performed (with the names of the librettists deleted). Lehar could hardly be blamed for the fact that his realm of dreams had been overtaken by the nightmare of the Third Reich, and he considered following friends like Richard Tauber into emigration. However, Austro-Hungarian patriotism left a profound imprint on his music, and during the years 1939–45 his songs again helped to sustain the war effort. What could be more topical, his biographer asked in 1940, than Lehar's ballad about a soldier buried in an unmarked grave in Poland?[31] Meanwhile, Beda-Löhner was deported first to Dachau and then to Auschwitz, where he perished in December 1942 (the composer made unavailing attempts to save him).[32] Louis Treumann, the Danilo whom Hitler had so admired, was deported to Theresienstadt and died there in 1943; but, as Germany faced military defeat, Lehar actually displaced Wagner as Hitler's favourite composer.[33]

Kraus's critique of the era of Lehar is a blend of jokes, irony and deeper significance. He gives a differentiated account of the operetta cultures of Germany and Austria, showing that the greatest dangers arise when chauvinism and sentimentality are combined. The fundamental question, which echoes through *Die letzten Tage der Menschheit*, is why fighting men should be so inspired by melancholy songs. Kraus did not live to experience the vogue for 'Lily Marlene', the ballad about love and death that conquered the airwaves of Europe during the Second World War. But he was familiar with the 'Volga Song' from Lehar's *Der Zarewitsch* (1927), which was revived in Munich in 1941. This was taken up by German radio as the Sixth Army advanced towards Stalingrad, and Lehar's song about a solitary Russian sentinel became the anthem of doomed German youth, defending the fatherland on the banks of the Volga: 'Es steht ein Soldat am Wolgastrand, / Hält Wache für sein Vaterland'.[34]

Wagner and the Total Art Work

Kraus recognized that national identity may be shaped by both popular and orchestral music. Ironizing the pride of the Austrians in their achievements, he recalled that original composers had usually been received with incomprehension both by the public and by reviewers, notably Eduard Hanslick, the music critic of the *Neue Freie Presse*. Following the death of Hugo Wolf, the sufferings of musical geniuses inspired a satirical dialogue in *Die Fackel*, which frames Kraus's lifelong campaign against philistinism (F 131, 1–4).[35] He took the fate of Wolf seriously, defending his reputation against the insinuations of another influential critic, Max Kalbeck of the *Neues Wiener Tagblatt* (F 158, 1–13). In February 1909, after songs by Wolf had provoked a riot in a provincial theatre, Kraus stressed the need to collect such 'features from the life of audiences' (F 272–3, 35). He was sensitive to the antisemitic prejudices of the right-wing press, including the campaign against Mahler.[36] A revealing example was provided by Hans Puchstein, music critic of the *Deutsches Volksblatt*, who systematically sneered at Jewish singers while praising the performances of non-Jews. Reviewing Mahler's production of *Hoffmanns Erzählungen* in autumn 1901, Puchstein failed to realize that there had been a last-minute change in casting and that the female lead whom he extravagantly praised was Marie Gutheil-Schoder, a singer of Jewish origin whom he had earlier condemned. Kraus, who was impressed by Gutheil-Schoder in the role of Antonia, was incensed by this blatant form of prejudice (F 86, 28–9). Two years later Puchstein criticized Mahler as a conductor for failing to do justice to Wagner's *Tannhäuser* in a performance at the Vienna Opera. In fact, Mahler had been called away to give a concert in Frankfurt, and the conductor whom Puchstein condemned was Franz Schalk. No wonder Kraus ridiculed both the 'ferocious antisemite' and the efforts of German-nationalist groups to boycott the music of Mendelssohn, Offenbach and Mahler (F 149, 20–2).

Kraus lived through a period when the work of Wagner was a dominant force in public life, exerting a fascination at every point in the ideological spectrum. Wagner's mythopoeic imagination created a sense of national destiny that anticipated the politics of Bismarck, and critics of German society in the Wilhelminian period were aware of operatic undertones. 'It is scarcely comprehensible', wrote Walther Rathenau in 1918, 'how completely the previous generation succumbed to the spell of Richard Wagner. [. . .] The Wagnerian gesture was the expression of a kind of primitive theatrical pageant of virtue.'[37] In Austria the composer became a cult figure in both progressive and nationalistic circles. Even Theodor Herzl succumbed, although Wagner was notorious for his hostility towards the Jews. Notable converts to Wagnerism included Otto Weininger, who was taken at the age of seven to a performance of *The Flying Dutchman* – a detail which is noted in *Die Fackel* (F 169, 12). For Weininger, Wagner was the greatest artist in the history of mankind, partly because he created in Siegfried the 'least Jewish' figure imaginable.[38] Wagner's music dramas appeared manly and dynamic, setting up heroic ideals of conquest and self-sacrifice, and Austrians with an inferiority complex responded ecstatically to his rituals of salvation. This resulted in a 'Dionysian' form of politics – an irrationalism that fused national pride with artistic inspiration.[39]

Mahler made his reputation as director of the Vienna Opera through his full-scale versions of Wagner operas, including the productions of *Tristan* and

The Flying Dutchman which so impressed the young Hitler during his first visit to Vienna.[40] Kraus was among those who welcomed Mahler's appointment, emphasizing the success of his *Lohengrin* in May 1897 and commending the energy with which he committed himself to reforming the opera (FS 2, 69 & 142). But he remained immune to the lure of Wagner's music, and the production by Mahler which he himself recalled with special pleasure was Offenbach's *Hoffmanns Erzählungen* (F 632–9, 78). Looking back over his career towards the end of his life, he recalled that when he was taken to a Wagner performance as a child, he had fallen asleep. In his list of 'diseases of childhood' which he miraculously escaped, Wagner features together with Marx, Nietzsche and Freud (F 890–905, 46 & 279). His resistance was strengthened by the writings of the Viennese satirist Daniel Spitzer, who published a series of glosses ridiculing Wagner's pretensions. For Kraus, these captivating satires showed how Wagner's art initiated 'an age of delusion' (F 912–15, 6). Kraus had had an opportunity to observe the Wagner cult at first hand, since around 1900 he had enjoyed close contacts with Houston Stewart Chamberlain, one of the champions of the cause. At Chamberlain's invitation he visited Bayreuth, but returned to Vienna unconverted.[41] He respected Wagner's artistic commitment, but the references to the composer in early numbers of *Die Fackel* remain cool and detached. The picture is complicated by the fact that he shared Wagner's hostility towards the commercialization of art and the undue influence of the press. In November 1902 he quoted a substantial passage on this theme from Wagner's *Gesammelte Schriften und Dichtungen*, an edition which may well have been in his library (F 122, 5–7).[42] However, Wagner's music dramas failed to measure up to Kraus's criteria for dramatic verse. In December 1906 he criticized Wagner's alliterative internal rhymes ('Stabreime'), ironizing the 'Wagner religion' and the 'incense-laden' atmosphere of the Festival Theatre (F 213, 21). In an irreverent allusion to the Wagnerian concept of 'music of the future', he suggests that a more down-to-earth equivalent would be 'unpleasant noise' (F 370–1, 36).

For Kraus, one of Wagner's flaws was his treatment of relations between the sexes. The cult of manliness epitomized by Siegfried, which Weininger so extravagantly admired, is anathema for the satirist, while he has grave reservations about Brunnhilde, the ideal of Germanic womanhood. In May 1908 Kraus set out his objections in an aphoristic analysis of Brunnhilde's declaration to Siegfried from the Prologue to *Götterdämmerung*:

'How would I love you, valiant hero, did I not send you forth to new deeds!' This is the voice of Wagner's woman. Such an attitude must surely diminish the hero's desire both for deeds and for woman. For the desire for deeds arises from the desire for woman. She should inspire not deeds but love: then the deeds will follow. (F 254–5, 33)

Kraus was doubtless aware of passages in *Tannhäuser*, *Lohengrin* and *Parsifal*, as well as the *Ring* cycle, where the heroic male forswears sexual love in order to dedicate himself to great deeds. He sees this as the wrong kind of action: vainglorious male heroics unrefined by sensuous femininity. The eroticism of *Tristan*, which so appealed to Thomas Mann, is ignored in this account, but the thrust of the argument is clear. Rejecting that puritan strain in Wagner that so appealed to Weininger, Kraus celebrates sensuous experience as the source of creativity, assigning to women the inspirational role in a bisexual universe.[43]

As a child, Kraus was immunized against Wagner's music by a healthy dose of Offenbach (F 890–905, 46). In poems like 'Jugend' (F 462–71, 182), he recalled the operettas that were revived in Vienna during the 1880s, including *La Belle Hélène, La Grande Duchesse de Gerolstein, Barbe-Bleue* and *La Princesse de Trébizonde*, together with Audran's *Gilette de Narbonne* and Lecocq's *La Fille de Madame Angot*.[44] His passion for Offenbach has been analysed in a fine monograph by Georg Knepler, one of the musicians who accompanied his recitals. This book contains valuable documentation, but it fails to engage with the significance of the Wagner–Offenbach antagonism. Kraus introduced the contrast between the two composers in his seminal essay 'Grimassen über Kultur und Bühne' (January 1909). For Kraus the function of music is 'to alleviate the rigidity of life, to bring refreshment to the rational mind and through relaxation to reactivate the processes of thought'. The operettas of Offenbach create 'realms of irrationality which stimulate the imagination' (F 270–1, 8–10). True operetta makes a conscious merit of its artificiality as an aesthetic form, and Offenbach is invoked to deflate the pretensions of the Wagnerian 'Gesamtkunstwerk' – the synthesis of the arts. In opera, Kraus argues, conspirators who sing become absurd because they take themselves so seriously; their solemnity is at odds with the fact that they are singing. In operetta, by contrast, the singing is sanctioned by the self-conscious irony of the genre. It is Offenbach who succeeds in creating the authentic 'Gesamtkunstwerk', in which action is integrated with song. By contrast, 'the devotional exercises of a Wagner opera are a theatrical absurdity' (F 270–1, 9–10). Returning to this theme almost twenty years later, Kraus again applied Wagner's favourite concept to Offenbach. The texts by his librettists Meilhac and Halévy may appear trivial, but their 'music-theatrical' flair constitutes the essential element in a 'Gesamtkunstwerk' (F 757–8, 43–4).

Kraus also sensed the political dangers, quoting a passage about Wagner by André Gide: 'Germany has perhaps never created anything so great and at the same time so barbaric' (F 244, 9). A systematic study has shown that imperialist rivalries impinged so strongly on the concert halls that 'national identity was being fought out on musical terrain'.[45] Wagner was among the cultural heroes invoked by Hermann Bahr to justify German military expansion in autumn 1914 (F 423–5, 41). The German mobilization, he claimed in another passage cited in *Die Fackel*, was exactly like 'a Richard Wagner score: complete ecstasy combined with complete precision' (F 706–11, 32). Like Rathenau, Kraus was aware of the ideological significance of the concept of 'Nibelung loyalty' ('Nibelungentreue'). This phrase was coined by Chancellor Bülow in a

Reichstag speech of 29 March 1909 to denote the bond of loyalty linking Germany with Austria-Hungary.[46] This seductive myth conflated the ethos of the *Nibelungenlied*, a medieval epic of conquest and love, with the passionate emotionalism of Wagner's cycle of music dramas, *Der Ring der Nibelungen*. The figure of Siegfried, Wagner's paragon of manliness, is fundamental to the cult of martial valour which forms a leitmotif of Kraus's anti-war satire. In January 1917 he attributes the food-shortages to an obsession with 'Nibelungen' and 'Valhalla' (F 445–53, 118), and his indictment of imperialism in January 1919 describes the Kaiser's ideology as a 'Gesamtkunstwerk', shaped by the Wagner operas he had attended at the Königliches Schauspielhaus (F 501–7, 9). Wagner remained a cult figure for German nationalists, and in October 1923 Kraus noted that arias from *Tannhäuser* continued to inspire reactionaries in the Tyrol (F 632–9, 27–8).

There is one aspect of Wagner that Kraus appears to ignore – his anti-semitism. He was doubtless familiar with the notorious tract 'Das Judentum in der Musik' ('Jews in Music'), since his satire on the failure of German-speaking Jews to achieve complete acculturation echoes Wagner's arguments. Wagner also asserted that music composed by European Jews is shallow and superficial because they have no roots in the national community, while true art is nourished by the instinctual life of the people ('das Volk').[47] Kraus too alludes to the Jewish milieu from which some of the most successful Austrian composers emerged, including Erich Korngold, the child prodigy whose ballet pantomime *Der Schneemann* was performed at the Imperial Opera in October 1910. Since he was the son of Julius Korngold, Hanslick's successor as music critic of the *Neue Freie Presse*, Kraus was convinced that the composer's success was due to his father's connections (F 313–14, 1–4).[48] Such comments echo Wagner's view of the undue influence exerted by the press over musical life, but in one fundamental respect their views diverged. Kraus argues, not that Jewish composers and writers lack roots in the people, but that they have assimilated too completely to the ethos of sybaritic Vienna. His position is thus quite distinct from the organized campaign against Jewish art which developed during the late nineteenth century, as a result of Wagner's legacy. The aim of the Jubiläumstheater, set up in Vienna in 1898 under the patronage of Karl Lueger, was to promote authors and composers of 'Aryan' descent and create an ensemble 'free of Jewish influence'. The programme of this theatre is recorded in a memorandum by its first director, Adam Müller-Guttenbrunn, published in *Die Fackel* in November 1903 (F 146, 12–21). Although Kraus had some sympathy with this challenge to the cultural establishment, he ridiculed the whole idea of an 'antisemitic theatre' (F 146, 10–11). The problem with 'Aryan' art, he observed, is that it is generally so inferior to the works by Jewish or foreign authors denounced by the nationalists (F 146, 18). He found these works far more entertaining than the Aryan alternative, repudiating the attempt to exclude Jewish artists as the 'excrescence of brains paralysed by party politics' (F 147, 5–6).

For German nationalists from Wagner onwards, it was Offenbach who represented 'Frenchified' and 'Jewish' art in its most insidious form. In 'Eine Kapitulation', a satire written in 1870 to celebrate the defeat of France, Wagner sneered at him in crude rhyming couplets as 'Jack von Offenback', whose music goes 'Krak! Krak! Krackerakrak'. And in another context he described the warmth of Offenbach's music as 'the warmth of the dunghill: all the pigs of Europe were able to wallow in it'.[49] He went on to argue that admirers of 'calamities à la Offenbach' had succumbed to a 'purely Jewish form of musical beauty'.[50] For Kraus, however, the spirit of irony was the source of Offenbach's appeal. He never developed the antithesis between Offenbach and Wagner into a systematic theory, and, after the Nazi seizure of power in Germany, he repudiated the suggestion that his primary intention was to denigrate Wagner. At the same time he made it clear that he regarded Offenbach, not Wagner, as 'the greatest music-dramatist of all times' (S 12, 46). Nietzsche was the first to see Offenbach as the most effective antidote to the genius of Wagner.[51] Kraus took this argument further, celebrating Offenbach's gift for undermining heroic myths by means of erotically charged musical fantasies with feminist undertones. Moreover, he also helped to inspire one of the most radical musical explorations of women's sexual power, Alban Berg's *Lulu*.

Musical Ideas: From the Harmonielehre to Lulu

Kraus's influence was greatest where it was unintended, but he failed in his conscious attempts at patronage. He particularly admired the 'Dafnis-Lieder', a song cycle by Herwarth Walden based on poems by Arno Holz, even arranging for the composer to give a private recital during one of his visits to Vienna. While claiming to know nothing of musical matters, he made repeated efforts to promote Walden's music, enlisting his contacts with Schoenberg, Zemlinsky and the music publisher Emil Hertzka, and suggesting the mezzo soprano Marie Gutheil-Schoder for a performance of Walden's songs. When Kraus printed the text and music of a Schoenberg song in *Die Fackel* (F 300, 9), he intended it to be accompanied by Walden's setting of a poem by Else Lasker-Schüler. In July 1911 he published a laudatory review of Walden's ballet *Fiametta* (F 326–8, 48–9), and his 'love' for Walden's music is repeatedly stressed in their correspondence.[52] Distancing himself in June 1912 from the artistic programme of *Der Sturm*, he still singled out the 'Dafnis-Lieder' for special praise (F 351–3, 53–4). But by that date Walden, ignoring his advice, had opted for a career in literature and the visual arts.

It was the School of Schoenberg that owed Kraus the most significant debt, even though he disowned their innovations. Early in 1909, after the scandal provoked by a performance of Schoenberg's string quartet, *Die Fackel* published an Open Letter in which the composer defended his position (F 272–3, 34–5). While supporting the principle of artistic experiment, Kraus distanced himself from Schoenberg's work in a letter to the composer dated 26 January 1909.[53] A concert conducted by Schoenberg in March 1913, which included

Alban Berg's 'Peter Altenberg Songs' and Webern's aphoristic 'Six Pieces for Orchestra', proved so provocative that members of the audience disrupted the performance. Even Schnitzler, who attended the concert with his wife, regarded Berg's songs as 'absurd' (AST 31 March 1913). Kraus responded by condemning the philistinism of the protesters, while reiterating that he understood nothing about music (F 374–5, 24). However, in 1911, when Schoenberg completed his *Harmonielehre*, he presented a copy to Kraus with the handwritten dedication: 'I have perhaps learnt more from you than one ought to learn, if one is to retain any independence.'[54] The annotated volumes of *Die Fackel* that survive in Schoenberg's library show that he was an attentive reader, but, while he saw himself as a 'student of Kraus', he prided himself on his own 'aesthetic discoveries'. Towards the end of his career, in a note written in California in June 1940, he recorded that despite certain disagreements he had always regarded Kraus as a 'truly great man'.[55]

The implications of Kraus's theories for Schoenberg have been elucidated in an article by Alexander Goehr, which is centred on the concepts of 'musical logic' and the 'musical idea': 'We may think in words', Schoenberg wrote, 'and obey the rules for the combining of words, and equally we may think in tones and obey the rules for the combining of tones.'[56] Such passages bear the imprint of Kraus's thinking, but Schoenberg's attitude was based on a fruitful misunderstanding. He took Kraus's theory of language to imply that 'form' may become autonomous in poetry and in music, just as colours become autonomous in abstract painting. In the *Blue Rider Almanac* of 1912 he made this point explicitly: 'When Karl Kraus calls language the mother of thought, and Wassily Kandinsky and Oskar Kokoschka paint pictures, the objective theme of which is hardly more than an excuse to improvise in colours and forms and to express themselves as only the musician expressed himself until now, these are symptoms of a gradually expanding knowledge of the true nature of art.'[57] Alluding to the proposition that language is 'the mother, not the handmaiden, of thought' (F 288, 14), Schoenberg takes this to imply that language has its own system of rules which generate meaning autonomously; but for Kraus this impersonal model of creativity coexists with a more traditional conception of authorship. Language may be the mother of thought, but it takes a 'thinker' to make her pregnant (F 300, 17). However, Schoenberg and Webern derived from his writings an aesthetic of autonomous form, in which music was stripped of merely decorative elements, and this misconception inspired compositions generated by the 'logic' of musical language, anticipating the minimalism of the 1970s. Wagner's mistake, according to Schoenberg, was to place 'drama in the foreground', achieving musical greatness against his own intentions. 'The natural reaction against Wagner, the theatre-musician,' he continues, 'produced a flowering of so-called absolute music.'[58]

The concept of 'absolute music' did not preclude an alliance with texts, and Schoenberg played with the idea of a composition based on Kraus's visionary satire 'Traum ein Wiener Leben' ('Viennese Life as a Dream'; BSN 1, 367). But it was Webern who composed the most significant settings of Kraus poems. During his early phase, Webern was influenced by the concept of a timeless 'origin', as expressed in Kraus's poem 'Zwei Läufer'. The double movement of this poem with its unexpected reversals became linked in his mind with the transcendent realm of memory. 'Reminiscence', he explained in a poignant letter of 23 April 1914 to Schoenberg, 'is not a look back, it is a look into the timeless, from where it is also forward towards the "origin". (That is a wonderful idea of Kraus. He speaks so often of the "origin".)'[59] This mystical conception is reflected in Webern's fondness for palindromic structures, in which the 'reversibility' of the materials (as Krenek observed) suggests 'a mysterious possibility of circumventing the one-way direction of time'.[60] Webern combined this quest for timelessness with a quasi-mystical love of the Austrian landscape, and his settings of poems by Kraus are suffused with religious associations. In his setting of 'Wiese im Park' (Opus 13, completed in 1917) he uses both harp and glockenspiel to accentuate the paradisiacal timbre of Kraus's lines. This forms part of a series of songs on the theme of the lost 'Heimat' which includes texts by Georg Trakl. Webern also wrote musical accompaniments for the most ontological of Kraus's nature poems, 'Vallorbe', highlighting the luminosity of Kraus's lines about the 'sheer blue' of the creation; and for the verse monologue 'Vision des Erblindeten', in which a blinded soldier is comforted by his mother's touch and the devastations of war are miraculously assuaged.[61] His manuscripts include three further sketches based on poems by Kraus: 'Flieder' ('Lilac'), 'Mutig trägst du die Last' ('Boldly you carry the burden') and 'In tiefster Schuld vor einem Augenpaar' ('Deeply indebted to a pair of eyes').[62]

Webern's interest in Die Fackel can be traced back to 1909, although his early comments were sceptical: 'This Kraus! Professional satyrist! [. . .] With hooves and horns!'[63] It was the world war that led him to take the satirist more seriously, and Kraus's ideas subsequently became absorbed into his theorizing. In the early 1930s, when he delivered his celebrated lectures on atonal music, Der Weg zur neuen Musik (The Path to the New Music), Kraus is again cited as an authority. To elucidate abstract conceptions of musical form, Webern takes as the starting-point the theory of language advanced in Kraus's essay 'Die Sprache' (F 885–7, 1–4). He suggests that the Schoenbergian 'musical idea' follows the logic of composition, just as according to Kraus the 'verbal idea' is generated by the logic of language. In his second lecture, however, Webern recalls Kraus's early suggestion that music should not be overloaded with ideas, but 'washes against the shores of thought'. Although claiming to revere Kraus, he sees this proposition as a 'problem', since it suggests that Kraus 'is quite incapable of imagining that music can have an idea, a thought, hidden in it'.[64] Webern is evidently quoting from the selection of Kraus's aphorisms published in Sprüche und Widersprüche.[65] If he had read the aphorism in the original number of Die Fackel, he would have realized that Kraus's primary target was not musical modernism, but the programmatic compositions of Richard Strauss (F 229, 12). The 'shores of thought' in Webern's work are far more abstract, and his late compositions have been aptly described as 'landscapes of the mind'.[66] In contrast to the melodramatic orchestration of Strauss, Webern's serial technique conveys abstract patterns with exceptional economy. The idea that his music puts time into reverse lies behind the quip attributed to Schoenberg: 'If a programme is too long, add a piece by Webern.'[67]

Kraus's impact on the work of Schoenberg's followers reverberates through their letters, diaries and notebooks. Webern's mystical temperament led him to respond to the nature motifs in the poetry of Kraus and Trakl in a religious spirit, celebrating in his late work an explicitly Christian idea of the 'Mater Gloriosa'.[68] Alban Berg's response led him in a very different direction – towards a musical exploration of the crisis of masculinity. His finest work was inspired not by any abstract 'musical idea', but by literary themes transposed into operatic terms. His first great success, *Wozzeck*, performed in Berlin in 1925, was based on Georg Büchner's early nineteenth-century tragedy about a soldier who is driven to distraction both by heartless superiors and by a faithless girlfriend, whom he murders in a final gesture of despair. Berg's opera, composed between 1918 and 1922, can be seen as a critique of the inhumanity of the First World War. Given his admiration for Kraus, it has been plausibly suggested that this work contains echoes of *Die letzten Tage der Menschheit*, especially in its use of the 'dance of death' motif.[69]

Berg's career culminated in *Lulu*, the opera based on Wedekind's *Erdgeist* and *Die Büchse der Pandora*. Its genesis provides the clearest illustration of the contribution of *Die Fackel* to musical culture, since both theme and structure were shaped by the ideas of Kraus and his circle. Berg's attitude to Kraus is reflected in a wealth of documentation, which has been analysed by Susanne Rode. She shows that throughout his career Berg was a dedicated reader of *Die Fackel*, regularly attending Kraus's readings. Since Berg (like Webern) was not of Jewish origin, his library has survived and his reception of Kraus's work can be reconstructed in detail, particularly as between 1903 and 1907 he kept a personal logbook with the title 'Von der Selbsterkenntnis' ('Towards Self-Knowledge'). In this he recorded excerpts from his reading, including many passages from *Die Fackel* both by Kraus and by Altenberg, Strindberg and Wedekind. *Lulu* owes its inception to the private production of *Die Büchse der Pandora*, organized by Kraus in 1905 at a time when Wedekind's play was banned by the censor.[70] Theodor Adorno, who in the mid-1920s accompanied Berg to many of Kraus's readings, testifies that the composer approached Wedekind's play 'in the spirit of Karl Kraus'.[71] Berg's interest in the satirist amounted to a lifelong obsession, which scarcely diminished in intensity between 1903, when he began to read *Die Fackel*, and 1934, when he wrote to congratulate Kraus on his sixtieth birthday. Only at one point, in autumn 1914, did his faith in the satirist falter. 'Kraus is behaving very badly,' he noted in a patriotic letter, disgusted by his protest against the war. The subsequent vindication of Kraus's position strengthened Berg's belief in the infallibility of the satirist's judgement, and by 1919 he had become a 'committed anti-militarist'.[72]

His attitude is epitomized by a comment in a letter to Webern of 14 August 1920: 'Oh the Fackel! I know it off by heart! I worship every line by this man Kraus – even if it's printed on the cover!'[73]

Kraus's view of relations between the sexes prompted Berg to devote a section of his logbook to the 'Eternal Feminine' ('Ewig-Weibliche'). Pride of place is given to a comment by Peter Altenberg about *Erdgeist*, the first part of Wedekind's *Lulu* tragedy, culled from *Die Fackel* (F 142, 19; Logbook No. 118). Berg was impressed by Kraus's idea that 'the male spirit is nourished by female desire' (F 229, 12; Logbook No.1065). He particularly admired 'Apokalypse', Kraus's visionary indictment of western civilization, and the critique of sexual hypocrisy in 'Die chinesische Mauer', which the composer read 'three times with ever increasing interest', clearly contributed to the radicalism of *Lulu*.[74] But it was Kraus's essay 'Die Büchse der Pandora' which made the decisive impact. Excerpts from this essay, first published in June 1905 (F 182, 1–14), were promptly transcribed by Berg.[75] He had already heard Kraus read the text on stage, as prelude to his production of Wedekind's play. Twenty years later Kraus recalled that memorable production, reading the text again and reprinting it in *Die Fackel* (F 691–6, 43–55). This number of the magazine, which survives in Berg's library, must have rekindled his interest in Lulu as subject for an opera. For a time, he considered Hauptmann's *Und Pippa tanzt!*, a neo-Romantic play that was drawn to his attention by Soma Morgenstern, but the impulse received from Kraus's circle tipped the balance in favour of Lulu.[76] Kraus himself supported the project by lending Berg a manuscript of Wedekind's play that had been presented to him by the author.[77]

Wedekind presents Lulu simultaneously as childlike ingenue and destructive *femme fatale*, but he leaves it unclear whether Lulu is a woman more sinned against than sinning. Does she not perhaps deserve the final retribution she receives at the hands of Jack the Ripper? This suggestion is emphatically repudiated in Kraus's essay, which interprets the play as an indictment of male attitudes towards sexuality. *Die Büchse der Pandora* is described as 'the vengeance of a male world which does not even shrink from avenging its own guilt' ('die Revanche einer Männerwelt, die noch die eigene Schuld zu rächen sich erkühnt'; F 189, 5). This reading of the play as a critique of repressive masculinity shaped Berg's libretto, which reduces Wedekind's text to about one-fifth of its original length. The characters from the tragedy lose their individuality and become – as Kraus suggested – 'types of masculinity' (F 182, 1). Berg also simplifies the structure, giving his opera a compelling symmetry. His repudiation of undisciplined emotionalism in his polemic against Pfitzner echoes Kraus's insistence on formal rigour.[78] A letter of 18 August 1924 from Berg to Webern (quoted by Douglas Jarman) shows how much he admired the symmetrical construction of *Die Fackel*.[79]

The most intriguing parallel between Kraus and Berg lies in their 'shared use of stylistic juxtaposition as a compositional technique'.[80] The structure of *Lulu* echoes Kraus's conception of a 'male world' that 'avenges its own guilt'. Berg

Gestatten Sie mir

Verehrter Herr Karl Kraus

Sie an Ihrem sechzigsten Geburtstag als den zu begrüßen, als der Sie zu Ihrem hundertsten von der ganzen Welt — auch von der deutschsprechenden und auch von der österreichisch denkenden — gefeiert werden werden : als einen der größten österreichischen Künstler, als einen der größten deutschen Meister.

In unwandelbarer Treue Ihr

Alban Berg

44   Alban Berg's setting of a line from *Lulu*, dedicated to Kraus

reduces the active male characters to six, conceived symmetrically as 'double roles'. The three men who 'avenge' the male world, destroying Lulu during the second half of the opera, are played by the same singers as the three men who die during the first half as a result of self-destructive attitudes to sexuality. Thus the role of Dr Schön, whose hypocrisy provokes Lulu to shoot him, is echoed at the end of the opera by that of Jack the Ripper. These contrasts are underscored by musical ironies that discredit the ethos of male domination.

Lulu, as the composer observed in a letter to Willi Reich, called for a 'leitmotif treatment' associated with the 'personalities which run through the work',
but in place of the cumulative emotions built up by the Wagnerian leitmotif,
he develops a network of ironic recurrences. A poignant example occurs in Act
I, scene 3, when Lulu turns the tables on her protector Dr Schön, forcing him
to write a letter breaking his engagement to another woman. As he breaks into
tears, she triumphantly sings the reprise: 'He is weeping. The man of authority is weeping!' to the music which had earlier accompanied Schön's attempt
to impose his will on her. Jarman suggests that the structure of *Lulu* expresses
'a fatalistic attitude to life'.[81] But this ignores the critical implications of Berg's
treatment of the 'feudalism of love', another phrase from Kraus's essay of 1905
which he transcribed into his logbook.[82] The man of authority weeping sub-
verts the dominance of masculinity, while Lulu retains her integrity: 'A soul in
the beyond who is rubbing the sleep from her eyes' (Fig. 44). Berg dedicated
his setting of this phrase to Kraus as a final tribute.[83]

CHAPTER 22

Offenbach and the Aryans

Although he was kept informed about the progress of *Lulu*, Kraus devoted his final years to Offenbach, whose musical comedies had made such an impression on him as a child. Indeed, he published his own adaptations of *Madame l'Archiduc* (1927), *Périchole* (1931) and *Vert-Vert* (1932). The performing rights were administered by Universal-Edition, stimulating stage and radio productions not only in Berlin, Vienna and Prague, but also in provincial cities like Essen, Düsseldorf and Cologne. Kraus carefully monitored these productions, complaining vociferously to Universal-Edition about unauthorized changes, but it was above all through his own recitals that he revived the spirit of Offenbach, accompanied at the piano by talented musicians like Otto Janowitz, Franz Mittler and Georg Knepler. He had contacts with some of the most gifted performers of his day, from Egon Kornauth, founder of the Vienna Trio, to Friedrich Hollaender, creator of the film music for *The Blue Angel*. In all, he worked with forty different musicians, a number of whom were composers in their own right.[1] Since Kraus did not own a piano, rehearsals would take place at the home of the accompanist, at the beginning of his nocturnal work schedule. Although he could not read music, he had (as Mittler recalls) an 'uncanny skill' that enabled him to sing any melody once he had heard it played on the piano, and Knepler confirms that he combined 'natural musicality' with a 'phenomenal memory'.[2]

Double-Tonguing and Role Reversal

Between February 1926 and April 1936 Kraus gave over 120 recitals of works by Offenbach, who overtook Shakespeare as the leading figure in his repertoire. During rehearsals the accompanist would take him through the musical score, and Kraus was able to perform complete operettas with only the text in his hand (Fig. 45). A total of fourteen Offenbach operettas were committed to memory in this way, and on one occasion he achieved the extraordinary feat of performing a cycle of seven different operettas on successive evenings

45   Kraus reciting Offenbach: sketch by Alfred Hagel

(F 811–19, 59). He gave the first of his Offenbach recitals in February 1926, when his struggle with Bekessy was approaching its climax, and in 1929, during his campaign against Schober, he gave no fewer than thirty such recitals. His passion for Offenbach can be calibrated against the changing political scene, and Knepler's study distinguishes three main phases. During the years 1926–9, musical motifs were actively integrated into Kraus's satirical crusade, but this was followed by a period of increasing resignation, during which Offenbach's fantasy world provided an escape from the pressure of events. Finally, in the years 1934–6, the triumph of Hitler virtually silenced this alternative musical culture, with only ten recitals in the last phase.[3]

   Kraus saw Offenbach as a kindred spirit, and his sense of the 'timelessness' of the operettas did not prevent him from making topical connections.

A programme note by Ernst Krenek, quoted in *Die Fackel* with approval, suggested that Kraus found in the figures of Offenbach 'unchanging prototypes of human behaviour' (F 864–7, 15). Thus the German Kaiser is identified as a caricature of Bobeche, the pompous potentate in *Barbe-Bleu* (F 657–67, 28), while Schober finds a multitude of musical reincarnations (F 781–6, 105–21). It was the link with Schober that led Kraus to describe the parade of the booted policemen, which forms the climax of *Les Brigands*, as the greatest of Offenbach's finales. In his eyes *Les Brigands* with its anti-militarist motifs was a 'Schober-Operette', and he was delighted to find anticipations of his satire on the Police Chief's obsession with 'duty' in *Les Bavards* (F 811–19, 81, 97 & 99). Offenbach represented 'a philosophy of life which provokes revulsion among the cave-dwellers' (F 811–19, 102). In his programme notes, the ideologies challenged by Offenbach are clearly defined: antisemitism, clericalism and the Christian-Germanic ideal (F 800–5, 64).

Kraus's scattered comments on this genre cannot be condensed into a coherent theory, but his attitude is framed by the contrast he drew in 1907 between the self-conscious art of Offenbach and the portentous solemnity of Wagner. Building on the scattered observations in *Die Fackel*, it is possible to draw up a series of tabular oppositions in the manner of Brecht's 'Notes on Mahagonny', in order to bring out the archetypal opposition:

Wagner's music dramas	*Offenbach's operettas*
passionate emotion	playful humour
audience swept away	audience stimulated to thought
mythological heroes	satirical types
nationalistic	cosmopolitan
prejudice against Jews	pride in Jewish origins
cult of military valour	satire on militarism
manliness	femininity
problematization of sexuality	celebration of erotic experience
music intensifies the text	music ironizes the text

Thematically, the contrast is clearest if we set the heroic Siegfried (Fig. 46a) against the satire on militarism in *Les Brigands* (Fig. 46b). To pinpoint Offenbach's irony, Kraus adapts from musicology the word 'double-tonguing' ('Doppelzunge') – the technique used by players of wind instruments to facilitate rapid note-repetitions. This concept is used to highlight the subtleties of Offenbach's *La Vie parisienne* (*Pariser Leben*): 'the inimitable double-tonguing of this music, which says everything simultaneously in a positive and a negative spirit, betraying idyll to parody, mockery to lyricism' (F 757–8, 47).

This argument is set out most forcefully in 'Offenbach Renaissance' (April 1927), the essay in which Kraus contrasts stage revivals of the French composer's works with the standards set by his own adaptations and recitals, reiterating his view that the combination of Henri Meilhac and Ludovic Halévy's witty texts with Offenbach's dazzling music forms an authentic

46   Martial valour: costume designs for (a) Wagner's *Götterdämmerung* (b) Offenbach's *Les Brigands*

'Gesamtkunstwerk'. By contrast, the artistically distinguished music of Johann Strauss in *Die Fledermaus* has no rapport with the operetta's prosaic text (F 757–8, 40–6). In a period dominated by patriotic music, Kraus's defence of the cosmopolitan Offenbach acquired political significance. In autumn 1927 a group of right-wing fanatics, infuriated by Kraus's campaign against Schober, threatened to disrupt one of his recitals of *Madame l'Archiduc*. He responded with a polemical essay contrasting the spirit of Offenbach with the ideology of German nationalism. Punning on the similarity in German between the words 'Arien' and 'Arier' ('arias' and 'Aryans'), he condenses this polemic into the incisive insight: 'There are no Offenbach Aryans' ('Es gibt keine Offenbacharier'; F 806–9, 56). These prophetic words were to be confirmed after Hitler's seizure of power, when Offenbach's works were banned in Germany and the composer was condemned as 'morally depraved' by contrast with the 'healthy, native music' of Johann Strauss.[4]

It may seem surprising that Kraus, who regarded the operettas of Strauss and Lehar with such distaste, should have praised Offenbach so extravagantly. But his claim that La Vie parisienne is artistically superior to Die Fledermaus has been endorsed by more systematic historians of the genre, who have shown how contrived the Strauss operetta is compared with Offenbach's sparkling celebration of the voice of the people. The reasons for Kraus's preference become even clearer when we recall the contrasting treatments of militarism by the two composers. In Der Zigeunerbaron (1885), Strauss uses militaristic motifs to create a spurious sense of Habsburg unity, based on patriotic and paternalistic values. Hungarian martial music is used to whip up recruitment fever, and civilians are transformed into fighting men to the refrain of 'Komm zu den Husaren'. The antithesis is provided by Offenbach's La Grande Duchesse de Gerolstein (1867), which exploits the principle of inversion to subvert all systems of oppressive authority, especially the military.[5]

The most prominent feature in Offenbach's dramaturgy, as Knepler has shown, is 'social role-reversal'.[6] Simple people are transformed into aristocrats and carry off their new identities with panache, providing a source of hilarious comedy and subversive social criticism. It is clear that Offenbach's sympathies lie with the underprivileged, like the servants in La Vie parisienne who pretend to be aristocrats in order to entertain visitors from Sweden, Baron and Baroness de Gondremark. The satire, by contrast, is directed against those in authority: the courtiers in Barbe-Bleu toadying to King Bobeche or the jingoistic General Bumbum in La Grande Duchesse de Gerolstein, a work that appealed to Kraus through its 'mockery of a world of militaristic delusions' (F 757–8, 45). These comments show how consciously Kraus exploited Offenbach's musical comedy in order to ridicule his own contemporaries.

The distinctive feature of his recitations of Offenbach (as of Nestroy) was his delight in adding topical verses, and some of his sharpest insights are formulated in this melodic medium. Schober as Bumbum chortles with delight as he 'hacks them all to pieces' in an Offenbachian reprise of the events of July 1927.[7] The courtiers in Barbe-Bleu prostrate themselves at the feet – not of King Bobeche – but of stock-exchange speculators, press barons and venal ministers of finance. Kraus adds to Offenbach's repertoire a whole gallery of rogues and villains: socialists and clericals, journalists and blackmailers, Nazis and Heimwehr commanders. In this world of musical marionettes we encounter Schober and Bekessy, Seipel and Hainisch, Krupnik and Castiglioni, Starhemberg, Papst and Pfrimer, Kerr and Lippowitz, Krupp and Thyssen, Reinhardt, Toller and Piscator. If their power cannot be broken by polemics, then at least they can be discredited by the recital of satirical songs. Kraus regarded these topical verses as an integral part of his oeuvre, printing many of them in Die Fackel and publishing a selection in book form.[8]

Kraus valued French operetta for its critique of an unjust social order based on male domination. Hence his fondness for Lecocq's La Fille de Madame Angot, a musical satire set among Paris market workers who triumph over their oppressors under the leadership of the indomitable Clairette. In January 1928 he adapted motifs from one of Clairette's songs to satirize Schober (F 781–6, 54 & 112–13). His favourite Offenbach characters are social outcasts who combine feminine charm with a resolute spirit that enables them to triumph over adversity, like the impoverished street singer who is the heroine of *Périchole*. This critique of patriarchy is prominent in the works he adapted for stage performance. His version of *Madame l'Archiduc*, in which the waitress Marietta assumes political authority, was performed in half-a-dozen different cities. Offenbach's heroines, even in a socially insouciant work of this kind, have a knack of imposing their will, but like Marietta they intervene with such melodic delicacy that few of their male counterparts can resist. Even more significant was Kraus's adaptation of *Périchole*, staged in March 1931 at the Kroll Opera in Berlin, with a programme note by Walter Benjamin emphasizing the topical implications (F 852–6, 25–7). One of the rehearsals was attended by Brecht, who watched with a stony face, sceptical about the claim that women make the world go round: 'Um Frauen, um Frauen / Alles sich dreht' (to quote Kraus's version of the chorus; S 13, 186). At this point in the rehearsal Brecht reportedly 'raised a finger and said very severely: "I contest that thesis." Kraus and Brecht looked at each other and suddenly both burst into laughter.'[9]

With the aid of his gifted librettists, Offenbach created a world in which women displace men as prime movers of the social and emotional action. This is evident in the works Kraus recited most frequently: *La Vie parisienne* (twenty times), *Barbe-Bleu* (fifteen), *La Grande Duchesse de Gerolstein* (fourteen), *Madame l'Archiduc* (thirteen), *Perichole* (thirteen), *Les Brigands* (ten), *Les Bavards* (nine) and *La Princesse de Trébizonde* (eight). The very first operetta he recited, *Barbe-Bleu*, sets the tone for this subversion of masculinity. Bluebeard, who has already poisoned five wives, has designs on Boulotte, a simple peasant girl, but she turns the tables on him, rescuing the other five wives – for Bluebeard has been deceived and they are not really dead. They dance their way to freedom in a triumphant finale that discredits one of the darkest myths of male domination – a blend (as Kraus saw it) of 'authentic horror and romanticism' (F 270–1, 9–10). This displacement of masculinity is reflected in the language of Kraus's adaptations, as well as their themes. In passages of self-reflection he stresses the qualitative difference between the rigour of formal German and the 'deeper mysteries of words entwined with music' (F 845–6, 35). He regarded the adaptations as an essential part of his oeuvre, paying tribute to the 'eternal value' of the original texts by Henri Meilhac and Ludovic Halévy, not for their literary qualities, but for their integration with the music. This 'melodic magic' creates what he calls 'the other sphere' ('die andere Sphäre'), in which conventional causality no longer applies, since it is governed by the 'logic of the irrational' (F 757–8, 43–6). It may seem fanciful to compare Kraus's 'other sphere' with Musil's concept of the 'other condition', but the ideas of the two authors are moving in similar directions: away from the universe of male rationality towards an emotional utopia that transcends gender differences.[10]

This subversion of causality is reflected in the language of Kraus's adaptations, which take liberties with German syntax that he would never have permitted himself in other contexts. He particularly admired the letter aria in which Périchole explains why she has to be unfaithful to her beloved Piquillo, but his rendering of the French libretto has been criticized for being too obviously a translation.[11] The following lines may serve as an illustration:

Ich fühl, wie dich schmerzt dieses Schreiben.
Was ich tue, ich kann nichts dafür.
Ich werde die Deine stets bleiben
Im Innern – das glaube mir. (S 13, 157)

I know you'll be hurt by this letter,
For my deeds I'm not really to blame.
But the things that essentially matter,
Trust me, will be always the same.[12]

Here Kraus's disruption of conventional syntax forms part of a conscious aesthetic strategy (he was so proud of this aria that he included it in the final volume of *Worte in Versen*).[13] It is only from the perspective of formal grammar that the word order is faulty. Writing within the 'other sphere' of Périchole's discourse, he freely infringes the linguistic conventions he defends so fiercely in his 'Sprachlehre'. In the introduction to his edition of *Madame l'Archiduc* he notes that German versification is 'more ponderous' than French (S 13, 9). Hence his readiness to waive the rules of syntax in order to adapt his linguistic medium to the playfulness of the French librettists' rhymes and the delicacy of Offenbach's rhythms. The facility of French, which he had repudiated in his pre-war writings, was now a quality to be emulated, and he no longer insisted that a writer of German had to be a 'real man' (F 329–30, 7). Conscious of the destructive effects of a specifically masculine language of command and control, he sympathized with Périchole's view that men are stupid: 'die Männer sind Idioten!' ('que les hommes sont bêtes!'; S 13, 194 & 247). Thematically, he affirmed Offenbach's 'satire on authority' (F 845–6, 9), while stylistically his adaptations enabled him to introduce a precocious element of *écriture féminine*, liberated from the constraints of logical control and deterministic causality.[14]

Kraus's revival of these satirical operettas made an impact in other quarters. When he recited *Barbe-Bleu* in Berlin on 25 March 1928, he was surprised to see the most powerful theatrical impresarios of the day in the audience, Alfred and Fritz Rotter (F 811–19, 66). The following year, when the Rotters staged *Barbe-Bleu* at the Metropole Theatre with Leo Slezak as Bluebeard and Käthe Dorsch as Boulotte, Kraus was prompted to attend by his 'longing to hear Offenbach's music played by an orchestra' (F 827–33, 42). He cherished *Barbe-Bleu* for its captivating 'mixture of styles' (F 811–19, 107), but the crudity of this Berlin production led him to feel that his efforts to promote an Offenbach renaissance had been in vain (F 834–7, 21–3). He found Reinhardt's grandiose production of *The Tales of Hoffmann* – with 35 soloists and 112 dancers – particularly disappointing (F 868–72, 6), and could not refrain from hissing from his seat in the stalls during a performance of Walter Mehring's adaptation of *La Grande Duchesse de Gerolstein*, directed by Karlheinz Martin. Kraus insisted that a 'north German version of Offenbach is a contradiction in terms', since this form of musical satire can be re-created only 'in the traditional style of the Paris and early Viennese operetta'. His own recital of *La Grande Duchesse* in Berlin on 12 January 1932 was designed to rehabilitate the work (F 868–72, 6 & 38–43).

There is some dispute about the musical quality of Kraus's recitals, since their appeal lay in the use of 'spoken song'. For purists, this mixed mode was unacceptable, and Paul Amadeus Pisk, the Schoenberg pupil who became music critic of the *Arbeiter-Zeitung*, argued that Kraus's 'Sprechgesang' lacked melody and rhythm, so that in purely musical terms the effect was 'very inadequate'. Against this we must set the testimony of three other members of Schoenberg's circle, Eduard Steuermann, Alban Berg and Rudolf Kolisch, who responded with an adulatory open letter. After praising the 'purely musical effect' of Kraus's recitals, including his rendering of the Frascata Letter Aria and the duet of Brazilian and Glove-Maker in *La Vie parisienne*, Steuermann observes that in operetta 'the unsung word may also be an essential part of the music' (F 811–19, 91–3). In conventional terms Pisk may have been right, but he failed to recognize the affinity between Kraus's 'Sprechgesang' and the aesthetic of dissonance which Schoenberg had pioneered in *Pierrot Lunaire*. Here, too, the soloist was instructed to speak, rather than sing the words – a challenging task, as Erika Stiedry-Wagner recalled in her account of rehearsals at the Society for Private Musical Performances: 'Singing is easy but to speak this way is very difficult.'[15]

In the work of Offenbach, the technique of double-tonguing corresponds to the double action – domestic servants masquerading in *La Vie parisienne* as ladies intoxicated with champagne (F 757–8, 47). An impression of this technique can be formed from the surviving recording of Kraus performing the Frascata Letter Aria in the voice of Metella the courtesan. To modern ears Kraus's singing voice is more beguiling than his polemical declamations.[16] In this aria, Frascata's memories of the days when he enjoyed Metella's favours become entwined with his appeal to her, in a letter which she reads out, to give his friend Gondremark an equally good time when he arrives in Paris. This exemplifies what Kraus most admired in Offenbach's art – its tongue-in-cheek quality. Femininity and irony go hand in hand, with the female voice mellifluously articulating male expectations in Kraus's poignant rendering. We simultaneously hear Frascata *speaking* (formulating a request) and Metella *singing* (her reprise of his memories) – an exemplary instance of 'double-tonguing'. No wonder Walter Benjamin cited this concept in his review of Kraus's performance, observing that he 'speaks the inner music rather than sings it'. The combination of lyricism and mockery transformed Metella's song into a 'requiem'.[17]

Operatic Politics: From Richard Strauss to Ernst Krenek

The corollary to Kraus's passion for Offenbach was his resistance to grand opera, and he made no secret of his scepticism about the composer hailed as Wagner's successor, Richard Strauss. In 1919 Strauss was appointed director of the Vienna Opera, a position which he held for six years, adopting a cautiously revivalist policy. Hofmannsthal, his friend and collaborator, suspected that Strauss was likely to put the interests of his own work above those of the institution – a hunch that was confirmed by events.[18] But the fact that the most famous living German composer had taken up residence in Vienna elicited acres of press coverage. In 1924, to mark his sixtieth birthday, the Austrian authorities presented him with a building plot in the Belvedere Gardens, so that he could construct a town house (in addition to his country residence in Bavaria). Kraus was incensed, launching into a forceful attack when Strauss took advantage of his position at the Opera to stage a work of his own with a characteristically Viennese flavour, *Schlagobers* (*Whipped Cream*).

Strauss's two most ambitious works of this period, the ballet *Schlagobers* and the opera *Intermezzo*, were based on texts by the composer himself, and this placed him in the satirist's field of fire. The première of *Schlagobers*, staged as part of the composer's birthday celebrations, took place at the Opera on 9 May 1924. The theme of the ballet was scarcely original. A boy preparing for confirmation is taken to a fashionable cake-shop in the Kärntnerstrasse and allowed to consume quantities of delicacies. As the boy sinks into an uneasy slumber, the cakes miraculously come to life, performing a succession of exotic dances with symbolic undertones. The climax is reached when a group of uncouth biscuits from the suburbs invade the city centre and start a revolution (the boy is suffering from indigestion). The revolt is finally suppressed by a flood of Bavarian beer. Kraus was evidently well briefed, since he comments on an episode that was removed before the first night. According to his analysis, the revolutionary activities of the mob were to be led by 'intellectual matzahs' – wafers of unleavened bread – implying that Jewish agitators are responsible for working-class discontent. Thus Kraus traduces the composer for his anti-semitism, as well as his disparaging treatment of the working class. The beer motif implies that Strauss expects 'all political salvation from Munich' – a reference to the beer-hall politics of Hitler. Kraus responded with a diatribe about the composer's face, familiar through countless press photographs: those shifty eyes, that clipped moustache, this 'face that expresses a whole new Germany of the Will to Power and skilful packaging, of boom before the collapse'. The composer is a 'high-class apocalyptic horseman' (F 649–56, 54–6). Kraus acknowledges that he is unqualified to pronounce on the musical merits of *Schlagobers* (one of the most meretricious of Strauss's compositions).[19] But satirical intuition led him to identify the composer with the new – authoritarian – Germany. During the Schubert Festival of 1928, Strauss shared with conservatively inclined friends like Hofmannsthal his ideas about the 'need for a dictatorship'.[20] Five years later the composer was to meet his nemesis as president (from 1933 to 1935) of the Reich Chamber of Music, with Furtwängler as his vice-president. For attentive readers of *Die Fackel*, Strauss's support for the Nazi cause would hardly have come as a surprise. When Strauss and Furtwängler raised their right arms, Kraus observed after Hitler's seizure of power, they were not about to conduct a concert (S 12, 164).

In December 1924 *Die Fackel* carried an equally stinging attack on *Intermezzo*, which had been premièred in Dresden in November. Strauss based his libretto on motifs from his private life – his stormy marriage to the singer Pauline de Ahna and her fit of jealousy on discovering that he had received a letter from a Berlin prostitute asking for opera tickets. The platitudinous plot provided Kraus with another field-day, and he ridiculed the dialogue between husband and wife, thinly disguised as Herr and Frau Storch. The composer portrayed himself as long-suffering husband, his wife as an embittered shrew. Worse still (in Kraus's eyes) was the episode about the prostitute, whose real-life identity was disclosed through leaked reports to the press. The Mietze Meier of the opera, members of Strauss's circle explained, was based on a 'lady of easy virtue' named 'Mietze Mücke, Berlin, Lüneburgerstraße 5'. Kraus was appalled by the salacious gossip, having actually met Mietze Mücke many years earlier, and far preferred her to the Strauss clique (F 668–75, 133–6).[21] He was by no means the only commentator to find this whole episode distasteful.[22] The furore about *Intermezzo* coincided with the news that Strauss was resigning as director of the Opera. For the critic Max Graf, this meant the departure of 'Vienna's greatest intellectual phenomenon'. Denouncing this view (F 668–75, 17–18), Kraus read his critique of *Intermezzo* from the stage of the Konzerthaus.

After Strauss's resignation in 1926, the new director of the Opera, Franz Schneiderhahn, introduced a more avant-garde programme. The sensation of 1927 was *Jonny spielt auf* (*Jonny Strikes Up the Band*), an experimental work by Ernst Krenek. The plot hinges on the contrast between Max, a white European composer, and Jonny, a black jazz musician. Max is conceived as an inhibited European intellectual, while Jonny is a child of nature who rejoices in his attractiveness to white women. The opera provoked strong reactions through its vivid stage-set, incorporating telephones, loudspeakers and a railway engine. Although not strictly a jazz opera, it uses jazz motifs to establish Jonny's character and accentuate his sexual potency. The Leipzig première in February 1927 proved such a success that the work soon went into production in Vienna. When it opened on 31 December, conservative critics argued that such a vulgar modern work had no place on the stage of the Opera House. Austrian Nazis reacted even more forcefully, disrupting performances with stink-bombs and organizing a mass meeting on 13 January in protest against 'artistic bolshevism'. Their poster denounced a 'racially alien gang of commercial Jews and freemasons' for reducing the Vienna Opera to 'a public convenience for their Jewish-Negroid perversities' (Fig. 47). Kraus responded at a public reading of 9 February with an acid comment (F 781–8, 87), and on

47   Nazi poster denouncing the production of Krenek's *Jonny spielt auf*

at least four occasions he condemned the Nazi protests in topical verses.[23] Demonstrations against the alleged 'negro take-over of the Opera', he explained, betrayed the same primitive mentality as the Aryan hostility to Offenbach (F 806–9, 56).

American jazz was perceived as an even graver threat than Offenbach. Paris in the 1920s was the centre from which the new music flowed, but it was Berlin that became the European capital of jazz, provoking a reaction which blended aesthetic arguments with xenophobia. In nationalist circles, hostility towards jazz was intensified by the presence of troops from Senegal during the French occupation of the Ruhr, which was seen as part of the Jewish conspiracy to defile the Aryan race by exposing German maidens to African hordes. The Jews were also blamed for the spread of jazz – an allegation linked with the success of *Showboat*, the American musical that presented black performers as heroes. Although Kraus had no ear for syncopated rhythm, he was one of the spiritual fathers of Jonny the jazz musician, for Krenek, like Berg and Webern, was a dedicated reader of *Die Fackel*. In 1923 he was introduced to Kraus, whom he regarded as his greatest teacher, effusively acknowledging his influence.[24] After he returned to Vienna in October 1928, the links between them became closer and more creative. However, his memoirs fail to mention the most significant debt: the link with *Jonny spielt auf*. The contrast between black vitality and white effeteness forms a leitmotif in *Die Fackel*, and even during his most conservative phase Kraus condemned western prejudices against blacks. The desire to 'string the niggers up', because white women find them sexually attractive, is seen as characteristic of the mentality of imperialism and denounced with visionary fervour in August 1912 in 'Weiße Frau und schwarzer Mann' ('White Woman and Black Man'; F 354–6, 1–4). In another early satire, 'Der Neger' ('The Negro'; October 1913), he acknowledged that he knew only two coloured people, compared with two hundred German authors – but he had no doubt which race has 'more intelligence, reliability and kindness'. His comic dialogue mocks the reactions of the Viennese when confronted with a black chauffeur, whose presence makes whites feel insecure. Taking issue with the theory that regards the 'negro' as an 'inferior being' ('Untermensch'), the satirist associates blacks with elemental 'forces of nature' (F 384–5, 42–4). This cult of the vitality of coloured people becomes a recurrent motif, culminating in the final number of *Die Fackel*, which affirms the superiority of African and Chinese culture to the barbarism of Europe (F 917–22, 82).

There are few references in *Die Fackel* to events in the United States, but Kraus makes an exception in cases of racially motivated violence. His visionary satire 'Die chinesische Mauer' (July 1909) is a response to American hysteria about the sexual potency of the Chinese, and reports about the lynching of blacks form a crucial motif in his apocalyptic panorama. In Illinois, he notes in 'Apokalypse' (October 1908), a white woman has had an affair with a negro. The consequences are transcribed from a newspaper report. A crowd of whites 'seized a negro, riddled him with bullets and strung the corpse up on a tree' (F 261–2, 6). Seventeen years later, in August 1925, he quoted a report from New York about a black man accused of a similar misdemeanour, who was 'tarred and feathered and dragged through the streets of the town astride a pole, before finally being hanged from a tree in the main square'. Such episodes inspire Kraus's frequent invocations of the non-white races as being 'naturally superior' to Europeans (F 697–705, 131–2), and he carried his campaign to the public platform. 'Der Neger' featured in nineteen public readings between 1913 and 1928, and he also repeatedly read 'Weiße Frau und schwarzer Mann'. Krenek must have been familiar with these texts, which were republished in 1922 in *Untergang der Welt durch schwarze Magie*. The connections in *Jonny spielt auf* between colour and sexuality bear clear traces of the satirist's influence, and Krenek, in a lecture of 1928, drew a similar contrast between stagnant European culture and his operatic embodiment of 'natural principle and primal force'.[25]

Kraus also ridiculed the paranoia provoked by Josephine Baker, the singer who embodied the vogue for black culture that swept Europe during the 1920s. After years of hardship as an aspiring dancer, first in St Louis (Missouri) and later in New York, she rose to fame in 1925 as star of the Paris *Revue Nègre*. Kraus had the opportunity to see her on stage during his visits to Paris in April 1926 and December 1927, and he had no hesitation in taking up her cause in 1928, when she began her tour of central Europe. Her arrival in Vienna at the end of January coincided with the scandal caused by *Jonny spielt auf*, provoking a furious reaction. Jonny, after all, was only an actor in blackface (Fig. 48a), while Josephine was there in the flesh (Fig. 48b). Christian morality and Aryan manhood were equally affronted when this coffee-coloured dancer appeared on stage, dancing in a banana-skirt (F 781–6, 88). There was a chorus of indignation from scandalized clerics in the *Reichspost*, tub-thumping Pan-Germans in the *Wiener Neueste Nachrichten* and racists in the *Deutschösterreichische Tageszeitung*. Kraus tackled these three papers during his public reading of 9 February in a scathing critique of the troglodytes, defending the divinely inspired Josephine against 'darkest central Europe' (F 781–6, 86–9).

His most eloquent response occurs in topical verses inserted in Offenbach operettas. On 11 February he slipped into a recital of *Barbe-Bleu* a line attacking the Austrian Deputy Chancellor, Karl Hartleb, for his hostility to the dancer (F 781–6, 57). He returned to the fray on 15 March, after one of the leaders of the Christian Social Party, Anton Jerzabek, had denounced Josephine in parliament, inserting in *La Vie parisienne* a telling repartee:

48 'Degenerate Music': (a) Jonny the jazz musician (cover of *Entartete Musik*) (b) Josephine Baker (illustration from *Das kleine Blatt*)

Baroness:
Das find' ich äußerst ennuyant: I certainly am not a prude,
Weil eine Negerin auftanzt nackt,   But in Vienna on the stage
Die Christen dort am Donaustrand   A negress dancing in the nude
Die sittliche Empörung packt.   Makes Christian people seethe with rage.

Joseph:
Ja die Erscheinung ist bekannt.   Bearing the evidence in mind,
Die Gründe liegen auf der Hand.   The reason is not hard to find.

Baroness:
Ich weiß, man ist gewohnt in Wien   The Viennese himself prefers

Joseph:
Die Fremden selber auszuziehn.   To rip off foreign visitors.

                                                      (F 781–6, 60)

This wittily synthesizes two characteristic attitudes towards foreigners: cupidity and xenophobia.

The Paris press had praised Josephine's 'magnificent animality', celebrating her as 'the black Venus that haunted Baudelaire'.[26] Kraus avoided these stereotypes, having met Josephine in person. A cryptic billet-doux survives, dated Vienna 1928 and inscribed in English with the words: 'For so very charming Monsieur Karl Kraus, with best wishes, sincere[ly] Josephine Baker'. This personal contact led him to praise her personal integrity, associating her with the heroines of Offenbach, who turn the tables on their male oppressors (F 788–80, 12). He was particularly impressed by her performance in one of Offenbach's less well-known works, *Die Kreolin* (*La Créole*), revived in Paris in 1934. At a time when racists were directing their most venomous abuse against 'cross-breeds', her decision to appear in *La Créole* was a courageous protest against Nazism. She was inspired by her hatred of racism, which can be traced back to a pogrom against blacks witnessed during her childhood in Missouri. Baker rose triumphantly to the challenge of Offenbach's role, even though she had never previously appeared in an operetta. A radio broadcast enabled Kraus to hear excerpts from her performance, which he enthusiastically commended (F 916, 2). This inspired him to prepare his own version of *Die Kreolin*, carefully collating earlier translations. His two recitals of this operetta, in Vienna on 11 November and 9 December 1935, constitute a final act of musical defiance, in which his cult of the French composer converged with his defence of black culture against a common enemy.

While Josephine Baker made a temporary sensation, Krenek's impact was more sustained, since he was a prolific essayist as well as a gifted composer. In 1929 he was invited by the literary editor, Friedrich Gubler, to become a regular contributor to the *Frankfurter Zeitung*, and his fine articles, accompanied by his correspondence with Gubler, have been republished under the title *Der hoffnungslose Radikalismus der Mitte*. The concept of a 'radicalism of the centre', which derives from Kraus, defines the position which Krenek defended against the extremes of communism and fascism.[27] In 1930 he produced a further work with Krausian undertones, the satirical opera *Kehraus um St. Stephan* (Last Dance around St Stephen's Cathedral), which portrays the chaos in Vienna after the collapse of November 1918.[28] As disorientated people from all social classes struggle to come to terms with the bleak post-war world, a brash entrepreneur arrives from Berlin with plans to absorb Austria into the German Reich. In a speech reminiscent of Kraus's 'Song of the Pan-German' he declares: 'First we'll smash the Poles, then we'll conquer France. [. . .] Then we'll march into Russia and put an end to Bolshevism.' Plans to stage this work at the Leipzig Opera were abandoned in 1931, since its political message was too provocative.[29]

Krenek was a politically conscious musician with a Christian conscience, and after the Nazi seizure of power in Germany he became an outspoken advocate of Austrian independence, contributing regular articles to the *Wiener Zeitung* and *Der christliche Ständestaat*. Of all the avant-garde composers of the inter-war period, he was Kraus's most vociferous supporter, and he set seven of his poems to music in a sequence entitled 'Durch die Nacht' ('Through the Night'), premièred in Dresden on 10 April 1931. After attending this concert incognito, Kraus praised the 'delicate unity of a musical–poetic art work' (F 852–6, 58–60).[30] In 1932, when Krenek, Willi Reich and Rudolf Ploderer founded their avant-garde journal *23*, it was welcomed by Alban Berg as 'a musical version of *Die Fackel*'. Kraus followed the fortunes of the journal with interest, conveying his compliments to Krenek.[31] The composer reciprocated by stressing, in an article published in *23* in November 1936, that Kraus's theory of language had anticipated the new 'musical thinking'.[32]

Krenek was at the vortex of the crisis of musical culture, which culminated in the exhibition of 'Degenerate Music', organized by Goebbels in Düsseldorf in 1938 as part of a Reich Music Festival. Richard Strauss, an outspoken opponent of atonal music, composed the Festival Prologue, hastening back from a holiday in Italy to provide a fanfare to introduce Goebbels's keynote speech. 'The fight against Judaism in German music,' Goebbels proclaimed, 'which Richard Wagner once took upon himself, quite alone, is [. . .] the never-to-be-surrendered fight of our own time [. . .] fought by a whole people.'[33] We know from Strauss's private notebooks how much he owed to Jewish colleagues: 'I have received so much support, so much self-sacrificing friendship, so much generous help and intellectual inspiration from Jews that it would be a crime not to acknowledge it with all gratitude,' he had written a few years earlier.[34] But he now became an outspoken supporter of Goebbels's policies.[35] The cover of the 'Degenerate Music' catalogue featured a black saxophonist wearing a Jewish star on his lapel. This was an allusion to *Jonny spielt auf*, even though Krenek, who was born in Vienna in 1900, came from a Christian family of Czech origin. The exhibition, designed by the Nazi musicologist Hans Ziegler, ridiculed the work of the modernists, including Schoenberg, Stravinsky, Hindemith, Korngold, Eisler, Berg and Hauer, but Krenek's popular success made him the target of particular venom. A photograph of the composer was accompanied by a caption accusing him of making propaganda in *Jonny spielt auf* for 'racial disgrace'. The centrepiece of the exhibition was a poster depicting Jonny as the epitome of 'cultural bolshevism'.[36]

Male-Voice Choirs and Barbaric Melodies

Opponents of musical modernism made a cult of choral singing. In 1843 the Vienna Male-Voice Choir (Männergesangsverein) was set up to promote 'German' singing, and its activities, which received acres of press coverage, formed a source of delightful comedy in early numbers of *Die Fackel* (F 226, 1–11). Kraus doubted whether they would succeed in spreading peace among the nations by singing songs like 'Därf i's Dirndl liaben?' (F 341–2, 9), especially as they identified themselves emphatically as 'German singers' (F 343–4, 9). The First World War intensified his scepticism. If soldiers sing on their way to death, choral singing must have a collective psychological function – as a means of obliterating the capacity for dissent. This critical view of music is suggested by his epigram on the function of the overture in the theatre: the audience is absorbed into a 'general haze' and its intellectual scruples 'overwhelmed by music' (F 472–3, 23). In *Die letzten Tage der Menschheit* he repeatedly shows how music enhances military propaganda, as the streets of Vienna surge with crowds singing the 'Die Wacht am Rhein'.

During the 1920s he intensified his focus on the politics of music, highlighting the significance of public singing. He was fascinated by the irony that both 'Deutschland über alles' and the Habsburg anthem 'Gott erhalte' were sung to the same Haydn melody. After 1918, 'Gott erhalte' was banned in Austria, since its text (by Johann Gabriel Seidl) incorporated militaristic slogans like 'Gut und Blut fürs Vaterland!' This created a vacuum, since it was difficult to devise a replacement that would command the loyalty of all factions in the Republic. Karl Renner wrote the text of a new anthem with music by Wilhelm Kienzl, but this 'Renner-Hymne' was never officially adopted as the national anthem. Kraus realized that Kienzl's tune could never displace Haydn's melody in popular consciousness, and he responded in autumn 1920 by writing his own anti-Habsburg version of Seidl's anthem, which he recited to Haydn's tune (F 552–4, 57–60). However, this anti-monarchist anthem was too negative in conception to capture the popular imagination. The lack of a national anthem reflected Austria's fractured identity during the 1920s. The Social Democrats sang not only the 'Renner-Hymne' but also 'Deutschland über alles', to emphasize their solidarity with Germany, prompting Kraus to suggest that they should stick to the 'Internationale'. The confusions over Haydn's tune, he observed in the same context, were leading Christian Socials and Nazis to sing in harmony (F 697–705, 120). Hearing this melody emanating from a pub in the suburbs of Vienna, the passer-by could only guess whether the singers were Pan-Germans or Habsburg loyalists. Kraus excelled in analysing the consequences when socialists from Klein Neusiedl tried to dissuade German-nationalist gymnasts from Schwechat from singing monarchistic songs – with musical instruments wielded as weapons (F 697–705, 123–4). Finally, in January 1930, Schober's right-wing coalition adopted a song by Ottokar Kernstock, 'Sei gesegnet ohne Ende', as the Austrian national anthem, again using Haydn's tune. Kernstock was an unrepentant militarist whose chauvinistic songs had earned him a scene in *Die letzten Tage der Menschheit* (III, 32). Kraus reacted by appealing to Social Democrats to avoid occasions when this anthem was sung (F 834–7, 44–5).

During the 1920s there were competing efforts to define Austrian identity through music festivals. The Music and Theatre Festival of the City of Vienna, organized by David Josef Bach in September 1924, provided a showcase for modernists like Schoenberg, provoking hostile responses in the conservative and antisemitic camps. The Christian Socials, inspired by the musicologist Guido Adler, replied in March 1927 with a festival to mark the centenary of the death of Beethoven, presenting him as a symbol of international reconciliation. The success of the festival could not conceal the underlying ideological tensions: the Social Democrats saw Beethoven as herald of revolutionary change, the nationalists praised his expression of German 'Volkstum', while local patriots claimed him as an Austrian – after all, he was buried in Vienna.[37] Kraus responded by quoting a laconic report from the London *Times* of April 1827: 'The file of carriages at the funeral of Beethoven, at Vienna, was said to be endless. A little more attention to him on the part of the owners, while living, would have been more to the purpose' (F 759–65, 19).

The mobilization of music reached its climax at the Tenth Festival of the German Choral Federation (Deutsche Sängerbundfest), held in Vienna to mark the centenary of the death of Schubert. The Sängerbund, founded in Nuremberg in 1862, was a nationalistic federation of Male-Voice Choirs with a total of over 600,000 members. It was defiantly male and middle-class, and its 'German' ethos had antisemitic implications – workers' choral associations were excluded, together with choirs that had female or Jewish members. About 150,000 singers, including thousands of visitors from the Reich, gathered in Vienna in July 1928, but their festival was dedicated less to the memory of Schubert than to nationalistic agitation. A wooden concert hall was constructed in the Prater with a capacity of 120,000, and a million spectators lined the streets to watch the parade.[38] Musically the festival was mediocre, but the political impact was enormous. The unity of the German 'Volk' was proclaimed by choirs 40,000 strong, as well as by spokesmen from all political parties, and a concert on 21 July was specifically designed as a 'demonstration for Anschluss'. Foreign observers reacted with alarm, and a Czech newspaper warned that Anschluss would involve 'a very different kind of music – the music of artillery and machine guns'.[39] Kraus analysed the event from the public platform in September, ridiculing the attempt to promote a 'consolidation of nationalistic feeling' by mixing beer and sausage with the music of the spheres. He found it absurd that solid citizens should spend a whole week excitedly assuring each other 'that they were Germans' (F 795–9, 15–17).

The Sängerbundfest served as a reminder that the nationalists had to be beaten at their own game. Kraus felt that if political tactics failed to discredit Schober, there might be 'no recourse other than music' (F 781–6, 106). After one of the Police Chief's admirers had composed a Schober March, Kraus responded with his 'Schober-Lied', a song about constabulary duty which deconstructs the dominant musical culture by incorporating motifs from the Radetzky March. This song, initially conceived as a musical interlude in *Die Unüberwindlichen*, was recited on numerous occasions, and in July 1928 he republished it as a broadsheet. He did not hesitate to carry his musical crusade on to the streets, aiming to flood the city with 150,000 copies of the song and establish it among the workers of Vienna as a popular ballad. When the Social Democratic bureaucracy refused to co-operate, he called on the support of the more radical Rote Hilfe, issuing a second edition of the broadsheet for the Workers' Choral Festival of August 1928. By September, approximately 19,000 copies had been sold (F 795–9, 27–9).

Kraus recognized that popular music generates compelling forms of group cohesion – an insight that is lacking in studies of Nazi music policy which focus on the concert hall, as if the debates about Hindemith, Pfitzner and Fürtwängler were the decisive factor.[40] It was Lehar, not Richard Strauss, whose music moved 'the masses', as Goebbels shrewdly observed; hence he promoted the 'musical bonding' of the *völkisch* community.[41] Music, according to Nazi aesthetics, was to be prized for its 'virility', and even Strauss was suspect – not only because of his Jewish librettists, but because his work was felt to be 'feminine'.[42] In Vienna every faction had its marching songs, from the Zionists to the Heimwehr, making an indelible impression on youthful minds.[43] Kraus sensed that music becomes a political force when it takes over the streets, and monitored these developments attentively. He noted that the Christian Socials sang the refrain 'Wir sind und bleiben christlich-sozial', while Front-line Veterans favoured the 'Seipel Anthem', composed in honour of the Chancellor (F 640–8, 19). He was shocked when the Social Democratic Schutzbund began to revive traditional marches in the spirit of Old Austria, condemning the 'renaissance of military music' (F 838–44, 66–7). In Germany, he observed, the fascists were using music even more effectively: thousands of patriotic voices sang 'Deutschland über alles' and 'Ich hatt' einen Kameraden' to welcome Hitler and Ludendorff to Nuremberg in 1923 (F 632–9, 451–3), while the Stahlhelm warmed up its audience with military marches played by its own band (F 743–50, 21). The 'Horst Wessel Lied' owed its impact to its stirring music as well as its strident text, blending the aggressive rhythm of marching feet with the lament for a fallen comrade. And Kraus did not fail to cite the most vicious of all Nazi songs, prominently featured in the Vienna election campaign of April 1932: 'When Jewish blood spurts from the knife, we all feel twice as good' (F 890–905, 183).[44]

The politicization of music was intensified by the advent of radio, and the pro-Anschluss concert staged in Vienna by the Deutscher Sängerbund in July 1928 was broadcast by radio networks throughout Germany, with a potential audience of seventy million.[45] In 1931, when the conductor Arturo Toscanini defied Mussolini by refusing to play the fascist anthem 'Giovinezza', he was physically assaulted – an event which provoked Kraus's protest both in prose and in song, contrasting the conductor's baton with the ruffian's cosh in verses adapted from Offenbach (F 857–63, 67 & 70–1). It was not only in Italy that music was being used as a means of creating fascist culture. In 1938 a German musicologist observed that the Third Reich had been 'not only fought but sung into existence'.[46] Meanwhile, Viennese musicians of Jewish origin were being deported to Nazi concentration camps, including Hermann Leopoldi, composer of 'Erst kommt Österreich', an eloquent plea for Austrian independence. He was fortunate to be released nine months later, after composing for his captors a barbaric melody that exemplifies the musical sadism of the Third Reich – the 'Buchenwald Song'.

PART SIX

INTO THE
THIRD REICH

CHAPTER 23

Twilight of Democracy

Frequent visits to Germany during the late 1920s involved Kraus in the crisis of Weimar democracy, as well as the defence of Austria. He found himself fighting a war on several fronts: 'In addition to the exploration of many artistic worlds, above all that of the divine Offenbach, in addition to the theory of language and the stimuli of everyday life, I am at the moment also [. . .] fighting against the power of the troglodytes, who after all represent the clear case of murder turned into newsprint and the possibility of newsprint turning into murder' (F 781–6, 22). The troglodytes in question were the staff of the *Völkischer Beobachter*, against whom he took legal action, securing a court conviction (F 800–5, 50). But, as he pointed out early in 1931, there was no point in trying to trap Nazi newspapers by means of literary hoaxes: Hitler had to be defeated 'politically' (F 852–6, 44). By June 1931 thugs on the streets of Vienna were wielding truncheons and screaming 'Death to the Jews!' ('Judaa varreeckee!'). If Austria was to assert its sovereignty, he insisted, two things were necessary: to bring these gangs under control (F 857–63, 6) and distance itself from the 'national madness' in Germany (F 876–84, 20). This led him to repudiate one of the main planks of Austrian policy, both on the right and on the left: the agitation for Anschluss.

A German–Austrian Communal Destiny?

Relations between Austria and the Weimar Republic were transformed by the German elections of 14 September 1930, in which the National Socialists obtained more than six million votes, winning 107 seats. From this point onwards Kraus's scepticism towards the Anschluss movement hardened into outright opposition. Since Austria was dependent on the western powers for financial credits, the government could not afford to make direct overtures to Germany, but the leadership remained committed to Anschluss as a long-term goal. Reviewing the campaign for Anschluss in 1927, Otto Bauer distinguished three main phases: the first revolutionary socialist, the second reactionary

nationalist, the third bourgeois capitalist.[1] However, in practice the three tendencies converged, creating strange bedfellows, since the Social Democrats
were just as enthusiastic as the Pan-Germans, although for different reasons. So
universal was the identification with Germany that many conservative politicians, including Schober and Schuschnigg, emphasized their solidarity with the
German 'Volk', while the only groups seriously opposed were the Habsburg
loyalists and the communists.[2] The campaigners for Anschluss ranged from
pragmatists like Gustav Stolper, who argued that an independent Austria was
not economically viable, to nationalists like Heinrich Srbik, who insisted that
Habsburg culture was Germanic. This issue undercut the polarization between
left and right, since fascist groups funded from Germany were committed to
Anschluss, whereas those supported by Mussolini were opposed. Some segments of Catholic opinion, led by Seipel, were also sceptical, but Karl Renner
and Otto Bauer were emphatically in favour. In his seminal study of the nationalities problem, first published in 1907, Bauer had used the phrase 'communal
destiny' ('Schicksalsgemeinschaft') to express solidarity with Germany.[3] The
Social Democrats, as Kraus observed, were in the absurd position of seeking
political support from countries apprehensive about the growing power of
Germany, while at the same time organizing rallies in support of Anschluss
(F 876–84, 8). Such demonstrations were held in Vienna throughout the
1920s, with vast crowds thronging the Heldenplatz.[4] Hitler's triumph in March
1938 was well rehearsed (Fig. 49).

In autumn 1930 Schober, who as chancellor had tried to steer a middle
course, formed a right-wing alliance including not only Pan-Germans and
Agrarians, but also a faction of the Nazi Party.[5] After the election of 9 November this 'Schoberblock' (with nineteen seats) held the balance of power,
forming a coalition with the Christian Socials (sixty-two seats), while the Social
Democrats (with seventy-two seats) remained in opposition. In his new role
as foreign minister, Schober now began to campaign for closer links with
Germany. Responding to the escalating economic crisis, which caused widespread unemployment in both countries, he embarked on secret negotiations
for a customs union with the German Foreign Minister, Julius Curtius. By
March 1931 discussions had reached an advanced stage, but, when the news
leaked out, there was an international furore, since the proposal undermined
the Franco-German rapprochement that had been promoted by Briand and
Stresemann. The French government exerted its political and financial muscle
to block the union, which was seen as a form of Anschluss in disguise. Austria
was financially so vulnerable that it succumbed to international pressure, but
the affair provoked a nationalistic reaction in the press, where it was claimed
that the country was being treated like a French colony. While the Nazis
exploited this surge of resentment, the Social Democrats also felt obliged to
affirm the 'Germanness' of their cause.

Kraus had been consistently sceptical about the Anschluss movement,
which he associated with German imperialism. The First World War, with its

49   Well rehearsed: Anschluss demonstration on the Heldenplatz, 1925

propaganda about fighting 'shoulder to shoulder', had left him with a rooted aversion to the Pan-German movement, and in the early 1920s he scathingly repudiated the arguments for Anschluss advanced by chauvinists like Professor Diehl in Innsbruck (F 531–43, 144–5). His attitude is clear, even when the reasons he gives are not entirely serious. While the Entente feared that Anschluss would strengthen German power, he pretended to believe that Germany would be weakened if it had to absorb a territory 'where not even muddle functions properly' (F 795–9, 17). It was not only fanatics like Diehl who accused him of maligning the German cause. In 1928 the journalist Alfred Kerr joined the chorus of denunciation, claiming during a protracted court action that Kraus was anti-German. In a legal submission quoted in *Die Fackel*, Kerr cited the 'Song of the Pan-German' as an example of Kraus's 'repulsively anti-German verses', describing it as a 'hymn of hate against Germany'. By playing the patriotic card, Kerr hoped to discredit him in the eyes of the court, but Kraus insisted that his target was German chauvinism, not the German people. How strange to find Kerr, a leftist author of Jewish origin, attempting to impress the court by presenting himself 'as patriotic German nationalist' (F 787–94, 171–6 & 200).

Kraus was an internationalist who believed in European co-operation and had a particular affection for France. Although he made a point of not joining political organizations, the International Anti-War Congress was an exception, and his name is listed, with those of Rolland, Barbusse, Gorky, Bertrand Russell, Einstein and Heinrich Mann, as a member of the committee for the Amsterdam Congress of August 1932 (F 876–84, 53–4). He welcomed the fact that Austrian rearmament was restricted by the League of Nations (F 868–72, 52) and described the ban on Anschluss as one of the few positive elements in the post-war peace treaties (F 876–84, 26). In March 1931, after news broke about the negotiations between Schober and Curtius, there was an outpouring of Pan-German enthusiasm in the Austrian press. Kraus responded with a gloss sarcastically entitled 'And Thus the Two German Brothers Stride Hand in Hand towards the Sun'. He repudiated the identification with 'German soil' and 'German being', mocking slogans like 'Grenzmark, Ostmark, Reichsmark, Blutsbrüderschaft, Singen und Sagen'. Citing the concept popularized by Otto Bauer, he ironizes those who hold forth about 'communal destiny', while behind the scenes trained economists are getting down to 'brass tacks' ('Tachles'). He also cites an effusion by Schober about 'the pulsing heart in the great realm of our German brothers' (F 847–51, 13–15). The economic crisis made Austria dependent on international credits, which blocked the proposed customs union, provoking resentment in both Germany and Austria, where Kraus detected an increasing xenophobia. In August 1931 he published an article on 'National Honour' ('Die nationale Ehre'), contrasting his own functional attitude to the state with the regressive attitudes of the 'cave-dwellers' – shorthand for the proto-fascist groups. He was shocked to see the Social Democrats joining the flag-waving – an 'abomination in the sight of the Lord'. It was Otto Bauer who claimed that Austria was being treated like one of the 'African negro tribes under the domination of the French colonial power'. Kraus countered that the Germans and Austrians were becoming so savage that they might benefit by being governed from abroad (F 857–63, 1–4).

During the following months the situation in Germany deteriorated, despite Brüning's emergency measures, and 1932 became the year of decision, especially for the beleaguered Jews.[6] Kraus's visits, which included public appearances in Berlin, Leipzig, Munich and Breslau, enabled him to judge the situation at first hand. In April 1932 he criticized both the German and the Austrian Social Democrats for their creed of 'a united *Volk* of brothers', drawing attention to the nationalistic overtones (F 873–5, 8–9). On 20 July, after Brüning had been dismissed by President Hindenburg, his successor Franz von Papen used the growing street violence as a pretext to suspend the constitution of Prussia, removing the Social Democrats from power (in Kraus's words) by means of 'a Prussian lieutenant and a couple of men from the Reichswehr'. Ten days later, in the Reichstag elections, the Nazis won a spectacular victory, with over 36 per cent of the vote and 230 seats. Kraus's judgement on the situation was unequivocal: 'all hell has been let loose' (F 876–84, 22–6). However, the Austrian Social Democrats were reluctant to abandon their German dreams. Austerlitz had died in July 1931, much lamented by Kraus, and the new editor of the *Arbeiter-Zeitung*, Oskar Pollak, lacked the integrity of his predecessor. In an editorial published during the election campaign, Pollak claimed (in a phrase highlighted in *Die Fackel*) that an 'indissoluble communal destiny unites the German working class on both sides of the border' (F 876–84, 1).

Kraus responded with 'Both Sides of the Border' ('Hüben und Drüben'), a political broadside delivered in public on 29 September to coincide with a mass Nazi rally. Emboldened by their electoral successes, the National Socialists held a 'Gauparteitag' in Vienna, culminating on 2 October with a demonstration on the Heldenplatz addressed by both Goebbels and Röhm. Sensing that the Social Democrats were playing into their hands by using the language of 'communal destiny', Kraus condemned this 'nationalistic slogan', arguing that if communal destiny were a serious principle, it ought equally to 'unite the Austrian and the French working class' (F 876–84, 22). The socialist strategy of 'muddling through' is contrasted with the immediate threat of a Nazi 'seizure of power' ('Machtergreifung'). Germany, he argues – six months before the Nazis finally seized power – is threatened by an irruption of barbarism which will lead to the demise of freedom. The outcome will depend on the speed and violence of Nazi tactics, since compromises may weaken their momentum. But socialist intellectuals still tremble with emotion when they hear the word 'Deutschland', and the mentality of Marxist theoreticians is reduced to the level of an 'inscription on a beer mug' (F 876–94, 6 & 14). They are dreaming of a socialist Greater Germany, when what is needed is resolute resistance. When the *Arbeiter-Zeitung* claims that the German working class is invincible, Kraus points out that it has capitulated 'without resistance'. He was dismayed that Carl Severing, the Prussian Minister of the Interior, allowed himself to be removed from office by a detachment of three soldiers, implying that the Social Democrats should have responded to Papen's coup by calling a general strike. Since the Prussian government had at its disposal a police force of 90,000 men, together with trade unionists and other groups committed to the defence of the Republic, some historians have seen Severing's capitulation as a disastrous failure of nerve, while others argue that resistance would have been useless, given the refusal of the communists to support a popular front.[7] Kraus offers a different interpretation, attributing the failure to the patriotic ethos of the German Social Democrats, inculcated during the First World War. It is their 'pride as military veterans' that inhibits them from opposing Papen and the Hindenburg clique. On this point at least the Austrian Social Democrats have a better record: under the leadership of Austerlitz, they had challenged the power of 'military judges and the general staff' (F 876–84, 22–9).

Kraus paints a grim picture of Germany under the shadow of Nazism, where 'people pass through life doing the goose-step and would rather be dead than not be slaves'. The situation is so scary that it would be preferable for Austria to be 'colonized by France' (F 876–84, 12). The Austro-Marxists had often chided the Christian Socials for their half-heartedness towards Germany, but after the Nazi triumph in the Reichstag election of July 1932 the boot was on the other foot, since opposition to Anschluss could be presented as a defence of democratic values. However, the socialists had tactical reasons for maintaining their pro-German stance. At the Lausanne Conference of July 1932 the new Chancellor, Engelbert Dollfuss, had secured a loan designed to stabilize the Austrian economy, conditional on the renunciation of union with Germany. When he returned to Vienna, he faced stormy debates in parliament, as he struggled to pass a package of painful measures that included a ban on Anschluss. In their efforts to unseat the coalition government and force a general election, the Social Democrats made common cause with their antagonists, the Pan-Germans, and on 17 August this unholy alliance came within an ace of winning a motion of no confidence.[8] This subordination of socialist principles to a Pan-German agenda led Kraus, in his declaration of 29 September, to accuse the Social Democrats of 'cowardice towards the enemy within' (F 876–84, 29).

The Enemy Within

National Socialism did not march into Austria in jackboots. Although there was an intermittent use of terror tactics, the dominant strategy was 'gradual infiltration'.[9] Put more bluntly, Austria was betrayed from within as a result of the German sympathies of leading politicians and the intrigues of closet Nazis. Kraus grasped the nettle in October 1927 when he drew attention to a long list of fascist organizations located in a government building and asked the public prosecutor to intervene (P 1, 81). Thus he was fully justified in inverting the concept of the enemy within, so often directed against socialists and Jews, and applying it to those who were undermining the independence of Austria. His documentation shows that the Nazi mentality filtered in through the most obscure cultural networks: choral societies and church parades, veterans' associations and gymnastic clubs, lecture theatres and school textbooks, military memoirs and writers' associations. The success of Austria's footballers – the 'Wunderteam' – may have given a much-needed boost to national pride.[10] But the athletes of the 'Deutscher Turnerverband', as Kraus repeatedly noted, were a threat to democracy. The process of 'newsprint turning into murder' was exemplified by the *Deutschösterreichische Tageszeitung*, which gleefully reported suicides by displaced eastern Jews under titles like 'Oh, if only they all did the same!' (F 838–44, 137). The problem, in Kraus's eyes, was the vulnerability of public opinion, and in countless glosses he exposes the susceptibility of the newspaper-reading public to nationalistic slogans. In December 1926 he summed up his position in the provocative words: 'If the *Neue Freie Presse* were to be taken over by the Nazis, the oldest subscriber would not allow his morning ritual of reading the editorial to be disturbed' (F 743–50, 158).

The fundamental danger derived from creeping fascism. Kraus's prime example is the Kulturbund, a cultural association founded in 1922 by Karl Anton Rohan, an aristocratic follower of the German philosopher Hermann Keyserling. Kraus's comments on the proceedings of this circle, which brought avant-garde poets together with unfrocked aristocrats, are scathing from the start (F 608–12, 23–5). In October 1923, glossing an article by Rohan in the *Neues Wiener Journal*, he drew attention to the dangers lurking behind the pretentious philosophical discourse, highlighting a remark about intellectual leaders of European youth like Artur Zickler being '*Fascists in their thinking*' (F 632–9, 138–42). When Rohan and Zickler attended Keyserling's School of Wisdom in Darmstadt, an event recorded by a woman reporter in fulsome detail, Kraus drew attention to the 'swastika' which she 'failed to notice' (F 640–8, 123). Rohan's barely concealed fascist sympathies did not prevent him from developing the Kulturbund into the leading cultural organization in Vienna, attracting subsidies from both German industrialists and the Austrian government. Although allegedly non-political, the association numbered many of the conservative elite among its members, including Hofmannsthal, Seipel, Wildgans, Schreyvogl and Srbik. Its programme featured eminent speakers from abroad like Martin Buber, Friedrich Gundolf, Paul Valéry, Leo Baeck, Thomas Mann and André Maurois. But by the mid-1930s, while still banking government subsidies, Rohan had become a member of the illegal Nazi Party, in cahoots with Papen to undermine the independence of Austria.[11]

Kraus denounced the 'force of a hybrid intellectualism' (F 781–6, 22): the writers, journalists and demagogues who conspired to make right-wing movements intellectually respectable. It was a sign of the confusion of the age that right-wing ideologists even tried to enlist Goethe in their cause. From the *Deutschösterreichische Tageszeitung* of 20 March 1932 he cited an article by Mirko Jelusich, an 'aesthete of the Swastiklers' admired by Mussolini, even though he had written a story advertising a brand of beer.[12] In this article, Jelusich claimed that Eckermann's *Conversations with Goethe* showed that Goethe would joyfully have joined the war against the French in 1812, if he had been a younger man. To refute this misreading, Kraus cited further passages in which Goethe distances himself from the war and praises France as one of the most cultivated nations on earth. Thus Jelusich was deceiving his 'völkisch' readers in claiming that Goethe shared their values, when the poet actually condemned national hatred as a feeling that occurs 'on the lowest levels of civilization'. The culture of Goethe definitely does not lead 'into the third Reich' ('ins dritte Reich'; F 873–5, 33–5).

Kraus was adept at dealing with pseudo-intellectuals like Jelusich, who was soon to emerge as one of the most prominent Austrian Nazis.[13] Fascism was not only the province of uneducated troglodytes, since the universities were a breeding-ground for antisemitism, especially in Vienna, where there was a large contingent of students from the German Reich, many of them fanatical Nazis.[14] The failure of the universities to resist the militancy of racist students is repeatedly condemned in *Die Fackel*. Discrimination against members of an ethnic or religious minority was prohibited by the Treaty of Saint-Germain, but this did not prevent the Senate of the Technical University from trying to exclude Jewish students by means of the 'numerus clausus' quota system.[15] Kraus responded in January 1923, during a Nestroy recital, with lines mocking the racist agitation: 'Now numerus clausus is making the news, / which means universities want fewer Jews!' ('Vom Numerus clausus ist viel jetzt die Red', / das heißt auf deutsch: weniger Juden für die Fakultät!'; F 613–21, 56). Academic life was continually disrupted by antisemitic demonstrations, and in January 1924 Kraus alluded to the German campaign against Einstein, noting that in Austria, too, the Christian Socials were incapable of 'imagining an Einstein without a kaftan'. The universities welcomed donations from Jewish benefactors, while poisoning the atmosphere with their protests against impoverished Jews who actually wanted to study (F 640–8, 137–9). In a characteristic riposte, Kraus observes that eastern Jews may have more feeling for the German language than the nationalistic professors who are trying to exclude them (F 640–8, 153). In February 1930 he reprinted a report of violence at the University medical school by cockade-wearing Heimwehr supporters: 'The cockaders first tested out their valour on women, who were beaten up and thrown down the stairs. Then, armed with pieces of the banister, clubs and knives, they attempted to storm the lecture theatre.' Since the victims included students from England and America, he contrasted this with a second report describing a reception by the America–Austria Society, with speeches about Viennese hospitality towards students from abroad (F 827–33, 43–4).

Racism on campus was nourished by reactionary attitudes among schoolteachers. The Nazi Party numbered many educators among its members, notably Richard Suchenwirth, a teacher from Carinthia who joined the Hitler faction after one of the many splits in the Austrian Nazi Party.[16] In July 1924, during one of his sorties into the realm of the *Deutschösterreichische Tageszeitung*, Kraus's eye was caught by the programme of a 'Midsummer Festival' ('Sonnenwendfeier'), a neo-pagan revival featuring song recitals, gymnastic displays, group singing, a bowling competition, quoits and even 'Humsti-Pumsti'. The highlight was a 'fire sermon' delivered by 'Pg. Professor Suchenwirth'. Kraus was well aware that 'Pg.' was the abbreviation for 'Parteigenosse' (Nazi Party Comrade), but after speculating about the mysteries of 'Humsti-Pumsti' he begins to wonder whether 'a Pg. Professor is perhaps a teacher of Pogroms' (F 657–67, 87–90). Suchenwirth's fervently pro-Nazi publications, including *Vom Ersten zum Dritten Reich*, prepared the ground for the annexation of Austria, and his speeches featured prominently in election propaganda. The name of 'Pg. Dr. Suchenwirth' was clearly visible, in April 1932, on the notorious election poster which anticipated the day when, in the words of the Nazi song, 'Jewish blood spurts from the knife' (Fig. 50).

Even more alarming was the militarization of the police force. The activities of thugs in uniform were copiously documented in the aftermath of the

50 Vienna, April 1932: Nazi election poster calling for 'Jewish blood'

massacre of July 1927, when Kraus devoted ten pages of small type to reports of brutality at police stations. A typical case was that of a tailor's apprentice, arrested on 15 July for remonstrating with the police for 'shooting people down like dogs'. A report sent to Kraus by an unnamed lawyer described how the apprentice was dragged to Police Headquarters, where the policemen beat him with fists and rifle-butts 'until his face and the upper part of his body were swollen and bleeding'. At another police station, political suspects were put through a jocularly named 'thrashing machine' ('Watschenmaschine'): a line of policemen who set about them with truncheons (F 771–6, 5–6 & 10). This was the police station in the Elisabethstrasse, about three blocks from Kraus's apartment. He sees the 'thrashing machine' as the first step towards the systematic use of torture, as practised by the police in Hungary. Inverting the notorious comment made by Chancellor Seipel about the demonstrators, Kraus insisted that there should be 'no mercy for such a system of policing'. However, when prosecutions for assault were brought against the police, they were blocked by reactionary judges like Hofrat Czerny, who was interested only in evidence which compromised the demonstrators. According to the police, anyone believed to have been in the vicinity of parliament on 15 July must be a socialist – and probably a Jew (F 771–6, 3–9 & 17)!

The use of armed police against left-wing demonstrators made headlines again in May 1929, when the Police Chief of Berlin, Karl Zörgiebel, brutally suppressed a communist-led May Day parade. Although Zörgiebel was a Social Democrat, he sent rifles and armoured cars into action against the demonstrators, and twenty-five were killed. Zörgiebel now joined Schober as one of the heroes of the bourgeois press, prompting Kraus to denounce his actions the following month. However, it was Schober he most forcefully attacked – the 'generalissimo' parading the streets of Vienna (F 811–19, 5). This alludes to the parade to mark the sixtieth anniversary of the founding of the Vienna police force, scheduled for the following day. Kraus goes on to analyse the political implications. As a chorus chanted the refrain 'Hail to the saviour of Vienna!', Schober consecrated the banners of the police force amid the ecstatic cheers of the crowd. These ceremonies were accompanied by an orgy of patriotism in the press, led by the *Neues Wiener Journal*. While Schober pontificated about the 'iron fist' of the police, Kraus suggested that it looked more like an army, equipped not only with revolvers and rubber truncheons, but with rifles and machine guns. Moreover the people whose job was to catch burglars and control the traffic were apparently defending the interests not only of their Austrian fatherland, but also of the German *Volk*. For Kraus this nightmarish atmosphere was reminiscent of an army on parade, jubilantly celebrated by war correspondents. The principal cheerleader was the socialist renegade Sandor Weiss, formerly editor of *Der Abend*, who had been imprisoned for blackmail during the Bekessy affair (F 811–19, 21–9). Released under an amnesty in 1928, he had renounced his leftist leanings and become a spokesman for political reaction.

The Heimwehr as Pacemakers of Fascism

The militarization of public life was intensified by the right-wing militias. At a date when Austrian National Socialists were still a disorganized minority, the Heimwehr had a broad popular base, especially in the provinces. There were three main groupings: the patriots led by the aristocratic Ernst Rüdiger Starhemberg, who formed a loose alliance with the Christian Socials; the radicals led by Richard Steidle, who campaigned for authoritarian government; and the extremist Heimatschutz led by Walter Pfrimer, linked with the Nazis. To understand their impact it is important to differentiate between the rival factions. Steidle, a patriotic Austrian who narrowly survived a Nazi assassination attempt in June 1933, perished in Buchenwald in 1940, while Starhemberg escaped into exile; but Pfrimer was a Nazi sympathizer who survived into old age. However, all three were committed to the defeat of Marxism, and after the burning of the Palace of Justice it was the resistance of the Heimwehr that forced the Social Democrats to call off the general strike. Chancellor Seipel, initially a critic of right-wing militias, now welcomed the Heimwehren as his allies, anticipating the 'decisive battle' in which they would defeat 'the enemies of Jesus Christ'.[17]

When the British government expressed alarm at the activities of these paramilitaries, Seipel gave an interview to Gedye, published in the *Daily Telegraph* on 3 September 1929, in which he compared the Heimwehr to the British Legion, whose members, after all, also enjoyed 'an occasional parade'. Under pressure from Gedye, he admitted that the Heimwehr had weapons, but blandly maintained that they were 'all deposited with the police'.[18] This statement, even if true, was not very reassuring, since it implied that Heimwehr and police were hand in glove. Responding to this article, Kraus challenged Seipel's statements about the location and control of weapons, suggesting that the British journalist should interview Seipel again in the light of all the contradictions. The 'solidarity of dishonesty', which affected all parties including the Social Democrats, made it virtually impossible to get through 'to the facts' (F 820–6, 15–16).

The Heimwehr movement could never have become a power in the land without foreign support, above all from Mussolini. Details of these transactions have been described by the Hungarian scholar Lajos Kerekes in his richly documented study, 'Twilight of a Democracy'.[19] This shows that in April 1928 Mussolini began secretly to supply the Heimwehr with weapons and funds, using Prime Minister Bethlen of Hungary as his intermediary. These resources enabled the Heimwehr to confront the socialist Schutzbund in a series of bloody battles which undermined the Republic.[20] The aim was to construct a fascist axis between Rome, Vienna and Budapest that would put an end to Austrian democracy. This agitation reached its peak in 1929, after the unexpected resignation of Seipel as chancellor on 3 April had destabilized the parliamentary system. After an interim government had been formed, led by the industrialist Ernst Streeruwitz, the Heimwehr leaders, backed by Mussolini's agents, embarked on the destruction of democracy. On 18 August a pitched battle between Heimwehr and Schutzbund units took place in the Styrian town of St Lorenzen, leaving four people dead and approximately two hundred injured. In mid-September the Heimwehr leaders published their 'final warning': unless a pro-Heimwehr cabinet was formed they would seize power by force. It was at this juncture that Schober took over as chancellor, backed by Mussolini.[21]

Kraus observed these developments with growing dismay. During the mid-1920s the campaign against Bekessy had absorbed his main energies, and he had paid relatively little attention to the Heimwehr. The activities of Austrian backwoodsmen seemed less of a threat than the violence of the Nazis, and the emblem of the Heimwehr, the 'Hahnenschwanz' cockade, never acquired the sinister implications of the swastika. But the emergence of the Heimwehr during the summer of 1929 as a mass movement led him to revise his views. After Schober's appointment as chancellor, he responded with a series of short glosses, asking how it was possible for a gang of desperadoes to dictate terms to the government. He was appalled not simply by the violence on the streets, but by the collusion of democratically elected politicians and the liberal press.

It is in this context that he concluded that an exaggerated fear of 'creeping bolshevism' was impelling Austria towards 'creeping fascism' (F 820–6, 16).

It was hardly surprising that the *Reichspost* supported the right-wing militias, but they were also backed by liberal newspapers under Jewish ownership. The key figure was Jakob Lippowitz, editor of the *Neues Wiener Journal*, a paper noted for its sensational news coverage rather than a clearly defined political line. Although it claimed to be a family paper, it was notorious for its small ads for the services of 'masseuses', a form of hypocrisy which the satirist repeatedly traduced. However, in the autumn of 1929 the paper played a more sinister role, as Lippowitz acted as king-maker in the creation of a new regime. In collaboration with the Heimwehr leadership, he was instrumental in installing Schober as chancellor. In an editorial of 26 September Lippowitz claimed credit for this appointment. The Chancellor (he wrote) had been 'carried to the pinnacle of power by an all-powerful popular movement, a movement of the *Volk* whose mouthpiece, now as in days gone by, is the *Neues Wiener Journal*'. Responding to this claim, Kraus asks what can have induced Lippowitz to put his newspaper in the service of such a reactionary movement. Parodying the language of the Heimwehr movement, he mocks the 'consolidated Aryan masses' for responding to the propaganda of a 'Prussian Israelite'. And he denounces Lippowitz for first encouraging the Heimwehr to organize 'marches around Vienna', and then denying foreign reports that they constitute a threat (F 820–6, 2–4 & 27–8). Lippowitz and Weiss were not the only Jewish journalists to support the Heimwehr, betraying a wholesale 'collapse of convictions'. Kraus also cites the case of Edmund Wengraf, one of the first to defend Schober's ruthless tactics in July 1927 (F 766–70, 8). Now this 'democratic Jew', formerly president of Concordia, has become such an admirer of the Heimwehr that he is cultivating the 'instincts of a front-line veteran' (F 820–6, 54–5). A further target is Maximilian Schreier, a 'liberal-minded Israelite' slightly more cautious in his sympathies. Kraus identifies him as a 'pacemaker of fascism', even though he is still not sure how seriously to take this movement in its Austrian form. The tendency of Jewish journalists to place an attractive gloss on fascism led him to anticipate the appearance of an Austrian 'Schmusolini' (F 820–6, 105) – a pun on the word 'Schmus' (Yiddish for 'chat' or 'gossip').

Jews were far more prominent in the socialist and democratic camps than on the far right, but a movement committed to the struggle against 'red terror' was bound to attract support from the bourgeoisie. Kraus had drawn attention to the phenomenon of Jewish subsidies for racist groups in the swastika sequence of *Wolkenkuckucksheim*.[22] He held the unholy alliance of clericalism, the press and the stock exchange responsible for the right-wing electoral victory of autumn 1920 (F 554–6, 2). While the Heimwehr received only intermittent financial backing during the early 1920s, the funds now came flooding in. They were subsidized by the Hauptverband der Industrie, an organization of industrialists and bankers which included prominent Jewish members, such as

Fritz Mandl and Rudolf Sieghart. In November 1929 Baron Louis Rothschild gave secret assurances that if the Heimwehr succeeded in seizing power with relatively little bloodshed, his banks would guarantee the stability of the Austrian Schilling.[23] Thus leading members of the Jewish community colluded with the anti-democratic factions led by Rintelen and Pfrimer, Starhemberg and Steidle. Kraus must have had good sources of information, for he noted Rothschild's support for the Heimwehr in one of his satirical songs (S 14, 206).[24]

The readiness of wealthy Jews to support right-wing militias was not as irrational as it now seems, for they felt more threatened by bolshevism than by fascism. The Russian Revolution had abolished capitalism and confiscated private property, closed the stock exchange and ruined foreign investors. The thought that the same thing might happen in Berlin or Vienna, Budapest or Rome filled businessmen with apprehension. Mussolini, on the other hand, was prepared to co-operate with leading industrialists, regardless of their origins, and even allowed fugitives from Nazi Germany to settle in Italy. He thus became a focus of admiration for Jews in other countries. A pamphlet written in English by Eli Rubin ('Sozius'), published in Vienna in 1936 under the title *The Jews in Italy*, emphasizes 'the atmosphere of equality and fraternity in which the Jews are living in the fascist Italy of Mussolini'.[25] It was not until 1938 that Jews were excluded from membership of the Italian fascist movement. In Austria, too, Seipel and Starhemberg co-operated with Jewish businessmen and financiers, without whose support they could not have built their political careers.[26] Seipel insisted in an interview reported in *Neue Freie Presse* that his antisemitism was directed against 'Asiatics' like Hugo Breitner, not against Jewish capitalists. In conversation with Pan-German political leaders in June 1930, Schober confided that he had used his influence with Jewish banks to obtain funding for the Heimwehr. Like Seipel, he hoped that by holding the purse-strings he could use the militias for his own purposes.[27]

The Heimwehr leaders were shocked to discover Schober's double game. In May 1930 they organized a mass rally at Korneuburg in a further attempt to destabilize Austrian democracy, but their bluff was called in September, when the President used his new powers to appoint Starhemberg as minister of the interior. Inspired by Hitler's electoral success in Germany, the Heimwehr gambled on gaining power through the ballot box, but in the November general election they won a mere eight seats. This forced them to rethink their tactics and contemplate a putsch. Rumours began to circulate that the Heimwehr's long-heralded 'march on Vienna' would take place towards the end of the year, but it was not until September 1931 that the Pfrimer faction finally made their move. A poorly organized putsch centred in Styria collapsed within twenty-four hours, but the government's counter-measures were so half hearted that Pfrimer was able to escape abroad and the Heimwehr retained most of their weapons.[28] At a trial in Graz in December, the jury was packed with Heimwehr supporters and all the accused were acquitted, including

Pfrimer, who was so confident about his position that he had returned to
Austria. After the verdict was announced, five members of the jury raised
their arms to give the fascist salute.[29] Kraus's comments on this episode are
embedded in the strophes he added to Offenbach's *Vert-Vert*, recited on 29
November. His scathing allusions to the coup underscore the weakness of the
government, the failure of the jury system, and the ominous influence of
Pfrimer's financial backers, the Alpine-Montan industrial combine (F 868–72,
45–7).

Under these circumstances, Kraus's ambivalent attitude towards Starhemberg becomes comprehensible. The Prince represented the patriotically
Austrian wing of the Heimwehr movement, opposed to the pro-Nazi tendencies of the Pfrimer faction. Moreover, Kraus and Starhemberg had another
thing in common: their scorn for Schober. Thus Kraus could not suppress a
twinge of admiration as he watched Starhemberg embark on a campaign to
expose Schober for having first supported the Heimwehr and later prevented
a putsch. In newspaper articles published in autumn 1931, Starhemberg called
Schober a 'crook', and, playing on the name of John the Baptist ('Johannes der
Täufer'), he dubbed him 'Johannes der Täuscher' ('John the Deceiver').[30] In an
article of December 1931, Kraus applauded this formulation, even though
he acknowledged that those who are planning treason have no right to complain when they are betrayed (F 864–7, 1–4). Although Schober compelled
Starhemberg to retract in court, his political reputation was damaged by the
customs-union debacle. Forced out of office in May 1932, Schober defended
his record in the short-lived journal *Gegenwart*, identified in one of Kraus's
satirical rhymes as a 'doughty Greater-German rag' (F 868–72, 56). But
Schober's health was broken, and on 19 August 1932 at the age of fifty-seven
he died of a heart attack. Kraus claimed, in a legal submission, that Schober too
had been 'a pacemaker of the Nazi movement in Austria' (P 4, 108). However,
he was hardly to blame for the fact that his traditional style of German
nationalism had been overtaken by a more lethal brand.[31]

The Limits of Satire

The twilight of democracy brought a crisis of satirical discourse, in both Vienna
and Berlin, and Kraus was not the only one to find himself almost at a loss for
words. In an article in *Die Weltbühne* of 8 March 1932 Kurt Tucholsky, the
most formidable left-wing critic of the Weimar Republic, succinctly observed:
'Satire has an upper limit. Buddha is beyond it. Satire also has a lower limit. In
Germany it is the prevailing fascist forces. It doesn't pay – you can't shoot that
low.'[32] In practice, Tucholsky had withdrawn from the fray several years
earlier, relocating first to France and finally to Sweden. His articles in *Die
Weltbühne* continued to provoke controversy, but the scourge of the Weimar
bourgeoisie and the imperial military caste found it difficult to gauge the Nazi
threat. His articles of the early 1930s presented Hitler as a pawn of the
Nationalists, underestimating his charismatic appeal. He failed to grasp the

revolutionary drive of the Nazis, since their blend of 'beer, gossip and anti-semitism' seemed to him beneath contempt.[33] However, there was some force in his observation that satire has a 'lower limit'. Even the most vocal verbal aggression presupposes constraints imposed by law, but this was undermined by the violence of the fascist gangs and the inability of the authorities to contain it. Appeals to reason tended to be drowned by the anarchy on the streets, even when they were as eloquent as the speech calling for an alliance between bour-geois parties and the Social Democrats, delivered by Thomas Mann in Berlin on 17 October 1930.[34]

For Jewish critics there was a further catch: the more resolutely they opposed the *völkisch* movement, the more they appeared to confirm the myth of a Jewish plot against the German people. This was the main reason why the efforts of defence organizations like Centralverein deutscher Staatsbürger jüdischen Glaubens proved so ineffective. They had more success through the covert operations undertaken by the Büro Wilhelmstrasse, a non-denominational information centre set up in Berlin in autumn 1929, which monitored right-wing activities and supplied republican opponents of Nazism with copious information. The centre's most imaginative move was to launch a supposedly independent satirical magazine entitled *Alarm*, published weekly between October 1929 and the spring of 1933, which was widely distributed in the Berlin area.[35] The idea was to beat Goebbels at his own game through humorous character assassinations, mocking satirical verses and crude cartoons, aimed primarily at a working-class readership. The theory, developed by the left-wing biologist Serge Chakotin, was that this type of 'sensual propaganda' ('Senso-Propaganda') would make a greater impact than traditional styles of 'rational propaganda' ('Ratio-Propaganda'). But Goebbels had an easier task, appealing in *Der Angriff*, the rabble-rousing journal of the Nazi movement, to the 'primitive instincts of the masses'. While *Der Angriff* directed its barbs against the discredited 'system' of the Weimar Republic, the counter-propaganda, co-ordinated by Walter Gyssling, was in the more awkward posi-tion of being 'Anti-Anti', the title of the leaflets produced by the Centralverein to discredit antisemitic myths.[36]

Although the crisis in Vienna was less acute, Kraus too was forced on the defensive. The legal system had been reduced to a farce by the jury in the Pfrimer trial, while the deaths of both Seipel and Schober in August 1932 marked the end of old-school diplomacy. The contrast between their self-righteous pronouncements and their devious policies had provided a rewarding target for the satirist, but words were wasted on a brutal cut-throat like Waldemar Pabst, chief of staff of the Heimwehr. Realizing that his ironic focus was no longer commensurate with events, Kraus suggested that satire was wasted on 'Heimatwehr, Heimatbund, -block, -schutz, -trutz und -schmutz' (F 845–6, 1). This makes it easier to understand why he has so little to say about a whole sequence of disruptive political events: the mass rallies that threatened the parliamentary system, the panic triggered by the collapse of the

Creditanstalt Bank, the escalating unemployment, and the provincial elections of April 1932. In Vienna that spring the National Socialists won over 200,000 votes (17 per cent of the total), mainly at the expense of the Christian Socials, who were blamed for the harsh austerity measures. This provoked a parliamentary crisis that remained unresolved, even after Dollfuss took office as chancellor on 20 May, since his wafer-thin majority depended on Starhemberg and the Heimwehr. At the beginning of October, inspired by the strategies of Brüning and Papen, Dollfuss introduced a system of government by decree, exploiting an obscure Enabling Act dating from the First World War, the 'Kriegswirtschaftliche Ermächtigungsgesetz'. Although parliament was not dissolved, this provided the basis for an increasingly authoritarian regime. In the face of this crisis, Kraus became reluctant to speak in his own voice, either from the public platform or in the pages of *Die Fackel*, and his occasional 'Zeitstrophen' scarcely constituted an adequate response. Confronted by the Nazi threat, he needed time to rethink his position, keeping a wary eye on the deteriorating situation in Germany, since he was convinced that the worst that could befall Austria would be annexation by force (F 876–84, 10).

Goodbye to Berlin

In mid-November 1932 Kraus paid a final visit to Berlin, giving three public readings. There could hardly have been a greater contrast to the thriving city where he had felt so much at home three years earlier. Admittedly, his prediction that the National Socialists would lose momentum if they delayed their seizure of power had been partially fulfilled, since they lost two million votes in the Reichstag election of 6 November, compared with their triumph in July. Middle-of-the-road voters had been shocked by the spectacle of SA units (Nazi stormtroopers) joining the communists in the Berlin public transport strike, organized on the eve of the elections in an attempt to destroy the system. The election result created new uncertainties, since there was little prospect of a stable coalition. Characteristically avoiding direct political comment, Kraus chose instead to include in one of his recitations a set of regulations promulgated by Papen's reconstituted Prussian police force, which banned nudist beaches and insisted that both men and women should wear full-length bathing-costumes. Responding to this ludicrous attempt to control incipient anarchy, he read a series of satirical ballads by Wedekind, as well as the love poem 'Kranich und Wolke' from Brecht's *Mahagonny* (F 885–7, 11–15).

Visitors to Berlin were shocked to find the dynamics of the city so changed. The successes of the Stresemann era had led Kraus to take a more optimistic view of German affairs during the mid-1920s, discounting the threat of anti-semitism. This is reflected in a text published in *Die Fackel* in December 1924, which portrays a woman with a broad Berlin accent peddling an antisemitic broadsheet entitled *Fridericus*. The title of Kraus's gloss is provided by the slogan which the woman was chanting as she tried to attract the custom of passers-by: 'Why does the Jew earn big bucks faster than the Christian?' ('Warum vadient der Jude schneller und mehr Jeld als der Christ?'). He recalls finding the scene so irresistible that he lingered in the Friedrichstrasse for a quarter of an hour, listening to the melody with which this slogan was chanted by an 'unadulterated Germanic newspaper woman'. She didn't earn a cent, although the passers-by were eager to buy salacious magazines reporting on sexual orgies, transvestites and nightclubs. Two hours later he returned to find the woman still at her post, an 'envious gob frozen into a symbol of unquenched Aryan longing'. Even more striking is his account of the response to her plaintive question: No one wanted to know the answer, everyone took the fact for granted, realizing that non-Jews would be just as keen to make money as Jews – if they weren't too dumb to do so! This impressionistic street scene gained weight through being framed by quotations from the Austrian Nazi daily, documenting the primitive mindset of its readers and the blend of envy and resentment that inspired them (F 668–75, 151).

Kraus recited this witty and perceptive text several times, sharing it with his Berlin audience in March 1925. During the Stresemann period there were good reasons to regard the Nazi movement as a marginal phenomenon, lacking appeal for the average German city-dweller. The success of Jewish businessmen was not particularly resented when economic recovery meant that prosperity was becoming more widely shared. With Hitler under lock and key, the National Socialists made no impact in the Reichstag election of May 1924, and in the elections of 1928 the Party won a mere twelve seats. But by the time Kraus paid his final visit to Berlin four years later, the country was gripped by economic crisis and the scene on the streets had been transformed, with Nazis and communists competing and at times even combining in their efforts to overthrow the democratic system. Moreover, neither the government nor the police force was taking effective steps to contain the violence.

The new mood was memorably described by Christopher Isherwood in *Goodbye to Berlin*. The young English author had been drawn to Weimar Germany by its atmosphere of interpersonal freedom, particularly the nudist beaches and homosexual bars. But the sensuous utopia fell apart before his eyes, and a section entitled 'Berlin Diary (1932–3)' records his observations of the conflict between extremist groups. One evening he saw three SA men in the Bülowstrasse, returning from a rally carrying rolled-up Nazi banners with sharp metal points. 'That's him!' one of them suddenly shouted, as they encountered a youth of seventeen or eighteen, and they jostled him into the shadow of a house entrance, standing over him, kicking him and stabbing him with the points of their banners. The men made their escape, leaving their victim with 'his left eye half poked out, and blood pouring from the wound'. Even more striking is Isherwood's observation of the behaviour of the bystanders: 'By this time dozens of people were looking on. They seemed surprised, but not particularly shocked – this sort of thing happened too often, nowadays. '*Allerhand* . . .' ['Whatever next!'] they murmured. Twenty yards away, at the Potsdamerstrasse corner, stood a group of heavily armed policemen. With their chests out, and their hands on their revolver belts, they magnificently disregarded the whole affair.'[37]

It is not clear whether Kraus witnessed this kind of violence during his final visit to Berlin, but he was certainly aware of the Potempa affair, which announced the impending reign of terror. Early in August 1932 a group of five stormtroopers broke into the home of a communist miner in the Silesian town of Potempa, kicking him to death before his mother's eyes. This time the men were arrested and the courts acted promptly, sentencing the murderers to death. However, Hitler very publicly intervened, sending his comrades a telegram saying he felt linked to them 'in boundless loyalty' and promising that they would soon be released.[38] The sentence was commuted to life imprisonment, and no one doubted that, once in power, Hitler would set the criminals free. Given Kraus's commitment to the rule of law, it is hardly surprising that he saw this episode as a portent. It became connected in his mind with an article in a highly regarded legal journal, the *Deutsche Juristenzeitung*, arguing that violent crimes should not be punished if they were 'motivated by the national interest' (cited DW 264/*289–90*). Although there are groups of violent thugs in every society, Weimar Germany was unique in voting them into power, giving them control of the police, and freeing them from penal sanctions. Against this background, it is easy to understand why Kraus ruled out the idea of co-operation between Vienna and Berlin. Denouncing the Social Democrats in September 1932 for their pipedream of a Greater Germany, he endorsed the stance of their conservative opponents: 'The Christian Socials – even if it is their own Austria they are defending and their own ambitions they are pursuing in their opposition to Hitler's Germany – are of course absolutely right to become more active now against Anschluss' (F 876–84, 16). This hints at the reorientation that was to lead him to declare for Dollfuss.

CHAPTER 24

Dollfuss and the Defence of Austria

Dollfuss was a politician in the Seipel tradition, devoutly Catholic and implacably anti-Marxist. Born in 1892 at Texing in Lower Austria, he was a patriot who had served on the Italian front during the First World War, rising to the rank of lieutenant in the prestigious Kaiserschützen. After abandoning the idea of training for the priesthood, he studied law at the University of Vienna. With the backing of Catholic organizations, he quickly made his mark as an administrator, first in the Lower Austrian Chamber of Agriculture and later as president of the Federal Railways. In March 1931 he entered the Cabinet of Karl Buresch as minister of agriculture, and a year later, in May 1932, he was appointed chancellor. During the following two years he made an extraordinary impact on Austrian politics, suspending parliament, crushing the Social Democrats, banning the Nazis, and establishing a corporate state, described by his biographer as an attempt 'to erect the Kingdom of God upon earth'.[1] It is scarcely surprising that Dollfuss was seen by conservatives as the saviour of Austria, but the question is: how did Kraus reach the same conclusion?

Bad Timing

Dollfuss made his first appearance in *Die Fackel* as a blurred figure in the top left-hand corner of a photograph of the Buresch Cabinet, reproduced by Kraus in March 1932 to accentuate his disdain for the Austrian political leadership (F 868–72, 53). That autumn, while commending the Christian Socials for opposing Anschluss, Kraus reserved the right to continue his attacks on the right-wing coalition – 'an irksome government which no failure can remove from the helm' (F 876–84, 30). Dollfuss is not mentioned by name, although by that date he had been chancellor for four months. In that same declaration Kraus also expressed a guarded admiration for communism – as a 'final hope' born of despair, after the dismal failures of the Social Democrats (F 876–84, 6). Thus his audience might have expected him to support the radical left, and at least one of his admirers assumed that he was evolving 'from a pacifist into a

communist'.[2] Politically, Kraus remained virtually silent between the end of
1932 and summer 1934, provoking rumours that alarmed admirers like the
Czech Social Democrat Wolfgang Brügel.[3] But the majority of his readers were
unprepared for the declaration of support for Dollfuss contained in his long
essay of July 1934, 'Warum die Fackel nicht erscheint' ('Why the Torch does
not appear'). Although Kraus's argument fills over three hundred pages, everything hinges on his claim that Dollfuss's resistance to Nazi Germany justifies his
authoritarian measures, which must be accepted as the 'lesser evil' (pp. 176–7).[4]
Summing up his position, he declared: 'I fully agree with Dollfuss that parlia-
mentarianism is ineffective against the resurrection of Wotan, democracy fails
when confronted by the mystery of Blood and Soil' (pp. 276–7).

As a satirist committed to ethical radicalism, Kraus had always scorned 'lesser
evils', but the threat from Nazi Germany required a more pragmatic response.
In supporting Dollfuss, he acted as a citizen defending the survival of his country rather than a satirist committed to some ideal 'higher order'. There is a
striking parallel with his conservative phase before the First World War, when
this dualism first emerged.[5] In 'Warum die Fackel nicht erscheint', Kraus
acknowledges the limits of satire. Living in times of terror constrains literary
expression, since 'violence is no target for polemic, madness no subject for
satire' (p. 26). Satire may still be an appropriate response to 'insolence and
especially stupidity' (p. 167), but it would be irresponsible to adopt the same
attitude to matters of life and death. Now that the existence of Austria is threatened, it is no longer permissible to mock the tourist trade. In May 1933 Hitler
imposed the 'thousand-Mark blockade' – a tax on German tourists visiting
Austria – in an attempt to strangle the economy. This compelled Kraus to
acknowledge that tourism had become indispensable for Austria's survival.
Satirical intransigence was appropriate only 'in opulent times' (p. 270).

In the first 169-page section of this essay, written in January and early
February 1934 (but not published until July), Kraus alludes to Dollfuss as the
'little saviour from great danger' (p. 14). This same passage contains a cryptic
reference to 'Aspern', a village near Vienna which had been the scene of a
celebrated battle in May 1809, when the Austrians checked the advance of
Napoleon's army. Later in the essay Kraus praises Dollfuss for qualities which
have become apparent 'since that second battle of Aspern' (p. 181). Hitler's
destruction of German democracy after the elections of 5 March 1933 led
many people to assume that within a matter of months the Nazis would also
seize power in Vienna. On 18 March the Bavarian Minister of Justice, Dr Hans
Frank, made a broadcast on Munich Radio calling for the overthrow of the
Austrian government. On 13 May Dr Frank arrived in Vienna on a propaganda
mission, using the 250th anniversary of the liberation of Vienna from the Turks
as a pretext for a rabble-rousing speeches. Aspern was the name of the airport
where his plane landed, and Frank was met by Dr Michael Skubl, Deputy
Police Chief, who informed him on behalf of the Austrian government that
his visit was 'unwelcome' ('unerwünscht').[6] This phrase so caught Kraus's

imagination that he highlighted it in *Die Fackel* (p. 14). To declare that the emissary of the German Reich was 'unwelcome' in Austria was an act of political courage, expressing Dollfuss's decision to defy Hitler. There was also a philosemitic subtext: the phrase 'Juden unerwünscht' had for decades been the slogan of popular antisemitism. By turning this phrase against their tormentors, Dollfuss signalled his determination to protect Austria's Jewish citizens. When Frank attempted to turn his speaking tour into a campaign for insurrection in Austria, he was arrested and 'escorted across the frontier'.[7] Hitler was so enraged that he imposed the punitive aforementioned 'thousand-Mark blockade'. This episode transformed Kraus's attitude towards Dollfuss, and sceptical reserve during the first twelve months of his chancellorship was followed by a sudden burst of admiration, as Dollfuss's resistance to Nazi pressure led him to be seen as a 'life-saver' (p. 33). And after the civil war of February 1934, Kraus savaged Dollfuss's left-wing critics, finally paying tribute to him as a 'hero inspired by faith', who fought for 'future freedom' (F 912–15, 71).

Kraus's readers remained unaware that his silence after Hitler's seizure of power did not signify inactivity. He was hard at work on *Dritte Walpurgisnacht*, a critique of Nazi Germany begun in May 1933, continued in the summer during a visit to Janowitz, and completed in draft by September (S 12, 333–6). But in September 1933, after agonized deliberations, he decided to refrain from publishing this text, so his readers were left in the dark. A number of excerpts from 'Dritte Walpurgisnacht' were included in 'Warum die Fackel nicht erscheint', but they take up only forty pages in this 315-page issue. Kraus had to acknowledge his anomalous position as a writer 'who remains silent towards Hitler [but] has no compunction in speaking out for Dollfuss' (p. 181). One half of the equation is missing, and the balance of Kraus's argument is further impaired by the harshness with which he harries the Social Democrats. While drafting 'Dritte Walpurgisnacht', Kraus did express reservations about the Dollfuss cult, which threatened to degenerate into 'obsequiousness'. Not wishing to overvalue the Chancellor's achievements, he nevertheless praised his commitment to the 'main concern': the defeat of Nazism. The confrontation between Frank and Skubl marked the start of an 'astonishing campaign' to save Austria from the swastika (DW 208 & 214–16/*231 & 236–8*). Austrian resistance to Nazi Germany has indeed been described by one historian as Hitler's 'first major foreign policy defeat'.[8]

Initially, it seemed that Dollfuss's policies were directed against the Social Democrats. On 7 March 1933, two days after the Nazi election victory in Germany, he took advantage of a breakdown in parliamentary procedure to suspend the Austrian constitution and assume powers of government by decree. Political meetings and marches were banned, press censorship was introduced, and on 1 May the streets of central Vienna were sealed off by the army to prevent the traditional May Day parade. However, these were not simply anti-socialist measures, since they were accompanied by a clampdown on the Austrian Nazis, and after the confrontation with Hans Frank the anti-Nazi campaign entered a new phase. In May Dollfuss banned the wearing of paramilitary uniforms, and in June the *Völkischer Beobachter* was prohibited. A pretext was also found for closing down the Nazi regional headquarters throughout Austria. The Nazis, supplied with weapons and explosives from Germany, reacted with what has been described as an 'unparalleled wave of terror'.[9] This reached a first climax in June 1933, when a bomb destroyed a Jewish-owned jeweller's shop in Vienna, killing both its proprietor and a passer-by. Scores of minor bomb attacks followed, damaging shops and causing panic in cinemas. The government responded by arresting 2,500 Nazis, including all Party officials, and on 19 June the National Socialist Party was banned, after SA men had murderously attacked a Christian youth organization in Krems with handgrenades – an episode that provoked Kraus's revulsion (p. 267). Purges of the army, the police and the civil service were also carried out to eliminate Nazis from positions of influence, and elected members of provincial governments were removed from office. A total of more than a thousand Nazis were expelled from Austria, including Theo Habicht, Hitler's principal lieutenant.

The campaign of terror continued for over a year, with further bomb attacks on department stores and coffee-houses, cinemas and railway trains. After Habicht had been deported, he launched a propaganda war against the Austrian government by means of numerous radio broadcasts from Munich, and an Austrian Legion of exiled Nazis was deployed along the German frontier, threatening armed incursions into Austrian territory. The pressure was intensified when on 3 October Dollfuss narrowly escaped an assassination attempt by a young Nazi, who fired at him from close range with a revolver. The Chancellor responded by declaring a state of emergency backed by martial law, reintroducing the death penalty for murder and arson (Fig. 51). As the terrorist attacks escalated, even the possession of explosives was made a capital offence. So many Nazis were arrested that in October 1933 a camp for political detainees had to be set up at Wöllersdorf near Wiener Neustadt, and by April 1934 about 50,000 Nazis had been convicted of political or civil offences. Kraus praised this campaign as a 'resistance against barbarism' (p. 218). It was this that inspired his own 'defence of Austria's essential being' (p. 242). His mistake lay not in his political judgement, but in his failure to explain his position until it was too late.

In May 1933 Dollfuss announced the formation of the Vaterländische Front (Fatherland Front), calling on all loyal citizens to support this organization for the defence of Austria. In his indictment of the Social Democrats, Kraus suggested that much human suffering would have been avoided, if only the opportunity provided by the Fatherland Front had been seized 'in good time' (p. 181). But his own support could not have been more badly timed. After all, he could have followed the example of his ally Ernst Krenek, who promptly joined the Fatherland Front in May and wrote a series of intensely pro-Austrian articles for *Der christliche Ständestaat*, the weekly magazine founded in

51   Poster announcing the reintroduction of the death penalty in Austria

1933 to support Dollfuss's cause. It was Kraus, after all, who inspired Krenek's attempts to chart a 'middle way' that was both 'conservative and radical', and he was doubtless familiar with the composer's article in the *Wiener Zeitung* on this theme.[10] It is understandable that Kraus, as a resolute non-joiner, needed more time to think through his response, but in private he was already praising Dollfuss's policy in June 1933 as 'surprisingly good and energetic' (BSN 1, 646). If he had publicly declared his position, this could have strengthened the campaign for Austrian independence. In September Dollfuss made two further appeals, one at a mass rally in Vienna and the other at the League of Nations in Geneva, calling on men of good will to support his defence of Austria. At that date, despite the government's authoritarian policies, some of Kraus's left-wing admirers might have been swayed by an appeal for an anti-Nazi alliance.

The value of cross-party alliances is exemplified by Hermynia Zur Mühlen, the communist author of aristocratic origin singled out for special praise in 'Warum die Fackel nicht erscheint'. Forced to flee from Nazi Germany, Zur Mühlen returned in May 1933 to Vienna, her place of birth, with the aim of creating an anti-fascist front. Her denunciation of a pro-Nazi German publisher, which appeared in the *Arbeiter-Zeitung* on 26 October 1933, caught Kraus's eye, leading him to praise her courage (pp. 110–12). He went on to quote a passage from her memoirs, *Ende und Anfang*, published in 1929, describing how she had asserted her authority over an armed and drunken Prussian thug through the commanding power of the words 'Rechtsum! Kehrt! Marsch!' ('Right about turn! Quick march!'). For Kraus, this exemplified the resolute stand that should be taken by the statesmen of Europe. He evidently recognized in Zur Mühlen a kindred spirit – an Austrian patriot who was prepared to set aside factional differences in order to resist the fascist threat. There are striking parallels between his critique of Nazism and her novel *Unsere Töchter, die Nazinen* ('Our Daughters, the Nazi Girls'), which portrays the attractions of the movement for the population of a small German town. The difference is that Zur Mühlen was determined to get her ideas into print: her novel appeared in instalments in summer 1934 in *Deutsche Freiheit*, a radical daily published in Saarbrücken while it was still under French administration. At the end of 1935 she arranged for a book edition to be published by the Catholic Gsur-Verlag in Vienna, provoking such outrage at the German embassy that the Austrian government felt obliged to ban it.[11] If Kraus had published his polemic against National Socialism at the end of 1933, he would have made a significant contribution to the popular front against fascism which Zur Mühlen and her allies were trying to promote. Instead, he contented himself with the publication in October 1933 of a ten-line poem announcing his decision to remain silent (F 888, 4).

War on Two Fronts

Dollfuss was fighting on two fronts: against the reality of Nazi terror and against the threat of Marxist insurrection. On 18 January 1934 he made a final attempt to enlist the support of moderate Social Democrats, inviting them (in a speech reported in the *Arbeiter-Zeitung*) to abandon the class struggle and join a 'grand alliance of the defenders of Austrian independence' (AZ 20 January 1934). While leaders like Renner were willing to compromise, the radicals of the Schutzbund were stockpiling arms and explosives for an armed confrontation, incensed that Dollfuss was confiscating their weapons while conniving at the arming of the Heimwehr. At the end of January the police discovered a cache of socialist weapons in Schwechat, and this was followed by further raids on Schutzbund strongholds in the provinces. It was this that provoked Schutzbund units in Linz to launch their desperate revolt.[12] Their comrades in Vienna responded to the call for action, even though they were ill equipped for a confrontation with the army. Using both Heimwehr and regular army units, Dollfuss crushed the insurrection within forty-eight hours. Working-class housing estates, including the Karl-Marx-Hof, were bombarded by artillery and mortar fire, and approximately two hundred socialists were killed. There were also many casualties on the government side, including over a hundred dead, while numerous civilians were caught in the crossfire.[13] In the aftermath of the revolt, hundreds of socialists were arrested, while their leaders, including Otto Bauer and Julius Deutsch, fled to Czechoslovakia. Eight of those arrested were executed under martial law, including a Social Democratic member of parliament, Koloman Wallisch. If Dollfuss had really wished to construct an anti-Nazi pact, he would have acted with greater clemency (there had been no executions in Austria since 1918). This 'unnecessary harshness', as Starhemberg observes in his memoirs, caused such bitterness that the possibility of co-operation with the Social Democrats was destroyed.[14]

In the aftermath of this catastrophe, Kraus's support for Dollfuss seemed an act of treachery. Indeed, he had the worst of both worlds, forfeiting the respect of left-wing friends while failing to speak out in defence of Dollfuss until it was too late. On 25 July 1934 the Nazis attempted a putsch. The poorly organized socialist revolt had shown how important it was to seize the centres of power, and on 25 July several lorryloads of Nazis disguised in army uniforms stormed both the headquarters of Austrian radio and the Chancellery on the Ballhausplatz, where a Cabinet meeting was in progress. Forewarned by the police, Dollfuss insisted that his Cabinet colleagues should leave the building. By this decision, according to a classic account, 'Dollfuss sealed his own fate but probably saved that of Austria,' since the order to scatter meant that most members of the government remained at liberty.[15] But the Chancellor himself was intercepted by the intruders and shot at close range. Refusing requests for either a doctor or a priest, the desperadoes left him to bleed to death, while their comrades at the radio station announced that the government had been overthrown. But the army, supported by the Heimwehr, once again rallied to the support of the government, laying siege to the Nazi positions in the capital and crushing further revolts in the provinces. The German ambassador, Dr Kurt Rieth, tried to negotiate a safe conduct that would have enabled the Nazis to escape to Germany, but the killing of Dollfuss prompted the government to take a sterner stance. The putschists were put on trial and their ringleaders executed. The complicity of Nazi Germany in the abortive coup was so blatant that Hitler felt obliged to replace his ambassador with the more emollient Papen and to abandon terror tactics in favour of a strategy of gradual subversion. Austria, for the time being, was saved.

When Kraus heard the news of Dollfuss's death, copies of his long-delayed number of Die Fackel were already being despatched to subscribers, and it was too late to halt distribution.[16] His text alluded to Dollfuss's courage in risking his life for the patriotic cause, and he reminded his readers that in a period of political turmoil the most carefully formulated argument runs the risk of being discredited 'in the very hour when it appears' (p. 307): prophetic words, since the events of 25 July transformed his eulogy into an epitaph. The assassination of Dollfuss virtually silenced Kraus as a political commentator, and the final numbers of *Die Fackel*, like his readings of the years 1933–6, relate almost exclusively to literary and musical subjects, particularly Offenbach and Shakespeare. In November 1934, introducing his reading of *Macbeth*, he found moving words to pay tribute to the heroic life of the Austrian Chancellor (F 912–15, 69–71). We also know that in July he sent a telegram of condolence to Dollfuss's widow, which shows how deeply his feelings were involved. Kraus was captivated by Dollfuss's personal charisma, as well as by his political courage. The Chancellor's boyish features (Fig. 52) were highly photogenic, a fact that government propaganda did not hesitate to exploit, and Kraus used to carry a photograph of Dollfuss in his pocket. He would proudly show this picture to his friends, as if the diminutive Chancellor were some kind of child prodigy, asking: 'Doesn't he look like Jackie Coogan?' – an allusion to the child actor who appeared with Charlie Chaplin in the silent film *The Kid*.[17] The fact

52   Chancellor Engelbert Dollfuss: an official portrait

that Coogan, who had visited Vienna in 1924 (F 668–75, 34–7), was of Jewish origin, gives this association an additional piquancy. It seems that the longing for a saviour blinded Kraus to the defects of an authoritarian regime. A more balanced epitaph is offered by Gedye: 'The real tragedy is that Dollfuss, with his unusual personal courage, energy and determination, his political agility and personal charm, should have destroyed Austrian liberty in the name of Austrian independence.'[18]

Double Book-keeping

The final years of Kraus's career were overshadowed by recriminations against the Social Democrats. He insisted that they should have supported Dollfuss against the Nazis, denouncing the discrepancy between the theory and prac-tice of their Marxism as 'double book-keeping' (p. 185). But Kraus himself was applying double standards, since he refused to acknowledge the responsibility of the government for the failure to construct an anti-Nazi coalition. More-over, he gave no indication of the date at which a coalition could – and should – have been achieved. In the years before the suppression of the National Assembly, the Social Democrats had certainly had their opportunities. In June 1931 Seipel attempted to form a government of national unity, with Otto Bauer as vice-chancellor, but the Social Democrats refused to join a coalition whose primary aim was to prop up the capitalist system.[19] In July, after the Social Democrats had been criticized in the *Neue Freie Presse* for their failure to accept the responsibilities of government, Kraus referred to such a coalition as a 'despicable act' (F 857–63, 27). Thus if the Social Democrats had made a deal with Seipel, Kraus would probably have condemned them for making pacts. A final opportunity for a grand coalition occurred in May 1932, when Dollfuss faced the task of constructing a parliamentary majority without the support of the Pan-Germans. He considered the possibility of reaching 'a working agree-ment with the socialists', but Bauer refused to co-operate and called for a general election instead.[20] In retrospect, Bauer saw this as a costly mistake, since it prompted Dollfuss to make a deal with Starhemberg and the Heimwehr.[21] But if the Social Democrats had come to terms with Dollfuss in May 1932 it is by no means certain that Kraus would have approved. His essay 'Hüben und Drüben' (September 1932) makes no reference to the need for an alliance.

It was Hitler's seizure of power that transformed Kraus's attitude towards coalitions. His letter of June 1933 praising Dollfuss's energetic measures added: 'only the stupidity of the Social Democrats [is] obstructive' (BSN 1, 646). A few days earlier, in a statement published in the *Wiener Zeitung* of 1 June, Dollfuss had emphatically rejected a demand by Habicht that National Social-ists should be included in a new coalition government.[22] Kraus seems unaware that, behind closed doors, Dollfuss had been negotiating with Nazi leaders about the possibility of an anti-Marxist front.[23] Kraus's letter implies that he now expected Bauer to come out in support of Dollfuss's anti-Nazi strategy, and he later bitterly reproached the Social Democrats for failing in their patriotic duty. The historical evidence shows that opinion among the Social Democrats was divided. While left-wingers like Max Adler and Ernst Fischer demanded revolutionary action, the right wing led by Renner and Seitz inclined towards compromise. The weakness of the Social Democrats once again lay in their dithering, and even at the final party conference, held in Vienna in October 1933, the question was left unresolved. Bauer attempted to hold the two wings together, but his concluding speech merely disguised the Party's failure of nerve behind the rhetoric of anti-fascism. 'The Austro-Marxist sheep', as a historian has put it, 'was being dressed up as a militant wolf, but this failed to impress Dollfuss.' No wonder they were mocked by critics on the far left like Jura Soyfer.[24]

During 1933 the Social Democrats, led by a conciliatory faction from Lower Austria, made repeated efforts to negotiate with the government. On 7 January 1934 the Party authorized Renner and the Lower Austrian leader Oskar Helmer to put forward plans for co-operation.[25] But these approaches were ultimately blocked by Dollfuss, who was caught in a dilemma of his own. Although he was inclined towards compromise, his secret agreements with Mussolini committed him to the complete elimination of Marxism.[26] A further obstacle is revealed in a confidential briefing of Christian Social members of parliament on 12 January 1934, in which Dollfuss summed up his position: 'If a compromise were to be made today with the Socialists in any form, that would be the most favourable breeding ground for Nazism.'[27] Of course, Kraus can hardly be expected to have inside information about Dollfuss's decisions, although he may have been unduly influenced by the Chancellor's conciliatory speech of 18 January, reported in the *Arbeiter-Zeitung*. But he too readily swallowed the official line about the sins of the Social Democrats.

After the insurrection of February 1934, the full force of government propaganda was deployed against Austro-Marxism. The official position was that while the government and the Heimwehr were engaged in a heroic struggle against the Nazis, the treacherous socialists had attempted a putsch. It was even claimed that Dollfuss 'had offered the Social Democrats a partnership in the government, but that this had been turned down'.[28] Bauer and Deutsch, now safely in exile, were castigated as cowards who had left their comrades in the lurch. Although Kraus is normally a perceptive critic of propaganda, his satirical impulse was now suspended. In the section of *Die Fackel* written between April and early July 1934, he ignored the errors of the Dollfuss government, bitterly denouncing the Social Democrats. He acknowledged the courage of workers who took up arms to defend their cause, expressing sympathy with the victims on both sides. But the tendentiousness of his argument becomes clear when he refers to them as 'victims of the Social Democratic crime' (p. 277). Judicial investigations revealed that leaders like Renner, Seitz and Helmer had done their best to avoid armed conflict and were not guilty of any crime. Only in the case of Schutzbund commanders did the state prosecutor succeed in obtaining convictions.[29]

Kraus's critique is more convincing when he addresses a more pervasive phenomenon: the disabling effects of '"Kampf"-Publistik' – the rhetoric of 'struggle' (p. 48). *Der Kampf* was the title of the leading journal of Austro-Marxism, and theoreticians like Bauer and Pollak saw fascism in terms of a dialectical conception of 'struggle' which presaged the socialist revolution of the future. Kraus trenchantly dissects this pseudo-revolutionary verbiage, showing how it blinded the Social Democrats to the realities of practical politics. In an incisive passage he denounces Bauer for 'explaining everything, rationalizing everything, ultimately hoping for a world-revolutionary war from which, amid a hundred million gassed corpses, lo and behold the Executive Committee of the Second International will arise like a phoenix' (p. 179). In Bauer's speeches it is never entirely clear whether the much-vaunted struggle is a call for armed insurrection or merely an appeal for electoral support, and he was also mocked by communist critics for his fondness for 'military metaphors'.[30] Kraus argues that the Social Democrats have played into the hands of the Nazis by blurring the concept of 'struggle' and thus making it politically respectable. The difference is that, when Bauer speaks of struggle, his metaphor creates a spurious sense of militancy; but when the Nazi regime declares that it will destroy anyone who opposes it 'with complete brutality' (pp. 95–6) that is exactly what it means.

Austria as an Orderly State

Kraus insisted on a qualitative distinction between Dollfuss's authoritarian measures and Hitler's seizure of power. The Social Democrats tended to use a catch-all concept of 'fascism' to identify both regimes, but this terminological confusion is ironized in the very first pages of 'Warum die Fackel nicht erscheint' (p. 3). Kraus takes issue with articles by Bauer and Pollak which defined developments in Germany and Austria in terms of 'two fascisms', both equally dangerous. He acknowledges that there are moments when Bauer recognizes the need to distinguish between 'clerico-fascism' and National Socialism, but insists that his position is riddled with inconsistencies (pp. 173–92). After denouncing the regime of Dollfuss and Schuschnigg as a 'Catholic fascistic dictatorship', Bauer ultimately did come to recognize that it was only a form of 'semi-fascism' ('Halbfaschismus').[31] This insight did not prevent him from declaring, in a passage cited in *Die Fackel* after the failure of the February 1934 insurrection, that the bestialities of Austro-fascism were 'in no way less grievous than those committed by Hitler-fascism in Germany' (p. 192).

Kraus had no patience with the use of 'fascism' as a generalized 'political formula' ('politische Formel', p. 123). Throughout his polemic he places the words 'Austro-fascism' and 'clerico-fascism' in quotation marks, identifying the key features that distinguish totalitarian Germany from authoritarian Austria: political violence, racial persecution and the perversion of religion. He reserves the word 'totalitarian' for the unprecedented horror of the Nazi regime (p. 24), emphasizing that Nazism is based on vengeance against all who deviate from prescribed norms of 'belief or birth' (p. 71). Its fundamental principle is not simply 'violence' but 'murder' (p. 115). Since this wave of terror threatens the existence of Austria, the authoritarian measures taken by the Dollfuss government are justified by the principle of 'self-defence' (p. 218). He even finds words to commend Emil Fey, the commander of the Heimwehr units that bombarded the socialists into submission (p. 262). And he argues that the executions carried out after the revolt of February 1934 are limited in scale, compared with the disproportionate violence of Nazi Germany (p. 173). Austrian socialists involved in the insurrection have, he claims, been subjected to 'lenient penal sanctions' (p. 288).

This contrast is reinforced by the distinction between German concentration camps and the Austrian internment camp at Wöllersdorf. To illustrate the difference between Dachau and Wöllersdorf, Kraus recalls a live interview with prisoners in a concentration camp, broadcast on German radio on 8 April 1933 as a propaganda exercise. A Jewish socialist named Maron, who seized this opportunity to protest against Nazi brutality, was dragged screaming from the microphone and subsequently killed. For Kraus this was moment when you could hear 'the gates of hell clanging shut' (p. 273). To underline the contrast, he cites a newspaper item about Wöllersdorf, published in the socialist press under the heading 'Barbarism in Austria'. While prisoners are being tortured at Oranienburg by being locked up in 'vertical coffins' ('Stehsärge'), the worst that can be said about Wöllersdorf is that someone had been refused a blanket (p. 172). Kraus was accused of minimizing the horrors of 'Austrian concentration camps'.[32] But his claim that conditions at Wöllersdorf were relatively humane is confirmed by a witness who was no friend of the Dollfuss regime, the British journalist Gedye. After a visit to Wöllersdorf in April 1934, Gedye reported that life there was easy, if boring: 'There was no hard labour to be done, as in the German camps. The inmates had to rise at six, clean their own hutments, do one hour's compulsory gymnastics and put out their lights by 9 p.m. Otherwise the time was their own, and seemed to be devoted chiefly to football, sunbathing or reading under the trees.'[33] However harsh the anti-socialist measures of 1934, the government was even more resolute in the campaign against the Nazis. Rank-and-file socialists involved in the February revolt were in many cases released by the courts, while Nazi terrorists were treated with commendable firmness.[34] A survey of Wöllersdorf in October 1934 showed that over 4,700 of its inmates were Nazis (as against 550 socialists). They included Eduard Frauenfeld, Gauleiter of Vienna, who was held at Wöllersdorf for over two years. No government in Weimar Germany had ever acted with such determination.[35]

If the persecution of ethnic minorities is a defining feature of fascism, then the term can hardly be applied to the regimes of Dollfuss and Schuschnigg, since, as Kraus rightly observes, they were mercifully free of 'racial mania' (p. 183). He repeatedly draws attention to the linkage between the two Nazi slogans 'Deutschland erwache! Juda verrecke!' ('Germans awake! Let the Jews croak!'), leaving his readers in no doubt that the essential aim of Nazism is 'destruction' (p. 158), above all the destruction of the Jews. His support for Dollfuss reflects the fact that the Austrian state protected Jewish citizens against Nazi attacks and resisted arguments for antisemitic legislation. Although the authoritarian constitution of May 1934 defined Austria as a 'Christian' state, it also stipulated that 'all citizens are equal before the law' and that 'civil and political rights and access to public positions, offices and dignities are independent of religious belief'.[36] These fine principles were not always put into practice, but it was not illogical for Austrian Jews to admire Dollfuss as a 'mini-Mussolini' who offered protection against the twin dangers of Nazism and bolshevism. This spectacle was ridiculed by radical socialists, and Kraus quotes articles from the *Arbeiter-Zeitung* referring to supporters of Dollfuss as a 'Jewish prayer-meeting' and mocking the 'Jewish bourgeoisie' (pp. 185 & 188) for being scared of Nazism. Wealthy Jews who support Dollfuss, he replies, are acting far more rationally than socialists who oppose him, and it would be absurd for Jews *not* to support Austrian Catholics in their struggle against Hitler (pp. 222–4).

For Kraus, the Catholic opposition to Nazism is more than welcome. In the constitution promulgated by Dollfuss on 1 May 1934 for the Christian Corporate State, political authority was affirmed 'in the name of God, the Almighty', while the Christian Social Party was fused with the Fatherland Front.[37] Since Kraus during the Seipel era had consistently opposed the politicization of religion, his support for the Corporate State represents a remarkable volte-face, but the unprecedented gravity of the crisis led him to welcome resistance to Nazism from whatever quarter. In a series of provocative formulations he suggests that 'the resistance of the Church' (p. 183) has been more sustained and courageous than that of the free-thinkers, suggesting that the social policies of Catholics like Cardinal Innitzer deserve more credit than those of Hilferding, Bauer or Blum (p. 181). Since Innitzer notoriously came to terms with the Nazis after the Anschluss, this judgement scarcely seems tenable, but in the context of the debate about 'Austro-fascism' Kraus's tribute was not entirely undeserved. The Church inhibited the governments of Dollfuss and Schuschnigg from developing into full-blown fascist regimes, and Kraus had grounds for placing the concept of 'Austro-fascism' in quotation marks, even in the final number of *Die Fackel* (F 917–22, 99). Historically, his analysis shows a grasp of practical politics, while at a theoretical level it anticipates the conclusions of political scientists who have drawn a clear distinction between 'authoritarian' and 'fascist' regimes.[38]

Admiration for Dollfuss led Kraus to identify himself in July 1934 as an 'optimist' for Austria (p. 183). One cartoonist even published a sketch showing him lecturing from a platform embellished by the symbol of the Fatherland Front (Fig. 53). He was also targeted in a sketch written by Hans Weigel for the satirical cabaret 'Die Stachelbeere' ('The Gooseberries'), which featured

53   Cartoon of Kraus as a supporter of the Fatherland Front

two luxury hotels, one named 'Zur schönen Aussicht' (for fellow travellers of
Nazism), the other named 'Zum goldenen Kreuz' (for those toadying to the
clerical regime in Austria). The joke was that Kraus was among those who had
booked in at the clerical hotel, and that he would be given a room next to
Franz Werfel, the Schuschnigg supporter who was his arch rival. The satire was
accentuated by placing the scene in Canossa, the Italian city where a medieval
German emperor had famously been humiliated by the Pope. For a moment
Kraus was speechless, especially when one of his friends at the Café Parsifal
enthused about the show, but two days later he set out his counter-arguments
with considerable vigour.[39] After receiving a strong letter from his lawyer Oskar
Samek, the cabaret group agreed to omit all reference to Kraus from future performances. The issue, as he explained in Die Fackel, was not simply his personal
reputation, but the cabaret's failure to distinguish between supporters of
Austrian independence and apologists for Nazi terror (F 912–15, 12–19).
    Kraus certainly endorsed the firm measures taken by the government against
the Nazi campaign in Austria.[40] But at certain points he seems to be defending
– not some 'lesser evil' – but a positive conception of authoritarian government.[41] There was a conservative streak in his longing for a statesman capable
of saving Austria, and his support for Dollfuss echoes his praise of Franz

Ferdinand twenty years earlier. In an oblique allusion to the constitution promulgated by Dollfuss in May 1934, he admittedly distances himself from prevailing 'conceptions of the state'. But in the same breath he congratulates Dollfuss for having 'abolished politics' (p. 184) – a reference to the suspension of parliament and the postponement of elections. In a sustained polemic against the socialists, the slogans of 'freedom' and 'democracy' are challenged in a style reminiscent of his assault on the rhetoric of liberalism before the First World War. Kraus, as he declared in legal submissions drafted during the final year of his life, was sceptical about 'democracy' and 'never made a secret of the fact that he rejected the liberal position in politics, economic life and the expression of opinion' (P 4, 276 & 290). He seems in 1934, as in 1915, positively to welcome both the abolition of trial by jury and the curbing of freedom of the press.

One of the most striking passages in 'Warum die Fackel nicht erscheint' suggests that controlling the irresponsibility of mass-circulation newspapers might provide the basis for constructing an 'orderly state' ('ein Ordnungsstaat', p. 280). Kraus does not comment in any detail on the innumerable controls imposed during 1933–4 by decrees designed to restrict journalistic sensationalism as well as political dissent. Through a process that began with occasional confiscations and culminated in systematic pre-censorship, editors were compelled to respect the principles of the Corporate State. Banner headlines and irresponsible rumours were prohibited, as were salacious photographs and intrusive reports about people's private lives, much to the discomfort of editors like Hans Habe, the son of Bekessy.[42] Kraus had repeatedly criticized the unrestricted freedom of the press, suggesting that an enlightened form of censorship might be preferable (F 712–16, 99–100). There was thus a significant convergence between his long-standing critique and the new controls. Indeed, the director of the Government Press Office responsible for enforcing the regulations, Bundespressechef Eduard Ludwig, was a reader of *Die Fackel* who had evidently sympathized with Kraus's efforts to curb the excesses of papers like *Die Stunde*.[43] Ludwig, who was responsible for stemming the flood of Nazi publications, was among the first to be deported to Dachau after the Anschluss.

The Austria that Kraus supported was an authoritarian anti-Nazi state. Official propaganda may have presented Dollfuss – and later Schuschnigg – as the 'Führer'.[44] But in practice they both relied on a traditional system of cabinet government, where decisions were taken by majority vote in accordance with emergency legislation, with President Miklas, as head of state, exercising a restraining influence. Although parliament was suspended, the stenographic record of Cabinet meetings shows that there were wide-ranging policy discussions, inconceivable under a dictatorship.[45] Even the decision to postpone parliamentary elections was less an anti-democratic than an anti-Nazi measure, designed to prevent Hitler's supporters from making sweeping gains (on 23 April 1933 the Nazis won 41 per cent of the vote in local elections at Innsbruck). Moreover, the curbing of the press was directed in the first instance against the *Völkischer Beobachter*, not the *Arbeiter-Zeitung*, which was not banned until the insurrection of February 1934. Kraus supported this system because he recognized that force had to be met with force. If Hitler was be overthrown, he argued, the statesmen of Europe must act in unison, committing themselves to an 'authoritarian decision'. Hence his claim that Dollfuss's resistance to Nazism prefigured the 'salvation of Europe' (pp. 112 & 206).

Propaganda Trips to Prague

If Kraus had really been a fascist sympathizer, he would have followed the example of Starhemberg and cultivated his contacts in Rome. Instead, he undertook the more difficult task of pleading the cause of Austria in Prague. During the years 1933–6 he paid at least ten visits to Czechoslovakia, frequently using the newly established air service between Vienna and Prague. Visits to Sidonie Nadherny in Janowitz provided a lifeline during the darkest days, although she later recalled that at one point he suggested a suicide pact: 'He could no more endure what happened under Hitler, he foresaw no future & doubted the sense of his past work, he could not bear to condemn himself to silence.'[46] However, he did not remain entirely silent, and his activities in Prague show that he never abandoned hope. The most significant visit took place early in March 1934, barely two weeks after the crushing of the socialist revolt. It was not Dollfuss whom he blamed for the bloodshed but the Social Democratic leadership, as he explained in a letter from the Palace Hotel in Prague to his French friend Marcel Ray. Early in February there had also been violent confrontations between left-wing and right-wing demonstrators in Paris, and this led Kraus to condemn Blum as well as Bauer for failing to mobilize support against 'the real enemy' – Nazism.[47] In France, too, internal divisions were tearing the country apart, undermining resistance to the power of Germany. Writing to Sidonie Nadherny, Kraus summarized his attempts to convince his friends in Prague of the justice of Dollfuss's cause and the treachery of the Austrian Social Democrats (BSN 1, 652–8), and he was later to describe this visit to Prague as an 'unpaid propaganda trip' (F 917–22, 74). Those involved in the discussions included Heinrich Fischer, two young socialists named Emil Franzel and Erich Heller, and the Czech authors Jan Münzer, Ferdinand Peroutka and Karel Čapek (P 4, 93–5 & 108–9). Fischer, who visited him in his hotel, found him 'physically worn out, though his reasoning was as sharp as ever'. When his socialist friends argued that he should condemn that 'bloodhound' Major Fey, Kraus replied: 'If a bloodhound is trained against Hitler, the bloodhound becomes my friend.'[48] As a result of these discussions, his friends were able to explain his political position before he did so himself. Erich Heller offered a summary of Kraus's arguments in an article published on 28 April 1934 in the Prague *Sozialdemokrat*, and Jan Münzer followed this with an article in Czech on 'The Silence of Karl Kraus', published on 2 May in *Pritomnost* (cited F 890–905, 219–20 & 235–52).[49]

Czechoslovakia formed an island of democracy, granting asylum to refugees from Germany and Austria, but Kraus observed their activities with scepticism, continuing to criticize Otto Bauer and his followers after they had transferred their headquarters to Brno. Even the journalistic projects of Willy Haas, formerly editor of Die literarische Welt, seemed to him suspect, and he wrote a letter to President Masaryk warning him not to support them.[50] However, Kraus himself benefited from the liberal policies of the Czech government. When his supporters devised a plan to save stocks of his books in Leipzig from being destroyed by the Nazis, it was to Prague that they brought them. Jan Münzer initiated the transfer, which resulted in considerable friction with the new distributor (P 4, 24–62). Kraus had a great affection for the Czech Republic. However strong his antipathy towards politicians and littérateurs of every nation, he insisted that he found among the Czechs 'more understanding even for matters relating to the German language than among officials of Germandom' (P 4, 30). To keep in touch with Czech opinion, he arranged for the Prager Tagblatt to be delivered to him in Vienna every morning, and references to this paper became increasingly frequent in his writings. He had friends on the staff of the paper, including the young Friedrich Torberg, whose writings he admired, and the erudite Ludwig Steiner, whose pronouncements he loved to parody.[51]

The Tagblatt was the most highly regarded German-language newspaper in Prague, attempting – at a time when the press in Germany and Austria was strictly censored – to maintain an independent line. Its office was located close to the Palace Hotel, and during Kraus's visits the editor, Dr Sigmund Blau, conversed with him about ways of raising journalistic standards.[52] Kraus responded with lengthy letters urging the paper to take a more critical view of events in Germany, in one of which he described himself with gentle irony as a 'loyal reader'.[53] In reality, his response was ambivalent, and in his correspondence with Sidonie Nadherny the code-word for the Prager Tagblatt is that 'wretched rag' ('Schandblatt'; BSN 1, 662). He was entertained by the paper's notorious misprints. 'Whaat treasures – !' ('Schäätze – !'), he declared, echoing Nestroy, finding both the paper's content and its orthography 'intresting' ('intressant' [sic]; F 917–22, 75 & 80). More seriously, he tried to persuade the Czechs to adopt a more positive attitude towards the Dollfuss government, welcoming the Tagblatt as a potential ally. The Czech-language press was less accessible, but he was delighted when, early in 1936, an editorial appeared in Ceske Slovo praising Dollfuss and Schuschnigg for their defence of Austrian independence. Kraus felt that his propaganda trip was at last paying dividends (F 917–22, 73–4).

The most difficult task was to explain why he was 'against Schober and for Dollfuss'. A passage in the final number of Die Fackel (F 917–22, 96–7) explains that Kraus would not have opposed Schober 'if he had had to resist Hitler (instead of smoothing his path)'. This implies that Schober's use of armed police against the demonstrators in July 1927 had prepared the ground for a Nazi take-over. A further explanation of his support for Dollfuss can be found in his court testimony. During the years 1934–6, Kraus initiated more than a dozen legal actions, of which the most significant were heard in Prague. His opponents ridiculed him for fighting court cases about faulty punctuation – the notorious 'Contest about a Comma'.[54] But the most important of these actions were political, designed to refute the charge that he supported Dollfuss for opportunistic reasons. The submissions to Czech courts, drafted in consultation with his lawyers Oskar Samek in Vienna and Jan Turnovsky in Prague, had the further objective of promoting a rapprochement between Austria and Czechoslovakia. Kraus used the courts to emphasize that the Hitler regime threatened 'not only Austria but the whole of Europe, especially Czechoslovakia' (P 4, 205). While the political formulations of *Die Fackel* are notoriously oblique, the submissions to the Czech courts are expressed in plainer language. A declaration of May 1936, intended for publication in the *Prager Tagblatt*, clarifies the contradictions in his position by explaining 'that he attacked the Heimwehr in its earlier phase and did not attack the Heimwehr when it actively resisted Hitler, that he attacked Schober's police at the time of Bekessy's domination, but acknowledged Dollfuss's police in its fight against assassination attempts with explosives' (P 4, 149). He argued that it was in the Czech interest to support Austria's resistance against Hitler, recalling that one of the spokesmen of Czech democracy – Ferdinand Peroutka – had praised him in March 1934 for his grasp of *Realpolitik* (F 917–22, 74).[55]

Kraus was sensitive to German nationalist undertones in the discourse of both Vienna and Prague. He despised the 'Teutomania' of the Sudeten Germans (F 657–67, 74), identifying the movement led by Konrad Henlein as a particular danger (F 917–22, 75). One of his most incisive polemics deals with the author Johannes Urzidil, press attaché at the German embassy in Prague, whom he accused of anti-Czech propaganda, first in *Die Fackel* in 1931 (F 864–7, 40–9), later – in February 1936 – in the courts (P 4, 293–4). But the acrimony caused by Kraus's attacks on the Austrian Social Democratic leadership made it difficult for him to justify himself in the eyes of Czech socialists. The journal *Sozialdemokrat*, official German-language organ of the Czech party, had for years been among his most resolute supporters. As late as April 1934, it published a tribute by Emil Franzel to mark his sixtieth birthday. But on 10 August, after Kraus's defence of Dollfuss, the same journal carried an anonymous article denouncing *Die Fackel* as a 'fascist' publication. Kraus responded with an action for defamation which appeared to have every prospect of success, since *Sozialdemokrat* had described him as an 'accomplice of the Austrian hangman'. It was not possible to identify the author of this virulent attack, although Samek suspected Emil Frankel (P 4, 125) – an ambiguous figure who later joined the Nazis. The case dragged on for eighteen months (P 4, 63–132), and in April 1936 Kraus, who was present in court, lost on a technicality. Turnovsky, when accepting a compromise relating to a secondary action, had failed to reserve the right to continue the case for defamation. The outcome may also have been influenced by ideological factors, and Turnovsky warned Samek that the judges were supporters of the Social Democrats (P 4, 68). This bitter court battle overshadowed the final months of Kraus's life, leaving him physically and emotionally exhausted.

In diplomatic terms, however, Kraus's interventions were vindicated. At a time when relations between Austria and Czechoslovakia were extremely tense, he made a determined effort to convince opinion-formers in Prague that the policies of Dollfuss, Starhemberg and Schuschnigg were justified. In May 1935 he commented that the Beneš government, which used the Viennese newspaper *Der Tag* as its mouthpiece, was still equivocating about Austria's 'defensive war' (F 909–11, 58–9). But in January 1936 there was a thaw in Austro-Czech relations, marked by Schuschnigg's visit to Prague, followed by return visits to Vienna by the Prime Minister of Czechoslovakia, Milan Hodza. At last there was a prospect of a 'normalisation of relations between the Danube states', as Hodza put it.[56] This provided Kraus with his cue for that 'defence of the Danube' which forms a leitmotif in the final number of *Die Fackel* (F 917–22, 77). An article published in the *Prager Tagblatt* raised further hopes of a rapprochement. Praising the Austrian government for its humane treatment of political prisoners, the author – Alfred Polgar – observed 'that once again this peculiar, small, powerless, and in a thousand ways lovable country has made us aware what a disgrace and disaster it would be, if it were nailed to the crooked cross' (cited F 917–22, 78). Czechoslovakia, too, was in Kraus's eyes a 'lovable country', and he was delighted by the dawning realization that a Nazi take-over in Austria would be a disaster for the Czechs. Even socialists like Erich Heller, who had dared to contradict him, were finally 'converted' – although 'too late to tell him'.[57] Kraus insisted that Hitler had to be resisted as a force of absolute evil. When in November 1934 he paid his final tribute to Dollfuss, his audience rose to their feet as a sign of respect. They understood what he meant in describing Dollfuss as the guardian standing 'at the gates of Walpurgis Night' (F 912–15, 71).

CHAPTER 25

Third Walpurgis Night

Dritte Walpurgisnacht was written between March and September 1933 in response to Hitler's seizure of power. This remarkable anti-Nazi polemic was typeset and scheduled to appear in a special number of *Die Fackel*, but in autumn 1933 Kraus decided against publication. The text, which has aptly been described as 'work in progress', survives in the form of corrected proofs with many emendations.[1] After Kraus's death, the most complete set of proofs was smuggled out of Austria by his lawyer Oskar Samek and taken to New York. It was not until 1952 that the book finally appeared, edited by Heinrich Fischer for the Kösel Verlag. A second edition, incorporating minor corrections, was published in 1967 with a fifty-page commentary, but it was not until 1989 that a more comprehensive version, edited by Christian Wagenknecht and incorporating textual variants, was published by Suhrkamp.[2] Critical opinion about *Dritte Walpurgisnacht* is divided. It was hailed by the Swiss dramatist Friedrich Dürrenmatt as a definitive analysis, but dismissed by Fritz Raddatz, editor of the works of Tucholsky, as a 'declaration of intellectual bankruptcy'.[3] This conflict of opinion arises from the intricacy of the text, which addresses reactionary politics through the prism of literary modernism, highlighting the difficulty of turning terror into form. The most poignant effects are achieved through a documentary technique modified by intertextuality and montage. Consequently, the argument appears to be decentred and to lack a progressive logic, reflecting the author's awareness of the limits of language in the face of catastrophe.

Language and Silence

'All words fail,' wrote Christopher Isherwood in a letter from Berlin to his friend Stephen Spender, after Hitler was appointed chancellor. The young English authors, deeply in love with Germany, found it impossible to comprehend how a progressive democracy could be transformed into a reactionary dictatorship. Events were so radically at odds with conventional modes of representation that they felt compelled to abandon the novels they were writing about their formative experiences. Moreover, they were baffled by the contradictory Nazi attitudes towards sexuality, which combined intense male bonding with vicious homophobia. Isherwood's conversations with Berthold Viertel, whom he met in London in autumn 1933 while working on the film *Little Friend*, may have provided him with new insights, especially as he learnt for the first time about Viertel's 'own elected Socrates', Karl Kraus.[4] But he had to resign himself to publishing *Goodbye to Berlin* as a collection of fragments, and it was a further fifty years before Spender succeeded in completing his novel about the rise of Nazism, *The Temple*. Viewing events from the security of Sweden, Kurt Tucholsky experienced the crisis in an even more acute form. His notebook from this period closes with a graphic representation of the progression from speech through writing to silence. After 1932 he did not write another word for publication, and in December 1935 he took his own life.[5]

Kraus, too, appeared in 1933 to be at a loss for words. After spending the summer partly in Janowitz, struggling to complete *Dritte Walpurgisnacht*, he decided against publication, stressing the 'manifest inadequacy' of his efforts (F 890–905, 35). He also shared with Heinrich Fischer a fear that his polemic might provoke reprisals against helpless victims of National Socialism in Germany, and he had reason to be concerned for his own safety after the radical publicist Theodor Lessing was assassinated by Nazi thugs on 31 August, after escaping to Czechoslovakia (308/*336*). He must have been aware that members of his pre-war circle, including Kurt Hiller and Erich Mühsam, were enduring the brutality of Nazi prisons.[6] In exile in London during the early 1940s, Fischer described Kraus's reactions: 'I remember how he would turn pale, how the veins in his forehead would swell, how he gazed with a look of uncomprehending astonishment at the newspaper in which he now read day after day of things more frightening than the worst carnage of the last war. Concentration camp, torture, persecution of Jews, pillory – all these things he would experience in imagination with an intensity that brought on physical decline and final collapse.'[7]

Returning to Janowitz in September 1933, Kraus wrote the poem that proclaimed his silence, 'Man frage nicht' (F 888, 4):

Man frage nicht, was all die Zeit ich machte.
Ich bleibe stumm;
und sage nicht, warum.
Und Stille gibt es, da die Erde krachte.
Kein Wort, das traf;
man spricht nur aus dem Schlaf.
Und träumt von einer Sonne, welche lachte.
Es geht vorbei;
nachher war's einerlei.
Das Wort entschlief, als jene Welt erwachte.

Don't ask about the actions I've been taking.
I'll not speak out,
nor say what it's about.
And there is silence when the earth's been quaking.
No word that fits;
you speak with drowsy wits,
and dream of smiling suns when morning's breaking.
It cannot last;
later it all was past.
The Word expired on Hitler's world's awaking.

The crisis of communication is stated in the plainest terms, framed by basic rhymes and brusque changes of tense. Two lines carry a particular imaginative charge. The fourth blends apocalyptics with geophysics, recalling the 'earthquake' from the Book of Revelation and the 'silence' that followed the breaking of the Seventh Seal.[8] The final line sets Nazi evangelism against biblical *logos*. The surface meaning may be that – in the face of Nazi violence – 'writing is useless'.[9] However, it is not simply 'words' that have failed but 'the Word' – the fundament of western civilization.

It was nine months before the next number of *Die Fackel* appeared, after the delays caused by the abortive socialist revolt of February 1934. Kraus's long-winded justification of his silence in 'Warum die Fackel nicht erscheint' is offset by dazzling excerpts from the manuscript of *Dritte Walpurgisnacht*, including the defiant opening statement: 'Hitler brings nothing to my mind' ('Mir fällt zu Hitler nichts ein'; F 890–905, 153). But the principal target is the obtuseness of the Social Democrats, and Canetti was reportedly so incensed that he tore that number of the magazine to pieces before Kraus's eyes.[10] The following year Berthold Viertel visited Kraus in Vienna in an effort to persuade him that his support for authoritarian Austria was mistaken. After a discussion that lasted through the night, they parted without reaching agreement. It was not that Kraus was mistaken about Hitler, indeed he saw only too clearly that the new barbarism would claim an 'infinite burden of victims'. But the catastrophe, as Viertel recalls, had reduced him to a state of hopelessness: 'Here the apocalyptic satirist, who had seen and suffered so much before the event, had reached the limits of his visionary power, just as the human being had reached the limits of his life.'[11] However, Viertel failed to realize that it was not a single author who had fallen silent, but a whole language that had reached its 'breaking point'.[12]

This crisis of communication is reflected in the response of Robert Musil, the only Austrian author of comparable critical intelligence. In 'Bedenken eines Langsamen' ('Laggardly Doubts'), an essay drafted during 1933, Musil attempted to analyse National Socialism by rational means, using statistics to show that German intellectual life had *not* been dominated by Jews. As an Aryan author he felt a 'duty to speak', since silence would lay him open to misunderstandings. Although his opposition to the Hitler regime was beyond question, this text shows that the lucid analytical discourse at which Musil excelled was wholly inadequate to the crisis, and it is not surprising that he left the essay unpublished, indeed unfinished. The only moment of Krausian insight occurs in a comment on the two main tendencies of the German leadership. The first, seen as 'conservative', attempts to persuade independent-minded authors to join the Nazi bandwagon; the second, defined as 'revolutionary', is epitomized by the words: 'If you won't be my brother I'll bash your skull in!'[13]

The person who came closest to appreciating Kraus's position was Bertolt Brecht. Seeking refuge in Vienna from the Nazi threat, he met Kraus in March 1933 at his favourite coffee-house, only to be greeted with the apodictic words: 'The rats are boarding the sinking ship.'[14] Their contacts during those days in Vienna helped to cement their friendship, but Austria was scarcely a safe haven for left-wing refugees. Brecht resettled in a fisherman's cottage in Denmark, and in autumn 1933 he invited Kraus to join him there, if the situation in Austria no longer appealed to him.[15] His letters and poems show that their conversations in Vienna had left a deep impression. After the publication of 'Man frage nicht', he wrote an elegy 'On the significance of the ten-line poem in number 888 of Die Fackel', commending Kraus's eloquent silence.[16] He had second thoughts when he heard that Kraus had supported Dollfuss against the socialists, penning a far more critical poem lamenting 'The rapid fall of the ignorant man of virtue'.[17] But their relationship survived the rift, and in November 1934 Brecht wrote to Helene Weigel in Vienna advising her to 'be nice' to Kraus and asking her to purchase his Shakespeare adaptations. It must have been at this time that Weigel presented him with Brecht's second, sharply critical poem.[18] The most significant of Brecht's letters to Kraus, dating from the same period, urges him to continue his study of language: 'The most frightful devastations have been caused by language. You have disclosed the atrocities of intonation and created an ethics of language' ('eine Sittenlehre der Sprache'). To stress the importance of this subject at times of crisis, he cites the examples of Confucius and Lao-tzu, as if Kraus were a Chinese sage who had to be coaxed into sharing his wisdom with the world.[19]

Dritte Walpurgisnacht can be seen as the fulfilment of Brecht's wish for an 'ethics' that interprets atrocities in linguistic terms. Kraus may feel that individual protest has been silenced, but this did not prevent him from immersing himself in the war of words, at the risk of being swamped by the surge of material. The stance he assumes is that of 'Wortregisseur' (238/259), a stage director orchestrating a cacophony of voices. The resulting acoustic montage juxtaposes the beguiling doublespeak of Goebbels with the raucous chanting of the SA, while a poignant counterpoint is provided by the plaintive cries of their victims: socialists and communists being dragged off to concentration camps, lawyers and shopkeepers whose existence has been destroyed. Liberals line up with nationalists, time-serving journalists with Nazi broadcasters, while cringing aristocrats conspire with petit-bourgeois usurpers. The impact of the tragedy is heightened by a range of discordant registers, from the exalted tones of patriotic intellectuals to advertising slogans and popular songs. Moreover, in Kraus's *Walpurgisnacht*, as in Eliot's *Waste Land*, the babble of a benighted civilization is blended with the discourse of the poets. The language of Goethe and Shakespeare forms a foil to the jargon of Goebbels and Benn, while there are undertones of biblical discourse. These polyphonic techniques enable Kraus to express not simply his own opinions, but the struggle for the soul of Germany.

The challenge was far greater than it had been in autumn 1914, when he had also reacted with a provisional declaration of silence (F 404, 2). Then the adversaries had been more evenly matched, since sensational news was still reported by 'cold' media: special editions of newspapers and proclamations posted in public squares. But in 1933 it is no longer the newsvendor whose voice signals catastrophe, but the massed ranks of stormtroopers chanting anti-semitic slogans. The bumbling staff officer who provided such rewarding material for *Die letzten Tage der Menschheit* has now been displaced by the hyper-efficient Propaganda Minister, and the media are 'hot': spoken words transformed into piercing slogans by radio broadcasts and the apparatus of mass communications.[20] But Kraus responds with great resourcefulness, orchestrating official declarations and snippets from political speeches into a composition that attunes us to the religious rhetoric underlying the Hitler cult. Moreover, fascist propaganda is correlated with liberal journalism, so that the conventional black-and-white picture of the seizure of power becomes fraught with ambiguity, as the book offers an indictment not simply of National Socialism, but of the deeply compromised civilization from which it emerged.

Dritte Walpurgisnacht incorporates over a thousand excerpts from the political discourse of 1933, interwoven with more than two hundred literary allusions. It also refers to about two hundred individuals by name, many of them extremely obscure, and footnotes are needed to elucidate a lexicon which extends from Auwi and Futterweit to Schweppermann and Uschla.[21] Other figures not mentioned by name, like the children of the American ambassador (200/*221*), also deserve to be identified so that the atrocities they witnessed can be authenticated.[22] The text is so densely woven that it threatens to lose the reader in a 'maze of thousands of antithetical allusions' (15/*24*). The literary references have never been fully elucidated, despite promising preliminary studies, and an annotated edition of this prophetic political text is long overdue.[23] Moreover the density of the text resists translation (only short excerpts are available in English).[24] It may be helpful to start with a synopsis, designed to elucidate Kraus's attempt to integrate 'formal prolixity' (20/*33*) into a 'plot' (289/*324*).

Prolixity and Plot

The book begins with that defiant statement of speechlessness: 'Hitler brings nothing to my mind,' hinting at 'das Nichts' – 'nothingness'. The brain is paralysed by events that defy explanation, since the Nazi system is based on violence and its ultimate aim is 'annihilation' (15/23). Kraus's response oscillates between Goethe's invocation of 'the indescribable' (*Faust*, l. 12108) and Shakespeare's painfully consoling principle that 'the worst is not / So long as we can say "This is the worst"' (*King Lear*, Act IV, scene 1, 28–9). However, he approaches his subject obliquely, switching the focus 'from the apocalyptic to the journalistic' (27/40), while repudiating the suggestion that there is any parallel between the suppression of press freedom by the Nazis and his own 'anti-journalistic thinking' (24/37). A Viennese newspaper has claimed that Hitler has fulfilled Kraus's wildest dreams by eliminating 'hack journalists' and expelling from Germany enemies of *Die Fackel* like Reinhardt and Kerr. Kraus points out that his aversion to journalism is fundamentally different from that of the Nazis. Indeed, his satire on reactionary Germany has been so outspoken that it is surprising his own work has not been included in the book-burnings.

To show that journalistic attitudes are still thriving under the Nazis, Kraus focuses on one of his adversaries from the liberal press, Bernhard Diebold of the *Frankfurter Zeitung*. He accuses Diebold of attempting to ingratiate himself with Goebbels in an article denouncing Kraus, Brecht and Tucholsky as 'destroyers of culture' (36/49). Diebold has also argued that radicals who prefer Offenbach to Wagner are responsible for 'cultural confusion' (33/46). In a scathing rejoinder, Kraus reaffirms his admiration for Offenbach, whose music has been banned in Germany, denouncing Diebold as 'the type who has sold himself to the devil' (39/52).

The extreme example of journalistic manipulation is provided by Goebbels, the Propaganda Minister who masters all linguistic registers, from the jargon of the liberal press to the visionary rhetoric of Expressionism. This gift for blending modernity and myth underlies Goebbels's appeal for a new German art based on 'steely romanticism' (42/54). This phrase is cited from the speech of 8 May on 'The Tasks of the German Theatre', in which Goebbels called for a heroic art to express the soul of the *Volk*.[25] What this means in practice is exemplified by poems on the theme 'Throw the Jews out!' by an unidentified author (Johann von Leers). With mock seriousness Kraus evaluates these appalling verses, emphasizing the link between poetry and politics. The precept 'Juden raus!' is being implemented 'by our wonderful stormtroopers' (49/62), assaulting Jews on the streets before dragging them off to the concentration camps. Hitler is celebrated in the Nazi press as an 'artistic connoisseur' (51/64). Ironizing this claim, Kraus shows that Goebbels's programme for artistic renewal has produced third-rate imitations of Heine, the Jewish poet whom the Nazis have banned. However, modern versions of Heine's most famous poem, 'Die Lorelei', conceal the fact that there are real corpses in the 'peacefully flowing Rhine'.

In an efficiently functioning Walpurgisnacht, according to Mephisto, 'the philosopher is also welcome' (*Faust*, l. 7844). But what philosophy could sanction horrors like 'the use of steel-rods' for 'the transformation of naked, even female bodies into lumps of bleeding flesh' (55/68)? Wagner has become a cult figure for the Nazis, but he despised the shallowness of German nationalism. Nietzsche's role is more problematic, since so much damage has been done by the concept of the 'superman', but the murderous activities of Nazi gangs come closer to the 'herd morality' he abhorred. Nietzsche preferred Jews to Germans and despised the antisemites. Only Heidegger and Spengler really qualify as 'verbal accomplices of violence' (59/72). Of the poets, it is Gottfried Benn who has offered the most extravagant justification for Nazism. This erstwhile left-wing intellectual epitomizes the 'sacrifice of intellect' (66/78). Quoting from one of the diatribes Benn delivered on Berlin radio, Kraus exposes his irrationalism, which blends heroic myth with pseudo-scientific jargon. Benn claims that the Nazi vision would still survive, even 'if ten wars were to erupt from the east and the west' to destroy it. This prompts Kraus to reflect on the irrepressible spirit of militarism, which he attributes to mistakes made during the post-war settlement. German paranoia about the 'stab in the back' has resulted in a longing for a 'war of revenge' against the 'enemy within' (76/88).

The problem of militarism leads to an analysis of the role of Papen, Hitler's Vice-Chancellor. Papen is one of those aristocrats whose function is to make conciliatory speeches which 'endow criminal affairs with an internationally acceptable veneer'. The utterances of this 'Janus-faced politician' (82/94) are juxtaposed with excerpts from a play by 'our national poet' (the xenophobic *Schlageter* by Hanns Johst), culminating in the notorious declaration: 'When I hear the word culture, I release the safety-catch on my revolver' (85/96). An even more astonishing phenomenon is the organization of German-nationalist Jews, which has published a book denouncing reports of Jewish persecution as 'atrocity propaganda'. Stories in the foreign press, so they claim, are damaging the interests of Jews living in Germany. Kraus ridicules this type of 'double-liar', the cringing apologist of German infamy. Wealthy German-nationalist Jews, he argues, have miscalculated 'the profit margins of cowardice' (86/98).

The liberal press in Austria is also trying to give the impression that for German Jews it is business as usual, despite the boycott of Jewish shops on 1 April 1933. Jewish doctors and lawyers may have been barred from their professions, but – according to the *Neue Freie Presse* – 'tranquillity and order prevail' and 'every German citizen of the Jewish faith' can carry on his business undisturbed (91/103). Kraus exposes the deviousness of these attempts to minimize the disaster. He attributes this delusion to four main factors. First, poverty of imagination: one could hardly function as a social being if one really faced such horrors. Secondly, deceit: the Nazis are systematic practitioners of lying. Thirdly, fear: people are unwilling to protest for fear of retaliation. Finally, incredulity: events really are 'unbelievable', so people are gripped by 'the urge not to believe what they know to be true' (99/110). Reports are quoted recording the brutality of the SA towards women and children, as well as Jews. Since it seems inconceivable that any human being could behave in this way, such reports are discounted as atrocity propaganda. 'Far worse than murder', Kraus concludes, 'is murder plus mendacity' (98/*110*). Some German intellectuals, including the psychologist Wolfgang Koehler and the author Ricarda Huch, have had the courage to distance themselves from Nazism, but refugee authors have tended to lament the damage to culture, rather than the destruction of human life. Kraus's scepticism about such apostles of culture is reinforced by events at the PEN Club congress in Dubrovnik. The Austrian delegates, led by Felix Salten and Grete Urbanitzky, have tried to block a resolution condemning the persecution of writers in Germany. He contrasts their evasiveness with the reality of concentration camps, alluding to a photograph (Fig. 54) which shows colleagues from Berlin Radio, including Hans Flesch and Alfred Braun, surrounded by wolf-like Nazis.

Kraus cites the slogan 'Against the mutilation of the German language!' used by the Nazis to justify the burning of books, and goes on to show how

54   'Former Radio Chiefs in the Concentration Camp', August 1933

grievously they themselves have abused the language. It is not simply their grammar that is faulty. Building on the worst practices of journalism, they have developed a system of euphemisms designed for 'the concealment of shameful facts' (113/127). Goebbels combines a command of journalistic jargon with a genius for coining new concepts and acronyms. This 'verbal imperialism' reduces language to a rigid system of predetermined categories and renders flexible thinking impossible (115/130). This analysis is confirmed by further passages from Benn's radio broadcast, which are so confused that they result in 'the refutation of his thought by his language' (116/132). Behind his rhetoric lurks the awkward fact, reported in the same newspaper that published his text, that under the Nazis the price of butter has gone up by almost 50 per cent.

The focus on language is intensified through an analysis of how phrases like 'running the gauntlet' are regaining their physical meaning in the Third Reich. The process is epitomized by a metaphor that, as we have noted, had a literal basis, 'rubbing salt in the wound'. Kraus quotes a report describing how an elderly socialist in a Nazi prison cut his hand while peeling potatoes, and then experienced the agony of having his hand thrust into a bag of salt (123/140). In the literary field, too, it is hard to distinguish metaphor from fact. The writer who longs to win poetic 'laurels' may now be able to help himself to a handful from the plot of land he has grabbed with the help of the SA. Kraus comments ironically on a black list of authors whose works are banned in Germany. They include a pornographic novel by Hans Heinz Ewers, an Austrian Nazi who in younger days was an admirer of Jewish culture and produced a poem against the pogroms in Russia. As antidote to Ewers's new-found enthusiasm for Nazism, Kraus quotes poems by Platen about the oppression of Poland during the nineteenth century, recalling that Platen, like Hölderlin, regarded the Germans as 'barbarians' (131–2/150–1). However, not every Jewish writer has been banned in Germany. An exception has been made for the Zionist author Emanuel bin Gorion, praised by the Nazis for opposing Jewish assimilation and supporting the 'Jewish-*völkisch* principle' (135/154). Since this decree is issued under the authority of the Prime Minister of Prussia, Kraus remarks that 'Gorion has made a hit with Goering' (136/155). Every book by a Jewish author must now be identified as a 'translation from the Hebrew'. Responding to a letter from a German broadcasting company, Kraus suggests that logically this must also apply to his own translation of Shakespeare's sonnets.

Nazi propaganda achieves its most insidious effects through 'tricks' or 'snares' of intonation (142/163). With Mephistophelian ingenuity (an allusion to *Faust*, l. 1976), 'sense' is turned into 'nonsense' and back again. To illustrate this process, Kraus quotes prize examples of the 'national-socialist communiqué', including self-contradictory declarations about Germany's expansionist aims. Supported by patriotic authors like Rudolf Binding, the wily Goebbels knows how to endow 'devious treachery' with an air of 'unimpeachable honesty'. The victims of Nazi violence are presented as if they were perpetrators, according to the principle of 'inverted causality' (153/*174*). National Socialism is distinguished from earlier forms of tyranny by its self-righteousness. The Party claims that its actions are designed to save Germany from communism, and Hitler has promised that Germany will pay the expenses of any Jew who wants to emigrate. Bloodthirsty deeds, in short, are clothed in a 'halo of sanctity'. According to the logic of the new civilization 'the murderer has not committed murder, if he denies his crime' and 'the cowardice of the murder gives him the stature of a hero' (165/*185*).

In Austria, as in Germany, the Nazis minimize their crimes by speaking of 'alleged' atrocities. The death of the Viennese jeweller Futterweit must surely have been suicide, even after it was proved that Nazis had planted the bomb (168–9/*188–90*). Austria's government is accused of atrocities – for sending terrorists to prison. These allegations lead Kraus to recall the concept he had coined for German propaganda during the First World War: 'innocent victimizers' (173/*194*). In a review of official attitudes towards both Austria and the Jews, he shows that the Nazis have perfected the art of aggressive self-righteousness, exemplified by the institution of 'protective custody'. Kraus contrasts the claim that social deviants are being detained for their own protection with documents showing what this really implies: gruesome injuries frequently resulting in death. With Swiftian irony he pretends to accept the official line that the concentration camps are enlightened reformatories. He is thus at a loss to explain why so many inmates seem to injure themselves or die of heart failure. Irony turns into invective as he records dozens of incidents of self-righteous sadism and perverted cruelty. Much of this takes place in public, with the victims paraded through the streets of Germany. Why are foreign powers ignoring what is happening?

Since this sadism has sexual undertones, the focus shifts to the treatment of women. Nazi regulations prescribe that 'gentlemen are to prefer blondes' (199/*219*). If a German girl fancies a Jew, she is likely to be dragged through the streets by a howling mob, wearing a placard proclaiming her shame. Such incidents are endorsed by the police as 'justifiable outbreaks of popular fury', while Jews denounced for lechery are sent to concentration camps (203/*226*). Meanwhile Hitler is celebrated with religious fervour and the antisemitic Hans Frank identifies National Socialism with humanism. Kraus contrasts this hypocrisy with the directness of Dollfuss, who, as noted, informed Frank at Aspern airport that his visit was unwelcome. Hence Dollfuss is praised for his resistance to Nazism, which shows wisdom, stamina and courage, and Kraus commits himself to the cause of Austria, acknowledging the need to restrain the satirical impulse in the face of mortal danger. His support is by no means diminished by the 'restriction on freedom of the press', which is justified on the basis of national security, and the Social Democrats are censured for opposing the very man who is trying to save their lives.

The tragedy of the Social Democrats is attributed to failures of leadership. In Germany the party was so obsessed with legality that it failed to take determined action against the Nazis while it still had the power to do so. In Austria it refuses to support Dollfuss's anti-democratic methods, not realizing that the use of emergency decrees is the only way to keep the Nazis out. The Party is denounced for its short-sighted policies and platitudinous propaganda, especially the editorials of Oskar Pollak in the *Arbeiter-Zeitung*. Politics should be assessed in terms not of ideology but of practical value ('Nutzen'; 239/*260*). Kraus contrasts the hollow rhetoric of Bauer and Pollak, the advocates of 'freedom', with the pragmatic attitudes of Starhemberg and Kunschak, defenders of the Austrian 'fatherland'. If left and right, *Arbeiter-Zeitung* and *Reichspost*, were willing to learn from each other, both sides might come closer to 'telling the truth' (244/*271*). The defenders of the fatherland are doing a greater service for freedom than the advocates of freedom are for the fatherland (245/*272*).

The focus reverts to Germany, where the nationalism of the new regime is at odds with its purported socialism, its racial arrogance with its desire to attract foreign visitors. There was even a proposal that the life of Hitler should be enacted in place of the Oberammergau passion play; after all, 'Adolf Hitler has a divine mission' (254/*280*). Kraus lists some of the martyrs of this new religion: from an ex-soldier who was beaten till his body was a mass of wounds to a venerable rabbi executed as a joke. Meanwhile the Nazi press reports that Hitler has presented a signed photograph of himself to children at a school for the blind. Kraus sums up the 'Führer principle' in Gloucester's words from *King Lear* (Act IV, scene 1, 46): "'Tis the time's plague when madmen lead the blind.' He goes on to cite a convoluted passage from *Mein Kampf* in which Hitler tries to differentiate the 'material' value of labour from its 'ideal' value (260/*286*). This is contrasted with reports that Aryan doctors are grabbing the jobs of their debarred Jewish colleagues and Aryan commissars confiscating Jewish businesses. A driving force behind antisemitism is economic envy (263/*288*), a leitmotif linked with the prophetic sketch of a Berlin street scene published in 1924.

According to the *Deutsche Juristenzeitung*, assault and murder are not to be treated as crimes if they are committed 'in the national interest'. Ancient Germanic traditions permit 'the complete extermination of the enemy within' (264/*290*). A double murderer from Austria has been rewarded with a staff appointment at Dachau, and there are reportedly 100,000 people in protective custody. This systematic perversion of justice leads Kraus to describe Germany as the country 'where lawlessness makes law its instrument' (273/*299*; an allusion to a prophetic passage from *Faust*, l. 4785). The indictment of legalized criminality culminates in a collage of excerpts from Goethe's Classical Walpurgisnacht. Kraus sees National Socialism not as a reaction against the journalistic civilization he despises, but as confirmation of his long-standing critique of 'empty words and loaded weapons' (282/*310*). Goebbels is the quintessential Berlin journalist, peddling primitivism through a modern terminology. Kraus concedes that his own critique of the press was admired by

Liebenfels, the apostle of Aryanism; but he also recalls that his pacifism led him to be denounced as a 'syphilitic' Jew. It is the convergence of political violence with media manipulation that has caused the catastrophe. The literary subtext resurfaces in this final section, hinting at a Shakespearean 'plot' (289/*324*). Hitler, like Macbeth, shall 'sleep no more', since a system based on violence invites apocalyptic retribution.

Goethe and the Laws of Nature

Such unprecedented events could scarcely be reconciled with a traditional plot, in which villains are brought to book and the moral order is restored. Language has imploded and causality become inverted, while a new epistemology deprives actors of the knowledge of their own deeds. Thus Kraus's Shakespearean paradigms come into conflict with a Faustian dramaturgy, in which crimes appear to be legitimized by the energy with which they are committed. From the title through to the final words, *Dritte Walpurgisnacht* is permeated by a sense that the 'most German of events' is prefigured in *Faust*, the 'most German of poems' (F 890–905, 81). In Goethe's tragedy the hero's journey towards redemption plunges him into daemonic realms of nature, first in the witches' sabbath celebrated on Walpurgis Night in Part I, then in the primitive pre-Hellenic limbo explored in the Classical Walpurgis Night of Part II, from which the majority of Kraus's *Faust* quotations are taken. The concept of a 'Third' Walpurgis Night implies that the horrors of the Third Reich are anticipated in the poet's vision. Moreover, Goethe's play, like Hitler's regime, raises fundamental questions about the relationship between nature, violence and morality. The theme is introduced at the very beginning of *Dritte Walpurgisnacht*, when Kraus quotes a panegyric celebrating Hitler's mission as 'naturgewaltig' ('empowered by nature'; 13/*19*).

The question whether the natural world originated in violence so fascinated Goethe that he made it a central theme of his Classical Walpurgis Night. The Vulcanists (represented by Anaxagoras) claim that the world came into existence through a single violent seismological event, while the Neptunists (represented by Thales) maintain that life emerged gradually from the oceans. This philosophical debate, forerunner of the antithesis between 'big bang' and 'steady state' models of the universe, fascinated thinkers of the eighteenth century. In Kraus's mind these ideas became connected with the Nazi seizure of power, which had occurred with such sudden and unpredictable force that he likened it to an 'excess of geodynamic nature' (10/*15*). He had long been aware of the vitalistic strain in German thought, which pictured nature in terms of conquest and violence, not harmony and balance, and his aim is now to bring out the ideological implications of this controversy, which are only hinted at by Goethe.[26] 'Natur, Natur!' (59/*72*) is the slogan he borrows from *Faust* (l. 7837) to characterize the philosophical dilemma raised by National Socialism – the question which of the two antagonistic conceptions of nature is to gain supremacy:

Nie war Natur und ihr lebendiges Fließen
Auf Tag und Nacht und Stunden angewiesen;
Sie bildet regelnd jegliche Gestalt,
Und selbst im Großen ist es nicht Gewalt.
Hier aber war's!

(62/75)

Nature, endowed with smooth creative powers,
never defers to days and nights and hours,
forming all beings with her shaping hand.
No violence lies even within what's grand.
But here it did![27]

These lines from Goethe's dialogue between Anaxagoras and Thales, embedded in a text dealing with thugs like Manfred von Killinger, raise the question: does nature sanction creativity or cruelty? Kraus suggests that this dialectic can be resolved only by taking account of human interventions which subordinate nature's creative powers to political domination.[28] The aptly named Killinger described in his memoirs how he thrashed a young woman with a horsewhip.[29] 'A Faustian nature [Faustnatur], perhaps,' Kraus observes, 'but a superman?' (63/76). The play on words equates the energy of 'Faust' with the use of the 'fist'. Kraus also reminds us that the cult of the 'superman' derives – through the mediation of Nietzsche – from Goethe's *Faust* (60/72). He further emphasizes that the conduct of these 'supermen' is unrelated to any 'measure of good and evil' (156/177). Although the ruthless aspect of the Faustian religion of nature appealed to German imperialists, Goethe's drama contains its own critique, showing how this philosophy of nature blurs the distinction between men and animals. Thus Kraus highlights Goethe's explorations of a subhuman realm in his polemic, borrowing from *Faust* (l. 7163) to observe that the Nazi predators include 'a hawk with gruesome talons' ('Habichtskrallen', 215/237) – an allusion to Theo Habicht, organizer of the terror campaign in Austria. Moreover, Hitler's feigned friendliness towards Hindenburg (156/177) is associated with Goethe's lines about Mephisto's 'ravenous intimacy' ('Rabentraulichkeit', l. 10702). Kraus's repeated emphasis on the concept of 'Faustnaturen' (273/299) identifies the vitalism portrayed in the play as one of the ideological antecedents of fascism.[30] Goethe departs from precedent in portraying a hero who escapes eternal damnation, and the redemption of Faust is associated with the principle of 'Streben' – dynamic striving. For Kraus, the Classical Walpurgis Night scene becomes the place where 'in the delirious dance over the abyss every form of wisdom and warning can be found' (214/236). He values Goethe's insight into the anarchic implications of primitive nature cults and their destructive consequences.

A further source of literary allusions is the Civil War sequence in Acts I and IV, from which battlefield motifs are borrowed to highlight the brutality of Hitler's seizure of power. Faust and Mephisto achieve military victory by magical means, calling on the aid of predatory animals. The predominant mood is expressed by one of the minor characters in a telling phrase: 'Onward to victory! Everything's allowed' (l. 10536). In citing this phrase (278/*304*), Kraus uses Goethe's words to identify the ruthlessness of the regime, while in Mephisto's 'Three Men of Violence', Raufebold, Habebald and Haltefest (l. 10323) he finds prototypes for Hitler's stormtroopers, ready to smash in the face of anyone who offends them. A speech by Raufebold is glossed as a report of what the SA have been doing in Breslau (278/*304*), the scene of outrageous assaults on Jewish lawyers. The crimes of these stormtroopers are prefigured in Act V by the gruesome killing of Philemon and Baucis, the elderly couple whose humble dwelling stands in the way of Faust's grandiose land-reclamation schemes. This becomes an image of the nameless victims of Nazi tyranny, whose houses and gardens have been confiscated and whose existence has been destroyed (125/*143*). In Goethe's tragedy this forms the crux of the moral action, since it involves Faust in guilt which he is unwilling to acknowledge. Even more chilling is the response of Mephisto, who claims that Philemon and Baucis are merely being resettled: 'Once the violence has been done, / They'll settle in a pretty home' ('Nach überstandener Gewalt / Versöhnt ein schöner Aufenthalt', l. 11280). These words form the very first *Faust* quotation in *Dritte Walpurgisnacht* (11/*16*), where Mephisto's words are applied to the fate of people dragged off to concentration camps.[31]

Shakespeare and Secret Murder

Kraus creates a counterpoint between literature and politics, juxtaposing Nazi communiqués with the diction of the poets. Goethe is cited more than a hundred times, while there are approximately thirty quotations from Shakespeare.[32] But frequency should not be confused with function, and the Shakespearean subtext becomes almost as significant as the motifs from Goethe. After *Faust*, the play cited most often is *Macbeth*, 'Shakespeare's bloodiest vision' (280/*306*). This is more clearly a tragedy of ambition, framed by a supernatural setting and haunted by witches, but here the similarity ends, since Macbeth's ambitions are political, while Faust's are existential, and the two plays inhabit different moral universes. The pact which Macbeth makes with natural forces leads him to commit actions that are unambiguously criminal, whereas Faust is rewarded, despite his crimes. Shakespeare certainly does not shrink from the idea that violence might be sanctioned by nature, since *Macbeth*, like *King Lear*, explores two philosophies of nature, one brutal, the other beneficent.[33] But Shakespeare's characters are haunted by a sense that their actions will be judged in *moral* terms. Kraus quotes Lady Macbeth's reflections on her crime: 'What need we fear who knows it when none can call our power to account?' (156/*177*). Despite these defiant words, Macbeth and his wife cannot escape the knowledge that they *will* be called to account for their misdeeds. In Shakespeare's symbolic climax, also cited by Kraus (291/*326*), nature becomes the moral force that defeats the usurper, as Birnam Wood comes to Dunsinane. In short, Shakespeare provides an ethical frame of reference that distinguishes between just and criminal actions, while Goethe's play explores a demonic realm in which immoral acts appear to be sanctioned by the cynical manipulations of Mephisto and the deluded arrogance of Faust.

Kraus brings these distinctions to bear on the obsession with racial purity. Antisemitic legislation of April 1933, designed to purge the professions, made it essential for all Germans to establish that they were 'Aryan', since the discovery of an unsuspected Jewish grandparent could lead to dismissal. After a Nazi newspaper had helpfully suggested that its readers should consult their aunts, Kraus responded with a blend of motifs from Shakespeare and Goethe: 'That way madness lies, says Shakespeare? No, the matter is becoming Faustian' (151/172). There follow lines from Goethe's play describing how Faust descends to the Mothers, embodiments of chthonic depths, and Kraus sets up a ludicrous contrast between grandiose earth goddesses and mundane aunts. In moral terms, however, the Shakespearean and Goethean paradigms diverge. The line about madness from *King Lear* (Act III, scene 4, 21) suggests that the bonds of kinship are treacherous and that to expose oneself to the forces of nature is insane, while the lines from *Faust* imply that an encounter with primal ancestors offers self-discovery through immersion in the 'depths' (l. 6220).

The tension between the two perspectives reaches its climax in the final section of *Dritte Walpurgisnacht*, where Kraus imperceptibly blends his prose with Shakespeare's verse. After listing some of the most gruesome horrors of Nazism, he suggests that for Hitler (as for Macbeth) the action has reached a point of no return:

> The plot is approaching the point where, should he wade no more, returning were as tedious as go o'er. [. . .] Now does he feel his secret murders sticking on his hands; now minutely revolts upbraid his faith-breach; those in command move only in command, nothing in love. Now does he feel his title hang loose about him, like a giant's robe upon a dwarfish thief. Methought I heard a voice cry: 'Sleep no more. Macbeth does murder sleep!' (289–90/*324–5*).

In this collage of motifs from three different scenes, Kraus attempts to bring together the political and the moral strands of his Shakespearean plot.[34] Writing in 1933, he sensed that Hitler's power, like Macbeth's, was threatened by his erstwhile allies. At crucial points in *Dritte Walpurgisnacht* it is suggested that the revolutionary violence of the SA will inevitably clash with Hitler's desire to consolidate his power by evolutionary means – a prophetic insight, since in June 1934 the fear of revolt did indeed lead Hitler to massacre Röhm and his confederates. Thus Kraus had good grounds for reproducing this Macbeth section in *Die Fackel* in July 1934, implying that his prophecy of a Shakespearean outcome might still be fulfilled (F 890–905, 315). The fact that Macbeth is defeated by an army assembled in England forms another suggestive motif. After quoting Ross's lament for Scotland ('Alas, poor country', 256/*282*), Kraus adds in parenthesis a line from Act III, scene 6: 'Some holy angel fly to the court of England and unfold his message!' The Shakespearean dramaturgy makes it clear that German events have universal implications. Of all Kraus's writings, *Dritte Walpurgisnacht* most explicitly invokes an international audience. He was shocked by the failure of Britain, France and the United States to take a stand against Hitler, realizing that the defeat of Nazism would require the intervention of foreign powers.

The final sentence of *Dritte Walpurgisnacht* anticipates that the crimes of Nazi Germany will ultimately provoke retribution (292/*327*). But the argument is inconclusive, since Kraus never succeeds in reconciling his Shakespearean plot with the very different perspective suggested by the references to Goethe. In 1918 he had been able to end *Die letzten Tage der Menschheit* with Horatio's words from the final scene of *Hamlet*, affirming the restoration of moral order; but the circumstances of 1933 precluded this kind of Shakespearean closure. *Dritte Walpurgisnacht* ends with an expression of wishful thinking – the lines from Act IV of *Faust II* (l. 10469) in which the Emperor piously hopes that the usurper will be defeated. When we turn to Goethe's play, we realize that these lines form part of the subplot which fails to resolve the fundamental conflicts between nature, morality and violence. Goethe himself, acknowledging that his tragedy resists rational explanation, described *Faust* as 'incommensurable'.[35] Kraus repeatedly uses Goethe's word to define his own sense of the impossibility of giving a coherent account of National Socialism (14/*21*).[36]

This dilemma is reflected in Kraus's own use of the word 'Natur'. Since National Socialism defies analysis in rational categories, he suggests in his introduction that it should be seen as some kind of 'natural' cataclysm, identifying 'retributive nature' ('die Richterin Natur') as the agent that will punish this eruption (13/*20*). Later he suggests that the Hitler regime must ultimately succumb to the 'laws of nature' which it has infringed (249/*275*). This strand in Kraus's argument has led one critic to describe his attitude as fatalistic.[37] But this ignores the philosophical dualism underlying the debate about nature. For Kraus, as for Adalbert Stifter, there is a gentle law of nature that endures every cataclysm. *Dritte Walpurgisnacht* may be dominated by ruthless human predators, Habicht the hawk and Hitler the raven, but its unsung hero is a dog, descendant of those faithful hounds who kept his faith alive during the First World War. He reverently reprints a press report about a dog shot and mortally wounded, after resisting Nazi intruders (255–6/*281*). This kind of wishful thinking is balanced by the pragmatism of his political analysis. On the same page that refers to 'natural laws', he asks how it was all possible. It was possible, he replies, because a minority seized control of the available weapons, creating new weapons so as to establish itself as the dominant majority (248/*275*). Repeatedly he suggests that such a totalitarian system can be defeated only by an appeal to foreign powers, in the final resort by an 'SOS to the USA' (114/*130*). Indeed, the threat to his own safety prompted him in May 1933 to have his passport extended 'for travel to the United States of America'.[38]

Hitler's Lethal Synthesis

Nazi propaganda was particularly successful in exploiting the longing for a leader which had suffused political German debates.[39] Despite Kraus's opening ploy, 'Hitler brings nothing to my mind,' the cult of the Führer forms a central theme of *Dritte Walpurgisnacht*. Hitler is referred to approximately a hundred times, twice as frequently as Goebbels. We have seen that Hitler had been identified in *Die Fackel* as an exceptional threat as early as September 1923, several weeks before the Munich putsch (F 632–9, 43). In Kraus's writings of the following decade we find a pervasive analysis of creeping fascism, and in October 1932 he issued a particularly timely warning. Although Hitler, on becoming a German citizen, had taken an oath of loyalty to the Weimar constitution, Kraus warned that if he succeeded in founding the 'third Reich' he would sweep all legal constraints aside (F 876–84, 43–4). Although the suddenness of the seizure of power took him by surprise, he had no illusions about what was in store for Germany once the Nazis were in control. After his election victory of March 1933, Hitler adopted the stance of the statesman, making speeches about international reconciliation and distancing himself from the thuggery on the streets. Echoing Bismarck, he even referred to himself on 10 May as an 'honest broker', uniquely qualified to resolve political and social conflicts.[40] Seizing on this pronouncement (44/57), Kraus demolishes the ideological façade of National Socialism by contrasting the public pronouncements of its leaders with their actions. He exposes the attempts to dismiss violence as merely 'unfortunate incidents' or 'unavoidable side-effects of the revolution' (149/170). Violence forms the essence of National Socialism and its fundamental aim is 'annihilation' ('Vernichtung', 15/23). Moreover, the violence is all the more insidious because of its 'ethical instrumentation' (156/177). The interaction between idealistic ethos and brutal action leads him to describe the Nazis as 'cut-throats with a loyal gaze, gangsters with saintly haloes' (170/191).

This analysis anticipates the judgement of Hitler's biographer Joachim Fest that the Nazi regime was based, not simply on the 'deliberate application of cruelty by murderers and sadists', but on 'perverted moral energy'.[41] Although Kraus's examples of Nazi propaganda date almost exclusively from the year 1933, he grasped the principle of aggressive self-righteousness underlying Hitler's speeches. Politically, the most significant was his address of 6 July to the newly appointed Nazi governors of the regions. Hitler argued that it was now time to channel the liberated river of revolution 'into the safe bed of evolution'.[42] Responding to this speech, Kraus integrates the concept of 'evolution' into the network of ironic allusions, contrasting Hitler's 'evolutionary' programme with the violence of his henchmen, especially the SA (156/177, 262/288, 267/293). The 'safe bed of evolution,' he concludes, 'does not permit peaceful sleep' (273/299). A similar dualism informs Hitler's pronouncements about war and peace. On 17 May he made a speech in the Reichstag about disarmament, designed to placate international opinion.[43] So moderate was his tone that even Roosevelt was delighted, while Britain, France and Italy began negotiations with Germany for a four-power pact.[44] Hitler's theme throughout 1933, even in his announcement on 14 October that Germany was leaving the League of Nations, is that war would be madness.[45] Glossing one such utterance (159/*180*), Kraus contrasts it with the glorification of death in battle and the militarization of German life. Goebbels's endorsement of the Führer's claim that Germany has 'not the slightest warlike intention' (146/*167*) makes it even more suspect. The failure of foreign powers to offer any resistance to the Nazis is repeatedly lamented, since their crimes are so horrific that they would justify the intervention of a 'European police force' (98/*109*).

How is it possible that people are so easily duped, both at home and abroad? The answer is suggested by the concept of 'synthesis', which Kraus identifies as one of the most insidious Nazi slogans, derived from a philosophical jargon that blurs vital distinctions. Kraus notes that the Führer has repeatedly appealed for a 'synthesis of tradition and innovation' (261/*287*), and he ironizes Hitler's appeal for a 'synthesis' between idealistic National Socialism and practical politics (275/*300*). This alludes to a speech delivered by Hitler on 13 July to a gathering of Nazi Gauleiters, stressing the importance of economic realism.[46] This concept of 'synthesis' had a certain basis in reality, reflecting Hitler's ability to reconcile competing interests. It was the alliance he constructed between the Nazi Party and the traditional elite – bankers and industrialists, aristocrats and officer corps – that enabled him to consolidate his power. His economic policy even placated Krupp and Thyssen (267/*293*), and Kraus notes how quickly the 'socialist' element was dropped from the Nazi programme (250/*276*). One of his most perceptive sections deals with the manipulation of aristocrats like Papen and Neurath, who have been reduced to 'robots', liable to be sent to a concentration camp the moment they step out of line (82/*94*). The symbol of this alliance between old and new is Hitler's relationship with Hindenburg. 'What an abdication of the marshal's baton before the knapsack!' Kraus remarks, inverting Napoleon's dictum (83/*95*). He goes on to show how the old guard have been outmanoeuvred, while Hindenburg is virtually a prisoner of the man he appointed chancellor (155/*175*).

A fundamental shift in Hitler's public image occurred during the course of 1933. He began that year in the office of chancellor, sanctioned by both Hindenburg and the Reichstag, but he ended it as Führer, his authority based on popular acclaim, expressed through a referendum.[47] At one level, 'Führertum' denotes a type of leadership that is dynamically modern: Hitler as the 'new man', his authority based on personal commitment, not membership of a traditional elite. But the concept of the Führer fuses the progressive with the primitive, endowing Hitler with the archaic aura of a tribal chieftain or medieval warrior. Underlying these two levels is a third, archetypal dimension: the messianic longing for a saviour. Kraus anticipates the phenomenon of 'redemptive antisemitism' – the combination of 'fear of racial degeneration' with 'religious belief in redemption'.[48] The language used to celebrate Hitler's birthday in April 1933 blends religious discourse with nature myths to create the illusion that his mission is 'divinely ordained'. Even demands for the destruction of (Jewish) 'parasites' express a faith in the Führer which, as Kraus ironically observes, is 'deeply religious' (12/19). That Hitler is fulfilling a 'divine mission' is proclaimed by Catholic priests (160/181) as well as Nazi propagandists, and the German Christians describe themselves as 'the stormtroopers of Jesus Christ' (291/326). It is widely accepted that Hitler has Christ-like qualities. The idea of staging his life story at Oberammergau may have been postponed, but soon it should be possible to celebrate the 'life of the man from Nazireth' (254/280).

The Führer, according to the *Völkischer Beobachter*, was to be adored rather than merely respected, renouncing 'all intellectual differentiation' (15/24). For Kraus, this was the crux of the matter. Repeatedly, he showed how intellectual, moral and legal criteria were swept aside by a stream of emotively charged propaganda, so that the agents of secular civilization were transformed into 'fire-worshippers'. Above all, it was the 'staging of Hitler' ('die Hitlerregie', 103/114) that sustained the Aryan creed, and Kraus recognized that the Führer had an instinctive understanding of the emotional power of symbols, especially the swastika.[49] Archaic symbols, flags and fireworks combine with saturation coverage by radio and the press to produce an epidemic of 'cerebral concussion' (11/17–18). In an exemplary passage about the Führer's alleged common touch, he ironized the images of Hitler smiling, shaking hands and arranging a birthday party for a little girl. Such pictures, disseminated through illustrated magazines (Fig. 55), were responsible for his 'gigantic peacock's tail' of popularity (181/201).

When Hitler was portrayed as chancellor, it was often in association with Hindenburg, the venerated German President. But when the concept of the Führer was invoked, the implication was that all power should be concentrated in his hands (155/176). Speaking in his statesmanlike voice, Hitler may insist that Germany has not the slightest warlike intention; but this contrasts with another policy document, described by Kraus as 'the expression of the inner desires of the Führer': the annexation of Austria, Alsace-Lorraine, German-speaking Switzerland, Liechtenstein, Luxemburg, Danzig and Memel (145–6/165–7). He was not fooled by the repeated references in the press to the Chancellor's 'great speech about peace' (157/187). In that speech of 17 May, Hitler even compared the function of the SA and the SS to that of a fire brigade.[50] After ironizing this phrase, Kraus juxtaposes it with another Hitler speech, delivered to SA men in Kiel, which stresses that their organization is dedicated to 'force' and 'violence' (81/93). There can be no harmonious synthesis, since the Chancellor publicly dedicated to peace cannot be reconciled with the Führer secretly intent on war. Thus *Dritte Walpurgisnacht* exposes the apocalyptic implications concealed by the well-staged pageant of orderly demonstrations and peaceful festivals: political tyranny, military conquest and racial annihilation.

55   Hitler at Berchtesgaden, surrounded by youthful admirers

Inferiority Complexes and Machismo

Kraus's documentation gains added force from his analysis of motives. Anti-semitism is seen as the expression of that 'irreparable emotion' which has dominated German life since Versailles: the feeling of having been cheated and betrayed. The peace settlement dealt a blow to national pride that could be assuaged only by a war of revenge against the inner enemy (76/88). Despite his scepticism about psychoanalysis, Kraus here uses the concept of the 'inferiority complex' as an analytical tool. In 1925, the Freudian analyst Siegfried Bernfeld had anticipated that 'the unconscious anxiety of the Germans, which is deep-rooted in a sense of inferiority', might be transformed into aggression by making them 'believe that they have an immensely powerful common enemy'. This should not be a real enemy like the French, for that would produce a real fear, but an enemy who does not really exist, and yet must be credible – the Jews! By this means, according to the right-wing strategy Bernfeld envisages, it will be possible to put young people and then the whole public 'in a state of panic fear: a sinister power threatens them and we come forward as their sav-iour and leader'. Similar arguments were developed in Arnold Zweig's *Caliban* (1927), a text that draws on the work of both Freud and Kraus in order to explain how German nationalists came to blame the Jews for the collapse of 1918.[51] In *Dritte Walpurgisnacht* Kraus's word for this sense of having been 'sold short' is 'Verkürzung', and he interprets the obsession with 'race' as a sign of the German sense of 'inferiority' (283/*311*). Hence their obsessive insistence that they are 'German'. He had already mocked this cult of 'Germanness' during the First World War, but under the Nazis the word acquired a superlative suffix, so that the new form of nationalism became the 'Germanest of virtues' (56/*69*).

Hitler was among those who observed that during the Weimar Republic the Germans had acquired 'inferiority complexes'.[52] Kraus may ironize this use of Freudian terminology by a reader of Karl May (42/*55*), but he subsequently develops his own version of this argument, attributing the various forms of German – and German-Jewish – nationalism to 'the conjunction of two complexes of inferiority' (88/*100*). Economic envy is seen as the most fundamental factor, and the sense of being inferior at making money is crystallized by the plaintive cry of that Berlin newspaper-vendor about Jews earning 'big bucks faster' (263/*288*). When Kraus first analysed this phenomenon in December 1924, he pointed out that the 'Germanic ideal' was an expression of resentment about 'cut-price Jewish competition' (F 668–75, 149–52). The economic crisis of the early 1930s transformed the need to find a scapegoat into a national obsession, and the boycott of Jewish businesses in April 1933 confirmed this diagnosis. The ostensible motive was to deter Jewish organizations abroad from publishing 'atrocity propaganda' by means of political blackmail: unless the international community abandoned its hostility towards the regime, the German Jews would be subjected to even greater hardships. The Nazis produced carefully staged photographs, incorporating slogans in English, designed to convey the impression of a dignified national protest (Fig. 56). A chemist in Berlin, who refused to close down his business, was murdered by Nazi thugs so that his trade could be taken over by a non-Jewish competitor; and a shopkeeper in a village in Hessen was terrorized by stormtroopers with rifles (60–1/*73–4*). Even an impoverished rag-dealer was subjected to obscene humiliations when he was unable to produce 500 Marks demanded by the SA (97–8/*109*). Another Jewish shop was looted while the police stood by (175/*195*); and German doctors have few inhibitions about grabbing the jobs of Jewish colleagues who have been forbidden to practise (258/*284*). Kraus even notes advertisements in the *Völkischer Beobachter* which reveal that connections with leading members of the Nazi Party are essential if you want to make money (272/*297*). Economic rivalry was also involved in the campaign against Jewish lawyers. The positions of well-qualified judges are now being taken over by 'champions of the national cause' (264/*290*), and he records the murders of two lawyers, Günther Joachim and Alfred Strauss (194/*215*), both of Jewish origin.[53]

Since economic envy offered only a partial explanation, Kraus quotes eyewitness reports that reveal a sinister blend of sadism and greed. Echoing the theories of Freud, he suggests that the Nazi with his jackboots and whip may be compensating for sexual inadequacy, so that a philosophical analysis of

Deutsche, verteidigt Euch
gegen die jüdische
Greuelpropaganda,
kauft
nur bei Deutschen!

Germans defend
yourselves against jewish
atrocity propaganda
buy only at German shops!

Deutsche!
Wehrt Euch!
Kauft nicht bei Juden!

56   Nazi boycott of Jewish-owned businesses, April 1933

Nazism would have to take account of 'perverted sexuality' (56/69). The cowardly monsters who run the concentration camps may be compensating for the erotic frustration of their marriages (61/74), and there seems to be a mysterious connection between inflicting pain and experiencing pleasure (196/216). This insight can be confirmed from other sources. Even hardened police officers like Rudolf Diels, first head of the Gestapo, were shocked by the brutality with which the SA treated defenceless prisoners. During the year 1933 Diels had ample opportunity to observe what was taking place inside German prisons, and the following year he explained to a member of the British embassy in private conversation: 'It was only after a number of instances of unnecessary flogging and meaningless cruelty that I tumbled to the fact that my organization had been attracting all the sadists in Germany.' Freud, he adds, might be able to explain why 'corporal chastisement ultimately arouses sadistic leanings in apparently normal men and women'.[54] Kraus's treatment of the theme of sexual sadism culminates in the collage of documents recording the outrages provoked by love relationships between Germans and Jews (199–204/*219–27*). He reprints gruesome details of more than twenty cases where men and women have been publicly denounced for choosing sexual partners of the wrong race. In Nuremberg a German girl who slept with a Jew has been dragged through the town by uniformed Nazis, with her head shaved and a placard around her neck proclaiming her shame. The official line is that young people who sabotage the Nazi cause in bed should be sent to concentration camps. Kraus, by contrast, suggests that intermarriage between different ethnic groups may produce exceptionally gifted children (88/*100*). Quoting a Nazi author who has confessed to an obsessive hatred for women, Kraus borrows a phrase from *Faust* (l. 1323) to suggest that this is 'the tail that wags the political dog' (*124*).[55] Homosexuality has become the norm among Nazi groups that favour 'the sultry interpenetration of mysticism and machismo' (131/*149*). This view can also be correlated with contemporary sources. 'The explanation of this outbreak of sadistic cruelty', observed R. T. Smallbones, who was British consul in Frankfurt from 1932 to 1939, 'may be that sexual perversion, and in particular homosexuality, are very prevalent in Germany.'[56] Even sexual intercourse has become 'co-ordinated' ('gleichgeschaltet'), Kraus observes, recalling the Prussian tradition propagated by Frederick the Great (197/*218*). Although he had been one of the advocates of the rights of homosexuals, what he discerns in the conduct of Nazi thugs is less attraction to men than fear of women. The German woman is to be desexualized, becoming a demure 'Germanic spouse' (199/*219–20*).

The whip becomes the symbol of displaced sexual phobias, especially in the passage quoted from the memoirs of Killinger. Confronted by a defiant woman during the post-war disorders in Munich, this hero of the Freikorps had ordered her to be horsewhipped. In one of the most revealing passages cited in *Dritte Walpurgisnacht*, Killinger proudly recalls that the woman was whipped until her buttocks were a mass of bruises (62–3/*75–6*). For a fuller account, we may turn to the study by Klaus Theweleit, which shows that manic attitudes towards women dominated the culture of the proto-fascist Freikorps. In his commentary on Killinger's memoirs, Theweleit points out that whipping is presented as an act of magnanimity; according to the code of the Freikorps, the woman deserved far more brutal treatment.[57] There is one significant detail, stressed by Theweleit, that Kraus omits: the defiant woman was a communist. His aim is to highlight the sadistic subtext concealed beneath the political confrontation. His final word on this subject is contained in the cryptic analogy he draws between Hitler's supposedly divine mission and Haarmann's sexual violence (291/*326*). Fritz Haarmann was a homosexual Jack the Ripper, a serial killer who terrorized the citizens of Germany during the 1920s. Kraus was not the only person to be struck by the uncanny resemblance between Haarmann and Hitler. When the mass murderer was finally apprehended, people found it hard to believe that a little man with a moustache could have committed such horrendous crimes.[58]

CHAPTER 26

National Socialism and the Ethics of Language

The text of *Dritte Walpurgisnacht* is so rich in insight that Kraus's readers had every reason to feel cheated by his decision not to publish. It must have been frustrating for those who attended his recital of Offenbach's *Madame l'Archiduc* in December 1934 to be teased by the musical interpolation: 'Topical rhymes aren't hard to find, / but Hitler brings nothing to my mind' (S 14, 505). Kraus despaired of finding readers capable of appreciating his attempt to 'observe the fallen state of German life from the perspective of linguistic theology' (F 890–905, 87). But the question remains: were his readers too obtuse, or was his project misconceived? There was little hope of convincing the defeated socialists, dreaming of action plans that would undermine Hitler's popularity with the German working class. Hence the spate of anti-fascist publications by exiled authors, especially in France, where Leopold Schwarzschild founded his journal *Das neue Tagebuch* with Joseph Roth as one of the contributors. Kraus must have read some of these writings during his visit to Paris in August 1933, since there are echoes in *Dritte Walpurgisnacht* of passages from the July number of *Das neue Tagebuch*. But his approach was on a different plane, avoiding the black-and-white paradigms of anti-fascism and insisting on a return to first principles – to language as the defining feature of the human condition.

Modernity, Technology and Newspeak

In January 1933 Edgar Ansel Mowrer, one of the shrewdest of American foreign correspondents, published an account of the demise of the Weimar democracy entitled *Germany Puts the Clock Back*. Denouncing the failure of the socialist-led government of Prussia to resist the Papen coup, he portrays a country in the clutches of reactionaries – generals and land-owners, judges and civil servants. Although the book became a best-seller, its reliance on a schematic model of 'progress versus reaction' made it a poor guide to the dynamic events of the following year. Although the threat of National Socialism is analysed in considerable detail, Hitler is conceived as a 'reactionary' who

– by November 1932 – has been outmanoeuvred by Papen and his clique of 'barons'.[1] A more compelling picture was provided by Mowrer's colleague H. R. Knickerbocker, writing in the *New York Evening Post* after Hitler's seizure of power. In April 1933 he invited his readers to imagine that, as a result of the Depression, the Ku Klux Klan had gained such popular support that they were able to capture a majority of seats in Congress. A fire on Capitol Hill, allegedly the work of communists, provided a pretext for arresting their principal opponents and replacing all state governors by Klan appointees. Judges, lawyers, doctors and police chiefs who refused to join the movement were forced out of their jobs, and, as thousands of refugees poured into Mexico and Canada, the constitution was rewritten and the Republic replaced by a dictatorship.[2] This certainly conveyed the overwhelming impact of Hitler's seizure of power, but the idea of the Nazis as fire-worshipping weirdos in white hoods was misleading. Both Mowrer and Knickerbocker failed to acknowledge the *modernity* of the Nazi movement.

At first sight Nazi policies certainly seemed retrograde, a 'return to the middle ages' according to a French newspaper quoted in *Dritte Walpurgisnacht* (50/63). Conservative ideologists contributed to this idea by celebrating Hitler as the longed-for 'nobleman' ('Herzog', cited 12/19), destined to liberate Germany from foreign bondage in accordance with ancient prophecy.[3] Pseudo-medievalism had long been one of Kraus's targets, but in the Nazi movement he perceived something far more sinister: 'primitive existence' sustained by the 'resources of radio technology' (11/16). During the First World War he had coined the phrase 'techno-romantic' for reactionary modernism, describing the Germans as 'barbarians equipped with electric lighting', and he had every reason to recall that formulation (28/41). But now the synthesis between old and new has reached the ultimate extreme: 'the simultaneous existence of electrodynamics and myth, splitting atoms and burning at the stake' (20/34). 'Romanticism incorporates chemistry,' and the knights and emperors from *Faust* (l. 10559) have become bomber pilots equipped with phosgene gas (278/304). Goethe's hero is a time-traveller whose longing for authentic being takes him back to the realms of myth. Modern Germany, powered by 'technology out of control' (283/313), has embarked on a similar journey in search of its Aryan ancestry, and the Third Reich is a synthesis of sophisticated technology and charismatic leadership.

Kraus anticipates the theories of Zygmunt Bauman about the modernity of the political system that sustained Hitler's regime and culminated in the Holocaust.[4] It is the combination of 'ink, technology and death' that makes Nazism so lethal (282/310). If Goebbels and Benn are cited at such length, it is because their discourse combines modern jargon with archaic myth. Radio technology supplies the medium, biology and geology the vocabulary for propagating pseudo-scientific fantasies and implementing primitive policies by modern methods. The Nazis use terms from science and business management, like 'incorporation' ('Überholung') and 'co-ordination' ('Gleichschaltung',

113/*128*), as euphemisms for the confiscation of property and the suppression of opposition.[5] A compelling blend of technical jargon and patriotic pathos was required to mobilize both the nationalistic middle classes and the frustrated masses. Thus National Socialism is seen not as a contradiction to – but a continuation of – the ills of modernity, including the journalistic culture represented by Alfred Kerr and Max Reinhardt (both now in exile). Goebbels is portrayed not as a *völkisch* ideologist, but as a sophisticated exponent of 'asphalt writing', whether 'modern German or modern Jewish' (40–1/*54*–6).

After stressing technological efficiency, Kraus analyses the acronyms and neologisms introduced for the control of political processes and the reorganization of industrial production. 'Are you a pedant panicked by new words?' he asks in the voice of Mephisto, the arch manipulator of language (*Faust*, l. 6267). As the author of innumerable neologisms Kraus had no such anxiety, since he himself coins new compounds for the impact of political propaganda, including 'Untergangster' (for followers of Spengler, 65/*78*), and 'irrnational' (for 'nutty nationalism', 79/*91*). Nazi neologisms like 'Reichsfachschaftsleiter' and 'Gaukulturwart' are objectionable not because they are new, but because they 'disrupt the limits of linguistic thinking', establishing a dehumanizing system of 'verbal imperialism'. To illustrate this process, he cites terms like 'Osaf' and 'NSBO', suggesting that this terminology echoes the acronyms introduced by modern commercial enterprises like HAPAG and WIPAG (113–15/*127*–30).[6] Efficient communication was a decisive factor, and it was apparently the Post Office that came up with the acronym Gestapo for Geheime Staatspolizei (Secret State Police).[7] In analysing such dehumanizing abbreviations, Kraus anticipates the insights of Orwell's 'Principles of Newspeak': 'The words Communist International, for instance, call up a composite picture of universal human brotherhood, red flags, barricades, Karl Marx, and the Paris Commune. The word Comintern, on the other hand, suggests merely a tightly-knit organization and a well-defined body of doctrine.'[8] Moreover, Kraus's critique penetrates beyond the externals of newspeak to the more intimate sphere of 'doublethink'. The psychology of Nazi murderers cannot be reduced to rational categories, he observes, since the Party member 'doesn't believe the things he has seen, indeed he doesn't even believe the things he has done' (162–3/*183*–4). According to the logic of the new civilization 'the murderer has not committed murder, if he denies his crime' (165/*185*). This anticipates another passage from *Nineteen Eighty-Four*, which defines 'doublethink' as 'the power of holding two contradictory beliefs in one's mind simultaneously, and accepting both of them. [. . .] The essential act of the Party is to use conscious deception while retaining the firmness of purpose that goes with complete honesty.'[9]

Dritte Walpurgisnacht cites numerous examples of newspeak and doublethink, but Kraus also shows how 'oldspeak' infuses the rhetoric of National Socialism. Orwell suggests that traditional concepts 'such as honour, justice, morality' will cease to exist under the new totalitarian regime.[10] Kraus, on the contrary, shows how reassuringly familiar old words are given a new force, so that 'Wille' no longer means 'free will', but the submission of the individual to the authority of Hitler – the 'Führerwille' (249/276). Nazi propaganda has no difficulty in adapting the pre-existing vernacular of the Weimar period as a vehicle for the mobilization of the masses. The 'mentality' that emerged from the First World War has produced a militaristic spirit which exacerbates both aggressive individual behaviour and international economic competition, giving new currency to the proverb 'viel Feind viel Ehr' (78–9/90) – 'the bigger your enemy, the harder he falls'. In *Language and Silence*, George Steiner observes that 'Hitler heard inside his native tongue the latent hysteria, the confusion, the quality of hypnotic trance [. . .] half nebulous jargon, half obscenity'. By virtue of recent history, the 'reservoirs of venom and moral illiteracy' found in any language were in Germany nearer to the 'surface of common speech'. Hence the popularity of that song about Jewish blood 'spurting' from the knife.[11] However, Kraus's essential point is that Hitler's hysteria could never have carried the day if it had not been supplemented by the guile of Goebbels.

Violence, Duplicity and Hit Tunes

This pervasive use of doublespeak, in the press and on the radio, is illustrated throughout *Dritte Walpurgisnacht*. Goebbels was continuously issuing directives to journalists, instructing them not only what to say but how to express it. In a sustained critique of the language of Nazi propaganda (112–15/125–31), Kraus points out that the Propaganda Minister has a thorough knowledge of 'journalistic dialect'. He has banned from reports of official functions clichés like 'the cream of society', which betray outdated social attitudes. At the same time insidious euphemisms are being deployed to disguise the use of violence. The model, derived from the terminology of the First World War, is the definition of soldiers sent into battle as 'human material'. Kraus shows that the principal concepts of the Nazi ideology have deceptive double meanings, like 'züchten', a word which hints at the connection between selective breeding and corporal punishment ('züchtigen', 71/83). Even an apparently innocent word like 'Elemente' is highlighted. When shopowners are tortured and citizens are robbed, the Nazi press speaks of unauthorized actions by unidentified 'elements' (249/275). The image of an altruistic movement threatened by 'irresponsible elements' (266/292) is repeatedly ironized. Hitler's plan for Germany may sound idealistic, but Kraus suggests in a subtle play on words that when 'elements' appear on the scene, they 'trample on the plan' ('Elemente treten auf den Plan', 273/299).

The pervasive contradictions of Nazi propaganda prompt Kraus to denounce the 'duplicitous German tongue' (207/230). The most compelling example, already cited in other contexts, is 'Schutzhaft' – 'protective custody'. According to a statement issued by Heinrich Himmler on 14 March 1933 (not cited by Kraus), those taken into 'protective custody' were 'under the direct protection of the police', whose task was to save them from the wrath of the mob. According to another version, the aim was to 'protect the people from asocial elements'.[12] In an exemplary analysis, Kraus exposes the brutal realities concealed behind this duplicitous phrase. 'Protective custody' is shown to be a contradiction in terms, since prisoners are at risk of being tortured and killed. The section describing the fate of a Breslau city councillor, Ernst Eckstein (184–6/204–7), is constructed around a collage of quotations – from Nazi propaganda and from eyewitness reports – for which Kraus uses smaller type:

> Dr Ernst Eckstein, who was taken into protective custody as one of the first political func-tionaries

– virtually an act of protection, then –

> had trouble coping with the conditions of his confinement.

The rumour had been circulating that these conditions were forced labour amid blows with rifle butts, whiplashings in the face, dosings with castor oil, participation in speaking choruses, and misunderstandings of that nature. After all, there were also occasional tours of the city in an open van, allegedly amid the jeers of nationalistic fighters, while other spectators were shaken and wept.

> Just two weeks ago he was busy working for the Breslau concentration camp.

Certainly not *in* the concentration camp: a kind of office work. Not, of course, without the physical exercise that the assiduous Edmund Heines, who once set an example himself, provides for his charges. One of them states:

> He had to cart heavy rocks, and when we others could relax, he was detailed to clean latrines. While he was forced to rummage around in there, he was displayed to camp visitors.

Yet, as such things will happen, despite diversions of this kind he surrendered to dejection and depression, states to which he evidently inclined. In a fit of

> depression he attempted to commit suicide in his cell. Finally, he refused food so that

– because they wanted to keep him alive and working –

> he had to be fed intravenously.

They spared no efforts. Doctors were sent for. They attribute his death

> primarily to his losing the will to live.

[. . .] The low resistance of prisoners often gives rise to complaints. No sooner has a person been in a concentration camp for a few hours than

> he had to be taken to hospital.

Some prove to be 'unfit for protective custody' on the way to the camp and have to be rerouted to the hospital. [. . .] Most people die of natural causes.[13]

In this passage Swiftian irony enhances the Krausian art of quotation, endow-ing individual destinies with exemplary significance (Eckstein was an idealistic socialist, Heines the brutish Chief of Police in Breslau).

The destruction of the rule of law is exemplified by the maltreatment of an unnamed Munich solicitor (Dr Michael Siegel). In March 1933, after protest-ing on behalf of a client who had been taken into protective custody, Siegel was physically assaulted and paraded through the streets with his clothes in tatters and an antisemitic placard around his neck declaring: 'I am a Jew and I will never again complain to the police' (Fig. 57).[14] As the group neared the main station, Siegel was photographed by an American visitor, and this image was soon making headlines around the globe. Kraus assumes that Siegel was taken to a concentration camp and then shot 'while trying to escape', and this

57 Complaining to the police: the fate of a Munich lawyer

leads him to compare this picture to the photograph of Battisti's corpse, which he had reprinted as the frontispiece of *Die letzten Tage der Menschheit* to epitomize the horrors of the First World War (50/63). In fact, Siegel was released and returned home with his bloodstained clothes in tatters, to the horror of his seven-year-old daughter. The Siegels, deeply attached to their Bavarian homeland, failed to read the signs of the times, remaining in Munich for a further seven years, although they sent their children to England. It was not until 1940 that Michael Siegel and his wife Mathilde succeeded in emigrating.[15]

Although Kraus was mistaken about the fate of Siegel, he was right to see such incidents as apocalyptic portents. The Gestapo regarded protective custody as its 'most important weapon', and Himmler was soon to bar lawyers from access to anyone arrested under this pretext.[16] Protective custody was used to silence opposition from all quarters, and the Catholic author Theodor Haecker narrowly escaped arrest for criticisms of the cult of the swastika published in the December 1932 number of *Der Brenner*.[17] Kraus quotes government statistics recording that there are 12,000 people in protective custody in Prussia. Not to be outdone, the authorities in Saxony claimed to have imprisoned twice as many, while a foreign news report suggested that the total for Germany as a whole might be 100,000 (270/295). The reports that were taken from the press were sometimes inaccurate, but this should not lead us to discount the documentary value of *Dritte Walpurgisnacht* or to conclude that many details 'cannot be verified'.[18] The reference to protective custody in Saxony, like other details in his documentation, is based on a report in the *Arbeiter-Zeitung* (3 July 1933), and he praised the paper for its reporting from

Germany (226/247).[19] Moreover, surviving records from the first year of the Hitler regime show that Kraus's figures were not far off the mark. Official statistics for 31 July 1933 put the number in protective custody at 26,789. Since individuals were continuously being arrested, sent to a camp for a short stint, and then released, it is likely that 100,000 people did indeed spend time in a concentration camp during 1933, of whom an estimated 500 to 600 were killed.[20]

The sadism of the camps had a grotesque musical accompaniment. The laughing hangman, so prominently featured in *Die letzten Tage der Menschheit*, reappears in *Dritte Walpurgisnacht* in Nazi uniform, singing as he performs his duties. There is an unforgettable vignette of a 'hangman' lounging at the prison door, singing a folksong that foreshadows early death ('Morgenrot, Morgenrot, / leuchtest mir zum frühen Tod', 192/213). Other musical motifs are more dynamic, as thugs reduce their victims to pulp with whips and steel rods, singing 'cheerful marching songs' (55/68), while music inspires the students in Frankfurt am Main to participate in the burning of books (132/151). Martial music and choral singing reinforced the mass rallies. It is worth recalling the text of the most extraordinary example – the marching song with the refrain: 'When Jewish blood spurts from the knife, / We all feel twice as good' ('Wenn's Judenblut vom Messer spritzt, / Geht's uns noch mal so gut', 159-60/180). These lines occur in the final strophe of 'Sturmsoldaten', an example of steely romanticism which incorporates the traditional motif of the soldier leaving his sweetheart behind ('Leb wohl mein allerliebster Schatz, wir seh'n uns nimmermehr'). The opening line suggests that it was designed to be sung not only by the SA, but also by youth groups: 'Stormtroopers young and old, take your weapon in your hand / For the Jew is wreaking havoc in the German fatherland' ('Ihr Sturmsoldaten jung und alt, nehmt die Waffe in die Hand / Denn der Jude hauset fürchterlich im deutschen Vaterland').[21] Kraus suggests that those who sing such songs experience an 'emphatic Coué effect' (159/180). Emile Coué was the psychologist responsible for the vogue for 'auto-suggestion' – the collective chanting of uplifting maxims to relieve distressing symptoms. This ritual purportedly liberates repressed energies, since the unconscious 'is credulous and accepts with unreasoning docility what it is told'.[22] The idea that 'we'll all feel twice as good' is a grotesque echo of the Coué principle, spiced with racial hatred, and the song could still be heard in the late 1930s, chanted by cheerful groups of ten-year-olds from Catholic families as they marched through the streets of Cologne.[23]

The association of political irrationalism with romantic music can be found in many writings of this period, notably those of Thomas Mann, whose interpretation of Wagner's 'Germanness' provoked such controversy.[24] Particular significance has also been attached to Hitler's passion for Wagner as a source of his political vision. But Kraus, after noting the razzmatazz at Bayreuth, brings this argument down to earth by linking Nazi violence – in a cryptic play on words – with 'hit tunes' ('Schlagermelodien'). Concentration-camp victims are simultaneously made to suffer and to sing – a motif that foreshadows the Buchenwald song and the Auschwitz orchestra. Further examples include prisoners forced to sing as they are paraded through the streets of Breslau, and communists tortured until they sing patriotic songs like the 'Horst Wessel Lied' and 'Ich hatt' einen Kameraden' (190–4/*210–15*). In *Dritte Walpurgisnacht* the ubiquitous 'Horst Wessel Lied', for which Gerhart Hauptmann has composed a prologue (*215*), crops up half-a-dozen times.[25] The combined effect of choral singing and hypnotic rhythm had a whole nation leaping to its feet and thrusting right arms into the air, after this song was adopted in July 1933 as a second German national anthem. Commenting on a tourist brochure designed to attract foreign visitors, Kraus sarcastically observes that in Germany 'the air is filled with music'. Unfortunately, American tourists who fail to respond when the 'Horst Wessel Lied' is played are knocked down and trampled underfoot (251–2/*278*).[26] The song is even featured during the Passion Play at Oberammergau, and the actor who plays the role of Christ is to sport a swastika. While the loyal apostles are to be unmistakably Aryan, Goebbels reinforces the antisemitic message by insisting that the Judas figure should be a 'markedly Jewish type' (253–4/*279*).[27]

Kraus's analysis of the language of National Socialism is exemplified by his critique of protective custody and his account of the hypnotic Coué effect. His analysis of propaganda avoids the mistake of isolating the so-called 'power of language' from the social nexus.[28] By focusing on performative aspects of controlled mass communications, he shows how social and verbal practices interact and reinforce each other within a ritualized public space. Thus he notes that half a million farm workers were mobilized in September 1933 for Goebbels's grandiose Harvest Festival near Hamlyn and that fifty searchlights illuminated the performance (141/*162*). The staging of Hitler fuses political menace with religious charisma, and atrocities are made palatable by being encoded in 'mendacious words' (19/*32*), while the lifting of the rule of law creates a vacuum in which aggressive behaviour is promoted by 'verbal violence' (115/*131*). Language on its own may not cause anything, but its function within the dominant system of communications yields a wealth of insight to a satirist 'sensitive to symptoms' (288/*322*). He shows that there is no uniform language sustaining the Nazi system, but a proliferation of duplicitous discourses, from discordant jargon and seductive euphemisms to religious exaltation and lofty philosophical utterance.

Goebbels the Spin Doctor

Kraus has little to say about the mind of the Führer, whose view of the world has been formed by the adventure stories of Karl May (42/*55*). He quotes a turgid passage from *Mein Kampf* to contrast Hitler's thinking with a biblical tradition that consigns evil men to the torments of hell, while the righteous are taken into Abraham's bosom (Luke 16: 22–6). Hitler shall cry in vain for 'his tongue to be cooled', for 'between us and you there is a great gulf fixed'

(260/*286*). Here Kraus draws the sharpest possible contrast between the discourses of Judaism and fascism. But the case of Goebbels is different, since his style derives from a modern journalistic milieu. As an intellectual, an aspiring man of letters who studied at Bonn under Friedrich Gundolf, he has even written a play that has won cautious praise in the liberal press (32/*45*). Hitler could never have consolidated his power without Goebbels's control of communications, and Kraus notes that this process is conceived as a spiritual renewal that encompasses private life (45/*57*). Where conventional accounts of his methods as Minister of Propaganda tend to concentrate on his control of policy, Kraus focuses on the medium rather than the message, showing how Goebbels exploits a spectrum of rhetorical nuances, blending journalistic jargon with nationalistic fervour. The 'intelligent' Propaganda Minister gives priority to the 'emotional realm' (148/*169*), and in his speeches Kraus identifies a convergence of three ideologies: reactionary nationalism, liberal journalism and visionary Expressionism.

Far from renouncing his early admiration for the movement, Goebbels emphasized in his 'steely romanticism' speech that 'Expressionism had healthy opinions, for its age was Expressionist'.[29] Several passages cited in *Dritte Walpurgisnacht* show how Nazi rhetoric exploits the Expressionist ideal of the 'new man'. Goebbels calls for a 'comprehensive spiritual renewal of German man' (cited 45/*57*). After noting the connection with the Nietzschean axiom that 'man' is to be transcended by 'superman' (59/*73*), Kraus suggests that the links with racist biology are even more sinister, since Gottfried Benn claims that history is about to produce 'a new biological type' (70/*82–3*). Repeated invocations of the rebirth of 'German man' (179/*200*) provide a framework for multiple ironies, as Kraus shows how far the reality falls short of the ideal. The aim of the Nazi movement, as he notes in his summary, is 'to create the new man' (290/*325*), but Goebbels has to acknowledge the gulf between this exalted goal and the mediocrity of Nazi culture. This cult was coupled with a negative myth of equal potency. Since the Germans found it impossible to believe that they had lost the war, the collapse could only be explained as a 'stab in the back'. The acceptance of the humiliating peace terms imposed at Versailles was blamed on the 'enemy within', the catchphrase for socialists, pacifists and Jews. Kraus denounces this 'satanic humbug', which now dominates the feelings of the whole nation, concluding that Germany suffers far less from the arbitrary actions of foreign powers than from 'the ideological rationalization that invented the enemy within' (76–7/*88–9*). This myth transformed the Jews into scapegoats for a whole cluster of fears and anxieties, not only political and economic but also psychological and sexual. The new man of Nazi mythology was assigned the task not merely of defeating world Jewry, but also of overcoming the 'Jew within himself'.[30]

These ideas were echoed at a popular level by the rabble-rousing slogan 'Deutschland erwache! Juda verrecke!' Reverberating through the streets of Germany, this slogan inspired a series of antisemitic excesses, even before the seizure of power. During the Berlin riots of 12 September 1931 it was chanted by the Nazi thugs on the Kurfürstendamm who 'assaulted every Jewish-looking person they could lay hands on'.[31] The slogan is difficult to translate, but the version 'Germans awake! Let the Jews croak!' does convey something of its hypnotic rhythm (although it is hard to convey the vindictiveness of 'verrecke', which hints at the death-throes of vermin). 'Juda' (literally 'Jewry') also sets up associations with Judas Iscariot, linking modern Nazi propaganda with traditional Christian antisemitism. Critics have complained that Kraus's analysis of National Socialism lacks an intellectual centre, but this double imperative forms the axis of his elliptical argument. The slogan epitomizes the power of doublethink: an appeal to spiritual values that sanctions bestial vindictiveness. The first part of the slogan, Kraus argues, would be ineffective without the second (16/25). The slogan on the streets was echoed at the highest levels of government. After claiming that National Socialism is committed 'to the principle of humanity', Hans Frank, as Minister of Justice, declares that Jews must be excluded 'from every aspect of the legal system' (cited 207/230). Writing in 1933, Kraus unerringly grasped the links between Nazism and the destruction of the Jews. Acknowledging the paranoid tendency to see enemies in every quarter, Jews, Marxists, bicyclists and supporters of relativity theory (250/276), he also gives due weight to the persecution of socialists and communists. But with prophetic insight he suggests that the 'immediate aim' (250/276) is the elimination of the Jews from German life. He anticipates that by the time Germany finally does awake – from the nightmare of Nazism – the second half of the slogan will have been shamefully fulfilled (280/306).

Kraus shows how carefully this campaign is being orchestrated by Goebbels. Conventional wisdom, now as in 1933, sees National Socialism as a system that destroyed freedom of the press, with the burning of the books signalling the onset of intellectual tyranny, but Kraus plays down the importance of these events, suggesting that too much honour has been accorded to authors who have been banned. By contrast with more sinister events like the boycott of Jewish businesses, the book-burnings are mere 'pantomime' (104/116). Black-and-white images of political tyranny are rejected, since the liberal press – in Kraus's view – has not been 'eliminated', but merely 'co-ordinated' (13/19). Existing journalistic practices have been adapted to the demands of the new ideology. The section on Diebold shows how those who remained in Germany colluded with the new regime. The *Frankfurter Zeitung* may try to remain liberal in tone, but its cultural columns help to enhance the prestige of fanatical Nazis like Goebbels and Hanns Johst (37/50).[32] Kraus draws a parallel between Goebbels's discourse and the techniques of mystification pioneered by Bekessy (142/163). An Austrian Nazi newspaper actually prided itself on methods of misreporting derived from so-called 'Jewish spin' ('jüdischer Dreh', 170/190). For Kraus, there is ample evidence of the connection between the 'two evils' of journalism and Nazism. National Socialism may *seem* to be a reaction against the modern system of mass communications, but in reality it is the fulfilment of that system, with the troglodytes occupying the editorial offices (280–1/ 307–8).

Dritte Walpurgisnacht portrays Goebbels as the quintessential journalist, adapting sophisticated communication techniques to a nationalistic ideology. We know from other sources that his early writings were coloured by socialist sympathies, while his ambition was to write for the *Berliner Tageblatt*, the leading Jewish-owned liberal newspaper. During the early 1920s Goebbels submitted nearly fifty articles to the paper, all of which were rejected, and as late as January 1924 he applied for an editorial post, once again being turned down. His resentment about the alleged Jewish domination of German culture was reinforced by further experiences of rejection. His novel *Michael*, issued in 1929 by a Nazi publisher, was initially rejected by Ullstein.[33] It was in September 1924, on the rebound from these rejections, that Goebbels accepted the editorship of the *Völkische Freiheit*, a nationalistic paper published in the Rhineland. Instead of producing liberal copy for the *Tageblatt*, he began to churn out antisemitic diatribes. This was the job that launched him on a career in journalism, leading in 1927 to the founding of *Der Angriff*, the rabble-rousing weekly that helped to capture Berlin for the Nazi cause. Goebbels is often pictured haranguing enormous crowds in the Berlin Sportpalast about the need for 'fanatical loyalty' and 'total war'. But this ignores the professionalism of his journalism, aptly reflected in the photograph showing him studying the latest edition of his paper (Fig. 58), and he was to end his life amid the ruins of Berlin writing editorials for *Das Reich*. After noting the links with the *Berliner Tageblatt*, Kraus concludes that his skills as 'Minister for

58   Goebbels the journalist, photographed with a copy of *Der Angriff*

Atrocity Propaganda' might easily have been employed by the opposite camp (42/55).

This picture of Goebbels as a journalist seems at odds with his fanaticism, but it is clear from his early diaries that he was essentially an opportunist who hitched his career to Hitler's cause. Goebbels, in the words of one biographer, 'sold National Socialism the way other people sell soap or refrigerators'.[34] Others have emphasized that even his antisemitism 'did not come naturally'.[35] It seems to have been a propagandistic strategy rather than a passionately felt obsession. As a young man he admired Jewish writers, including Heine, and even had an affair with a girl whose mother was Jewish. He was 'far too calculating', as one of his close collaborators observed, to be an 'instinctive antisemite'.[36] The propagandist who claims to despise Jewish culture is actually, in Kraus's view, the product of the liberal press:

> Goebbels is familiar with all the trendy terminology which rootless intellectual authors are no longer able to use. He has attitude and empathy, he knows about stimulus and impetus, application and implication, dramatic presentation, filmic transposition, flexible formulation and the other aids to radical renewal, he has experience and perspective, indeed for both reality and vision, he has life-dynamics and world-philosophy, he approves of ethos and pathos, but also mythos, he supplies subordination and integration into the living-space and working-space of the nation, he embraces the emotional realm of community and the vitalism of personality, he professes loyalty to kith and kin and international solidarity and favours synthesis, he transmits stimuli and tentatively explores parameters before arriving at the central modality, in order to fathom latent potential and accentuate the problematics of intellectuality, he knows all about fossilized tradition and burgeoning creativity, he values will-power, recognizes purposive achievement, such as the artifice inherent in artistry, he acknowledges fluidity, accessibility and significant form, and can distinguish between the expansive and the convulsive, indeed I suspect that he is orientated in the cosmic; at all events he recognizes potential for development and defines emotionally the type that, inescapably, in the final analysis must surely eventuate in trend-setting hegemony, and knows that when the build-up of will-power precipitates willed conformity and hence collective action and cultural symbiosis, dynamism and rhythm form prominent parameters, and that then the goal is totality, though in the first instance steely romanticism – in short, you can't fool him about anything that was previously to be found in the cultural ragbag of the *Berliner Tageblatt* or *Berliner Zeitung* and that, whether modern German or modern Jewish, denoted a world sucked dry by those who saw the rest as suckers.

This pen-portrait is a collage of motifs from a variety of sources, most notably the speech of 8 May 1933 in which Goebbels defined his programme of steely romanticism.[37] It has often been pointed out that Nazi techniques for mobilizing popular opinion were modelled on revolutionary Marxism, but Goebbels himself, in a speech about propaganda delivered on 9 January 1928, gave pride of place to the liberal press: 'For example, when I consider the newspapers, I have to say that I learn most from the *Berliner Tageblatt*. It is edited in exemplary Jewish fashion. I have never discovered anything there that – from the Jewish viewpoint – could be considered a blunder.'[38]

It was this multiplicity of styles that made Goebbels's propaganda so potent. *Der Angriff* owed its popularity to caricatures of bumbling bureaucrats and rapacious politicians, and Goebbels aspired to be a 'satirist' (43/56). His most effective ploy was to create stock characters like 'Isidor', the nickname with which he taunted the Vice-President of the Berlin Police, Dr Bernhard Weiss. The portrayal of his plodding policemen as 'St Bernards' ('Bernhardiner') reveals a beguiling lightness of touch, and Goebbels's polemics, boldly illustrated by the cartoonist Mjoelnir, were designed to make Jew-baiting seem amusing.[39] This slickness enabled Goebbels to captivate the intellectuals and reassure the middle classes, placate foreign diplomats and soothe nervous industrialists, while holding in reserve the slogans designed for the thugs on the streets. When he attended the League of Nations in September 1933, we are told that Goebbels adopted 'the Geneva jargon'. Addressing foreign correspondents, he blandly described the antisemitic violence in Germany as 'certain excesses committed by uncontrollable elements'.[40] It was not simply the content of his statements that seduced the foreign press, but his suave personal style. The correspondent of the London *Times* reported that the tone of Dr Goebbels was 'extremely mild and clearly intended as a useful conciliatory gesture'.[41]

Unlike foreign observers, Kraus was not deceived, identifying Goebbels as the paradigmatic spin doctor with a gift for soundbites. After Toscanini, protesting against the exclusion of Jews from German cultural life, had refused to conduct at Bayreuth, Goebbels calmed the ensuing furore through a series of plausible communiqués. The subtlety of his technique, reminiscent of the distortions of the Bekessy era, led Kraus to coin the word 'Tonfallstricke' (142/163), a triple pun which combines the meanings of 'sound trap' ('Ton-Fallstricke'), 'tonic constraints' ('Tonfall-Stricke') and 'intonation tricks' ('Tonfalls-Tricke'). The function of the Propaganda Minister, according to his summary, is to equip a primitive environment with a 'terminological décor' (282/310). As the most modern mind in a regressive movement, he is the true protagonist of the Third Walpurgis Night. Lines from *Faust* (ll. 7237–8) are used to suggest the parallel between his club-foot and the devil's cloven hoof (53/66). The dominant figure in Kraus's polemic, as in Goethe's play, is not the would-be superman but his diabolical companion, 'the totally cynical Mephistopheles'.[42] Other Nazi leaders are mentioned only in passing – Himmler once, Streicher twice, Rosenberg three times. Even the brutish Göring, who authorizes his uniformed thugs to pump bullets into their opponents, remains a shadowy figure. It is Goebbels, master of the arts of media, technology and death, who is most compellingly portrayed. Perhaps, if he had landed that job on the *Berliner Tageblatt*, the world would have been spared the Third Reich (282/310).

Heidegger's House of Being

The seizure of power also attracted intellectual support, notably from Martin Heidegger. In his Rectoral Address of May 1933 at the University of Freiburg, he defined the spiritual world of a nation as 'the power that comes from preserving at the most profound level the forces that are rooted in the soil and blood of a *Volk*, the power to arouse most inwardly and shake most extensively its existence'. In quoting this passage, Kraus shows how plausibly Heidegger blends his philosophy of 'Dasein' with the ideology of 'Blut und Boden', denouncing him as one of the 'verbal accomplices of violence'. This is illustrated by a further quotation from the Freiburg lecture, proclaiming that one must act 'in the sense of questioning, unsheltered steadfastness in the midst of the uncertainty of the totality of being'. This prompts Kraus to raise the disturbing question whether German 'transcendental' philosophy has served as a 'training school for the Hitler-idea' (58–9/71–2).

The linkage between Heidegger's existentialism and his idealization of National Socialism has preoccupied commentators ever since.[43] Like Kraus, the philosopher had been exempted from military service during the First World War because of ill health, and it has been argued that he compensated for this through a philosophy of 'resoluteness' ('Entschlossenheit'), 'toughness' ('Härte'), 'struggle' ('Kampf') and 'discipline' ('Zucht'). Such concepts, already prominent in his writings of the late 1920s, suffuse the rhetoric of his Rectoral Address.[44] At a more fundamental level, his thinking was driven by the quest for 'authenticity', so memorably formulated in *Being and Time* (*Sein und Zeit*, 1927). Modern intellectual disciplines provide no answer, according to his lecture 'What is Metaphysics?' (1929), because they have 'lost their roots in their essential ground'. Given that the longed-for authenticity should be a shared experience, it was logical to develop a nationalistic philosophy that sought salvation in the *völkisch* community ('Volksgemeinschaft'), the dominant concept in his political texts. In addition to indoctrinating his students about the virtues of the Nazi revolution, he gave a series of lectures in November 1933 in support of Hitler's decision to take Germany out of the League of Nations, which was to be sanctioned by a plebiscite. Invoking the concept of 'self-responsible *völkisch* existence', he produced arguments just as twisted as those of Goebbels. In Hitler's Germany, he declared, there is no 'irruption of lawlessness' or 'reversion into barbarism'. Moreover, the decision to leave the League of Nations is '*not* a turning away from the community of peoples'.[45] Although Heidegger subsequently doubted whether National Socialism was living up to his ideals, he remained an unrepentant Party member until 1945, combining post-Nietzschean disillusionment with the cult of the national community.

Heidegger's later writings offer a rather different view of what constitutes the ground of being. It is no longer *the Germans* as a metaphysical nation who are seen as the embodiment of collective authenticity, but *German* as a philosophical language with expressive resources comparable to those of Ancient Greek. The reader of texts of the late 1940s and early 1950s like the 'Letter on Humanism' and 'Building Dwelling Thinking' will be struck by surprising parallels with Kraus's philosophy of language. We think of Kraus when we are told that it is wrong to act as if we were the 'master of language', since essential understanding comes to us 'out of language'. We think of Heidegger when we read of the harmony which emerges out of the 'metaphysical necessity of verbally founded ideas' ('aus der metaphysischen Notwendigkeit worthaltender Vorstellungen'). In fact, the first passage is from 'Building Dwelling Thinking', while the second is from *Die Fackel* of June 1921, subsequently reprinted in *Die Sprache* (S 7, 293). Both writers value language as a repository of wisdom, highlighting its metaphorical fundus, but Kraus's idea of dwelling in the 'house of language' anticipates by thirty years Heidegger's definition of language as the 'house of Being' ('Haus des Seins').[46] The linguistic turn in his later work leads him, in the essay 'Poetically Man Dwells', to introduce the very Krausian idea that 'strictly it is language that speaks'.[47] Heidegger, too, renouncing the technocratic values of modernity with its debased modes of communication, seeks to create out of language a vision of authentic being. Although he has been rightly criticized for failing to retract his support for National Socialism, he deserves credit for the rethinking that distinguishes his later work. In his eloquent writings of the 1950s he reinscribes the Rilkean theme of an authentic rapport with 'things', privileging the language of poetry in his commentaries on Friedrich Hölderlin and Stefan George. However, the Krausian precedents remain unacknowledged.

In short, what language 'speaks' depends on the mind of the locutor and the tradition that inspires him. Heidegger's vocabulary of 'being' ('Sein'), 'existence' ('Dasein') and 'essence' ('Wesen') is remote from the heritage of the Enlightenment which inspires Kraus's appeal to 'humanity' ('Menschheit', 12/18), 'humaneness' ('Menschlichkeit', 104/115) and 'human dignity' ('Menschenwürde', 196/216). Even the later Heidegger remains committed to the anarchic energy of pre-Socratic nature philosophy, whereas Kraus's essential ground lies within a Judaeo-Christian tradition that privileges moral precept and intertextual allusion. There is no denying the brilliance of Heidegger's reflections on poetry, but the sad truth is that an exceptional feeling for language provides no protection against racial prejudice or political delusion. The interwar period abounds in examples of gifted stylists who developed fascist sympathies, from Benn and Yeats to Pound and Céline. Kraus certainly demonstrates the value of 'linguistic scepticism' ('der sprachliche Zweifel'), as defined in his essay 'Die Sprache', but his suggestion that the German language might serve as a moral 'arbiter' ('Ordonnanz') is impossible to sustain (F 885–7, 2–3). After all, the Aryan myth emerged from the speculations of historical philology, while modern linguistics was founded by an antisemite. Language became a fetish for *völkisch* poets like Josef Weinheber, whose 'Hymnus auf die deutsche Sprache' ('Hymn to the German Language'), written in autumn 1933, equated German with the values of 'Heimat' and 'Vaterland'. We know from his letters that he modelled his 'linguistic conscience' on Kraus.[48]

Diaries in the Night

In his lectures of the 1930s Heidegger repudiated the 'humanizing, Christian ideas' which were allegedly suffocating the spirit of National Socialism.[49] This led him in his 'Introduction to Metaphysics' (1935) to condemn the author primarily responsible for introducing Kierkegaard's Christian existentialism to German readers, Kraus's friend Theodor Haecker. In autumn 1933 Haecker published a small book entitled *Was ist der Mensch?* ('What is Man?'), an eloquent appeal to Christian humanism that infuriated the philosopher by ignoring the National Socialist movement. Heidegger responded by mocking Haecker and his admirers for failing to realize where 'the authentic decisions must fall'.[50] With public discourse in the grip of this decisionist gobbledegook, the ethically responsible use of German was forced underground. The most significant heirs to Kraus's ethics of language were those who continued to write in secret, and Hitler's reign of terror provoked a Europe-wide revival of diary-writing. Some victims of persecution, from Anne Frank in the secret annexe in Amsterdam to Arnold Daghani in the slave-labour camp of Mikhailowka, abandoned the use of German as a protest against Nazi barbarism.[51] For others, like Avraham Tory in the Kovno Ghetto, writing in Yiddish represented a despairing affirmation of Jewish solidarity. Keeping a diary in German involved a more complex process of self-reflection, since the language of the perpetrators had to be turned against itself. With the possibilities of publication restricted for a radical Catholic author, the diary also became Haecker's favoured medium. After narrowly escaping imprisonment in 1933, he was continuously at risk of arrest, especially as his Munich circle included the students of the White Rose resistance group, and it is a miracle that his diary survived, given the double threat of house searches by the Gestapo and bombing raids by the Royal Air Force.

The evocatively titled *Tag- und Nachtbücher* ('Diaries in the Night') were first published in 1947, two years after Haecker's death. They include lucid reflections on his friendship with Kraus, distinguishing the impassioned scepticism of the satirist from the redemptive faith of the Christian. It is not German culture but holy scripture that constitutes the primary focus of Haecker's soul-searching, and the New Testament provides the norm against which he measures the abominations of Nazism, as in the entry for 24 December 1940:

> In the same night that Christ was born the leaders of the German people spoke of the *German* Christmas. Can God still be called God after this horrifying desecration of his name? Woe unto your children and grandchildren! And everywhere that appalling arrogance, above all in the words of Field Marshal von Brauchitsch: 'The sea provides England with a protective wall only as long as we please.' God can enclose no one with a protective wall if Hitler is opposed to it. 'God has blessed us.' That is what the Field Marshal said and he continued: 'God will not forsake us *if* – well, if what? Will the Field Marshal continue with that age-old formula which since the very beginning of prayer has been the only possible final phrase: if we remain faithful to God – no, I knew with dead certainty that he would not say that, but what did he say instead? He said: 'if we remain faithful to ourselves'. So that is now the condition which we impose on God: If we remain faithful to ourselves, i.e. in their opinion if we remain faithful to Hitler, God *must* help us. That is the arrogant German faith.[52]

This is a passage that Kraus would have admired for its use of quotation to create an ethically inspired intertextuality, but it also indicates the limitations of Haecker's writing. As a devotional diary it remains within the private sphere, hearkening to an inner voice rather than opening out to a wider world.

A more compelling example is provided by the diarist who may be regarded as Kraus's *Doppelgänger*, Victor Klemperer, a Jewish-born Romance philologist. As a young man, Klemperer had converted to Protestantism, but he ultimately renounced all forms of religious faith. After serving in the German army during the First World War, he became professor of French literature at the Technical University in Dresden. He survived during the Nazi period, living under atrocious conditions and wearing the Yellow Star, mainly because his loyal wife Eva was an 'Aryan'. After 1945, a significant number of diaries were published by German authors opposed to National Socialism, but Klemperer's diary, the greatest of them all, did not appear until 1995. It became an unexpected best-seller, translated into English in two volumes under the titles *I Shall Bear Witness* and *To the Bitter End*. This, too, is a work written under conditions of secrecy and danger, since he and his wife would certainly have been executed if the diary had been discovered during the frequent house searches.

Despite its focus on daily life in Dresden, the diary creates a panorama of everyday life under the Nazi regime. Where Haecker was strengthened by his reading of Kierkegaard, Klemperer's style can be correlated with that of the French Encyclopédistes, whose writings remained the focus of his research. Schooled by his reading of Diderot, he developed a mode of notation that is vividly impressionistic, perceptively psychological, and encyclopaedic in scope, transforming the personal into the political. His explicit assumption is that we ṃay understand human affairs by focusing not on great events, such as the inva-
e texture of social life and words and actions
xchange on 8 April 1944 with his friend
ian wife:

'I shall bear witness.' – 'The things you write
ig things, Kiev, Minsk, etc., you know nothing
ich are important to me but the everyday life of
ousand mosquito bites are worse than a blow to
mosquito bites. . .' Stühler, a little later: 'I once
read that fear of something is worse than the event itself. How I dreaded the house search. And when the Gestapo came, I was quite cold and defiant. And how our food tasted afterwards! All the good things, which we had hidden and they had not found.' – 'You see, I'm going to note that down!'[53]

This passage shows what a resourceful writer Klemperer was – arguably the most important diarist of the twentieth century (he kept a diary continuously from 1918 until his death in 1960). His gift for dialogue extends the range of his observations beyond the personal, draws his readers into the action. Anne Frank, in hiding in Amsterdam, could only describe what she saw from her window. Klemperer's diary encompasses a broad social world, from the

claustrophobic interiors of the Jewish community through vivid accounts of factory work to terrifying encounters with the German authorities and the degradations of imprisonment. Every detail counts, every snatch of conversation, every odd phrase overheard on a tram, read in a newspaper or noted from a radio broadcast.

It is this focus on language that makes the work so intriguing. Shortly after the end of the war, Klemperer published a study of the language of the Third Reich, based on his diaries, entitled *LTI: Notizbuch eines Philologen*.[54] By focusing on key terms like 'fanatisch' (for the power of the German people) and 'jüdisch' (for any force opposed to it), the book demonstrates the crudity of the dominant ideology. But Klemperer's ear for the nuances of colloquial expression also enables him to show how people – even persecuted Jews – succumb to what he calls the 'language of the victor'. This lies not simply in racist terminology, but in less fully conscious processes of brainwashing like the 'exorbitant use of the superlative'. In this view, the strength of totalitarianism derives from a combination of political force and linguistic programming, and he repeatedly cites the dictum, derived from Schiller, that 'language thinks and writes for you'.[55]

There are remarkable parallels between Klemperer's conclusions, based on precise observations over a period of twelve years, and the diagnosis so incisively formulated by Kraus in 1933. Since Klemperer makes no reference to *Die Fackel*, it is all the more remarkable that he offers similar psycholinguistic insights. The transformation of the sinister word 'fanatisch' into a positive virtue, already highlighted in *Dritte Walpurgisnacht* (119/136), forms the theme of one of Klemperer's most cogent chapters. Equally remarkable are the similarities in their view of Goebbels, identified as a quintessentially modern figure with a command of all conceivable 'registers'.[56] Of course, it is possible that both Kraus and Klemperer were mistaken – misled into overvaluing the impact of words by their obsession with speech acts. Klemperer's original analysis of the language of National Socialism was received with considerable scepticism, especially by academic linguists, one of whom concluded that he was attacking the Nazi regime under the *pretence* of criticizing its language, while another suggested that his arguments were impaired by his 'understandably biased view' as a victim of antisemitism.[57]

The publication of Klemperer's diaries, with their wealth of exemplification, has shown up the limitations of these judgements. The diaries constitute a uniquely valuable corpus of linguistic practices from the Nazi era, illuminated by a sensitive and humane observer living under the threat of deportation. Klemperer's dilemma as a persecuted Jew, compounded by his cultural conservatism, may at times make him oversensitive to harmless neologisms, but he shows how a totalitarian system can deprive language of its civilizing function and pervert it into an instrument for inciting hatred and condoning violence. Some of the passages he records are comparable to the hate sessions in *Nineteen Eighty-Four*, where Orwell describes how the state forces all citizens to watch

a Two Minutes Hate: 'a hideous, grinding speech, as of some monstrous machine running without oil. [. . .] As usual, the face of Emmanuel Goldstein, the Enemy of the People.'[58] The difference is that Klemperer did not need to invent anything, since hate speech had become a dominant feature of German journalism and broadcasting. On 29 May 1943, aware that Jews deported to the east were being systematically killed, he summarizes a tirade from a Nazi newspaper entitled 'The Jew is to blame' ('Schuld ist der Jude'): 'The Jews prepared the First World War. [. . .] Thus *only* the Jew is to blame for everything, we must *exterminate* him in Europe' ('Die Juden haben den Ersten Weltkrieg vorbereitet. [. . .] An allem also *nur* der Jude schuld, wir müssen ihn in Europa *ausrotten*').[59] This genocidal language would not have surprised Kraus, for the article cited in the diary is by Dr Johann von Leers, one of Goebbels's spokesmen on Jewish affairs. Ten years earlier the satirist had included verses by Leers in *Dritte Walpurgisnacht*, noting that his slogan 'Throw the Jews out!' was already being implemented (48–9/61–2).[60]

Linguistic–Theological Observations

Klemperer was a rationalist who took a strictly secular view of events. Even when held in solitary confinement, he was not tempted to resort to prayer, unlike other victims of the Nazi regime.[61] His lifeline in prison was a stub of pencil, given him by a kindly warder, which enabled him to continue writing. However, he was aware that the way people spoke about Hitler was suffused with religious feeling, devoting a whole chapter to this phenomenon in his book on the language of National Socialism and concluding that it was a 'language of faith' with its roots in Christianity.[62] This insight, too, is anticipated in *Dritte Walpurgisnacht*, which opens with quotations that reveal the messianic fervour of the Hitler myth. Strong men fold their hands in prayer to thank the Lord for the Führer, while women reportedly rend their clothes in rapture (12/18). This sensitivity to religious language reveals the source of the fascination exerted by Hitler until the bitter end. The examples cited by Klemperer from conversations with ordinary Germans who still passionately 'believed' in the Führer in the spring of 1945 may appear impressionistic, but they are confirmed by a more systematic source: the reports of the German Security Service. These show that Goebbels never achieved his goal of complete control over hearts and minds, since there were plenty of grumbles about the hardships of war and the failings of the Party. But the Hitler myth was so potent that it defied the facts, even after the failure of the Russian campaign and the bombing of German cities. After the attempt on Hitler's life in July 1944, the Security Service noted that many people connected 'mystical, religious notions with the person of the Führer'.[63]

Kraus goes beyond Klemperer in developing the approach he defines as 'sprachtheologisch' (F 890–905, 87). *Dritte Walpurgisnacht* concludes with a reference to a comet similar to a cross, of which it is written that if it is 'twisted to the right' ('rechtsgeflügelt'), it signifies death (291/326). The allusion is to

the Emperor Constantine's vision of a radiant cross in the sky, which inaugurated the Christian era in Europe – but which has now been blotted out by the
swastika. Kraus cannot summon up the religious faith which enabled Haecker
to endure persecution, and instead he turns inwards towards his beloved language. This involves not some irrational faith in 'the Word' as an antidote to
Nazi propaganda, but a focus on the hidden dimensions of metaphor.

Metaphors, he argues in one of the defining passages of *Dritte Walpurgisnacht*,
constitute the 'measure of the human world' (123/*141*). This theme is fore-
grounded on the first page of the book, where he observes that anyone who
'sticks his neck out' ('die Stirn bieten') in the struggle against Nazism is likely
to have his brains bashed in (9/*12*). Civilized expressions relating to parts of the
body have been made redundant by the regime of violence, and when the
Nazis announce that the impact of the boycott will be 'stunning' ('schlagartig',
113/*128*) they really mean it. Expressions that have been re-literalized, like
'licking someone's boots' (61/*74*) provide linguistic symptoms of political barbarism. The principle of proportionality enshrined in the phrase 'an eye for an
eye', a residue from the practice of penal maiming, becomes in Göring's mouth
a call for unrestrained physical assaults (122/*139*). The question is how far the
dynamic drive towards primitivism will carry. 'Progress', Kraus had written
many years earlier, 'makes purses out of human skin' (F 287, 11).

His most cogent examples, as Werner Welzig observes, have theological
overtones.[64] The announcement of the boycott of Jewish businesses in April
1933 proclaimed that not a hair on a Jew's head would be harmed – a phrase
that doubtless derived from Goebbels.[65] This precept implies a consensus about
the sanctity of human life, but for Kraus it had become a hollow phrase,
connected – in his epitaph to the First World War – with the paradox that
people who supposedly 'wouldn't harm the hair on a fly' are capable of sadistic cruelty (F 501–8, 102). Citing in *Dritte Walpurgisnacht* the assertion that 'not
a hair on a Jew's head has been harmed', he observes that it could be justified
only if one ignored the fact that some victims had lost part of their scalp as their
hair was shaved into swastika-shaped patterns (123/*142*). Here he places an
incident involving the maltreatment of communists in Leipzig, reported in the
Arbeiter-Zeitung (12 & 13 April 1933), in the very different perspective created
by his linguistic theology with its scriptural associations. When Jesus foretells
the destruction of Jerusalem in Luke chapter 21, he warns that 'some of you
they shall cause to be put to death [. . .] but there shall not a hair of your head
perish'. For orthodox Jews the sanctity associated with untouched hair derives
from the prohibition on shaving in Leviticus 19: 27. Kraus's sensitivity to this
motif led him to insist – on the prophetic final page of *Dritte Walpurgisnacht* –
on remembering 'every harmed hair on the head of all those who committed
no crime, apart from being born!' (292/*327*). He clearly has the persecution of
Jews in mind, though even he can hardly have envisaged the sequel. After the
pogrom of November 1938, in which scores of civilians were killed, the claim
that 'not a hair of a Jew's head' had been touched was again widely reported.[66]

Two years later, after the conquest of Poland, German soldiers gleefully hacked off the beards of orthodox believers, while the SS set about recycling the hair of concentration-camp victims for industrial purposes.[67]

Kraus's focus on metaphor recalls that passage from Maimonides, cited by Gershom Scholem, which stresses the ambiguity of prophetic language: 'Only in the days of the Messiah will everyone know what the metaphors mean.'[68] As the Germans greeted Hitler as their longed-for redeemer, the question arose what he and his minions really meant when they spoke of 'ruthlessly cleansing' their enemies ('säubern, unerbittlich!') and indeed 'exterminating' them ('ausrotten'; cited 157/178). The fact that these phrases were used by the intemperate Göring might lead one to discount them.[69] After all, 'ausrotten' was another metaphor that had become hollow from overuse by politicians unaware of its biblical echoes, to which Kraus draws attention in recalling gruesome passages from the Old Testament (139–40/160).[70] Most observers assumed that when the Nazis spoke of 'destroying' communists and 'exterminating' Jews, they were using language metaphorically, in the sense of expelling them from positions of influence. When such statements were reported in the British press, they were interpreted 'in a figurative sense'.[71] But Kraus makes it clear that physical destruction is the essence of the Nazi movement. He quotes a passage in which Nazi jurists invoke ancient Germanic laws which allegedly sanctioned 'the *complete extermination* of the enemy within'. The passage goes on to explain that traditionally any member of the *Volk* 'was entitled *publicly to slay*' their enemy (264/290). Kraus's source for this document is the *Arbeiter-Zeitung* of 20 June 1933, but – unlike the socialist paper – he places these propositions in emphatic type, making it clear that the warning should be taken literally, since it has been confirmed by the release of the Potempa murderers. In short, he saw that Nazism was driven by an 'exterminationist mentality'.[72]

The fact that Kraus left his polemic unpublished suggests that he was unsure how far to carry his account of the restitution of metaphor. Could language be the chimera that devours its own children by rendering them incapable of distinguishing the literal from the symbolic? The clearest example is provided by the ideology of 'blood'. Even in times of peace, Kraus had noted back in 1913, the imagery of blood is ubiquitous (F 374–5, 3). But blood has a multiplicity of meanings, from family membership and biological inheritance to physical excitement and courage in battle. The life-giving fluid containing red and white corpuscles is transformed into an ideological matrix, endlessly invoked by racists and warmongers. Kraus's reflections on this theme led him, during the First World War, to identify the driving force behind German propaganda as 'bloodthirstiness of language' ('die Blutbereitschaft des Worts'; F 406–12, 102). In Die letzten Tage der Menschheit (V, 42) he reminds us that it is real blood that is being shed, not that of the propagandists but the 'blood of the others' – the conscripts sent into battle. In the aftermath of the war, revanchist German writing was dominated by a cult of 'blood' that fused the ideas of military courage and racial purity. Essentially, it was a debate about how the war should

be remembered. Was it – as Ernst Jünger insisted – a national crusade led by heroic stormtroopers, or was it – as Kraus argued – a humanitarian disaster, for which the unrepentant militarists were themselves to blame? Each faction developed its own mode of commemoration, with pacifists striving to counteract the pagan cults of *völkisch* authors. While Kraus was haunted by the cost in human suffering, Jünger claimed that redemption could be attained only through 'the shedding of blood'.[73]

In *Dritte Walpurgisnacht* this 'blood myth' (11/17) is noted dozens of times, from Heidegger's endorsement of 'blood-driven forces' (58/70) to the exceptional 'value of blood' for the SS (290/325). Nazi propaganda exploits both the belief that blood determines genetic inheritance and the fear that 'Aryan blood' may be polluted by sexual intercourse with strangers (202/224). In the German press and radio, Kraus concludes, the word 'blood' occurs more often in a single day than it does in a whole year in other countries. Blood in this metaphorical sense suggests racial purity and pulsating energy, irrational drives and brutal actions, carried out by a 'leadership elite defined by blood' (179–80/199–200). The situation would be happier, Kraus observes, if 'blood' were indeed merely a metaphor, but a 'miracle of transubstantiation' has taken place, since a 'surge of physical blood is beginning to flow through the crust of language' (121/138). The concept of the 'crust' of language implies that words have a healing power, provided they are properly used, forming a protective tissue around the all-too-vulnerable body. Metaphors, properly used, contribute to a culture of argument in which physical conflict has been displaced on to a symbolic plane.

The Nazi appropriation of the language of blood reverses the process of civilization. Lurking behind it is a barely repressed delight in violence, articulated by Spengler in a passage describing 'the ecstasy of feeling when the knife slices into the enemy's body' (cited 64/77). Hence the 'eruption of empty phrases into violent actions' (123/141). Despite the denials, real blood is flowing in German prisons (162/182), since bloodthirsty metaphors create a climate that encourages the infliction of real wounds. Kraus cites the case of a victim of Nazi torture who escaped across the border to a Refugee Reception Centre in Saarbrücken, then under French administration. The severity of his injuries prompts a representative of the Centre to say: 'We have seen the man and his wounds' (254/280). The allusion to the wounds of Christ is all the more poignant for remaining unspoken.[74]

Language reaches its limit when it is reduced to the rhythm of torture. Kraus quotes the testimony of two victims of the SA in Hamburg, one a Jew, the other an Austrian, forced to chant the words: 'I – am – a – stinking – Jew!' and 'I – want – to – become – a – German!' The moment their voices falter, they are beaten with rubber truncheons (193/213–14). He links this with the form of torture known as 'Grammophonspielen'. The victim's prostrate body forms the gramophone record, and a sharp instrument is applied to produce sounds that satisfy his captors. We know from other sources, including the memoirs of

Kurt Hiller, that such dehumanizing techniques were widely used with the aim of enforcing total submission. Nazi methods of torture were unusual in being designed not to elicit information, but to inflict humiliation, pushing their victims to the limits of body and mind, depriving them even of speech. Thus Jean Améry, an Auschwitz survivor, introducing the chapter on 'Torture' in his memoir *At the Mind's Limits*, had reason to recall Kraus's dictum: 'The Word expired on Hitler's world's awaking.'[75] For former camp inmates, he adds, that metaphysical concept of the Word had died long before. Like Paul Celan, he was haunted for the rest of his life by the struggle for adequate expression. After Auschwitz, as Adorno observed, poetic language is no longer able to 'sublimate suffering', and 'Celan's poems articulate unspeakable horror by being silent'.[76]

Kraus anticipates these post-Holocaust positions by foregrounding the impossibility of writing conclusively about the Nazi reign of terror. A rounded picture runs the risk of reconciling the reader with disaster through the pleasures of literary form, while journalistic fluency may lapse into a pornography of power that endows the figure of Hitler with perverse glamour. Hence Kraus's angular, refractory style, his allusive intertextuality, his determination to make the reader struggle every inch of the way, slipping in puns so poignant that we don't know whether to laugh or cry. Snippets of quotation displace coherent narrative, but truth slips through the mesh of metaphor, revealing hidden impulses which conscious speech denies. This prismatic approach, infused with irony, avoids the melodramatic effects found in the works of contemporaries who attempted to emulate his apocalyptic style: the purple prose of Joseph Roth's diatribe *Der Antichrist* or the stilted dialogues of Dosio Koffler's *German Witches' Sabbath*.[77] Kraus's guiding principle is understatement, decentring historical events in a style that anticipates Aharon Appelfeld's novels about Austrian Jews drifting towards their doom. Setting aside the temptations of grand narrative, the satirist creates a diffuse panorama of linguistic fragments and broken voices.

Kraus's eschatology culminates in the simplest of phrases – an idiom that had haunted him throughout his career: 'letzten Endes' ('at the end of the day' or 'in the final reckoning'). The focus on 'atrocities of intonation', which Brecht so admired, made him specially sensitive to adverbial modifiers. This is illustrated by the statements he quotes about two prisoners who died while in protective custody: 'His death was "*primarily* due to *losing the will to live*"' and '"He died of heart failure and in any case he was stateless"' (185–6/*205–7*). Phrases like 'primarily' or 'in any case' encourage us not to think too hard about what is actually happening. The throwaway phrase that he most frequently puts into scare-quotes is 'letzten Endes'. The German phrase, meaning literally 'at the final end', is more obviously a tautology than its English equivalent, but the heedlessness of modern usage has obscured the traditional associations with 'death'.[78] In the introduction to *Dritte Walpurgisnacht* Kraus restores that original meaning by making it clear that the 'final end' of National Socialism is 'annihilation' (15/*23–4*).

As this phrase 'letzten Endes' evolves into a leitmotif, readers attuned to religious overtones will pick up the allusion to biblical passages prophesying the 'End of Days'. When Kraus, at the outbreak of the First World War, declaimed prophetic verses from Isaiah, they included disturbing visions of what 'shall come to pass in the last days' (Isaiah 2: 2). Thus 'letzten Endes' is both a cliché to make readers wince and a prophecy inspiring apprehension. By the end of *Dritte Walpurgisnacht* this phrase has come to signal an unprecedented catastrophe – the combination of journalistic cliché with cataclysmic violence. The phrase occurs at least twenty-five times, culminating in a 'Terrifying Revelation of the Final End' that includes 'new, completely stifling waves of poison gas' (291/*326*). Although this passage remained unpublished, Kraus never allows his readers to forget the threat of poison gas. In the final year of *Die Fackel*, as Mussolini's troops are massing on the border of Eritrea, he quotes a report that engineers from IG Farben are supplying gas canisters for use during the invasion of Abyssinia. The gas is being transported with characteristic efficiency 'by German technicians and Gestapo'. Noting these developments in the introduction to an excerpt from his memoirs, he fears the consequences for defenceless populations, describing the toxic effects of the new chemical weapons on the human body. Max Reinhardt may be about to conquer Hollywood, but the weary world is unlikely to survive the 'apocalypse' that will result from the 'double effect of poison gas and the press' (F 912–15, 34–5). He also cites a suggestion by H. R. Knickerbocker that people may be safer from gas attacks if they spend their lives in cellars. Neither of them realized that poison gas would prove most effective when released in a confined space.

Writing and Erasure

The encroaching horror deprived Kraus of his powers of expression. Even Offenbach recitals seemed problematic, since he felt that Hitler's seizure of power 'strangles laughter, as it suffocates one's breath' (F 909–11, 25). The 'global stupidity', he wrote to Sidonie in May 1936, was making 'all work impossible – apart from adapting Shakespeare' (BSN 1, 687). Retranslating dramatic verse took his mind off other things, and he produced two handsome volumes of Shakespeare adaptations, before the series was cut short by his death from a heart attack on 12 June 1936. The final numbers of *Die Fackel* are damp squibs, containing only occasional flashes of illumination, but the loss of control over words is most obvious in a manuscript: Kraus's last will and testament. Dimly aware that his days were numbered, he sat down at Janowitz during the night of 27–28 August 1935 and drafted a new four-page testament indicating how his property should be dispersed after his death. One does not need to be a graphologist to see that this handwriting betrays acute anxiety.[79]

Several commentators have drawn attention to the Freudian slip on the final page, where he wrote 'mein Leben' ('my life') instead of 'mein Ableben' ('my decease'), betraying a fear of death that may be intrinsic to the satirical temperament.[80] Moreover, in naming his literary executors he wrote the word 'aber' ('but') instead of 'außer' ('except'), creating a nonsense that caused legal complications. He failed to notice these mistakes when he revised his will on 9–10 February 1936, and his corrections merely made the manuscript more difficult to read, since he vehemently deleted the names of several people originally included among his beneficiaries. Unaware that his illness was so advanced, he failed to take the precaution of having his will typed by a secretary or solicitor's clerk. It is clear from the desolate state of the manuscript that he no longer felt syntactically secure, and there was no magic writing pad to smooth out the erasures, which reflected the bitter disputes that clouded the final months of his life.

The oppressive political climate of the mid-1930s impacted on Kraus's personal relationships. It was not merely that his support for Dollfuss had cost him the respect of left-wing friends. Personal jealousies were also involved, and his lifelong companion Helene Kann was drawn into a dispute with other members of his circle over the use of the insulting phrase 'Jewish insolence'.[81] Feeling obliged to take Helene's side, Kraus became embroiled in arguments that led to the breaking of long-standing friendships with the publisher Franz Glück and the art historian Ludwig Münz. A planned edition of the letters of Peter Altenberg had to be abandoned, and Glück was required to return the precious letters from Altenberg which Kraus had lent him. His anger is evident from the amended manuscript of his will, in which the names of Glück and Münz, together with several others, are emphatically deleted. He seems to have endured these tribulations with fortitude, for Walter Benjamin, on hearing details of the final weeks of his life, associated the tragedy of Kraus's death with the 'Shakespearean world spirit'.[82]

The erasures in Kraus's testament were followed less than two years after his death by a more spectacular blank – the referendum on the independence of

59   Austrian posters: (a) warning against Nazi terrorism (b) urging support for Austrian
     independence

Austria. The 'Gentlemen Agreement' (sic!) of July 1936 between Germany and Austria provided only a temporary respite for the beleaguered Alpine Republic, and in January 1938 Hitler summoned Schuschnigg to Berchtesgaden for a showdown. Reporting back to his Cabinet in Vienna, the Austrian Chancellor decided to defy the Nazi threat (Fig. 59a) by announcing that there would be a referendum on the future of the country. Ballot papers were printed, boldly inviting a 'Yes' vote for Austria (Fig. 59b). Although there was no systematic sampling of public opinion, historians believe there would have been a majority in favour of Austrian independence. There was a dynamic publicity campaign organized by the Fatherland Front, and even the Social Democrats responded to the patriotic appeal. The streets were transformed by slogans urging a 'Yes' vote, plastered on walls and painted on pavements. This was the last chance to stave off the Nazi threat by means of the written word, and Kraus would certainly have supported the campaign.

However, Austria was abandoned by the allies that had so recently guaranteed its independence, including Britain and France. The decisive factor was the stance of Italy, which had leapt to Austria's defence in June 1934. Italy was now embroiled in the war in Abyssinia, which earned it the hostility of the League of Nations and pushed Mussolini into an alliance with Hitler. In 1938 the Austrian government stood alone, and resistance was undermined both by pro-Nazi members of the Cabinet and by fascist demonstrations in the provinces.[83] Through a combination of political propaganda and military menace, Hitler forced Schuschnigg to cancel the referendum, and on 12 March German troops crossed the border. The scenes that followed shocked the

60   Vienna, March 1938: Jews forced to scrub the streets

world, but the satirist would hardly have been surprised, since he had so often pictured the mentality of Kasmader, the quintessential Austrian reactionary. There was an outburst of sadism, orchestrated not by the new German Gauleiter but by Austria's homegrown Nazis, who gleefully forced Jews to scrub the streets (Fig. 60). There was no longer any public space for writing hostile to the regime, and the erasure of words prefigured the extermination of defenceless victims. As the Kasmaders gathered in their thousands to welcome Hitler to the Heldenplatz, Austrian patriots – both Christian and Jewish – had nowhere to hide. On 16 March, Egon Friedell, Kraus's friend from the early days of *Die Fackel*, jumped to his death from the window of his apartment to escape the Gestapo. The suicide rate rose so rapidly that the municipal gas company reportedly cut off supplies to its Jewish customers. It was not hard to imagine how the satirist would have glossed the news in *Die Fackel*. Commenting on this report in a letter of summer 1939, Walter Benjamin observed: 'So Karl Kraus died too soon, after all.'[84]

Apocalypse and After

served in an essay published in 1963, 'after
values and hopes by the political bestiality
f coming 'after' had already begun in 1919,
pitaph on the First World War. His phrase
otted down in an unpublished notebook,
when taken together with prophetic scenes
eit: the mob defacing the shopfronts of
y, the critique of the bombing of civilian
rine warfare, the indictment of the execu-
tions at Kragujevac, the portrayal of factories run on forced labour, the
intuitions about the use of poison gas. No text could have been more topical
in the concentration-camp universe created by National Socialism.

Karl Kraus in Dachau

No doubt Kraus, like other Austrian patriots, would have been on the first
train to Dachau, had he lived two years longer. Even if he had escaped to
Czechoslovakia, he would probably have shared the fate of his brother Rudolf
Kraus and his publisher Richard Lanyi, who were deported to their deaths in
Auschwitz. But the spirit of the satirist survived in the concentration camps, as
we know from the memoirs of the Austrian cultural politician Viktor Matejka.
As a Catholic student in the early 1920s, Matejka had fallen under Kraus's spell,
vainly attempting to persuade his contacts in the Christian Social Party that *Die
letzten Tage der Menschheit* should be staged at the Burgtheater. During the
1930s he used his position as an educational adviser for the Dollfuss government to promote reconciliation between socialist and Catholic factions. The
tragedy of the First Austrian Republic lay in irreparable polarizations: the
patriots were not democrats and the democrats were not patriots. These attitudes were modified by the experience of the camps, where anti-Nazis of all
persuasions – socialists and monarchists, communists and clericals – found

themselves incarcerated cheek by jowl. Matejka, who was deported to Dachau, contributed to this new spirit by organizing the library. Conditions were not as extreme as in the extermination camps in the east, and books were provided with the aim of converting the prisoners to Nazi values. In his memoirs Matejka describes his delight at discovering Kraus's writings among a consignment of books for the library, including bound copies of Die Fackel, the nine volumes of Worte in Versen, and Die letzten Tage der Menschheit. Since Kraus's writings were banned in Germany, Matejka altered the title to Tage der Menschheit, fearing that if the book were discovered it might imply that the days of the Third Reich were numbered. The books circulated clandestinely among the prisoners, and he was pleased to introduce Kraus's work to German readers.[2]

After his return to Vienna, Matejka was among those who welcomed the Red Army as liberators, joining the Communist Party and being appointed Cultural Councillor for the City of Vienna. One of his aims was to revive Austro-Jewish culture, but his efforts were frustrated by more conservative colleagues. Political refugees who had fled from Nazi tyranny were not welcomed back to post-war Austria, and Jews who had escaped the Holocaust were excluded from positions of influence. Matejka gives an illuminating account of the obscurantism that frustrated his efforts to have Arnold Schoenberg honoured on his seventy-fifth birthday.[3] His attempts to rehabilitate Karl Kraus were equally unsuccessful, since so many of his fellow citizens lived in a state of denial. The myth that Austria, in the words of the Moscow Declaration, had been the 'first victim' of Hitlerite aggression was welcomed as an alibi, and the official line (anticipated by Kraus's poem of November 1918) was: 'We're innocent as fleecy lambs.' In short, the new national identity was the 'product of forgetfulness'.[4] There were few signs of repentance, as Karl Renner, the target of Kraus's subtle barbs, became head of the state which he had betrayed in 1938.

During the occupation by the four Allied Powers, Social Democrats and former Christian Socials closed ranks in an effort to restore Austrian independence. The coalition government, led by Catholic politicians like Leopold Figl, frustrated claims for the compensation of Jewish victims of Nazism, while Leopold Kunschak declared, no less stridently in 1945 than in 1919, that there was no place in Austria for Jews.[5] Friedrich Funder, renowned for his diatribes in Die Reichspost, was able to resume his journalistic career as editor of the Catholic weekly Die Furche, although Dachau had tempered his virulence, while the reactionary Rudolf Henz, director of the state-owned Austrian Radio and Television, ensured that subversives like Kraus were passed over in silence. Instead, the government promoted backwoodsmen like Nabl, Strobl and Waggerl, rewarding them with state prizes while excluding authors who had emigrated.[6] It was conveniently forgotten that many of the prize-winners, led by the Catholic dramatist Max Mell, had welcomed the destruction of Austria in 1938, celebrating the sacred union of the German Volk and praising Hitler for his humanity.[7] When the Reinhardt-Seminar was reopened, the person responsible for its aryanization in 1938 was soon back at his post as director, reminiscing about the good old days without mentioning the fate of his colleague Emil Geyer, murdered in Mauthausen.[8] After an interlude of denazification, literary historians like Heinz Kindermann and Josef Nadler were able to continue their careers, while independent spirits like Friedrich Heer were condemned for suggesting that Austrians were still infected by the Nazi mentality.[9] Some attempt was made to develop a more radical style of journalism, especially in the pages of *Neues Österreich*, and Oskar Pollak returned from British exile to resume the editorship of the *Arbeiter-Zeitung*. But Pollak shared Henz's phobia about anti-establishment satire, and attempts to found a Karl Kraus Society were frustrated by combined pressures from left and right. Only through the work of Friedrich Torberg, who returned from California to found *Das Forum* with American support, were the achievements of *Die Fackel* recalled. Deep in the recesses of the City Library, an archivist was cataloguing Kraus's papers, which had survived in Switzerland during the war, but the contents of his library, preserved by Oskar Samek after Kraus's death, were looted by Nazi thugs in 1938. After the war there was no public space in Austria for a revival of his writings, and it was in Germany that the renaissance began.

The Post-War German Revival

The apocalyptic visions of *Die letzten Tage der Menschheit* became reality in the 1940s, as fire rained down from heaven over the cities of Germany. The obliteration bombing carried out by the British and American air forces failed in the aim of crippling Germany's military capacity, of undermining support for Hitler and bringing the war to a speedy conclusion. But after the unconditional surrender, as people began to rebuild their country out of the ruins, the longer-term effects became clear. There was no longer any support for the militaristic ethos that had sustained national identity for so long. In a memorable account of what it felt like to be at the mercy of the nightly bombardment, Jakov Lind described the destruction of Ludwigshafen in 1944 as an 'apocalyptic' experience: 'The day of justice has come. The earth opens up to swallow all that breathes.' Lind was a Viennese-born Jew who survived the war in Germany and the Netherlands under an assumed name, masquerading as a Dutch sailor on a cargo-boat on the Rhine. His eyewitness account, first published in 1969, records the moment of truth:

> The Allied bombers were the doves of peace. The bombs and only the bombs destroyed the arrogance of the burgher who had believed for far too long that one can get away with murder. Nothing in the history of modern Germany equalled this catharsis straight from heaven; it made West Germany more democratic than it has ever been, and more pacifist than anyone can recall.[10]

This vision of cosmic retribution suggests that the suffering inflicted upon German civilians was legitimized by its moral consequences. Lind was by no means the only author to compare this bombing of German cities to the 'Day of Judgement'.[11]

Lind's memoirs make it clear that the post-war German mentality after 1945 was very different from that which Kraus diagnosed in 1919. In place of embittered revanchism, there was a desire for reconciliation with France, a welcome for the Marshall Plan, and a willingness to participate in the peaceful reconstruction of Europe. The transformation was brought about by suffering on an apocalyptic scale, while the concept of a Day of Judgement gained substance through the revelations about concentration camps and the verdicts of the Nuremberg War Crimes Tribunal. The trials established a concept of 'crimes against humanity' that Kraus (like Kant) would have emphatically endorsed. Anti-militarist models of modern Germany emerged on both sides of the Iron Curtain, programmatically anti-fascist in the east, systematically denazified in the west. This was accompanied by a revitalization of cultural life, initiated in the Federal Republic by Heinrich Böll, Günter Grass and the authors of the Gruppe 47. This was reinforced by the rehabilitation of the German-Jewish intellectual tradition which had flourished between the wars: from Adorno, Benjamin and Canetti through Kafka and Lasker-Schüler to Roth, Schoenberg, Tucholsky, Wittgenstein and the Zweigs. Since the minds of these creative spirits had been shaped by their reading of Die Fackel, the Kraus revival was implicit before it actually occurred.

The first post-war Kraus editions appeared in Switzerland, provoking a dispute about copyright that was resolved by a compromise between Heinrich Fischer, who returned to Munich from his exile in London, and Oskar Samek, who remained in New York. The Kösel editions of Kraus's writings, which Fischer launched with Die Dritte Walpurgisnacht in 1952, contributed to the new critical climate, while inexpensive reprints of Die Fackel were eagerly acquired by the generation of 1968. In the German Democratic Republic, the satirist's reputation was revived through the efforts of Kurt Krolop and Georg Knepler, and the launching of Wagenknecht's Suhrkamp paperback edition placed Kraus in the pantheon of modern classics alongside Benjamin and Brecht. A new generation of German academics, led by Helmut Arntzen, began to explore the nuances of Kraus's writings, while Friedrich Pfäfflin of the German Literary Archive in Marbach showcased his work through a series of exhibitions and publications. The satirist began to be taken seriously even in Austria, after productions of Die letzten Tage der Menschheit were staged at the Vienna Festival, and government funding enabled Werner Welzig to launch his ambitious 'Wörterbuch der Fackel' project.

Kraus's writings entered the electronic age when Suhrkamp published the complete text of Die Fackel on compact disk. This electronic version has introduced his ideas to a new internet-orientated generation, offering reading experiences that are segmented rather than sequential. Gone are the days when a researcher might feel moved to spend the better part of a lifetime poring over the pages of a little magazine. At a touch of the keyboard it is now possible to retrieve every reference in *Die Fackel* to a specific theme, from Anschluss to Zionism. Systematic searches incorporating word counts will bring the satirist's principal themes into a sharper focus than could be achieved by traditional reading, and a more comprehensive account of his critique of the press may be facilitated by the knowledge that there are 2,312 occurrences of the word 'Zeitung' and 4,728 of the word 'Presse'. However, the implications for our own day can be succinctly summarized by reference to a concept that occurs only once: 'counterfeit reality' ('vorgetäuschte Wirklichkeit').

Virtual Reality

Although Kraus realized that difficulties of translation would restrict his international readership, he claimed in an epigram that 'Only those distant in time and nation / will grasp my satire's implication.'[12] If his ideas have indeed made an impact far beyond Germany and Austria, it is because the globalization of communications and the intensified impact of the media have given the modern world a distinctly Krausian turn. In France his conception of wars as 'media events' has been taken up by critics like Bourdieu and Bouveresse. Indeed, he has been identified as 'a guiding spirit for all subsequent theorists and practitioners of radical media criticism', posing penetrating questions for any 're-workings of history which foreground language and culture'.[13]

This kind of prophetic insight is exemplified by an article of May 1926, which foreshadows the phenomenon of virtual reality in the sense of media-generated images that create a world of plausible delusion. Responding to press headlines about the possibility of 'Anschluss' between Austria and Germany, Kraus suggests that the hypnotic power of newsprint has created a 'counterfeit reality' in which 'nothing is real except for lies'. Newspapers in Berlin and Vienna, by quoting each other's use of the concepts 'Volkstum', 'das deutsche Volk' and 'das Volk Deutschösterreichs', generate a circular discourse that has no basis in any actual political or diplomatic event. The Austrian Chancellor is on a visit to Berlin, but he and his German counterpart haven't yet met, let alone released a communiqué. To fill the vacuum, the press is recycling slogans deriving from 'the latest beer-hall conversations of the two realms'. Through their emphasis on the word 'Volk', a tendentious concept implying both political solidarity and biological homogeneity, the media are creating a frame of reference that is essentially fictitious. The problem is that this gigantic apparatus has the capacity to turn 'non-events' into 'action and death' (F 726–9, 59–61).

'Volk', with its populist, nationalistic and racist implications, shows how a single word can shape a destructive world, especially when set against 'Menschheit', the humanistic principle that sustains Kraus's vision. As we rely on such keywords to compose our thoughts, our comprehension becomes distorted by slogans, clichés and conceptual muddles. The attempt to justify barbaric atrocities by invoking the concept of 'holy war' is repudiated both in *Die Fackel* and in *Die letzten Tage der Menschheit*, and Kraus would have been among the first to point out that the concept of a 'war on terror' involves a conceptual muddle of a comparable kind, substituting emotive metaphor for rational policy. Terrorists, then as now, are criminals who should be brought to justice, and there was a modicum of logic in the Austro-Hungarian invasion of Serbia, since the plot to assassinate Franz Ferdinand was indeed hatched in Belgrade. But how can an act of terrorism committed by Saudis trained in Afghanistan justify the invasion of Iraq? This is counterfeit reality on a global scale, recalling Kraus's dictum that wars begin when diplomats tell lies to journalists – and believe them when they see them in print. The media mogul has been reborn in modern guise, controlling global communications empires of unprecedented power; but there is no Kraus or Kipling to denounce the irresponsible power of the harlot.

When the neo-conservative Heinrich Friedjung, claiming that Austria was 'in danger', cited forged documents in an attempt to stage a war, his lies were exposed in court and he was publicly humiliated.[14] Sadly, as Kraus observed in January 1910, the political lesson was not learnt, and the warmongers ultimately had their way. The evidence used to justify the invasion of Iraq proved to be just as fraudulent as that cited – in all sincerity – by Friedjung; but no court has succeeded in impeaching the political leaders responsible for an unreal scenario that has cost countless lives. The photographs of enemy bases, displayed by the American Secretary of State at the United Nations to justify the attack on Iraq, owed more to slick public relations than to reliable intelligence, contributing to a strategy of mass deception. It is now America that is said to be 'in danger' and Britain that is standing 'shoulder to shoulder' with the dominant military power. Modern governments have a far more sophisticated propaganda apparatus than in Kraus's day, and the phantom enemies created by the spin doctors seem as remote from reality as the fantasy realms of adolescent computer games.

In short, word and world have become detached in a way that the satirist anticipated. When the concept 'word-world' ('Wortwelt') was introduced in *Die Fackel*, it initially related to the realm of poetry, exemplified by the densely woven texture of Lasker-Schüler's poem 'Ein alter Tibetteppich' (F 321–2, 50). But in October 1911 we find Kraus using the same neologism to describe the impact on his imagination of a multiplicity of 'voices and grimaces, apparitions and memories, quotations and posters, newspapers and rumours, discarded rubbish and fortuitous events'. For an author attuned to this 'word-world', he concludes, a 'war report' ignored by his contemporaries becomes an urgent 'cry for help' (F 333, 11). This foreshadows the irresponsible media coverage of the Balkan War of 1912, which Kraus analysed so incisively, while the propaganda of the First World War led him to develop a more sophisticated critique of communications. In the brave new world of mass communications, he insisted, the 'report *is* the reality' (F 366–7, 32) and the telegram 'an instrument of war like the grenade' (F 404, 12).

This analysis of the relationship between politics and language is far more radical than Orwell's essay on the same theme. 'The world', Kraus observed, 'is sieved through the sieve of language' (F 443–4, 29). Far from advocating a uniform system of communication such as Esperanto, he urges us to use our own language with the greatest possible sensitivity, alert to its inherent wisdom while remaining open to other cultures. Hence the endless hours he devoted to finding expressive equivalents for Offenbach's witty librettos and Shakespeare's inspirational plays. Insisting on the value of poetry in the conversation of mankind, he never tired of reading the scene in which Faust, fleeing from his bleak Nordic climes to the sunlit world of Helen of Troy, is united with her through the medium of rhyme. The language of the poets suggested to him that difference can be overcome through rhyme, and in Lasker-Schüler he admired an author who brought together east and west, Jewish and Arab worlds.

This faith in the inner resources of language is counterbalanced by a rigorous call for 'linguistic scepticism' ('sprachliche Zweifel'; F 885–7, 2). Kraus identified what we now know as 'soundbites' and 'spin' as an insidious means of converting events into propaganda, arguing that the vacuous 'chatter' of peacetime journalism renders public opinion vulnerable to more malign forms of manipulation. He did not live to witness the emergence of the media-generated myths of the television age, but his ideas have been taken up by more recent critics of the nexus between mass communications, global corporations and the military–industrial complex. Thus the spirit of Kraus, like that of Nestroy, transcends its own times, and his condemnation of those who believe they have God on their side applies to all who see war as a crusade, whether German Kaiser or American President.[15] Religious language may enhance our ethical sense, but it can also be used to justify cataclysmic conflict – the two-edged sword of the apocalypse.

There are, of course, more hopeful signs. The impact of Kraus's work has been reinforced by performances of *Die letzten Tage der Menschheit* in many parts of Germany, including the spectacular production in a Nazi bunker near Bremen, directed in 1999 by Johann Kresnik, which remained in the repertoire for five years and attracted a total audience of 35,000. In 1990 an almost equally ambitious Italian production, directed by Luca Ronconi, was staged at the disused Fiat car factory in Turin, while the new French translation by Jean-Louis Besson and Henri Christophe, published by Éditions Agone in 2005, is likely to enhance the play's impact in the francophone world. Although poets and satirists will never be acknowledged as the legislators of mankind, it is the work of Wilfred Owen and Siegfried Sassoon that has revolutionized attitudes towards what used to be known as the 'Great War', while Orwell's essays and novels enhance our resistance to propaganda. In Austria, critical spirits like Helmut Qualtinger confronted their audiences with the reality of their Nazi past, while the Waldheim controversy prompted public acknowledgements of Austrian complicity in war crimes. And the award of the Nobel Prize for Literature to Elfriede Jelinek has honoured an author who continues the Kraus tradition of anti-establishment satire and radical media criticism.[16] In Germany, despite the problems created by unification, the critique of militarism has transformed the climate so radically that in autumn 2002 the electorate chose a government opposed to the impending war, despite the unpopularity of its domestic policies. Further developments include the introduction of Peace Studies in schools and universities and the adoption of programmes of Holocaust education by the nations of the European Union.

Although no City of God has emerged from the apocalypse, there are islands of sanity in a world swamped by xenophobia. After centuries of devastating warfare, sites of memory have been created in many parts of Europe to serve as centres of reconciliation. In Berlin, the design of Daniel Libeskind's Jewish Museum retraces the topography of that vibrant culture with which Kraus so vigorously engaged. In Vienna, the Holocaust monument by Rachel Whiteread uses the motif of books turned away from the viewer to symbolize the closing of the Austrian mind during the Nazi period, while in the adjacent annexe of the Jewish Museum the names of those who perished can be accessed through an electronic databank. The sixtieth anniversary of the ending of the Second World War is being commemorated by public ceremonies across the globe, not least in a Europe united as never before. There are also more secluded places of remembrance, especially – for those attuned to the work of Kraus – Schloss Janowitz (Janovice) in Bohemia. In May 1999 the mortal remains of his beloved Sidonie Nadherny, who died in England, were reinterred in the park at Janowitz, which she had tended with such devotion. That ceremony, jointly organized by the governments of Germany, Austria and the Czech Republic, acted as a symbol of reconciliation. The present book will enhance this process if it succeeds in showing how the writings of a satirist committed to peace illuminate the dilemmas of our own conflictual world.

Reference Notes

PART ONE

Chapter 1

1   Thomas Mann, *Tagebücher 1918–1921*, ed. Peter de Mendelssohn (Frankfurt, 1979), pp. 23–4.

2   G. E. R. Lloyd, *Demystifying Mentalities* (Cambridge, 1990), pp. 1–6.

3   The 'Ideas of 1914' are reviewed in Hew Strachan, *The First World War*, vol. 1: *The Call to Arms* (Oxford, 2001), pp. 1114–39.

4   John Horne and Alan Kramer, *German Atrocities, 1914: A History of Denial* (New Haven and London, 2001), esp. pp. 57–8 and 113–20.

5   See Friedrich Hiller von Gaertringen, '"Dolchstoß"-Diskussion und "Dolchstoß-legende" im Wandel von vier Jahrzehnten' in *Geschichte und Gegenwartsbewußtsein: Historische Betrachtungen und Untersuchungen*, ed. Waldemar Besson and Friedrich von Gaertringen (Göttingen, 1963), pp. 122–60.

6   Richard Bessel, *Germany after the First World War* (Oxford, 1993), p. 89.

7   See Peter Pulzer, *The Rise of Political Anti-Semitism in Germany and Austria*, revised edn (London, 1988), pp. 240–50.

8   Strachan, *The First World War*, 1, pp. 1115–16.

9   Norman Cohn, *Warrant for Genocide: The Myth of the Jewish World Conspiracy and the 'Protocols of the Elders of Zion'* (Chico CA, 1981), pp. 134–5.

10   Fritz J. Raddatz, *Verwerfungen: Sechs literarische Essays* (Frankfurt, 1972), pp. 9–42: 'Der blinde Seher: Karl Kraus'; first published in *Merkur*, 22, No. 6 (June 1968), pp. 517–32.

11   Gisela Brude-Firnau, *Die literarische Deutung Kaiser Wilhelms II. zwischen 1889 und 1989* (Heidelberg, 1998), pp. 98–104. For a judicious review of 'what was wrong with Wilhelm II', see John C. G. Röhl, *Wilhelm II: The Kaiser's Personal Monarchy 1888–1900*, tr. Sheila de Bellaigue (Cambridge, 2004), pp. 1040–67.

12   See Hermann Wilhelm, *Dichter Denker Fememörder: Rechtsradikalismus und Antisemitismus in München von der Jahrhundertwende bis 1921* (Berlin, 1989), p. 57.

13   See Friedrich Pfäfflin, 'Fackelrot am Münchener Himmel: Karl Kraus und Ludwig Thoma 1903–1921', in *Festschrift für Werner Goebel* (Munich, 1980), pp. 94–130; Wilhelm, *Dichter Denker Fememörder*, pp. 112–17; Gertrud M. Rösch, *Ludwig Thoma als Journalist* (Frankfurt, 1989), pp. 313–18.

14   See David Clay Large, '"Out with the Ostjuden": The Scheunenviertel Riots in Berlin, November 1923' in *Exclusionary Violence: Antisemitic Riots in Modern German History*, ed. Christhard Hoffmann, Werner Bergmann and Helmut Walser Smith (Ann Arbor, 2002), pp. 123–40.

15   On the significance of the swastika, see Malcolm Quinn, *The Swastika: Constructing the*

Symbol (London, 1994); Nicholas Goodrick-Clarke, *The Occult Roots of Nazism* (London, 1985).

16 An electronic word-search has identified seventy-nine references to the words 'Hakenkreuz' and 'Hakenkreuzler' in *Die Fackel* between 1921 and 1932, documenting Kraus's sensitivity to this threat.

17 In this book 'Nazis' is generally used as the English equivalent for 'Hakenkreuzler', although occasionally, where Kraus is emphasizing the visual impact of the symbol, 'Swastiklers' is preferred.

18 See also the analysis of Kraus's response to Nazism in Kurt Krolop, *Sprachsatire als Zeitsatire bei Karl Kraus* (Berlin, 1987), esp. pp. 210–12.

19 Credit is due to Friedrich Pfäfflin for deciphering further phrases from this notebook, which is now in the Kraus Archive, including (on the left) 'Hofrathskäschen = Romadour', 'Die Deutschen wollten viele Niederlagen' and 'Kunst war nur Dienstbote beim Kaufmann, gehört entlassen'. Several of these motifs occur in the October 1915 number of *Die Fackel* (F 406–12, 101 & 116).

20 See Gerhard Botz, *Gewalt in der Politik: Attentate, Zusammenstöße, Putschversuche, Unruhen in Österreich 1918 bis 1938* (Vienna, 1976), p. 260.

21 For the significance of 'Fronterlebnis', see J. P. Stern, *Hitler: The Führer and the People* (London, 1978), chapter 2. For examples of Hitler's artistic talent, including his sketches of scenes from the western front, see Frederic Spotts, *Hitler and the Power of Aesthetics* (London, 2002).

22 Norbert Elias, 'The Decay of the State Monopoly of Violence in the Weimar Republic' in Elias, *On Civilization, Power and Knowledge: Selected Writings*, ed. Stephen Mennell and Johan Goudsblom (Chicago, 1998), pp. 150–60 (p. 155).

23 Klaus Theweleit, *Male Phantasies*, tr. Stephen Conway, 2 vols (Cambridge, 1987).

24 See *Lyrik der Deutschen, für seine Vorlesungen ausgewählt von Karl Kraus*, ed. Christian Wagenknecht (Munich, 1990), pp. 63–9.

25 See Edward Timms, '"Rächer der Natur": Zur Ästhetik der Satire bei Karl Kraus und Rosa Luxemburg' in *Karl Kraus: Ästhetik und Kritik*, ed. Stefan Kaszynski and Sigurd Paul Scheichl (Munich, 1989), pp. 55–69. These ideas have been further developed by Irina Djassemy, who draws parallels with Adorno's critique of the domination of nature in her book *Der 'Produktivgehalt kritischer Zerstörererarbeit': Kulturkritik bei Karl Kraus und Theodor W. Adorno* (Würzburg, 2002), pp. 108–62.

26 See Edward Timms, *Karl Kraus – Apocalyptic Satirist: Culture and Catastrophe in Habsburg Vienna* (New Haven and London, 1986), pp. 192–4.

27 'Zu den Nationalsozialisten ist ihm als Satiriker wohl wirklich nichts eingefallen.' Sigurd Paul Scheichl, '"Hüben und Drüben": 1918–1936 in der "Fackel"' in *'Was wir umbringen': 'Die Fackel' von Karl Kraus*, ed. Heinz Lunzer, Victoria Lunzer-Talos and Marcus G. Patzka (Vienna exhibition catalogue, 1999), pp. 134–9 (p. 138).

28 See F. L. Carsten, *Fascist Movements in Austria: From Schönerer to Hitler* (London, 1977); Gilbert Allardyce, 'What Fascism is Not: Thoughts on the Deflation of a Concept', *American Historical Review*, 84 (April 1979), pp. 367–98.

29 See Joachim G. Fest, *Hitler*, tr. Richard and Clara Winston (London, 1975), pp. 172–3.

30 The artist was Mechtilde Lichnowsky, one of Kraus's closest friends. See *Mechtilde Lichnowsky 1879–1958*, ed. Wilhelm Hemecker, *Marbacher Magazin 64* (Marbach am Neckar, 1993), pp. 42–4; and *Karl Kraus und Mechtilde Lichnowsky: Briefe und Dokumente 1916–1958*, ed. Friedrich Pfäfflin and Eva Dambacher (Marbach, 2000), pp. 62, 123–4 & 211.

31 See Bruce F. Pauley, *Der Weg in den Nationalsozialismus: Ursprünge und Entwicklung in Österreich* (Vienna, 1988).

32 See Kurt Krolop, *Reflexionen der Fackel: Neue Studien über Karl Kraus* (Vienna, 1994), pp. 98–102.

33 An extreme example, which uses the phrase 'syphilitischer Judenbub', is provided by the anonymous typewritten letter of 30 September 1930 (Kraus Archive, IN 161.970), reproduced in Michael Horowitz, *Karl Kraus: Bildbiographie* (Vienna, 1986), pp. 86–7.

Chapter 2

1 Marsha L. Rozenblit, *Reconstructing a National Identity: The Jews of Habsburg Austria during World War I* (Oxford, 2001), p. 126.

2 The comparable figures for France were 73 per cent, for Germany 65 per cent and for the British Empire 34 per cent. See Augustin M. Prentiss, *Chemicals in War: A Treatise on Chemical Warfare* (New York, 1937), p. 651.

3 The concept of an 'improvised' revolution derives from an article by the German constitutional lawyer Hugo Preuss entitled 'Die Improvisierung des Parlamentarismus', originally published in the *Norddeutsche Allgemeine Zeitung* on 26 October 1918. See Hugo Preuss, *Staat, Recht und Freiheit* (Hildesheim, 1964), pp. 361–4.

4 Manfred Jochum, *Die Erste Republik in Dokumenten und Bildern* (Vienna, 1983), pp. 10–12.

5 See György Borsányi, *The Life of a Communist Revolutionary, Béla Kun*, tr. Mario D. Fenyo (Columbia NY, 1993), pp. 80–1.

6 See Hans Hautmann, 'November 1918 – eine Revolution?' in *Österreich November 1918: Die Entstehung der Ersten Republik*, ed. Isabella Ackerl and Rudolf Neck (Vienna, 1986), pp. 158–67.

7 Map drawn by H. Auner on the basis of the decisions of the Austrian National Assembly, reproduced in Karl Bednarik and Stephan Horvath, *Österreich 1918* (Vienna, 1968), p. 112.

8 Otto Bauer, *Die österreichische Revolution* (Vienna, 1923), pp. 110–15.

9 See Karl Renner, *Die Gründung der Republik Deutschösterreich, der Anschluß und die Sudetendeutschen*, ed. Eduard Rabofsky (Vienna, 1990), p. 36; Walter Goldinger and Dieter A. Binder, *Geschichte der Republik Österreich 1918–1938* (Vienna, 1992), p. 19.

10 *Außenpolitische Dokumente der Republik Österreich 1918–1938* (= ADÖ), ed. Klaus Koch, Walter Rauscher and Arnold Suppan, vol. 1 (Munich, 1993), p. 71.

11 See Erich Scheithauer and others, *Geschichte Österreichs in Stichworten* (Vienna, 1983), 5, pp. 61–5 & 108–11.

12 Hans Kelsen, 'Die völkerrechtliche Stellung des Staates Deutsch-Oesterreich', reprinted in ADÖ, 1, pp. 206–9.

13 ADÖ, 1, pp. 24–5.

14 Bauer, *Die österreichische Revolution*, p. 157.

15 ADÖ, 2, pp. 435–88.

16 The official name of the party was 'Sozialdemokratische Arbeiterpartei Deutschösterreichs'.

17 Scheithauer and others, *Geschichte Österreichs in Stichworten*, 5, pp. 77–9. For a more detailed account, see Wilhelm Brauneder, *Deutschösterreich 1918: Die Republik entsteht* (Vienna, 2000).

18 The most significant exception was Steyr, which enjoyed local autonomy in policing matters as a result of a privilege granted in the nineteenth century. See Charlie Jeffrey, *Social Democracy in the Austrian Provinces, 1918–1934: Beyond Red Vienna* (London, 1995), p. 115.

19 See Paul Julian Weindling, *Epidemics and Genocide in Eastern Europe 1890–1945* (Oxford, 2000), chapter 4; *The 1918–1919 Pandemic of Influenza: The Urban Impact in the Western World*, ed. Fred R. van Hartesveldt (Lewiston NY, 1993), esp. chapter 2: 'Frankfurt' (by Stephen G. Fritz).

20 'Nach diesem Ereignis hat der große Krieg auch den letzten Sinn für uns verloren'. *Neue Freie Presse* (Morgenblatt), 2 November 1918.

21 ADÖ, 1, pp. 507–8.

22 Renner, *Die Gründung der Republik*, p. 47. For further details, see Michael John, '"We Do Not Even Possess Our Selves": On Identity and Ethnicity in Austria, 1880–1937',.in *Austrian History Yearbook*, 30 (1999), pp. 17–64.

23 Jakob Wassermann, *Mein Weg als Deutscher und Jude* (Berlin, 1921), p. 102.

24 The abbreviation AST, followed by date, refers to Arthur Schnitzler, *Tagebuch*, ed. Werner Welzig (Vienna, 1981–2000).

25 Austrian production of wheat and rye fell by almost 50 per cent in 1915, compared with the previous year. See David F. Strong, *Austria (October 1918–March 1919): Transition from Empire to Republic* (New York, 1974), p. 49.

26 Beatrix Hoffmann-Holter, *'Abreisendmachung': Jüdische Kriegsflüchtlinge in Wien 1914 bis 1923* (Vienna, 1995), pp. 36–7, 59, 65, 69 & 143.

27 Hoffmann-Holter, *Jüdische Kriegsflüchtlinge*, pp.129–34.

28 Weindling, *Epidemics and Genocide*, p. 114.

29 Hoffmann-Holter, *Jüdische Kriegsflüchtlinge*, pp. 123–4, 130, 134 & 143.

30 Hoffmann-Holter, *Jüdische Kriegsflüchtlinge*, pp. 127 & 170–1.

31 Hoffmann-Holter, *Jüdische Kriegsflüchtlinge*, pp. 145–6.

32 Hoffmann-Holter, *Jüdische Kriegsflüchtlinge*, p. 168.

33 Tony Kushner and Katharine Knox, *Refugees in an Age of Genocide: Global, National and Local Perspectives during the Twentieth Century* (London, 1999), pp. 73–88.

34 See Jacob Rosenthal, 'The "Counting of the Jews" by the German Army in the First World War: The Background, the Controversy and its Historical Impact' (doctoral dissertation, Hebrew University, 2002).

35 See Christian Schölzel, 'Fritz Rathenau (1875–1949). On Antisemitism, Acculturation and Slavophobia: An Attempted Reconstruction', *Leo Baeck Institute Yearbook*, 48 (2003), pp. 135–62 (p. 149).

36 For the concept of an 'antisemitic consensus', see Evan Burr Bukey, *Hitler's Austria: Popular Sentiment in the Nazi Era 1938–1945* (Chapel Hill, NC, 2000), pp. 22–4.

37 Ignaz Seipel, 'Minoritätenschutz und Judenfrage nach dem christlichsozialen Programm' in *Volkswohl*, 9 (1918), pp. 49ff.; quoted in Anton Staudinger, 'Christlichsoziale Judenpolitik in der Gründungsphase der Ersten Republik', in *Jahrbuch für Zeitgeschichte 1978*, ed. Karl Stuhlpfarrer (Vienna, 1979), pp.17–18. Cf. Gerhard Botz, Ivar Oxaal and Michael Pollak (eds), *Eine zerstörte Kultur: Jüdisches Leben und Antisemitismus in Wien seit dem 19. Jahrhundert* (Buchloe, 1990), pp. 253–5.

38 'Volksbundflugschriften, No. 4' quoted in Herwig Würtz (ed.), *Wahljahr 1919* (Vienna, 1989), p. 20.

39 Cf. Staudinger, 'Christliche Judenpolitik', p. 30.

40 Hoffmann-Holter, *Jüdische Kriegsflüchtlinge*, pp. 166 & 174.

41 'Die Juden!', unsigned article in the *Volkssturm*, Vienna, 24 August 1919 ('Wer hat diesen Weltkrieg, wer hat dieses Massenmorden über uns heraufbeschwört? *Die Juden!* … Wer trägt die Schuld an unserer furchtbaren Not? *Die Juden!*').

42 Hoffmann-Holter, *Jüdische Kriegsflüchtlinge*, pp. 177–8.

43 See reports in the Viennese press in autumn 1919, especially *Der Abend*, 6 October 1919, p. 2.

44 Soma Morgenstern, *Alban Berg und seine Idole: Erinnerungen und Briefe*, ed. Ingolf Schulte (Berlin, 1999), pp. 344–6.

45 Hoffmann-Holter, *Jüdische Kriegsflüchtlinge*, p. 217.

46 Bruno Frei, *Jüdisches Elend in Wien: Bilder und Daten* (Vienna, 1920). Frei was editor of the left-wing paper *Der Abend*, which had published some of his data in journalistic form.

47 David Rechter, *The Jews of Vienna and the First World War* (London, 2001), pp. 120–1 & 165–6; Harriet Pass Freidenreich, *Jewish Politics in Vienna, 1918–1938* (Bloomington IN, 1991), pp. 63–7.

48 Rozenblit, *Reconstructing a National Identity*, p. 11.

49 Samuel Krauss, *Die Krise der Wiener Judenschaft* (Vienna, 1919), pp. 2 & 15; quoted in Rechter, *The Jews of Vienna*, p. 73.

50   Joseph Roth, *The Wandering Jews*, tr. Michael Hofmann (London, 2001), p. 22 (adapted); Roth, *Das journalistische Werk 1924–1928*, ed. Klaus Westermann (Cologne, 1990), pp. 838–9.

51   Anton Kuh, *Juden und Deutsche* (Berlin, 1921), reprinted with an introduction by Andreas B. Kilcher (Vienna, 2003); Theodor Lessing, *Der jüdische Selbsthaß* (Berlin, 1930), reprinted with an introduction by Boris Groys (Munich, 1984). See also Sander L. Gilman, *Jewish Self-Hatred: Anti-Semitism and the Secret Language of the Jews* (Baltimore MD, 1986).

52   Berthold Viertel, *Karl Kraus: Ein Charakter und die Zeit* (Leipzig, 1921), p. 60. For confirmation that 'self-hatred' is 'not a specifically Jewish problem', see Ritchie Robertson, 'The Problem of "Jewish Self-Hatred" in Herzl, Kraus and Kafka', *Oxford German Studies*, 16 (1985), pp. 81–108 (p. 84).

53   Robert Musil, 'Der Anchluss an Deutschland' in *Die neue Rundschau*, March 1919, No. 8, pp. 1033–42 and 'Buridans Österreicher' in *Der Friede*, 14 February 1919, No. 8, pp. 1030–2; see Musil, *Precision and Soul*, pp. 90–101 (p. 99).

54   Gabriele Johanna Eder, *Wiener Musikfeste zwischen 1918 und 1938: Ein Beitrag zur Vergangenheitsbewältigung* (Vienna, 1991), p. 287.

55   See Margarete Grander, 'Staatsbürger und Ausländer: Zum Umgang Österreichs mit den jüdischen Flüchtlingen nach 1918' in *Asylland wider Willen: Flüchtlinge in Österreich im europäischen Kontext seit 1914*, ed. Gernot Heiss and Oliver Rathkolb (Vienna, 1995), pp. 60–85 (p. 65).

56   Lukas Langhoff, *Staatsbürgerrecht und Heimatrecht in Österreich* (Vienna, 1920), p. 22; cf. Grander, 'Staatsbürger und Ausländer', pp. 75–7.

57   Grander, 'Staatsbürger und Ausländer', p. 79.

58   Hoffmann-Holter, *Jüdische Kriegsflüchtlinge*, p. 253.

59   Hoffmann-Holter, *Jüdische Kriegsflüchtlinge*, pp. 218n., 257 & 263.

60   *Between Hitler and Mussolini: The Memoirs of Ernst Rüdiger Prince Starhemberg* (London, 1942), p. 25.

61   See Kurt Skalnik, 'Auf der Suche nach der Identität' in *Österreich 1918–1938: Geschichte der Ersten Republik*, ed. Erika Weinzierl and Kurt Skalnik, 2 vols (Graz, 1983), 1, pp. 11–24: 'von wirtschaftlicher Not bedrängt und von geistiger Orientierungslosigkeit gezeichnet' (p. 24).

62   Staudinger, 'Christlichsoziale Judenpolitik', pp. 36–8.

63   For systematic accounts, see Paul Fussell, *The Great War and Modern Memory* (New York and London, 1975); J. M. Winter, *The Experience of World War I* (London, 1988), esp. Part 6: 'The Memory of War'.

64   Richard Schaukal, *Karl Kraus – Versuch eines geistigen Bildnisses* (Vienna, 1933).

65   For further details of the Kragujevac case, see R. G. Plaschka, H. Haselsteiner and A. Suppan, *Militärassistenz, Widerstand und Umsturz in der Donaumonarchie 1918*, 2 vols (Vienna, 1974), 1, 388–400; photographic documentation, 2, plates 24–6.

66   *Vernichtungskrieg: Verbrechen der Wehrmacht 1941 bis 1944* (exhibition catalogue), ed. Hannes Heer and Birgit Otte (Hamburg, 1997), pp. 48–54. Böhme committed suicide in May 1947 while awaiting trial as a war criminal.

67   See Sonja Niederacher, 'The Myth of Austria as Nazi Victim' in *'Hitler's First Victim?' Memory and Representation in Post-War Austria* (Austrian Studies, vol. 11), ed. Judith Beniston and Robert Vilain (Leeds, 2003), pp. 14–32.

68   See Armin Mohler, *Die konservative Revolution in Deutschland 1918–1932* (Stuttgart, 1950); George Mosse, *The Myth of the War Experience* (New York, 1988).

69   See Ficker, letters to Kraus of 10 October 1919 and 12 February 1920 in Ludwig von Ficker, *Briefwechsel 1914–1925*, ed. Ignaz Zangerle and others (Innsbruck, 1988), pp. 191–3 and 233–5.

Chapter 3

1   Karl Kraus, *Weltgericht*, 2 vols (Leipzig, 1919).

2   This phrase first occurs in Schiller's poem 'Resignation' (1786) and was popularized by Hegel in his *Grundlinien der Philosophie des Rechts* (1821), para. 340.

3   Quoted in Wilhelm Hennis, *Max Weber: Essays in Reconstruction* (London, 1988), p. 146.

4   *Kant's Schriften* (Akademieausgabe), vol. 8 (Berlin, 1912), p. 357n.; cf. *Kant's Political Writings*, ed. Hans Reiss, tr. H. B. Nisbet (Cambridge, 1970), p. 105n.

5   'Über den Gemeinspruch: "Das mag in der Theorie richtig sein, taugt aber nicht für die Praxis"' in *Kant's Schriften*, 8, pp. 311–12; cf. *Kant's Political Writings*, pp. 63 & 90–2 (translation modified).

6   *Kant's Schriften*, 8. p. 309; cf. *Kant's Political Writings*, pp. 87–8.

7   *Kant's Schriften*, 8, p. 309; cf. *Kant's Political Writings*, p. 89 (translation modified).

8   *Kant's Schriften*, 8, pp. 346 & 356; cf. *Kant's Political Writings*, pp. 96 & 104.

9   For a discussion of this paradox, see Robert Kagan, *Paradise and Power: America and Europe in the New World Order* (London, 2003), pp. 13–14 & 57–8.

10 See Reinhard Merkel, *Strafrecht und Satire im Werk von Karl Kraus* (Baden-Baden, 1994), pp. 230–1.

11 Horne and Kramer, *German Atrocities*, pp. 340–55; Franz Exner and Georg Lelewer, *Krieg und Kriminalität in Österreich, mit einem Beitrag über die Kriminalität von Militärpersonen* (Vienna, 1927), pp. 139–40.

12 See Hannah Arendt, *Eichmann in Jerusalem: A Report on the Banality of Evil*, revised and enlarged edn (Harmondsworth, 1994).

13 Winston S. Churchill, *The World Crisis*, vol. 4 (London, 1931), p. 54.

14 Exner and Lelewer, *Krieg und Kriminalität in Österreich*, pp. 119–25.

15 *AZ*, 21 December 1918, p. 1 & 31 December 1918, pp. 5–6.

16 Edward Timms, 'Mr Lukacs changes trains', *London Review of Books*, 9, No. 4 (19 February 1987), pp. 8–9. For a more detailed account of his activities as a commissar, see Arpad Kadarkay, *Georg Lukács: Life, Thought, and Politics* (Cambridge MA, 1991), pp. 202–31.

17 See V. I. Lenin, *Collected Works*, 47 vols (Moscow, 1960–80), 31, pp. 17–118 and 165–7. Lenin's critique of 'purely verbal' Marxism (p. 165) relates to an article by Lukács in the Viennese journal *Kommunismus*, No. 6 (1 March 1920).

18 See *Georg Lukács: Sein Leben in Bildern, Selbstzeugnissen und Dokumenten*, ed. Eva Fekete and Eva Karádi (Stuttgart, 1981), p. 120.

19 Borsányi, *Life of a Communist Revolutionary*, pp. 193 & 471.

20 Ezra Mendelsohn, *The Jews of East Central Europe between the Wars* (Bloomington IN, 1983), p. 23.

21 Mann, *Tagebücher 1918–1921*, p. 63.

22 Borsányi, *Life of a Communist Revolutionary*, p. 245. For a more critical view of Korvin's activities, see Bennett Kovrig, *Communism in Hungary: From Kun to Kádár* (Stanford CA, 1979), pp. 51–2.

23 For further details of Bettelheim's activities, see Julius Braunthal, *In Search of the Millennium* (London, 1945), p. 232; and Borsányi, *Life of a Communist Revolutionary*, pp. 180–2.

24 Anton Lehár, *Erinnerungen: Gegenrevolution und Restaurationsversuche in Ungarn 1918–1921*, ed. Peter Broucek (Munich, 1973).

25 For further details, see the section 'Karl Kraus und Ungarn' in János Szabó, *Untergehende Monarchie und Satire: Zum Lebenswerk von Karl Kraus* (Budapest, 1992), pp. 139–47.

26 *Kant's Schriften*, 8, p. 377; cf. *Kant's Political Writings*, p. 122.

27 Weindling, *Epidemics and Genocide*, pp. 150–66.

28   Karl Kraus, *Frühe Schriften*, ed. J. J. Braakenburg, 3 vols (Munich, 1979), 2, pp. 115 & 128.

29   See Kurt Krolop, 'Die Tschechen bei Karl Kraus – Karl Kraus bei den Tschechen' in Krolop, *Reflexionen der Fackel: Neue Studien zu Karl Kraus* (Vienna, 1994), pp. 179–98; also Krolop, 'Zur Frühgeschichte der tschechischen Karl Kraus-Rezeption um 1910' in *Brücken: Germanistisches Jahrbuch Tschechien-Slowakei* (Berlin, 1996), pp. 19–31.

30   After the riot in Prague on 16 November 1920, Kafka wrote to his Czech friend Milena Jesenská that he was 'swimming in hatred of Jews'. Kafka, *Briefe an Milena* (Frankfurt, 1966), p. 184. Cf. Christoph Stölzl, *Kafkas böses Böhmen* (Frankfurt, 1989), p. 99.

31   See the memoirs of the Marxist critic Paul Reimann, *Ve dvacatych letech* (1966), quoted in Krolop, *Reflexionen der Fackel*, pp. 199–200. See also Jaromir Louzil and Zdenek Solle, 'Karl Kraus und die Tschechoslowakei', *Kraus-Hefte*, 15 (July 1980), pp. 1–8.

32   Kurt Krolop, 'Karl Kraus-Rezeption in den böhmischen Ländern' in *Reading Karl Kraus: Essays on the Reception of 'Die Fackel'*, ed. Gilbert J. Carr and Edward Timms (Munich, 2002), pp. 147–62.

33   Friedrich Torberg, *Die Tante Jolesch, oder der Untergang des Abendlandes in Anekdoten* (Munich, 1975), pp. 161–7.

34   The firm of Jakob Kraus provided the source of his private income, which was revalued in the aftermath of the currency reforms. See the Kraus Archive, IN 169.775.

35   Johann Wolfgang Brügel, *Tschechen und Deutsche 1918–1938* (Munich, 1967), p. 23.

36   On Masaryk's efforts to promote a 'tschechisch-deutsche Symbiose', see Brügel, *Tschechen und Deutsche*, pp. 184–5.

37   Hillel J. Kieval, *Languages of Community: The Jewish Experience in the Czech Lands* (Berkeley CA, 2000), pp. 210–16.

38   Quoted in Kieval, *Languages of Community*, p. 207.

39   T. G. Masaryk, *Die Weltrevolution: Erinnerungen und Betrachtungen*, tr. Camillo Hoffmann, pp. 66ff. (quoted in F 697–705, 111).

40   See Peter Demetz, 'Masaryks Faust' in Demetz, *Böhmische Sonne, Mährischer Mond: Essays und Erinnerungen* (Vienna, 1996), pp. 107–27.

41   See Elizabeth Wiskemann, *Czechs and Germans: A Study of the Struggle in the Historic Provinces of Bohemia and Moravia* (London, 1938), pp. 118–23; Brügel, *Tschechen und Deutsche*, pp. 129–35.

42   Wiskemann, *Czechs and Germans*, p. 126. See also Kurt Krolop, 'Karl Kraus und die bömischen Länder' in *Karl Kraus – in Jičin geboren, in der Welt zu Hause* (supplement 9 to *Z ceskeho raje podkrkonosi*, 2005), pp. 13–28 (p. 22).

43   The draft of this letter to the *Prager Tagblatt*, dated 22 October 1926, was published in *Kraus-Hefte*, 12 (October 1979), pp. 1–4.

44   Quoted in Brügel, *Tschechen und Deutsche*, pp. 138–9.

45   Bruno Kafka (1881–1931) was the son of Franz Kafka's father's cousin. See Anthony Northey, *Kafka's Relatives: Their Lives and his Writing* (New Haven and London, 1991), p. 89–90.

46   See the *Deutsche Zeitung Bohemia* file in the Austrian National Library, 394.109. C-D.Per.

47   For a more sympathetic account of Winder's career, see Jürgen Serke, *Böhmische Dörfer: Wanderungen durch eine literarische Landschaft* (Vienna, 1987), pp. 143–61. Serke acknowledges (p. 146) that the pro-German policy of *Bohemia* placed Winder in a difficult position.

48   Kamil Krofta and Bruno Kafka, *Die Deutschen in der Tschechoslowakei* (Prague, 1928), p. 49.

49   *Feinde in Scharen. Ein wahres Vergnügen dazusein: Karl Kraus-Herwarth Walden Briefwechsel 1909–1912*, ed. George Avery (Göttingen, 2002), pp. 45–6 & 69.

50   See Gerald Stieg, '"Wir wollen weniger zitiert und mehr gelesen sein": Karl Kraus in Frankreich', in *Reading Karl Kraus*, pp. 206–18.

51   Jean-Paul Sartre, *Les Mots*, ed. David Nott (London, 1981), p. 26.

52   Heinz Gollwitzer, *Die gelbe Gefahr: Geschichte eines Schlagworts. Studien zum imperialistischen Denken* (Göttingen, 1962), esp. pp. 206–18.
53   Ku Hung-Ming, *Papers from a Viceroy's Yamen: Chinese Plea for the Cause of Good Government and True Civilization in China* (Shanghai, 1901).
54   Hung-Ming, *Papers*, pp. 141 & 181–90.
55   Wolfram Eberhard, *A History of China* (Berkeley CA, 1969), p. 300.
56   Joseph Needham, letter of 9 March 1977 to Edward Timms (Timms Collection).
57   See Kuei-Fen Pan-Hsu, *Die Bedeutung der chinesischen Literatur in den Werken Klabunds* (Frankfurt, 1990), pp. 198–213.
58   Letters to Sidonie Nadherny, 2 April 1915, 29 July 1915, 12/13 November 1915, 13 November 1916, 17/18 November 1916, 14 November 1917, 14/15 February 1922.
59   Kraus had second thoughts about this concept, which occurs in Act I, scene 12 of the 1919 edition of *Die letzten Tage* but is omitted from the corresponding passage in the book edition of 1922 (Act I, scene 29).
60   Samuel P. Huntington, *The Clash of Civilizations and the Remaking of World Order* (New York, 1996), pp. 20–1 and 229–45 (p. 238).
61   Hung-Ming, *Papers*, p. 92.

Chapter 4

1   For an English translation, see *In These Great Times: A Karl Kraus Reader*, ed. Harry Zohn (Manchester, 1984), pp. 70–83.
2   Edith Dörfler and Wolfgang Pensold, *Die Macht der Nachricht: Die Geschichte der Nachrichtenagenturen in Österreich* (Vienna, 2001), pp. 272–3, quoting from Meister (no first name), *Kabelkrieg und Lügenfeldzug* (Münster, 1914): 'die mächtigste Waffe der englischen Regierung'.
3   Dörfler and Pensold, *Die Macht der Nachricht*, pp. 283–5.
4   For an overview of these episodes and the climate of opinion they created, see Jeffrey Verhey, *The Spirit of 1914: Militarism, Myth, and Mobilization in Germany* (Cambridge, 2000), esp. pp. 77–86.
5   See the analysis of the 'phantom army' episode in Vincent Sherry, *The Great War and the Language of Modernism* (Oxford, 2003), pp. 56–7.
6   Verhey, *The Spirit of 1914*, p. 85.
7   Arthur Ponsonby, *Falsehood in Wartime: Containing an Assortment of Lies Circulated throughout the Nations during the Great War* (London, 1928), pp. 57–62.
8   One of the few commentaries on the epilogue can be found in Wilhelm Hindemith, *Die Tragödie des Nörglers* (Frankfurt, 1985), pp. 109–30.
9   Hindemith, *Tragödie des Nörglers*, p. 103.
10   Page references in the text refer to the first edition of *Die letzte Nacht* (Sonderheft der Fackel, Vienna, 1918); cf. S 10, 731–70.
11   Bertha von Suttner, *Die Waffen nieder!* (Hildesheim, 1982), pp. 182–4.
12   Fyodor Dostoevsky, *The Brothers Karamazov*, tr. David Magarshack (Harmondsworth, 1988), p. 307.
13   The Wagnerian name Siegfried was much favoured by patriotic German Jews, as Kraus had pointed out in October 1911 (F 333, 9). 'Abendrot' echoes the 'poetic' surnames adopted by German and Austrian Jews under the legislation making surnames compulsory.
14   A summary of Haber's career can be found in Morris Goran, *The Story of Fritz Haber* (Oklahoma City, 1967).
15   Goran, *The Story of Fritz Haber*, p.74.
16   See Paul Günther, *Fritz Haber: Ein Mann der Jahrhundertwende* (Munich, 1969), p. 21.
17   Günther, *Fritz Haber*, pp. 23–4.
18   Richard Rhodes, *The Making of the Atomic Bomb* (New York, 1986), p. 91.

19   Augustin M. Prentiss, *Chemicals in War: A Treatise on Chemical Warfare* (New York, 1937), p. 662. Mustard gas, invented by Haber's colleagues Lommel and Steinkopf, was named 'Lost' in their honour.

20   See Goran, *The Story of Fritz Haber*, pp. 74–5.

21   Rhodes, *The Making of the Atomic Bomb*, p. 94.

22   Quoted in Dietrich Stoltzenberg, *Fritz Haber: Chemiker, Nobelpreisträger, Deutscher, Jude* (Weinheim, 1994), pp. 310–13 (p. 311).

23   Prentiss, *Chemicals in War*, pp. 679–80.

24   Haber, who died in exile in 1934, was forced to resign his position as director of the Berlin Institute after the Nazi seizure of power. His biographer records that his one consolation in 1919 was the thought that 'Germany would rise again' and that there would be 'another war in twenty years' (Goran, *The Story of Fritz Haber*, p. 80).

25   Weindling, *Epidemics and Genocide*, pp. 128–30; Stoltzenberg, *Fritz Haber*, p. 467.

26   Adolf Hitler, *Mein Kampf* (Munich, 1939), p. 772; *Hitler's Mein Kampf*, tr. D. C. Watt (London, 1987), p. 620.

27   Sherry, *The Great War and the Language of Modernism*, pp. 239 & 257; cf. *The Diaries of Virginia Woolf*, vol. 1, *1915–1919*, ed. Anne Olivier Bell (New York, 1977), p. 138.

28   Anton C. Zijderveld, *On Clichés: The Supersedure of Meaning by Function in Modernity* (London, 1979), pp. 46–7.

29   For a comprehensive picture of Kraus's permutations on formulaic expressions, including 'das Kind mit dem Bade ausschütten', 'Perle vor die Säue werfen', 'Schulter an Schulter' and 'last not least', see *Wörterbuch der Redensarten zu der von Karl Kraus 1899 bis 1936 herausgegebenen Zeitschrift 'Die Fackel'*, ed. Werner Welzig (Vienna, 1999).

30   See Timms, *Karl Kraus – Apocalyptic Satirist* (1986), pp. 273–80 & 319–33.

31   Kraus, *Die Unüberwindlichen* (1928), pp. 112–13.

32   Hitler, *Mein Kampf* (Munich, 1939), p. 198: 'jede wirkungsvolle Propaganda [hat sich] auf nur sehr wenige Punkte zu beschränken und diese schlagwortartig so lange zu verwerten, bis auch bestimmt der Letzte unter einem solchen Worte das Gewollte sich vorzustellen vermag'; *Mein Kampf*, tr. D. C. Watt, p. 165.

33   See Sherry, *The Great War and the Language of Modernism*, esp. pp. 64–70.

34   Chris Hedges, *War is a Force that Gives us Meaning* (New York, 2002), pp. 142–3.

35   Erwin Chargaff, *Vermächtnis: Essays* (Stuttgart, 1992), pp. 267, 270 & 283: '"Die letzten Tage der Menschheit" [. . .] dauern noch immer an'. Excerpts from this lecture, which was never delivered, are reprinted in *Karl Kraus: Marbacher Kataloge 52*, ed. Friedrich Pfäfflin and Eva Dambacher (Marbach am Neckar, 1999), p. 348.

36   John Theobald, *The Media and the Making of History* (Aldershot, 2004), pp. 2–15.

37   Noam Chomsky, *Language and Responsibility* (Hassocks, 1979), p. 38.

38   Phillip Knightley, *The First Casualty: The War Correspondent as Hero and Myth-Maker from the Crimea to Kosovo* (London, 2000), pp. 483–500; Jean Baudrillard, *La Guerre du Golfe n'a pas eu lieu* ('The Gulf War Did Not Take Place'; Paris, 1991).

39   Richard Keeble, *Secret State, Silent Press: New Militarism, the Gulf and the Modern Image of Warfare* (Luton, 1997), p. 5.

40   *Desert Storm and the Mass Media*, ed. Bradley S. Greenberg and Walter Gantz (Cresskill NJ, 1993). See in particular 'Public Relations as a Weapon of Modern Warfare' by Ray Eldon Hiebert, pp. 29–36 (p. 36) and 395–6, 'The Crisis in the Gulf and the Lack of Critical Media Discourse' by Douglas Kellner, pp. 37–47 (p. 41) and 'Media Coverage and U.S. Public Opinion on the Persian Gulf' by David P. Fan, pp. 125–42.

41   Keeble, *Secret State, Silent Press*, pp. 8 and 24.

42   *Die letzten Tage der Menschheit*, Act I, scene 29; for a partial translation of this exchange, see Karl Kraus, *The Last Days of Mankind*, abridged and ed. by Frederick Ungar (New York, 1974), p. 34.

43   G. K. A. Bell, 'Obliteration Bombing' in Bell, *The Church and Humanity 1939–1946* (London, 1946), pp. 129–41.

44   Sheldon Rampton and John Stauber, *Weapons of Mass Deception: The Uses of Propaganda in Bush's War on Iraq* (London, 2003). See also Imad Khadduri, *Iraq's Nuclear Mirage: Memoirs and Delusions* (Richmond Hill, Ont., 2003).

45   The original advertisement, which Kraus reprinted in facsimile (F 577–82, facing p. 96), is reproduced and translated in Karl Kraus, *In These Great Times*, pp. 90–1.

46   Quoted in *Times Literary Supplement*, 22 June 2001, p. 16.

47   The word 'Mördergrube' derives from Luther's translation of Jeremiah 7: 11, echoed in Matthew 21: 13. This is rendered in the Authorized Version as 'den of thieves'. The translation by Harry Zohn, taken from *In These Great Times*, has been modified accordingly.

48   Umberto Eco, 'Apocalyptic and Integrated Intellectuals: Mass Communications and Theories of Mass Culture' in Eco, *Apocalypse Postponed*, ed. Robert Lumley (Bloomington IN, 1994), pp. 17–35 (19 & 25).

49   See the critique of 'apocalyptic' approaches to the dilemma of Austro-German Jewry in Michael André Bernstein, *Foregone Conclusions: Against Apocalyptic History* (Berkeley CA, 1994), pp. 16–41.

PART TWO
Chapter 5

1   Ludwig Wittgenstein, letter of 3 October 1931 to G. E. Moore, in Wittgenstein, *Letters to Russell, Keynes and Moore* (Oxford, 1974), p. 139.

2   See Peter Eppel, *'Concordia soll ihr Name sein . . .': 125 Jahre Journalisten- und Schriftstellerverein 'Concordia'* (Vienna, 1984), pp. 178–259; Dörfler and Pensold, *Die Macht der Nachricht*, pp. 309–19.

3   While Helmut Arntzen, in *Karl Kraus und die Presse* (Munich, 1975), stresses the unchanging nature of newspaper phraseology ('Die Unveränderlichkeit der Presse als Phrase', p. 51), Djassemy, in *Der 'Produktivgehalt kritischer Zerstörerarbeit'*, concludes that the phraseology of the new journalism appealed to lower instincts ('niedere Instinkte', p. 275).

4   For an analysis of the June 1911 elections, see John W. Boyer, *Culture and Political Crisis in Vienna: Christian Socialism in Power, 1897–1918* (Chicago, 1995), pp. 268–84.

5   For a more detailed documentation and analysis, see *Wahljahr 1919* (Katalog der Wiener Stadt- und Landesbibliothek), ed. Herwig Würtz (Vienna, 1989); Gabriele Melischek and Josef Seethaler, 'Zwischen Gesinnung und Markterfolg: Zum politischen Spektrum der Wiener Tagespresse der Ersten Republik' in *Politisches Raisonnement in der Informationsgesellschaft*, ed. Kurt Imhof and Peter Schulz (Zurich, 1996), pp. 61–78.

6   See Edward Timms, 'Ambassador Herzl and the Blueprint for a Modern State' in *Theodor Herzl and the Origins of Zionism* (Edinburgh, 1997), pp. 16–17.

7   Compare the account of Bahr's reactionary politics in Kurt Ifkovits, 'Hermann Bahrs *Tagebücher* aus den Jahren 1927 bis 1931' with the view of him as a figure from a 'soap opera' in Alfred Pfabigan, 'Hermann Bahr als Opfer'; both in *Hermann Bahr – Für eine andere Moderne*, ed. Jeanne Benay and Alfred Pfabigan (Berne, 2004), pp. 3–14 and 205–20.

8   Ludwig Ullmann, 'Heimat in der Fremde: Ein Buch der Erinnerung und der Gegenwart' (unpublished typescript, completed in New York in 1948, now in the archive of the Literaturhaus, Vienna), p. 72.

9   Roth, *Das journalistische Werk 1915–1923*, pp. 27–282.

10   Siegfried Jacobsohn to Karl Kraus, 20 December 1919 (Kraus Archive, IN 140.867).

11   *Der Volkssturm*, Wochenzeitung des deutschen Christenvolkes für christlich-nationale Kultur, gegen Judaismus, Materialismus, Kapitalismus, ed. Anton Orel, No. 34 (20 July 1919), p.1. Kraus alludes to this incident in F 800–5, 73. The very first number of *Der*

Volkssturm (1 December 1918) had denounced the newly founded Republic as 'die Judenrepublik'.

12 See Dr Joseph Eberle, *Großmacht Presse: Enthüllungen für Zeitungsgläubige, Forderungen für Männer* (Vienna, 1920), esp. chapter 4: 'Presse und Judentum'.

13 See Robert Harris, *GOTCHA! The Media, the Government and the Falklands Crisis* (London, 1983), chapter 3.

14 The lack of precision in Kraus's use of the term 'Jewish' is rightly criticized by John Theobald in his study *The Paper Ghetto: Karl Kraus and Anti-Semitism* (Frankfurt-am-Main, 1996), esp. pp.109–11. But it is misleading to claim (p. 152) that the 'Judenpresse' remained his 'chief target' after 1919.

15 For further details, see Josef Seethaler and Gabriele Melischek, *Demokratie und Identität: Zehn Jahre Republik in der Wiener Presse 1928* (Vienna, 1993); also, by the same authors, *Die Wiener Tageszeitungen: Eine Dokumentation*, vol. 3: *1918–1938* (Frankfurt am Main, 1992).

16 For an overview of the daily press in Berlin, see Peter de Mendelssohn, *Zeitungsstadt Berlin: Menschen und Mächte in der Geschichte der deutschen Presse* (Berlin, 1959), pp. 306–8.

17 Cf. Karl Emil Franzos, *Der Pojaz* (Königstein, Taunus, 1979), p. 94: 'Dreh (= 'talmudische Spitzfindigkeit'); also the Yiddish idiom 'Dray nicht mein kopf' ('don't twist my head around'), quoted by Howard Jacobson, *Times Literary Supplement*, 21 January 2000, p. 20. 'Dreh' may also be linked with 'Dreidel', the spinning top used in the Jewish children's game.

18 The song had no title when first published in Kraus's magical operetta *Literatur oder Man wird doch da sehn* (Vienna, 1921), pp. 59–60, where the speaker has the fictional name Schwarz-Drucker (literally Black-Printer). The conventional German title is 'Lied des Schwarz-Druckers'.

19 See Toni Stolper, *Ein Leben im Brennpunkt unserer Zeit – Wien, Berlin, New York: Gustav Stolper 1888–1947* (Tübingen, 1960), p. 154.

20 Burkhard Müller, *Karl Kraus: Mimesis und Kritik des Mediums* (Stuttgart, 1995), pp. 59–62.

21 *Diana, the Making of a Media Saint*, ed. Jeffrey Richards, Scott Wilson and Linda Woodhead (London, 1999), p. 157.

22 For an overview of antisemitic caricature, including grotesque examples from *Kikeriki*, see Eduard Fuchs, *Die Juden in der Karikatur* (Munich, 1921).

23 See the anthology *Die gezeichnete Republik: Österreich 1918–1938 in Karikaturen*, ed. Peter Malina (Vienna, 1988), which relies primarily on left-wing sources. For right-wing Austrian caricature, see *Die Muskete: Kultur- und Sozialgeschichte im Spiegel einer satirisch-humoristischen Zeitschrift 1905–1941*, ed. Murray G. Hall (Vienna, 1983). The work of the more extreme antisemites has not been reprinted.

24 For further details, see Leo Lensing, 'Die Fotoporträts' in *'Was wir umbringen': 'DIE FACKEL' von Karl Kraus*, ed. Heinz Lunzer, Victoria Lunzer-Talos and Marcus G. Patka (Vienna 1999), pp. 55–61.

25 Kraus, *Literatur und Lüge* (Vienna, 1929), pp. 328–9 (cf. S 3, 301–2).

26 Torberg, *Die Tante Jolesch*, pp. 186–7.

27 In December 1896 Lueger's henchman Ernst Schneider had proposed that all Jewish property should be confiscated. See the report headed 'Ernst oder Scherz?' in *Sonn- und Montagszeitung*, 14 December 1896, p. 5 (Austrian National Library, 399340–E Period.).

28 Eppel, *'Concordia'*, p. 166.

29 Karl Ausch, *Als die Banken fielen: Zur Soziologie der politischen Korruption* (Vienna, 1968), p. 133.

30 See Ausch, *Als die Banken fielen*, pp. 134–7.

31 See Dörfler and Pensold, *Die Macht der Nachricht*, pp. 330–3.

32 *Beiträge zur Geschichte und Vorgeschichte der Julirevolte* (Vienna, 1934), pp. 26–8.
33 Dörfler and Pensold, *Die Macht der Nachricht*, pp. 245–50 & 316.
34 Ullmann, 'Heimat in der Fremde', pp. 38–9 & 71–3.
35 Eppel, *'Concordia'*, p. 252.
36 See Philip Williamson, *Stanley Baldwin: Conservative Leadership and National Values* (Cambridge, 1999), pp. 39–44 & 231–4.

Chapter 6

 1 Helmut Gruber, *Red Vienna: Experiment in Working-Class Culture 1919–1934* (New York, 1991), p. 64; cf. Helmut Weihsmann, *Das rote Wien: Sozialdemokratische Architektur und Kommunalpolitik 1919–1934* (Vienna, 1985), p. 112.
 2 Josef Weidenholzer, *Auf dem Weg zum Neuen Menschen: Bildungs- und Kulturarbeit der österreichischen Sozialdemokratie in der Ersten Republik* (Vienna, 1981).
 3 For a review of attempts to create the 'New Human Being' in Steyr, see Jeffrey, *Social Democracy in the Austrian Provinces*, pp. 129–62. On Salzburg, see Ingrid Bauer, *Von der alten Solidarität zur neuen sozialen Frage: Ein Salzburger Bilderlesebuch* (Vienna, 1988).
 4 See the section on 'Red Vienna' in Nancy Cartwright and others, *Otto Neurath: Philosophy between Science and Politics* (Cambridge, 1996), pp.56–9.
 5 See Burkhardt Rukschcio and Roland Schachel, *Adolf Loos: Leben und Werk* (Salzburg, 1987), pp. 229–30.
 6 Rukschcio and Schachel, *Adolf Loos*, pp. 258–66 & 290.
 7 See Timms, *Karl Kraus – Apocalyptic Satirist* (1986), pp. 7–9.
 8 Under the authoritarian regime of Engelbert Dollfuss, all these Social Democratic associations were banned. See Joseph Buttinger, *Am Beispiel Österreichs: Ein geschichtlicher Beitrag zur Krise der sozialistischen Bewegung* (Frankfurt, 1972), pp. 29–30.
 9 *Ostdeutsche Rundschau*, 18 January 1919, quoted in Rukschcio and Schachel, *Adolf Loos*, pp. 230–1.
10 *Wien, Stadt der Juden: Die Welt der Tante Jolesch*, ed. Joachim Riedl (Vienna, 2004), esp. pp. 43–84.
11 Pierre Bourdieu, *The Field of Cultural Production: Essays on Art and Literature*, ed. Randal Johnson (Cambridge, 1993), pp. 37–40.
12 For the concept of 'empowered marginality', see Timms, 'Ambassador Herzl', pp. 12–15.
13 Robert E. Norton, *Secret Germany: Stefan George and his Circle* (Ithaca and London, 2002); Quentin Bell, *Bloomsbury* (London, 1990); for the Fugitive Poets, who flourished at Vanderbilt University during the inter-war period, see Michael P. Farrell, *Collaborative Circles: Friendship Dynamics and Creative Work* (Chicago, 2001), pp. 68–113.
14 Karl Popper, *Unended Quest: An Intellectual Autobiography* (London, 1976), chapters 8, 9, 11 & 16.
15 See Murray G. Hall, *Österreichische Verlagsgeschichte 1918–1938*, 2 vols (Vienna, 1985).
16 Eppel, *'Concordia'*, Part II, chapter 1: 'Die "Concordia" in der Ersten Republik'.
17 Compare the discussion of the coffee-houses of the Enlightenment in Jürgen Habermas, *The Structural Transformation of the Public Sphere* (Cambridge MA, 1989).
18 For a selection of these writings in English translation, see *The Vienna Coffeehouse Wits 1890–1938*, tr., ed. and with an introduction by Harold B. Segel (West Lafayette IN, 1993).
19 Heimito von Doderer, *Tagebücher 1920–1939*, ed. Wendelin Schmidt-Dengler and others, 2 vols (Munich, 1996), 1, p. 231.
20 For an account of one of Kessler's breakfasts, including a discussion of foreign policy with Gustav Stresemann, see Harry Graf Kessler, *Tagebücher 1918–1937*, ed. Wolfgang Pfeiffer-Belli (Frankfurt, 1961), p. 232: entry for 25 June 1920.

21   Torberg, *Die Tante Jolesch*, p. 296.

22   For a comprehensive account of the exile community, see Lee Congdon, *Exile and Social Thought: Hungarian Intellectuals in Germany and Austria 1919–1933* (Princeton NJ, 1991).

23   See Szabó, *Untergehende Monarchie und Satire*, pp. 143–4 & 168.

24   Kadarkay, *Georg Lukács*, pp. 264–5.

25   See *Georg Lukács: Sein Leben in Bildern, Selbstzeugnissen und Dokumenten*, pp. 122–5; Borsányi, *Life of a Communist Revolutionary*, pp. 318, 325 & 356.

26   Morgenstein, *Alban Berg*, pp. 79–80 & 386.

27   See Ludwig Reichold, 'Die christlich inspirierten Jugendorganisationen in Österreich' in *Geistiges Leben im Österreich der Ersten Republik*, ed. Isabella Ackerl and Rudolf Neck (Vienna, 1986), pp. 313–30.

28   See Judith Beniston *'Welttheater': Hofmannsthal, Richard von Kralik, and the Revival of Catholic Drama in Austria 1890–1934* (London, 1998), p. 195.

29   See Judith Beniston, 'Cultural Politics in the First Republic: Hans Brečka and the "Kunststelle für christliche Volksbildung"' in *Catholicism and Austrian Culture*, ed. Ritchie Robertson and Judith Beniston (Edinburgh, 1999), pp. 101–18.

30   Rudolf G. Ardelt, *Zwischen Demokratie und Faschismus: Deutschnationales Gedankengut in Österreich 1919–1930* (Salzburg, 1972), pp. 98–102

31   *Deutscher Geist in Österreich*, ed. Karl Wache (Vienna, 1933), p. 62.

32   See Oskar Waas, *Die Pennalie: Ein Beitrag zu ihrer Geschichte* (Graz, 1967), pp. 185–6. I am grateful to Sigurd Paul Scheichl for drawing my attention to this source.

33   Eckart Früh, 'Vom Wiener "Stürmer" und antisemitischen Dränger im Theater der dreißiger Jahre' in *Verspielte Zeit: Österreichisches Theater der dreißiger Jahre*, ed. Hilde Haider-Pregler and Beate Reiterer (Vienna, 1997), pp. 322–34 (p. 323).

34   The announcement of Pogatschnigg's appointment as 'Propagandaleiter der N. S. D. A. P. (Hitler-Bewegung)' appeared in the *Österreichischer Nationalsozialist* on 12 February 1927. Details of his career have been reconstructed from press cuttings in the *Tagblatt* Archive in Vienna, and I am grateful to Dr Eckhart Früh for his assistance.

35   Ernst Fischer, 'Literatur und Ideologie in Österreich 1918–1938' in *Internationales Archiv für Sozialgeschichte der deutschen Literatur: Forschungsreferate*, ed. Wolfgang Frühwald, Georg Jäger and Alberto Martino (Tübingen, 1985), p. 191. The prejudices promoted by chess clubs are recalled in Edwin Hartl, *Wenn ich so zurückdenke: Hintergedanken an die gute alte Zeit* (Vienna, 1991), pp. 30–5.

36   Ludwig Hirschfeld, *Das Buch von Wien* (Vienna, 1927), pp. 43–4, quoted in Martin Lichtfuss, *Operette im Ausverkauf: Studien zum Libretto des musikalischen Unterhaltungstheaters im Österreich der Zwischenkriegszeit* (Vienna, 1989), p. 53.

37   See *Leben mit provisorischer Genehmigung: Leben, Werk und Exil von Dr. Eugenie Schwarzwald*, ed. Hans Deichmann (Berlin, 1988).

38   For further details, see *Aufbruch in das Jahrhundert der Frau? Rosa Mayreder und der Feminismus in Wien um 1900*, ed. Reingard Witzmann (Vienna, 1990).

39   See Friedrich Stadler, *Studien zum Wiener Kreis* (Frankfurt am Main, 1997), pp. 627–39.

40   Karl Fallend, *Wilhelm Reich in Wien: Psychoanalyse und Politik* (Vienna, 1988), pp. 28–34 & 115–27.

41   Wilhelm Reich, *Die Sexualität im Kulturkampf: Zur sozialistischen Umstrukturierung des Menschen* (Copenhagen, 1936), p. 133.

42   Wilhelm Reich, *Passion of Youth: An Autobiography 1897–1922*, tr. Philip Schmitz and Jerri Tompkins (London, 1989), p. 161.

43   For further details, see Ulrich Weinzierl, 'Die Kultur der "Reichspost"' in *Aufbruch und Untergang: Österreichische Kultur zwischen 1918 und 1938*, ed. Franz Kadrnoska (Vienna, 1981), pp. 325–44; and Alfred Pfoser and others, *Schnitzlers 'Reigen'*, 2 vols (Frankfurt, 1993).

44   See Kristine von Soden, *Die Sexualberatungsstellen der Weimarer Republik 1919–1933* (Berlin, 1988).

45　See the report in *Der Morgen (Wiener Montagsblatt)*, 5 February 1923, p. 1: 'Hakenkreuzler-Attacke bei dem Vortrag von Magnus Hirschfeld'.

46　Friedrich Koch, *Sexuelle Denunziation: Die Sexualität in der politischen Auseinandersetzung* (Hamburg, 1995), pp. 13–35.

47　For a detailed account of Bettauer's publications, see Murray G. Hall, *Der Fall Bettauer* (Vienna, 1978), pp. 20–69.

48　See Hall, *Der Fall Bettauer*, pp. 43–4, 47–8, 56–7, 64 & 166.

49　See Max Winter, 'Zum Tode Hugo Bettauers' in *Die Unzufriedene*, No. 15 (1925), quoted in *Wien, Stadt der Juden*, pp. 168–9.

50　Hall, *Der Fall Bettauer*, pp. 75 & 100–5.

51　Hall, *Der Fall Bettauer*, pp. 116–26.

52　Robert Musil, *Tagebücher*, ed. Adolf Frisé (Hamburg, 1976), 2, pp. 1156–7.

53　Reprinted in facsimile in Ernst Glaser, *Im Umfeld des Austromarxismus: Ein Beitrag zur Geistesgeschichte des österreichischen Sozialismus* (Vienna, 1981), p. 19.

54　See *Der hoffnungslose Radikalismus der Mitte: Der Briefwechsel Ernst Krenek–Friedrich T. Gubler 1928–1939*, ed. Claudia Maurer Zenck (Vienna, 1989), pp. 8 (note) & 190.

Chapter 7

1　Derrida, 'Freud et la scène de l'écriture', *Tel Quel*, No. 26 (summer 1966); English translation by Alan Bass in Derrida, *Writing and Difference* (London, 2002), p. 285.

2　For the parallel with Mallarmé, see Luis Migul Isava, *Wittgenstein, Kraus, and Valéry: A Paradigm of Poetic Rhyme and Reason* (New York, 2002), p. 74. The idea of 'hammering away' at language is implied by Nietzsche's principle of 'working on a page of prose as if one were working on a sculpture'; cited F 254–5, 25; 293, 27–8).

3　For a differentiated account of German crowd behaviour in July and August 1914, see Verhey, *The Spirit of 1914*, pp. 22–96 (p. 32). Cf. Alice Freifeld, *Nationalism and the Crowd in Liberal Hungary, 1848–1914* (Washington DC, 2000).

4　See Alisa Douer, *Wien Heldenplatz: Mythen und Massen 1848–1998*, photographic documentation with texts in German and English (Vienna, 2000); Jeffrey, *Social Democracy in the Austrian Provinces*, pp. 32–4 & 67–9.

5　Peter Fritzsche, *Germans into Nazis* (Cambridge MA, 1998), pp. 106 & 171–2.

6　Peter Fritzsche, *Reading Berlin 1900* (Cambridge MA, 1996), p. 20.

7　Report in the *Tägliche Rundschau*, quoted in Verhey, *The Spirit of 1914*, p. 27.

8　See the note on this scene by Friedrich Pfäfflin in *Karl Kraus: Marbacher Kataloge 52*, p. 208.

9　H. D. [= Hilda Doolittle], *Tribute to Freud* (London, 1985), pp. 58–9.

10　See Timms, *Karl Kraus – Apocalyptic Satirist* (1986), pp. 310–11.

11　*Tagebuch der Straße: Geschichte in Plakaten*, ed. Bernhard Denscher (Vienna, 1981), pp. 145–203.

12　See Kraus's letter of 25 July 1909 to Walden in *Kraus–Walden Briefwechsel*, pp. 24–5; cf. Stoessl's essay 'Kameraderie', published in *Die Fackel* in December 1908 (F 267–8, 16–22).

13　Ludwig von Ficker, *Briefwechsel 1926–1939* (Innsbruck, 1991), pp. 117 & 383.

14　For example 'Lundi Rue Christine' in Guillaume Apollinaire, *Calligrammes: Poems of Peace and War (1913–1916)*, with English translations by Anne Hyde Greet (Berkeley CA, 1991), pp. 52–7.

15　James Boyd White, *Justice as Translation: An Essay in Cultural and Legal Criticism* (Chicago, 1990), p. 267.

16　For a detailed analysis, see Jörg Schönert, '"Wir Negativen" – Das Rollenbewußtsein des Satirikers Kurt Tucholsky in der ersten Phase der Weimarer Republik (1918–1924)' in Irmgard Ackermann (ed.), *Kurt Tucholsky: Sieben Beiträge zu Werk und Wirkung* (Munich, 1981), pp. 46–88.

17 Paul Reiter, 'Mimesis, Modernism and Karl Kraus's "Jewish Question"' in *Reading Karl Kraus*, pp. 55–73 (p. 59).

18 See Katerina Clark and Michael Holquist, *Mikhail Bakhtin* (Cambridge MA, 1984), pp. 9–13.

19 See Sigurd Paul Scheichl, 'Der Stilbruch als Stilmittel bei Karl Kraus' in *Karl Kraus in neuer Sicht*, ed. Sigurd Paul Scheichl and Edward Timms (Munich, 1986), pp. 128–42.

20 Musil is identified as author of the article quoted from the *Prager Presse* in Krolop, 'Karl Kraus und die böhmischen Länder', p. 19. The compact disc of 'Karl Kraus und Jacques Offenbach' (MONO 91058), issued by the Schiller-Nationalmuseum in Marbach in 1999, includes a recording made in 1930 of the 'Eating Scene' from *Die Schwätzerin von Saragossa*, in which Kraus gives a differentiated performance of five different voices.

21 For a full (unrhymed) English translation, see 'To my Printer', tr. Elizabeth M. Wilkinson, first published in her 'Festschrift', *Tradition and Creation* (Leeds, 1978), p. 177.

22 Marshall McLuhan, *The Gutenberg Galaxy: The Making of Typographic Man* (London, 1962).

23 A large number of proofsheets survive, with multiple manuscript corrections, in the Vienna City Library (Kraus Archive) and the Austrian National Library. A pioneering analysis has shown how meticulously Kraus revised and refined his texts – down to the last dash and exclamation mark! See Djassemy, *Der 'Produktivgehalt kritischer Zerstörerarbeit'*, pp. 345–57.

24 See the facsimile reproduced in S 17, 407.

25 *Das Notwendige und das Überflüssige*, bearbeitet von Karl Kraus (Vienna, 1920). For a differing interpretation of Kraus's choice of fonts, with accompanying facsimiles, see S 14, 485 & 558–9.

26 The original manuscript, corrected proof and printed page are reproduced by Christian Wagenknecht in S 16, 384–7.

27 Gershom Scholem, *Walter Benjamin: The Story of a Friendship* (London, 1982), p. 107; cf. the German original *Walter Benjamin: Die Geschichte einer Freundschaft* (Frankfurt, 1976), p. 136.

28 See *The Bible as Book: The First Printed Editions*, ed. Paul Saenger and Kimberly van Kampen (London, 1999), esp. the chapter on *Glossa Ordinaria* by Karlfried Froehlich (pp. 15–21). For the secularization of the 'Glosse' in Germany from Lichtenberg to Kraus, see Burckhard Spinnen, *Schriftbilder: Studien zu einer Geschichte emblematischer Kurzprosa* (Münster, 1989).

29 For a fuller account, see Müller, *Karl Kraus: Mimesis und Kritik des Mediums*, pp. 47–240.

30 *Worte in Versen*, vols 1 (1916) and 2 (1917) were printed by Drugulin in Leipzig, while vols 3 (1918), 4 (1919) and 5 (1920) were printed by Jahoda & Siegel, although still published in Leipzig. Vol. 6 (1922) was the first in this series to be published by the Verlag 'Die Fackel'.

31 Kraus to Walden, 23 March 1910, in *Kraus–Walden Briefwechsel*, pp. 187–90.

32 Cf. Lynne Truss, *Eats, Shoots & Leaves: The Zero Tolerance Approach to Punctuation* (London, 2003).

Chapter 8

1 Paul Engelmann, *Letters from Ludwig Wittgenstein with a Memoir*, tr. L. Furtmüller (Oxford, 1967), pp. 122–31.

2 Quoted in Nancy Cartwright, *Otto Neurath* (Cambridge, 1996), p. 65.

3 Otto Neurath, *International Picture Language: The First Rules of Isotype* (London, 1936), pp. 51 & 64–5.

4 Ludwig Wittgenstein, *Philosophical Investigations*, tr. G. E. M. Anscombe (Oxford, 1996), pp. 194–6 and 207–9.

5   Cf. *Travels into Several Nations of the World. By Lemuel Gulliver*, Part IV, chapter 4, in Swift, *Gulliver's Travels and Selected Writings*, ed. John Hayward (London, 1934), p. 234.

6   Ernst Gombrich, *The Sense of Order: A Study of the Psychology of Decorative Art* (Oxford, 1979), p. 138. See also Gombrich, *Art and Illusion: A Study of the Psychology of Pictorial Representation* (London, 1977), pp. 4–5.

7   Ritchie Robertson, *The 'Jewish Question' in German Literature, 1749–1939* (Oxford, 1999), p. 185.

8   *Collins Dictionary of the English Language* (London, 1979), p. 264; cf. the definition in *Duden:Deutsches Universalwörterbuch* (Mannheim, 1989), p. 303: 'Organismus, der aus verschiedenen Zellen aufgebaut ist'.

9   There is only one reference to Kraus in Popper, *Unended Quest: An Intellectual Biography*, p. 106. For a perceptive account of the Popper–Wittgenstein antagonism, see David Edmonds and John Eidington, *Wittgenstein's Poker: The Story of a Ten-Minute Argument between Two Great Philosophers* (New York, 2002).

10 See the proofs for this number of *Die Fackel* (F 632–9) in the Vienna City Library.

11 Christian Wagenknecht, *Das Wortspiel bei Karl Kraus* (Göttingen, 1965), esp. pp. 23–31 (for the increasing frequencies in Kraus's later work).

12 J. Langdon, *Wordplay: Ambigrams and Reflections on the Art of Ambigrams* (New York, 1992).

13 Quoted in *The Era of Expressionism*, ed. Paul Raabe (London, 1963), p. 49.

14 John Felstiner, *Paul Celan: Poet, Survivor, Jew* (New Haven, 1995), pp. 32–3 and 297, n. 22. Felstiner notes that the original title of Celan's poem, 'Death Tango', echoes that of Kraus's poem 'Tod und Tango' (F 386, 18).

15 *The Complete Works of Lewis Carroll*, ed. Alexander Woollcott (London, 1939), p. 198 (*Through the Looking Glass*, chapter 6).

16 See Edmonds and Eidinow, *Wittgenstein's Poker*, p. 231.

17 Wittgenstein, *Philosophical Investigations*, p. 2 (para. 1).

18 For a systematic account, see Anne Barton, *The Names of Comedy* (Oxford, 1990).

19 Twelve different categories of the play on names are identified in Rolf Max Kully, 'Namensspiele: Die erotische, die polemische und die poetische Verwendung der Eigennamen in den Werken von Karl Kraus' in *Karl Kraus: Diener der Sprache, Meister des Ethos*, ed. Joseph P. Strelka (Tübingen, 1990), pp. 139–66.

20 See Benzion C. Kaganoff, *A Dictionary of Jewish Names and their History* (New York, 1977); Dietz Bering, *The Stigma of Names: Antisemitism in German Daily Life, 1812–1933*, tr. Neville Plaice (Cambridge, 1992).

21 David Lodge, *The Modes of Modern Writing: Metaphor, Metonymy, and the Modes of Modern Literature* (London, 1977), p. 75.

22 George Lakoff and Mark Johnson, *Metaphors We Live By* (Chicago, 1980), pp. 81 & 110.

23 J. P. Stern, 'Karl Kraus's Vision of Language' in *Modern Language Review*, 61 (January 1966), p. 84; cf. George Orwell, 'Politics and the English Language' in *Collected Essays* (London, 1961), pp. 337–51.

24 'Slogan' derives from the Gaelic 'sluagh-ghairm' – 'battle cry'.

25 Wagenknecht, *Das Wortspiel*, p. 93.

26 See *Wörterbuch der Redensarten*, pp. 273–80 & 651–6.

27 Norbert Elias, 'The Decay of the State Monopoly of Violence in the Weimar Republic' in Elias, *On Civilization, Power, and Knowledge: Selected Writings*, ed. Stephen Mennell and Johan Goudsblom (Chicago, 1998), pp. 150–60 (pp. 155–6).

28 Norbert Elias, *The Civilizing Process: The History of Manners*, tr. Edmund Jephcott (Oxford, 1978), pp. 153–60.

29 Ella Freeman Sharpe, 'Psycho-Physical Problems Revealed in Language: An Examination of Metaphor' in Sharpe, *Collected Papers on Psycho-Analysis*, ed. Marjorie Brierley (London, 1950), pp.155–69 (pp. 156–7).

30 *Brewer's Dictionary of Phrase and Fable* (London, 2001), p. 1020.

31 Edward Timms, 'Language and the Satirist in the Work of Karl Kraus' (doctoral dissertation, University of Cambridge, 1967), pp. 210–73.

32 Wilhelm von Humboldt, *On Language: The Diversity of Human Language-Structure and its Influence on the Mental Activity of Mankind*, tr. Peter Heath (Cambridge, 1988), p. 49.

33 'Kulturkonservatismus' is the label used for Kraus's 'Epigonen-Begriff' in Jens Malte Fischer, *Karl Kraus: Studien zum 'Theater der Dichtung' und Kulturkonservatismus* (Kronberg, 1973), pp. 171–6.

34 David Welch, *Germany, Propaganda and Total War, 1914–1918: The Sins of Omission* (London, 2000), p. 247.

35 Peter von Polenz, *Deutsche Sprachgeschichte vom Spätmittelalter bis zur Gegenwart*, vol. 3 (Berlin, 1999), pp. 306–15.

36 Hans Jürgen Heringer, 'Karl Kraus als Sprachkritiker', *Muttersprache*, 77 (1967), pp. 256–62 (p. 260).

37 Bill Dodd, 'Karl Kraus's Reputation as Language Critic in the Light of "Linguistically Grounded Language Criticism"' in *Reading Karl Kraus: Essays on the Reception of 'Die Fackel'*, ed. Gilbert J. Carr and Edward Timms (Munich, 2001), pp. 231–46 (p. 245).

38 See the discussion of Heidegger in Paul Ricoeur, *The Rule of Metaphor: Multi-disciplinary Studies in the Creation of Meaning in Language*, tr. Robert Czerny (London, 1978), pp. 280–9 & 310–13.

39 Wittgenstein, *Philosophical Investigations*, p. 20 (para. 43).

40 Eduard Engel, *Sprich Deutsch! Ein Buch zur Entwelschung* (Leipzig, 1917).

41 *Wie sagt man in Österreich? Wörterbuch der österreichischen Besonderheiten* (Mannheim, 1969).

42 See Kurt Krolop, 'Die "Hörerin" als Sprecherin: Sidonie von Nadherny und ihre "Sprachlehre"' in *Brücken: Germanistisches Jahrbuch Tschechien – Slowakei* (Berlin, 1999), pp. 43–53.

43 Ludwig Wittgenstein, *Tractatus Logico-Philosophicus* (London, 1961), pp. 114–15.

44 Wittgenstein, *Philosophical Investigations*, p. 48 (para. 119).

45 For a more detailed review of the parallels between Kraus and Wittgenstein, see Luis Miguel Isava, *Wittgenstein, Kraus, and Valéry* (New York, 2002), esp. pp. 69–73.

46 Moses Maimonides, *The Guide for the Perplexed*, translated from the original Arabic text by M. Friedländer (London, 1956), pp. 2 & 34–5.

47 Maimonides, 'Laws Concerning the Installation of Kings', quoted in Gershom Scholem, *The Messianic Idea in Judaism and other Essays on Jewish Spirituality* (London, 1971), p. 29.

48 J. Ramsey Michaels, *Interpreting the Book of Revelation* (Grand Rapids MI, 1992), pp. 89 & 107.

49 Bernard McGinn, *Visions of the End: Apocalyptic Traditions in the Middle Ages* (New York, 1979).

50 D. H. Lawrence, *Apocalypse and the Writings on Revelation*, ed. Mara Kalnins (Cambridge, 1980), pp. 19 & 142.

51 Jacques Derrida, 'Of an Apocalyptic Tone Recently Adopted in Philosophy', tr. John P. Leavey Jr, in the *Oxford Literary Review*, 6, No. 2 (1984), pp. 3–37 (esp. pp. 29–30).

52 This summary of Derrida's position is indebted to Christopher Norris, 'Versions of Apocalypse: Kant, Derrida, Foucault' in *Apocalypse Theory and the Ends of the World*, ed. Malcolm Bull (Oxford, 1995), pp. 227–49.

53 Timms, *Karl Kraus – Apocalyptic Satirist* (1986), pp. 374–80.

54 Albert Ehrenstein, 'An Karl Kraus' in *Die Gefährten*, No. 7 (Vienna, 1920); reprinted in *Die Belagerung der Urteilsmauer: Karl Kraus im Zerrspiegel seiner Feinde*, ed. Franz Schuh and Juliane Vogel (Vienna, 1986), pp. 67–81 ('[die] heilige Schrift geschändet', p. 72).

55 Berthold Viertel, *Karl Kraus: Ein Charakter und die Zeit* (Dresden, 1921), p. 61,

56 Scholem, *Friendship*, p. 107; *Freundschaft*, p. 136.

57   Scholem, *Friendship*, p. 175n.; *Freundschaft*, p. 219n.
58   GST = Gershom Scholem, *Tagebücher nebst Aufsätzen und Entwürfen bis 1923*, ed. Karlfried Gründer and Friedrich Niewöhner, 2 vols (Frankfurt, 1995 & 2000).
59   Gershom Scholem, *Briefe I: 1914–1947*, ed. Itta Shedletzky (Munich, 1994), pp. 126–7 (letter of 30 November 1917 to Werner Kraft).
60   Franz Werfel, 'Die Metaphysik des Drehs' in *Die Aktion*, 3 March 1917, pp. 124–8; reprinted in *Die Belagerung der Urteilsmauer: Karl Kraus im Zerrspiegel seiner Feinde*, ed. Franz Schuh and Juliane Vogel, pp. 58–62.
61   Klaus Vondung, 'Geschichte als Weltgericht: Genesis und Degradation einer Symbolik' in *Kriegserlebnis: Der Erste Weltkrieg in der literarischen Gestaltung und symbolischen Deutung der Nationen*, ed. Vondung (Göttingen, 1980), pp. 62–84 ('Deutschland wird in die Rolle des "Werkzeugs Gottes" zum Vollstrecker des Weltgerichts erhoben', p. 67).
62   For a more detailed account of that 'apocalyptic' conception of German destiny, see Richard Steigmann-Gall, *The Holy Reich: Nazi Conceptions of Christianity 1919–1945* (Cambridge, 2003).

PART THREE
Chapter 9

1   Cf. Freud's use of the word 'nachträglich', see J. Laplanche and J.-B. Pontalis, *The Language of Psychoanalysis*, tr. Donald Nicholson-Smith (London, 1980), pp. 111–14.
2   Larry Wolff, *Postcards from the End of the World: An Investigation into the Mind of Fin-de-Siècle Vienna* (London, 1989), p. 61.
3   See Merkel, *Strafrecht und Satire*, p. 513.
4   Wolff, *Postcards*, p. 122.
5   Wolff, *Postcards*, pp. 89–91.
6   Heinrich Lammasch to Karl Kraus, 8 December 1899 (Kraus Archive, IN 158.804). Cf. Merkel, *Strafrecht und Satire*, p. 512.
7   Wolff, *Postcards*, pp. 196–8.
8   Wolff, *Postcards*, pp. 210–15; Freud, '"A Child Is Being Beaten"', SE 17, 175–204.
9   See Edward Timms, 'New Approaches to Child Psychology: From Red Vienna to the Hampstead Nursery' in *Intellectual Migration and Cultural Transformation: Refugees from National Socialism in the English-Speaking World*, ed. Edward Timms and Jon Hughes (Vienna, 2003), pp. 219–39.
10 See Eckart Früh, 'Jugend in Wien um 1900' in *Zeitungen im Wiener Fin de Siècle*, ed. Sigurd Paul Scheichl and Wolfgang Duchkowitsch (Oldenbourg, 1997), pp. 257–67 (p. 261).
11 See the card from Lammasch to Kraus (probably dating from 1899/1900) acknowledging a donation of 20 Crowns to the Kinderschutz- und Rettungsgesellschaft (Kraus Archive, IN 158.823).
12 On the deficiencies of the law regulating child abuse, see Merkel, *Strafrecht und Satire*, pp. 507–11.
13 Boyer, *Culture and Political Crisis in Vienna*, p. 428.
14 See 'Die Auslandshilfe nach dem Kriege' in General [Ottokar] Landwehr, *Hunger: Die Erschöpfungsjahre der Mittelmächte* (Zurich, 1931), pp. 315–23; Max Winter, *Das Kind und der Sozialismus* (Vienna, 1924), pp. 100–2.
15 Felix Kanitz, *Kämpfer der Zukunft: Eine systematische Darstellung der sozialistischen Erziehungsgrundsätze* (Vienna, 1929), pp. 3–7 and 90–4.
16 Jeffrey, *Social Democracy in the Austrian Provinces*, pp. 95–9.
17 Erich Scheithauer and others, *Österreichs Geschichte in Stichwörtern* (Vienna, 1983), 4, p. 146. For a detailed study, see Helmut Utitz, *Die österreichischen Kinderfreunde und Roten Falken 1908–1938* (Salzburg, 1975).

18 Winter, *Das Kind und der Sozialismus*, pp. 108–12.

19 Konrad Algermissen, *Sozialistische und christliche Kinderfreundbewegung* (Hanover, 1931), pp. 27–36 and 219–21.

20 See Charles A. Gulick, *Austria from Habsburg to Hitler* (Berkeley CA and Los Angeles, 1948), vol. 1: *Labor's Workshop of Democracy*, p. 599.

21 *Geschichte der österreichischen Kinder- und Jugendliteratur von 1800 bis zur Gegenwart*, ed. Hans-Heino Ewers and Ernst Seibert (Vienna, 1997), p. 95.

22 Bertrand Russell, 'Free Thought and Official Propaganda' (Moncure Conway Lecture for 1922), reprinted in Russell, *Sceptical Essays* (London, 1935), p. 114 (italics in the German translation added by Kraus).

23 Quoted in Peter Singer, *Pushing Time Away: My Grandfather and the Tragedy of Jewish Vienna* (London, 2003), p. 135.

24 Letter of 12 June 1913 from Thomas Mann to Ludwig Ficker, in Ludwig von Ficker, *Briefwechsel 1909–1914* (Salzburg, 1986), p. 159. For the significance of Jean Paul texts in Kraus's public readings, see Kurt Krolop, 'Bewahrer, Zeugen und Rächer der Natur – Richter der Menschheit: Jean Paul bei Karl Kraus' in Kurt Krolop, *Reflexionen der Fackel* (Vienna, 1994), pp. 105–18.

25 See Timms, *Karl Kraus – Apocalyptic Satirist* (1986), pp.111 & 222.

26 Caroline Kohn, *Karl Kraus* (Stuttgart, 1966), p. 19.

27 Germaine Goblot, 'Les Parents de Karl Kraus', in *Études Germaniques*, 5 (1950), 1, pp. 43–53.

28 Paul Schick, *Karl Kraus* (Reinbek bei Hamburg, 1993), pp.10–28; Sophie Schick, 'Kindheit und Lehrjahre' (unpublished typescript in the Kraus Archive).

29 Kurt Rosner, *Damals – Bilderbuch einer Jugend* (Düsseldorf, 1948), pp. 75–7.

30 Heinrich Sedlmayr, 'Aus der Kindheit großer Menschen: Karl Kraus', in *Die Mutter*, 5 (1925), pp. 5–6.

31 Hugo Bettauer, 'Das Geburtstaggeschenk', in *Der Tag*, 27 April 1924, p. 4.

32 Sophie Schick, 'Kindheit und Lehrjahre', p. 18.

33 Goblot, 'Les parents de Karl Kraus', p. 53.

34 *Minutes of the Vienna Psychoanalytical Society*, tr. M. Nunberg, ed. Herman Nunberg and Ernst Federn, 4 vols (New York, 1962–75), 2, pp. 382–93.

35 The letters cited are in the Kraus Archive.

36 Karl Kraus to Richard Kraus, 4 September 1897 (Friedrich Pfäfflin Collection, Marbach).

37 Margarete Mitscherlich, 'Sittlichkeit und Kriminalität: Psychoanalytische Bemerkungen zu Karl Kraus', in *Text + Kritik: Sonderband Karl Kraus*, ed. Heinz Ludwig Arnold (Munich, 1975), p. 27.

38 The envelope containing these relics is inscribed in Kraus's hand: '*Familiensache!* gehört meiner lieben Schwester Marie nach meinem Tode' (Kraus Archive, IN 171.277).

39 Bettauer in *Der Tag*, 27 April 1924, p. 4.

40 For a fuller account, see Edward Timms, 'Kokoschka's Pictographs – A Contextual Reading' in *Word & Image*, 6, No. 1 (January–March 1990), pp. 4–17.

41 Oskar Kokoschka, *My Life*, tr. David Britt (London, 1974) pp. 38–9.

42 Werner Kraft, *Karl Kraus: Beiträge zum Verständnis seines Werkes* (Salzburg, 1956), p. 265.

43 Virginia Woolf, *Moments of Being: Unpublished Autobiographical Writings*, ed. Jeanne Schulkind (London, 1986), p. 77.

44 Freud's policy of ignoring Kraus's criticisms dates back to April 1910 (*Minutes of the Vienna Psychoanalytical Society*, 2, p. 476).

45 Wilhelm Stekel, 'Über Psychoanalyse, Psychotherapie, medizinische Psychologie und Sozialwissenschaft' in *Medizinische Klinik*. No. 11 (22 March 1923), p. 361.

46 See *The Freud/Jung Letters*, tr. Ralph Manheim and R. C. F. Hull (London, 1974), p. 480.

47   Laplanche and Pontalis, *The Language of Psychoanalysis*, p. 211. The term 'Father-Imago' was first used by Jung in *Wandlungen und Symbole der Libido* (1911).
48   Carl Spitteler, *Gesammelte Werke* (Zurich, 1945), 5, esp. pp. 286–98.
49   'Die Erinnerung ist das einzige Paradies, aus welchem wir nicht getrieben werden können' (FS 2, 121 & 3, 141)

Chapter 10

1   Karl Kraus, *Worte in Versen*, vol. 3 (Leipzig, 1918), p. 23 (= S 9, 149).
2   For a preliminary discussion, which anticipates some of the findings of this section, see Edward Timms, 'The "Child-Woman": Kraus, Freud, Wittels and Irma Karczewska' in *Vienna 1900: From Altenberg to Wittgenstein* (Austrian Studies 1), ed. Edward Timms and Ritchie Robertson (Edinburgh, 1990), pp. 87–107.
3   Timms, *Karl Kraus – Apocalyptic Satirist* (1986), pp. 75–80 & 99.
4   The story, 'Ladislaus Posthumous', appeared in *Die Fackel* in February 1907 (F 218, 4–20).
5   Page references introduced by the letter M refer to *Freud and the Child Woman: The Memoirs of Fritz Wittels*, ed. Edward Timms (New Haven and London, 1995), which is based on the typescripts by Wittels in A. A. Brill Library, New York. For a discussion of the difficulties of shaping these materials for publication, see Leo Lensing, '"Freud and the Child Woman" or "The Kraus Affair"? A Textual "Reconstruction" of Fritz Wittels's Psychoanalytic Autobiography' in *German Quarterly*, 69, No. 3 (1996), pp. 322–32.
6   In Wittels's memoirs Irma Karczewska is referred to throughout by the name of Mizerl (the name he used for her fictional reincarnation in the first edition of his novel *Ezechiel der Zugereiste*).
7   The first reference to Irma (code-name 'die Kleine') in the correspondence in the Kraus Archive occurs in a postcard to Kraus from Erich Mühsam dated 2 May 1906 (IN 138.043). Only one letter survives from Mühsam to Irma herself, dated 5 March 1908 (IN 138.085).
8   'Und wie ich Dich aus dem Bett des Kraus herauszerrte [. . .]', Fritz Wittels, letter to Irma Karczewska, 27 July 1907 (IN 102.561).
9   Cf. *Die Hetärengespräche von Lukian*, with fifteen drawings by Gustav Klimt (Leipzig, 1907).
10   See the letter from Fritz Wittels to Irma Karczewska, 21 July 1907 (IN 102.561)
11   *Minutes of the Vienna Psychoanalytic Society*, 1, p. 195n.
12   Erich Mühsam, postcards to Kraus dated 5 May 1906 (IN 138.044) and 7 May 1906 (IN 138.045). Cf. Mühsam, *In meiner Posaune muß ein Sandkorn sein: Briefe 1900–1934*, ed. Gerd W. Jungblut, 2 vols (Vaduz, 1984), 1, pp. 60–2. The first reference to 'die Kleine' in the extensive unpublished correspondence from Hauer to Kraus occurs in a letter dated 29 June [1906] (IN 140.905).
13   Kete Parsenow, postcard to Kraus dated 3 July 1918 (IN 139.618).
14   Paul Schick, *Karl Kraus in Selbstzeugnissen und Bilddokumenten* (Reinbek, 1965), p. 53.
15   Handwritten letter dated 3 October 1908 from Kraus to Kurt Rosner, Kraus Archive, IN 216.606.
16   Kraus Archive, undated draft, IN 167.344.
17   See the handwritten notes by Kraus with comments by Frieda Wacha which are preserved in the Kraus Archive, Ib 159.627.
18   These details have been traced with the help of the Information Service (Meldeauskunft) of the Vienna Municipal and Provincial Archive (Wiener Stadt- und Landesarchiv), on the basis of the reference in Kraus's will to 'das [. . .] Grab der armen Frau Maria Christoduloff'. The official record confirms the date of her birth as 30 January 1890 and her death as 1 January 1933, both in Vienna.

19   Quotations are based on the original of Irma's diary, which is preserved in the Kraus Archive.

20   Under Austrian law, fourteen was the age of consent for sexual intercourse.

21   This suggestion was made by Sophie Schick during an interview with the author.

22   'So schafft man sich selber sein Haus-Nemesiserl zur Privat-Marterey'. Johann Nestroy, *Frühere Verhältnisse*, scene 7.

23   These documents are published in *Karl Kraus: Marbacher Kataloge 52*, pp. 143–59.

24   There is no reference to Yerta in Wittels's memoirs. For further information about her tragically curtailed life (she died of leukaemia in 1913) see Rudolf von Urban, *Myself Not Least: Memoirs of a Psychoanalyst* (London, 1958), pp. 112–15.

25   See *Karl Kraus: Marbacher Kataloge 52*, pp. 145–9.

26   For further details, see Sigurd Paul Scheichl, 'Der Berliner Prozeß Wittels-Kraus (1910): Prager Zeitungsberichte' in *Kraus-Hefte*, 65 (1993), pp. 1–8.

27   Fritz Wittels, *Ezechiel der Zugereiste*, 5th edn (Vienna, 1911).

28   For further details, see Leo A. Lensing, 'Karl Kraus as "Volksklassiker"? Upton Sinclair and the Translation of *Die letzten Tage der Menschheit*', in *Deutsche Vierteljahresschrift für Literaturwissenschaft und Geistesgeschichte*, 58 (1984), pp. 156–87.

29   Letter of 13 October 1932 from the Verlag to Mieczlaw R. Frenkel; quoted in Michael Worbs, *Nervenkunst: Literatur und Psychoanalyse im Wien der Jahrhundertwende* (Frankfurt, 1983), p. 170.

30   Fritz Wittels, *Sigmund Freud: His Personality, his Teaching, and his School*, tr. Eden and Cedar Paul (London, 1924), p. 212.

31   The text of this letter is quoted from Wittels's English translation in his memoirs. It has been checked against the original in the Library of Congress.

32   Sigmund Freud, letter of 20 April 1928 to Fritz Wittels (Library of Congress).

33   See Susan Quinn, *A Mind of her Own – The Life of Karen Horney* (London, 1987), pp. 337–40.

34   Undated letter from Altenberg to Kraus, published in Andrew Barker and Leo A. Lensing, *Peter Altenberg: Rezept die Welt zu sehen* (Vienna, 1995), p. 265.

35   Kete Parsenow, postcard to Kraus postmarked 25 January 1924 (IN 139.649): 'Wie geht es dir u. deiner Familie? Du weißt was ich meine.'

36   See Dagmar Malone, 'Gina Kaus' in *Deutsche Exilliteratur seit 1933*, vol. 1: *Kalifornien*, Part 1, ed. John M. Spalek and Joseph Strelka (Berne, 1976), pp. 751–61 (p. 758); and Hartmut Vollmer, 'Vicki Baum und Gina Kaus: Ein Porträt zweier Erfolgsschrift-stellerinnen der Zwischenkriegszeit' in *Wien–Berlin*, ed. Bernhard Fetz and Hermann Schlösser (Vienna, 2001), pp. 45–57.

37   Gina Kaus, *Und was für ein Leben* (Hamburg, 1979), pp. 122–42.

38   For a detailed account of her career, see *Mechtilde Lichnowsky 1879–1958*, ed. Wilhelm Hemecker.

39   *Karl Kraus und Mechtilde Lichnowsky*, pp. 14 & 26.

40   *Karl Kraus und Mechtilde Lichnowsky*, p. 81.

41   'Doppelbeleuchtung' – the concept used in the commentary on their letters in *Karl Kraus und Mechtilde Lichnowsky*, p. 45.

42   *Karl Kraus und Mechtilde Lichnowsky*, pp. 104 & 192.

43   *Karl Kraus und Mechtilde Lichnowsky*, pp. 93–8.

44   Mary Dobrzensky's papers are located at the Academy of Sciences in Budapest; the Oblastni Archive in Zamrsk, Czech Republic; the Brenner Archive, Innsbruck; and the German Literature Archives, Marbach. Copies of many of her letters to Kraus are also in the Vienna Kraus Archive.

45   See *Karl Kraus und Mechtilde Lichnowsky*, pp. 205–6.

46   *Karl Kraus und Mechtilde Lichnowsky*, pp. 31, 35, 44 & 52–3.

47   For infromation about Dobrzensky's circle, see 'Der literarische Kreis von Maria Dobrzensky und deren Kontakte mit tschechischen Schriftstellern (Zusammenfas-

sung)', German summary of an article in Czech in *Studie o rukopisech*, vol. 15 (Prague, 1976), pp. 97–8.

48   Typewritten transcripts of these letters of 17 & 20/21 November 1920 are in the Kraus Archive, IN 174.732. The word 'Blaustrumpf', which had figured a dozen times in Kraus's early anti-feminist satire, is no longer used in *Die Fackel* after 1915, the final instance being F 406–12, 102.

49   Letter of 27/28 December 1920 to Mechtilde Lichnowsky. *Karl Kraus und Mechtilde Lichnowsky*, p. 39.

50   Letter from Kraus to Mary Dobrzensky, 28/29 May 1921, German Literature Archive, Marbach.

51   Dobrzensky to Kraus, 21 July 1925 (copy in the Kraus Archive).

52   'Ist es nicht Zeit, daß wir liebend / uns vom Geliebten befrein und es bebend bestehn'; Rainer Maria Rilke, *Duino Elegies: The German Text with an English Translation* by J. B. Leishman and Stephen Spender (London, 1957), pp. 26–7 (translation modified).

53   Rainer Maria Rilke, *New Poems: The German Text with a Translation* by J. B. Leishman (London, 1964), pp. 142–7.

54   See the retrospective account by Lichnowsky in *Karl Kraus und Mechtilde Lichnowsky*, pp. 72–4.

55   See note 72 for further details of Sidonie's diaries.

56   'Der Geist müsse die Macht haben, den Tod zu verhindern.' Helene Kann in the Basle *National-Zeitung*, 22 April 1944, quoted in Paul Schick, 'Der Satiriker und der Tod: Versuch einer typologischen Deutung', *Festschrift zum hundertjährigen Bestehen der Wiener Stadtbibliothek* (Vienna, 1956), p. 215.

57   *Karl Kraus und Mechtilde Lichnowsky*, pp. 84 & 108.

58   'Vorstellungen, durch die [. . .] eine Erkrankung abgesagt werden könnte', Vorlesungsprogramm, 9 & 12 January 1935 (collection in the Vienna City Library).

59   See *Die Frauen der Wiener Moderne*, ed. Lisa Fischer and Emil Brix (Vienna, 1997).

60   Sofie Lazarsfeld, *Wie die Frau den Mann erlebt: Fremde Bekenntnisse und eigene Betrachtungen* (Vienna, 1931).

61   Sidonie Nadherny to Albert Bloch, 18 November 1947, in Elke Lorenz, *'Sei Ich ihr, sei mein Bote': Der Briefwechsel zwischen Sidonie Nadherny und Albert Bloch* (Munich, 2002), p. 162.

62   See Timms, *Karl Kraus – Apocalyptic Satirist* (1986), pp. 75–80.

63   See the letter from Bertha Maria Mayr to Karl Kraus dated 5 October 1935, in which she thanks him for his inquiry about her husband's health, Kraus Archive, IN 144.012.

64   Helga Malmberg, *Widerhall des Herzens: Ein Peter Altenberg-Buch* (Munich, 1961), p. 228.

65   Else Lasker-Schüler, letters of 17 December 1923 and 5 March 1924, in *Briefe an Karl Kraus*, ed. Astrid Gehlhoff-Claes (Cologne, n. d.), pp. 91–100 (p. 92).

66   *Karl Kraus: Marbacher Kataloge 52*, p. 198.

67   Peter Altenberg, *Auswahl aus seinem Werk von Karl Kraus* (Vienna, 1932), pp. 406–7 and 521. For a fuller account of Altenberg's androgynous ideal, see Edward Timms, 'Peter Altenberg: Authenticity or Pose' in *Fin-de-Siècle Vienna*, ed. G. J. Carr and Eda Sagarra (Dublin, 1985), pp. 126–42.

68   Mechtilde Lichnowsky, *Der Kampf mit dem Fachmann* (Vienna, 1925), pp. 169–72.

69   *Karl Kraus und Mechtilde Lichnowsky*, pp. 152–4.

70   Lorenz, *Briefwechsel*, p. 57.

71   Alena Wagnerova, *Das Leben der Sidonie Nadherny: Eine Biographie* (Hamburg, 2003), p. 8: 'eine außergewöhnliche, nicht leicht faßbare Frau'.

72   A total of fourteen of Sidonie Nadherny's handwritten diaries are preserved in the Statni Oblastni Archive, Prague. They take the form of plain notebooks or exercise books with irregular dated entries. The personal diaries (AC 47/1–3) are written mainly (but not exclusively) in English, the travel journals (AC 46/1–11) mainly in German.

73 Approximately one hundred of Sidonie's letters survive in the Rilke Archive at Fischerhude. Only one example is included (incomplete) in Rilke, *Briefe an Sidonie Nadherny von Borutin*, ed. Bernhard Blume (Frankfurt, 1973), pp. 341 & 370.

74 Lorenz, *Briefwechsel*, p. 47.

75 Rilke, *Briefe an Sidonie Nadherny*, p. 87 (14 October 1908).

76 Sidonie to Johannes Nadherny, 15/16 December [1908], quoted in Lorenz, *Briefwechsel*, p. 48.

77 Sidonie Nadherny to Albert Bloch, 30 January 1948, in Lorenz, *Briefwechsel*, p. 194.

78 Kurt Krolop, 'Die "Hörerin" als Sprecherin: Sidonie von Nadherny und "ihre Sprachlehre"' in *Brücken: Germanistisches Jahrbuch Tschechien-Slowakei 1999* (Berlin, 2000), pp. 43–53.

79 See the story 'Der Zeichner' in Lichnowsky's collection *Zum Schauen bestellt* (Esslingen, 1953), pp. 105–11.

80 Wagnerova, *Das Leben*, p. 44.

81 Sidonie Nadherny, letter of 10 August 1914, cited in Rilke, *Briefe an Sidonie Nadherny*, p. 365.

82 See Wagnerova, *Das Leben*, pp. 69–77 and 191, n. 16.

83 See Koraljka Kos, 'Die kroatische Komponistin Dora Pejacevic und ihre Beziehung zu Karl Kraus' in *Kraus-Hefte*, 9 (January 1979), pp. 2–7.

84 'blumengeschmückte Altäre', Sidonie Nadherny to Albert Bloch, 22 May 1948, in Lorenz, *Briefwechsel*, p. 308.

85 Sidonie Nadherny to Albert Bloch, 26 January 1948, in Lorenz, *Briefwechsel*, p. 189.

86 Sidonie Nadherny to Albert Bloch, 30 January 1948, in Lorenz, *Briefwechsel*, p. 193.

87 Timms, *Karl Kraus – Apocalyptic Satirist* (1986), pp. 250–1.

88 According to information provided by Friedrich Pfäfflin (letter of 24 August 2001 to Edward Timms), Josef Kalixt Stanislaus Graf Rzyszczewski-Stadion was born on 30 October 1893 in Dalsko Turisko/Wolhynien. Little is known about him apart from the observations in his Austrian military dossier, which records that he was intelligent, serious, calm, ambitious, reliable and popular with his comrades ('intelligent, ernst, ruhig; ambitioniert und zuverlässig [. . .] beliebter Kamerad'). By profession he was presumably a land-owner since, after serving as an officer in the Austrian army from 1914 to 1916, he was 'released from military service for agricultural purposes' ('für landwirtschaftliche Zwecke vom Militärdienst enthoben').

89 Rilke, *Briefe an Sidonie*, pp. 193–4.

90 Sidonie Nadherny to Albert Bloch, 28/29 February 1948, in Lorenz, *Briefwechsel*, p. 259.

91 Sidonie Nadherny, *Chronik über Vrchotovy Janovice*, ed. Friedrich Pfäfflin (Marbach, 1995), p. 41.

92 See Jaromir Louzil, 'Der Lebensabend der Sidonie Nadherny von Borutin in ihren Briefen an Vaclav Wagner' in *Wissenschaftliche Zeitschrift der Universität Halle*, 41 (1992), pp. 19–29 ('Bestien', p. 28). The reference to 'beastly Germans' occurs in Sidonie Nadherny, letter to Albert Bloch, 30 January 1948, in Lorenz, *Briefwechsel*, p. 194.

93 'Mut zum Ertragen', letter of 10 February 1944 to Vaclav Wagner; cited in Wagnerova, *Das Leben*, pp. 153–62.

94 Wagnerova, *Das Leben*, p. 163.

Chapter 11

1 Ernst Krenek, *Im Atem der Zeit: Erinnerungen an die Moderne*, tr. Friedrich Saathen (Hamburg, 1998), pp. 163–4 ('eine christliche Haltung [. . .] in der störenden Verkleidung eines weltstädtischen jüdischen Journalisten').

2 For example, Carl Dallago, Ferdinand Ebner, Ludwig Ficker, Theodor Haecker, Ludwig Hänsel, Edwin Hartl, Karl Borromäus Heinrich, Aurel Kolnai, Leopold

Liegler, Viktor Matejka, Georg Moenius, Carl Muth, Sigismund von Radecki, Richard von Schaukal, Emil Schönauer, Paula Schlier, Karl Thieme, Leopold Ungar, Ignaz Zangerle and August Zechmeister.

3   *Wörterbuch der Redensarten.*

4   John Theobald, *The Paper Ghetto: Karl Kraus and Anti-Semitism* (Frankfurt, 1996), p.196; Wilma Abeles Iggers, *Karl Kraus: A Viennese Critic of the Twentieth Century* (The Hague, 1967), pp. 171 & 181.

5   The exception is the study by Alexander Lang, '*Ursprung ist das Ziel': Karl Kraus und sein 'Zion des Wortes'* (Frankfurt, 1998).

6   Harry Zohn, *Karl Kraus and the Critics* (Columbia DC, 1997), p. 27.

7   Gerald Stieg, *Der Brenner und die Fackel: Ein Beitrag zur Wirkungsgeschichte von Karl Kraus* (Salzburg, 1976); see also Heike Fischer, *In gebrochenem Deutsch . . . : Sprachtheologie und Gestaltästhetik bei Karl Kraus* (Frankfurt, 1998).

8   Timms, *Karl Kraus – Apocalyptic Satirist* (1986), p. 242.

9   Ludwig von Ficker, letter of 18 October 1927 to Theodor Haecker, in Ficker, *Briefwechsel 1926–1939.*

10 Richard Hess, *Joshua* (Leicester: Tyndale Old Testament Commentaries, 1996), pp. 42 & 52.

11 Timms, *Karl Kraus – Apocalyptic Satirist* (1986), p. 340.

12 Hess, *Joshua*, p. 23.

13 Bernhard W. Anderson, *The Living World of the Old Testament*, 4th edn (London, 2000), pp. 112 & 134.

14 The issues are carefully reviewed in Anderson, *The Living World*, pp. 131–41.

15 Anderson, *The Living World*, p. 123.

16 Louis Jacobs, *The Jewish Religion: A Companion* (Oxford, 1995), p. 459.

17 Ficker, *Briefwechsel 1926–1939*, p. 303.

18 Stieg, *Der Brenner und Die Fackel*, pp. 232–4.

19 Jacobs, *The Jewish Religion*, pp. 459–60 (article on 'Shekhinah').

20 Dan Cohn-Sherbok, *Messianic Judaism* (London, 2000), p. 87.

21 Ficker, letter of 9 May 1928 to Paula Schlier, in Ficker, *Briefwechsel 1926–1939*, p. 117.

22 Sigismund von Radecki, *Wie ich glaube* (Cologne, l953), p. 36: '"Man kann ja auch Christ bleiben, ohne in der Kirche zu sein"'.

23 See Stieg, *Der Brenner und die Fackel*, pp. 168–75; Edward Timms, 'The Christian Satirist: A Contradiction in Terms?' in *Forum for Modern Language Studies*, 31 (1995), pp. 101–16.

24 Ludwig von Ficker, *Denkzettel und Danksagungen* (Munich, 1967), pp. 45–52.

25 Stieg, *Der Brenner und die Fackel*, pp. 65 & 217.

26 Werner L. Hohmann, *Ferdinand Ebner: Bedenker und Ebner des Wortes in der Situation der 'geistigen Wende'* (Essen, 1995), p. 173.

27 Compare the discussion of 'Schöpfung' in Jochen Schmidt, *Die Geschichte des Genie-Gedankens in der deutschen Literatur, Philosophie und Politik 1750–1945*, 2 vols (Darmstadt,1985).

28 Stieg, *Der Brenner und die Fackel*, pp. 227–8.

29 *The Ethics of the Fathers*, quoted in Jacobs, *The Jewish Religion*, p. 105.

30 Northrop Frye, *The Great Code: The Bible and Literature* (New York, 1981), p. 106.

31 Jacobs, *The Jewish Religion*, p. 104.

32 Martin Heidegger, 'Brief über den "Humanismus"' in *Wegmarken*, ed. Friedrich-Wilhelm von Herrmann (Frankfurt, 1996), pp. 313–64 (esp. pp. 334–6); cf. Heidegger, *Basic Writings*, ed. David Farrell Krell (London, 2002), pp. 337–40.

33 Kraus, *Literatur*, p. 59 (= S 11, 57).

34 'Neue Apologie des Buchstaben h' (1773) in Johann Georg Hamann, *Sämtliche Werke* (Historisch-kritische Ausgabe, Vienna, 1951), 3, pp. 89–108. See also Michael West,

Transcendental Wordplay: America's Romantic Punsters and the Search for the Language of Nature (Athens OH, 2000), p. 113.

35   Ficker, *Denkzettel*, p. 126.
36   Ficker, *Briefwechsel 1926–1939*, pp. 298–300.
37   Cf. Timms, *Karl Kraus – Apocalyptic Satirist* (1986), p. 182.
38   See C. J. Thornhill, *Walter Benjamin and Karl Kraus: Problems of a 'Wahlverwandtschaft'* (Stuttgart, 1996), pp. 6–31.
39   Scholem, *Friendship*, pp. 227–30; *Freundschaft*, pp. 283–7.
40   For an English translation, which has been modified in what follows, see Walter Benjamin, *Reflections*, tr. Edmund Jephcott (New York, 1976), pp. 239–73.
41   Benjamin, *Gesammelte Schriften*, ed. Rolf Tiedemann and Hermann Schweppenhäuser (Frankfurt, 1977), vol. 2, part 1, pp. 335, 349, 363 & 367.
42   Scholem, *Friendship*, p. 230; *Freundschaft*, p. 286.
43   Gershom Scholem, *Walter Benjamin und sein Engel: Vierzehn Aufsätze und kleine Beiträge* (Frankfurt, 1983), pp. 44–8.
44   Scholem, *Engel*, p. 59.
45   Scholem, *Friendship*, p. 82; *Freundschaft*, p. 105.
46   Timms, *Karl Kraus – Apocalyptic Satirist* (1986), pp. 231–6.
47   Benjamin, *Ursprung des deutschen Trauerspiels* (Frankfurt, 1963), pp. 29–31; *The Origin of German Tragic Drama*, tr. John Osborne (London, 1990), pp. 45–6.
48   Benjamin, *Schriften*, 2, pp. 363 & 367.
49   Walter Benjamin, *Gesammelte Briefe VI: 1938–40*, ed. Christoph Gödde and Henri Lonitz (Frankfurt, 2000), p. 123.

Chapter 12

1   See *Visions and Blueprints: Avant-Garde Culture and Radical Politics in Early Twentieth-Century Europe*, ed. Edward Timms and Peter Collier (Manchester, 1988).
2   See *Die Expressionismusdebatte*, ed. Hans-Jürgen Schmitt (Frankfurt, 1973).
3   See John Dixon Halliday, *Karl Kraus, Franz Pfemfert and the First World War: A Comparative Study of 'Die Fackel' and 'Die Aktion'* (Passau, 1986).
4   Kraus to Walden, 19/20 March 1910, in *Kraus–Walden Briefwechsel*, pp. 180–1.
5   *Rundfrage über Karl Kraus*, ed. Ludwig von Ficker (Innsbruck, [1917]), p. 17.
6   For a selection of polemics against Kraus, see *Die Belagerung der Urteilsmauer: Karl Kraus im Zerrspiegel seiner Feinde*, ed. Franz Schuh and Juliane Vogel.
7   See Kraus's draft letter to Walden of early 1912, published in *Kraus–Walden Briefwechsel*, pp. 396–9.
8   The rallying-point for avant-garde authors disenchanted with the war was Pfemfert's journal *Die Aktion*. See Eva Kolinsky, *Engagierter Expressionismus: Politik und Literatur zwischen Weltkrieg und Weimarer Republik* (Stuttgart, 1970).
9   See Timms, *Karl Kraus – Apocalyptic Satirist*, chapter 16.
10 See *Deutsche Dichtung im Weltkrieg*, ed. Ernst Volkmann (Leipzig, 1934).
11 Rilke, *Sämtliche Werke*, 6 vols (Wiesbaden, 1956), 2, pp. 86–92.
12 See Lore B. Foltin and Josef Pfeifer, 'Franz Werfel und die politischen Umwälzungen des Jahres 1918 in Wien', *Études Germaniques*, 26 (1971), pp. 194–207.
13 See Franz Blei, *Schriften in Auswahl* (Munich, 1960), which includes a pseudo-psychological attack on Kraus (pp. 283–7).
14 For a more positive view, see Karl-Markus Gauß, 'Karl Kraus und seine "kosmischen Schieferln". Zur Rehabilitation von Albert Ehrenstein, Hugo Sonnenschein und Georg Kulka', in *Zeitgeschichte*, 10 (1982–3), pp. 43–59; Uwe Laugwitz, *Albert Ehrenstein: Studien zu Leben, Werk und Wirkung eines deutsch-jüdischen Schriftstellers* (Frankfurt, 1987), pp. 218–35; and Serke, *Böhmische Dörfer*, pp. 345–75.
15 Ralf Georg Reuth, *Goebbels*, tr. Krishna Winston (London, 1993), pp. 40–1 & 50.

16 Joseph Goebbels, *Michael: Ein deutsches Schicksal in Tagebuchblättern*, 32–6 thousand (Munich: Zentralverlag der NSPAD, 1936), p. 77.

17 Goebbels, *Michael*, pp. 101–2.

18 See Reuth, *Goebbels*, p. 64.

19 Goebbels, *Michael*, p. 102, 113 and 149; the references to the (unnamed) Hitler are unmistakable.

20 See Claus-Ekkehard Bärsch, *Erlösung und Vernichtung: Dr. phil. Joseph Goebbels: Zur Psyche und Ideologie eines jungen Nationalsozialisten 1923–1927* (Munich, 1987).

21 Joseph Goebbels, *Tagebücher*, ed. Ralf Georg Reuth (Munich, 1992), 1, pp. 49–87 ('Ich bin deutscher Kommunist'; p. 85).

22 Goebbels, *Tagebücher*, 1, pp. 87–8 & 162.

23 'Judas Iscariot: Eine biblische Tragödie' (1918), 'Heinrich Kämpfert: Ein Drama' (1919), 'Kampf der Arbeiterklasse: Drama' (1919–20), 'Die Saat: Ein Geschehen in drei Akten' (1920), and 'Der Wanderer: Spiel mit einem Prolog, elf Bildern und einem Epilog' (1923).

24 Renate Gisela Braimah, 'Goebbels and German Modernism' (MA dissertation, University of Sussex, 1994), pp. 29–44.

25 Kraus, *Dritte Walpurgisnacht*, p. 41/54.

26 Kurt Lenk, *Volk und Staat: Strukturwandel politischer Ideologien im 19. und 20. Jahrhundert* (Stuttgart, 1971).

27 For this simplistic view, see Ulrich Nill, *Die 'geniale Vereinfachung': Anti-Intellektualismus in Ideologie und Sprachgebrauch bei Joseph Goebbels* (Frankfurt, 1991).

28 Goebbels, *Tagebücher*, vol. 1, pp. 89–90.

29 Quoted in Helmut Heiber, *Goebbels*, tr. John K. Dickinson (New York, 1972), p.55.

30 Joseph Goebbels, *Der Angriff: Aufsätze aus der Kampfzeit*, ed. Hans Schwarz van Berk, 7th edn (Munich, 1939); *Wetterleuchten: Aufsätze aus der Kampfzeit (2. Band 'Der Angriff)*, ed. Georg-Wilhelm Müller (Munich 1939)

31 Max Weber, 'Der Beruf zur Politik', in Weber, *Soziologie, Weltgeschichtliche Analysen, Politik*, ed. Eduard Baumgarten (Stuttgart, 1968), pp. 167–85.

32 See *Weltfreunde: Konferenz über die Prager deutsche Literatur*, ed. Eduard Goldstücker (Prague, 1967).

33 Kurt Wolff, *Autoren, Bücher, Abenteuer: Betrachtungen und Erinnerungen eines Verlegers* (Berlin, n.d.), p. 94.

34 Franz Werfel, 'Die Metaphysik des Drehs', in *Die Aktion*, 3 March 1917, columns 124–8; reprinted in the Zionist journal *Die Selbstwehr (Unabhängige jüdische Wochenschrift)*, 11, No. 16 (20 April 1917); and in *Die Belagerung der Urteilsmauer: Karl Kraus im Zerrspiegel seiner Feinde*, ed. Franz Schuh and Juliane Vogel (Vienna, 1986), pp. 58–64.

35 Kraus's judgement has tended to be endorsed by more recent analyses of Expressionist poetry. See Hellmut Thomke, *Hymnische Dichtung im Expressionismus* (Berne, 1972).

36 Franz Kafka, *Briefe 1902–1924*, ed. Max Brod (Frankfurt, 1958), p. 425.

37 See *Hirnwelten funkeln: Literatur des Expressionismus in Wien*, ed. Ernst Fischer and Wilhelm Haefs (Salzburg, 1988), p. XVIII.

38 See Patrick Bridgwater, *The German Poets of the First World War* (London, 1985).

39 *Modern German Poetry 1910–1960*, ed. Michael Hamburger and Christopher Middleton (London, 1963), p. xxxvii ('idealistic humbug'); Ernst Fischer, 'Expressionismus – Aktivismus – Revolution' in *Expressionismus in Österreich: Die Literatur und die Künste*, ed. Klaus Amann and Armin A. Wallas (Vienna, 1994), pp. 19–48 ('nützliche Idioten'; p. 43).

40 Werfel, 'Die Metaphysik des Drehs', in *Die Belagerung der Urteilsmauer*, pp. 58–64.

41 Timms, *Karl Kraus – Apocalyptic Satirist* (1986), chapter 9.

42 'Ich was wirklich darauf gefaßt, diesen jungen Menschen einfach zu umarmen; aber ich sah sofort, daß dies in keinem Fall möglich sei. [. . .] Der Jude, der Judenjunge, um es

geradeaus zu sagen, hätte mir nichts verschlagen, aber es mochte mir doch wohl auch die durchaus jüdische Einstellung zu seiner Produktion fühlbar geworden sein, dieses connaitre les choses pour ne pas les avoir eu [. . .]'. Rainer Maria Rilke, *Briefwechsel mit Hugo von Hofmannsthal*, ed. Rudolf Hirsch and Ingeborg Schnack (Frankfurt, 1978), p. 77.

43 'A Hellerau et à Drèsde j'ai beaucoup vu Franz Werfel. C'était triste, "ein Judenbub" sagte Sidie Nadherny (die von Janowitz herübergekommen war, ganz erschrocken) et elle n'avait pas complètement tort. [. . .] un esprit juif qui connait par trop la marchandise. [. . .] la mentalité juive [. . .] cet esprit qui pénètre les choses pour ne les avoir eues, comme le poison qui entre partout en se vengeant de ne pas faire partie d'un organisme'. *Rainer Maria Rilke und Marie Thurn und Taxis – Briefwechsel*, ed. Ernst Zinn, 2 vols (Zurich, 1951), 1, pp. 323–4.

44 Franz Werfel, 'Begegnungen mit Rilke', in *Das Tagebuch*, 8, No. 4 (22 January 1927).

45 Rilke, *Briefe an Sidonie Nadherny*, pp. 214–16.

46 Joachim W. Storck, 'Rilke und Karl Kraus', in *Literatur und Kritik*, 211/212 (February–March 1987), pp. 40–54.

47 Rilke, *Briefe an Sidonie Nadherny*, p. 216.

48 Rilke, *Briefwechsel mit Hofmannsthal*, p. 78.

49 T. S. Eliot, *After Strange Gods: A Primer of Modern Heresy* (New York, 1934), p. 20.

50 'Er hat mit einer List, zu der ihn die Selbsterhaltung erzog, sein Unbefestigtsein aus einem Unglück in eine Überlegenheit gewandelt [. . .] da ist er zum Schädling, zum Eindringling, zum Auflöser geworden.' Rainer Maria Rilke, *Briefe aus Muzot 1921–1926* (Leipzig, 1935), pp. 130–4 (letter of 25 April 1922 to Ilse Blumenthal-Weiss).

51 Ingeborg Schnack, *Rainer Maria Rilke – Chronik seines Lebens und Werkes*, 2 vols (Frankfurt, 1975), 1, p. 207.

52 Otto Weininger, *Geschlecht und Charakter*, 3rd impression (Vienna and Leipzig, 1904), chapter 13: 'Das Judentum', pp. 414 ('der Mensch haßt nur, durch wen er sich unangenehm an sich selbst erinnert fühlt') & 442 ('Duplizität, ja Multiplizität').

53 Franz Werfel, 'Eine Erklärung', in *Die Selbstwehr*, 11, No. 20 (15 May 1917).

54 Page references are to the first edition of *Spiegelmensch*, published by Kurt Wolff Verlag (Munich, 1920).

55 'armverschlungene Freunde schreiten [. . .]' in magischer Vereinigung' (*Spiegelmensch*, pp. 68 & 74); the allusions are to the poems 'Der schöne strahlende Mensch' and 'An den Leser' from *Der Weltfreund*.

56 See Peter Stephan Jungk, *Franz Werfel – Eine Lebensgeschichte* (Frankfurt, 1987), pp. 114–22; Jungk, *A Life Torn by History: Franz Werfel 1890–1945*, tr. Anselm Hollo (London, 1990), pp. 75–9.

57 For a detailed analysis, see Timms, *Karl Kraus – Apocalyptic Satirist*, pp. 232–7.

58 The 'Solo' was not written until January 1920, when the first draft of *Spiegelmensch* was almost complete. See Jungk, *Franz Werfel*, pp. 121–2; *A Life Torn by History*, p. 79.

59 Page references are to Karl Kraus, *Literatur oder Man wird doch da sehn* (Vienna and Leipzig, 1921). Kraus's own recording of Schwarz-Drucker's song, 'Das Lied von der Presse', is available on Preiser Records, PR 3017.

60 See *Karl Kraus' 'Literatur oder Man wird doch da sehn': Genetische Ausgabe und Kommentar*, ed. Martin Leubner (Göttingen, 1996), pp. 289 & 337–45.

61 See Leubner's judicious commentary in *'Literatur oder Man wird doch da sehn'*, pp. 213–66.

62 Scholem, *Friendship*, p. 82; *Freundschaft*, p. 105 ('Erstickungsanfälle vor Lachen').

63 Blei, who shared Schmitt's nostalgia for 'pre-democratic' institutions, supported clerical politics while conceding that he had no Christian faith. See Franz Blei, *Briefe an Carl Schmitt 1917–1933*, ed. Angela Reinthal (Heidelberg, 1995), pp. 9 & 32.

64 Kafka, *Briefe 1902–1924*, pp. 336–8.

65 See Jungk, *Franz Werfel*, pp. 167–9; *A Life Torn by History*, pp. 112–13.
66 For the context of the passages quoted by Kraus, see Franz Werfel, *Paulus unter den Juden* (Berlin, Vienna and Leipzig, 1926), pp. 119–20, 155 & 180.

PART FOUR
Chapter 13

1 See Glaser, *Im Umfeld des Austromarxismus*, p. 19.
2 Julius Braunthal, *In Search of the Millennium* (London, 1945), pp. 249–51.
3 Letter from Siegfried Jacobsohn to Karl Kraus, 27 June 1920, Kraus Archive, IN.140.872.
4 'temperamentvoll'; Karl Kraus to Friedrich Austerlitz, 6 November 1924, Kraus Archive, Ib159.626/35.
5 See Andrew G. Whiteside, *The Socialism of Fools: Georg Ritter von Schönerer and Austrian Pan-Germanism* (Berkeley CA, 1975).
6 See Julius Carlebach, *Karl Marx and the Radical Critique of Judaism* (London, 1978).
7 *Verhandlungen des sechsten österreichischen sozial-demokratischen Parteitages* (Vienna, 1897), pp. 87 & 103; quoted in Robert S. Wistrich, 'Social Democracy, Antisemitism and the Jews of Vienna', in *Jews, Antisemitism and Culture in Vienna*, ed. Ivar Oxaal, Michael Pollak and Gerhard Botz (London and New York, 1988), pp. 118–19.
8 See Walter B. Simon, 'The Jewish Vote in Austria', in *Leo Baeck Institute Yearbook*, 16 (1971), pp. 97–123.
9 See Bruce F. Pauley, 'Political Antisemitism in Interwar Vienna', in *Jews, Antisemitism and Culture*, pp. 152–73 (p. 158).
10 In British English, public ownership of the means of production is normally known as 'nationalization'. In this chapter the word 'socialization' is used to denote Bauer's model of public ownership as the prelude to a classless society. Cf. Robert Danneberg, *Vienna under Socialist Rule*, tr. H. J. Stenning (London, 1925), p. 20.
11 Bauer, *Die österreichische Revolution*, pp. 166–78.
12 See Eduard März and Fritz Weber, 'Sozialdemokratie und Sozialisierung nach dem Ersten Weltkrieg' in *Österreich November 1918*, pp. 101–23 (p. 113).
13 Bauer, *Die österreichische Revolution*, pp. 159–61 & 178–82.
14 Richard Swedberg, *Joseph A. Schumpeter: His Life and Work* (Cambridge, 1991), p. 68.
15 Swedberg, *Joseph A. Schumpeter*, pp. 67–8.
16 See the handwritten draft of a letter from Kraus to Bauer, Kraus Archive IN 167.354.
17 Bauer's letter to Béla Kun, dated 'Wien, am 16. Juni 1919', is reprinted in *Ungarn 1919 und Österreich* (Vienna, 1979), pp. 99–105.
18 See März and Weber, 'Sozialdemokratie und Sozialisierung nach dem Ersten Weltkrieg', pp. 106–7.
19 See the 'Linz Programme' of the Austrian Social Democratic Party, *Protokoll des Sozialdemokratischen Parteitages* (Vienna, 1926), p. 248.
20 Sonnenschein's critique, 'Karl Kraus oder die Kunst der Gesinnung' (11 March 1920), published in the *Neues Wiener Journal*, is reprinted in part in F 531–43, 99–133. For a fuller account of Sonnenschein's career, see Serke, *Böhmische Dörfer*.
21 See Georg Knepler, *Karl Kraus liest Offenbach* (Berlin, 1984), pp. 86–7, for a discussion of Kraus's use of the word 'bürgerlich'.
22 See the Kraus Archive, IN 169.775.
23 See the following articles in *Der Kampf*: Oskar Pollak, 'Ein Künstler und Kämpfer', 16, No. 1 (January 1923), pp. 31–6; D. J. Bach, 'Der unpopuläre Kraus', 16, No. 2 (February 1923), pp. 77–9; Oskar Pollak, 'Noch einmal Karl Kraus', 19, No. 6 (June 1926), pp. 261–7; Friedrich Austerlitz, 'Der wahre Kraus', 19, No. 7 (July 1926), pp. 309–14; Oskar Pollak, 'Noch einmal die Karl Kraus Anhänger', 19, No. 8 (August 1926), p. 353.

24   For a detailed account of the tax system, see Danneberg, *Vienna under Socialist Rule*, pp. 11–18.

25   See Rudolf Spitzer, *Karl Seitz: Waisenknabe – Staatspräsident – Bürgermeister von Wien* (Vienna, 1994), esp. pp. 33, 37 & 55–6.

26   At the opening of the European Ice-skating Championship in Vienna in January 1930, Seitz had invited hostile comment by remaining seated during the playing of the newly introduced Austrian national anthem. See Spitzer, *Karl Seitz*, p. 82.

27   For a documentation of the seven hundred public readings Kraus gave during his career as editor of *Die Fackel*, see Christian Wagenknecht, 'Die Vorlesungen von Karl Kraus: Ein chronologisches Verzeichnis', in *Kraus-Hefte*, 35/36 (October 1985), pp. 1–30.

28   According to Helmut Gruber, the Kunststelle 'failed because it set itself an impossible task'. See Gruber, *Red Vienna*, p. 102.

29   About two thousand volumes from David Josef Bach's collection are now in Cambridge University Library.

30   See Elke Mühlleitner, *Biographisches Lexikon der Psychoanalyse: Die Mitglieder der psychologischen Mittwoch-Gesellschaft und der Wiener Psychoanalytischen Vereinigung 1902–1938* (Tübingen, 1992), pp. 29–31.

31   This copy is now in the Cambridge University Library, S746.d.93.10.

32   This remarkable collection ('Geschenkcassette') passed into the possession of Dr Philip Marriot, the great-nephew (by adoption) of David Josef Bach, who has donated it to Gonville and Caius College, Cambridge.

33   For further details of readings and performances for working-class audiences, see Hans Eberhard Goldschmidt, 'Die Vorlesungen für Arbeiter', in Knepler, *Karl Kraus liest Offenbach*, pp. 233–7.

34   Kraus indicates that, for technical reasons, his manuscripts were not actually displayed (F 679–85, 82). They were returned to him on 3 January 1925 (Kraus Archive, Ib159.626/37).

35   The (unnamed) Bach is described as '[ein Mann], der alles das, was er öffentlich vertreten hat, hinterher privatim preisgibt mit dem Versprechen, dass er es auch öffentlich tun werde, und der dieses Versprechen nicht hält' (Ib159.626/35).

36   Kraus Archive, Ib159.626/36.

37   Kraus's letter to Austerlitz of 6 November 1924 contains a second paragraph complaining about Seitz.

38   Kiesler's most celebrated architectural design is the Shrine of the Book in Jerusalem.

39   Henriette Kotlan-Werner, *Kunst und Volk: David Josef Bach, 1874–1947* (Vienna, 1977), pp. 74–7 ('unter Judenhänden wird alles zum Geschäft').

40   'völlige Standpunktslosigkeit [. . .] in der Führung und Vertretung von Angelegenheiten, die ich im Gegensatz [. . .] zu Ihrer Partei für lebenswichtig halte': Kraus Archive, Ib159.626/35.

41   See Gruber, *Red Vienna*, pp. 97–8.

42   Alfred Pfoser, *Literatur und Austromarxismus* (Vienna, 1980), pp. 63–4.

43   Danneberg, *Vienna under Socialist Rule*, p. 43.

44   See Norbert Leser, *Zwischen Reformismus und Bolschewismus: Der Austromarxismus als Theorie und Praxis* (Vienna, 1968); Anson Rabinbach, *The Crisis of Austrian Socialism: From Red Vienna to Civil War 1927–1934* (Chicago, 1983); J. Wiedenholzer, *Auf dem Weg zum 'Neuen Menschen': Bildungs- und Kulturarbeit der österreichischen Sozialdemokratie in der Ersten Republik* (Vienna, 1981).

45   For further details, see Alfred Pfabigan, *Karl Kraus und der Sozialismus* (Vienna, 1976), pp. 220–3.

46   For a summary of Gruener's chequered career, see Ficker, *Briefwechsel 1926–39*, p. 438.

47   See Eckart Früh, 'Karl Kraus und der Kommunismus' in *Zeitgeschichte*, 15, No. 8 (May 1988), pp. 315–45.

Chapter 14

1 See Klemens von Klemperer, *Ignaz Seipel: Christian Statesman in a Time of Crisis* (Princeton NJ, l972), pp. 120–39.

2 In 1923 there were 9,268 registered defections from the Catholic Church in Vienna; in 1924 (after a vigorous anti-clerical campaign) there were 22,888. See Klemperer, *Ignaz Seipel*, p. 229.

3 Quoted in Alfred Diamant, *Austrian Catholics and the First Republic: Democracy, Capitalism, and the Social Order 1918–1934* (Princeton NJ, 1960), p. 169n.

4 See Friedrich Heer, *God's First Love: Christians and Jews over Two Thousand Years*, tr. Geoffrey Skelto (London, 1967).

5 *Civiltà cattolica*, 1921, 1, pp. 472–3; 1922, 4, pp. 369–71; 1938, 2, pp. 76–82; cited in David I. Kertzer, *Unholy War: The Vatican's Role in the Rise of Modern Anti-Semitism* (London, 2001), pp. 272–3 & 278.

6 For the continuities with National Socialism, see Erika Weinzierl, *Prüfstand: Österreichs Katholiken und der Nationalsozialismus* (Mödling, 1988); Stefan Moritz, *Grüß Gott und Heil Hitler: Katholische Kirche und Nationalsozialismus in Österreich* (Vienna, 2002).

7 Hedwig Pfarrhofer, 'Dr. Friedrich Funder: Sein Leben und sein Werk' (doctoral dissertation, University of Salzburg, 1976), pp. 188–9.

8 See Edward Timms, 'Antisemitism in the Universities and Student Fraternities: The "numerus clausus" Debate' in *The German-Jewish Dilemma: From the Enlightenment to the Shoah*, ed. Edward Timms and Andrea Hammel (Lampeter, 1999), pp. 137–52.

9 'fortschreitenden Levantinisierung Wiens'; quoted in Robert Koerber, *Rassesieg in Wien, der Grenzfeste des Reiches* (Vienna, 1939), p. 230.

10 See John Theobald, *The Paper Ghetto: Karl Kraus and Anti-Semitism* (Frankfurt, 1996), pp. 163–7.

11 See Nina Scholz and Heiko Heinisch, *'Alles werden sich die Christen nicht gefallen lassen': Wiener Pfarrer und die Juden in der Zwischenkriegszeit* (Vienna, 2001).

12 See *Geschichte Österreichs in Stichworten*, 5, pp. 130–3; Klemperer, *Ignaz Seipel*, pp. 206–19.

13 Diamant, *Austrian Catholics*, pp. 92–3.

14 Quoted in Anton Staudinger, 'Christlichsoziale Judenpolitik in der Gründungsphase der Österreichischen Republik' in *Jahrbuch für Zeitgeschichte* (Vienna), 1978, p. 18.

15 Klemperer, *Ignaz Seipel*, pp. 255–7.

16 Ignaz Seipel, 'Die Seelensanierung' (speech of 16 January 1924) in *Seipels Reden in Österreich und anderwärts*, ed. Josef Gessl (Vienna, 1926), pp. 95–7.

17 Klemperer, *Ignaz Seipel*, pp. 274–92.

18 Diamant, *Austrian Catholics*, p. 253.

19 Judith Beniston, *'Welttheater': Hofmannsthal, Richard von Kralik and the Revival of Catholic Drama in Austria, 1890–1934* (London, 1998), p.158.

20 *Neu Österreich: Seine Kultur, Bodenschätze, Wirtschaftsleben und Landschaftsbilder*, ed. Eduard Stepan (Amsterdam and Vienna, 1923), pp. 157–64: 'Österreichs Dichtung seit dem Umsturz'.

21 Hermann Bahr, 'Tagebuch' in *Neues Wiener Journal*, 26 October 1930; quoted in Ifkovits, 'Hermann Bahrs *Tagebücher* aus den Jahren 1927 bis 1931', p. 14.

22 For a more systematic account of Kralik's eccentric views and his narcissistic conviction that his beliefs must prevail, see Bernhard Doppler, '"Ich habe diesen Krieg immer sozusagen als meinen Krieg angesehen": Der katholische Kulturkritiker Richard von Kralik (1852–1934)' in *Österreich und der Große Krieg 1914–1918*, ed. Klaus Amann and Hubert Lengauer (Vienna, 1989), pp. 96–104.

23 Richard von Kralik, 'Die Hauptakte', RP, 21 March 1915; quoted in Beniston,

'Welttheater', p. 160. See also Günther Ramhardter, *Geschichtswissenschaft und Patriotismus: Österreichische Historiker im Weltkrieg 1914–1918* (Munich, 1973), pp. 118–33.

24   For a more detailed assessment of Kralik's 'megalomaniac tendencies', see Beniston, *'Welttheater'*, pp. 180–99 (p. 181).

25   See Beppo Beyerl, 'Wein aus Welschlandfrüchten' in *Mit der Ziehharmonika*, 15, No. 1 (March 1998), pp. 59–60. For the full text of the 'Hakenkreuzlied', set to music by Sepp Rosegger, see Helmut Brenner, *Musik als Waffe? Theorie und Praxis der politischen Musikverwendung, dargestellt am Beispiel der Steiermark 1938–1945* (Graz, 1992), p. 46.

26   See Albert Berger, 'Lyrische Zurüstung der "Österreich"-Idee: Anton Wildgans und Hugo von Hofmannsthal' in *Österreich und der große Krieg* 1914–1918, pp.144–52.

27   First published in Anton Wildgans, *Österreichische Gedichte* (Leipzig, n.d. [1915]), pp. 4–7.

28   Ferdinand Avenarius, 'Aussprachen mit Juden', *Der Kunstwart*, 25, No. 22 (August 1912), p. 225. See Steven E. Aschheim, 'Moritz Goldstein's "The German-Jewish Parnassus"' in *Yale Companion to Jewish Writing and Thought*, ed. Sander L. Gilman and Jack Zipes (New Haven, 1997), pp. 299–305.

29   This may have been the 'Totentanz' scene, published in the *Prager Presse* on 20 August 1922. See Karl Kraus, *Dramen*, ed. Christian Wagenknecht (Frankfurt, 1989), pp. 370–1 (n. 9).

30   For a fuller account of the relationship between Kraus and Hofmannsthal, see Reinhard Urbach, 'Karl Kraus und Hugo von Hofmannsthal: Eine Dokumentation' in *Hofmannsthal Blätter* 12 (1974), pp. 272–424; and Edward Timms, 'Hofmannsthal, Kraus and the *Theatrum Mundi*' in *Hugo von Hofmannsthal: Commemorative Essays*, ed. W. E. Yuill and Patricia Howe (London, 1981), pp. 123–32.

31   Ferdinand Ebner, 'Das Ärgernis der Repräsentation', reprinted in Ebner, *Schriften* (Munich, 1963), vol. 1, pp. 506–21. See also Gerhard Stieg, 'Ferdinand Ebners Kulturkritik am Beispiel der Salzburger Festspiele' in *Gegen den Traum vom Geist: Ferdinand Ebner*, ed. Walter Mathlagl and others (Salzburg, 1985), pp. 237–45.

32   See Beniston, *'Welttheater'*, pp.156–7; Michael P. Steinberg, *The Meaning of the Salzburg Festival: Austria as Theater and Ideology, 1890–1938* (Ithaca NY, 1990), p. 209.

33   'Verfälschung deutscher Kunst durch jüdische Dilettanten', *Deutscher Volksruf*, 19 March 1921; 'Kirchenschändung durch jüdische Schauspieler', *Der Eiserne Besen*, 7 August 1924; quoted in Günther Fellner, *Antisemitismus in Salzburg 1918–1938* (Vienna, 1979), pp. 103–4.

34   Karl Kraus, *Wolkenkuckucksheim* (Vienna, 1923), pp. 56–62 (= S 11, 151–5).

35   Kraus, *Wolkenkuckucksheim*, pp. 105–7 (= S 11, 191–2).

36   Kraus, *Wolkenkuckucksheim*, pp. 68 & 104 (= S 11, 160 & 190).

37   See Richard Steigmann-Gall, *The Holy Reich: Nazi Conceptions of Christianity 1919–1945* (Cambridge, 2003).

38   Kraus, *Wolkenkuckucksheim*, p. 120 (= S 11, 203).

Chapter 15

1   Elias Canetti, *Das Gewissen der Worte: Essays* (Munich, 1978), p. 41; *The Conscience of Words*, tr. Joachim Neugroschel (New York, 1979), p. 36.

2   Jonathan Swift, No. 38, in *The Examiner and Other Pieces* (Oxford, 1940), p. 141.

3   Rudolf von Ihering, *Der Kampf um's Recht*, 10th edn (Vienna, 1891), pp. 45–9.

4   Ihering, *Kampf um's Recht*, pp. 54–5.

5   Merkel, *Strafrecht und Satire*, pp. 280–1 & 332–3.

6 Reinhard Merkel, 'Zum Verhältnis zwischen Strafrecht und Satire im Werk von Karl Kraus', in *Literatur und Kritik*, 219–20 (November–December 1987), pp. 444–59 (p. 446).

7 For further details, see Merkel, *Strafrecht und Satire*, pp. 491–8.

8 See Ingo Müller, *Hitler's Justice: The Courts of the Third Reich*, tr. Deborah Lucas Schneider (London, 1991), pp. 36–9.

9 Kurt Tucholsky, 'Das Buch der deutschen Schande' in *Gesammelte Werke*, ed. Mary Gerold-Tucholsky and Fritz Raddatz, 3 vols (Reinbek bei Hamburg, 1960), 1, pp. 818–24 (p. 824).

10 Tucholsky, 'Prozess Harden' in *Gesammelte Werke*, 1, pp. 1070–8 (p. 1078).

11 See Emil Julius Gumbel, *Vier Jahre politischer Mord* (Berlin, 1922). For an account of the campaign against Gumbel, see Edgar Ansel Mowrer, *Germany Puts the Clock Back* (London, 1933), pp. 172–4.

12 Tucholsky, 'Deutsche Richter' in *Gesammelte Werke*, 2, pp. 771–83 (p. 775).

13 For a more detailed account, see Harold L. Poor, *Kurt Tucholsky and the Ordeal of Germany, 1914–1935* (New York, 1968), chapter 6: 'Tucholsky and the Communists'.

14 See Timms, *Karl Kraus – Apocalyptic Satirist* (1986), pp. 47–9.

15 *Karl Kraus contra . . . Die Prozeßakten der Kanzlei Oskar Samek*, ed. Hermann Böhm, 4 vols (Vienna, 1995–7). References to this edition are identified by the letter P (followed by the volume and page number).

16 White, *Justice as Translation*, pp. xiii-xiv.

17 This typology derives from Zygmunt Bauman, *Legislators and Interpreters: On Modernity, Post-Modernity and Intellectuals* (Ithaca NY, 1987), pp. 120–4.

18 Canetti, *Das Gewissen der Worte*, p. 41; *The Conscience of Words*, p. 31.

19 Franz Kafka, *Amtliche Schriften*, ed. Klaus Hermsdorf (Berlin, 1984), pp. 95–120 (p. 102).

20 *The Complete Short Stories of Franz Kafka*, ed. Nahum N. Glatzer, tr. Willa and Edwin Muir (Harmondsworth, 1983), p. 247; Kafka, *Die Erzählungen* (Frankfurt, 1961), pp. 289–90.

21 Ritchie Robertson, *Kafka: Judaism, Politics, and Literature* (Oxford, 1987), p. 175.

22 Elias Canetti, *Die Fackel im Ohr: Lebensgeschichte 1921–1931* (Frankfurt, 1982), p. 151; *The Torch in My Ear*, tr. Joachim Neugroschel (New York, 1982), p. 159.

23 Canetti, *Gewissen der Worte*, p. 40; *Conscience of Words*, p. 31.

24 Canetti, *Gewissen der Worte*, pp. 46–7; *Conscience of Words*, p. 36.

25 Walter Benjamin, *Gesammelte Schriften*, II, 1, p. 349. In this chapter the word 'Recht' is variously translated as 'right', 'law' and 'justice', depending on the ideological context.

26 Benjamin, *Gesammelte Schriften*, II, 2, p. 624.

27 Only in a later context does Kraus refer to Padajaunig by name (F 691–5, 113).

28 Tucholsky, 'Deutsche Richter' in *Gesammelte Werke*, 2, pp. 771–83 (p. 774).

29 Franz Kobler, 'The Contribution of Austrian Jews to Jurisprudence' in *The Jews of Austria: Essays on their Life, History and Destruction*, ed. Josef Fraenkel (London, 1967), pp. 25–40.

30 Georg Glockemeier, *Zur Wiener Judenfrage* (Leipzig and Vienna, 1936), p. 77; Steven Beller, *Vienna and the Jews 1867–1938: A Cultural History* (Cambridge, 1989), pp. 20 & 37.

31 Reported in *Die Stunde*, 1 February 1925, p. 6.

32 Ludwig Mitteis, *Reichsrecht und Volksrecht in den östlichen Provinzen des Römischen Kaiserreichs* (Leipzig, 1891).

33 See for example Helmut Nicholai, *Grundlagen der kommenden Verfassung: Über den staatsrechtlichen Aufbau des Dritten Reiches* (Berlin, 1933).

34 Othmar Spann, *Der wahre Staat* (Leipzig, 1921).

35 Helmut Nicholai, *Die rassengesetzliche Rechtslehre: Grundzüge einer nationalsozialistischen*

Rechtsphilosophie (Munich, 1933).

36   Manfred Baldus, 'Habsburgian Multiethnicity and the "Unity of the State": On the Structural Setting of Kelsen's Legal Thought' in *Hans Kelsen and Carl Schmitt: A Juxtaposition*, ed. Dan Diner and Michael Stolleis (Gerlingen, 1999), pp. 13–25.

37   Carl Schmitt, 'Das gute Recht der Revolution' in *Westdeutscher Beobachter*, 12 May 1933; quoted in Bernd Rüthers, 'On the Brink of Dictatorship: Hans Kelsen and Carl Schmitt in Cologne 1933' in *Hans Kelsen and Carl Schmitt: A Juxtaposition*, pp. 115–22 (p. 121).

38   Quoted in Raphael Gross, '"Jewish Law" and "Christian Grace": Carl Schmitt's Critique of Hans Kelsen' in *Hans Kelsen and Carl Schmitt: A Juxtaposition*, p. 103.

39   Carl Schmitt, *Der Begriff des Politischen* (Berlin, 1932), p. 55. The first edition of the book appeared in 1927.

40   In Franz Blei, *Das große Bestiarium der modernen Literatur* (Berlin, 1922). Kraus, in his comments on this book (F 601–7, 84–8), held Blei responsible for the caricature. For evidence of Schmitt's authorship, see Blei, *Erzählung eines Lebens*, ed. Ursula Pia Jauch (Vienna, 2004), p. 466.

41   See Horst Göppinger, *Juristen jüdischer Abstammung im 'Dritten Reich'* (Munich, 1990), pp. 34–41.

42   Josef Lang, *Erinnerungen des letzten Scharfrichters im k. k. Österreich*, ed. Oskar Schalk (Vienna, 1920); reprinted as *Die Erinnerungen des österreichischen Scharfrichters: Erweiterte, kommentierte und illustrierte Neuauflage*, ed. Harald Seyrl (Vienna, 1996).

43   Merkel, *Satire und Strafrecht*, p. 215.

44   Act V, scene 50: 'Magog: Rechtsordnung? Wir haben Gas!'

45   Hitler, *Mein Kampf* (Munich, 1939), p. 588. The number of German soldiers executed for desertion during the First World War was 48, compared with 346 in the British army, according to Müller, *Hitler's Justice*, p.182,

46   See the figures given in Müller, *Hitler's Justice*, pp. 184 & 196.

47   Gross, '"Jewish Law" and "Christian Grace"', pp. 104–7.

48   Dr Lothar Kreyssig, a member of the Confessional Church who protested against the euthanasia programme and was allowed to take early retirement. See Müller, *Hitler's Justice*, pp. 193–6.

49   Felix Frankfurter, *The Case of Sacco and Vanzetti* (Boston, March 1927), p. 43.

Chapter 16

1   Jansci Bekessy was so affected by his father's fall from grace that he changed his name to Hans Habe. His memoirs, *Ich stelle mich: Meine Lebensgeschichte*, 2nd edn (Munich, 1986), are an important source.

2   For an outline of Bekessy's early years, see the unsigned article of 22 April 1927 in the Hungarian weekly *Hetiujsag*, ed. Franz Falus (German translation in the Samek Collection, Vienna City Library, C 147.950).

3   Bekessy's personality is eloquently portrayed by his son Hans Habe in *Ich stelle mich*, which includes vivid accounts of the 'mental illness' episode (pp. 42–5) and the escape along the Danube (pp. 66–70).

4   Article of 22 April 1927 in the Hungarian weekly *Hetiujsag* (p. 7 of the German translation in the Samek Collection).

5   Emmerich Bekessy, 'Meine Freundschaft und Feindschaft mit Camillo Castiglioni', *Bekessy's Panoptikum*, No. 1 (April 1928), pp. 83–127. References to this compendium (only one number of which ever appeared) are identified in the text by the abbreviation BP, followed by page number.

6   Eduard März, *Österreichische Bankpolitik in der Zeit der großen Wende 1913–1923* (Vienna, 1981), p. 468.

7   For a detailed analysis of Kraus's view of Castiglioni, see Claudia Attlmayr, 'Die

Verwandlung des Bankiers Camillo Castiglioni in eine satirische Figur von Karl Kraus' (MA dissertation, Innsbruck, 1990).

8   Ernst Hanisch, *Der lange Schatten des Staates: Österreichische Gesellschaftsgeschichte im 20. Jahrhundert* (Vienna, 1994), pp. 282–3.

9   Karl Ausch, *Als die Banken fielen: Zur Soziologie der politischen Korruption* (Vienna, 1968), pp. 133–5.

10 Anna Eisenmenger, *Blockade: The Diary of an Austrian Middle-Class Woman 1914–1925* (New York, 1932), p. 222.

11 Ausch, *Als die Banken fielen*, p. 158.

12 Hugo Portisch, *Österreich I: Die unterschätzte Republik* (Vienna, 1989), p. 244.

13 Fritz Weber, 'Vor dem großen Krach: Die Krise des österreichischen Bankwesens in den zwanziger Jahren' (inaugural dissertation, Salzburg, 1991), p. 8; quoted in Hanisch, *Der lange Schatten des Staates*, p. 279.

14 Ausch, *Als die Banken fielen*, p. 170.

15 Ausch, *Als die Banken fielen*, pp. 192–6.

16 Ausch, *Als die Banken fielen*, p. 165.

17 Portisch, *Österreich I*, p. 122.

18 Ausch, *Als die Banken fielen*, pp. 124–7.

19 Habe, *Ich stelle mich*, p. 88.

20 See Attlmayr, 'Die Verwandlung des Bankiers', pp. 36–42.

21 'Der Prozess Bekessy: Stenographisches Protokoll der Schwurgerichtsverhandlung über die Privatanklage der Herausgeber des "Österreichischen Volkswirt" Walther Federn u. Dr Gustav Stolper gegen Emmerich Bekessy Herausgeber der "Börse" und der "Stunde" am 18. und 19. Jänner 1924' (Vienna, 1924), p. 30.

22 For an account of Stolper's campaign against Bekessy, see Stolper, *Ein Leben im Brennpunkt unserer Zeit*, pp. 151–8.

23 Anton Kutschera, '"Die Stunde" unter der Leitung ihres Herausgebers Emmerich Bekessy. Ein Beitrag zum Studium der Inflationspresse in Österreich' (doctoral dissertation, Vienna, 1952), pp. 312–13.

24 Karl Tschuppik, *Von Franz Joseph zu Adolf Hitler – Polemiken, Essays und Feuilletons*, ed. Klaus Amann (Vienna, 1982).

25 Letter of 6 April 1925 from Rechtsanwalt Dr Bruno Kurzweil (Graz) to Karl Kraus, confirming that 'die Ihnen nach dem Leibrentenvertrag vom 1.III.1912 zustehende Lebensrente von monatlich K 1000. - - gegenüber den Herren Alfred, Josef und Rudolf Kraus ab 1.III.1925 auf S 400. - - aufgewertet wurde'. Kraus Archive, IN 169.774.

26 'Aufzeichnung über die Besprechungen mit Herrn Arnold Rolleder in der Angelegenheit gegen Ely und die "Stunde"', Vienna, 26 May 1927, Samek Collection, Kraus Archive.

27 For a further account of this episode, see Ernst Spitz, *Bekessy's Revolver* (Vienna, 1926), pp. 33–5: 'Der Fall Reitzes'.

28 Kuh, *Luftlinien – Feuilletons, Essays und Publizistik* (Vienna, 1981), pp. 151–201; cf. the transcripts in the Samek Collection, C 147.950, Folder 10.

29 Kuh, *Luftlinien*, pp. 156, 167 & 172.

30 Samek Collection, C 147.950, Folder 4.

31 See Gulick, *Austria from Habsburg to Hitler*, 1, pp. 326–9.

32 Stolper expressed his dismay at the 'enfeeblement of public morality' in a valedictory article entitled 'Abschied von Österreich', published in the *Österreichische Volkswirt* on 26 September 1925; see Stolper, *Ein Leben im Brennpunkt unserer Zeit*, pp. 171–2.

33 See 'Protokoll mit Herrn Billie Wilder in den Redaktionsräumen der "Stunde"' (undated) and 'Protokoll über die Sitzung des Betriebsrates am 2. März in Angelegenheit des Ernst Spitz', copies of which are in the Samek Collection, C 147.950, Folder 17. Ernst Spitz, who made contact with Samek after his dismissal from

Die Stunde, evidently provided him with these stenographic records of discussions within the rival camp.

34   Spitz,*Bekessy's Revolver*, pp. 31–2: 'Bekessys Kaffeehaussteuer'.

35   Deposition by Josef Heller in the Samek Collection, C 147.950, Folder 15.

36   'Anläßlich der an Ihnen verübten beispiellosen Schuftentat und für deren männliche Abwehr drückt Ihnen in alter Achtung und Treue die Hand – Karl Kraus'; undated draft in Kraus's hand, Kraus Archive, IN 167.360.

37   Kraus fails to mention that Waldegg was sentenced to two years' imprisonment for banking fraud. See Ausch, *Als die Banken fielen*, pp. 168–72.

38   Habe, *Ich stelle mich,*, pp. 120–38; 'Rechtsanwälte [. . .] und Wahrsager', p. 122.

39   Robert Musil, *Tagebücher*, ed. Adolf Frisé, 2 vols (Reinbek bei Hamburg, 1976), 1, p. 634.

40   See Peter Chippindale and Chris Horrie, *Stick It up your Punter! The Rise and Fall of the 'Sun'* (London, 1990).

41   Tschuppik claimed to be following his conscience ('seinem Gewissen'), in so far as this was possible in writing for the capitalist press, in an article of 17 November 1923 in *Die Stunde* (Tschuppik, *Von Franz Joseph zu Adolf Hitler*, p. 29).

42   'Aufzeichnung über die Besprechungen mit Herrn Arnold Rolleder', dated 23 May and 26 May 1927 (Samek Collection). Rolleder, who had been a freelance at *Die Stunde*, suggested that 'Tschuppik und Kuh zu einander homosexuelle Beziehungen gehabt haben'. He also noted that, according to Ernst Ely, another journalistic colleague, Tschuppik's work as editor was impaired when he was under the influence of cocaine ('kokainisiert'). For Bekessy's reported comments on Kuh and Tschuppik as 'teils Säufer, teils Pederasten', see P 1, 177.

43   'Der Prozess Bekessy: Stenographische Protokoll', p. 5.

44   Kuh, *Luftlinien*, pp. 175–7.

45   Hans Habe, *Erfahrungen* (Freiburg, 1973), p. 44.

46   See Kierkegaard, *The 'Corsair' Affair and Articles Related to the Writings*, ed. and tr. by Howard V. Hong and Edna H. Hong (Princeton NJ, 1982), pp. ix & xviii.

47   One of Goldschmidt's reasons for giving up the *Corsair* was that he wished to avoid the implication that his writings were inspired by his 'caustic Jewish nature'. See *The 'Corsair' Affair*, p. 151.

48   When in December 1927 Bekessy is finally identified as 'ungarischer Jude', the phrase conveys the perspective of the Pan-German politician and Police Chief Johann Schober (F 771–6, 81).

49   Theodor Adorno, 'Sittlichkeit und Kriminalität' in *Gesammelte Schriften*, vol. 11 (Frankfurt, 1984), p. 372.

50   Maurice Zolotow, *Billy Wilder in Hollywood* (London, 1977), p. 29.

51   See Johann Georg Keith, 'A Comparison of Jonathan Swift's and Karl Kraus's Prose Satire' (doctoral dissertation, University of Cambridge, 1973), chapter IV (b): 'The Quantity of Ideas per Square Inch'.

52   Habe, *Ich stelle mich*, p. 112.

53   *Camillo Castiglioni oder die Moral der Haifische*, director Peter Patzak, script by Dieter Stiefel, Austria 1988.

54   Roth, *Das journalistische Werk*, 3, p. 723.

Chapter 17

1   Gulick, *Austria from Habsburg to Hitler*, 1, pp. 245–6 & 702–8.

2   The power of Kraus's reading of 'Weg damit!' can be judged from the gramophone recording he made in 1934, reissued by Preiser Records (PR 3017).

3   Cited in Norbert Leser, 'Der 15. Juli als Peripetie des Austromarxismus und der österreichischen Demokratie der Ersten Republik' in *1927 als die Republik brannte: Von*

Schattendorf bis Wien, ed. Norbert Leser and Paul Sailer-Wlasits (Vienna, 2002), pp. 53–92 (p. 70); cf. Rabinbach, *The Crisis of Austrian Socialism*, pp. 46–7.

4 Norbert Leser, 'Das Linzer Programm und der 15. Juli als Höhepunkt austromarxistischer Politik' in *Die Ereignisse des 15. Juli 1927*, ed. Rudolf Neck and Adam Wandruszka (Vienna, 1979), pp. 150–68 (p. 156).

5 Statement in the *Neue Freie Presse*, 14 January 1927, quoted in Klemperer, *Ignaz Seipel*, p. 255.

6 For details of this 'Kampf um [. . .] die Dorfstraße und das Wirtshaus', see Gerhard Botz, 'Der "Schattendorfer Zusammenstoß": Territorialkämpfe, Politik und Totschlag im Dorf' in *1927 als die Republik brannte*, pp. 11–31 (p. 18).

7 See Viktor Liebscher, 'Die österreichische Geschworenengerichtsbarkeit und die Juliereignisse 1927' in *Die Ereignisse des 15. Juli 1927*, pp. 60–99.

8 Gerald Stieg, *Frucht des Feuers: Canetti, Doderer, Kraus und der Justizpalastbrand* (Vienna, 1990), p. 28 ('das prekäre Gleichgewicht').

9 Norbert Leser, 'Der 15. Juli 1927, pp. 53–92 ('Ratlosigkeit und Inkompetenz', p. 77).

10 See Gerhard Botz, *Krisenzonen einer Demokratie: Gewalt, Streik und Konfliktunterdrückung in Österreich seit 1918* (Frankfurt, 1987), pp. 65–70.

11 Rainer Hubert, *Schober: 'Arbeitermörder' und 'Hort der Republik'* (Vienna, 1990), p. 207 ('Kette von Fehlern').

12 For the conflicting accounts of this episode given by Schober and Seitz, see Hubert, *Schober*, pp. 200–01.

13 See Winifried R. Garscha and Barry McLoughlin, *Wien 1927: Menetekel für die Republik* (Vienna, 1987), p. 125.

14 Karl Renner, 'Die Partei, die Koalition und die innere Abrüstung' in *Neues Wiener Tagblatt*, 12 November 1927; cited in Stieg, *Frucht des Feuers*, pp. 66–7.

15 Garscha and McLoughlin, *Wien 1927*, p. 156.

16 Klemperer, *Ignaz Seipel*, p. 269.

17 The closest parallel is provided by Los Angeles in April 1992. The acquittal of four policemen, who had been videoed as they beat up a black car driver, provoked several days of rioting, during which sixty protestors were killed.

18 Garscha and McLoughlin, *Wien 1927*, p. 132.

19 Garscha and McLoughlin, *Wien 1927*, p. 164.

20 Garscha and McLoughlin, *Wien 1927*, pp. 227–6; cf. Jacques Hannak, *Johannes Schober – Mittelweg in die Katastrophe. Porträt eines Repräsentanten der verlorenen Mitte* (Vienna, Frankfurt and Zurich, 1966), pp. 101–2.

21 *Ausschreitungen in Wien am 15. und 16. Juli 1927: Weissbuch herausgegeben von der Polizidirektion in Wien* (Vienna, October 1927); Robert Danneberg, *Die Wahrheit über die 'Polizeiaktion' am 15. Juli: Der Bericht der vom Wiener Gemeinderat zur Untersuchung der Ereignisse vom 15. Juli eingesetzten Kommission* (Vienna, 1927).

22 Erich Fried, *Mitunter sogar lachen: Erinnerungen* (Frankfurt, 1996), pp. 33–4.

23 Frank Field, *The Last Days of Mankind: Karl Kraus and his Vienna* (London, 1967), pp. 177–8.

24 See Timms, *Karl Kraus – Apocalyptic Satirist* (1986), pp. 332–3.

25 Arendt, *Eichmann in Jerusalem*, p. 54.

26 Cf. Christopher R. Browning, *Ordinary Men: Reserve Police Battalion 101 and the Final Solution in Poland* (New York, 1998), pp. 55–8 & 217–19; Ernst Klee, Willi Dressen and Volker Riess, *'Schöne Zeiten': Judenmord aus der Sicht der Täter und Gaffer* (Frankfurt, 1988); English translation by Deborah Burnstone under the title *'Those Were the Days'* (London, 1991), pp. 8–22 (with facsimile of the German logbook).

27 *Ausschreitungen in Wien am 15. und 16. Juli 1927*, p. 20.

28 G. E. R. Gedye, 'Some Aspects of the Vienna Disorders', *Contemporary Review*, 122, No. 741 (September 1927), pp. 305–11.

29 G. E. R. Gedye, *Fallen Bastions: The Central European Tragedy* (London, 1939), pp. 31–4.

30 For a lucid review of this question, see Stieg, *Frucht des Feuers*, pp. 39–65.
31 'Verlangen Sie nichts vom Parlament und von der Regierung, das den Opfern und Schuldigen an den Unglückstagen gegenüber milde scheint, aber grausam wäre gegenüber der verwundeten Republik'. Garscha and McLoughlin, *Wien 1927*, p. 242; cf. Klemperer, *Ignaz Seipel*, pp. 266–7.
32 For confirmation of this trend, which led Seipel to align himself with the Heimwehr, see Klemperer, *Ignaz Seipel*, pp. 289–92.
33 The two posters are reproduced side by side in *Tagebuch der Strasse: Geschichte in Plakaten*, ed. Bernhard Denscher (Vienna, 1981), pp. 176–7.
34 Canetti, *The Torch in my Ear*, pp. 244–6; *Die Fackel im Ohr*, p. 232.
35 For a fuller account of the context, see Stieg, *Frucht des Feuers*, pp. 65–9.
36 Stieg, *Frucht des Feuers*, pp. 60–5.
37 See Eckart Früh, 'Karl Kraus und der Kommunismus', *Zeitgeschichte*, 15, No. 8 (May 1988), pp. 315–36 (p. 319).
38 *Rotbuch gegen Schobers Weißbuch*, ed. Rote Hilfe (Vienna [1927]).
39 Quoted in Früh, 'Karl Kraus und der Kommunismus', p. 324.
40 See Borsányi, *Life of a Communist Revolutionary*, pp. 325–42.
41 Quoted in Früh, 'Karl Kraus und der Kommunismus', p. 324.
42 Hubert, *Schober*, pp. 251–9 (p. 255).

PART FIVE
Chapter 18

1 Heinrich Fischer, *Ungeschminkt: Ein Vortrag über Theater* (Vienna, 1932), pp. 6–10.
2 The abbreviation FS refers to the three volumes of Karl Kraus, *Frühe Schriften* (Munich, 1979–88), edited by the Dutch scholar Johannes J. Braakenburg with explanatory notes.
3 Cf. Hans Weigel, *Karl Kraus oder die Macht der Ohnmacht* (Vienna, 1968), p. 21; Manfred Schneider, *Die Angst und das Paradies des Nörglers*, p. 68.
4 Goblot, 'Les Parents de Karl Kraus', pp. 47 & 53.
5 For a review of these issues, see Gilbert J. Carr, 'The "Young" Kraus and the "Old" Burgtheater: Sources and Interpretations' in *Reading Karl Kraus: Essays on the Reception of 'Die Fackel*, pp. 23–39.
6 See *Burgtheater Wien 1776–1986: Ebenbild und Widerspruch*, ed. Reinhard Urbach and Achim Benning (Vienna, 1986), pp. 17–21; and W. E. Yates, *Theatre in Vienna* (Cambridge, 1997), p. 84.
7 See 'Sonnenthals Rollen im Burgtheater' in *Adolf von Sonnenthals Briefwechsel*, ed. Hermine von Sonnenthal, 2 vols (Stuttgart, 1912), 2, pp. 239–49 (p. 247). Sonnenthal first appeared in *King Lear* on 17 November 1889, a production which Kraus recalls in F 191, 22.
8 Simon Williams, *Shakespeare on the German Stage*, Vol. 1: *1586–1914* (Cambridge, 1990), p. 155.
9 Yates, *Theatre in Vienna*, p.76.
10 See Heinz Kindermann, *Shakespeare und das Burgtheater* (Vienna, 1964), pp. 17–21. Dingelstedt's stage design for *Antony and Cleopatra* (Fig. 19) resembles a Hollywood film set.
11 Burckhard's repertoire included Ibsen's *Enemy of the People* (October 1890), *The Pretenders* (April 1891), *The Feast at Solhaug* (November 1891) and *The Wild Duck* (January 1897); Hauptmann's *Einsame Menschen* (December 1891), *College Crampton* (February 1892), *Hanneles Himmelfahrt* (December 1893), *Die versunkene Glocke* (March 1897) and *Fuhrmann Henschel* (January 1899); and Schnitzler's *Liebelei* (October 1895).
12 Kari Grimstad, *Masks of the Prophet: The Theatrical World of Karl Kraus* (Toronto, 1982), pp. 49–50.

13   Ludwig Speidel, *Schauspieler* (Berlin, 1911), p. 170; see also 'Sonnenthal als Wallenstein', pp. 224–9.

14   *Sonnenthals Briefwechsel*, 2, pp. 98, 112–13, 117 and 170.

15   Immanuel Kant, *Kritik der Urteilskraft*, ed. Karl Vorländer (Leipzig, 1922), p. 122.

16   See also FS 2, 22; F 78, 22.

17   *Sonnenthals Briefwechsel*, 2, pp. 67–9 (Sonnenthal cites the phrase 'hot tears' in English).

18   The numerous sources cited in *Die Fackel* include Ludwig Speidel, *Schauspieler*; Auguste Wilbrandt-Baudius, *Erinnerungsskizzen einer alten Burgtheaterschauspielerin*; Ludwig Hevesi, *Zerline Gabillon: Ein Künstlerleben*; Helene Bettelheim-Gabillon, *Im Zeichen des alten Burgtheaters*; Jakob Minor, *Aus dem alten und neuen Burgtheater*; Adolf Wilbrandt, *Erinnerungen*; Heinrich Anschütz, *Erinnerungen*; Hermann Schöne, *Aus den Lehr- und Flegeljahren*; and Josef Lewinsky, *Kleine Schriften dramaturgischen und theatergeschichtlichen Inhalts*.

19   Aleida Assmann, *Erinnerungsräume: Formen und Wandlungen des kulturellen Gedächtnisses* (Munich, 1999).

20   The text of *Die Klabriaspartie* by Adolf Bergmann is reprinted in *Luftmenschen spielen Theater: Jüdisches Kabarett in Wien 1890–1938*, ed. Hans Veigl (Vienna, 1992).

21   Nahma Sandrow, *Vagabond Stars: A World History of Yiddish Theatre* (Syracuse NY, 1996), pp. 58 & 85.

22   See Georg Wacks, *Die Budapester Orpheumgesellschaft: Ein Varieté in Wien 1899–1919* (Vienna, 2002), pp. 40–55: 'Der jüdische Jargon'.

23   Karl Kraus to Otto Stoessl, 1 February 1909, in Karl Kraus and Otto Stoessl, *Briefwechsel 1902–1925*, ed. Gilbert J. Carr (Vienna, 1996), p. 95.

24   Wacks, *Die Budapester*, pp. 106–32.

25   See Wacks, *Die Budapester*, pp. 86–91.

26   Kokoschka, *My Life*, p. 47.

27   See Wacks, *Die Budapester*, pp. 65–6 & 205.

28   Gilman, *Jewish Self-Hatred*, p. 242.

29   See Timms, *Karl Kraus – Apocalyptic Satirist* (1986), p. 179.

30   For a further discussion of this motif, see Leo A. Lensing, 'Tiertheater: Textspiele der jüdische Identität bei Altenberg, Kraus und Kafka' in *Das jüdische Echo: Europäisches Forum für Kultur und Politik*, 48 (October 1999), pp. 79–86.

31   Robertson, *Kafka: Judaism, Politics, and Literature*, p. 34.

32   Evelyn Torton Beck, *Kafka and the Yiddish Theatre: Its Impact on his Work* (Madison WI, 1971), p. 30.

33   See Brigitte Dalinger, *Verloschene Sterne: Geschichte des jüdischen Theaters in Wien* (Vienna, 1998).

34   Beck, *Kafka and the Yiddish Theatre*, pp. 28 & 43 (on his 'difficulties' with Yiddish); Sandrow, *Vagabond Stars*, p. 160.

35   For a detailed commentary, see *Karl Kraus' 'Literatur oder Man wird doch da sehn'*, ed. Martin Leubner.

36   Max Brod, *Streitbares Leben* (Munich, 1960), p. 98.

37   Franz Kafka, *Briefe 1902–1924* (Frankfurt, 1958), pp. 336–7.

38   Kraus, *Literatur* (Vienna, 1921), p. 9: 'Alles spricht durcheinander, gestikuliert heftig'.

39   André Németh, *Kafka ou le mystère juif* (Paris, 1947), pp. 160–8; Mark Anderson, *Kafka's Clothes: Ornament and Aestheticism in the Habsburg Fin de Siècle* (Oxford, 1992), pp. 205–7.

40   From the tone of Kafka's comments, it seems unlikely that the book was *Untergang der Welt durch schwarze Magie*, as suggested in the recently published edition of Klopstock's papers, *Kafkas letzter Freund: Der Nachlaß Robert Klopstock*, ed. Hugo Wetscherek (Vienna, 2003), pp. 59–61 & 260.

41   Kafka, *Briefe 1902–1924*, pp. 380, 458–9 & 477.

42   *Kraus–Herwarth Walden Briefwechsel*, pp. 393–4.

43   Siegfried Jacobsohn to Karl Kraus, 20 December 1919, Kraus Archive, IN 140.867.

44 See further letters from Jacobsohn to Kraus in the Kraus Archive, esp. IN 140.841 (15 February 1918) and IN 140.846 (undated).
45 Berthold Viertel, 'Erinnerungen an Karl Kraus' in *Lynkeus* (Vienna, 1948–51), No. 3, pp. 16–20; reprinted in Viertel, *Kindheit eines Cherub: Autobiographische Fragmente* (Vienna, 1991), pp. 184–92.
46 For further details see 'Heinrich Fischer zum 22. August 1971', Sonderheft der Nachrichten aus dem Kösel-Verlag (Munich, 1971).
47 See 'Werbeschrift für die Gründung eines Theaters in Berlin' and 'Wege zur Truppe', two manuscripts written by Viertel in this period, published in Bertold Viertel, *Schriften zum Theater*, ed. Gert Heidenreich (Munich, 1970), pp. 247–54.
48 The première of the *Merchant of Venice* was followed by Kurt Hamsun's *Vom Teufel geholt* (6 October 1923); Georg Kaiser's *Nebeneinander* (15 November, with a set designed by George Grosz); Robert Musil's *Vinzenz und die Freundin bedeutender Männer* (2 December, with designs by Friedl Dicker); Eugene O'Neill's *Emperor Jones* (17 January 1924, designed by Friedrich Kiesler); and J. M. Synge's *The Playboy of the Western World* (directed by Heinz Hilpert), followed by Wedekind's *Liebestrank* (6 March 1924, also directed by Hilpert).
49 See Klaus Völker, 'Berthold Viertels dramatische Opposition und sein Bemühen um ein Theater der Ensemblekunst im Berlin der Zwanziger Jahre' in *Traum von der Realität: Berthold Viertel*, ed. Siglinde Bolbecher, Konstantin Kaiser and Peter Roessler (Vienna, 1998), pp. 99–120.
50 Unpublished letter of 12 February 1924 from Jacobsohn to Kraus, Kraus Archive, IN 138.006.
51 Gilbert J. Carr, '"Organic" Contradictions in Alfred Kerr's Theatre Criticism', *Oxford German Studies* 14 (1983), p. 120; see also Carr, 'Alfred Kerr, Theodor Wolff und Max Reinhardt' in *Kraus-Hefte*, 69 (January 1994), pp. 9–12.
52 In the five years 1928–33 Kraus gave eighty-five readings in Austria (all of them in Vienna) compared with eighty-eight in Germany (including fifty-one in Berlin). See Wolfgang Hink, *Die Fackel: Bibliographie und Register* (Munich, 1994), 2, pp. 214–16.
53 Marcel Reich-Ranicki, *Mein Leben* (Munich, 1999), p. 115; cf. *The Author of Himself: The Life of Marcel Reich-Ranicki*, tr. Ewald Osers (London, 2001), p. 77.
54 Heinrich Fischer, 'Some Personal Memories on Karl Kraus, Else Lasker-Schüler and Bertolt Brecht', unpublished typescript dated Oxford, 30 November 1964 (Timms Collection), p. 17.
55 See F 595–600, 52; F 806–9, 65; and F 885–7, 16–17.
56 Erwin Piscator, *Das politische Theater* (Reinbek, 1963), p. 227.
57 Heinrich Fischer, 'Die Unüberwindlichen' in *Stichwort: Zeitung des Theaters am Schiffbauerdamm*, No. 1 (September–December 1928).
58 Like Nestroy, Kraus had a gift for creating speaking names: 'Barkassy' suggests taking cash ('Bargeld') from the till ('Kasse').
59 Weigel, *Karl Kraus oder die Macht der Ohnmacht*, p. 231; Grimstad, *Masks of the Prophet*, p. 213.
60 Benjamin, *Gesammelte Schriften*, IV, 1, pp. 552–4.
61 For further details of the Sklareks, see Otto Friedrich, *Before the Deluge: A Portrait of Berlin in the 1920s* (London, 1974), pp. 314–15.
62 In 1929 Kraus's total earnings of over 120,000 Schilling from publications and recitals, offset by production costs of approximately 92,000 Schilling, yielded a taxable income of 28,836 Schilling. The losses incurred during the 1930s meant that the Verlag Die Fackel had to be subsidized from his earnings from recitals and broadcasts, supplemented by his private income. See Friedrich Pfäfflin, '"Meine materielle Sorge wurzelt in Prag": Revision einer Fehleinschätzung' in *Karl Kraus – in Jičin geboren*, pp. 71–82.
63 The play was taken up by left-wing companies, led by the 'Workers Theatre' section of the Leipzig Komödienhaus in November 1931, which also gave performances at the

Berlin Volksbühne the following month, watched by Kraus from the gallery (F 868–72, 13 & 27). There was a further production by the Vienna 'Proletarian Theatre' in May 1932 (S 11, 367).

Chapter 19

1 Goethe, 'Shakespeare und kein Ende' in *Werke*, ed. Erich Trunz (Munich, 1982), 12, pp. 288–9.
2 See Paul Stefanek, 'Karl Kraus versus Max Reinhardt' in *Max Reinhardt: The Oxford Symposium*, ed. Margaret Jacobs and John Warren (Oxford, 1986), pp. 112–23. See p. 193, n. 3 for Reinhardt's comment.
3 Leonhard M. Fiedler, 'Reinhardt, Shakespeare and the "Dreams"' in *Max Reinhardt: The Oxford Symposium*, p. 82.
4 Stefanek in *Max Reinhardt: The Oxford Symposium*, p. 121.
5 Reinhardt, 'Autobiographische Aufzeichnungen', quoted in Leonhard M. Fiedler, *Max Reinhardt* (Reinbek, 1975), p. 15.
6 Williams, *Shakespeare on the German Stage 1586–1914*, pp. 203–10 (p. 208).
7 Wilhelm Hortmann, *Shakespeare on the German Stage: The Twentieth Century* (Cambridge, 1998), pp. 30–4.
8 Friederike Hagel, 'Der Vorleser Karl Kraus' in *Kraus-Hefte*, 37 (January 1986), pp. 1–5.
9 See *Lyrik der Deutschen für seine Vorlesungen ausgewählt von Karl Kraus*.
10 T. S. Eliot, 'Tradition and the Individual Talent' (1919) in *Selected Prose*, ed. John Hayward (Harmondsworth, 1963), pp. 21–30.
11 From *Rundfrage über Karl Kraus* (Innsbruck, 1917), p. 14.
12 The statutes of 'Theater der Dichtung, Karl Kraus, Vorbereitende Vereinigung', which are located in the Allgemeines Verwaltungsarchiv: Bundeskanzleramt / Generaldirektion für die öffentliche Sicherheit (Geschäftszeichen 15/4 Wien/99), were reprinted by Eckart Früh in *Noch mehr* (Vienna, May 1986), pp. 14–18. A copy of the printed appeal is in the Kraus Archive.
13 See Peter Roessler, 'Das Reinhardt-Seminar 1928–1938' in *Ambivalenzen: Max Reinhardt und Österreich*, ed. Edda Fuhrich, Ulrike Dembski and Angela Eder (Vienna, 2004), pp. 161–83.
14 Kurt Krolop, 'Ebenbild und Gegenbild: Goethe und "Goethes Volk" bei Karl Kraus' in Krolop, *Sprachsatire als Zeitsatire*, pp. 192–209.
15 See also F 668–75, 154; F 686–90, 20; F 697–705, 64; F 717–23, 68; F 743–50, 116; F 751–6, 29; F 759–65, 77; F 912–15, 5.
16 *Helena: Klassisch-romantische Phantasmagorie. Zwischenspiel zu Faust*, published in volume 4 of the 'Ausgabe letzter Hand'.
17 Goethe's comments on the language of *Pandora* were reprinted in *Die Fackel* (F 554–6, 24), quoted at Kraus's recitations (F 726–9, 74) and included in his programme notes (F 668–75, 54).
18 Gottfried Diener, *Pandora – Zu Goethes Metaphorik: Entstehung, Epoche, Interpretation des Festspiels* (Bad Homburg, 1968), p. 8.
19 Kurt Wolff, *Autoren/Bücher/Abenteuer: Betrachtungen und Erinnerungen eines Verlegers* (Berlin, 1965), p. 86; Kurt Wolff, *A Portrait in Essays and Letters*, ed. Michael Ermarth, tr. Deborah Lucas Schneider (Chicago, 1991), pp. 93–4.
20 See *Goethes Werke* (Sophien-Ausgabe), vol. 50 (Weimar, 1900), pp. 339 & 451–6.
21 Goethe in conversation with the composer Zelter, 6 June 1825, cited in Manfred Osten, *'Alles veloziferisch' oder Goethes Entdeckung der Langsamkeit* (Frankfurt, 2003), p. 11.
22 'fremdartige Versmaße'; Eduard Engel, *Goethe: Der Mann und das Werk*, 2 vols (Braunschweig, 1923), 2, p. 652.
23 *Karl Kraus liest Eigenes und Angeeignetes* (Supplement to *Marbacher Kataloge 52* incorpo-

rating three CDs of historical recordings), ed. Friedrich Pfäfflin and Eva Dambacher (Marbach, 1999), p. 16.

24   The words, so well known that Kraus does not need to quote them directly, are usually printed in the form 'er kann mich – – – '; see *Goethes Werke* (Hamburger Ausgabe in 14 Bänden), 4, p. 139.

25   Paul Eisner, 'Karl Kraus liest Goethes Pandora', *Prager Presse*, 12 November 1932 (cited F 885–7, 9).

26   See Irmgard Schartner, *Karl Kraus und die Musik* (Frankfurt, 2002), for a systematic account of the role of music in Kraus's public readings; especially pp. 289–317 (for the memoirs of his accompanists); also Knepler, *Karl Kraus liest Offenbach*, pp. 15–18.

27   *Karl Kraus liest Eigenes und Angeeignetes*, pp. 40–2.

28   *Karl Kraus liest Eigenes und Angeeignetes*, p. 48.

29   Mittler's score is reproduced in Schartner, *Karl Kraus und die Musik*, pp. 182–4. For further details of his career, see Diana Mittler-Battipaglia, *Franz Mittler: Austro-American Composer, Musician, and Humorous Poet* (New York, 1993).

30   All seven adaptations are available in one volume in Karl Kraus, *Theater der Dichtung: Shakespeare* (Schriften, vol. 15), ed. Christian Wagenknecht (Frankfurt, 1994), abbreviated in the text as S 15.

31   Compare William Shakespeare, *The Complete Works*, ed. Stanley Wells and Gary Taylor (Oxford, 1988), pp. 936 and 969.

32   See Schartner, *Karl Kraus und die Musik*, pp. 174–7.

33   Schartner, *Karl Kraus und die Musik*, pp. 192–9 & 223–4; cf. Timms, *Karl Kraus – Apocalyptic Satirist* (1986), p. 384.

34   Schartner, *Karl Kraus und die Musik*, pp. 361–2.

35   Brecht, *Werke*, ed. Werner Hecht and others (Berlin and Frankfurt, 1989–2000) 21, pp. 153–5; and 26, p. 237.

36   James K. Lyon, 'Das dialektische Verhältnis Karl Kraus–Bertolt Brecht' in *Karl Kraus: Diener der Sprache, Meister des Ethos*, ed. Joseph P. Strelka, pp. 267–85 (p. 270).

37   Fischer, 'Some Personal Memories', p. 31.

38   Ernst Josef Aufricht, *Erzähle, damit du dein recht erweist* (Berlin, 1966), p. 73. The typescript in the Brecht Archive confirms that the second strophe did not form part of the original script, but was added at a later stage. See Lyon, 'Das dialektische Verhältnis Karl Kraus–Bertolt Brecht', p. 271.

39   Kurt Krolop, 'Bertolt Brecht und Karl Kraus' in Krolop, *Sprachsatire als Zeitsatire*, pp. 252–303 (p. 255).

40   Canetti, *Die Fackel im Ohr*, p. 259; *The Torch in my Ear*, p. 278.

41   Bertolt Brecht, *Arbeitsjournal*, 3 vols (Frankfurt, 1973), 1, p. 493.

42   Krolop, *Sprachsatire als Zeitsatire*, p. 352, n. 42.

43   Brecht, *Werkausgabe*, 19, p. 431.

44   Heinrich Fischer, 'Karl Kraus und seine "Fackel": Zum 25. Todestag' in *Süddeutsche Zeitung*, 3/4 June 1961: '"Das halte ich für witziger als zehn deutsche Lustspiele"'.

45   Canetti, 'Karl Kraus – Schule des Widerstands' in *Das Gewissen der Worte*, pp. 39–49 (p. 42).

46   Canetti in 'Akustische Maske und Maskensprung', an interview with Manfred Durzak, in *Zu Elias Canetti*, ed. Manfred Durzak (Stuttgart, 1983), pp. 17–30 (p. 22).

47   Fischer, 'Some Personal Memories', pp. 19–20.

48   The alleged 'alliance' ('Bündnis') with communism is emphasized in Friedrich Rothe, *Karl Kraus: Die Biographie* (Munich, 2003), pp. 17–22.

49   See Leo Lensing, '"Kinodramatisch": Cinema in Karl Kraus' *Die Fackel* and *Die letzten Tage der Menschheit*', *German Quarterly*, 55, No. 4 (1982), pp. 480–98.

50   Fischer, 'Some Personal Memories', p. 31.

51   António Joaquim Coelho de Sousa Ribiero, 'Karl Kraus e Shakespeare: Uma Poética da Citação' (doctoral dissertation, University of Coimbra, 1991), pp. 799–800.

52 Richard Flatter, *Karl Kraus als Nachdichter Shakespeares: Eine sprachkritische Untersuchung* (Vienna, n.d.).

53 See Michael Rogers, 'Kraus and Shakespeare: A Dramaturgical Investigation', *Modern Language Review*, 88 (1993), pp. 912–22 (p. 920).

54 See Williams, *Shakespeare on the German Stage*, chapter 5: 'Shakespeare at the Weimar Court Theatre'.

55 Flatter, *Karl Kraus als Nachdichter Shakespeares*, pp. 53–71.

56 See Hortmann, *Shakespeare on the German Stage*, pp. 5–7 (for the influence of Friedrich Gundolf) and pp. 51–2 (for a summary of the 'battle for Shakespeare').

57 See Hedges, *War is a Force that Gives us Meaning*, pp. 25–30 and 90. *Troilus and Cressida* is quoted at length by Hedges, who had a volume of Shakespeare in his pocket when he was captured at Basra in 1991 by the Iraqi Republican Guard.

58 H. A. L. Fisher, *A History of Europe* (London, 1936), p. v.

Chapter 20

1 Karl Kraus, *Zeitstrophen* (Vienna, 1931). The abbreviation S 14 (followed by page number) refers to Kraus, *Theater der Dichtung / Nestroy / Zeitstrophen*, ed. Christian Wagenknecht (Frankfurt, 1992), which also contains previously unpublished verses from Kraus's literary estate.

2 See Paul Peters, *Die Wunde Heine: Zur Geschichte des Heine-Bildes in Deutschland* (Bodenheim, 1997).

3 Gustav Karpeles, 'Heinrich Heine', *Ost und West*, 6, No. 1 (1906), p. 28; quoted in *The Jewish Reception of Heinrich Heine*, ed. Mark H. Gelber (Tübingen, 1992), pp. 143–4.

4 For a systematic interpretation of Kraus's hostility towards Heine as a response to the crisis of modernity, see Dietmar Goltschnigg, *Die Fackel ins wunde Herz: Kraus über Heine* (Vienna, 2002), pp. 15–110.

5 *Heinrich Heines Sämtliche Werke*, ed. Oskar Walzel, 10 vols (Leipzig, 1911), 2, pp. 139–40: 'Das neue Israelitische Hospital zu Hamburg'.

6 Robertson, *The 'Jewish Question' in German Literature 1749–1939*, p. 319.

7 F. R. Leavis, *Revaluation: Tradition and Development in English Poetry* (London, 1936, repr. 1957), pp. 203–32.

8 See Goltschnigg, *Die Fackel ins wunde Herz*, pp. 71–2 (for an example of misleading quotation) and 87 (on the question of antisemitic stereotypes).

9 Andreas Disch, *Das gestaltete Wort: Die Idee der Dichtung im Werk von Karl Kraus* (Zurich, 1969), p. 118.

10 Mechtild Borries, *Ein Angriff auf Heinrich Heine: Kritische Betrachtungen zu Karl Kraus* (Stuttgart, 1971), p. 56.

11 Theodor Adorno, *Noten zur Literatur* (Berlin and Frankfurt, 1958), pp. 144–52.

12 Timms, *Karl Kraus – Apocalyptic Satirist* (1986), pp. 320–1.

13 See Jens Malte Fischer, *Studien zum 'Theater der Dichtung' und Kulturkonservatismus* (Kronberg, 1973), pp. 153–70.

14 Borries, *Ein Angriff*, pp. 62–3.

15 Borries, *Ein Angriff*, pp. 80–7.

16 An earlier version of this argument was published in *Heine und die Weltliteratur*, ed. T. J. Reed and Alexander Stillmark (Oxford, 2000), pp. 168–81.

17 *Heines Werke*, 3, p. 362.

18 *Heines Werke*, 3, p. 357.

19 *Heines Werke*, 2, p. 285.

20 'ein wortspielerischer, kreativer Anarchismus, den [. . . Karl Kraus . . .] zeit seines Lebens heftig bekämpfen wird'; Goldschnigg, *Die Fackel ins wunde Herz*, p. 34.

21 Morgenstern, *Alban Berg*, p. 70.

22   Compare 'Das goldene Kalb' in *Heines Werke*, 3, p. 38.

23   Quoted in Stieg, *Der Brenner und Die Fackel*, p. 210.

24   The first volume of what was planned as a twenty-volume edition was *Eine Wohnung ist zu vermieten* (Johann Nestroys ausgewählte Werke), ed. von L. Liegler (Vienna: R. Lanyi, 1925). See also Gerald Stieg, 'Ist Nestroy ein Wiener Dialektdichter?' in *Johann Nestroy 1801–1862: Vision du monde et écriture dramatique*, ed. Gerald Stieg and Jean-Marie Valentin (Asnières, 1991), pp. 157–64.

25   See Junk's memoirs, quoted in Schartner, *Karl Kraus und die Musik*, pp. 298–300.

26   See the discussion of J. L. Austin's ideas in Judith Butler, *Excitable Speech: The Politics of the Performative* (New York, 1997), pp. 2–10.

27   See the tribute to Kraus's recitals in Soyfer's essay 'Vom lebendigen Nestroy: Zum 75. Todestag' (1937) in Jura Soyfer, *Die Ordnung schuf der liebe Gott: Eine Auswahl*, ed. Werner Martin (Leipzig, 1979), p. 56.

28   For a full account, see Schartner, *Karl Kraus und die Musik*, pp. 13–91.

29   Memoirs of Viktor Junk, quoted in Schartner, *Karl Kraus und die Musik*, p. 302.

30   'Autorgut der musikalischen Idee'; draft letter in Kraus's hand, quoted in Schartner, *Karl Kraus und die Musik*, pp. 303–6; Kraus Archive IN 169.199.

31   Letter of 4/5 December 1922 from Kraus to Lichnowsky in *Karl Kraus und Mechtilde Lichnowsky*, p. 135.

32   See Otto Rommel, 'Johann Nestroy: Der Satiriker auf der Altwiener Komödien-bühne' in Nestroy, *Gesammelte Werke in sechs Bänden* (Vienna, 1962), 1, p. 175; Franz H. Mautner, *Nestroy* (Heidelberg, 1974), p. 13.

33   *Karl Kraus und Mechtilde Lichnowsky*, p. 108 (letter of 29/30 March 1922).

34   In Knepler, *Karl Kraus liest Offenbach*, p. 212, the capacities of the halls used for Kraus's recitals are listed as follows: 'Architektenvereinssaal 270, Großer Konzerthaussaal etwas über 2000, Mittlerer Konzerthaussaal 890, Kleiner Konzerthaussaal 420, Kleiner Musikvereinssaal 520, Offenbachsaal 567, Gewerbevereinssaal etwa 300, Ehrbarsaal 419'.

35   Friedrich C, Heller and Peter Revers, *Das Wiener Konzerthaus: Geschichte und Bedeutung 1913–1983* (Vienna, 1983), pp. 148–60.

36   Canetti, *Die Fackel im Ohr*, pp. 67–70; cf. *The Torch in my Ear*, pp. 69–71; Canetti, *Das Gewissen der Worte*, pp. 39–49; cf. *The Conscience of Words*, pp. 29–39; *Zu Elias Canetti*, ed. Manfred Durzak, p. 18.

Chapter 21

1   See Marc A. Weiner, *Arthur Schnitzler and the Crisis of Musical Culture* (Heidelberg, 1986).

2   Julian Johnson, 'The Reception of Karl Kraus by Schönberg and his School' in *Reading Karl Kraus: Essays on the Reception of 'Die Fackel'*, p. 100.

3   Ernst Krenek, *Zur Sprache gebracht* (Munich, 1958), p. 224.

4   Harry Zohn, 'Das Wienerlied als Psychogramm einer Bevölkerung' in *Literatur und Kritik*, 239–40 (November–December 1989), pp. 452–65 (p. 457).

5   The original title of the Strauss waltz was not 'An der schönen blauen Donau' but 'Wiener seid froh', and the text mocking the Jews for transforming the Ringstrasse into 'ein neues Jerusalem' was by Josef Weyl. See *quasi una fantasia: Juden und die Musikstadt Wien*, ed. Leon Botstein and Werner Hanak (Vienna, 2003), p. 23.

6   *Wiener Lieder und Tänze* (Im Auftrage der Gemeindevertretung der Stadt Wien), ed. Eduard Kremser (Vienna, 1912), 1, p. 6.

7   See Camille Crittenden, *Johann Strauss and Vienna: Operetta and the Politics of Popular Culture* (Cambridge, 2000), p. 104.

8   See *Sag zum Abschied. . . Wiener Publikumslieblinge in Bild und Ton* (exhibition catalogue of the Historical Museum of the City of Vienna, 1992).

9   'Der kleine Kohn' by J. Einödshofer (Verlag H. Augustin, Berlin) is quoted from a brochure circulated during the Munich Oktoberfest entitled *Andenken an die 'Bräuros'l*. I am grateful to Dr Gertraud Pressler of the Archiv Wiener Volksliedwerk for tracing the text.

10 See Stekel's essay 'Der "kleine Kohn"', reprinted in *Aus dem Kreis um Sigmund Freud*, ed. Ernst Federn and Gerhard Wittenberger (Frankfurt, 1992), pp. 220–7.

11 Dietz Bering, *The Stigma of Names*, tr. Neville Plaice (Cambridge, 1992), pp. 149–54.

12 Stefan Frey, *Franz Lehar oder das schlechte Gewissen der leichten Musik* (Tübingen, 1955), pp. 32 & 36.

13 For an analysis of this technique of quotational satire, see Helmut Arntzen, 'Exkurs über Karl Kraus' in *Deutsche Literatur im 20. Jahrhundert*, ed. Hermann Friedmann and Otto Mann (Heidelberg, 1961), 1, pp. 244–55.

14 'We don't want to fight, but, by jingo, if we do, / We've got the ships, we've got the men, we've got the money too.' Song by G. W. Hunt, *Oxford Dictionary of Quotations* (Oxford, 2001), p. 395.

15 Robert Service, *Rhymes of a Red Cross Man* (New York, 1916), quoted in Glen Watkins, *Proof through the Night: Music and the Great War* (Berkeley CA, 2003), p. 74.

16 Hugo Zuckermann, a lawyer who volunteered for military service in 1914 and died of his wounds on 23 December of the same year.

17 Stan Czech, *Franz Lehar: Weg und Werk* (Berlin, 1940), pp. 149–64.

18 See Martin Lichtfuss, *Operette im Ausverkauf: Studien zum Libretto des musikalischen Unterhaltungstheaters im Österreich der Zwischenkriegszeit* (Vienna, 1989), p. 30.

19 See Peter Conrad, *Modern Times, Modern Places* (London, 1998), chapter 2: 'The End of the World in Vienna', esp. p. 51.

20 See Peter Hawig, *Dokumentarstück – Operette – Welttheater: 'Die letzten Tage der Menschheit' in der literarischen Tradition* (Essen, 1984); Elgin Bohnenkamp, 'Kommentare zur Musik in den "Letzten Tagen der Menschheit"', *Kraus-Hefte*, 46 (April 1988), pp. 1–8; Gerald Stieg, '*Die letzten Tage der Menschheit* – Eine negative Operette?' in *Österreich und der große Krieg*, pp. 180–5.

21 The sources of many of the songs alluded to in *Die letzten Tage der Menschheit* are identified in Schartner, *Karl Kraus und die Musik*, pp. 200–14. In 'Rosa, wir fahren nach Lodz', a marching song written by Fritz Beda-Löhner, a soldier abandons his bride for a 30.5cm mortar (nicknamed 'Rosa').

22 Bernard Grun, *Prince of Vienna: The Life, the Times and the Melodies of Oscar Straus* (London, 1955), pp. 45–53.

23 Moritz Csaky, *Ideologie der Operette und Wiener Moderne: Ein kulturhistorischer Essay zur österreichischen Identität* (Vienna, 1996), pp. 48, 54, 64–5 & 101.

24 Csaky, *Ideologie der Operette*, pp. 25–7 & 291–3.

25 Frey, *Franz Lehar*, p. 168.

26 Lichtfuss, *Operette im Ausverkauf*, pp. 108–9 & 134–40.

27 'Du, nur du' was the title of a popular song of the inter-war period, with music by Ernst Arnold. See Christian Seiler, *Die beliebtesten Schlager der 20er Jahre*, ed. Christian Seiler (Vienna, n.d.), p. 176.

28 Lichtfuss, *Operette im Ausverkauf*, pp. 31–3.

29 For a detailed analysis of the *Friederike* libretto, see Lichtfuss, *Operette im Ausverkauf*, pp. 285–91.

30 Joseph Wulf, *Musik im Dritten Reich: Eine Dokumentation* (Frankfurt, 1983), pp. 437ff.

31 Czech, *Franz Lehar*, p. 160.

32 Frey, *Franz Lehar*, pp. 138–44.

33 Robert Dachs, *Sag beim Abschied. . .* (Vienna, 1997), pp. 195–8; Spotts, *Hitler and the Power of Aesthetics*, p. 263.

34 See the memoirs of German veterans, cited in Antony Beevor, *Stalingrad* (London, 1999), p. 307. For details of the operetta, see Norbert Linke, *Franz Lehar* (Reinbek bei

Hamburg, 2001), pp. 86–7 & 119; and Czech, *Franz Lehar*, p. 226.

35   This dialogue, 'Ist die Folter in Österreich abgeschafft?' ('Torture in Austria'), was written by the music critic Robert Hirschfeld and revised by Kraus. See Kraus and Stoessl, *Briefwechsel 1902–1925*, p. 183.

36   See Henry-Louis de la Grange, *Gustav Mahler*, vol. 2: *Vienna: The Years of Challenge (1897–1904)* (Oxford, 1995), esp. chapters 5 & 7.

37   Walter Rathenau, *An Deutschlands Jugend* (Berlin, 1918), p. 83.

38   Weininger, *Geschlecht und Charakter*, p. 414: 'sein Siegfried das Unjüdischeste ist, was erdacht werden konnte'.

39   See William J. McGrath, *Dionysian Art and Populist Politics in Austria* (New Haven, 1974).

40   Brigitte Hamann, *Hitlers Wien: Lehrjahre eines Diktators* (Munich, 1996), pp. 43–4.

41   See Hans-Heinrich Wilhelm, 'Houston Stewart Chamberlain und Karl Kraus: Ein Bericht über ihren Briefwechsel 1901–1904' in *Zeitgeschichte*, 10, Nos 11–12 (August–September 1983), pp. 405–34.

42   Richard Wagner, 'Wollen wir hoffen?' in *Sämtliche Schriften und Dichtungen* (Leipzig: Breitkopf & Härtel, Volksausgabe, Sechste Auflage, n.d.), 10, pp. 132ff.

43   For a more detailed discussion, see Timms, *Karl Kraus – Apocalyptic Satirist* (1986), pp. 91–3.

44   Yates, *Theatre in Vienna*, pp. 155f.

45   Watkins, *Proof through the Night*, p.18.

46   Henry and Mary Garland, *The Oxford Companion to German Literature* (Oxford, 1976), p. 636.

47   Wagner, *Sämtliche Schriften und Dichtungen*, 5, pp. 75–9. Cf. *Wagner on Music and Drama: A Compendium of Richard Wagner's Prose Works*, tr. H. Ashton Ellis (New York, 1981), pp. 54–8.

48   Kraus was not alone in harbouring these suspicions. See Brendan G. Carroll, *The Last Prodigy: A Biography of Erich Wolfgang Korngold* (Portland OR, 1997), pp. 47, 61 & 65–7.

49   Wagner, *Sämtliche Schriften und Dichtungen*, 9, pp. 35 & 57.

50   Wagner, *Sämtliche Schriften und Dichtungen*, 8, pp. 252.

51   Friedrich Nietzsche, *Werke in drei Bänden*, ed. Karl Schlechta (Munich, 1966), 3, p. 441.

52   *Kraus–Walden Briefwechsel*, p. 387. See also pp. 139, 162 & 190.

53   Quoted in Friedrich Pfäfflin, 'Karl Kraus und Arnold Schönberg' in *Text + Kritik: Sonderband Karl Kraus*, ed. Heinz Ludwig Arnold (Munich, 1975), p. 135.

54   *Rundfrage über Karl Kraus* (Innsbruck, 1917), p. 21.

55   See 'Arnold Schönberg und Karl Kraus: Künstler und Kritiker', in *Marbacher Kataloge 52*, ed. Ulrich Ott and Friedrich Pfäfflin, pp. 361–73.

56   Alexander Goehr, 'Schoenberg und Karl Kraus: The Idea behind the Music' in *Music Analysis*, 4, Nos 1–2 (March–July 1985), pp. 59–71 (p. 62).

57   Arnold Schoenberg, 'The Relationship to the Text' in Schoenberg, *Style and Idea*, tr. D. Newlin (London, 1951), pp. 141–5.

58   Schoenberg, *Style and Idea*, pp. 105 & 193.

59   Quoted in Julian Johnson, *Anton Webern and the Transformation of Nature* (Cambridge, 1999), p. 83.

60   Ernst Krenek, 'Anton Webern: A Profile'; quoted in Johnson, *Anton Webern*, p. 233.

61   Johnson, *Anton Webern*, pp. 134–8 & 146.

62   Anne C. Shreffler, *Webern and the Lyrical Impulse: Songs and Fragments on Poems by Georg Trakl* (Oxford, 1994), pp. 59–61.

63   Letter of 25 July 1909 from Webern to Helene Nahowski; letter of 7 May 1912 from Webern to Alban Berg; quoted in Susanne Rode, *Alban Berg und Karl Kraus* (Frankfurt, 1988), p. 131.

64   Anton Webern, *The Path to the New Music*, ed. Willi Reich (Bryn Mawr PA, 1963), pp. 9–10 & 13–15; cf. the German edition *Der Weg zur neuen Musik*, (Vienna, 1960).
65   Kraus, *Sprüche und Widersprüche* (Munich, 1909), p. 133; revised and republished (with different pagination) by Verlag 'Die Fackel' in 1924.
66   Johnson, *Anton Webern*, p. 211.
67   Quoted in Robert Craft, 'Rondo with primroses: The musical and botanical life of Anton Webern', *Times Literary Supplement*, 12 November 2004, p. 14.
68   Johnson, *Anton Webern*, pp. 159–60.
69   See Watkins, *Proof through the Night*, chapter 13: 'The Last Days of Mankind', esp. pp. 233–40.
70   Willi Reich, *The Life and Work of Alban Berg*, tr. Cornelius Cardew (London, 1965), pp. 156–9.
71   Rode, *Alban Berg und Karl Kraus*, pp. 79 & 349.
72   Compare Alban Berg's letter of November 1914 to Paul Hohenberg with his letter of 27 November 1919 to Erwin Schulhoff; quoted in Rode, *Alban Berg und Karl Kraus*, pp. 134 & 140.
73   Quoted in Rode, *Alban Berg und Karl Kraus*, p. 62.
74   Rode, *Alban Berg und Karl Kraus*, pp. 92, 111, 122, 141 & 204.
75   Rode, *Alban Berg und Karl Kraus*, p. 401.
76   Morgenstern, *Alban Berg und seine Idole*, pp. 392–3.
77   Rode, *Alban Berg und Karl Kraus*, pp. 224–33.
78   Rode, *Alban Berg und Karl Kraus*, pp. 192–203 & 302–7.
79   Douglas Jarman, *The Music of Alban Berg* (Berkeley CA, 1979), pp. 140–1.
80   Johnson, 'The Reception of Karl Kraus by Schönberg and his School', p. 104.
81   Jarman, *Music of Alban Berg*, pp. 208 and 233.
82   Rode, *Alban Berg und Karl Kraus*, p. 215.
83   *Stimmen über Karl Kraus* (Vienna, 1934), p. 43.

Chapter 22

1   For details of Kraus's accompanists, see Schartner, *Karl Kraus und die Musik*, pp. 145–70 & 378.
2   Knepler, *Karl Kraus liest Offenbach*, p. 17; Franz Mittler, '"Es war nicht leicht, aber schön . . ."', *Forum*, 3, No. 30 (1956), p. 295; cf. Mittler-Battipaglia, *Franz Mittler*.
3   Knepler, *Karl Kraus liest Offenbach*, p. 111.
4   Kurt Arnold Findeisen, *Das Leben ein Tanz, der Tanz ein Leben: Der Walzerkönig Johann Strauß und seine Zeit* (Leipzig, 1941), p. 41; quoted in Crittenden, *Johann Strauss and Vienna*, p. 107.
5   Volker Klotz, *Operette: Porträt und Handbuch einer unerhörten Kunst* (Munich, 1991), pp. 25–41 & 109–26.
6   'sozialer Rollentausch'; Knepler, *Karl Kraus liest Offenbach*, p. 20.
7   Knepler, *Karl Kraus liest Offenbach*, pp. 130–8.
8   Kraus, *Zeitstrophen* (Vienna, 1931).
9   Fischer, 'Some Personal Memories', pp. 31–2.
10   For a fine account of Musil's ideas, see David S. Luft, *Eros and Inwardness in Vienna: Weininger, Musil, Doderer* (Chicago, 2003), pp. 91–134.
11   Hans Weigel, *Karl Kraus oder Die Macht der Ohnmacht* (Vienna, 1968), pp. 240–2. For an appreciation of Kraus's version of the letter aria in *Perichole*, see Werner Kraft, *Karl Kraus: Beiträge zum Verständnis seines Werkes* (Salzburg, 1956), pp. 146–59.
12   Kraus encouraged his readers to study his translations, which were partly based on earlier German versions, by including extensive passages from the French libretti as appendices to his editions. In this case he took considerable liberties with the original: 'Ces paroles-là sont cruelles, / Je le sais bien . . . mais que veux-tu? / Pour les choses

essentielles / Tu peux compter sur mon vertu' (S 13, 239).

13 Kraus, *Worte in Versen*, vol. 9 (Vienna, 1930), p. 45 (= S 9, 608).

14 For parallel developments in English writing, especially Virginia Woolf's novel *Mrs Dalloway*, see Sherry, *The Great War and the Language of Modernism*, pp. 283–93.

15 Joan Allen Smith, *Schoenberg and his Circle: A Viennese Portrait* (New York, 1986), p. 99 (oral history interview).

16 *Karl Kraus liest Eigenes und Angeeignetes: Originaltonaufnahmen auf 3 CDS*, Marbach: Deutsches Literaturarchiv, 1999.

17 Benjamin, *Schriften*, II, 2, pp. 515–17.

18 Letter from Hofmannsthal to Strauss, quoted in Norman del Mar, *Richard Strauss: A Critical Commentary on his Life and Works*, vol. 2 (London, 1969), pp. 221–2.

19 Cf. del Mar, *Richard Strauss*, 2, p. 235; Matthew Boyden, *Richard Strauss* (London, 1999), pp. 262–3.

20 See Kessler, *Tagebücher 1918–1937*, p. 563 (14 June 1928).

21 The name 'Gerda Mücke' had featured in an earlier satire on chauvinistic attitudes towards prostitutes (F 413–17, 14).

22 del Mar, *Richard Strauss*, 2, pp. 237–63. For an alternative view, see Michael Kennedy, *Richard Strauss: Man, Musician, Enigma* (Cambridge, 1999), pp. 229–34.

23 Kraus, *Zeitstrophen*, pp. 11, 29, 38 & 59.

24 Ernst Krenek, *Im Atem der Zeit: Erinnerungen an die Moderne*, tr. Friedrich Saathen (Hamburg, 1998), p. 393.

25 Quoted in *Ernst Krenek: Zeitgenosse des 20. Jahrhunderts*, ed. Matthias Schmidt (Vienna, 2000), p. 52 (article by Albrecht Dümling).

26 Phyllis Rose, *Black Cleopatra: Josephine Baker in her Time* (London, 1990), p. 31.

27 *Der hoffnungslose Radikalismus der Mitte*, pp. 8n. & 190.

28 For Krenek's own account, which stresses his use of 'Krausian dialogue', see *Im Atem der Zeit*, pp. 756–62.

29 For further details, see Meret Forster, *Reflexe kultureller Modernisierung: Ernst Kreneks Radikalismus der Mitte und der Einfluss von Karl Kraus* (Frankfurt, 2004), pp. 137–54. The entrepreneur's original (Jewish-sounding) name Goldstein was amended to Kabuleke for the planned performance.

30 Further settings of Kraus texts by avant-garde composers include 'Bange Stunde' by Josef Matthias Hauer and 'Die letzte Nacht' by Hanns Eisler. See *Kraus-Hefte*, 46 (April 1988), p. 12.

31 Rode, *Alban Berg und Karl Kraus*, p. 183.

32 Krenek, 'Erinnerung an Karl Kraus' in *23*, Nos 28–30 (1936), pp. 3–4.

33 Boyden, *Richard Strauss*, pp. 329–31.

34 Quoted in Kennedy, *Richard Strauss*, pp. 274–5.

35 Kennedy, *Richard Strauss*, pp. 284–5.

36 See *Ernst Krenek: Zeitgenosse des 20. Jahrhunderts*, pp. 42–5.

37 For a detailed account of these festivals, see Gabriele Johanna Eder, *Wiener Musikfeste zwischen 1918 und 1938: Ein Beitrag zur Vergangenheitsbewältigung* (Vienna, 1991), pp. 66–105 & 112–54.

38 Eder, *Wiener Musikfeste*, pp. 155–201.

39 Article from *Narodni Politiko*, as reported in the *Neue Freie Presse*, 25 July 1928; quoted in Eder, *Wiener Musikfeste*, p. 200.

40 Cf. Michael H. Kater, *The Twisted Muse: Musicians and their Music in the Third Reich* (New York, 1987); and Fred K. Prieberg, *Musik im NS-Staat* (Frankfurt, 1982).

41 'Lehar hat die Massen, Sie nicht!': Goebbels in conversation with Strauss, cited in Werner Egk, *Die Zeit wartet nicht* (Munich, 1981), p. 343; see also Kater, *The Twisted Muse*, pp. 26 & 130.

42 Kennedy, *Richard Strauss*, p. 290.

43 Musical memories from his childhood in the Vienna of the 1930s have been recorded

by Jakov Lind in 'Mein Wiener Liederbuch', Norddeutscher Rundfunk, first broadcast on 10 February 1987.

44 For the text of this song, 'Sturmsoldaten', see *10 S.A. Kampflieder zusammengestellt von Sturm 22/97* (Neuss, n.d.), Wiener Library microfilm B 10 (2) – B 487. It should not be confused with the 'Horst Wessel Lied': 'Die Fahnen hoch!'

45 Eder, *Wiener Musikfeste*, p. 176.

46 Josef Müller-Blattau, *Geschichte der deutschen Musik* (Berlin, 1938), p. 307; quoted in Alexander L. Ringer, *Arnold Schoenberg: The Composer as Jew* (Oxford, 1990), p. 221. For the politicization of music in the Austrian provinces, see Brenner, *Musik als Waffe?*

PART SIX
Chapter 23

1 Otto Bauer, 'Wandlungen und Probleme der Anschlußbewegung', in *Der Kampf*, July 1927, pp. 297ff., quoted in Otto Leichter, *Otto Bauer: Tragödie oder Triumph?* (Vienna, 1970), pp. 135–7.

2 Alfred D. Low, *The Anschluss Movement, 1931–1938, and the Great Powers* (Boulder CO, 1985), chapters 2–4.

3 Otto Bauer, *Die Nationalitätenfrage und die Sozialdemokratie* (Vienna, 1924), p. 135.

4 See 'Riesenkundgebung der Wiener Bevölkerung für den Anschluß', front-page report with full-page photograph in *Die Woche* (Berlin, 30 May 1925); reprinted in Alisa Douer, *Wien Heldenplatz: Mythen und Massen* (Vienna, 2000), p. 77.

5 Hubert, *Schober*, pp. 372–8.

6 See *Entscheidungsjahr 1932: Zur Judenfrage in der Endphase der Weimarer Republik*, ed. Werner E. Mosse and Arnold Paucker (Tübingen, 1965).

7 Compare Fest, *Hitler*, pp. 339–40, and *Berlin 1932: Das letzte Jahr der Weimarer Republik*, ed. Diethart Kerbs and Henrick Stahr (Berlin, 1992), p. 18.

8 The Lausanne proposals were passed by a single vote: 81 to 80. See *Geschichte Österreichs in Stichworten*, 5, pp. 212–13. The failure of the Social Democrats to recognize, after Nazi gains in the Austrian regional elections of April 1932, that the National Socialists represented the greatest danger, is analysed in Franz Schausberger, *Letzte Chance für die Demokratie* (Vienna, 1993), pp. 117–25.

9 Radomir Luza, *Austro-German Relations in the Anschluss Era* (Princeton NJ, 1975), p. 29.

10 Vienna, 16 May 1931: Austria 5, Scotland 0; Berlin, 24 May: Germany 0, Austria 6; Basel, 29 November: Switzerland 1, Austria 8.

11 Klaus Amann, *Zahltag: Der Anschluß österreichischer Schriftsteller an das Dritte Reich* (Bodenheim, 1996), pp. 168–91.

12 Mirko Jelusich, *Der Zauber von Wien* (Vienna, 1931), a sentimentalization of Vienna designed to advertise 'Dreher-Bier'. See *Kraus-Hefte*, 45 (January 1988), pp. 7–8.

13 See Johannes Sachslehner, *Führerwort und Führerblick: Mirko Jelusich* (Königstein/ Taunus, 1985).

14 See Pauley, *Der Weg in den Nationalsozialismus*, p. 67.

15 See Timms, 'Antisemitism in the Universities and Student Fraternities: The "numerus clausus" controversy'.

16 See Pauley, *Der Weg in den Nationalsozialismus*, pp. 52–5.

17 Quoted in C. Earl Edmondson, *The Heimwehr and Austrian Politics 1918–1936* (Athens GA, 1978), p. 51.

18 Klemperer, *Ignaz Seipel*, p. 355; Gedye, *Fallen Bastions*, pp. 41–4.

19 Lajós Kerekes, *Abenddämmerung einer Demokratie: Mussolini, Gömbös und die Heimwehr* (Vienna, 1966).

20 See Botz, *Gewalt in der Politik*, pp. 161–86.

21   See Edmondson, *The Heimwehr*, pp. 70–90.
22   Kraus, *Wolkenkuckucksheim*, p. 106.
23   Kerekes, *Abenddämmerung*, p. 59.
24   Kraus, *Zeitstrophen*, p. 12.
25   Sozius [Eli Rubin], *The Jews in Italy* (Vienna, 1936), p. 5.
26   Seipel's financial adviser was the banker Gottfried Kunwald, while Starhemberg relied
     on the support of the arms manufacturer Fritz Mandl. See Klemperer, *Ignaz Seipel*,
     pp. 118–19; Edmondson, *The Heimwehr*, pp. 145 & 172–3.
27   Klemperer, *Ignaz Seipel*, pp. 219 & 255; Hubert, *Schober*, pp. 352–3; Edmondson, *The
     Heimwehr*, pp. 63, 106 & 128.
28   Josef Hofmann, *Der Pfrimer-Putsch: Der steirische Heimwehrprozeß des Jahres 1931* (Vienna
     and Graz, 1965), pp. 69–78.
29   Edmondson, *The Heimwehr*, pp. 136–48; Hofmann, *Der Pfrimer-Putsch*, pp. 84–91.
30   *Reichspost*, 26 September 1931 and *Arbeiter-Zeitung*, 25 November 1931; cf. Hubert,
     Schober, p. 413.
31   Cf. Hubert, *Schober*, pp. 418–20.
32   Tucholsky, *Gesammelte Werke*, 3, p. 1029.
33   Poor, *Kurt Tucholsky*, pp. 194–9.
34   Reprinted under the title 'Appell an die Vernunft' in Thomas Mann, *Achtung Europa:
     Aufsätze zur Zeit* (Stockholm, 1938), pp. 41–69.
35   *Alarm: Kampfblatt gegen Volksbetrug und Volksverhetzung*, edited by Arthur Schweriner.
     For further details see Arnold Paucker, *Deutsche Juden im Kampf um Recht und Freiheit*
     (Teetz, 2003), esp. the chapter 'Kampf gegen den Nationalsozialismus', pp. 127–60.
36   Goebbels, *Tagebücher*, 2, p. 696 (4 September 1932); cf. Walter Gyssling, *Mein Leben in
     Deutschland* and *Der Anti-Nazi: Handbuch im Kampf gegen die NSDAP*, ed. Leonidas Hill
     (Bremen, 2002).
37   Christopher Isherwood, *Goodbye to Berlin* (London, 1952), pp. 307–8.
38   Fest, *Hitler*, pp. 341–3.

Chapter 24

1   Gordon Brook-Shepherd, *Dollfuss* (London, 1961), p. 156.
2   Franz Leschnitzer, 'Vom Pazifisten zum Kommunisten', in *Die Friedenswarte*, No. 8
     (August 1932); quoted in Früh, 'Karl Kraus und der Kommunismus', p. 328.
3   Dr J. W. Brügel, 'Antwort an Karl Kraus' (unpublished typescript, Prague, 1934), p. 7:
     'Schon vor mehr als einem Jahre habe ich gehört, auf Grund eines Privatgesprächs, daß
     Karl Kraus den Standpunkt vertritt, Dollfuss sei als das kleinere Übel Hitler gegenüber
     zu tolerieren.'
4   In this chapter, page numbers in brackets identify quotations from F 890–905.
5   See Timms, *Karl Kraus – Apocalyptic Satirist* (1986), p. 248.
6   The wording in the official account of this episode is 'nicht erwünscht'. See *Beiträge
     zut Vorgeschichte und Geschichte der Julirevolte*, p. 21.
7   Gedye, *Fallen Bastions*, p. 80.
8   Gottfried-Karl Kindermann, *Hitler's Defeat in Austria 1933–1934*, tr. Sonia Brough and
     David Taylor (London, 1988), p. xv. For a more detailed account, see Kindermann,
     Österreich gegen Hitler: Europas erste Abwehrfront 1933–1938 (Vienna, 2003).
9   Botz, *Gewalt in der Politik*, p. 216.
10   Krenek, 'Konservativ und radikal', *Wiener Zeitung*, 21 January 1934; see Forster, *Reflexe
     kultureller Modernisierung*, pp. 86–96.
11   See Hermynia Zur Mühlen, *Unsere Töchter, die Nazinen*, ed. Jörg Thunecke (Vienna,
     2000), with publication details in the 'Nachwort' (pp. 143–57).
12   Kindermann, *Österreich gegen Hitler*, pp. 152–64. For an account by one of the

participants, see Ilona Duczynska, *Workers in Arms: The Austrian Schutzbund and the Civil War of 1934* (New York and London, 1978).

13 See Martin Kitchen, *The Coming of Austrian Fascism* (London, 1980), chapter 9; Kindermann, *Österreich gegen Hitler*, pp. 170–1.

14 Starhemberg, *Between Hitler and Mussolini*, p. 132.

15 Brook-Shepherd, *Dollfuss*, p. 250.

16 'Dollfuss † 25.7.34; "Fackel" erschien 28.7.34': pencilled note, probably by the original purchaser, in Edward Timms's copy of F 890–905.

17 Leopold Ungar, *Die Weltanschauung Gottes*, ed. Franz Richard Reiter (Vienna, 1987), p. 192.

18 Gedye, *Fallen Bastions*, p. 65.

19 Klemperer, *Ignaz Seipel*, pp. 393–8.

20 Brook-Shepherd, *Dollfuss*, p. 88.

21 Rabinbach, *The Crisis of Austrian Socialism*, pp. 80–1.

22 See Ludwig Reichold, *Kampf um Österreich: Die vaterländische Front und ihr Widerstand gegen den Anschluß 1933–1938* (Vienna, 1984), p. 99.

23 For a more critical view of Dollfuss, see Gerhard Jagschitz, *Der Putsch: Die Nationalsozialisten 1934 in Österreich* (Graz, 1976); and Ulrich Kluge, *Der österreichische Ständestaat 1934–1938* (Vienna, 1984).

24 Kitchen, *The Coming of Austrian Fascism*, pp. 185–9; Soyfer, 'So starb eine Partei. Romanfragment' in *Die Ordnung schuf der liebe Gott*, pp. 225–376.

25 Everhard Holtmann, *Zwischen Unterdrückung und Bürgerkrieg: Sozialistische Arbeiterbewegung und autoritäres Regime in Österreich 1933–1938* (Vienna, 1978), pp. 84–92.

26 Rabinbach, *The Crisis of Austrian Socialism*, pp. 149–50 & 157–8.

27 *Protokolle des Klubvorstandes der Christlichsozialen Partei, 1932–1934*, ed. Walter Goldinger (Munich, 1980), p. 325; quoted in Pauley, *Der Weg in den Nationalsozialismus*, p. 112.

28 Kitchen, *The Coming of Austrian Fascism*, p. 210.

29 Holtmann, *Unterdrückung und Bürgerkrieg*, pp. 121–43.

30 Soyfer, *Die Ordnung schuf der liebe Gott*, p. 261 ('militärische Vergleiche').

31 For a critical summary of Bauer's theory of fascism, see Wolfgang Neugebauer, 'Der "Austro-Faschismus" in der Sicht von Sozialisten und Kommunisten' in *'Austro-Faschismus': Beiträge über Politik, Ökonomie und Kultur 1934–1938*, ed. E. Talos and W. Neugebauer (Vienna, 1984), pp. 199–221 (esp. pp. 201–2).

32 Brügel, *Antwort an Karl Kraus*, p. 18.

33 Gedye, *Fallen Bastions*, pp. 166–7.

34 Holtmann, *Zwischen Unterdrückung und Befreiung*, pp. 113–20.

35 Pauley, *Der Weg in den Nationalsozialismus*, pp. 105–22.

36 Cited in Kindermann, *Österreich gegen Hitler*, pp. 408–9.

37 Brook-Shepherd, *Dollfuss*, pp. 103–9.

38 Stanley G. Payne, *Fascism: Comparison and Definition* (Madison WI, 1980). Payne's insistence that the Austrian 'Ständestaat' cannot be regarded as 'fascist' has prompted a number of Austrian historians to reassess this question. See *'Austro-Faschismus'*.

39 The scene in the Café Parsifal is described in Krenek, *Im Atem der Zeit*, pp. 936–7 (it was his wife Berta who praised the show). For Werfel's support for Schuschnigg, see Jungk, *Franz Werfel*, pp. 224–5 & 239–40; *A Life Torn by History*, pp. 151–3 & 161–2.

40 For a detailed documentation, see Reichold, *Kampf um Österreich*.

41 The convergence between Kraus's thinking and the policies of Dollfuss is analysed in Norbert Frei, 'Karl Kraus und das Jahr 1934' in *Österreichische Literatur der dreißiger Jahre*, ed. Klaus Amann and Albert Berger (Vienna, 1985), pp. 303–19 (p. 312).

42 For details of the restrictions, see Eppel, *'Concordia'*, pp. 229–43; Habe, *Ich stelle mich*, pp. 261–8.

43 Ludwig, a specialist on the history of the Austrian press, was later to supervise the

doctoral dissertation by Anton Kutscher, '"Die Stunde" unter der Leitung ihres Herausgebers Emmerich Bekessy' (University of Vienna, 1953).

44 See *Unser Staatsprogramm: Führerworte* (Vienna: Bundeskommissiariat für Heimatdienst, 1935).

45 *Protokolle des Ministerrates der Ersten Republik: Kabinet Engelbert Dollfuss*, ed. Gertrude Enderle-Burcel, 7 vols (Vienna, 1980–6).

46 Sidonie Nadherny, letter of 30 January 1948 to Albert Bloch, in Lorenz, *Briefwechsel*, p. 195.

47 Kraus, letter of 27 March 1934 to Marcel Ray, in *Karl Kraus: Marbacher Kataloge 52*, pp. 476–9.

48 Fischer, 'Some Personal Memories', pp. 21–2.

49 For further information on Münzer, see Kurt Krolop, 'Karl-Kraus-Rezeption in den böhmischen Ländern' in *Karl Kraus und 'Die Fackel'*, pp. 151–5.

50 'An den Präsidenten der tschechoslowakischen Republik', typed carbon copy, 28 August 1933. Kraus Archive, Ib 156.626/173.

51 See Torberg, *Die Tante Jolesch*, p. 163.

52 For further details about the *Prager Tagblatt* under Blau's editorship, see Pavel Dolezal, *Tomas G. Masaryk, Max Brod und das 'Prager Tagblatt' (1918–1938)* (Frankfurt, 2004).

53 'An die Redaktion des "Prager Tagblatt"', typed carbon copy, 29 January 1935. Kraus Archive, Ib 159.626/206.

54 'Der Kampf um ein Komma oder Trauriges Ende des Karl Kraus', article by 'Isk' [= F. C. Weiskopf] in *Der Gegenangriff*, 14 January 1934 (cited F 889, 9–10).

55 See Krolop, 'Karl-Kraus-Rezeption in den böhmischen Ländern', pp. 148–51.

56 'Normalisierung der Beziehungen zwischen den Donaustaaten'; quoted in Reichold, *Kampf um Österreich*, p. 100.

57 Erich Heller in a letter to Edward Timms, 4 August 1989 (Timms Collection). See also Heller, *Flucht aus dem zwanzigsten Jahrhundert: Eine kulturkritische Skizze* (Vienna, 1938), pp. 21–2.

Chapter 25

1 Jochen Stremmel, *'Dritte Walpurgisnacht': Über einen Text von Karl Kraus* (Bonn, 1982), pp. 66–100 (p. 83). Copies of the proofs with corrections in Kraus's hand can be consulted in the Brenner Archive (Innsbruck) and the Jewish National Library (Jerusalem).

2 Numerals in brackets give page references both to the original Kösel edition (in roman type) and to the Suhrkamp edition (in italics after the slash). Wagenknecht incorporates textual variants, which are printed at the foot of the page, but the gain in philological accuracy results in a less readable text.

3 Details of the critical reception are given in Stremmel, *'Dritte Walpurgisnacht'*, pp. 162–219. Contrast Raddatz, *Verwerfungen*, p. 39, with the review of *Dritte Walpurgisnacht* in Friedrich Dürrenmatt, *Literatur und Kunst: Essays, Gedichte und Reden* (Zurich, 1998), pp. 38–41.

4 Isherwood, *Christopher and his Kind, 1929–1939* (London, 1977), pp. 94 & 121.

5 Poor, *Kurt Tucholsky*, p. 202.

6 Mühsam was tortured and finally murdered in Oranienburg on 11 July 1934. Hiller barely survived the brutality of his imprisonment, vividly recalled in his memoir *Leben gegen die Zeit* (Hamburg, 1967), pp. 250–86.

7 Heinrich Fischer, 'The Other Austria and Karl Kraus' in *In Tyrannos: Four Centuries of Struggle against Tyranny in Germany*, ed. H. J. Rehfisch (London, 1944), p. 326.

8 Revelation 8: 1 & 5 ('Stille' is the word used in Luther's translation).

9 For an alternative reading of this poem, see Theobald, *The Media and the Making of History*, p. 69 (the phrase 'No word that fits' was suggested by his translation).

10   See Sven Hanuschek, *Elias Canetti: Biographie* (Munich, 2005), pp. 220–1.
11   Notes written by Viertel about his visit to Vienna in December 1935, published in *Karl Kraus: Marbacher Kataloge 52*, pp. 479–81.
12   George Steiner, *Language and Silence: Essays 1958–1966* (Harmondsworth, 1969), p. 143.
13   This text, published in German in 1978, is translated under the title 'Ruminations of a Slow-witted Mind' in Musil, *Precision and the Soul*, pp. 214–34 (pp. 223 and 227).
14   See Ulrich Joost, 'Ein geflügeltes Wort' in *Kraus-Hefte*, 30 (April 1984), pp. 5–8.
15   Bertolt Brecht, *Letters*, tr. Ralph Manheim (London, 1990), p. 147.
16   First published in *Stimmen über Karl Kraus zum 60. Geburtstag* (Vienna, 1934), pp. 11–12.
17   See the fine article 'Bert Brecht und Karl Kraus' in Krolop, *Sprachsatire als Zeitsatire*, pp. 252–303.
18   Krolop, *Sprachsatire als Zeitsatire*, p. 298.
19   Brecht, *Letters*, pp. 139–40 & 187.
20   A distinction adapted from Marshall McLuhan, *Understanding Media: The Extensions of Man* (London, 1964), chapter 2: 'Media Hot and Cold'.
21   The Suhrkamp edition contains a useful index of names, which is unfortunately incomplete. Auwi was the nickname of August Wilhelm von Hohenzollern, one of Hitler's aristocratic supporters; Futterweit was a Viennese jeweller, killed by a bomb planted by a Nazi terrorist in June 1933; Schweppermann features in German folklore as the naive patriot who insisted on eating two eggs on the eve of battle; Uschla, which Kraus uses as an expletive, is an acronym for 'Untersuchungs- und Schlichtungsausschuß', a Nazi disciplinary body.
22   See the memoirs of Martha Dodd, *Through Embassy Eyes* (New York, 1939), pp. 28–9.
23   The most useful commentaries can be found in Stremmel, *'Dritte Walpurgisnacht'* and Krolop, *Sprachsatire als Zeitsatire*. See also Albrecht Betz, 'Die "Worthelfer der Gewalt" in der *Dritten Walpurgisnacht*' in *Karl Kraus et son temps*, ed. Gilbert Krebs and Gerald Stieg (Paris, 1989), pp. 155–71.
24   Karl Kraus, *In These Great Times*, pp. 105–14: 'Protective Custody', tr. Harry Zohn; 'From *Third Walpurgis Night*', tr. Ritchie Robertson, in *The German-Jewish Dialogue: An Anthology of Literary Texts 1749–1993*, ed. Ritchie Robertson (Oxford, 1999), pp. 257–63.
25   'Die Aufgaben des deutschen Theaters', reprinted in Dr Joseph Goebbels, *Revolution der Deutschen: 14 Jahre Nationalsozialismus – Goebbelsreden mit einleitenden Zeitbildern* (Oldenburg, 1933), pp. 175–201.
26   See *Goethes Faust* (Hamburg, 1957), ed. Erich Trunz, p. 570.
27   English versions of quotations from *Faust* are adapted from Theodore Martin's translation, revised by W. H. Bruford (London and New York: Everyman's Library, 1954).
28   Compare the discussion of this question in Djassemy, *Der 'Produktivgehalt kritischer Zerstörerarbeit'*, pp. 367–76. Citing a passage from *Dialektik der Aufklärung*, she goes on to show how Kraus's satire anticipates the critique of the fascist 'domination of nature' ('Naturbeherrschung', p. 394) by Adorno and Horkheimer.
29   Manfred von Killinger, *Ernstes und Heiteres aus dem Putschleben* (Berlin, 1928). After the seizure of power, Killinger was appointed prime minister of Saxony; see Krolop, *Sprachsatire als Zeitsatire*, pp. 219 and 342.
30   The link between 'Faustian' values and fascism is questioned in Stremmel, *'Dritte Walpurgisnacht'*, pp. 137–40. For the wider context, see Robert A. Pois, *National Socialism and the Religion of Nature* (London, 1986), pp. 38–9.
31   For a detailed analysis of Kraus's references to the Philemon and Baucis motif, see Krolop, *Sprachsatire als Zeitsatire*, pp. 222–7.
32   Stremmel, *'Dritte Walpurgisnacht'*, pp. 121 and 141.
33   See John F. Danby, *Shakespeare's Doctrine of Nature: A Study of King Lear* (London, 1956).
34   *Macbeth*, II, 2: 33–4; III, 5: 136–9; V, 2: 15–22.

35   *Goethes Faust*, ed. Trunz, p. 453.
36   Cf. F 890–905: 8, 72 & 157.
37   Borries, *Ein Angriff*, p. 92.
38   See *Karl Kraus: Marbacher Kataloge 52*, p. 470.
39   Ernest K. Bramsted, *Goebbels and National Socialist Propaganda* (East Lansing, 1965), pp. 197–229; Ian Kershaw, *The 'Hitler Myth': Image and Reality in the Third Reich* (Oxford, 1987), pp. 4 and 19–21.
40   Max Domarus, *Hitler: Reden und Proklamationen 1932–45*, 2 vols (Munich 1965), 1, p. 267 (Rede auf dem ersten Kongreß der Deutschen Arbeitsfront).
41   Fest, *Hitler*, p. 377.
42   Domarus, *Reden*, 1, p. 286.
43   Domarus, *Reden*, 1, pp. 270–9.
44   Fest, *Hitler*, p. 436.
45   Domarus, *Reden*, 1, p. 312.
46   *AZ*, 14 July 1933; quoted in Stremmel, *'Dritte Walpurgisnacht'*, p. 131.
47   See Kershaw, *The 'Hitler Myth'*, pp. 48–64.
48   Saul Friedländer, *Nazi Germany and the Jews: The Years of Persecution 1933–39* (London, 1998), p. 87.
49   Cf. Spotts, *Hitler and the Power of Aesthetics*, pp. 43–72.
50   Domarus, *Reden*, 1, pp. 266 and 275.
51   Siegfried Bernfeld, *Sisyphos oder Die Grenzen der Erziehung* (Leipzig and Vienna, 1925); cf. Bernfeld, *Sisyphus or The Limits of Education* (Berkeley CA, 1973), pp. 75–6; Arnold Zweig, *Caliban oder Politik und Leidenschaft* (reprinted Berlin, 1993).
52   Domarus, *Reden*, 1, p. 261.
53   See Horst Göppinger, *Juristen jüdischer Abstammung im 'Dritten Reich'*, 2nd edn (Munich, 1990), pp. 49–64.
54   Quoted in Philip Metcalfe, *1933* (New York, 1988), p. 240.
55   This phrase does not occur in the Kösel edition, which is based on the revised excerpt in F 890–905.
56   Quoted in Samuel Igra, *Germany's National Vice* (London, 1945), p. 7.
57   Klaus Theweleit, *Männerphantasien*, 2 vols (Hamburg, 1980), 1, pp. 179–80.
58   In his memoir *The Turning Point*, Klaus Mann describes the striking resemblance between Haarmann and Hitler. Quoted in Friedrich, *Before the Deluge*, pp. 349–50.

Chapter 26

1   Edgar Ansel Mowrer, *Germany Puts the Clock Back* (London, 1933), pp. 296–301.
2   See Metcalfe, *1933*, pp. 18–29 & 124.
3   See Jost Hermand, *Der alte Traum vom neuen Reich: Völkische Utopien und National-sozialismus* (Frankurt, 1988), pp. 180 and 289.
4   Zygmunt Bauman, *Modernity and the Holocaust* (Cambridge, 1989).
5   'Gleichschaltung' literally means switching machinery to the same electric current. See the Glossary in J. M. Ritchie, *German Literature under National Socialism* (London, 1983).
6   'Osaf = Oberster SA-Führer (Adolf Hitler)'; 'NSBO = Nationalsozialistische Betriebszellenorganisation', the organization used to smash the trade unions. See Karl-Heinz Brackmann and Renate Birkenhauer, *NS-Deutsch: 'Selbstverständliche' Begriffe und Schlagwörter aus der Zeit des Nationalsozialismus* (Straelen, 1988).
7   Metcalfe, *1933*, p. 132.
8   George Orwell, *Nineteen Eighty-Four* (Harmondsworth, 1974), pp. 247–8.
9   Orwell, *Nineteen Eighty-Four*, p. 171.
10   Orwell, *Nineteen Eighty-Four*, p. 246.
11   Steiner, *Language and Silence*, pp. 140–2 (Steiner confuses a line from 'Sturmsoldaten' with the more universally popular 'Horst Wessel Lied').

12   Robert Gellately, *Backing Hitler: Consent and Coercion in Nazi Germany* (Oxford, 2001), pp. 21 and 44.

13   The translation (by Harry Zohn) is taken from *In These Great Times*, pp. 105–7.

14   This wording, confirmed by Siegel to his daughter Bea Green, diverges from that in some reproductions of the photograph, where the illegible lettering was enhanced for publication. See letter of 5 February 2004 from Bea Green to Edward Timms (Timms Collection).

15   Michael Siegel had a second career in Peru as a legal adviser and a rabbi, living to the age of ninety-six. For the reminiscences of his daughter Beate (Bea Green), see Anja Salewsky, *'Der olle Hitler soll sterben!' Erinnerungen an den jüdischen Kindertransport nach England* (Munich, 2001), pp. 25–47.

16   Gellately, *Backing Hitler*, p. 40.

17   See Theodor Haecker, letter of 29 April 1933 to Richard Seewald, in *Theodor Haecker: Leben und Werk – Texte, Briefe, Erinnerungen, Würdigungen*, ed. Bernhard Hanssler and Hinrich Siefken (Esslingen, 1995), pp. 107–8.

18   Wilhelm Alff, 'Karl Kraus und die Zeitgeschichte' in Kraus, *Die Dritte Walpurgisnacht* (Munich, 1967), p. 324: 'Manche Einzelheit dürfte sich nicht verifizieren lassen.'

19   See the facsimiles from the *Arbeiter-Zeitung* reproduced in the documentation 'Dritte Walpurgisnacht und Arbeiter-Zeitung' in *Noch mehr*, ed. Kurt Faecher (Vienna, April 1983), pp. 1–47.

20   Gellately, *Backing Hitler*, p. 58.

21   Quoted from *10 S.A. Kampflieder zusammengestellt von Sturm 22/97* (Neuss, n.d.), Wiener Library microfilm B 10 (2) – B 487.

22   J. Louis Orton, *Emile Coué: The Man and his Work* (London, 1935), pp. 6 & 79.

23   Heinrich Böll, 'Brief an einen jungen Katholiken' in Böll, *Erzählungen, Hörspiele, Aufsätze* (Cologne, 1961), p. 308.

24   Mann's essay 'Leiden und Größe Richard Wagners' appeared in the *Neue Rundschau* in April 1933. A more sweeping account of the 'musicality of the German soul' can be found in his essay 'Deutschland und die Deutschen' (1945), which prefigures the allegorical novel *Doktor Faustus*.

25   This sentence is omitted from the Kösel edition; cf. Stremmel, *'Dritte Walpurgisnacht'*, p. 94.

26   Details of some of the thirty-two assaults reported to the American embassy are given in Metcalfe, *1933*, pp. 146–66 .

27   For an English translation of this section from *Dritte Walpurgisnacht* (by Ritchie Robertson), see *The German-Jewish Dialogue*, pp. 257–63.

28   The 'power of language' idea is questioned in Utz Maas, 'Sprache im Nationalsozialismus: Macht der Wortes oder Lähmung der Sprache' in *'Gift, das du unbewußt eintrinkst': Der Nationalsozialismus und die deutsche Sprache*, ed. Werner Bohleber and Jörg Drews (Bielefeld, 1991), pp. 25–37.

29   Goebbels, *Revolution der Deutschen*, p. 191: 'Der Expressionismus hatte gesunde Ansichten, denn seine Zeit war expressionistisch.'

30   'Das Judentum in und außer uns' was the title of a series of articles by Dietrich Eckart, published in 1919 in the journal *Auf gut deutsch*. See Geoffrey Stoakes, *Hitler and the Quest for World Domination* (Leamington Spa, 1986), pp. 9–10.

31   Report in the *Manchester Guardian* of 14 September 1931, quoted in Brigitte Granzow, *A Mirror of Nazism: British Opinion and the Emergence of Hitler 1929–1933* (London, 1964), pp. 154–5.

32   For Goebbels's view of the *Frankfurter Zeitung* as a channel for more subtle types of propaganda, see Bramsted, *Goebbels*, pp. 124–42.

33   See Viktor Reimann, *The Man Who Created Hitler: Joseph Goebbels*, tr. Stephen Wendt (London, 1977), pp. 21–9.

34   Helmut Heiber, *Goebbels*, tr. John K. Dickinson (London, 1972), p. 76.

35   Reimann, *The Man Who Created Hitler*, p. 97.
36   Werner Stephan, *Joseph Goebbels: Dämon einer Diktatur* (Stuttgart, 1949), p. 180.
37   Goebbels, *Revolution der Deutschen*, pp. 175–201.
38   Dr Goebbels, *Signale der neuen Zeit* (Munich, 1934), p. 45.
39   Mjoelnir and Dr Goebbels, *Das Buch Isidor: Ein Zeitbild voll Lachen und Hass* (Munich, 1929).
40   Reimann, *The Man Who Created Hitler*, p. 212.
41   *The Times*, 29 September 1933, quoted in Bramsted, *Goebbels*, p. 144.
42   Cf. Heiber, *Goebbels*, p. 134.
43   For a summary of the critical debate, see Tom Rockmore, *On Heidegger's Nazism and Philosophy* (Berkeley CA, 1992), pp. 282–8. For a translation of the Rectoral Address, see *The Heidegger Controversy: A Critical Reader*, ed. Richard Wolin (New York, 1991), pp. 29–39.
44   Hugo Ott, *Martin Heidegger – Unterwegs zu seiner Biographie* (Frankfurt, 1988) pp. 150–4.
45   *The Heidegger Controversy*, pp. 49–52.
46   See Martin Heidegger, 'Bauen Wohnen Denken' in *Vorträge und Aufsatze*, ed. Friedrich-Wilhelm von Hermann (Frankfurt, 2000), pp. 147–64 (p. 148); and 'Brief über den "Humanismus"' in *Wegmarken*, p. 313; cf. Heidegger, *Basic Writings* (London, 2002), pp. 217 and 348.
47   Heidegger, '". . . dichterisch wohnet der Mensch . . ."' in *Vorträge und Aufsatze*, pp. 191–208 (p. 194). For an account of the 'constitutive' conception of language, deriving from Herder and Humboldt, on which both Kraus and Heidegger draw, see Charles Taylor, 'Heidegger, Language, and Ecology' in *Heidegger: A Critical Reader*, ed. Hubert Dreyfus and Harrison Hall (Oxford, 1992), pp. 247–69.
48   Josef Weinheber, *Sämtliche Werke*, ed. Josef Nadler and Hedwig Weinheber, 5 vols (Salzburg, 1954–6), 2, pp. 92–3; and 5, pp. 67–74 (letter of 17 September 1932 to Friedrich Sacher).
49   *The Heidegger Controversy*, p. 44.
50   For further details, see Ott, *Martin Heidegger*, pp. 255–9. Although Haecker is not mentioned by name in Heidegger's 'Einführung in die Metaphysik', Ott's reconstruction of the aim of his polemic is clear and convincing.
51   Anne Frank, who wrote in Dutch, banned the speaking of German in the Secret Annex (entry of 17 November 1942). Arnold Daghani wrote his diary in English on the pages of a shorthand notebook. See Edward Timms, 'Memories of Mikhailowka: Labour Camp Testimonies in the Arnold Daghani Archive' in *Remembering for the Future: The Holocaust in an Age of Genocide*, ed. Yehuda Bauer and others (New York, 2001), 1, pp. 205–27.
52   Theodor Haecker, *Tag- und Nachtbücher 1939–1945*, ed. Hinrich Siefken (Innsbruck, 1989), p. 141.
53   Victor Klemperer, *Ich will Zeugnis ablegen bis zum letzten: Tagebücher 1942–1945*, ed. Walter Nowojski (Berlin, 1995), p. 503; *To the Bitter End: The Diaries of Victor Klemperer 1942–1945*, abridged and tr. Martin Chalmers (London, 1999), pp. 294–5.
54   Victor Klemperer, *LTI: Notizbuch eines Philologen* (Berlin, 1947); *The Language of the Third Reich: LTI – Lingua Tertii Imperii. A Philologist's Notebook*, tr. Martin Brady (London, 2000).
55   Klemperer, *Language of the Third Reich*, p. 61; see also chapter 28: 'The Language of the Victor' and chapter 30: 'The Curse of the Superlative'.
56   Klemperer, *Language of the Third Reich*, pp. 156 and 257; see also chapter 9: 'Fanatical'.
57   C. J. Wells, *German: A Linguistic History to 1945* (Oxford, 1987), p. 409; Roderick Watt, 'Victor Klemperer and the Language of National Socialism' in *The German-Jewish Dilemma*, pp. 243–54 (p. 244).
58   Orwell, *Nineteen Eighty-Four*, p. 13.
59   Klemperer, *To the Bitter End*, p. 223; *Tagebücher 1942–1945*, p. 385.

60   For further details of Leers's book of poetry, *Forderung der Stunde: Juden raus!* (Berlin, 1933) and his numerous antisemitic publications, see Krolop, *Sprachsatire als Zeitsatire*, pp. 218–20 and 341–2.

61   See the comparison by Wolfgang Grünberg, 'Die Schriftsteller Victor Klemperer und Jochen Klepper in ihren Tagebüchern aus der Kriegszeit' in *Unvollendetes Leben zwischen Tragik und Erfüllung*, ed. Miriam Gillis-Carlebach and Wolfgang Grünberg (Hamburg, 2002), pp. 109–27.

62   Klemperer, *Language of the Third Reich*, p. 109.

63   Kershaw, *The 'Hitler Myth'*, pp. 215–19.

64   See the discussion of 'kein Haar krümmen' in *Wörterbuch der Redensarten*, ed. Werner Welzig, pp. 405–12 & 1049–51.

65   The phrase 'kein Haar gekrümmt' also occurs in 'Wider die Greuelhetze des Weltjudentums', the speech delivered by Goebbels on 1 April 1933; see Goebbels, *Revolution der Deutschen*, pp. 155–61 (p. 158).

66   *Manchester Guardian*, 28 November 1938; cited in Andrew Sharf, *The British Press and Jews under Nazi Rule* (London, 1964), p. 83.

67   See the documentation about the activities of 'Haarverwertungsbetriebe' in Reimund Schnabel, *Macht ohne Moral: Eine Dokumentation über die SS* (Frankfurt, 1957), esp. pp. 259–63.

68   Maimonides, 'Laws Concerning the Installation of Kings', quoted in Scholem, *The Messianic Idea in Judaism*, p. 29.

69   For further details of Göring's speech see Fest, *Hitler*, p. 292.

70   Luther expresses the promise that the Lord will 'cast out many nations' (Deuteronomy 7: 1) as 'viele Völker ausrotten', and the motif recurs in his translation of Joshua 23: 4.

71   Sharf, *The British Press and Jews under Nazi Rule*, p. 98.

72   For a fuller account of the linguistic encoding of the 'exterminationist mentality', see Paul Lawrence Rose, '"Extermination/Ausrottung": Meanings, Ambiguities and Intentions in German Antisemitism and the Holocaust, 1800–1945' in *Remembering for the Future*, 2, pp. 726–50.

73   Ernst Jünger, *Feuer und Blut* (Magdeburg, 1925), p. 113; cited in Jürgen Brokoff, *Die Apokalypse in der Weimarer Republik* (Munich, 2001), p. 106.

74   Compare the passage in which Doubting Thomas touches the wounds of Jesus (John 20: 24–8).

75   Jean Améry, *At the Mind's Limits: Contemplations by a Survivor on Auschwitz and its Realities*, tr. Sidney and Stella P. Rosenfeld (New York, 1986), p. 20 (translation modified).

76   Theodor Adorno, *Aesthetic Theory*, tr. C. Lenhardt (London, 1984), p. 444.

77   Joseph Roth, *Der Antichrist* (1934), reprinted in *Das journalistische Werk 1929–1939*, pp. 563–665; Dosio Koffler, *Die deutsche Walpurgisnacht: Ein Spiel in fünf Szenen* (Mannheim, 1987), first published London, 1941; English translation by Graham Rowson, published in London in 1942 under the title *The German Witches' Sabbath: A Satire in Five Scenes*.

78   *Deutsches Wörterbuch* (Leipzig, 1839), vol. 3, column 452.

79   See the facsimile in Horowitz, *Karl Kraus: Bildbiographie*, pp. 160–1.

80   See Paul Schick, 'Der Satiriker und der Tod: Versuch einer typologichen Deutung' in *Festschrift zum hundertjährigen Bestehen der Wiener Stadtbibliothek* (Vienna, 1956), pp. 200–30.

81   Cited by Sidonie Nadherny in a letter of 25–26 February 1948 to Albert Bloch, published in Lorenz, *Briefwechsel*, p. 255.

82   Benjamin to Gershom Scholem, 4 April 1937, in Benjamin, *Gesammelte Briefe*, 5, p. 507.

83   The tactics used by Hitler's supporters in the Austrian Cabinet, Arthur Seyss-Inquart and Edmund Glaise von Horstenau, to force the cancellation of the referendum are

described in *Ein General im Zwielicht: Die Erinnerungen Edmund Glaises von Horstenau*, ed. Peter Broucek, 3 vols (Vienna, 1980–3), 2, pp. 252–6.

84 'Karl Kraus ist denn doch zu früh gestorben'. Benjamin, letter of June 1939 to Margarete Steffin, in *Gesammelte Briefe*, 6, p. 294.

Epilogue

1 Steiner, *Language and Silence*, p. 22.

2 Viktor Matejka, *Widerstand ist alles: Notizen eines Unorthodoxen* (Vienna, 1993), pp. 90–2, 122 & 209–10.

3 Matejka, *Widerstand*, pp. 189–200.

4 Ernst Bruckmüller, 'The Development of Austrian National Identity' in *Austria 1945–95: Fifty Years of the Second Republic*, ed. Kurt Richard Luther and Peter Pulzer (Aldershot, 1998), pp. 83–108 (p. 88).

5 *'Ich bin dafür, die Sache in die Länge zu ziehen': Die Wortprotokolle der Bundesregierung von 1945 bis 1952 über die Entschädigung der Juden*, ed. Robert Knight (Frankfurt, 1988); Oliver Rathkolb, 'Verhandlungen über Schuld und Geschichte: Materielle Restitution und Entschädigung in Österreich 1945–2002' in *Freuds verschwundene Nachbarn*, ed. Lydia Marinelli (Vienna, 2003), pp. 75–87 (Kunschak's speech of autumn 1945 is quoted on p. 77).

6 See the chapter 'Men for all Seasons: Österreichische Literaturpreisträger der fünfziger Jahre' in Klaus Amann, *Die Dichter und die Politik: Essays zur österreichischen Literatur nach 1918* (Vienna, 1992), pp. 219–22.

7 *Bekenntnisbuch österreichischer Dichter* (Vienna, 1938), pp. 68 (Max Mell), 102–3 (Karl Hans Strobl) and 112 (Karl Heinrich Waggerl).

8 Roessler, 'Das Reinhardt-Seminar' in *Ambivalenzen*, pp. 178–81.

9 Friedrich Heer, 'Nach 1945' in *Vom Reich zu Österreich: Kriegsende und Nachkriegszeit, erinnert von Augen- und Ohrenzeugen*, ed. Jochen Jung (Salzburg, 1983), pp. 166–77.

10 Jakov Lind, *Counting my Steps* (London, 1969), pp. 125–6 & 140.

11 Compare the account of the destruction of Hamburg by Hans Erich Nossack, first published under the title 'Der Untergang' in 1948, reprinted in *Hamburg 1943: Literarische Zeugnisse zum Feuersturm*, ed. Volker Hage (Frankfurt, 2003), pp. 63–81 (p. 70).

12 See the discussion of this motif in Timms, *Karl Kraus – Apocalyptic Satirist* (1986), pp. 50–1.

13 Theobald, *The Media and the Making of History*, pp. 68 & 76. For the impact on Kraus's ideas on the media criticism of Jacques Bouveresse and the late Pierre Bourdieu, see Gerald Stieg, 'Karl Kraus in der aktuellen französischen Medienkritik' in *Karl Kraus – in Jičin geboren*, pp. 113–25.

14 See Timms, *Karl Kraus – Apocalyptic Satirist* (1986), pp. 147–53.

15 See Hedges, *War is a Force that Gives us Meaning*, pp. 4–5.

16 See the documentation of Elfriede Jelinek's controversial career in *Die Nestbeschmutzerin: Jelinek & Österreich*, ed. Pia Janke (Salzburg, 2002).

Bibliographical Note

In the twenty years since the original volume of *Karl Kraus – Apocalyptic Satirist* was completed there have been important publications in this field, including new editions of Kraus's writings. Details of all works cited in this second volume are given in the notes. What follows is a check-list of the most significant sources.

A. Primary sources

(see also the List of Abbreviations, p. xx.)

1   Die Fackel

The text of *Die Fackel* (Vienna, 1899–1936) forms the staple of Kraus research. In addition to the reprints by Kösel Verlag and Zweitausendeins, an electronic edition is now available: *Die Fackel*, Volltextausgabe mit Bibliographie und Register von Wolfgang Hink, CD-ROM, ed. Friedrich Pfäfflin (Munich, 2002).

2   Editions of Kraus's writings

The original book editions have been consulted at every stage. The two-volume edition of Kraus's early writings, *Frühe Schriften*, edited by Johannes J. Braakenburg, has been completed by the publication of a third volume of annotations (Munich, 1988). The Kösel edition of Kraus's *Werke*, edited by Heinrich Fischer, has been superseded by the Suhrkamp Verlag paperback edition of the *Schriften*, edited by Christian Wagenknecht, which includes all the writings published by Kraus in book form, together with further selections from *Die Fackel*. This edition comprises the following twenty volumes:

S 1   *Sittlichkeit und Kriminalität* (1987)
S 2   *Die chinesische Mauer* (1987)
S 3   *Literatur und Lüge* (1989)

S 4 *Untergang der Welt durch schwarze Magie* (1989)
S 5 *Weltgericht I* (1988)
S 6 *Weltgericht II* (1988)
S 7 *Die Sprache* (1987)
S 8 *Aphorismen* (1986)
S 9 *Gedichte* (1989)
S10 *Die letzten Tage der Menschheit* (1986)
S11 *Dramen* (1989)
S12 *Dritte Walpurgisnacht* (1989)
S13 *Theater der Dichtung: Offenbach* (1994)
S14 *Theater der Dichtung: Nestroy, Zeitstrophen* (1992)
S15 *Theater der Dichtung: William Shakespeare* (1994)
S16 *Brot und Lüge: Aufsätze 1919–1924* (1991)
S17 *Die Stunde des Gerichts: Aufsätze 1925–1928* (1992)
S18 *Hüben und Drüben: Aufsatze 1929–1936* (1993)
S19 *Die Katastrophe der Phrasen: Glossen 1910-1918* (1994)
S20 *Kanonade auf Spatzen: Glossen 1920-1936; Shakespeares Sonette: Nachdichtung* (1994)

Each of these volumes contains an informative afterword. In addition, a pre-cisely transcribed and fully annotated edition of the manuscript of one of Kraus's plays has been published: *Karl Kraus' 'Literatur oder Man wird doch da sehn': Genetische Ausgabe und Kommentar*, ed. Martin Leubner (Göttingen, 1996).

3 Correspondence

Karl Kraus, *Briefe an Sidonie Nadherny von Borutin, 1913–36*, ed. Heinrich Fischer and Michael Lazarus, 2 vols (Munich, 1974)
Karl Kraus und Mechtilde Lichnowsky: Briefe und Dokumente 1916–1958, ed. Friedrich Pfäfflin and Eva Dambacher (Marbach, 2000)
Karl Kraus-Otto Stoessl, *Briefwechsel 1902-1925*, ed. Gilbert J. Carr (Vienna, 1996)
Feinde in Scharen. Ein wahres Vergnügen dazusein: Karl Kraus-Herwarth Walden Briefwechsel 1909–1912, ed. George C. Avery (Göttingen, 2002)
Ludwig von Ficker, *Briefwechsel*, ed. Ignaz Zangerle and others, 3 vols (Salzburg and Innsbruck, 1986–91)

4 Unpublished writings

The most important resource is the Karl Kraus Archive of the Vienna City Library (Wiener Stadt- und Landesbibliothek), a rich collection of letters, cor-rected proofsheets, manuscripts, photographs and biographical documents, including the diary of Irma Karczewska and the files of Oskar Samek. Further source material is available at the Brenner Archive in Innsbruck and the Deutsches Literaturarchiv in Marbach. Other unpublished sources include the diaries of Sidonie Nadherny at the Statni Oblastni Archive in Prague, the Fritz

Wittels papers at the Brill Library in New York, and the memoirs of Ludwig Ullmann at the Literaturhaus in Vienna. The artistic, literary and musical manuscripts presented to David Josef Bach in 1924 are currently in the library of Gonville and Caius College, while the books he brought with him to England, many of them with personal dedications, are in Cambridge University Library. The collection of Edward Timms contains a small number of unpublished items, including a typescript by Heinrich Fischer entitled 'Some Personal Memories on Karl Kraus, Else Lasker-Schüler and Bertolt Brecht'.

5   Voice recordings

Karl Kraus liest aus eigenen Schriften with Nachruf auf Karl Kraus, gesprochen von Alfred Polgar, digital remastering reissued on CD by Preiserrecords in 1989

Karl Kraus liest Eigenes und Angeeignetes, three CDs with texts published as a supplement to Marbacher Katalog 52, ed. Friedrich Pfäfflin and Eva Dambacher (Marbach, 1999)

6   Legal submissions and court proceedings

Karl Kraus contra . . . Die Prozeßakten der Kanzlei Oskar Samek, ed. Hermann Böhm, 4 vols (Vienna, 1995–7)

7   Newspapers and periodicals

The Austrian National Library and the Vienna City Library have comprehensive collections of the newspapers of Kraus's day, including the Arbeiter-Zeitung, the Deutschösterreichische Tageszeitung, the Neue Freie Presse, the Reichspost and Die Stunde, some of which can be consulted in the original bound editions. The Tagblatt Archive at the Vienna City Library is a further valuable resource.

8   Memoirs

Elias Canetti, Die gerettete Zunge: Geschichte einer Jugend (Munich, 1977); Die Fackel im Ohr: Lebensgeschichte 1921–1931 (Munich, 1982); Das Augenspiel: Lebensgeschichte 1931–1937 (Munich, 1985)

Ernst Krenek, Im Atem der Zeit: Erinnerungen an die Moderne, translated from the English original by Friedrich Saathen (Hamburg, 1998)

Viktor Matejka, Widerstand ist alles: Notizen eines Unorthodoxen (Vienna, 1983)

Gershom Scholem, Walter Benjamin – Die Geschichte einer Freundschaft (Frankfurt, 1975)

Leopold Ungar, Die Weltanschauung Gottes: Dokumente, Berichte, Analysen, ed. Richard Reiter (Vienna, 1987)

Freud and the Child Woman: The Memoirs of Fritz Wittels, ed. Edward Timms (New Haven and London, 1995)

B   Studies of Kraus's work

There is no comprehensive account of Kraus's achievements in the period between the First and the Second World Wars, but his work has been illuminated by a number of specialized studies, of which the following proved particularly helpful:

Gilbert J. Carr and Edward Timms (eds), *Karl Kraus und Die Fackel: Aufsätze zur Rezeptionsgeschichte / Reading Karl Kraus: Essays on the Reception of* Die Fackel (Munich, 2001)

Irina Djassemy, *Der 'Produktivgehalt kritischer Zerstörerarbeit': Kulturkritik bei Karl Kraus und Theodor W. Adorno* (Würzburg, 2002)

Meret Forster, *Reflexe kultureller Modernisierung: Ernst Kreneks Radikalismus der Mitte und der Einfluss von Karl Kraus 1928–1938* (Frankfurt, 2004)

Wolfgang Hink, *Die Fackel: Bibliographie und Register*, 2 vols (Munich, 1994)

Luis Miguel Isava, *Wittgenstein, Kraus and Valéry: A Paradigm for Poetic Rhyme and Reason* (New York, 2002)

Georg Knepler, *Karl Kraus liest Offenbach: Erinnerungen, Kommentare, Dokumentationen* (Vienna, 1984)

Kurt Krolop, *Sprachsatire als Zeitsatire bei Karl Kraus* (Berlin, 1987)

Kurt Krolop, *Reflexionen der Fackel: Neue Studien über Karl Kraus* (Vienna, 1994)

Alexander Lang, *'Ursprung ist das Ziel': Karl Kraus und sein 'Zion des Wortes'* (Frankfurt, 1998)

Elke Lorenz, *'Sei Ich ihr, sei mein Bote': Der Briefwechsel zwischen Sidonie Nadherny und Albert Bloch* (Munich, 2002)

Heinz Lunzer, Victoria Lunzer-Talos and Marcus G. Patka (eds), *'Was wir umbringen': 'DIE FACKEL' von Karl Kraus* (Vienna, 1999)

Reinhard Merkel, *Strafrecht und Satire im Werk von Karl Kraus* (Baden-Baden, 1994)

Burkhard Müller, *Karl Kraus: Mimesis und Kritik des Mediums* (Stuttgart, 1995)

Friedrich Pfäfflin and Eva Dambacher (eds), *Karl Kraus: Marbacher Kataloge 52* (Marbach am Neckar, 1999)

Susanne Rode, *Alban Berg und Karl Kraus* (Frankfurt, 1988)

Irmgard Schartner, *Karl Kraus und die Musik* (Frankfurt, 2002)

Sigurd Paul Scheichl and Christian Wagenknecht (eds), *Kraus-Hefte*, Nos 1–72 (Munich, January 1977–October 1994)

Gerald Stieg, *Der Brenner und Die Fackel: Ein Beitrag zur Wirkungsgeschichte von Karl Kraus* (Salzburg, 1976)

Gerald Stieg, *Frucht des Feuers: Canetti, Doderer, Kraus und der Justizpalastbrand* (Vienna, 1990)

Jochen Stremmel, *'Dritte Walpurgisnacht': Über einen Text von Karl Kraus* (Bonn, 1982)

Christopher Thornhill, *Walter Benjamin and Karl Kraus: Problems of a 'Wahlverwandtschaft'* (Stuttgart, 1996)

Alena Wagnerova, *Das Leben der Sidonie Nadherny: Eine Biographie* (Hamburg, 2003)

Werner Welzig (ed.), *Wörterbuch der Redensarten zu der von Karl Kraus 1899 bis 1936 herausgegebenen Zeitschrift 'Die Fackel'* (Vienna, 1999)

C   Bibliothek Janowitz

A new series of publications has been launched under this title by Friedrich Pfäfflin, the long-serving administrator of Kraus's literary estate. In addition to Karl Kraus, *Wiese im Park: Gedichte an Sidonie Nadherny*, ed. Friedrich Pfäfflin (Frankfurt, 2004), it will feature shorter publications by leading scholars such as Christian Wagenknecht and Leo A. Lensing. Three important new editions of correspondence have also been announced, which should enhance our understanding of Sidonie Nadherny and the ambience she created at Schloss Janowitz:

Karl Kraus, *Briefe an Sidonie Nadherny von Borutin 1913–1936*, ed. and extended by Friedrich Pfäfflin on the basis of the original edition by Heinrich Fischer and Michael Lazarus, 2 vols (Göttingen, autumn 2005)

Rainer Maria Rilke–Sidonie Nadherny von Borutin, *Briefwechsel 1906–1929*, ed. Joachim W. Storck in conjunction with Waltraud and Friedrich Pfäfflin (Göttingen, 2006)

Sidonie Nadherny, *Briefe an Vaclav Wagner: Schloss und Park Janowitz in den Jahren 1942 bis 1949*, ed. Friedrich Pfäfflin and Alena Wagnerova (forthcoming, 2007)

D   Translations

Kraus's principal writings are available in a number of other languages, including complete French translations of his two most important works: *Les derniers jours de l'humanité*, tr. Jean-Louis Besson and Henri Christophe (Marseilles, 2004); and *Troisième nuit de Walpurgis*, tr. Pierre Deshusses, with a preface by Jacques Bouveresse (Marseilles, 2005). Unfortunately, only limited selections of his writings have been translated into English, listed here in order of publication:

Poems: Authorized English translation from the German, tr. Albert Bloch (Boston, 1930)

The Last Days of Mankind, abridged by Frederick Ungar, tr. Alexander Gode and Sue Ellen Wright (New York, 1974)

In these Great Times: A Karl Kraus Reader, ed. Harry Zohn, tr. Joseph Fabry and others (Montreal, 1976; Manchester, 1984)

Half-Truths and One-and-a-Half Truths: Selected Aphorisms, ed. and tr. Harry Zohn (Montreal, 1976)

No Compromise: Selected Writings, ed. Frederick Ungar, tr. Sheema Z. Buehne and others (New York, 1977)

A short selection of Kraus's writings is included in *The Vienna Coffeehouse Wits 1890–1938*, ed. and tr. Harold B. Segel (West Lafayette IN, 1993). In addition, a new edition of Kraus's selected writings, translated by Patrick Healy, is scheduled for publication by Penguin Classics in 2006.

In the absence of standard English editions, quotations in this book have been translated by the author, except where otherwise indicated. There is clearly a need for new and improved English translations, especially of *Die letzten Tage der Menschheit*. A parallel-text edition of Kraus's poems might prove particularly illuminating, highlighting the tensions between the original and the translator's elusive goal. An amended version of his most enigmatic poem, discussed from a different angle in each volume of *Karl Kraus – Apocalyptic Satirist*, may serve as envoi for the completed book:

Zwei Läufer laufen zeitentlang,	Two runners down time's path are sped,
der eine dreist, der andere bang:	one bold, the other full of dread:
Der von Nirgendher sein Ziel erwirbt;	The one from nowhere acquires his goal;
der vom Ursprung kommt und am Wege stirbt.	the one from the origin expires on the road.
Der von Nirgendher das Ziel erwarb,	The nowhere man, his goal acquired,
macht Platz dem, der am Wege starb.	yields to the runner who expired.
Und dieser, den es ewig bangt,	For him, gripped by eternal fear,
ist stets am Ursprung angelangt.	the origin is always near.

Sources of Illustrations

I am grateful to the individuals and institutions listed below for permission to reproduce images. Special thanks are due to: Stuart Robinson of the Media Service Unit, University of Sussex, for his skilled assistance with the preparation of illustrations; and Marek Jaros, Photo Archivist of the Wiener Library, for professional guidance.

A. Public collections

Dokumentationsarchiv des österreichischen Widerstandes (Vienna), Figs 47 & 50; Gonville and Caius College (Cambridge), Fig. 42; Historisches Museum der Stadt Wien (Vienna), Fig. 25 (© DACS 2005); Israel Museum (Jerusalem), Fig. 23 (© DACS 2005); Österreichische Galerie (Vienna), Fig. 16 (© DACS 2005); Österreichisches Theatermuseum (Vienna), Figs 28, 38 & 43; Stadtbibliothek Monacensia (Munich), Fig. 20(a); Statni Oblastni Archive (Prague), Fig. 21; Wiener Library (London), Figs 48(a), 55, 56, 57 & 60; Wiener Stadt- und Landesbibliothek (Vienna City Library), Frontispiece, Figs 2, 12, 17, 18(a), 36(a) & 36(b).

B. Private collections

Tilbert Eckertz (Berlin), Cover Photograph, Fig. 8(b); Friedrich Pfäfflin (Marbach), Figs 19(a) & 19(b); Edward Timms (Brighton), 27.

C. Printed sources: Newspapers and periodicals

Arbeiter-Zeitung, Fig. 10; *Bekessy's Panoptikum*, Figs 30(a), 30(b), 33(a) & 33(b); *Das kleine Blatt*, Fig. 48(b); *Die Fackel*, Figs 22 & 39(b); *Gegen-Angriff*, Fig. 53; *Der Stürmer*, Fig. 13; *Die Stunde*, Figs 8(a), 31, 32(a), 32(b), 32(c), 32(d), 33(a) & 34; Illustrierte Kronenzeitung, Fig. 26.

D. Printed sources: Books

1938–1988: Ein Beitrag zum Gedenkjahr, Figs 59(a) & 59(b); Gordon Brook-Shepherd, *Dollfuss*, Fig. 52; Alisa Douer, *Wien Heldenplatz: Mythen und Massen*,

Fig. 49; Mjoelnir and Dr Goebbels, *Das Buch Isidor: Ein Zeitbild voll Lachen und Hass*, Fig. 29(b); Joseph Goebbels, *Revolution der Deutschen*, Fig. 58; *The Graphic Work of Felicien Rops*, Fig. 20(b); *Hetärengespräche*, illustrated by Gustav Klimt, 18(b); Oskar Kleinschmied, *Schober*, Figs 35 & 37; Georg Knepler, *Karl Kraus liest Offenbach*, Figs. 6 & 45; Robert Körber, ed., *Antisemitismus der Welt im Wort und Bild*, Fig. 11; Siegfried Kracauer, *Jacques Offenbach und das Paris seiner Zeit*, Fig. 46(b); Leopold Liegler, *Karl Kraus und sein Werk*, Fig. 15; Heinz Lunzer, ed., *'Was wir umbringen'*: Die Fackel *von Karl Kraus*, Fig. 40; Otto Neurath, *International Picture Language*, Fig. 14(a); Ernst Nolte, *Der Faschismus*, Fig. 3; Erwin Piscator, *Das politische Theater*, Fig. 39(a); Hugo Portisch, *Österreich I: Die unterschätzte Republik*, Fig. 54; Augustin M. Prentiss, *Chemicals in War*, Fig. 5(b); Harald Seyrl, ed., *Die Erinnerungen des österreichischen Scharfrichters*, Fig. 51; Rudolf Spitzer, *Karl Seitz*, Figs 24(a) & 24(b); *Stimmen über Karl Kraus zum 60. Geburtstag*, Fig. 44; Mary Tucholsky, ed., *Kurt Tucholsky und Deutschlands Marsch ins Dritte Reich*, Fig. 29(a); Hans Wilderotter, ed., *Die Extreme berühren sich: Walther Rathenau*, Fig. 1; Simon Williams, *Shakespeare on the German Stage*, Fig. 41; Ludwig Wittgenstein, *Philosophical Investigations*, Fig. 14(b).

Index